A History of World Societies

FOURTH EDITION

A HISTORY OF WORLD SOCIETIES

Volume B
From 1100
Through
the French
Revolution

John P. McKay
University of Illinois at
Urbana-Champaign

Bennett D. Hill
Georgetown University

John Buckler
University of Illinois at
Urbana-Champaign

HOUGHTON MIFFLIN COMPANY

Boston   Toronto
Geneva, Illinois   Palo Alto
Princeton, New Jersey

Senior Sponsoring Editor: Patricia A. Coryell
Senior Associate Editor: Jeffrey Greene
Manufacturing Manager: Florence Cadran
Marketing Manager: Clint Crockett

Credits: P. 588: From *Europe in the Seventeenth Century* by David
Ogg (New York: Macmillan, 1967), pp. 198–199.
Reprinted by permission of A & C Black, London. Pp.
685–686: From *The Selected Letters of Lady Mary Wortley
Montagu*, ed. R. Halsband (London: Longman Group,
1970), pp. 98–99, 106, 105, 96–97).

Cover image: School of Cuzco, *Manuela Thupa Amaru Nusta,*
18th century copy of a 16th century portrait, Museo
Arqueológico de Cuzco. Courtesy of Dr. Mauro
Concha-Péres, Rector, Universidad Nacional de San
Antonio Abad del Cusco

Printed in the U.S.A.
Library of Congress Catalog Card Number: 95-76999
ISBN Student Text: 0-395-75381-3
ISBN Examination Copy: 0-395-76592-7
  3456789-VH-99   98

John P. McKay Born in St. Louis, Missouri, John P. McKay received his B.A. from Wesleyan University (1961), his M.A. from the Fletcher School of Law and Diplomacy (1962), and his Ph.D. from the University of California, Berkeley (1968). He began teaching history at the University of Illinois in 1966 and became a professor there in 1976. John won the Herbert Baxter Adams Prize for his book *Pioneers for Profit: Foreign Entrepreneurship and Russian Industrialization, 1885–1913* (1970). He has also written *Tramways and Trolleys: The Rise of Urban Mass Transit in Europe* (1976) and has translated Jules Michelet's *The People* (1973). His research has been supported by fellowships from the Ford Foundation, the Guggenheim Foundation, the National Endowment for the Humanities, and IREX. His articles and reviews have appeared in numerous journals, including *The American Historical Review, Business History Review, The Journal of Economic History,* and *Slavic Review*. He edits *Industrial Development and the Social Fabric: An International Series of Historical Monographs*.

Bennett D. Hill A native of Philadelphia, Bennett D. Hill earned an A.B. at Princeton (1956) and advanced degrees from Harvard (A.M., 1958) and Princeton (Ph.D., 1963). He taught history at the University of Illinois at Urbana, where he was department chairman from 1978 to 1981. He has published *English Cistercian Monasteries and Their Patrons in the Twelfth Century* (1968) and *Church and State in the Middle Ages* (1970); and articles in *Analecta Cisterciensia, The New Catholic Encyclopaedia, The American Benedictine Review,* and *The Dictionary of the Middle Ages.* His reviews have appeared in *The American Historical Review, Speculum, The Historian, The Catholic Historical Review,* and *Library Journal*. He has been a fellow of the American Council of Learned Societies and has served on committees for the National Endowment for the Humanities. Now a Benedictine monk of St. Anselm's Abbey, Washington, D.C., he is also a Visiting Professor at Georgetown University.

John Buckler Born in Louisville, Kentucky, John Buckler received his B.A. (*summa cum laude*) from the University of Louisville in 1967. Harvard University awarded him the Ph.D. in 1973. From 1984 to 1986 he was an Alexander von Humboldt Fellow at the Institut für Alte Geschichte, University of Munich. He has lectured at the Fondation Hardt at the University of Geneva, and has participated in numerous international conferences. He is currently the professor of Greek history at the University of Illinois. In 1980 Harvard University Press published his *The Theban Hegemony, 371–362 B.C.* He has also published *Philip II and the Sacred War* (Leiden 1989), and co-edited *BOIOTIKA: Vorträge vom 5. International Böotien-Kolloquium* (Munich 1989). He has assisted the National Endowment for the Humanities, and reviews articles for journals in the United States and Europe. He has published substantially on Plutarch in *Aufstieg und Niedergang der römischen Welt* (Berlin, New York. 1992). His articles have appeared in journals both here and abroad, including the *American Journal of History, Classical Philology, Rheinisches Museum für Philologie, Classical Quarterly, Wiener Studien, Symbolae Osloenses*, and many others.

Contents in Brief

Contents

❧ CHAPTER 13

❧ CHAPTER 14

Maps

Timelines/Genealogies

* The comparative timeline, *A History of World Societies: A Brief
Overview,* begins on page 770.

Listening to the Past

Preface

A History of World Societies has grown out of our desire to infuse new life into the study of world civilization. We know full well that historians are using imaginative questions and innovative research to open up vast new areas of historical interest and knowledge. We recognize that these advances have dramatically affected economic, intellectual, and, especially, social history, and that new research and fresh interpretations are revitalizing the study of traditional, mainstream political, diplomatic, and religious developments. Despite history's vitality as a discipline, however, it seems to us that both the broad public and the intelligentsia have been losing interest in the past.

It is our conviction, based on considerable experience in introducing large numbers of students to the broad sweep of civilization, that a book reflecting current trends can excite readers and inspire a renewed interest in history and the human experience. Our strategy has been twofold.

First, we have made social history the core element of our work. We not only incorporate recent research by social historians but also seek to re-create the life of ordinary people in appealing human terms. A strong social element seems especially appropriate in a world history, for identification with ordinary people of the past allows today's reader to reach an empathetic understanding of different cultures and civilizations. At the same time we have been mindful of the need to give great economic, political, intellectual, and cultural developments the attention they deserve. We want to give individual students and instructors a balanced, integrated perspective so that they can pursue on their own or in the classroom those themes and questions that they find particularly exciting and significant.

Second, we have made every effort to strike an effective global balance. We are acutely aware of the great drama of our times—the passing of the era of Western dominance and the simultaneous rise of Asian and African peoples in world affairs. Increasingly, the whole world interacts, and to understand that interaction and what it means for today's citizens, we must study the whole world's history. Thus we have adopted a comprehensive yet manageable global perspective. We study all geographical areas and the world's main civilizations, conscious of their separate identities and unique contributions. We also stress the links between civilizations, for it is these links that have been transforming multicentered world history into the complex interactive process of different continents, peoples, and cultures that we see today.

CHANGES IN THE FOURTH EDITION

In preparing the fourth edition, we worked hard to keep *A History of World Societies* up-to-date and to strengthen our distinctive yet balanced approach. Six goals shaped our plan for this new edition.

More Concise Treatment of Western History

To achieve the optimal length, we shortened the text by approximately 10 percent overall. We accomplished this reduction primarily through cuts in Western-oriented material while adding important new information to our non-Western coverage. Thus the proportion of non-Western material has grown, but the overall length of the book has decreased. For this edition, two chapters on Rome were combined into one (Chapter 7), three chapters on medieval Europe were combined into two (Chapters 12 and 13), and three chapters on nineteenth-century Europe were combined into two (Chapters 25 and 26).

Updated Approach to Social History

In a thorough revision of our coverage of social developments we give greater attention to cultural and intellectual life and somewhat less to quantitative and demographic aspects. Increased emphasis on culture and attitudes invigorates our social history core and accurately reflects current scholarship and changing interests within the historical profession. Accordingly, this edition has expanded discussions of religious life, including the spread of Buddhism in ancient India (Chapter 3); popular religion in Mesopotamia (Chapter 1), in classical Greece (Chapter 5), in Aztec and Inca society (Chapter 14), and in revolutionary France (Chapter 23); the evolution of Jewish religion (Chapter 2), of Eastern monasticism (Chapter 8), and of Calvin's Geneva (Chapter 15); and the resurgence of Christianity (Chapter 31) and of Islam (Chapter 34) in the twentieth century.

Consistently greater attention to popular culture includes new sections on the experiences of Jews under Islam and Christianity (Chapter 9); on the cult of the royal mummies in Inca society (Chapter 14); on troubadour poets and recreation in the Middle Ages (Chapters 12 and 13); on community values in eighteenth-century Europe (Chapter 19); on Chinese attitudes toward wealth and consumption (Chapter 22); and on the counterculture in the 1960s (Chapter 33). New material on health and health care features recent research on medieval European practices and early hospitals (Chapter 12), on eighteenth-century practitioners in Europe (Chapter 19) and the Ottoman Empire (Chapter 21), and on declining birthrates in Asia and Latin America (Chapter 36).

Interactions between cultures are also highlighted: the relations between Egyptians and Nubians (Chapter 1), pagans and Christians (Chapter 7), Muslims and Jews (Chapter 9), European educated elites and popular classes (Chapters 18 and 19), Europeans and Africans in the slave trade (Chapter 20), Chinese and foreigners in the eighteenth century (Chapter 22), and rich and poor nations since 1945 (Chapter 36).

We also carefully revised sections on the life of the people to set social developments consistently in their broad historical context.

Incorporation of Recent Scholarship

We carefully revised every chapter to reflect recent scholarship. Because we are committed to a balanced approach, we once again incorporated important new findings on political, economic, and intellectual developments. Revisions of this nature include material on the Babylonian Captivity (Chapter 2), the spread of Buddhism in India (Chapter 3), living patterns in neolithic China (Chapter 4), democratic ideology in Athens and the political background of Plato and Aristotle's thought (Chapter 5), and Roman commerce and frontier relations between Romans and Germans (Chapter 7). Similar revisions in Chapter 8 through 17 incorporate new material on Islamic education in world perspective (Chapter 9), African geography (Chapter 10), the origins of European feudalism (Chapter 12), the Aztec practice of human sacrifice (Chapter 14), the political uses of pornography in early modern Europe (Chapter 15), and Louis XIV's relations with the nobility (Chapter 17).

There is important new material reflecting recent scholarship on the cultural impact of the Enlightenment (Chapters 18 and 19); the Swahili states and transatlantic slave trade (Chapter 20); the institutions of the Mughal state under Akbar (Chapter 21); Chinese foreign policy under the Qing (Chapter 22); banks in continental industrialization and the early labor movement (Chapter 24); the role of class conflict in nineteenth-century domestic politics, imperialism, and the origins of World War I (Chapters 26, 27, and 29); educational reforms and political culture in republican France (Chapter 26); the idea of race in the United States (Chapter 28); Nietzsche and his influence (Chapter 31); the Nazi state and the origins of Italian fascism (Chapter 32); and the growing diversity of life in the Third World (Chapter 35). Recent developments in Europe and the Western Hemisphere (Chapter 33) and in Asia and Africa, especially in China and South Africa (Chapter 34), are examined from an updated post–cold war perspective.

In short, recent research keeps the broad sweep of our history fresh and up-to-date.

Integrated Treatment of Women and Gender

We broadened our treatment of women's history and gender issues and integrated it into the main narrative rather than reserving it for separate sections. This approach reflects current scholarly thinking. Our updated discussion of Hellenistic women is integrated in the central narrative (Chapter 5). Gender roles and attitudes toward divorce are considered in the context of early Islam (Chapter 9). New material on European women in agriculture and commerce during the Middle Ages (Chapters 12 and 13), on gender roles in Aztec society (Chapter 14) and in early European arts and letters (Chapter 16), on women in the Ottoman Empire (Chapter 21), and on Japanese women in agriculture and family relations (Chapter 22) are appropriately positioned. Elite women and peasant women in village communities are reconsidered in the context of the Enlightenment (Chapters 18 and 19) and the French Revolution (Chapter 23). Women in twentieth-century European dictatorships are compared systematically (Chapter 32), and the place of women in Third World economic development and population growth is stressed (Chapter 35).

New "Problems of Historical Interpretation"

The addition of more "problems of historical interpretation" in the third edition was well received, so we increased their number in the fourth. We believe that the problematic element helps students develop the critical-thinking skills that are among the most precious benefits of studying history. New examples of this more open-ended, interpretive approach include the debate over the origins of Rome (Chapter 7), the impact of the Renaissance on the lives of ordinary and elite women (Chapter 15), the motives and legacy of Christopher Columbus (Chapter 16), popular reading habits in eighteenth-century Europe and their significance (Chapter 19), the question of racial identity in the United States and how it developed (Chapter 28), European social tensions and the origins of World War I (Chapter 29), the nature of twentieth-century dictatorships (Chapter 32), the validity of *Third World* as an analytical concept (Chapter 35), and prospects for the United Nations and world government (Chapter 36).

Revised Full-Color Art and Map Programs

Because the past can speak in pictures as well as in words, artwork remains an integral part of our book, and the illustrative component of our work was carefully revised. We added many new illustrations—our art program includes nearly two hundred color reproductions—letting great art and important events come alive. As in earlier editions, all illustrations were carefully selected to complement the text, and all carry captions that enhance their value. The use of full color throughout this edition clarifies the maps and graphs and enriches the textual material. The maps and their captions have been updated.

DISTINCTIVE FEATURES

Distinctive features, both new and revised, guide the reader in the process of historical understanding. Many of these features also show how historians sift through and evaluate evidence. Our goal is to suggest how historians actually work and think. We want the reader to think critically and to realize that history is neither a list of cut-and-dried facts nor a senseless jumble of conflicting opinions.

New Primary-Source Chapter Feature

One of our goals is to show how historians sift through and evaluate evidence—to suggest how historians actually work and think. We want to encourage students to think critically and to realize that history is neither a list of cut-and-dried facts nor a senseless jumble of conflicting opinions. To help students come to this realization, at the end of each chapter in the fourth edition we added a two-page passage from a primary source. This important new feature, entitled "Listening to the Past," extends and illuminates a major historical issue considered in the chapter. For example, in Chapter 3, a selection from the *Mahabharta* tells an ancient Indian creation story; and in Chapter 6, a selection from *Plutarch's Lives* recounts the sacrifice of a famous queen for her people. Chapter 12 presents a mind-opening Arab account of the First Crusade, and the German traveler Olearius provides a fascinating and influential picture of the Russian state and society in Chapter 17. A report on discussions with Africans concerning the abolition of the slave trade is found in Chapter 20, and a Jesuit priest's report on a trip to the Mughal court of Akbar is featured in Chapter

21. Writer Stephan Zweig probes the sexuality of young men and women in nineteenth-century Vienna in Chapter 26, and a reporter witnesses the bloody climax to Gandhi's civil disobedience in Chapter 30. A Jewish doctor who survived Auschwitz describes the horror of the Nazi death camps in Chapter 32, and poor rural women in today's Third World tell their stories in Chapter 35.

Each "Listening to the Past" section opens with a problem-setting introduction and closes with "Questions for Analysis" that invite students to evaluate the evidence as historians would. Drawn from writings addressing a variety of social, cultural, political, and intellectual issues, these sources promote active involvement and critical interpretation. Selected for their interest and importance and carefully fitted into their historical context, these sources do indeed allow students to listen to the past and to observe how history has been shaped by individual men and women, some of them great aristocrats, others ordinary folk.

Improved Chapter Features

Distinctive features from earlier editions have been retained but improved. To help guide students toward historical understanding, we again pose specific questions at the beginning of each chapter. These questions are answered in the course of each chapter, and each chapter ends with a concise summary. We re-examined and revised the questions and summaries to maximize their usefulness.

Once again in the narrative itself we quote extensively from a wide variety of primary sources, demonstrating in our use of these quotations how historians evaluate evidence. Thus the examination of primary sources is not only highlighted in the "Listening to the Past" material but is an integral part of the narrative as well. We believe that such extensive quotation from primary sources will help students learn to interpret and think critically.

Each chapter again contains an annotated listing of suggestions for further reading. Brief descriptions of each work will help readers know where to turn to continue thinking and learning about specific topics. These bibliographies have been revised and updated.

Revised Timelines

The chapter timelines that appeared in earlier editions are substantially improved, and the comparative timelines that were dispersed throughout the third edition have been brought together in an appendix at the end of the book. Comprehensive and easy to locate, this useful timeline will allow students to compare simultaneous political, economic, social, cultural, intellectual, and scientific developments over the centuries.

Flexible Format

World history courses differ widely in chronological structure from one campus to another. To accommodate the various divisions of historical time into intervals that fit a two-quarter, three-quarter, or two-semester period, *A History of World Societies* is published in three versions that embrace the complete work:

- One-volume hardcover edition: *A History of World Societies*
- Two-volume paperback edition: *A History of World Societies*, Volume 1, *To 1715* (Chapters 1–17), and Volume 2, *Since 1500* (Chapters 16–36)
- Three-volume paperback edition: *A History of World Societies*, Volume A, *From Antiquity Through the Middle Ages* (Chapters 1–14), Volume B, *From 1100 Through the French Revolution* (Chapters 13–23), and Volume C, *From the French Revolution to the Present* (Chapters 23–36)

Overlapping chapters in the two-volume and three-volume editions facilitate matching the appropriate volume with the opening and closing dates of a specific course.

ANCILLARIES

Our learning and teaching ancillaries enhance the usefulness of the textbook:

- *Study Guide*
- *Computerized Study Guide*
- *Instructor's Resource Manual*
- *Test Items*
- *Computerized Test Items*
- *Map Transparencies*

The excellent *Study Guide* has been thoroughly revised by Professor James Schmiechen of Central Michigan University. Professor Schmiechen has been a tower of strength ever since he critiqued our initial prospectus, and he has continued to give us many valuable suggestions as well as his warmly appreciated support. His *Study Guide* contains learning objectives, chapter summaries, chapter outlines, review questions, extensive multiple-choice exercises, self-check lists of important concepts and events, and a variety of study aids and suggestions. The fourth edition also retains the study-review exercises on the interpretation of visual sources and major political ideas as well as suggested issues for discussion and essay, chronology reviews, and sections on studying effectively. The sections on studying take the student through reading and studying activities like underlining, summarizing, identifying main points, classifying information according to sequence, and making historical comparisons. To enable both students and instructors to use the *Study Guide* with the greatest possible flexibility, the guide is available in two volumes, with considerable overlapping of chapters. Instructors and students who use only Volumes A and B of the textbook have all the pertinent study materials in a single volume: *Study Guide,* Volume 1 (Chapters 1–23). Those who use only Volumes B and C of the textbook also have all the necessary materials in one volume: *Study Guide*, Volume 2 (Chapters 13–36). The multiple-choice sections of the *Study Guide* are available in a *Computerized Study Guide*, a tutorial version that tells students not only which response is correct but also why each of the other choices is wrong; it also provides the number of the textbook page where each question is discussed. These "rejoinders" to the multiple-choice questions also appear in printed form at the end of the *Study Guide*. The *Computerized Study Guide* is available for IBM® computers.

The *Instructor's Resource Manual*, prepared by John Marshall Carter, contains instructional objectives, annotated chapter outlines, suggestions for lectures and discussion, paper and class activity topics, primary-source exercises, map activities, and lists of audio-visual resources. The accompanying *Test Items*, by Professor Charles Crouch of Georgia Southern University, offer identification, multiple-choice, map, and essay questions for a total of approximately 2,000 test items. These test items are available to adopters in both IBM® and Macintosh versions, both of which include editing capabilities.

In addition, a set of full-color *Map Transparencies* of all the maps in the textbook is available on adoption.

Acknowledgments

It is a pleasure to thank the many instructors who have read and critiqued the manuscript through its development.

Eva Baham
Southern University

Lester Bilsky
University of Arkansas, Little Rock

Kenneth Capalbo
Quincy University

Donald Clark
Trinity University

Frank Coppa
St. John's University

Francis Danquah
Southern University

Gloria-Thomas Emeagwali
Central Connecticut State University

Fuabeh Fonge
North Carolina Agricultural and Technical State University

Bruce Garver
University of Nebraska, Omaha

Ruth Hertzberg
Shippensburg University

Ahmed Ibriham
University of South Carolina

Michelle Scott James
MiraCosta College

Delmarie Klobe
Kapiolani Community College

David Kopf
University of Minnesota

Jim Norris
University of Arkansas, Monticello

Evelyn Rawski
University of Pittsburgh

Edward Reynolds
University of California, San Diego

Leila el-Tawil Sarieddine
Southern University

Cynthia Talbott
University of Northern Arizona

Colonel Steven Wager
United States Military Academy, West Point

Mary Watrous
Washington State University

Colonel James Scott Wheeler
United States Military Academy, West Point

Barbara Woods
South Carolina State University

It is also a pleasure to thank our editors at Houghton Mifflin for their effort and support over many years. To Elizabeth Welch, Senior Basic Book Editor, we owe a special debt of gratitude and admiration. To Jean Woy, Editor-in-Chief for History and Political Science, to Sean Wakely, Senior Sponsoring Editor, and to Jeff Greene, Senior Associate Editor, we express our sincere appreciation. And we thank most warmly Jan Fitter, Leslie Anderson Olney, and Carole Frohlich for their contributions in development, production, and art and photo research.

Many of our colleagues at the University of Illinois continued to provide information and stimulation for our book, often without even knowing it. N. Frederick Nash, Rare Book Librarian, made many helpful suggestions for illustrations, and the World Heritage Museum at the university allowed us complete access to its sizable holdings. James Dengate supplied information on objects from the museum's collection, and Caroline Buckler took many excellent photographs of the museum's objects. Such wide-ranging expertise was a great asset for which we are very appreciative. Bennett Hill wishes to express his sincere appreciation to Ramón de la Fuente for his patience, encouragement, and research assistance in the preparation of the fourth edition.

Each of us has benefited from the generous criticism of his co-authors, although each of us assumes responsibility for what he has written. John Buckler is the author of Chapters 1–7 and 11; Bennett Hill continues the narrative in Chapters 8–10, 12–16, 20–22, and 28; and John McKay is the author of Chapters 17–19, 23–27, and 29–36. Finally, we continue to welcome the many comments and suggestions that have come from our readers, for they have helped us greatly in this ongoing endeavor.

J.P.M.   B.D.H.   J.B.

CHAPTER

13

Creativity and Crisis in the Central and Later Middle Ages

Miniature of King
Charles VII presiding at
the trial of the Duc
d'Alençon. *(Source: Bay-
erische Staatsbibliothek,
Munich)*

The central Middle Ages witnessed some of the most remarkable achievements in the history of the Western world. Europeans displayed tremendous creativity in many facets of culture. The university, a unique Western contribution to civilization, came into being. The Gothic cathedral manifested medieval people's deep Christian faith, their sense of community, and their appreciation of the worlds of nature, humanity, and God.

In the medieval world, the nobility fought, the clergy prayed, and the peasantry worked to produce the food on which all depended. The lives of the vast majority of ordinary people continued to be conditioned by their local geography, climate, religion, and parish. For the peasantry, considerable social mobility existed in the central Middle Ages. Then, between 1300 and 1450, Europeans experienced a series of frightful shocks: economic dislocation, plague, war, and social upheaval. The last book of the New Testament—the Book of Revelation, dealing with visions of the end of the world, disease, war, famine, and death—inspired thousands of sermons and religious tracts. Death and preoccupation with death make the fourteenth century one of the most wrenching periods of Western civilization.

The progression from the vitality and creativity of the central Middle Ages to the crises of the later Middle Ages brings to mind a number of questions:

- How did the universities, the Gothic cathedrals, and troubadour poetry evolve, and what do they reveal about medieval ideals and society?
- How did people actually live, and what were their major preoccupations and lifestyles?
- What were the social and psychological effects of economic difficulties, disease, and war in the later Middle Ages?
- What impact did schism in the Christian church have on the lives of ordinary people?
- What political and social factors were reflected in the development of national literatures and in the expansion of literacy?

These are among the questions this chapter will explore.

MEDIEVAL UNIVERSITIES

Just as the first strong secular states emerged in the thirteenth century, so did the first universities. This was no coincidence. The new bureaucratic states and the church needed educated administrators, and universities were a response to this need.

Since the time of the Carolingian Empire, monasteries and cathedral schools had offered the only formal instruction available. Monasteries were geared to religious concerns. They wished to maintain an atmosphere of seclusion and silence and were unwilling to accept large numbers of noisy lay students. In contrast, schools attached to cathedrals and run by the bishop and his clergy were frequently situated in bustling cities, and in the eleventh century in Bologna and other Italian cities wealthy businessmen established municipal schools. Inhabited by peoples of many backgrounds and "nationalities," cities stimulated the growth and exchange of ideas. In the course of the twelfth century, cathedral schools in France and municipal schools in Italy developed into universities.

The growth of the University of Bologna coincided with a revival of interest in Roman law. The study of Roman law as embodied in Justinian's *Code* had never completely died out in the West, but this sudden burst of interest seems to have been inspired by Irnerius (d. 1125), a great teacher at Bologna. His fame attracted students from all over Europe. Irnerius not only explained the Roman law of Justinian's *Code* but applied it to difficult practical situations. An important school of civil law was founded at Montpellier in France, but Bologna remained the greatest law school throughout the Middle Ages.

At Salerno, interest in medicine had persisted for centuries. Greek and Muslim physicians there had studied the use of herbs as cures and experimented with surgery. The twelfth century ushered in a new interest in Greek medical texts and in the work of Arab and Greek doctors. Students of medicine poured into Salerno and soon attracted royal attention. In 1140, when King Roger II (r. 1130–1154) of Sicily took the practice of medicine under royal control, his ordinance stated:

Who, from now on, wishes to practice medicine, has to present himself before our officials and examiners, in order to pass their judgment. Should he be bold enough to disregard this, he will be punished by imprisonment and confiscation of his entire property. In this way we are taking care that our subjects are not endangered by the inexperience of the physicians.[1]

In the first decades of the twelfth century, students converged on Paris. They crowded into the cathedral school of Notre Dame and spilled over into the area later called the Latin Quarter—whose name probably reflects the Italian origin of many of the students. The cathedral school's international reputation had already drawn to Paris scholars from all over Europe. One of the most famous of them was Peter Abélard.

The son of a minor Breton knight, Peter Abélard (1079–1142) studied in Paris, quickly absorbed a large amount of material, and set himself up as a teacher. Fascinated by logic, which he believed could be used to solve most problems, Abélard used a method of systematic doubting in his writing and teaching. As he put it, "By doubting we come to questioning, and by questioning we perceive the truth." Other scholars merely asserted theological principles; Abélard discussed and analyzed them.

The influx of students eager for learning and the presence of dedicated and imaginative teachers created the atmosphere in which universities grew. In northern Europe—at Paris and later at Oxford and Cambridge in England—associations or guilds of professors organized universities. They established the curriculum, set the length of time for study, and determined the form and content of examinations. University faculties grouped themselves according to academic disciplines, or schools—law, medicine, arts, and theology. The professors, known as "Schoolmen" or "Scholastics," developed a method of thinking, reasoning, and writing in which questions were raised and authorities cited on both sides of a question. The goal of the Scholastic method was to arrive at definitive answers and to provide a rational explanation for what was believed on faith.

The Scholastic approach rested on the recovery of classical philosophical texts and on ancient Greek and Arabic texts that had entered Europe in the early twelfth century. Thirteenth-century philosophers relied on Latin translations of these texts, especially translations of Aristotle. The Scholastics reinterpreted Aristotelian texts in a Christian sense.

In exploration of the natural world, Aristotle's axioms were not precisely followed. Medieval scientists argued from authority, such as the Bible, Justinian's *Code,* or ancient scientific treatises, rather than from direct observation and experimentation, as modern scientists do. Thus the conclusions of medieval scientists were often wrong. Nevertheless, natural science gradually emerged as a discipline distinct from philosophy.

Many of the problems that Scholastic philosophers raised dealt with theological issues. For example, they addressed the question that interested all Christians, educated and uneducated: How is a person saved? Saint Augustine's thesis—that, as a result of Adam's fall, human beings have a propensity to sin—had become a central feature of medieval church doctrine. The church taught that it possessed the means to forgive the sinful: grace conveyed through the sacraments. The Scholastics held that one must also *decide* to use the grace received. In other words, a person must use his or her reason to advance to God.

Thirteenth-century Scholastics devoted an enormous amount of time to collecting and organizing knowledge on all topics. These collections were published as *summa,* or reference books. There were summa on law, philosophy, vegetation, animal life, and theology. Saint Thomas Aquinas (1225–1274), a professor at Paris, produced the most famous collection, the *Summa Theologica,* which deals with a vast number of theological questions.

Aquinas drew an important distinction between faith and reason. He maintained that, although reason can demonstrate many basic Christian principles such as the existence of God, other fundamental teachings such as the Trinity and original sin cannot be proved by logic. That reason cannot establish them does not, however, mean they are contrary to reason. Rather, people understand such doctrines through revelation embodied in Scripture. Scripture cannot contradict reason, nor reason Scripture:

The light of faith that is freely infused into us does not destroy the light of natural knowledge [reason] implanted in us naturally. For although the natural light of the human mind is insufficient to show us these things made manifest by faith, it is nevertheless impossible that these things which the divine principle gives us by faith are contrary to these implanted in us by nature [reason]. Indeed, were that the case, one or the other would have to be false, and, since both are given to us by God, God would have to be the author of untruth, which is impossible.[2]

Thomas Aquinas and all medieval intellectuals held that the end of both faith and reason was the knowledge of, and union with, God. His work later became the fundamental text of Roman Catholic doctrine.

At all universities, the standard method of teaching was the *lecture*—that is, a reading. The professor read a passage from the Bible, Justinian's *Code,* or one of Aristotle's treatises. He then explained and interpreted the passage; his interpretation was called a *gloss.* Students wrote down everything. Because books had to be copied by hand, they were extremely expensive, and few students could afford them. Students therefore depended for study on their own or on friends' notes accumulated over a period of years. Examinations were given after three, four, or five years of study, when the student applied for a degree. The professors determined the amount of material students had to know for each degree, and students frequently insisted that the professors specify precisely what that material was. Examinations were oral and very difficult. If the candidate passed, he was awarded the first, or bachelor's, degree. Further study, about as long, arduous, and expensive as it is today, enabled the graduate to try for the master's and doctor's degrees. Degrees were technically licenses to teach. Most students, however, did not become teachers. They staffed the expanding royal and papal administrations.

✣ FROM ROMANESQUE GLOOM TO "UNINTERRUPTED LIGHT"

It is difficult for twentieth-century people to appreciate the extraordinary amounts of energy, imagination, and money involved in building medieval churches. Between 1180 and 1270 in France alone, eighty cathedrals, about five hundred abbey churches, and tens of thousands of parish churches were constructed. This construction represents a remarkable investment for a country of scarcely 18 million people. More stone was quarried for churches in medieval France than had been mined in ancient Egypt, where the Great Pyramid alone consumed 40.5 million cubic feet of stone. All these churches displayed a new architectual style. Fifteenth-century critics called the new style

Gothic because they mistakenly believed the fifth-century Goths had invented it. It actually developed partly in reaction to the earlier Romanesque style, which resembled ancient Roman architecture.

The manner in which a society spends its wealth expresses its values. Cathedrals, abbeys, and village churches testify to the deep religious faith and piety of medieval people. If the dominant aspect of medieval culture had not been the Christian faith, the builder's imagination and the merchant's money would have been used in other ways.

✣ **Interior of La Sainte Chapelle, Paris**   The central features of the Gothic style—pointed arch, ribbed vaulting, and flying buttress—made possible the construction of churches higher than ever before and the use of stained glass to replace stone walls. King Louis IX built this church to house the crown of thorns and other relics that he brought back from the Crusades. The result is a building of breathtaking beauty, a jeweled reliquary. *(Source: Art Resource, NY)*

In the ninth and tenth centuries, the Vikings and Magyars had burned hundreds of wooden churches. In the eleventh century, the abbots wanted to rebuild in a more permanent fashion, and after the year 1000, church building increased on a wide scale. Because fireproofing was essential, ceilings had to be made of stone. Therefore, builders replaced wooden roofs with arched stone ceilings called vaults. The stone ceilings were heavy; only thick walls would support them. Because the walls were so thick, the windows were small, allowing little light into the interior of the church. In northern Europe, twin bell towers often crowned these Romanesque churches, giving them a powerful, fortresslike appearance. Built primarily by monasteries, Romanesque churches reflect the quasi-military, aristocratic, and pre-urban society that built them.

The inspiration for the Gothic style originated in the brain of one monk, Suger, abbot of Saint-Denis (1122–1151). When Suger became abbot, he decided to reconstruct the old Carolingian abbey church at Saint-Denis. Work began in 1137. On June 11, 1144, King Louis VII and a large crowd of bishops, dignitaries, and common people witnessed the solemn consecration of the first Gothic church in France.

Not unknown before 1137, the basic features of Gothic architecture—the pointed arch, the ribbed vault, and the flying buttress—allowed unprecedented interior lightness. Since the ceiling of a Gothic church weighed less than that of a Romanesque church, the walls could be thinner. Stained-glass windows were cut into the stone, flooding the church with light. The interior, Suger exulted, "would shine with the wonderful and uninterrupted light of most sacred windows, pervading the interior beauty."[3]

Begun in the Île-de-France, Gothic architecture spread throughout France with the expansion of royal power. French architects were soon invited to design and supervise the construction of churches in other parts of Europe, and the new style traveled rapidly.

The construction of a Gothic cathedral represented a gigantic investment of time, money, and corporate effort. The bishop and the clergy of the cathedral made the decision to build, but they depended on the support of all social classes. Bishops raised revenue from contributions by people in their dioceses, and the clergy appealed to the king

and the nobility. Above all, the church relied on the financial help of those with the greatest amount of ready cash, the commercial classes.

Money was not the only need. A great number of craftsmen had to be assembled: quarrymen, sculptors, stonecutters, masons, mortar makers, carpenters, blacksmiths, glassmakers, roofers. Unskilled laborers had to be recruited for the heavy work. The construction of a large cathedral was rarely completed in one lifetime; many cathedrals were never finished at all. Because generation after generation added to the building, many Gothic churches show the architectural influences of two or even three centuries.

Towns competed to build the largest and most splendid church. In northern France in the late twelfth and early thirteenth centuries, cathedrals grew progressively taller. The people of Beauvais exceeded everyone: their church, started in 1247, reached 157 feet. Unfortunately, the weight imposed on the vaults was too great, and the building collapsed in 1284. Medieval people built cathedrals to glorify God—and if mortals were impressed, so much the better.[4]

Cathedrals served secular as well as religious purposes. The sanctuary containing the altar and the bishop's chair belonged to the clergy, but the rest of the church belonged to the people. In addition to marriages, baptisms, and funerals, there were scores of feast days on which the entire town gathered in the cathedral for festivities. Local guilds met in the cathedrals to arrange business deals, plan recreational events and the support of disabled members. Magistrates and municipal officials held political meetings there. Pilgrims slept there, lovers courted there, and traveling actors staged plays there. The cathedral belonged to all.

First and foremost, however, the cathedral was intended to teach the people the doctrines of Christian faith through visual images. Architecture became the servant of theology. The west front of the cathedral faced the setting sun, and its wall was usually devoted to the scenes of the Last Judgment. The north side, which received the least sunlight, displayed events from the Old Testament. The south side, washed in warm sunshine for much of the day, depicted scenes from the New Testament. This symbolism implied that the Jewish people of the Old Testament lived in darkness and that the Gospel brought by Christ illuminated the world. Every piece of sculpture, furniture, and stained glass had some religious or social significance.

Stained glass beautifully reflects the creative energy of the central Middle Ages. It is both an integral part of Gothic architecture and a distinct form of painting. The glassmaker "painted" the picture with small fragments of glass held together with strips of lead. As Gothic churches became more skeletal and had more windows, stained glass replaced manuscript illumination as the leading kind of painting. Thousands of scenes in the cathedral celebrate nature, country life, and the activities of ordinary people. All members of medieval society had a place in the City of God, which the Gothic cathedral represented.

The drama, derived from the church's liturgy, emerged as a distinct art form during the same period. For centuries, skits based on Christ's Nativity and Resurrection had been performed in monasteries and cathedrals. Beginning in the thirteenth century, plays based on these and other biblical themes and on the lives of the saints were performed in the towns. Guilds financed these "mystery plays"—so called because they were based on the mysteries of the Christian faith. Performed first at the cathedral altar, then in the church square, and later in the town marketplace, mystery plays enjoyed great popularity. By combining comical farce based on ordinary life with serious religious scenes, they allowed the common people to understand and identify with religious figures and the mysteries of their faith.

❖ TROUBADOUR POETRY

In the twelfth and thirteenth centuries a remarkable literary culture blossomed in southern France. The word *troubadour* comes from the Provençal word *trobar*, which in turn derives from the Arabic *taraba*, meaning "to sing" or "to sing poetry." A troubadour was a poet of Provence who wrote lyric verse in his or her native language and sang it at one of the noble courts. Troubadour songs had a variety of themes. Men sang about "courtly love," the pure love a knight felt for his lady, whom he sought to win by military prowess and patience; about the love a knight felt for the wife of his feudal lord; or about carnal desires seeking satisfac-

tion. Women troubadours *(trobairitz)* focused on their emotions, their intimate feelings, or their experiences with men. Some poems exalted the married state, and others idealized adulterous relationships; some were earthy and bawdy, and others advised young girls to remain chaste in preparation for marriage. Many poems celebrate the beauties of nature; a few speak of the sexual frustrations of nuns. The married Countess Beatrice of Dia (1150–1200?) expresses the hurt she feels after being jilted by a young knight:

I've suffered great distress
From a knight whom I once owned.
Now, for all time, be it known:
I loved him-yes, to excess.
    His jilting I've regretted,
Yet his love I never really returned.
Now for my sin I can only burn:
    Dressed, or in my bed.

O if I had that knight to caress
Naked all night in my arms,
He'd be ravished by the charm
Of using, for cushion, my breast.
    His love I more deeply prize
Than Floris did Blancheflor's
Take that love, my core,
    My sense, my life, my eyes!

Lovely lover, gracious, kind,
When will I overcome your fight?
O if I could lie with you one night!
Feel those loving lips on mine!
    Listen, one thing sets me afire:
Here in my husband's place I want you,
If you'll just keep your promise true:
    Give me everything I desire.[5]

Because of its varied and contradictory themes, courtly love has been one of the most hotly debated topics in all medieval studies. One scholar concludes that it was at once "a literary movement, an ideology, an ethical system, an expression of the play element in culture, which arose in an aristocratic Christian environment exposed to Hispano-Arabic influences."[6] Another scholar insists there is no evidence for the practice of courtly love. If, however, the knight's love represented the respect of a vassal for his lady, a respect that inspired him to noble deeds, then perhaps courtly love contributed to an improvement in the status of women.

Troubadours certainly felt Hispano-Arabic influences. In the eleventh century, Christians of southern France were in intimate contact with the Arabized world of Andalusia, where reverence for the lady in a "courtly" tradition had long existed. In 1064 the Provençal lord Guillaume de Montreuil captured Barbastro and, according to legend, took a thousand slave girls from Andalusia back to Provence. Even if this figure is an exaggeration, those women who came to southern France would have been familiar with the Arabic tradition of sung poetry and continued it in their new land. Troubadour poetry thus represents another facet of the strong Muslim influence on European culture and life.[7]

The romantic motifs of the troubadours also influenced the northern French *trouvères,* who wrote adventure-romances in the form of epic poems. At the court of his patron Marie of Champagne, Chrétien de Troyes (ca 1135–1183) used the legends of the fifth-century British king Arthur to discuss contemporary chivalric ideals and their moral implications. Such poems as *Lancelot, Percival and the Holy Grail,* and *Tristan and Isolde* reveal Chrétien as the founding father of the Western romantic genre. The theme of these romances centers on the knight-errant who seeks adventures and who, when faced with crises usually precipitated by love, acquires new values and grows in wisdom.

The songs of the troubadours and trouvères were widely imitated in Italy, England, and Germany, and they spurred the development of vernacular languages (see pages 432–433). Most of the troubadours and trouvères came from and wrote for the aristocratic classes, and their poetry suggests the interests and values of noble culture in the central Middle Ages.

LIFE IN CHRISTIAN EUROPE IN THE CENTRAL MIDDLE AGES

In the late ninth century, medieval intellectuals described Christian society as composed of those who pray (the monks), those who fight (the nobles), and those who work (the peasants). According to this image of social structure, function determined social classification.[8] Reality, however, was somewhat different. In the eleventh and twelfth centuries, most clerics and monks descended from the noble class and retained aristocratic attitudes and values, and the lay brothers who did most of the agricultural labor on monastic estates came from the peasant classes. The division of society into fighters, monks, and peasants also presents too static a view of a world in which there was considerable social mobility. Moreover, such a social scheme does not take into consideration townspeople and the emerging commercial classes. That omission, however, is easy to understand. Traders and other city dwellers were not typical members of medieval society. Medieval people were usually contemptuous (at least officially) of profit-making activities, and even after the appearance of urban commercial groups, the ideological view of medieval Christian society remained the one formulated in the ninth century: the three-part division among peasants, nobles, and monks.

Those Who Work

According to one modern scholar, "Peasants were rural dwellers who possess (if they do not own) the means of agricultural production."[9] Some peasants worked continuously on the land. Others supplemented their ordinary work as brewers, carpenters, tailors, or housemaids with wage labor in the field. In either case, all peasants supported lords, clergy, townspeople, as well as themselves. The men and women who worked the land in the twelfth and thirteenth centuries made up the overwhelming majority of the population, probably more than 90 percent. Yet it is difficult to form a coherent picture of them. The records that serve as historical sources were written by and for the aristocratic classes.

It is important to remember that peasants' conditions varied widely across Europe and that geography and climate as much as human initiative and local custom determined the peculiar quality of rural life.[10] The problems that faced the farmer in Yorkshire, England, where the soil was rocky and the weather rainy, were very different from those of the Italian peasant in the sun-drenched Po Valley.

Another obstacle to the creation of a coherent picture of the peasants has been historians' tendency to group all peasants into one social class. Although medieval theologians lumped everyone who worked the land into the "those who work" category, there were many kinds of peasants— ranging from complete slaves to free and very rich

The Three Classes Medieval people believed that their society was divided among clerics, warriors, and workers, here represented by a monk, a knight, and a peasant. The new commercial class had no recognized place in the agrarian military world. (*Source: The British Library*)

farmers. The status of the peasantry fluctuated widely all across Europe. The period from 1050 to 1250 was one of considerable social mobility.

Slaves were found in western Europe in the central Middle Ages, but in steadily declining numbers. That the word *slave* derives from *Slav* attests to the widespread trade in men and women from the Slavic areas in the Middle Ages. Around the year 1200, there were in aristocratic and upper-middle-class households in Provence, Catalonia, Italy, and Germany a few slaves—blond Slavs from the Baltic, olive-skinned Syrians, and blacks from Africa. Legal language differed considerably from place to place,

and the distinction between slave and serf was not always clear. Both lacked freedom—the power to do as one wished—and both were subject to the arbitrary will of one person, the lord. A serf, however, could not be bought and sold like an animal or an inanimate object, as the slave could.

The serf was required to perform labor services on the lord's land. The number of workdays varied, but it was usually three days a week except in the planting or harvest seasons, when it increased. Serfs frequently had to pay arbitrary levies, as for marriage or inheritance (see page 355). The precise amounts of tax paid to the lord depended on local custom and tradition. A free person had to do none of these things. For his or her landholding, rent had to be paid to the lord, and that was often the sole obligation. A free person could move and live as he or she wished.

Serfs were tied to the land, and serfdom was a hereditary condition. A person born a serf was likely to die a serf, though many did secure their freedom. About 1187 Glanvill, an official of King Henry II and an expert on English law, described how *villeins* (literally, "inhabitants of small villages")—as English serfs were called—could be made free:

A person of villein status can be made free in several ways. For example, his lord, wishing him to achieve freedom from the villeinage by which he is subject to him, may quit-claim [release] him from himself and his heirs; or he may give or sell him to another with intent to free him. . . . No person of villein status can seek his freedom with his own money, . . . because all the chattels of a villein are deemed to be the property of his lord that he cannot redeem himself from villeinage with his own money, as against his lord. If, however, a third party provides the money and buys the villein in order to free him, then he can maintain himself for ever in a state of freedom as against his lord who sold him. . . . If any villein stays peaceably for a year and a day in a privileged town and is admitted as a citizen into their commune, that is to say, their gild, he is thereby freed from villeinage.[11]

Thus, with the advent of a money economy, serfs could save money and, through a third-person intermediary, buy their freedom.

The economic revival that began in the eleventh century (see pages 380–386) advanced the cause of individual liberty. Hundreds of new towns arose in Ireland, in Mecklenburg and Pomerania in northeastern Germany, and in reconquest Spain; their settlers often came from long distances. Some colonial towns were the offspring of colonial traders. For example, Venetian and Genoese merchants founded in the Crimean region trading posts that served as entrepôts on the routes to China. The thirteenth century witnessed enormous immigration to many parts of Europe that previously had been sparsely settled. Immigration and colonization provided the opportunity for freedom and social mobility.[12]

Another opportunity for increased personal freedom, or at least for a reduction in traditional manorial obligations and dues, was provided by the reclamation of waste and forest land in the eleventh and twelfth centuries. Marshes and fens were drained and slowly made arable. This type of agricultural advancement frequently improved the peasants' social and legal condition. A serf could clear a patch of fen or forest land, make it productive, and, through prudent saving, buy more land and eventually purchase freedom. Settlers on the lowlands of the abbey of Bourbourg in Flanders, who had erected dikes and extended the arable land, possessed hereditary tenures by 1159. They secured personal liberty and owed their overlord only small payments.

In the thirteenth century, the noble class frequently needed money to finance crusading, building, or other projects. For example, in 1240 when Geoffrey de Montigny became abbot of Saint-Pierre-le-Vif in the Senonais region of France, he found the abbey church in bad disrepair and needed revenues to rebuild it. Geoffrey also discovered that the descendants of families who had once owed the abbey servile obligations now refused to recognize their bondage. Some of these peasants had grown wealthy. When the abbot determined to reclaim these peasants in order to get the revenues to rebuild his church, a legal struggle ensued. In 1257 a compromise was worked out whereby Geoffrey manumitted 366 persons who in turn agreed to pay him £500 a year over a twelve-year period.[13]

In the central Middle Ages, most European peasants, free and unfree, lived on a *manor,* the estate of a lord. The manor was the basic unit of medieval rural organization and the center of rural life. All other generalizations about manors and manorial life have to be limited by variations in the quality of the soil, local climatic conditions, and methods of cultivation. Manors varied from several thousand acres to as little as 120 acres. Recent archaeological evidence suggests that a manor might include several villages, one village whose produce was divided among several lords, or an isolated homestead.

The arable land of the manor was divided into two sections. The *demesne,* or home farm, was cultivated by the peasants for the lord. The other, usually larger section was held by the peasantry. All the arable land, both the lord's and the peasants', was divided into strips, and the strips belonging to any given individual were scattered throughout the manor. All peasants cooperated in the cultivation of the land, working it as a group. All shared in any disaster as well as in any large harvest.

A manor usually held pasture or meadowland for the grazing of cattle, sheep, and sometimes goats. Often the manor had some forest land as well. Forests had enormous economic importance. They were the source of wood for building and fuel, resin for lighting, ash for candles, and ash and lime for fertilizers and all sorts of sterilizing products. The forests were used for feeding pigs, cattle, and domestic animals on nuts, roots, and wild berries.

The fundamental objective of all medieval agriculture was the production of an adequate food supply. Using the method that historians have called the *open-field system,* peasants divided the arable land of a manor into two or three fields without hedges or fences to mark the individual holdings of the lord, serfs, and freemen. Beginning in the eleventh century in parts of France, England, and Germany, peasants divided all the arable land into three large fields. In any one year, two of the fields were cultivated and one lay fallow. One part of the land was sown with winter cereals such as rye and wheat, the other with spring crops such as peas, beans, and barley. Each year the crop was rotated. Local needs, the fertility of the soil, and dietary customs determined what was planted and the method of crop rotation.

In the early twelfth century, the production of iron increased greatly. In the thirteenth century, the wooden plow continued to be the basic instrument of agricultural production, but its edge was strengthened with iron. Only after the start of the fourteenth century, when lists of manorial equipment began to be kept, is there evidence for pitchforks, spades, axes, and harrows.

The plow and the harrow (a cultivating instrument with heavy teeth that breaks up and smoothes the soil) were increasingly drawn by horses. The development of the padded horse collar, resting on the horse's shoulders and attached to the load by shafts, led to an agricultural revolution. The horse collar let the animal put its entire weight into the task of pulling. In the twelfth century, the use of horses, rather than oxen, spread because horses' greater strength brought greater efficiency to farming. Horses, however, were an enormous investment, perhaps comparable to a modern tractor. They had to be shod (another indication of increased iron production), and the oats they ate were costly. Although horses represent a crucial element in the improvement of husbandry, students of medieval agriculture are not sure whether the greater use of horses increased crop yields.

The thirteenth century witnessed a tremendous spurt in the use of horses to haul carts to market. Large and small farmers increasingly relied on horses to pull wagons because they could travel much faster than oxen. Consequently, goods

Boarstall Manor, Buckinghamshire In 1440, Edmund Rede, lord of this estate, had a map made showing his ancestor receiving the title from King Edward I (lower field). Notice the manor house, church, and peasants' cottages along the central road. In the common fields, divided by hedges, peasants cultivated on a three-year rotation cycle— winter wheat, spring oats, and fallow. Peasants' pigs grazed freely in the woods, indicated by trees. We don't know whether the peasants could hunt the deer. *(Source: Buckinghamshire Record Office, Aylesbury)*

reached a market faster, and the number of markets within an area to which the peasant had access increased. The opportunities and temptations for consumer spending on nonagricultural goods multiplied.[14]

Agricultural yields varied widely from place to place and from year to year. By twentieth-century standards, they were very low. Inadequate soil preparation, poor seed selection, lack of manure—all made low yields virtually inevitable. And, like farmers of all times and places, medieval peasants were at the mercy of the weather. Yet there was striking improvement over time. Researchers have tentatively concluded that between the ninth and early thirteenth centuries, yields of cereals approximately doubled, and on the best-managed estates farmers harvested five bushels of grain for every bushel of seed planted. Grain yields were probably greatest on large manorial estates, where there was more professional management.

A modern Illinois farmer expects to get 40 bushels of soybeans, 150 bushels of corn, and 50 bushels of wheat for every bushel of seeds planted. Of course, modern costs of production in labor, seed, and fertilizer are quite high, but this yield is at least ten times that of the farmer's medieval ancestor. Some manors may have achieved a yield of 12 or even 15 to 1, but the *average* manor probably got a yield of only 5 to 1 in the thirteenth century.[15]

Life on the Manor   For most people in medieval Europe, life meant country life. A person's horizons were not likely to extend beyond the manor on which he or she was born. True, peasants who colonized sparsely settled regions such as eastern Germany must have traveled long distances. But most people rarely traveled more than twenty-five miles beyond their villages. Their world was small, narrow, and provincial in the original sense of the

 Late Medieval Wheelless Plow   The sharp-pointed colter of this plow cut the earth while the attached moldboard lifted, turned, and pulverized the soil. As the man steers the plow, his wife prods the oxen. The caption reads, "God speed the plow, and send us corn [wheat] enough." *(Source: Trinity College Library, Cambridge)*

word: limited by the boundaries of the province. This way of life did not have entirely unfortunate results. A farmer had a strong sense of family and the certainty of its support and help in time of trouble. People knew what their life's work would be—the same as their mother's or father's. They had a sense of place, and pride in that place was reflected in adornment of the village church. Religion and the village gave people a sure sense of identity and with it psychological peace. Modern people—urban, isolated, industrialized, rootless, and thoroughly secularized—have lost many of these reinforcements.

But, even aside from the unending physical labor, life on the manor was dull. Medieval men and women must have had a crushing sense of frustration. Often they sought escape in heavy drinking. English judicial records of the thirteenth century reveal a surprisingly large number of "accidental" deaths. Strong, robust, commonsensical farmers do not ordinarily fall on their knives and stab themselves, or slip out of boats and drown, or get lost in the woods on a winter's night. They were probably drunk. Many of these accidents occurred, as the court records say, "coming from an ale." Brawls and violent fights were frequent at taverns.

Scholars have recently spent much energy investigating the structure of medieval peasant households. Because little concrete evidence survives, conclusions are very tentative. It appears, however, that a peasant household consisted of a simple nuclear family: a married couple alone, a couple of children, or a widow or widower with children. Peasant households were *not* extended families containing grandparents or married sons and daughters and their children. The simple family predominated in thirteenth-century England, in northern France in the fourteenth century, and in fifteenth-century Tuscany. Before the first appearance of the Black Death (see pages 419–421), perhaps 94 percent of peasant farmers married, and both bride and groom were in their early twenties. The typical household numbered about five people—the parents and three children.[16]

Women played a significant role in the agricultural life of medieval Europe. Historians often overlook this obvious fact. Women worked with men in wheat and grain cultivation, in the vineyards, and in the harvest and preparation of crops needed by the textile industry—flax and plants used for dyeing cloth, such as madder (which pro-

duces shades of red) and woad (which yields blue dye). Especially at harvest time women shared with their fathers and husbands the backbreaking labor in the fields, work that was especially difficult for them because of weaker muscular development and frequent pregnancies. Lords of great estates commonly hired female day laborers to shear sheep, pick hops (used in the manufacture of beer and ale), tend gardens, as well as do household chores such as cleaning, laundry, and baking. Servant girls in the country considered their hired status as temporary, until they married. Thrifty farm wives contributed to the family income by selling for cash the produce of their gardens or kitchen: butter, cheese, eggs, fruit, soap, mustard, cucumbers. In a year of crisis, careful management was often all that separated a household from starvation. And starvation was a very real danger to the peasantry down to the eighteenth century.

Women managed the house. The size and quality of peasants' houses varied according to their relative prosperity, and usually depended on the amount of land held. The poorest peasants lived in windowless cottages built of wood and clay or wattle and thatched with straw. These cottages consisted of one large room that served as the kitchen and living quarters for all. Everyone slept there. The house had an earthen floor and a fireplace. The lack of windows meant that the room was very sooty. A trestle table, several stools, one or two beds, and a chest for storing clothes constituted the furniture. A shed attached to the house provided storage for tools and shelter for animals. Prosperous peasants added rooms and furniture as they could be afforded, and some wealthy peasants in the early fourteenth century had two-story houses with separate bedrooms for parents and children.

Every house had a small garden and an outbuilding. Onions, garlic, turnips, and carrots were grown and stored through the winter. Cabbage was raised and pickled almost everywhere. Preserving and storing other foods were the basic responsibility of the women and children.

Women dominated in the production of ale for the community market. They had to know how to mix the correct proportions of barley, water, yeast, and hops in 12-gallon vats of hot liquid. Brewing was hard and dangerous work. Records of the English coroners' courts reveal that 5 percent of women who died lost their lives in brewing accidents, falling into the vats of boiling liquid.[17] Ale was the universal drink of the common people in northern Europe. By modern American standards the rate of consumption was heroic. Each monk of Abingdon Abbey in twelfth-century England was allotted 3 gallons a day, and a man working in the fields for ten hours probably drank much more.[18]

The mainstay of the diet for peasants everywhere—and for all other classes—was bread. It was a hard, black substance made of barley, millet, and oats, rarely of expensive wheat flour. The housewife usually baked the household supply once a week. If sheep, cows, or goats were raised, she also made cheese.

The diet of those living in an area with access to a river, lake, or stream was supplemented with fish, which could be preserved by salting. In many places there were severe laws against hunting and trapping in the forests. Deer, wild boars, and other game were strictly reserved for the king and nobility. These laws were flagrantly violated, however, and stolen rabbits and wild game often found their way to the peasants' tables.

Lists of peasant obligations and services to the lord, such as the following from Battle Abbey, commonly included the payment of chickens and eggs:

John of Coyworth holds a house and thirty acres of land, and owes yearly 2 p at Easter and Michaelmas; and he owes a cock and two hens at Christmas, of the value of 4 d.[19]

Except for the rare chicken or illegally caught wild game, meat appeared on the table only on the great feast days of the Christian year: Christmas, Easter, and Pentecost. Then the meat was likely to be pork from the pig slaughtered in the fall and salted for the rest of the year. Some scholars believe that, by the mid-thirteenth century, there was a great increase in the consumption of meat generally. If so, this improvement in diet is further evidence of an improved standard of living.

Breakfast, eaten at dawn before people departed for their farmwork, might well consist of bread, an onion (easily stored through the winter months), and a piece of cheese, washed down with milk or ale. Farmers, then as now, ate their main meal around noon. This was often soup—a thick *potage* of boiled cabbage, onions, turnips, and peas, seasoned with a bone or perhaps a sliver of meat. The evening meal, taken at sunset, consisted of leftovers from the noon meal, perhaps with bread, cheese, milk, or ale.

Once children were able to walk, they helped their parents in the hundreds of chores that had to be done. Small children were set to collecting eggs, if the family had chickens, or gathering twigs and sticks for firewood. As they grew older, children had more responsible tasks, such as weeding the family vegetable garden, shearing the sheep, helping with the planting or harvesting, and assisting their mothers in the endless tasks of baking, cooking, and preserving. Because of poor diet, terrible sanitation, and lack of medical care, the death rate among children was phenomenally high.

Health Care What medical attention was available to the sick person in Western Europe between 1050 and 1300? Scholars are only beginning to explore this question, and there are many aspects of public health that we know little about. The steady rise in population in these centuries is usually attributed to the beginnings of political stability, the reduction of violence, and the increases in cultivated land and food supply. It may also be ascribed partly to better health care. Survival to adulthood probably meant a tough people. A recent study of skeletal remains in the village of Brandes in Orisans in Burgundy showed that peasants enjoyed very good health: they were well built, they had excellent teeth, and their bones revealed no signs of chronic disease. This evidence comes from only one village, but preliminary research confirms the impression that is given by romantic literature: in the prime of life the average person had an innocent raw vitality that enabled him or her to eat, drink, and make love with great gusto.[20]

In recent years scholars have produced some exciting information relating to the natural processes of pregnancy and childbirth. But the acquisition of information has not been easy. Because modesty forbade the presence of men at the birth of a child, very few men could write about it, and there was general illiteracy among women. One woman who wrote extensively, the twelfth-century physician Trotula of Salerno, tended to explain problems of gynecology (women's health) and obstetrics (pregnancy and childbirth) in terms of the relative degree of heat and cold and moisture and dryness within the female body. On the potential difficulty of childbirth she wrote

There are, however, certain women so narrow in the function of childbearing that scarcely ever or never do they succeed. . . . Sometimes external heat comes up around the internal organs and they are straightened in the act of giving birth. Sometimes the exit from the womb is too small, the woman is too fat, or the foetus is dead, not helping nature by its own movements. This often happens to a woman giving birth in winter. If she has by nature a tight opening of the womb, the coldness of the season constricts the womb still more. Sometimes the heat all goes out of the woman herself and she is left without strength to help herself in childbearing. . . . Let her sides, abdomen, hips, and flanks be rubbed with oil of roses or oil of violets.[21]

Trotula believed that sneezing, which forced the woman to push her inner organs downward, should be induced. Her general knowledge cannot be called scientific.

Midwives learned their work through a practical apprenticeship, not through any sort of professional study. Most could not read, and even if they could, few medical texts existed. Because the first pregnancy of many women ended fatally, women of all social classes had a great fear of childbirth. Trotula, Hildegard of Bingen, and other writers on obstetrics urged pregnant women to pray that Christ would grant them a safe childbed.[22]

In the thirteenth century midwives began the practice of delivery by caesarean section—birth by an incision through the abdominal wall and uterus—so called from the traditional belief that the Roman statesman Julius Caesar had been born by means of this operation. Caesarean sections were performed only if the mother had died in labor; the purpose of the operation was the baptism of the child to assure its salvation.

Caesarean sections posed serious ethical problems. Who was to decide whether the mother was

A Caesarean Birth   The midwife lifts a male child from the abdominal opening in the mother's dead body. Her helper prepares a tub of water to bathe the child. Since few infants survived the procedure, midwives needed witnesses to assert that they had not bungled the birth or deliberately killed the infant. *(Source: The British Library)*

dead? (The stethoscope was not invented until 1819.) Who could decide whether the fetus was alive after the mother's death? In a very difficult birth should the life of the mother be sacrificed for the sake of the child? An Old English translation of Trotula's advice to midwives states that "whan the woman is feble and the chylde may noght comyn out, then it is better that the chylde is slayne than that the moder of the child also dye." The greatest theologian of the age, Saint Thomas Aquinas in his treatise on baptism is also explicit: "Evil should not be done that good may come. Therefore one should not kill the mother in order to baptize the child; if, however, the child be still alive in the womb after the mother has died, the mother should be opened in order to baptize the child."[23] Since caesarean sections were performed only after the mother was dead, the choice of the mother's life or the child's never arose.[24] About 1400, male surgeons, motivated by professional, scientific, and probably financial interests, began to perform caesarean sections. Thus through caesarean births men entered the field of obstetrics.[25]

Childhood diseases, poor hygiene, tooth decay, wounds received in fighting, and the myriad ail-ments and afflictions for which even modern medical science has no cure—from cancer to the common cold—must have caused considerable suffering. For the sick what care existed?

As in all ages, the sick everywhere depended above all on the private nursing care of relatives and friends. For public health, English sources provide the largest evidence to date. In the British Isles the twelfth century witnessed a momentous breakthrough in the establishment of institutional care in hospitals. In addition to the infirmaries run by monks and nuns, there were at least 113 hospitals in England with possibly as many as 3,494 beds. Medieval hospitals were built by the royal family, the clergy, barons, and ordinary people to alleviate the suffering of the sick, not just to house them. Hospitals attracted considerable popular support, and in their charitable contributions women played an especially strong role in the endowment of hospitals.[26]

As in the developed modern world, persons living in or near a town or city had a better chance of receiving some form of professional attention than did those in remote rural areas. English documents label at least ninety practitioners as *medicus,* mean-

Saint Maurus, Healing   A rich body of legend developed around Maurus, a noble-man's son given as an oblate to Saint Benedict. In the eleventh century, Maurus had a reputation, unsupported by evidence, for medical knowledge and curative powers. Here he is depicted giving a patient some kind of pharmaceutical preparation. *(Source: Bibliothèque municipale de Troyes)*

ing physician, surgeon, or medical man, but that is a pitifully small number in a population of perhaps 2 million. With so few doctors, only the largest cities—such as London, York, Winchester, and Canterbury, which all catered to pilgrims and travelers—had resident physicians. At other hospitals, physician consultants were brought in as the occasion required. Most people, of course, did not live in or near large towns. They relied for assistance on the chance presence of a local monk or nun with herb and pharmaceutical knowledge, a local person skilled in setting broken bones, or the wise village person experienced in treating diseases.

Since public morality and ancient tradition forbade the examination of female patients by men, women could practice obstetrics and gynecology. But although women played active roles as healers and in the general care of the sick, male doctors jealously guarded their status and admitted very few women to university medical schools when they were founded; "Francesca Romano, who was licensed as a surgeon in 1321 by Duke Carl of Calabria is the exception that proves the rule."[27] The medical faculty at the University of Paris in the fourteenth century penalized women who practiced medicine because they lacked a degree— which they were not allowed to get.

Popular Religion   Apart from the land, the weather, and the peculiar conditions that existed on each manor, the Christian religion had the greatest impact on the daily lives of ordinary people in the central Middle Ages. Religious practices varied widely from country to country and even from province to province. But nowhere was religion a one-hour-on-Sunday or High Holy Days affair. Christian practices and attitudes permeated virtually all aspects of everyday life.

As the Germanic and Celtic peoples were Christianized, their new religion became a fusion of Jewish, pagan, Roman, and Christian practices. In the central Middle Ages, all people shared as a natural and public duty in the religious life of the community.

The village church was the center of community life—social, political, and economic as well as religious. Most of the important events in a person's life took place in or around the church. A person was baptized there, within hours of birth. Men and women confessed their sins to the village priest there and received, usually at Easter and Christmas, the sacrament of the Eucharist. In front of the church, the bishop reached down from his horse and confirmed a person as a Christian by placing his hands over the candidate's head and making the sign of the cross on the forehead. (Bishops Thomas Becket of Canterbury and Hugh of Lincoln were considered especially holy men because they got down from their horses to confirm.) Young people courted in the churchyard and, so the sermons of the priests complained, made love in the church cemetery. Priests urged couples to marry publicly in the church, but many married privately, without witnesses (see page 429).

In the church, women and men could pray to the Virgin and the local saints. The stone in the church altar contained relics of the saints, often a local saint to whom the church itself had been dedicated. The saints had once lived on earth and thus, people believed, understood human problems. They could be helpful intercessors with Christ or with God the Father. They could perform miracles. The saint became the special property of the locality where his or her relics rested. Thus to secure the saint's support and to guarantee the region's prosperity, a busy traffic in relics developed—bones, articles of clothing, the saint's tears or saliva, even dust from the saint's tomb. The understanding that existed between the saint and the peasants rested on the customary medieval relationship of mutual fidelity and aid: peasants would offer the saint prayers, loyalty, and gifts to the shrine or church in return for the saint's healing and support. When saints failed to receive the attention they felt they deserved, they sometimes took offense and were vindictive. An English knight whose broken arm was healed by Saint James forgot to thank the saint at his shrine at Reading, whereupon the saint punished the knight by breaking his other arm.

What had been the saints' social background when alive? "The initiative in creating a cult (of a saint) always belonged to believers"[28] (ordinary people). Although papal authorities insisted that they had the exclusive right to examine the lives and activities of candidates for sainthood in a formal "trial," popular opinion declared people saints. Between 1185 and 1431, only seventy official investigations were held at Rome, but hundreds of new persons across Europe were venerated as saints. Church officials and educated clergy evaluated candidates according to the "heroic virtue" of their lives, but lay people judged solely by the candidates' miracles.

Modern research suggests a connection between the models of holiness and the social structures in different parts of Europe. Northern Europeans and southern Europeans chose saints of different social backgrounds or classes. In France and Germany, saints were primarily men and women of the nobility. In Italy and Mediterranean lands, saints tended to be *popolani*—non-nobles, nonaristocrats. The cult of the saints, which developed in a rural environment among uneducated people, is a central feature of popular culture in the Middle Ages.[29]

Popular religion consisted largely of rituals heavy with symbolism. Before slicing a loaf of bread, the good wife tapped the sign of the cross on the loaf with her knife. Before the planting, the village priest customarily went out and sprinkled the fields with water, symbolizing refreshment and life. Shortly after a woman had successfully delivered a child, she was "churched." Churching was a ceremony of thanksgiving based on the Jewish rite of purification. When a child was baptized, a few grains of salt were dropped on its tongue. Salt had been the symbol of purity, strength, and incorruptibility for the ancient Hebrews, and the Romans had used it in their sacrifices. It was used in Christian baptism to drive away demons and to strengthen the infant in its new faith.

The entire calendar was designed with reference to Christmas, Easter, and Pentecost. Saints' days were legion. Everyone participated in village processions. The colored vestments the priests wore at Mass gave the villagers a sense of the changing seasons of the church's liturgical year. The signs and symbols of Christianity were visible everywhere.

What did people actually *believe*? It is difficult to say, partly because medieval peasants left few written records of their thoughts, partly because in any age there is often a great disparity between what people profess to believe and their conduct or the ways they act on their beliefs. Peasants accepted what family custom and the clergy taught them. Recent research has shown that in the central Middle Ages a new religious understanding emerged. "Whereas early Christianity looked to holy men and women and early medieval society turned to saints to effect the connection between God and humankind through prayers of intercession," in the twelfth century a sacramental system developed. The seven sacraments—Baptism, Penance, Eucharist, Confirmation, Marriage, Holy Orders,

Extreme Unction—brought grace, the divine assistance or help needed to lead a good Christian life and to merit salvation. At the center of the sacramental system stood the Eucharist, the small piece of bread that through the words of priestly consecration at the Mass, became the living body of Christ and, when worthily consumed, became a channel of Christ's grace. The ritual of consecration, repeated at every altar of Christendom, became a unifying symbol in a complex world.[30]

The Mass was in Latin, but the priest delivered sermons on the Gospel in the vernacular—or he was supposed to. An almost universal criticism of the parish clergy in the twelfth and thirteenth centuries was that they were incapable of explaining basic Christian teaching to their parishioners. The growth of the universities did not improve the situation, because few diocesan clerics attended them and those who did obtain degrees secured administrative positions. The only parish priest to be canonized in the entire Middle Ages, the Breton lawyer and priest Saint Yves (d. 1303), had resigned a position as a diocesan judge to serve rural parishioners. At the trial for his canonization, laypeople stressed not only that he led a simple and frugal life but that he put his forensic skills to the service of preaching the Christian gospels. Saint Yves is the great exception that proves the rule that the medieval parish clergy were generally incapable of preaching in a rural milieu. Parish priests celebrated the liturgy and administered the sacraments, but they had other shortcomings. A thirteenth-century Alsatian chronicler said that the peasants of the region did not complain that their pastors lived in concubinage, because that made them less fearful for the virtue of their daughters.[31]

Christians had long had special reverence and affection for the Virgin Mary as the Mother of Christ. In the eleventh century, theologians began to emphasize the depiction of Mary at the crucifixion in the Gospel of John (19:25–27):

But standing by the cross of Jesus were his mother, and his mother's sister, Mary the wife of Clopas, and Mary Magdalene. When Jesus saw his mother and the disciple whom he loved standing near, he said to his mother, "Woman, behold, your son!" Then he said to the disciple, "Behold, your mother!"

Medieval scholars interpreted this passage as expressing Christ's compassionate concern for all humanity and Mary's spiritual motherhood of all Christians. The huge outpouring of popular devotions to Mary concentrated on her role as Queen of Heaven and, because of her special relationship to Christ, as all-powerful intercessor with him. Masses on Saturdays specially commemorated her, sermons focused on her unique influence with Christ, and hymns and prayers to her multiplied.

Those Who Fight

The nobility, though a small fraction of the total population, strongly influenced all aspects of medieval culture—political, economic, religious, educational, and artistic. For that reason, European society in the twelfth and thirteenth centuries may be termed aristocratic.

Members of the nobility enjoyed a special legal status. A nobleman was free personally and in his possessions. He was limited only by his military obligation to king, duke, or prince. As the result of his liberty, he had certain rights and responsibilities. He raised troops and commanded them in the field. He held courts that dispensed a sort of justice. Sometimes he coined money for use within his territories. As lord of the people who settled on his lands, he made political decisions affecting them, resolved disputes among them, and protected them in time of attack. The liberty and privileges of the noble were inheritable, perpetuated by blood and not by wealth alone.

The nobleman was a professional fighter. His social function, as churchmen described it, was to protect the weak, the poor, and the churches by arms. He possessed a horse and a sword. These, and the leisure time in which to learn how to use them in combat, were the visible signs of his nobility. He was encouraged to display chivalric virtues—courtesy, loyalty to his commander, and generosity. All nobles were knights, but not all knights were noble.[32]

Those who aspired to the aristocracy desired a castle, the symbol of feudal independence and military lifestyle. Through military valor, a fortunate marriage, or outstanding service to king or lord, poor knights could and did achieve positions in the upper nobility of France and England. Not so in Germany, where a large class of unfree knights, or *ministerials,* fought as warriors or served as stewards who managed nobles' estates or households. In the twelfth century, ministerials sometimes ac-

quired fiefs and wealth. The most important ministerials served the German kings and had significant responsibilities. Legally, however, they remained of servile status: they were not noble.[33]

Infancy, Childhood, and Youth   The rate of infant mortality (the number of babies who died before their first birthday) in the central Middle Ages must have been staggering. The limited information indicates that midwives had surely contributed to the death rate of both the newborn and the mother. Natural causes—disease and poor or insufficient food—also resulted in many deaths. Infanticide, however, which was common in the ancient world, seems to have declined in the central Middle Ages. Ecclesiastical pressure worked steadily against it. Infanticide in medieval Europe is another indication of the slow and very imperfect Christianization of European peoples.

On the other hand, the abandonment of infant children seems to have been the most favored form of family limitation, widely practiced throughout the entire Middle Ages. Abandonment was "the voluntary relinquishing of control over children by their natal parents or guardians, whether by leaving them somewhere, selling them, or legally consigning authority to some other person or institution."[34] Why did parents do this? What became of the children? What was the rate of abandonment? What attitudes did medieval society have toward this practice?

Poverty or local natural disaster led some parents to abandon their children because they could not support them. Thus Saint Patrick wrote that, in times of famine, fathers would sell their sons and daughters so that the children could be fed. Parents sometimes gave children away because they were illegitimate or the result of incestuous unions.

Sometimes parents believed that someone of greater means or status might find the child and bring it up in better circumstances than the natal parents could provide. Disappointment in the sex of the child or its physical weakness or deformity might also lead parents to abandon it. Finally, some parents were indifferent—they "simply could not be bothered" with the responsibilities of parenthood.[35]

The Christian Middle Ages witnessed a significant development in the disposal of superfluous children: they were given to monasteries as *oblates,* or "offerings." Boys and girls were given to

Children Given to Creditors Ecclesiastical laws against lending money at interest were widely flouted, and many nobles, having borrowed beyond their ability to repay, fell heavily into debt. The selling or giving of children to creditors, illustrated here, was one solution to indebtedness. *(Source: The Bodleian Library, Oxford)*

monasteries or convents as permanent gifts. By the seventh century, church councils and civil codes had defined the practice: "Parents of any social status could donate a child, of either sex, at least up to the age of ten." Contemporaries considered oblation a religious act, for the child was offered to God often in recompense for parental sin. But oblation also served social and economic functions. The monastery nurtured and educated the child in a familial atmosphere, and it provided career opportunities for the mature monk or nun despite his or her humble origins.[36] In the twelfth and thirteenth centuries, the incidence of noble parents giving their younger sons and daughters to religious houses increased dramatically; nobles wanted to preserve the estate intact for the eldest son. In

the early thirteenth century, the bishop of Paris observed that children were "cast into the cloister by parents and relatives just as if they were kittens or piglets whom their mothers could not nourish; so that they may die to the world not spiritually but . . . civilly, that is—so that they may be deprived of their hereditary position and that it may devolve on those who remain in the world." The abandonment of children remained a socially acceptable institution. Ecclesiastical and civil authorities never legislated against it.[37]

For children of aristocratic birth, the years from infancy to around the age of seven or eight were primarily years of play. Infants had their rattles, as the twelfth-century monk Guibert of Nogent reports, and young children their special toys. Guibert of Nogent speaks in several places in his autobiography of "the tender years of childhood"—the years from six to twelve. Describing the severity of the tutor whom his mother assigned to him, Guibert wrote:

Placed under him, . . . I was kept from ordinary games and never allowed to leave my master's company, or to eat anywhere else than at home, in everything I had to show self-control in word, look, and deed, so that he seemed to require of me the conduct of a monk rather than a clerk. While others of my age wandered everywhere at will and were unchecked in the indulgence of such inclinations as were natural at their age, I, hedged in with constant restraints and dressed in my clerical garb, would sit and look at the troops of players like a beast awaiting sacrifice. Even on Sundays and saints' days I had to submit to the severity of school exercises.[38]

Guibert's mother had intended him for the church. At about the age of seven, a boy of the noble class who was not intended for the church was placed in the household of one of his father's friends or relatives. There he became a servant to the lord and received his formal training in arms. He was expected to serve the lord at the table, to assist him as a private valet when called on to do so, and, as he gained experience, to care for the lord's horses and equipment. The boy might have a great deal of work to do, depending on the size of the household and the personality of the lord. The work that children did, medieval people believed, gave them experience and preparation for later life.

Training was in the arts of war. The boy learned to ride and to manage a horse. He had to acquire skill in wielding a sword, which sometimes weighed as much as twenty-five pounds. He had to be able to hurl a lance, shoot with a bow and arrow, and care for armor and other equipment. Increasingly, in the eleventh and twelfth centuries, noble youths learned to read and write some Latin. Still, on thousands of charters from that period, nobles signed with a cross (+) or some other mark. Literacy for the nobility became more common in the thirteenth century. Formal training was concluded around the age of twenty-one with the ceremony of knighthood. The custom of knighting, though never universal, seems to have been widespread in France and England but not in Germany. Once knighted, a young man was supposed to be

courteous, generous, and, if possible, handsome and rich. Above all, he was to be loyal to his lord and brave in battle. In a society lacking strong institutions of government, loyalty was the cement that held aristocratic society together. The greatest crime was called a *felony,* which meant treachery to one's lord.

Parents often wanted to settle daughters' futures as soon as possible. Men tended to prefer young brides. A woman in her late twenties or thirties had relatively few years in which to produce children; thus aristocratic girls in the central Middle Ages were married at around the age of sixteen.

The future of many young women was not enviable. For a girl of sixteen, marriage to a man in his thirties was not the most attractive prospect, and marriage to a widower in his forties and fifties was even less so. If there were a large number of marriageable young girls in a particular locality, their "market value" was reduced. In the early Middle Ages, it had been the custom for the groom to present a dowry to the bride and her family, but by the late twelfth century the process was reversed. Thereafter, the size of the marriage portions that brides and their families offered to prospective husbands rose higher and higher.

What was a young woman unhappily married to a much older man to do? The literature of courtly love is filled with stories of young bachelors in love with young married women. How hopeless their love was is not known. The cuckolded husband is a stock figure in masterpieces such as *The Romance of Tristan and Isolde,* Chaucer's *The Merchant's Tale,* and Boccaccio's *Fiammetta's Tale.*

Power and Responsibility   The responsibilities of a noble in the central Middle Ages depended on the size and extent of his estates, the number of his dependents, and his position in his territory relative to others of his class and to the king. As a vassal a noble was required to fight for his lord or for the king when called on to do so. By the mid-twelfth century, this service was limited in most parts of western Europe to forty days a year. The noble was obliged to attend his lord's court on important occasions when the lord wanted to put on great displays, such as at Easter, Pentecost, and Christmas. When the lord knighted his eldest son or married off his eldest daughter, he called his vassals to his court. They were expected to attend and to present a contribution known as a "gracious aid."

Until the late thirteenth century, when royal authority intervened, a noble in France or England had great power over the knights and peasants on his estates. He maintained order among them and dispensed justice to them. The quality of justice varied widely: some lords were vicious tyrants who exploited and persecuted their peasants; others were reasonable and evenhanded. In any case, the quality of life on the manor and its productivity were related in no small way to the temperament and decency of the lord—and his lady.

Women played a large and important role in the functioning of the estate (see Listening to the Past). They were responsible for the practical management of the household's "inner economy"—cooking, brewing, spinning, weaving, caring for yard animals. The lifestyle of the medieval warrior nobles required constant travel, both for purposes of war and for the supervision of distant properties. Frequent pregnancies and the reluctance to expose women to hostile conditions kept the lady at home and therefore able to assume supervision of the family's fixed properties. When the lord was away for long periods—on crusade, for instance, the lord could be gone from two to five years, if he returned at all—his wife often became the sole manager of the family properties. Between 1060 and 1080, the lady Hersendis was the sole manager of her family's properties in northern France while her husband was on crusade in the Holy Land.

Women Defending Castle Women shared with men the difficulties and dangers of defending castles. Armed with rocks and bows and arrows, and not hesitating to poke a finger through a chain-mail helmet and into the eye of a knight scaling the walls on a ladder, these noble ladies try to fight off attackers. *(Source: Bibliothèque royale Albert 1er, Brussels)*

Nor were women's activities confined to managing households and estates in their husbands' absence. Medieval warfare was largely a matter of brief skirmishes, and few men were killed in any single encounter. But altogether the number slain ran high, and there were many widows. Aristocratic widows frequently controlled family properties and fortunes and exercised great authority. Although the evidence is scattered and sketchy, there are indications that women performed many of the functions of men. In Spain, France, and Germany they bought, sold, and otherwise transferred property. Gertrude, labeled "Saxony's almighty widow" by the chronicler Ekkehard of Aura, took a leading role in conspiracies against the emperor Henry V.

Those Who Pray

Monasticism represented some of the finest aspirations of medieval civilization. The monasteries were devoted to prayer, and their standards of Christian behavior influenced the entire church. The monasteries produced the educated elite that was continually drawn into the administrative service of kings and great lords. Monks kept alive the remains of classical culture and experimented with new styles of architecture and art. They introduced new techniques of estate management and land reclamation. Although relatively few in number in the central Middle Ages, the monks played a significant role in medieval society.

Toward the end of his *Ecclesiastical History of England and Normandy*, when he was well into his sixties, Orderic Vitalis, a monk of the Norman abbey of Saint Evroul, interrupted his narrative to explain movingly how he happened to become a monk:

And so, O glorious God, you didst inspire my father Odeleric to renounce me utterly and submit me in all things to thy governance. So, weeping, he gave me, a weeping child, into the care of the monk Reginald, and sent me away into exile for love of thee, and never saw me again. And I, a mere boy, did not presume to oppose my father's wishes, but obeyed him in all things, for he promised me for his part that if I became a monk I should taste of the joys of Heaven with the Innocents after my death. . . . And so, a boy of ten, I crossed the English channel and came into Normandy as an exile, unknown to all, knowing no one.[39]

Orderic Vitalis (ca 1075–ca 1140) was one of the leading scholars of his time. As such, he is not a representative figure or even a typical monk. Intellectuals, those who earn their living or spend most of their time working with ideas, are never typical figures of their times. In one respect, however, Orderic was quite representative of the monks of the central Middle Ages: although he had no doubt that God wanted him to be a monk, the decision was actually made by his parents. Orderic was the third son of a knight who held lands in western England. Concern for the provision of his two older sons probably led the knight to give his youngest boy to the monastery.

Medieval monasteries were religious institutions whose organization and structure fulfilled the social needs of the feudal nobility. The monasteries provided noble children with both an honorable and aristocratic life and opportunities for ecclesiastical careers.[40] As medieval society changed economically, and as European society ever so slowly developed middle-class traits, the monasteries almost inevitably drew their manpower, when they were able, from the middle classes. Until that time, they were preserves of the aristocratic nobility.

Through the Middle Ages, social class also defined the kinds of religious life open to women. Kings and nobles usually established convents for their daughters, sisters, aunts, or aging mothers. Entrance was restricted to women of the founder's class. Since a well-born lady could not honorably be apprenticed to a tradesperson or do any kind of manual labor, the sole alternative to life at home was the religious life.

The founder's endowment and support greatly influenced the later social, economic, and political status of the convent. A few convents received large endowments and could accept many women. Amesbury Priory in Wiltshire, England, for example, received handsome endowments from King Henry II and his successors. In 1256 Amesbury supported a prioress and 76 nuns, 7 priests, and 16 lay brothers. The convent raised £100 in annual rents and £40 from the wool clip—very large sums at the time. By 1317 Amesbury had 177 nuns.[41] Most houses of women, however, possessed limited resources and remained small in numbers.

The office of abbess or prioress, the house's superior, customarily went to a nun of considerable social standing. Since an abbess or prioress had responsibility for governing her community and

Synagogue Hildegard of Bingen, the first major German mystic, developed a rich theology on the basis of her visions. Here Synagogue is portrayed as a tall woman commanded by God to prepare humanity for the coming of Christ. In her arms Moses holds up the stone tablets of the Ten Commandments; in her lap are the patriarchs and prophets who foretold the birth of Christ. The headband symbolizes the Virgin Mary: because Mary gave the world the savior, Hildegard makes Synagogue the Mother of the Incarnation. *(Source: Rheinische Bildarchiv)*

for representing it in any business with the outside world, she was a woman of local, sometimes national, power and importance. Although the level of intellectual life in the women's houses varied widely, the career of Hildegard of Bingen suggests the activities of some nuns in the central Middle Ages. The tenth child of a lesser noble family, Hildegard (1098–1179) was given when eight years old as an oblate to an abbey in the Rhineland, where she learned Latin and received a good education. In 1147 Hildegard founded the convent of Rupertsberg near Bingen. There she produced a body of writings including the *Scivias (Know the Ways),* a record of her mystical visions that incorporates vast theological learning; the *Physica (On the Physical Elements),* a classification of the natural elements, such as plants, animals, metals, and the movements of the heavenly bodies; a mystery play; and a medical work that led a distinguished twentieth-century historian of science to describe Hildegard as "one of the most original writers of the Latin West in the twelfth century." At the same time, she carried on a vast correspondence with scholars, prelates, and ordinary people and had such a reputation for wisdom that a recent writer has called her "the Dear Abby of the twelfth century to whom everyone came or wrote for advice or comfort."[42] An exceptionally gifted person, Hildegard represents the Benedictine ideal of great learning combined with a devoted monastic life. Like intellectual monks, however, intellectual nuns were not typical of the era.

In medieval Europe the monasteries of men greatly outnumbered those of women. The pattern of life within individual monasteries varied widely from house to house and from region to region. One central activity, however—the work of God— was performed everywhere. Daily life centered around the liturgy.

Seven times a day and once during the night, the monks went to choir to chant the psalms and other prayers prescribed by Saint Benedict. Prayers were offered for peace, rain, good harvests, the civil authorities, the monks' families, and their benefactors. Monastic patrons in turn lavished gifts on the monasteries, which often became very wealthy. Through their prayers the monks performed a valuable service for the rest of society.

Prayer justified the monks' spending a large percentage of their income on splendid objects to enhance the liturgy; monks praised God, they believed, not only in prayer but in everything connected with prayer. They sought to accumulate priestly vestments of the finest silks, velvets, and embroideries, as well as sacred vessels of embossed silver and gold and ornamented and bejeweled Gospel books. Every monastery tried to acquire the relics of its patron saint, which necessitated the production of a beautiful reliquary to house the relics. The liturgy, then, inspired a great deal of art, and the monasteries became the crucibles of art in Western Christendom.

The monks fulfilled their social responsibility by praying. It was generally agreed that they could best carry out this duty if they were not distracted by worldly needs. Thus great and lesser lords gave the monasteries lands that would supply the community with necessities.

The usual method of economic organization was the manor. Many monastic manors were small enough and close enough to the abbey to be supervised directly by the abbot. But if a monastery held and farmed vast estates, the properties were divided into administrative units under the supervision of one of the monks of the house.

The Cistercians, whose constitution insisted that they accept lands far from human habitation, were ideally suited to the agricultural needs and trends

Beekeeping at Monte Cassino   Because of the scarcity and expense of sugar, honey was the usual sweetener for pastries and liquids throughout the Middle Ages. This illustrator had never actually seen the process of gathering honey: without veils, nets, and gloves, the beekeepers would be badly stung. *(Source: Biblioteca Apostolica Vaticana)*

of their times. In the Low Countries they built dikes to hold back the sea, and the reclaimed land was put to the production of cereals. In the eastern parts of Germany they took the lead in draining swamps and cultivating wasteland. As a result of their efforts, the rich, rolling land of French Burgundy was turned into lush vineyards, and the rocky soil and damp downs of northern and central England were turned into sheep runs.

Some monasteries lent their surplus revenues to the local nobility and peasantry. In the twelfth century the abbey of Savigny in Normandy, for example, acted as a banking house, providing loans at interest to many noble families of Normandy and Brittany. Although church law opposed usury—lending at interest—one reliable scholar has recently written that "it was clerics and ecclesiastical institutions (monasteries and nunneries) that constituted the main providers of credit."[43]

Whatever work particular monks did and whatever economic activities individual monasteries were involved in, monks also performed social services and exerted an influence for the good. In addition to running schools and "hospitals," monasteries like Saint Albans, situated north of London on a busy thoroughfare, served as hotels and resting places for travelers. In short, monasteries performed a variety of social services in an age when there was no "state" and no conception of social welfare as a public responsibility.

✤ CRISES OF THE LATER MIDDLE AGES

In the later years of the thirteenth century, Europeans seemed to run out of steam. The crusading movement gradually fizzled out. Few new cathedrals were constructed, and if a cathedral had not been completed by 1300, the chances were high that it never would be. The strong rulers of England and France, building on the foundations of their predecessors, increased their authority and gained the loyalty of all their subjects. The vigor of those kings, however, did not pass to their immediate descendants. Meanwhile, the church, which for two centuries had guided Christian society, began to face grave difficulties. A violent dispute between the papacy and the kings of England and France badly damaged the prestige of the pope.

But religious struggle was only one of the crises that would face European society in the fourteenth century.

A Challenge to Religious Authority

In 1294, King Edward I of England and Philip the Fair of France declared war on each other. To finance this war, both kings laid taxes on the clergy. Kings had been taxing the church for decades. Pope Boniface VIII (r. 1294–1303), arguing from precedent, insisted that kings gain papal consent for taxation of the clergy and forbade churchmen to pay the taxes. But Edward and Philip refused to accept this decree, partly because it hurt royal finances and partly because the papal order threatened royal authority within their countries. Edward immediately denied the clergy the protection of the law, an action that meant its members could be attacked with impunity. Philip halted the shipment of all ecclesiastical revenue to Rome. Boniface had to back down.

Philip the Fair and his ministers continued their attack on all powers in France outside royal authority. Philip arrested a French bishop who was also the papal legate. When Boniface defended the ecclesiastical status and diplomatic immunity of the bishop, Philip replied with the trumped-up charge that the pope was a heretic. The papacy and the French monarchy waged a bitter war of propaganda. Finally, in 1302, in a letter entitled *Unam Sanctam* (because its opening sentence spoke of one holy Catholic church), Boniface insisted that all Christians, including kings, are subject to the pope. Philip's university-trained advisers, with an argument drawn from Roman law, maintained that the king of France was completely sovereign in his kingdom and responsible to God alone. French mercenary troops went to Italy and arrested the aged pope at Anagni. Although Boniface was soon freed, he died shortly afterward.

The Black Death

Economic difficulties originating in the later thirteenth century were fully manifest by the start of the fourteenth. In the first decade, the countries of northern Europe experienced considerable price inflation. The costs of grain, livestock, and dairy products rose sharply. Severe weather, which historical geographers label "the Little Ice Age," made a serious situation frightful. An unusual number of storms brought torrential rains, ruining the wheat, oat, and hay crops on which people and animals depended almost everywhere. Population had steadily increased in the twelfth and thirteenth centuries, and large amounts of land had been put under cultivation. The amount of food yielded, however, did not match the level of population growth. Bad weather had disastrous results. Poor harvests—one in four was likely to be poor—led to scarcity and starvation. Almost all of northern Europe suffered a terrible famine in the years 1315 to 1317. Then in 1318 disease hit cattle and sheep, drastically reducing the herds and flocks. Another bad harvest in 1321 brought famine, starvation, and death. The undernourished population was ripe for the Grim Reaper, who appeared in 1348 in the form of the Black Death.

In October 1347, Genoese ships traveling from the Crimea in southern Russia brought the bubonic plague to Messina, from where it spread across Sicily and up into Italy. By late spring of 1348, southern Germany was attacked. Frightened French authorities chased a galley bearing the disease from the port of Marseilles, but not before plague had infected the city. In June 1348 two ships entered the Bristol Channel and introduced it into England. All Europe felt the scourge of this horrible disease (Map 13.1).

The bacillus that causes the plague, *Pasteurella pestis,* likes to live in the bloodstream of an animal or, ideally, in the stomach of a flea. The flea in turn resides in the hair of a rodent, sometimes a squirrel but preferably the hardy, nimble, and vagabond black rat. In the fourteenth century, the host black rat traveled by ship, where it could feast for months on a cargo of grain or live snugly among bales of cloth. Fleas bearing the bacillus also had no trouble nesting in saddlebags.[44] Comfortable, well fed, and often having greatly multiplied, the black rats ended their ocean voyage and descended on the great cities of Europe.

The plague took two forms—bubonic and pneumonic. The rat was the transmitter of the bubonic form of the disease. The pneumonic form was communicated directly from one person to another.

Although by the fourteenth century urban authorities from London to Paris to Rome had begun to try to achieve a primitive level of sanitation, urban conditions remained ideal for the spread of disease. Narrow streets filled with mud, refuse, and human excrement were as much cesspools as thoroughfares. Dead animals and sore-covered beggars greeted the traveler. Houses whose upper stories

 Saint Dominic and the Inquisition The fifteenth-century court painter to the Spanish rulers Ferdinand and Isabella, Pedro Berruguete (d. 1504) here portrays an event from the life of Saint Dominic. Dominic presides at the trial of Count Raymond of Toulouse, who had supported the Albigensian heretics. Raymond, helmeted and on horseback, repented and was pardoned; his companions, who would not repent, were burned. Smoke from the fire has put one of the judges to sleep, and other officials, impervious to the human tragedy, chat among themselves. *(Source: Museo del Prado, Madrid)*

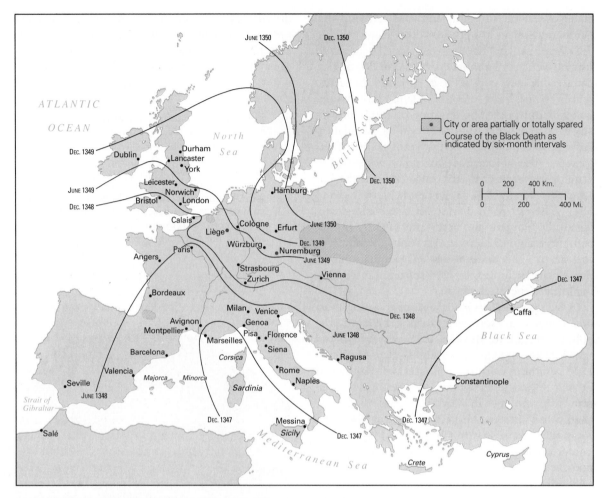

✻ **MAP 13.1 The Course of the Black Death in Fourteenth-Century Europe**
Notice the routes that the bubonic plague took across Europe. How do you account
for the fact that several regions were spared the "dreadful death"?

projected over the lower ones eliminated light
and air. And extreme overcrowding was commonplace. When all members of an aristocratic family
lived and slept in one room, it should not be surprising that six or eight persons in a middle-class
or poor household slept in one bed—if they had
one.

Standards of personal hygiene remained fright-
fully low. Fleas and body lice were universal afflictions: everyone from peasants to archbishops had
them. One more bite did not cause much alarm.
But if that nibble came from a bacillus-bearing flea,
an entire household or area was doomed.

The symptoms of the bubonic plague started
with a growth the size of a nut or an apple in the
armpit, in the groin, or on the neck. This was the
boil, or *buba,* that gave the disease its name and
caused agonizing pain. If the buba was lanced and
the pus thoroughly drained, the victim had a
chance of recovery. The secondary stage was the
appearance of black spots or blotches caused by
bleeding under the skin. Finally, the victim began
to cough violently and spit blood. This stage, indicating the presence of thousands of bacilli in the
bloodstream, signaled the end, and death followed
in two or three days. Rather than evoking compassion for the victim, a French scientist has written,
everything about the bubonic plague provoked
horror and disgust: "All the matter which exuded
from their bodies let off an unbearable stench;

sweat, excrement, spittle, breath, so fetid as to be overpowering; urine turbid, thick, black or red."[45]

Fourteenth-century medical literature indicates that physicians had no rational explanation for the disease, could sometimes ease the pain, but had no cure. Most people—lay, scholarly, and medical—believed that the Black Death was caused by some "vicious property in the air" that carried the disease from place to place. When ignorance was joined to fear and ancient bigotry, savage cruelty sometimes resulted. Many people believed that the Jews had poisoned the wells of Christian communities and thereby infected the drinking water. This charge led to the murder of thousands of Jews across Europe. According to one chronicler, sixteen thousand were killed at the imperial city of Strasbourg alone in 1349. That sixteen thousand is probably a typically medieval numerical exaggeration does not lessen the horror of the massacre.

The Italian writer Giovanni Boccaccio (1313–1375), describing the course of the disease in Florence in the preface to his book of tales, *The Decameron,* pinpointed the cause of the spread:

Moreover, the virulence of the pest was the greater by reason that intercourse was apt to convey it from the sick to the whole, just as fire devours things dry or greasy when they are brought close to it. Nay, the evil went yet further, for not merely by speech or association with the sick was the malady communicated to the healthy with consequent peril of common death, but any that touched the clothes of the sick or aught else that had been touched or used by them, seemed thereby to contract the disease.[46]

The highly infectious nature of the plague, especially in areas of high population density, was recognized by a few sophisticated Arabs. When the disease struck the town of Salé in Morocco, Ibu Abu Madyan shut in his household with sufficient food and water and allowed no one to enter or leave until the plague had passed. Madyan was entirely successful. The rat that carried the disease-bearing flea avoided travel outside the cities. Thus the countryside was relatively safe. City dwellers who could afford to move fled to the country districts.

Because population figures for the period before the arrival of the plague do not exist for most countries and cities, only educated guesses can be made about mortality rates. Of a total English population of perhaps 4.2 million, probably 1.4 million died of the Black Death in its several visits.[47] Densely populated Italian cities endured incredible losses. Florence lost between half and two-thirds of its 1347 population of 85,000 when the plague visited in 1348. The disease recurred intermittently in the 1360s and 1370s and reappeared many times down to 1700. Population losses in Bohemia and Poland seem to have been much less. Historians of medicine have recently postulated that people with blood type O are immune to the bubonic disease; since this blood type predominated in Hungary, that region would have been slightly affected. No estimates of population losses have ever been attempted for Russia and the Balkans.

Economic historians and demographers sharply dispute the impact of the plague on the economy in the late fourteenth century. The traditional view that the plague had a disastrous effect has been greatly modified. The clearest evidence comes from England, where the agrarian economy showed remarkable resilience. Although the severity of the disease varied from region to region, it appears that by about 1375 most landlords enjoyed revenues near those of the pre-plague years. By the early fifteenth century seigneurial prosperity reached a medieval peak. Why? The answer appears to lie in the fact that England and many parts of Europe suffered from overpopulation in the early fourteenth century. Population losses caused by the Black Death "led to increased productivity by restoring a more efficient balance between labour, land, and capital."[48] Population decline meant a sharp increase in per capita wealth. Increased demand for labor meant greater mobility among peasant and working classes. Wages rose, providing better distribution of income. The shortage of labor and steady requests for higher wages put landlords on the defensive. Some places, such as Florence, experienced economic prosperity as a long-term consequence of the plague.

Even more significant than the social effects were the psychological consequences. The knowledge that the disease meant almost certain death provoked the most profound pessimism. Imagine an entire society in the grip of the belief that it was at the mercy of a frightful affliction about which nothing could be done, a disgusting disease from which family and friends would flee, leaving one to die alone and in agony. It is not surprising that

Procession of Saint Gregory According to the *Golden Legend,* a thirteenth-century collection of saints' lives, in 590 when plague ravaged Rome, Pope Gregory I ordered a procession around the city to beg heaven to end the epidemic. As the people circle the walls, a deacon falls victim, and Pope Gregory sees an angel on top of Hadrian's tomb (thereafter called Castel Sant'Angelo), which Gregory interprets to mean the plague is ending. *(Source: Musée Condé, Chantilly/The Bridgeman Art Library, London)*

some sought release in orgies and gross sensuality while others turned to the severest forms of asceticism and frenzied religious fervor. Some extremists joined groups of *flagellants,* men and women who whipped and scourged themselves as penance for their and society's sins, in the belief that the Black Death was God's punishment for humanity's wickedness.

The literature and art of the fourteenth century reveal a terribly morbid concern with death. One highly popular artistic motif, the Dance of Death, depicted a dancing skeleton leading away a living person. No wonder survivors experienced a sort of shell shock and a terrible crisis of faith. Lack of confidence in the leaders of society, lack of hope for the future, defeatism, and malaise wreaked enormous anguish and contributed to the decline of the Middle Ages. A long international war added further misery to the frightful disasters of the plague.

The Hundred Years' War (ca 1337–1453)

Another phase of the centuries-old struggle between the English and French monarchies, the Hundred Years' War was fought intermittently from 1337 to 1453. Its causes were both distant and immediate. The English claimed Aquitaine as an ancient feudal inheritance. In 1329 England's King Edward III (r. 1327–1377) paid homage to Philip VI (r. 1328–1350) for Aquitaine. French policy, however, was strongly expansionist, and in 1337 Philip, determined to exercise full jurisdiction there, confiscated the duchy. This action was the immediate cause of the war. Edward III maintained that the only way he could exercise his rightful sovereignty over Aquitaine was by assuming the title of king of France.[49] As the grandson and eldest surviving male descendant of Philip the Fair, he believed he could rightfully make this claim.

For centuries, economic factors involving the wool trade and the control of Flemish towns had served as justifications for war between France and England. The wool trade between England and Flanders was the cornerstone of both countries' economies; they were closely interdependent. Flanders was a fief of the French crown, and the Flemish aristocracy was highly sympathetic to the monarchy in Paris. But the wealth of Flemish merchants and cloth manufacturers depended on English wool, and Flemish burghers strongly supported the claims of Edward III.

The governments of both England and France manipulated public opinion to support the war. Edward III issued letters to the sheriffs describing in graphic terms the evil deeds of the French and listing royal needs. Kings in both countries instructed the clergy to deliver sermons filled with patriotic sentiment. The royal courts sensationalized the wickedness of the other side and stressed the great fortunes to be made from the war. Philip VI sent agents to warn communities about the dangers of invasion and to stress the French crown's revenue needs to meet the attack.[50]

The Hundred Years' War was popular because it presented unusual opportunities for wealth and advancement. Poor knights and knights who were unemployed were promised regular wages. Criminals who enlisted were granted pardons. The great nobles expected to be rewarded with estates. Royal exhortations to the troops before battles repeatedly stressed that, if victorious, the men might keep whatever they seized. The French chronicler Jean Froissart wrote that, at the time of Edward III's expedition of 1359, men of all ranks flocked to the English king's banner. Some came to ac-

quire honor, but many came in order "to loot and pillage the fair and plenteous land of France."[51]

The period of the Hundred Years' War witnessed the final flowering of the aristocratic code of medieval chivalry. Indeed, the enthusiastic participation of the nobility in both France and England was in response primarily to the opportunity the war provided to display chivalric behavior. War was considered an ennobling experience: there was something elevating, manly, fine, and beautiful about it. Describing the French army before the Battle of Poitiers (1356), a contemporary said:

Then you might see banners and pennons unfurled to the wind, whereon fine gold and azure shone, purple, gules and ermine. Trumpets, horns and clarions—you might hear sounding through the camp; the Dauphin's [title borne by the eldest son of the king of France] great battle made the earth ring.[52]

This romantic and "marvelous" view of war holds little appeal for modern men and women, who are more conscious of the slaughter, brutality, dirt, and blood that war inevitably involves. Also, modern thinkers are usually conscious of the broad mass of people, while the chivalric code applied only to the aristocratic military elite. When English knights fought French ones, they were social equals fighting according to a mutually accepted code of behavior. The infantry troops were looked on as inferior beings. When a peasant force at Longueil destroyed a contingent of English knights, their comrades mourned them because "it was too much that so many good fighters had been killed by mere peasants."[53]

The war was fought almost entirely in France and the Low Countries (Map 13.2). It consisted mainly of a series of random sieges and cavalry raids. During the war's early stages, England was highly successful. At Crécy in northern France in 1346, English longbowmen scored a great victory over French knights and crossbowmen. Although the fire of the longbow was not very accurate, it allowed for rapid reloading, and English archers could send off three arrows to the French crossbowmen's one. The result was a blinding shower of arrows that unhorsed the French knights and caused mass confusion. The firing of cannon—probably the first use of artillery in the West—created further panic. Thereupon the English horsemen charged and butchered the French.

1337
(before the Battle of Crécy)
Held by the kings of England

1360
(after the Battle of Poitiers)
Held by the kings of England
✕ Major battles

ca 1429
(after the siege of Orléans)
Held by the kings of England
✕ Major battle

1453
(end of war)
Held by the kings of England

The Battle of Crécy, 1346
Pitched battles were unusual
in the Hundred Years' War.
At Crécy, the English scored a
spectacular victory. The longbow proved a more effective
weapon than the French
crossbow, but characteristically the artist concentrated
on the aristocratic knights.
(*Source: Bibliothèque Nationale,
Paris*)

Ten years later, Edward the Black Prince, using
the same tactics as at Crécy, smashed the French at
Poitiers, captured the French king, and held him
for ransom. Again, at Agincourt near Arras in
1415, the chivalric English soldier-king Henry V
(r. 1413–1422) gained the field over vastly superior numbers. By 1419 the English had advanced
to the walls of Paris. But the French cause was not
lost. Though England scored the initial victories,
France won the war.

The ultimate French success rests heavily on the
actions of an obscure French peasant girl, Joan of
Arc, whose vision and work revived French fortunes and led to victory. Born in 1412 to well-
to-do peasants in the village of Domrémy in

**MAP 13.2 English Holdings in France During
the Hundred Years' War**   The year 1429
marked the greatest extent of English holdings in
France. Why was it unlikely that England could
have held these territories permanently?

Champagne, Joan of Arc grew up in a religious
household. During adolescence she began to hear
voices, which she later said belonged to Saint
Michael, Saint Catherine, and Saint Margaret. In
1428 these voices spoke to her with great urgency,
telling her that the dauphin (the uncrowned King
Charles VII) had to be crowned and the English
expelled from France. Joan went to the French
court, persuaded the king to reject the rumor
that he was illegitimate, and secured his support
for her relief of the besieged city of Orléans (see
Map 13.2).

Joan arrived before Orléans on April 28, 1429.
Seventeen years old, she knew little of warfare and
believed that if she could keep the French troops
from swearing and frequenting brothels, victory
would be theirs. On May 8 the English, weakened
by disease and lack of supplies, withdrew from Orléans. Ten days later, Charles VII was crowned
king at Reims. These two events marked the turning point in the war.

In 1430 England's allies, the Burgundians, captured Joan and sold her to the English. When the English handed her over to the ecclesiastical authorities for trial, the French court did not intervene. The English wanted Joan eliminated for obvious political reasons, but sorcery (witchcraft) was the charge at her trial. Witch persecution was increasing in the fifteenth century, and Joan's wearing of men's clothes appeared not only aberrant but indicative of contact with the Devil. In 1431 the court condemned her as a heretic. Her claim of direct inspiration from God, thereby denying the authority of church officials, constituted heresy. She was burned at the stake in the marketplace at Rouen. A new trial in 1456 rehabilitated her name. In 1920 she was canonized and declared a holy maiden, and today she is revered as the second patron saint of France.

The relief of Orléans stimulated French pride and rallied French resources. As the war dragged on, loss of life mounted, and money appeared to be flowing into a bottomless pit, demands for an end increased in England. The clergy and intellectuals pressed for peace. Parliamentary opposition to additional war grants stiffened. Slowly the French reconquered Normandy and finally ejected the English from Aquitaine. At the war's end in 1453, only the town of Calais remained in English hands (see Map 13.2).

For both France and England, the war proved a disaster. In France the English had slaughtered thousands of soldiers and civilians. In the years after the sweep of the Black Death, this additional killing meant a grave loss of population. The English had laid waste to hundreds of thousands of acres of rich farmland, leaving the rural economy of many parts of France a shambles. The war had disrupted trade and the great fairs, resulting in the drastic reduction of French participation in international commerce. Defeat in battle and heavy taxation contributed to widespread dissatisfaction and aggravated peasant grievances.

The costs of the war were tremendous. England spent over £5 million on the war effort, a huge sum in the fourteenth and fifteenth centuries. Manpower losses had greater social consequences. The knights who ordinarily handled the work of local government as sheriffs, coroners, jurymen, and justices of the peace were abroad, and their absence contributed to the breakdown of order at the local level. The English government attempted to finance the war effort by raising taxes on the wool crop. Because of steadily increasing costs, the Flemish and Italian buyers could not afford English wool. Consequently, raw wool exports slumped drastically between 1350 and 1450.[54]

The long war also had a profound impact on the political and cultural lives of the two countries. Most notably, it stimulated the development of the English Parliament. Between 1250 and 1450, representative assemblies from several classes of society flourished in many European countries. In the English Parliaments, French Estates, German Diets, and Spanish Cortes, deliberative practices developed that laid the foundations for the representative institutions of modern liberal-democratic nations. Representative assemblies declined in most countries after the fifteenth century, but the English Parliament endured. Edward III's constant need for money to pay for the war compelled him to summon not only the great barons and bishops but knights of the shires and burgesses from the towns as well. Between the outbreak of the war in 1337 and the king's death in 1377, parliamentary assemblies met twenty-seven times. Parliament met in thirty-seven of the fifty years of Edward's reign.[55]

In England theoretical consent to taxation and legislation was given in one assembly for the entire country. France had no such single assembly; instead, there were many regional or provincial assemblies. Why did a national representative assembly fail to develop in France? The initiative for convening assemblies rested with the king, who needed revenue almost as much as the English ruler.

No one in France wanted a national assembly. Linguistic, geographic, economic, legal, and political differences were very strong. People tended to think of themselves as Breton, Norman, Burgundian, or whatever, rather than French. Through much of the fourteenth and early fifteenth centuries, weak monarchs lacked the power to call a national assembly. Provincial assemblies, highly jealous of their independence, did not want a national assembly. The costs of sending delegates to it would be high, and the result was likely to be increased taxation. Finally, the Hundred Years' War itself hindered the growth of a representative body of government. Possible violence on dangerous roads discouraged people from travel.

In both countries, however, the war did promote *nationalism*—the feeling of unity and identity that binds together a people who speak the same language, have a common ancestry and customs, and live in the same area. In the fourteenth century, nationalism largely took the form of hostility toward foreigners. Both Philip VI and Edward III drummed up support for the war by portraying the enemy as an alien, evil people. Edward III sought to justify his personal dynastic quarrel by linking it with England's national interests. As the Parliament Roll of 1348 states:

The Knights of the shires and the others of the Commons were told that they should withdraw together and take good counsel as to how, for withstanding the malice of the said enemy and for the salvation of our said lord the King and his Kingdom of England . . . the King could be aided.[56]

After victories, each country experienced a surge of pride in its military strength. Just as English patriotism ran strong after Crécy and Poitiers, so French national confidence rose after Orléans. French national feeling demanded the expulsion of the enemy not merely from Normandy and Aquitaine but from French soil. Perhaps no one expressed this national consciousness better than Joan of Arc, when she exulted that the enemy had been "driven out of *France.*"

Religious Crisis

In times of crisis or disaster, people of all faiths have sought the consolation of religion. In the fourteenth century, however, the official Christian church offered very little solace. In fact, the leaders of the church added to the sorrow and misery of the times.

From 1309 to 1376, the popes lived in the city of Avignon in southeastern France. In order to control the church and its policies, Philip the Fair of France pressured Pope Clement V to settle in Avignon. Critically ill with cancer, Clement lacked the will to resist Philip. This period in church history is often called the Babylonian Captivity (referring to the seventy years the ancient Hebrews were held captive in Mesopotamian Babylon).

The Babylonian Captivity badly damaged papal prestige. The Avignon papacy reformed its financial administration and centralized its government. But the seven popes at Avignon concentrated on bureaucratic matters to the exclusion of spiritual objectives. In 1377 Pope Gregory XI (r. 1370–

1378) brought the papal court back to Rome. Unfortunately, he died shortly after the return. At Gregory's death, Roman citizens demanded an Italian pope who would remain in Rome.

Urban VI (r. 1378–1389), Gregory's successor, had excellent intentions for church reform. He wanted to abolish simony, pluralism (holding several church offices at the same time), absenteeism, clerical extravagance, and ostentation, but he went about the work of reform in a tactless, arrogant, and bullheaded manner. He delivered blistering attacks on cardinals and threatened to excommunicate some of them. When he was advised that such excommunications would not be lawful unless the guilty had been warned three times, he shouted, "I can do anything, if it be my will and judgment."[57] Urban's quick temper and irrational behavior have led scholars to question his sanity. His actions brought disaster.

The cardinals slipped away from Rome, met at Anagni, and declared Urban's election invalid because it had come about under threats from the Roman mob. The cardinals then proceeded to elect Cardinal Robert of Geneva, the cousin of King Charles V of France, as pope. Cardinal Robert took the name Clement VII (r. 1378–1394) and set himself up at Avignon in opposition to the legally elected Urban. So began the Great Schism, which divided Western Christendom until 1417.

The powers of Europe aligned themselves with Urban or Clement along strictly political lines. France recognized the Frenchman, Clement; England, France's historic enemy, recognized Urban. The scandal provoked horror and vigorous cries for reform. The common people—hard-pressed by inflation, wars, and plague—were thoroughly confused about which pope was legitimate. The schism weakened the religious faith of many Christians and gave rise to instability and religious excesses. At a time when ordinary Christians needed the consolation of religion and confidence in religious leaders, church officials were fighting among themselves for power.

The English scholar and theologian John Wyclif (1329–1384) wrote that papal claims of temporal power had no foundation in the Scriptures and that the Scriptures alone should be the standard of Christian belief and practice. He urged the abolition of such practices as the veneration of saints, pilgrimages, pluralism, and absenteeism. Sincere Christians, Wyclif said, should read the Bible for themselves. Wyclif's views had broad social and economic significance. He urged that the church be stripped of its property. His idea that every Christian free of mortal sin possessed lordship was seized on by peasants in England during a revolt in 1381 and used to justify their goals.

Although Wyclif's ideas were vigorously condemned by ecclesiastical authorities, they were widely disseminated by humble clerics and enjoyed great popularity in the early fifteenth century. The teachings of Wyclif's followers, called Lollards, allowed women to preach and to consecrate the Eucharist. Women, some well educated, played a significant role in the movement. After Anne, sister of Wenceslaus, king of Germany and Bohemia, married Richard II of England, members of Queen Anne's household carried Lollard principles back to Bohemia, where they were spread by John Hus, rector of the University of Prague.

In response to continued calls throughout Europe for a council, the two colleges of cardinals—one at Rome, the other at Avignon—summoned a council at Pisa in 1409. A distinguished gathering of prelates and theologians deposed both popes and selected another. Neither the Avignon pope nor the Roman pope would resign, however, and the appalling result was the creation of a threefold schism.

Finally, because of the pressure of the German emperor Sigismund, a great council met at the imperial city of Constance (1414–1418). It had three objectives: to end the schism, to reform the church "in head and members" (from top to bottom), and to wipe out heresy. The council condemned the Lollard ideas of John Hus, and he was burned at the stake. The council eventually deposed the three schismatic popes and elected a new leader, the Roman cardinal Colonna, who took the name Martin V (1417–1431).

Martin proceeded to dissolve the council. Nothing was done about reform. The schism was over, and though councils subsequently met at Basel and at Ferrara-Florence, in 1450 the papacy held a jubilee, celebrating its triumph over the conciliar movement. In the later fifteenth century, the papacy concentrated on Italian problems to the exclusion of universal Christian interests. The schism and the conciliar movement, however, had exposed the crying need for ecclesiastical reform, thus laying the foundations for the great reform efforts of the sixteenth century.

 ## MARRIAGE AND THE PARISH IN THE LATER MIDDLE AGES

Marriage and the local parish church continued to be the center of the lives of most people. Scholars long believed that because peasants were illiterate and left very few statements about their marriages, generalizations could not be made about them. Recent research in English manorial, ecclesiastical, and coroners' records, however, has uncovered fascinating material. Evidence abounds of teenage flirtations, and many young people had sexual contacts—some leading to conception. Premarital pregnancy may have been deliberate: because children were economically important, the couple wanted to be sure of fertility before entering marriage.

"Whether rich or poor, male or female, the most important rite de passage for peasant youth was marriage."[58] Did they select their own spouses or accept their parents' choices? Church law stressed that for a marriage to be valid both partners had to freely consent to it. Nevertheless, the evidence overwhelmingly shows, above all where land or other property accompanied the union, that parents took the lead in arranging their children's marriages. Parents might have to depend on a son- or daughter-in-law for care in old age. Marriage determined the life partner, the economic circumstances in which the couple would live, and the son-in-law who might take on the family land. Most marriages were between men and women of the same village; where the name and residence of a husband are known, perhaps 41 percent were outsiders. Once the prospective bride or groom had been decided on, parents paid the lord's fee. To allow for objections to the union, parents saw that the parish priest published on three successive Sundays the banns—public announcements that the couple planned to marry. And parents made the financial settlement. The couple then proceeded to the church door. There they made the vows, rings were blessed and exchanged, and the ceremony concluded with some kind of festivity.[59]

The general pattern in late medieval Europe was marriage between men in their middle or late twenties and women under twenty.[60] Poor peasants and wage laborers, both men and women, did not marry until their mid or late twenties. In the later Middle Ages, as earlier—indeed, until the late nineteenth century—economic factors rather than romantic love or physical attraction determined whom and when a person married. The young agricultural laborer on the manor had to wait until he had sufficient land. Thus most men had to wait until their fathers died or yielded the holding. The late age of marriage affected the number of children a couple had. The journeyman craftsman in the urban guild faced the same material difficulties. Prudent young men selected (or their parents selected for them) girls who would bring the most land or money to the union.

With marriage for men postponed, was there any socially accepted sexual outlet? Municipal authorities in many European towns set up legal houses of prostitution or red-light districts either outside the city walls or away from respectable neighborhoods. For example, authorities in Montpellier set aside Hot Street for prostitution, required public women to live there, and forbade anyone to molest them. Prostitution thus passed from being a private concern to a social matter requiring public supervision.[61] Publicly owned brothels were more easily policed and supervised than privately run ones.

Prostitution was an urban phenomenon because only populous towns had large numbers of unmarried young men, communities of transient merchants, and a culture accustomed to a cash exchange. Although the risk of disease limited the number of years a woman could practice this profession, many women prospered. Some acquired sizable incomes. In 1361 Françoise of Florence, a prostitute working in a brothel in Marseilles, made a will in which she made legacies to various charities and left a large sum as a dowry for a poor girl to marry. Legalized prostitution suggests that public officials believed the prostitute could make a positive contribution to the society; it does not mean the prostitute was respected. Rather, she was scorned and distrusted. Legalized brothels also reflect a greater tolerance for male than for female sexuality.[62]

Once a couple married, the union ended only with the death of one partner. Deep emotional bonds knit members of medieval families. Most parents delighted in their children, and the church encouraged a cult of paternal care. Divorce did not exist. The church held that a marriage validly entered into, with mutual oral consent or promise of two parties, could not be dissolved. Annulments were granted in extraordinary circumstances, such

Shepherds Dancing   As in all ages, young people (and some not so young) enjoyed dancing, and the marriage or baptismal feast or harvest celebration provided an opportunity, perhaps accompanied by singing or the music of someone talented on the harmonica or as seen here (lower right) on a bagpipe. (*Source: Bibliothèque Nationale, Paris*)

as male impotence, on the grounds that a lawful marriage had never existed.[63]

Theologians of the day urged that the couple's union be celebrated and witnessed in a church ceremony and blessed by a priest. A great number of couples, however, treated marriage as a private act. They made the promise and spoke the words of marriage to each other without witnesses and then proceeded to enjoy the sexual pleasures of marriage. This practice led to a great number of disputes, because one or the other of the two parties could later deny having made a marriage agreement. The records of the ecclesiastical courts reveal evidence of marriages contracted in a garden, in a blacksmith's shop, at a tavern, and, predictably, in a bed.

Marriage and collective work on the land remained the focus of life for the European peasantry in the thirteenth century. Craft guilds, however, provided the small minority of men and women living in towns and cities with the psychological satisfaction of involvement in the manufacture of a superior product. The guild member also had economic security. The guilds looked after the sick, the poor, the widowed, and the orphaned. Masters and employees worked side by side.

In the fourteenth century, those ideal conditions began to change. The fundamental objective of the craft guild was to maintain a monopoly on its product, and to do so recruitment and promotion were carefully restricted. Some guilds required a high entrance fee for apprentices; others admitted only relatives of members. Restrictions limited the number of apprentices and journeymen to match the anticipated openings for masters. Women experienced the same exclusion. A careful study of the records of forty-two craft guilds in Cologne, for example, shows that in the fifteenth century all but six became virtual male preserves.[64] The decreasing number of openings created serious frustrations. Strikes and riots occurred in the Flemish towns, in France, and in England.

The recreation of all classes reflected the fact that late medieval society was organized for war and that violence was common. The aristocracy engaged in tournaments or jousts; archery and wrestling had great popularity among ordinary people. Everyone enjoyed the cruel sports of bull-baiting and bearbaiting. The hangings and mutilations of criminals were exciting and well-attended events, with all the festivity of a university town before a Saturday football game. Chroniclers exulted in describing executions, murders, and massacres. Here a monk gleefully describes the gory execution of William Wallace in 1305:

Wilielmus Waleis, a robber given to sacrilege, arson and homicide . . . was condemned to most cruel but justly deserved death. He was drawn through the streets of London at the tails of horses, until he reached a gallows of unusual height, there he was suspended by a halter; but taken down while yet alive, he was mutilated, his bowels torn out and burned in a fire, his head then cut off, his body divided into four, and his quarters transmitted to four principal parts of Scotland.[65]

Violence was as English as roast beef and plum pudding, as French as bread, cheese, and *potage.*

 ## Peasant Revolts

In the fourteenth century, economic and political difficulties, disease, and war profoundly affected the lives of European peoples. Decades of slaughter and destruction, punctuated by the decimating visits of the Black Death, made a grave economic situation virtually disastrous. In many parts of France and the Low Countries, fields lay in ruin or untilled for lack of labor power. In England, as taxes increased, criticisms of government policy and mismanagement multiplied.

Peasant revolts occurred often in the Middle Ages. Early in the thirteenth century, the French preacher Jacques de Vitry asked rhetorically, "How many serfs have killed their lords or burnt their castles?"[66] And in the fourteenth and fifteenth centuries, social and economic conditions caused a great increase in peasant uprisings.

In 1358, when French taxation for the Hundred Years' War fell heavily on the poor, the frustrations of the French peasantry exploded in a massive uprising called the *Jacquerie,* after a supposedly happy agricultural laborer, Jacques Bonhomme (Good Fellow). Two years earlier, the English had captured the French king John and many nobles and held them for ransom. The peasants resented paying for their lords' release. Recently hit by plague, experiencing famine in some areas, and harassed by fur-collar criminals, peasants erupted in anger and frustration in Picardy, Champagne, and the area around Paris. Crowds swept through the countryside slashing the throats of nobles, burning their castles, raping their wives and daughters, killing or maiming their horses and cattle. Artisans, small merchants, and parish priests joined the peasants. Urban and rural groups committed terrible destruction, and for several weeks the nobles were on the defensive. Then the upper class united to repress the revolt with merciless ferocity. Thousands of the "Jacques," innocent as well as guilty, were cut down.

The Peasants' Revolt in England in 1381, involving perhaps a hundred thousand people, was probably the largest single uprising of the entire Middle Ages. The causes of the rebellion were complex and varied from place to place. In general, though, the thirteenth century had witnessed the steady commutation of labor services for cash rents, and the Black Death had drastically cut the labor supply. As a result, peasants demanded higher wages and fewer manorial obligations. Thirty years earlier the parliamentary Statute of Laborers of 1351 had declared:

Whereas to curb the malice of servants who after the pestilence were idle and unwilling to serve without securing excessive wages, it was recently ordained . . . that such servants, both men and women, shall be bound to serve in return for salaries and wages that were customary . . . five or six years earlier.[67]

This attempt by landlords to freeze wages and social mobility could not be enforced. As a matter of fact, the condition of the English peasantry steadily improved in the course of the fourteenth century. Why then was the outburst in 1381 so serious? It was provoked by a crisis of rising expectations.

The relative prosperity of the laboring classes led to demands that the upper classes were unwilling to grant. Unable to climb higher, the peasants found release for their economic frustrations in revolt. But economic grievances combined with other factors. The south of England, where the revolt broke out, had been subjected to frequent and destructive French raids. The English government did little to protect the south, and villages grew increasingly scared and insecure. Moreover, decades of aristocratic violence, much of it perpetrated against the weak peasantry, had bred hostility and bitterness. In France frustration over the lack of permanent victory increased. In England the social and religious agitation of the popular preacher John Ball fanned the embers of discontent. Sayings such as Ball's famous couplet "When Adam delved and Eve span; Who was then the gentleman?" reflect real revolutionary sentiment.

The straw that broke the camel's back in England was the reimposition of a head tax on all adult males. Beginning with assaults on the tax collectors, the uprising in England followed much the same course as had the Jacquerie in France. Castles and manors were sacked; manorial records were destroyed. Many nobles, including the archbishop of Canterbury, who had ordered the collection of the tax, were murdered. Urban discontent merged with rural violence. Apprentices and journeymen, frustrated because the highest positions in the guilds were closed to them, rioted.

The boy-king Richard II (r. 1377–1399) met the leaders of the revolt, agreed to charters ensuring peasants' freedom, tricked them with false promises, and then proceeded to crush the uprising with terrible ferocity. Although the nobility tried to restore ancient duties of serfdom, virtually a century of freedom had elapsed, and the

John Ball Outdoors after Mass the priest from Kent preached his radical egalitarianism: "matters goeth not well . . . in England nor shall (they) till everything be common and . . . there be no villains (serfs) nor gentlemen . . . What have we deserved, or why should we be kept thus in servage (servitude)?" All contemporary writers blamed Ball for fomenting the rebellion of 1381. But the evidence shows that peasant demands were limited and local: hunting rights in the woods, freedom from miscellaneous payments, exemption from special work on the lord's bridges or parks. *(Source: Private Collection)*

commutation of manorial services continued. Rural serfdom had disappeared in England by 1550.

Conditions in England and France were not unique. In Florence in 1378, the *ciompi,* the poor propertyless workers, revolted. Serious social trouble occurred in Lübeck, Brunswick, and other German cities. In Spain in 1391, massive uprisings in Seville and Barcelona took the form of vicious attacks on Jewish communities. Rebellions and uprisings everywhere reveal deep peasant and working-class frustration and the general socioeconomic crisis of the time.

❧ Vernacular Literature in the Later Middle Ages

Few developments express the emergence of national consciousness more vividly than the emergence of national literatures. Across Europe people spoke the language and dialect of their particular locality and class. In England, for example, the common people spoke regional English dialects, and the upper classes conversed in French. Official documents and works of literature were written in Latin or French. Beginning in the fourteenth century, however, national languages—the vernacular—came into widespread use not only in verbal communication but in literature as well. Two masterpieces of European culture, Dante's *Divine Comedy* (1310–1320), and Chaucer's *Canterbury Tales* (1387–1400), brilliantly manifest this new national pride.

Dante Alighieri (1265–1321) descended from an aristocratic family in Florence, where he held several positions in the city government. Dante called his work a "comedy" because he wrote it in Italian and in a different style from the "tragic" Latin; a later generation added the adjective "divine," referring both to its sacred subject and to Dante's artistry. Each of the *Divine Comedy*'s three parts describes one of the three realms of the next world—Hell, Purgatory, and Paradise. Dante recounts his imaginary journey through these regions toward God. The Roman poet Virgil, representing reason, leads Dante through Hell, where he observes the torments of the damned and denounces the disorders of his own time, especially ecclesiastical ambition and corruption. Passing up into Purgatory, Virgil shows the poet how souls are purified of their disordered inclinations. From Purgatory, Beatrice, a woman Dante once loved

and the symbol of divine revelation in the poem, leads Dante to Paradise. In Paradise, home of the angels and saints, Saint Bernard—representing mystic contemplation—leads Dante to the Virgin Mary. Through her intercession he at last attains a vision of God.

The *Divine Comedy* portrays contemporary and historical figures, comments on secular and ecclesiastical affairs, and draws on Scholastic philosophy. Within the framework of a symbolic pilgrimage to the City of God, the *Divine Comedy* embodies the psychological tensions of the age. A profoundly Christian poem, it also contains bitter criticism of some church authorities. In its symmetrical structure and use of figures from the ancient world, such as Virgil, the poem perpetuates the classical tradition. But as the first major work of literature in the Italian vernacular, it is distinctly modern.

Geoffrey Chaucer (1340–1400), the son of a London wine merchant, was an official in the administrations of the English kings Edward III and Richard II and wrote poetry as an avocation. Chaucer's *Canterbury Tales* is a collection of stories in lengthy, rhymed narrative. On a pilgrimage to the shrine of Saint Thomas Becket at Canterbury (see page 378), thirty people of various social backgrounds each tell a tale. The Prologue sets the scene and describes the pilgrims, whose characters are further revealed in the story each one tells. For example, the gentle Christian Knight relates a chivalric romance; the gross Miller tells a vulgar story about a deceived husband; the earthy Wife of Bath, who has buried five husbands, sketches a fable about the selection of a spouse. In depicting the interests and behavior of all types of people, Chaucer presents a rich panorama of English social life in the fourteenth century. Like the *Divine Comedy, Canterbury Tales* reflects the cultural tensions of the times. Ostensibly Christian, many of the pilgrims are also materialistic, sensual, and worldly, suggesting the ambivalence of the broader society's concern for the next world and frank enjoyment of this one.

Perhaps the most versatile and prolific French writer of the later Middle Ages was Christine de Pisan (1363?–1434?). The daughter of a professor of astrology, Christine had acquired a broad knowledge of Greek, Latin, French, and Italian literature. The deaths of her father and husband left her with three small children and her mother to support, and she resolved to earn her living with her pen. In addition to poems and books on love, religion, and morality, Christine produced major historical works and many letters. *The City of Ladies* (1404) lists the great women of history and their contributions to society, and *The Book of Three Virtues* provides prudent and practical advice on household management for women of all social classes and at all stages of life. Christine de Pisan's wisdom and wit are illustrated in her autobiographical *Avison-Christine.* She records that a man told her that an educated woman is unattractive because there are so few, to which she responded that an ignorant man was even less attractive because there are so many.

From the fifth through the thirteenth century, the overwhelming majority of people who could read and write were priests, monks, and nuns. Beginning in the fourteenth century, a variety of evidence attests to the increasing literacy of laypeople. In England, as one scholar has recently shown, the number of schools in the diocese of York quadrupled between 1350 and 1500; information from the Flemish and German towns is similar: children were sent to schools and received the fundamentals of reading, writing, and arithmetic. The penetration of laymen into the higher positions of government administration, long the preserve of clerics, indicates the rising lay literacy.

The spread of literacy represents a response to the needs of an increasingly complex society. Trade, commerce, and expanding government bureaucracies required more and more literate people. Late medieval culture remained an oral culture in which most people received information by word of mouth. But by the mid-fifteenth century, even before the printing press was turning out large quantities of reading materials, the evolution toward a literary culture is already perceptible.[68]

The Wife of Bath The fame of medieval England's greatest poet, Geoffrey Chaucer, rests on *The Canterbury Tales,* consisting of a Prologue and the stories of twenty-four pilgrims on their way to Canterbury. The earthy, vivacious Wife of Bath, having had five husbands "not counting other company in youth," is very blunt about her charms and her power:

> *In wyfhode I wol use myn instrument*
> *As freely as my Maker hath it sent.*

Faithful to Chaucer's description, the artist shows her with wide-brimmed hat, hair in a net, and riding astride, not sidesaddle as ladies were expected to do. *(Source: Reproduced by permission of The Huntington Library, San Marino, California)*

SUMMARY

Universities—institutions of higher learning unique to the West—emerged from cathedral and municipal schools and provided trained officials for the new government bureaucracies. The soaring Gothic cathedrals that medieval towns erected demonstrate civic pride, deep religious faith, and economic vitality.

The performance of agricultural services and the payment of rents preoccupied peasants throughout the Middle Ages. Though peasants led hard lives, the reclamation of waste and forest lands, migra-tion to frontier territory, or flight to a town offered means of social mobility. The Christian faith, though perhaps not understood at an intellectual level, provided a strong emotional and spiritual solace.

By 1100 the nobility possessed a strong class consciousness. Aristocratic values and attitudes shaded all aspects of medieval culture. Trained for war, nobles often devoted considerable time to fighting, and intergenerational squabbles were common. Yet a noble might shoulder heavy judicial, political, and economic responsibilities, depending on the size of his estates.

The monks and nuns exercised a profound influence on matters of the spirit. In their prayers, monks and nuns battled for the Lord, just as the chivalrous knights clashed on the battlefield. In their chant and rich ceremonial, in their architecture and literary productions, and in the example of many monks' lives, the monasteries inspired Christian peoples to an incalculable degree. As the crucibles of sacred art, the monasteries became the cultural centers of Christian Europe.

Late medieval preachers likened the crises of their times to the Four Horsemen of the Apocalypse in the Book of Revelation, who brought famine, war, disease, and death. The crises of the fourteenth and fifteenth centuries were acids that burned deeply into the fabric of traditional medieval European society. Bad weather—beyond human control—brought poor harvests, which contributed to the international economic depression. Disease, fostered widespread depression and dissatisfaction. Population losses caused by the Black Death and the Hundred Years' War encouraged the working classes to try to profit from the labor shortage by selling their services higher. When peasant frustrations exploded in uprisings, the frightened nobility and upper middle class joined to crush the revolts. But events had heightened social consciousness among the poor.

The increasing number of schools leading to the growth of lay literacy represents a positive achievement of the later Middle Ages. So also does the development of national literatures. The first sign of a literary culture appeared.

Religion held society together. European culture was a Christian culture. But the Great Schism weakened the prestige of the church and people's faith in papal authority. The conciliar movement, by denying the church's universal sovereignty, strengthened the claims of secular governments to jurisdiction over all their peoples. The later Middle Ages witnessed a steady shift of loyalty away from the church and toward the emerging national states.

NOTES

1. Quoted in H. E. Sigerist, *Civilization and Disease* (Chicago: University of Chicago Press, 1943), p. 102.

2. Quoted in J. H. Mundy, *Europe in the High Middle Ages, 1150–1309* (New York: Basic Books, 1973), pp. 474–475.

3. E. Panofsky, trans. and ed., *Abbot Suger on the Abbey Church of St.-Denis and Its Art Treasures* (Princeton, N.J.: Princeton University Press, 1946), p. 101.

4. See J. Gimpel, *The Cathedral Builders* (New York: Grove Press, 1961), pp. 42–49.

5. Quoted in J. J. Wilhelm, ed., *Lyrics of the Middle Ages: An Anthology* (New York: Garland Publishers, 1993), pp. 94–95.

6. R. Boase, *The Origin and Meaning of Courtly Love* (Manchester, Eng.: 1977), pp. 129–130.

7. I have leaned on the very persuasive interpretation of M. R. Menocal, *The Arabic Role in Medieval Literary History* (Philadelphia: University of Pennsylvania Press, 1990), pp. ix–xv and 27–33.

8. G. Duby, *The Chivalrous Society,* trans. C. Postan (Berkeley: University of California Press, 1977), pp. 90–93.

9. B. A. Hanawalt, *The Ties That Bound: Peasant Families in Medieval England* (New York: Oxford University Press, 1986), p. 5.

10. E. Power, "Peasant Life and Rural Conditions," in J. R. Tanner et al., *The Cambridge Medieval History,* vol. 7 (Cambridge: Cambridge University Press, 1958), p. 716.

11. Glanvill, "De Legibus Angliae," bk. 5, chap. 5, in *Social Life in Britain from the Conquest to the Reformation,* ed. G. G. Coulton (London: Cambridge University Press, 1956), pp. 338–339.

12. See R. Bartlett, "Colonial Towns and Colonial Traders," in *The Making of Europe: Conquest, Colonization, and Cultural Change, 950–1350* (Princeton, N.J.: Princeton University Press, 1993), pp. 167–196.

13. See W. C. Jordan, *From Servitude to Freedom: Manumission in the Senonais in the Thirteenth Century* (Philadelphia: University of Pennsylvania Press, 1986), esp. Ch. 3, pp. 37–58.

14. See John L. Langdon, *Horses, Oxen, and Technological Innovation: The Use of Draught Animals in English Farming, 1066–1500* (New York: Cambridge University Press, 1986), esp. pp. 254–270.

15. G. Duby, *The Early Growth of the European Economy: Warriors and Peasants from the Seventh to the Twelfth Century* (Ithaca, N.Y.: Cornell University Press, 1978), pp. 213–219.

16. See Hanawalt, *The Ties That Bound,* pp. 90–100.

17. Ibid., p. 149.

18. On this quantity and medieval measurements, see D. Knowles, "The Measures of Monastic

Beverages," in *The Monastic Order in England* (Cambridge: Cambridge University Press, 1962), p. 717.

19. S. R. Scargill-Bird, ed., *Custumals of Battle Abbey in the Reigns of Edward I and Edward II* (London: Camden Society, 1887), pp. 213–219.

20. G. Duby, ed., *A History of Private Life,* vol. 2, *Revelations of the Middle Ages* (Cambridge, Mass.: Harvard University Press, 1988), p. 585.

21. Quoted in E. Amt, ed., *Women's Lives in the Middle Ages: A Sourcebook* (New York: Routledge, 1992), pp. 103–104.

22. See C. Klapisch-Zuber, ed., *A History of Women,* vol. 2, *Silences of the Middle Ages* (Cambridge, Mass.: Harvard University Press, 1992), p. 289 et seq.

23. See R. Blumenfeld-Kosinski, *Not of Woman Born: Representations of Caesarian Birth in Medieval and Renaissance Culture* (Ithaca, N.Y.: Cornell University Press, 1990), p. 27.

24. Ibid.

25. Ibid., p. 47.

26. E. J. Kealey, *Medieval Medicus: A Social History of Anglo-Norman Medicine* (Baltimore: Johns Hopkins University Press, 1981), p. 102.

27. Klapisch-Zuber, *Silences of the Middle Ages,* p. 299.

28. See A. Gurevich, *Medieval Popular Culture: Problems of Belief and Perception,* trans. J. M. Bak and P. A. Hollingsworth (New York: Cambridge University Press, 1990), Ch. 2, pp. 39–77, esp. p. 76.

29. Ibid.

30. See M. Rubin, *Corpus Christi: The Eucharist in Late Medieval Culture* (New York: Cambridge University Press, 1992), p. 13 et seq.

31. A. Vauchez, *The Laity in the Middle Ages: Religious Beliefs and Devotional Practices,* ed. D. E. Bornstein, trans. M. J. Schneider (Notre Dame, Ind.: University of Notre Dame Press, 1993), pp. 99–102.

32. Duby, *The Chivalrous Society,* p. 98.

33. J. B. Freed, "The Origins of the European Nobility: The Problem of the Ministerials," *Viator* 7 (1976): 214.

34. J. Boswell, *The Kindness of Strangers: The Abandonment of Children in Western Europe from Late Antiquity to the Renaissance* (New York: Pantheon Books, 1989), p. 24. This section relies heavily on this important work.

35. Ibid., pp. 428–429.

36. Ibid., pp. 238–239.

37. Ibid., pp. 297, 299, and the Conclusion.

38. J. F. Benton, ed. and trans., *Self and Society in Medieval France: The Memoirs of Abbot Guibert of Nogent* (New York: Harper & Row, 1970), p. 46.

39. M. Chibnall, ed. and trans., *The Ecclesiastical History of Orderic Vitalis* (Oxford: Oxford University Press, 1972), 2.xiii.

40. R. W. Southern, *Western Society and the Church in the Middle Ages* (Baltimore: Penguin Books, 1970), pp. 224–230, esp. p. 228.

41. See M. W. Labarge, *A Small Sound of the Trumpet: Women in Medieval Life* (Boston: Beacon Press, 1986), pp. 104–105.

42. J. M. Ferrante, "The Education of Women in the Middle Ages in Theory, Fact, and Fantasy," in *Beyond Their Sex: Learned Women of the European Past,* ed. P. H. Labalme (New York: New York University Press, 1980), pp. 22–24.

43. W. C. Jordan, *Women and Credit in Pre-Industrial and Developing Societies* (Philadelphia: University of Pennsylvania Press, 1993), p. 61.

44. W. H. McNeill, *Plagues and Peoples* (New York: Doubleday, 1976), pp. 151–168.

45. Quoted in P. Ziegler, *The Black Death* (Harmondsworth, Eng.: Pelican Books, 1969), p. 20.

46. J. M. Rigg, trans., *The Decameron of Giovanni Boccaccio* (London: J. M. Dent & Sons, 1903), p. 6.

47. Ziegler, *The Black Death,* pp. 232–239.

48. J. Hatcher, *Plague, Population and the English Economy, 1348–1530* (London: Macmillan Education, 1986), p. 33.

49. See G. P. Cuttino, "Historical Revision: The Causes of the Hundred Years' War," *Speculum* 31 (July 1956): 463–472.

50. J. Barnie, *War in Medieval English Society: Social Values and the Hundred Years' War* (Ithaca, N.Y.: Cornell University Press, 1974), p. 6.

51. Quoted ibid., p. 34.

52. Quoted ibid., p. 73.

53. Ibid., pp. 72–73.

54. M. M. Postan, "The Costs of the Hundred Years' War," *Past and Present* 27 (April 1964): 34–53.

55. See G. O. Sayles, *The King's Parliament of England* (New York: Norton, 1974), app., pp. 137–141.

56. C. Stephenson and G. F. Marcham, eds., *Sources of English Constitutional History,* rev. ed. (New York: Harper & Row, 1972), p. 217.

57. Quoted in J. H. Smith, *The Great Schism 1378: The Disintegration of the Medieval Papacy* (New York: Weybright & Talley, 1970), p. 141.

58. Hanawalt, *The Ties That Bound,* p. 197. This section leans heavily on Hanawalt's important work.

59. Ibid., pp. 194–204.

60. See D. Herlihy, *Medieval Households* (Cam-

bridge, Mass.: Harvard University Press, 1985), pp. 103–111.

61. L. L. Otis, *Prostitution in Medieval Society: The History of an Urban Institution in Languedoc* (Chicago: University of Chicago Press, 1987), p. 2.

62. Ibid., pp. 118–130.

63. See R. H. Helmholz, *Marriage Litigation in Medieval England* (Cambridge: Cambridge University Press, 1974), pp. 28–29 and passim.

64. See M. C. Howell, *Women, Production, and Patriarchy in Late Medieval Cities* (Chicago: University of Chicago Press, 1986), pp. 134–135.

65. A. F. Scott, ed., *Everyone a Witness: The Plantagenet Age* (New York: Thomas Y. Crowell, 1976), p. 263.

66. Quoted in M. Bloch, *French Rural History,* trans. J. Sondeimer (Berkeley: University of California Press, 1966), p. 169.

67. Stephenson and Marcham, *Sources of English Constitutional History,* p. 225.

68. See M. Keen, *English Society in the Later Middle Ages, 1348–1500* (New York: Penguin Books, 1990), pp. 219–239.

Suggested Reading

The achievements of the central and later Middle Ages have attracted considerable scholarly attention, and the curious student will have no difficulty finding exciting material. Three general surveys of the period 1050 to 1300 are especially recommended: D. Nicholas, *The Evolution of the Medieval World* (1992), explores the major themes of the age in depth; G. Holmes, ed., *The Oxford History of Medieval Europe* (1992), discusses the creativity of the period in a series of essays; and J. R. Strayer, *Western Europe in the Middle Ages* (1955), is a masterful synthesis.

N. Orme, *Education and Society in Medieval and Renaissance England* (1989), focuses on early education, schools, and literacy in English medieval society. J. Leclercq, *The Love of Learning and the Desire of God* (1974), discusses monastic literary culture. For the development of literacy among laypeople and the formation of a literate mentality, the advanced student should see M. T. Clanchy, *From Memory to Written Record: England, 1066–1307* (1979).

For the new currents of thought in the central Middle Ages, see C. Brooke, *The Twelfth Century Renaissance* (1970), a splendidly illustrated book with copious quotations from the sources; E. Gilson, *Héloise and Abélard* (1960), which treats the medieval origins of modern humanism against the background of Abélard the teacher; D. W. Robertson, Jr., *Abélard and Héloise* (1972), which is highly readable, com-monsensical, and probably the best recent study of Abélard and the love affair he supposedly had; C. H. Haskins, *The Renaissance of the Twelfth Century* (1971), a classic; and C. W. Hollister, ed., *The Twelfth Century Renaissance* (1969), a well-constructed anthology with source materials on many aspects of twelfth-century culture.

On the medieval universities, C. H. Haskins, *The Rise of the Universities* (1959), is a good introduction. H. De Ridder-Symoens, ed., *A History of the University in Europe,* vol. 1, *Universities in the Middle Ages* (1991) offers up-to-date interpretations by leading scholars. H. Rashdall, *The Universities of Europe in the Middle Ages* (1936), is the standard scholarly work. G. Leff, *Paris and Oxford Universities in the Thirteenth and Fourteenth Centuries* (1968), gives a fascinating sketch and includes a useful bibliography.

F. and J. Gies, *Cathedral, Forge, and Waterwheel* (1993), provides an exciting and illustrated survey of medieval technological achievements. The following studies are all valuable for the evolution and development of the Gothic style: P. Frankl, *The Gothic* (1960); O. von Simson, *The Gothic Cathedral* (1973); and J. Bony, *French Gothic Architecture of the 12th and 13th Centuries* (1983). H. Kraus, *Gold Was the Mortar: The Economics of Cathedral Building* (1979), describes how the cathedrals were financed. D. Grivot and G. Zarnecki, *Gislebertus, Sculptor of Autun* (1961), is the finest appreciation of Romanesque architecture written in English. For the actual work of building, see D. Macaulay, *Cathedral: The Story of Its Construction* (1961), which explores the engineering problems involved in cathedral building and places the subject within its social context. For the most important cathedrals in France, architecturally and politically, see A. Temko, *Notre Dame of Paris: The Biography of a Cathedral* (1968); G. Henderson, *Chartres* (1968); and A. Katzenellengoben, *The Sculptural Programs of Chartres Cathedral* (1959), by a distinguished art historian. E. Panofsky, *Abbot Suger on the Abbey Church of St.-Denis and Its Art Treasures* (1946), provides a contemporary background account of the first Gothic building. C. A. Bruzelius, *The Thirteenth-Century Church at St.-Denis* (1985), traces later reconstruction. J. Gimpel, *The Medieval Machine: The Industrial Revolution of the Middle Ages* (1977), an extremely useful book, discusses the mechanical and scientific problems involved in early industrialization and shows how construction affected the medieval environment.

On troubadour poetry, see, in addition to the titles by R. Boase and J. J. Wilhelm cited in Notes, M. Bogin, *The Women Troubadours* (1980).

For the Black Death, see P. Ziegler, *The Black Death* (1969), a fascinating and highly readable study. For the social implications of disease, see W. H. Mc-

Neill, *Plagues and Peoples* (1976); F. F. Cartwright, *Disease and History* (1972); and H. E. Sigerist, *Civilization and Disease* (1970). For the economic effects of the plague, see J. Hatcher, *Plague, Population, and the English Economy, 1348–1550* (1977).

The standard study of the long military conflicts of the fourteenth and fifteenth centuries remains E. Perroy, *The Hundred Years' War* (1959). J. Barnie's *War in Medieval English Society* treats the attitudes of patriots, intellectuals, and the general public. D. Seward, *The Hundred Years' War: The English in France, 1337–1453* (1981), tells an exciting story, and J. Keegan, *The Face of Battle* (1977), Ch. 2, "Agincourt," describes what war meant to the ordinary soldier. B. Tuchman, *A Distant Mirror: The Calamitous Fourteenth Century* (1980), gives a vivid picture of many facets of fourteenth-century life while concentrating on the war. The best treatment of the financial costs of the war is probably M. M. Postan, "The Costs of the Hundred Years' War," cited in the Notes. E. Searle and R. Burghart, "The Defense of England and the Peasants' Revolt," *Viator* 3 (1972), is a fascinating study of the peasants' changing social attitudes. R. Barber, *The Knight and Chivalry* (1982), and M. Keen, *Chivalry* (1984), give fresh interpretations of the cultural importance of chivalry.

For political and social conditions in the fourteenth and fifteenth centuries, see the works by Sayles, Bloch, Hanawalt, and Helmholz cited in the Notes. The following studies are also useful: P. S. Lewis, *Later Medieval France: The Polity* (1968); L. Romier, *A History of France* (1962); A. R. Meyers, *Parliaments and Estates in Europe to 1789* (1975); R. G. Davies and J. H. Denton, eds., *The English Parliament in the Middle Ages* (1981); I. Kershaw, "The Great Famine and Agrarian Crisis in England, 1315–1322," *Past and Present* (May 1973); K. Thomas, "Work and Leisure in Pre-industrial Society," *Past and Present* 29 (December 1964); R. Hilton, *Bond Men Made Free: Medieval Peasant Movements and the English Rising of 1381* (1973), a comparative study; M. Keen, *The Outlaws of Medieval Legend* (1961) and "Robin Hood—Peasant or Gentleman?" *Past and Present* 19 (April 1961): 7–18; and P. Wolff, "The 1391 Pogrom in Spain: Social Crisis or Not?" *Past and Present* 50 (February 1971): 4–18. Students are especially encouraged to consult the brilliant achievement of E. L.

Ladurie, *The Peasants of Languedoc,* trans. J. Day (1976). R. H. Hilton, ed., *Peasants, Knights, and Heretics: Studies in Medieval English Social History* (1976), contains a number of valuable articles primarily on the social implications of agricultural change. J. C. Holt, *Robin Hood* (1982), is a soundly researched and highly readable study of the famous outlaw.

For women's economic status in the late medieval period, see the important study of M. C. Howell, *Women, Production, and Patriarchy in Late Medieval Cities* (1986). B. Hanawalt, *The Ties That Bind,* cited in the Notes, gives a living picture of the family lives of ordinary people in rural communities. D. Nicholas, *The Domestic Life of a Medieval City: Women, Children, and the Family in Fourteenth-Century Ghent* (1985), focuses on an urban society. C. Klapisch-Zuber, ed., *A History of Women,* vol. 2, *Silences of the Middle Ages* (1992), contains useful essays on many aspects of women's lives and status. S. Shahar, *The Fourth Estate: Women in the Middle Ages* (1983), is a provocative work. J. M. Bennett, *Women in the Medieval English Countryside: Gender and Household in Brigstock Before the Plague* (1987), is a fascinating case study. E. Amt, ed., *Women's Lives in Medieval Europe: A Sourcebook* (1993), has fresh primary material on many aspects of the lives of noble, business, and peasant women.

The poetry of Dante and Chaucer may be read in the following editions: D. Sayers, trans., *Dante: The Divine Comedy,* 3 vols. (1963); and N. Coghill, trans., *Chaucer's Canterbury Tales* (1977). The social setting of *Canterbury Tales* is brilliantly evoked in D. W. Robertson, Jr., *Chaucer's London* (1968).

For the religious history of the period, F. Oakley, *The Western Church in the Later Middle Ages* (1979), is an excellent introduction. R. N. Swanson, *Church and Society in Late Medieval England* (1989), provides a good synthesis of English conditions. S. Ozment, *The Age of Reform, 1250–1550* (1980), discusses the Great Schism and the conciliar movement in the intellectual context of the ecclesio-political tradition of the Middle Ages. Students seeking a highly detailed and comprehensive work should consult H. Beck et al., *From the High Middle Ages to the Eve of the Reformation,* trans. A. Biggs, vol. 14 in the History of the Church series, ed. H. Jedin and J. Dolan (1980).

PAST

A Medieval Noblewoman

In 1115 Guibert (ca 1064?–1124), descendant of a noble family and abbot of Noyon in Picardy, wrote an autobiography, one of the rare examples in the Middle Ages of this literary genre. Cast in the form of a prayer to God, like Saint Augustine's Confessions, *on which it was modeled, Guibert's autobiography includes a sketch of his mother's life. Guibert deeply loved his mother, was dependent on her, and seems to have concentrated on her virtues. He thus gives us an informed, if perhaps idealized, picture of a twelfth-century French noblewoman.*

First and above all, therefore, I render thanks to Thee for that Thou didst bestow on me a mother fair, yet chaste, modest and most devout. . . .

Almost the whole of Good Friday had my mother passed in excessive pain of travail. . . . Racked, therefore, by pains long-endured, and her tortures increasing as her hour drew near, when she thought I had at last in a natural course come to the birth, instead I was returned within the womb. By this time my father, friends, and kinsfolk were crushed with dismal sorrowing for both of us, for whilst the child was hastening the death of the mother, and she her child's in denying him deliverance, all had reason for compassion. . . . So they ask[ed] counsel in their need and [fled] for help to the altar of the Lady Mary, and to her . . . this vow was made and in the place of an offering this gift laid upon the Gracious Lady's altar: that should a male child come to the birth, he should be given up to the service of God and of herself in the ministry, but if one of the weaker sex, she should be handed over to the corresponding calling. At once was born a weak little being, almost an abortion, and at that timely birth there was rejoicing only for my mother's deliverance, the child being such a miserable object. . . . On

that same day . . . I was put into the cleansing water [baptized, for fear of death]. . . .

Once I had been beaten in school—the school being no other than the dining-hall in our house, for he had given up the charge of others to take me alone, my mother having wisely required him to do this for a higher emolument and a better position. When, therefore, at a certain hour in the evening, my studies, such as they were, had come to an end, I went to my mother's knees after a more severe beating than I had deserved. And when she, as she was wont, began to ask me repeatedly whether I had been whipped that day, I, not to appear a tell-tale, entirely denied it. Then she, whether I liked it or not, threw off the inner garments which they call a vest or shirt, and saw my little arms blackened and the skin of my back everywhere puffed up with the cuts from the twigs. And being grieved to the heart by the very savage punishment inflicted on my tender body, troubled, agitated and weeping with sorrow, she said: "You shall never become a clerk, nor any more suffer so much to get learning." At that I, looking at her with what reproach I could, replied: "If I had to die on the spot, I would not give up learning my book and becoming a clerk." Now she had promised that if I wished to become a knight, when [I] reached the age for it, she would give me the arms and equipment.

She, when hardly of marriageable age, was given to my father, a mere youth, by provision of my grandfather. . . . Now it so happened that at the very beginning of that lawful union conjugal intercourse was made ineffective through the bewitchments of certain persons. For it was said that their marriage drew upon them the envy of a step-mother, who, having nieces of great beauty and nobility, was plotting to entangle one of them with my father.

Meeting with no success in her designs, she is said to have used magical arts to prevent entirely the consummation of the marriage. His wife's virginity thus remaining intact for three years, during which he endured his great misfortune in silence, at last, driven to it by his kinsfolk, my father was the first to reveal the facts. Imagine how my kinsmen tried hard in every way to bring about a divorce, and their constant pressure upon my father, young and raw, to become a monk. . . . This, however, was not done for his soul's good, but with the purpose of getting possession of his property. But when their suggestion produced no effect, they began to hound the girl herself, far away as she was from her kinsfolk and harassed by the violence of strangers, into voluntary flight out of sheer exhaustion under their insults, and without waiting for divorce. Meanwhile she endured all this, bearing with calmness the abuse that was aimed at her, and, if out of this rose any strife, pretending ignorance of it. Besides certain rich men perceiving that she was not in fact a wife, began to assail the heart of the young girl; but Thou, O lord, the builder of inward chastity, didst inspire her with purity stronger than her nature or her youth. . . .

In plainness of living there was nothing that she could do, for her delicacy and her sumptuous rearing did not admit of a meagre diet. In other matters no one knew what self-denial she practised. With these eyes I have seen and made certain by touch that whereas over all she wore garments of rich material, next to her skin she was covered with the roughest haircloth, which she wore not only in the daytime, but, what was a great hardship for a delicate body, she even slept in it at night.

The night offices she hardly ever missed, being as regular at the services attended by all God's people in holy seasons; in such fashion that scarcely ever in her house was there rest from the singing of God's praises by her chaplains. . . . A few years before her death she conceived a strong desire to take the sacred veil. When I tried to dissuade her, putting forward as authority the passage where it is written, "Let no prelate attempt to veil widows," saying that her most chaste life would be sufficient without the external veil . . . yet so

Medieval noblewoman at work, from a fifteenth-century manuscript. *(Source: The British Library)*

much more was she inflamed and by no reasoning could be driven from her resolve. So she prevailed, and when taking the veil in the presence of John, the Abbot of that place, gave satisfactory reasons for this act, and in the end she proved that . . . her consecration was invited by signs from heaven.

Questions for Analysis

1. What values shaped Guibert's representation of his mother?

2. How did her marriage come about, and how would you describe her married life?

3. What is the value of this picture of a noblewoman for a present-day historian?

Source: C. C. Swinton Bland, trans., *The Autobiography of Guibert of Nogentsous-Coucy* (New York, 1925); and E. Amt, ed., *Women's Lives in Medieval Europe* (New York: Routledge, 1993), pp. 142–149.

14

The Americas Before European Intrusion, ca 400–1500

This plate from the *Codex Mendoza* dipicts the Aztec legend of the founding of Mexico-Tenochtitlan on the spot where an eagle—an incarnation of Huitzilopochtli—perched on a cactus. *(Source: The Bodleian Library, Oxford)*

etween approximately A.D. 300 and 1500, sophisticated civilizations developed in the Western Hemisphere. But unlike most other societies in the world, which felt the influences of other cultures—sub-Saharan Africa, for example, experienced the impact of Muslims, Asians, and Europeans—Amerian societies grew in almost total isolation from other peoples. Then, in 1501–1502, the Florentine explorer Amerigo Vespucci (1451–1512) sailed down the eastern coast of South America to Brazil. Convinced that he had found a new world, Vespucci published an account of his voyage. Shortly thereafter the German geographer Martin Waldseemüller proposed that this new world be called "America" to preserve Vespucci's memory. Initially applied only to South America, by the end of the sixteenth century the term *America* was used for both continents in the Western Hemisphere.

To the peoples of the Americas, the notion of discovery meant nothing. They did not write about it, and most of the information we have about the Americas derives from European sources. Thus the "new world" was in a very real sense a European invention. Even for Europeans the concept of discovery presented problems. In matters of geography, as in other branches of knowledge, medieval Europeans believed that all human knowledge was contained in the Scriptures, the writings of the church fathers, and the Greek and Roman authors, none of whom mentioned a new world. The adventurous explorers of the fifteenth and sixteenth centuries sailed west searching for Asia and Africa because Europeans believed that those continents and Europe composed the only world that existed. They did not expect to find new continents. Long before the arrival of Europeans, however, sophisticated civilizations were flourishing in Central and South America.

- What is the geography of the Americas, and how did it shape the lives of the peoples?

- What patterns of social and political organization did Amerindian peoples display before the European intrusion?

- What are the significant cultural achievements of the Maya, the Aztecs, and the Incas?

This chapter considers these questions.

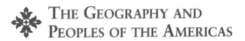

✤ THE GEOGRAPHY AND PEOPLES OF THE AMERICAS

The distance from the Bering Strait, which separates Asia from North America, to the southern tip of South America is about eleven thousand miles. A mountain range extends all the way from Alaska to the tip of South America, crossing Central America from northwest to southeast and making for rugged country along virtually the entire western coast of both continents.

Scholars use the term *Mesoamerica* to designate the area of present-day Mexico and Central America. Mexico is dominated by high plateaus bounded by coastal plains. Geographers have labeled the plateau regions "cold lands," the valleys between the plateaus "temperate lands," and the Gulf and Pacific coastal regions "hot lands." The Caribbean coast of Central America—modern Belize, Guatemala, Honduras, Nicaragua, El Salvador, Costa Rica, and Panama—is characterized by thick jungle lowlands, heavy rainfall, and torrid heat; it is an area generally unhealthy for humans. Central America's western uplands, with their more temperate climate and good agricultural land, support the densest population in the region.

Like Africa, South America is a continent of extremely varied terrain (see Map 14.3). The entire western coast is edged by the Andes, the highest mountain range in the Western Hemisphere. On the east coast another mountain range—the Brazilian Highlands—accounts for one-fourth of the area of modern-day Brazil. Three-fourths of South America—almost the entire interior of the continent—is lowland plains. The Amazon River, at 4,000 miles the second longest river in the world, bisects the north-central part of the continent, draining 2.7 million square miles of land. Tropical lowland rain forests with dense growth and annual rainfall in excess of 80 inches extend from the Amazon and Orinoco river basins northward all the way to southern Mexico.

Most scholars believe that people began crossing the Bering Strait from Russian Siberia between fifty thousand and twenty thousand years ago, when the strait was narrower than it is today. Skeletal finds indicate that these immigrants belonged to several ethnic groups now known collectively as American Indians, or Amerindians. Amerindians were nomadic and technologically

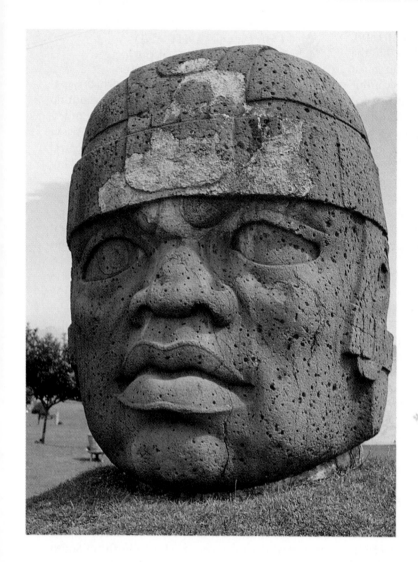

Colossal Head Monument from San Lorenzo Measuring 9 feet, 4 inches in height, and over 10 tons in weight, this basalt head is a superb example of Olmec sculpture intended as architecture. The facial features have led some scholars to suggest African influences, but that hypothesis has not been proven. *(Source: National Tarn/Photo Researchers, Inc.)*

primitive people who lived by hunting small animals, fishing, and gathering wild fruits. As soon as an area had been exploited and a group had grown too large for the land to support, some families broke off from the group and moved on, usually southward. Gradually the newcomers spread throughout the Americas, losing contact with one another.

At the time the Europeans arrived, most of the peoples of North America and the huge Amazon basin were Neolithic hunters and farmers, some migratory and some living in villages. Hunters of big game (bison, elk, boar) armed with heavy stone missiles, traveled in small groups. Sizable groups of people who had learned to cultivate the soil lived a more settled life. Archaeological excavations indicate that corn was grown in Mexico City around 2500 B.C. Before 2300 B.C. the Amerindians also were raising beans, squash, pumpkins, and, in the area of modern Peru, white potatoes.

Amerindians in central Mexico built *chinampas,* floating gardens. They dredged soil from the bottom of a lake or pond, placed the soil on mats of woven twigs, and then planted crops in the soil. Chinampas were enormously productive, yielding up to three harvests a year. So extensive was this method of agriculture that central Mexico became known as the chinampas region. In Peru, meanwhile, people terraced the slopes of the Andes with stone retaining walls to keep the hillsides from sliding. Both chinampas and terraced slopes required the large labor force that became available with stable settlement.

Agricultural advancement had definitive social and political consequences. Careful cultivation of the land brought a reliable and steady food supply, which contributed to a relatively high fertility rate and in turn to a population boom. Because corn and potatoes require much less labor than does grain, Amerindian civilizations had a large pool of people who were not involved in agriculture and thus were available to construct religious and political buildings and serve in standing armies.[1]

MESOAMERICAN CIVILIZATIONS FROM THE OLMECS TO THE TOLTECS

Several American civilizations arose between roughly 1500 B.C. and A.D. 900: the civilizations of the Olmecs, the Maya, Teotihuacán, and the Toltecs. Archaeological investigations of these civilizations are under way, and more questions than answers about them remain, but scholars generally accept a few basic conclusions about them.

Scholars believe that Olmec civilization is the oldest of the early advanced Amerindian civilizations. Olmec culture, based on agriculture, spread over regions in central Mexico that lie thousands of miles apart. The Olmec practice of building scattered ceremonial centers found its highest cultural expression in the civilization of the Maya. The Maya occupied the area of present-day Yucatán, the highland crescent of eastern Chiapas in Mexico, and much of Guatemala and western Honduras. In the central plateau of Mexico an "empire" centered at Teotihuacán arose. Scholars hotly debate whether the Teotihuacán territory constituted an empire, but they agree that Teotihuacán society was heavily stratified and that it exercised military, religious, and political power over a wide area. The Toltecs, whose culture adopted many features of Teotihuacán and Olmec civilizations, was the last advanced Amerindian civilization before the rise of the Aztecs.

The Olmecs

Population growth in the region of southern Veracruz and Tabasco (see Map 14.2) led to the development of the first distinct Mesoamerican civilization: the Olmec. Scholars estimate that the Olmecs thrived from approximately 1500 B.C. to A.D. 300. All subsequent Mesoamerican cultures derive from their culture. At present-day San Lorenzo, the center of Olmec society, were groups of large stone buildings where the political elite and the priestly hierarchy resided with their retainers. Peasant farmers inhabited the surrounding countryside. From careful study of the surviving architectural structures and their richly carved jade sculptures, scholars have learned that a small hereditary elite governed the mass of workers and that the clustered buildings served as sites for religious ceremonies and as marketplaces for the exchange of agricultural produce and manufactured goods. The Olmecs also possessed a form of writing.

Around 900 B.C. San Lorenzo was destroyed, probably by migrating peoples from the north, and power passed to La Venta in Tabasco. Archaeological excavation at La Venta has uncovered a huge volcano-shaped pyramid. Standing 110 feet high at an inaccessible site on an island in the Tonala River, the so-called Great Pyramid was the center of the Olmec religion. The upward thrust of this monument, like that of the cathedrals of medieval Europe, may have represented the human effort to get closer to the gods. Built of huge stone slabs, the Great Pyramid required, scholars estimated, some 800,000 man-hours of labor. It testifies to the region's bumper harvests, which were able to support a labor force large enough to build such a monument. Around 300 B.C., La Venta fell, and Tres Zapotes, 100 miles to the northwest, became the leading Olmec site.

Olmec ceremonialism, magnificent sculpture, skillful stone work, social organization, and writing were important cultural advances that paved the way for the developments of the Classic period (A.D. 300–900), the golden age of Mesoamerican civilization.

The Maya of Central America

In the Classic period the Maya attained a level of intellectual and artistic achievement equaled by no other Amerindian people and by few peoples anywhere. The Maya developed a sophisticated system of writing, perhaps derived partly from the Olmec. They invented a calendar more accurate than the European Gregorian calendar. And they made advances in mathematics that Europeans did not match for several centuries.

Who were the Maya, and where did they come from? What was the basis of their culture? What is the significance of their intellectual and artistic achievement? The word *Maya* seems to derive from

Zamna, the name of a Maya god. Linguistic evidence leads scholars to believe that the first Maya were a small North American Indian group that emigrated from southern Oregon and northern California to the western highlands of Guatemala. Between the third and second millennia B.C. various groups, including the Cholans and Tzeltalans, broke away from the parent group and moved north and east into the Yucatán peninsula. The Cholan-speaking Maya, who occupied the area during the time of great cultural achievement, apparently created the culture.

Maya culture rested on agriculture. The staple crop in Mesoamerica was maize (corn). In 1972, a geographer and an aerial photographer studying the Campeche region of the Yucatán peninsula (Map 14.1) proved that the Maya practiced intensive agriculture in raised narrow rectangular plots that they built above the low-lying, seasonally flooded land bordering rivers. Because of poor soil caused by heavy tropical rainfall and the fierce sun, farmers may also have relied on *milpa* for growing maize. Using this method, farmers cut down the trees in a patch of forest and set the wood and brush afire. They then used a stick to poke holes through the ash and planted maize seed in the holes. A milpa (the word refers to both the area and the method) produced for only two years, after which it had to lie fallow for between four and seven years. Throughout the Yucatán Peninsula, the method of burning and planting in the fertile ashes, known as *swidden agriculture,* remains the typical farming practice today.

In addition to maize, the Maya grew beans, squash, chili peppers, some root crops, and fruit trees. Turkeys were domesticated, but barkless

Cylindrical Vessel Because the Maya suffered a high death rate from warfare, sacrificial ritual, and natural causes, the subject of death preoccupied them. Many art objects depict death as a journey into Xibalba, the Maya hell, and to rebirth for the Maya in children and grandchildren who replace them. Here three Xibalbans receive a sacrificial head on a drum. The scrawny torso of one has the look of starvation, and the excrement implies a revolting smell. The next figure, with a skeletal head, insect wings, and a distended stomach, suggests a parasitic disease. A common if nauseating scene. (*Source: © Justin Kerr 1985. Courtesy Houston Art Museum*)

dogs that were fattened on corn seem to have been the main source of protein. In the Yucatán, men trapped fish along the shores. The discovery of rich Maya textiles all over Mesoamerica indicates that cotton was widely exported.

The raised-field and milpa systems of intensive agriculture yielded food sufficient to support large population centers. The entire Maya region could have had as many as 14 million inhabitants. At Uxmal, Uaxactún, Copán, Piedras Negras, Tikal, Palenque, and Chichén Itzá (see Map 14.1), archaeologists have uncovered the palaces of nobles, elaborate pyramids where nobles were buried, engraved steles (stone-slab monuments), masonry temples, altars, sophisticated polychrome pottery, and courts for games played with a rubber ball. The largest site, Tikal, may have had 40,000 people. Since these centers lacked industrial activities, scholars avoid calling them cities. Rather they were religious and ceremonial centers.

Public fairs accompanying important religious festivals in population centers seem to have been the major Maya economic institutions. Jade, obsidian, beads of red spiny oyster shell, lengths of cloth, and cacao (chocolate) beans—all in high demand in the Mesoamerican world—served as the medium of exchange. The extensive trade among Maya communities, plus a common language, promoted the union of the peoples of the region and gave them a common sense of identity. Merchants trading beyond Maya regions, such as with the Mije-speaking peoples of the Pacific coast, the post-Olmec people of the Gulf coast, the Zapotecs of the Valley of Oaxaca, and the Teotihuacanos of the central valley of Mexico were considered state ambassadors bearing "gifts" to royal neighbors who reciprocated with their own "gifts." Since this long-distance trade played an important part in international relations, merchants conducting it were high nobles or even members of the royal family.

The Maya were a Stone Age people. Lacking iron tools until a few centuries before the Spanish conquest and beasts of burden until after the conquest, how were goods transported to distant regions? The extensive networks of rivers and swamps were the main arteries of transportation; over them large canoes carved out of hardwood trees carried cargoes of cloth and maize. Wide roads also linked Maya centers; on the roads merchants and lords were borne in litters, goods and produce on human backs. Trade produced considerable wealth that seems to have been concen-

MAP 14.1 The Maya World, a.d. 300–900
Archaeologists have discovered the ruins of dozens of Mayan city-states. Only the largest of them are shown here. Called the "Greeks of the New World," the Maya perfected the only written language in the Western Hemisphere, developed a sophisticated political system and a flourishing trade network, and created elegant art.

trated in a noble class, for the Maya had no distinctly mercantile class. They did have a sharply defined hierarchical society. A hereditary elite owned private land, defended society, carried on commercial activities, exercised political power, and directed religious rituals. The intellectual class also belonged to the ruling nobility. The rest of the people were free workers, serfs, and slaves.

The Maya developed a system of hieroglyphic writing with 850 characters and used it to record chronology, religion, and astronomy in books made of bark paper and deerskin. The recent deciphering of this writing has demonstrated that inscriptions on steles are actually historical documents recording the births, accessions, marriages, wars, and deaths of Maya kings. An understanding of the civilization's dynastic history allows scholars to interpret more accurately Maya pictorial imagery and to detect patterns in Maya art. They are

Palace Doorway Lintel at Yaxchilan, Mexico Lady Xoc, principal wife of King Shield-Jaguar, who holds a torch over her, pulls a thorn-lined rope through her tongue to sanctify with her blood the birth of a younger wife's child—reflecting the importance of blood sacrifice in Maya culture. The elaborate headdresses and clothes of the royal couple show their royal status. *(Source: © Justin Kerr 1985)*

finding that the imagery explicitly portrays the text in pictorial scenes and on stelar carvings.[2]

In the sixteenth century, Spanish friars taught Maya students to write their language in the Roman script so that the friars could understand Maya culture. Maya deities and sacrificial customs, however, provoked Spanish outrage. To hasten Maya conversion to Christianity, the priests tried to extirpate all native religion by destroying Maya sculpture and books. Only one Maya hieroglyphic book survived: the *Popul Vuh,* or Book of Council, which was written in European script by a young Quiche noble. Scholars call this document the Maya "Bible," meaning that like the Judeo-Christian scriptures the *Popul Vuh* gives the Maya view of the creation of the world, concepts of good and

evil, and the entire nature and purpose of the living experience.

A method of measuring and recording time to arrange and commemorate events in the life of a society and to plan the agricultural and ceremonial year is a basic feature of all advanced societies. From careful observation of the earth's movements around the sun, the Maya invented a calendar of eighteen 20-day months and one 5-day month, for a total of 365 days. Using a system of bars (— = 5) and dots (∘ = 1), the Maya devised a form of mathematics based on the vigesimal (20) rather than the decimal (10) system. They proved themselves masters of abstract knowledge—notably in astronomy, mathematics, calendric development, and the recording of history.

Maya civilization lasted about a thousand years, reaching its peak between approximately A.D. 600 and 900, the period when the Tang Dynasty was flourishing in China, Islam was spreading in the Middle East, and Carolingian rulers were extending their sway in Europe. Between the eighth and tenth centuries, the Maya abandoned their cultural and ceremonial centers, and Maya civilization collapsed. Archaeologists and historians attribute the collapse to some combination of foreign invasions led by peoples attracted to the wealth of the great Maya centers, domestic revolts of subject peoples, disease, overpopulation resulting from crop failures, and the acquisition of so much territory by expansionist kings that rulers could not govern effectively. Just as scholars give no single reason for the decline and fall of the Roman Empire in Europe, so current scholarship holds that many factors were responsible for the fall of Maya civilization. The Maya, however, were not totally vanquished. Having resisted Indian invaders and the encroachments of Spanish American civilization, about 2 million Maya survive today on the Yucatán peninsula.

Teotihuacán and Toltec Civilizations

During the Classic period the Teotihuacán Valley in central Mexico witnessed the flowering of a remarkable civilization built by a new people from regions east and south of the Valley of Mexico. The city of Teotihuacán had a population of over 200,000—larger than any European city at the time. The inhabitants were stratified into distinct social classes. The rich and powerful resided in a special precinct, in houses of palatial splendor. Ordinary working people, tradespeople, artisans, and obsidian craftsmen lived in apartment compounds, or *barrios,* on the edge of the city. The inhabitants of the barrios seem to have been very poor and related by kinship ties and perhaps by shared common ritual interests. Agricultural laborers lived outside the city. Teotihuacán was a great commercial center, the entrepôt for trade and culture for all of Mesoamerica. It was also the ceremonial center of an entire society, a capital filled with artworks, a mecca that attracted thousands of pilgrims a year.

In the center of the city stood the Pyramids of the Sun and the Moon. The Pyramid of the Sun was built of sun-dried bricks and faced with stone. Each of its sides is 700 feet long and 200 feet high.

The smaller Pyramid of the Moon is similar in construction. In lesser temples, natives and outlanders worshiped the rain-god and the feathered serpent later called Quetzalcoatl. These gods were associated with the production of corn, the staple of the people's diet.

Although Teotihuacán dominated Mesoamerican civilization during the Classic period, other centers also flourished. In the isolated valley of Oaxaca at modern-day Monte Albán (see Map 14.2), for example, Zapotecan-speaking peoples established a great religious center whose temples and elaborately decorated tombs testify to the wealth of the nobility. The art—and probably the entire culture—of Monte Albán and other centers derived from Teotihuacán.

As had happened to San Lorenzo and La Venta, Teotihuacán collapsed before invaders. Around A.D. 700 semibarbarian hordes from the southwest burned Teotihuacán; Monte Albán fell shortly afterward. By 900 the golden age of Mesoamerica had ended. There followed an interregnum known as the "Time of Troubles" (ca A.D. 800–1000), characterized by disorder and extreme militarism. Whereas nature gods and their priests seem to have governed the great cities of the earlier period, militant gods and warriors dominated the petty states that now arose. Among these states, the most powerful heir to Teotihuacán was the Toltec confederation, a weak union of strong states. The Toltecs admired the culture of their predecessors and sought to absorb and preserve it. Through intermarriage, they assimilated with the Teotihuacán people. In fact, every new Mesoamerican confederation became the cultural successor of earlier confederations.

Under Toliptzin (ca 980–1000), the Toltecs extended their hegemony over most of central Mexico. Toliptzin established his capital at Tula. Its splendor and power became legendary during his reign. Apparently he took the name "Quetzalcoatl," signifying his position as high priest of the Teotihuacán god worshiped by the Toltecs. According to the "Song of Quetzalcoatl," a long Aztec glorification of Toliptzin,

he was very rich and had everything necessary to eat and drink, and the corn under his reign was in abundance, and the squash very fat, an arm's length around, and the ears of corn were so tall that they were carried with both arms. . . . And more than that the said Quetzalcoatl had all the wealth of the world, gold and silver and green stones jade and other precious things and a great abundance of coca trees in different colors, and the said vassals of the said Quetzalcoatl were very rich and lacked nothing. . . . Nor did they lack corn, nor did they eat the small ears but rather they used them like firewood to heat up their baths.[3]

Later, Aztec legends described a powerful struggle between the Toltecs' original tribal god, Tezcatlipoca, who required human sacrifices, and the newer Toltec-Teotihuacán god Quetzalcoatl, who gave his people bumper corn crops, fostered learning and the arts, and asked only the sacrifice of animals like butterflies and snakes. Tezcatlipoca won

Tezcatlipoca and Quetzalcoatl The Aztecs were deeply concerned with the passage of time, and like the Maya they had a solar year of 365 days divided into 18 months of 20 days each. The Aztec *tonalamatl*, or sacred "book of days," included a ritual calendar that portrayed thirteen Lords of the Day and nine Lords of the Night, each of them associated with a particular bird. This early-sixteenth-century illustration of a book of days shows Tezcatlipoca and Quetzalcoatl, who were major Lords of the Day. *(Source: Bibliothèque de l'Assemblée, Paris)*

this battle, and the priest-king Toliptzin-Quetzal-coatl was driven into exile. As he departed, he promised to return and regain his kingdom.

Whatever reality lies behind this legend, it became a cornerstone of Aztec tradition. It also played a profound role in Mexican history: by a remarkable coincidence, Quetzalcoatl promised to return in the year that happened to be 1519, the year in which the Spanish explorer Hernando Cortés landed in Mexico. Belief in the Quetzalcoatl legend helps explain the Aztec emperor Montezuma's indecisiveness about the Spanish adventurers and his ultimate fate (see pages 522–523).

After the departure of Toliptzin-Quetzalcoatl, troubles beset the Toltec state. Drought led to crop failure. Northern barbarian peoples, the Chichimec, attacked the borders in waves. Weak, incompetent rulers could not quell domestic uprisings. When the last Toltec king committed suicide in 1174, the Toltec state collapsed. In 1224 the Chichimec captured Tula.

The last of the Chichimec to arrive in central Mexico were the Aztecs. As before, the vanquished strongly influenced the victors: the Aztecs absorbed the cultural achievements of the Toltecs. The Aztecs—building on Olmec, Maya, Teotihuacán, and Toltec antecedents—created the last unifying civilization in Mexico before the arrival of the Europeans.

❈ AZTEC SOCIETY: RELIGION AND WAR

Although the terms *Aztec* and *Mexica* are used interchangeably here, *Mexica* is actually the more accurate word because it is a pre-Columbian term designating the dominant ethnic people of the island capital of Tenochtitlán-Tlalelolco. Aztec derives from *Aztlan,* the legendary homeland of the Mexica people before their migration into the Valley of Mexico, is *not* a pre-Columbian word, and was popularized by nineteenth-century historians.[4]

The Aztecs who appeared in the Valley of Mexico spoke the same Nahuatl language as the Toltecs but otherwise had nothing in common with them. Poor, unwelcome, looked on as foreign barbarians, the Aztecs had to settle on a few swampy islands in Lake Texcoco. From these unpromising beginnings they rapidly assimilated the culture of the

Toltecs and in 1428 embarked on a policy of territorial expansion. By the time Cortés arrived in 1519, the Aztec confederation encompassed all of central Mexico from the Gulf of Mexico to the Pacific Ocean as far south as Guatemala (Map 14.2). Thirty-eight subordinate provinces paid tribute to the Aztec king.

The growth of a strong mercantile class led to an influx of tropical wares and luxury goods: cotton, feathers, cocoa, skins, turquoise jewelry, and gold. The upper classes enjoyed an elegant and extravagant lifestyle; the court of Emperor Montezuma II (r. 1502–1520) was more magnificent than anything in western Europe. How, in less than two hundred years, had the Mexicans (from the Aztec word *mizquitl,* meaning "desolate land," or from *Mixitli,* the Aztec god of war) grown from an insignificant tribe of wandering nomads to a people of vast power and fabulous wealth?

The Aztecs' pictorial records attribute their success to the power of their war-god Huitzilopochtli and to their own drive and willpower. Will and determination they unquestionably had, but there is another explanation for their success: the Aztec state was geared for war. In the course of the fifteenth century, the primitive tribesmen who had arrived in the Valley of Mexico in 1325 transformed themselves into professional soldiers. Military campaigns continued; warriors were constantly subduing new states and crushing rebellions. A strong standing army was the backbone of the Aztec state, and war became the central feature of Mexica culture.

Warfare was a formal stylized ritual conducted according to rules whose goal was the capture, not the execution, of the enemy. Warriors hurled projectiles into their massed foes, intending to demoralize, not to kill. Then, a crippling blow with his obsidian "sword" to a foe's knees or to one of the muscles in the back of the thigh enabled the Aztec warrior to bring him to the ground. Once subdued, men with ropes tied the captive and took him to the rear of the battlefield.[5]

Religion and Culture

In Mexica society, religion was the dynamic factor that transformed other aspects of the culture: economic security, social mobility, education, and especially war. War was an article of religious faith. The state religion of the Aztecs initially gave them powerful advantages over other groups in central

MAP 14.2 The Aztec Empire, 1519   Aztecs controlled much of central Mexico. The Maya survived in the Yucatán Peninsula and some of present-day Guatemala. Notice the number of cities.

Mexico; it inspired them to conquer vast territories in a remarkably short time.[6] But that religion also created economic and political stresses that could not easily be resolved and that ultimately contributed heavily to the society's collapse.

Chief among the Aztecs' many gods was Huitzilopochtli, who symbolized the sun blazing at high noon. The sun, the source of all life, had to be kept moving in its orbit if darkness was not to overtake the world. To keep it moving, Aztecs believed, the sun had to be fed frequently precious fluids—that is, human blood. Human sacrifice was a sacred duty, essential for the preservation and prosperity of humankind. Black-robed priests carried out the ritual:

The victim was stretched out on his back on a slightly convex stone with his arms and legs held by four priests, while a fifth ripped him open with a flint knife and tore out his heart. The sacrifice also often took place in a manner which the Spanish described as gladiatorio: the captive was tied to a huge disk of stone . . . by a rope that left him free to move; he was armed with wooden weapons, and he had to fight several normally-armed Aztec warriors in turn. If, by an extraordinary chance, he did not succumb to their attacks, he was spared; but nearly always the "gladia-

tor" fell, gravely wounded, and a few moments later he died on the stone, with his body opened by the black-robed, long-haired priests.[7]

Mass sacrifice was also practiced:

Mass sacrifices involving hundreds and thousands of victims could be carried out to commemorate special events. The Spanish chroniclers were told, for example, that at the dedication in 1487, of the great pyramid of Tenochtitlán four lines of prisoners of war stretching for two miles each were sacrificed by a team of executioners who worked night and day for four days. Allotting two minutes for sacrifice, the demographer and historian Sherburne Cook estimated that the number of victims associated with that single event was 14,100. The scale of these rituals could be dismissed as exaggerations were it not for the encounters of Spanish explorers with . . . rows of human skulls in the plazas of the Aztec cities. . . . In the plaza of Xocotlan "there were . . . more than one hundred thousand of them."[8]

The Mexica did not invent human sacrifice; it seems to have been practiced by many Mesoamerican peoples. The Maya, for example, dedicated their temples with the blood of freshly executed victims. Anthropologists have proposed several explanations—none of them completely satisfactory—for the Aztecs' practice of human sacrifice and the cannibalism that often accompanied it. Some suggest that human sacrifice served to regulate population growth. Yet ritual slaughter had been practiced by earlier peoples—the Olmecs, the Maya, the dwellers of Teotihuacán, and the Toltecs—in all likelihood before population density had reached the point of threatening the food supply. Moreover, since almost all the victims were men—warriors captured in battle—population growth could still have exceeded the death rate. Executing women of child-bearing age would have had more effect on population growth.

According to a second hypothesis, the ordinary people were given victims' bodies as a source of protein.[9] These people lived on a diet of corn, beans, squash, tomatoes, and peppers. Wildlife was scarce, and dog meat, chicken, turkey, and fish were virtually restricted to the upper classes. The testimony of modern nutritionists that beans supply ample protein, and the evidence that, in an area teeming with wild game, the Huron Indians of North America ritually executed captives and feasted on their stewed bodies, weaken the validity of this theory.

A third, more plausible, theory holds that ritual human sacrifice was an instrument of state terrorism—that the Aztec rulers crushed dissent with terror. The Aztecs controlled a large confederation of city-states by sacrificing prisoners seized in battle; by taking hostages from among defeated peoples as ransom against future revolt; and by demanding from subject states an annual tribute of people to be sacrificed to Huitzilopochtli. Unsuccessful generals, corrupt judges, and careless public officials, even people who accidentally entered forbidden precincts of the royal palaces, were routinely sacrificed. When the supply of such victims ran out, slaves, plebeians, and even infants torn from their mothers suffered ritual execution. The emperor Montezuma II, who celebrated his coronation with the sacrifice of fifty-one hundred people, could be said to have ruled by holocaust. Trumpets blasted and drums beat all day long announcing the sacrifice of yet another victim. Blood poured down the steps of the pyramids. Death and fear stalked everywhere. Ordinary people appear to have endured this living nightmare by escaping into intoxicating drink and drugs.[10] Even this in-

terpretation, however, does not put the practice of human sacrifice in its full cultural context.

The Mexica state religion required constant warfare for two basic reasons. One was to meet the gods' needs for human sacrifice; and, secondly, warriors for the next phase of imperial expansion. ". . . the sacred campaigns of Huitzilopochtli were synchronized with the political and economic needs of the Mexica nation as a whole."[11] Nobles, warriors, and commoners who secured captives on the battlefield shared in the booty, lands, and the

The Goddess Tlazolteotl   The Aztecs believed that Tlazolteotl (sometimes called "Mother of the Gods"), by eating refuse, consumed the sins of humankind. As the goddess of childbirth, Tlazolteotl was extensively worshiped. Notice the squatting position for childbirth, then common all over the world. *(Source: Dumbarton Oaks Research Library and Collections, Washington, D.C.)*

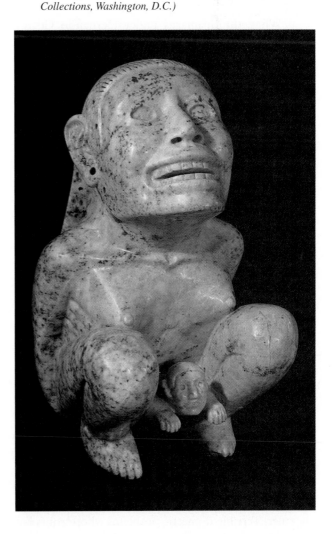

emperor's rich rewards of gold and silver jewelry, feathered costumes, and other articles of distinctive dress—depending on the number of captives they won. Nobles could grow wealthier, and the ordinary soldier could be promoted to the nobility. Social status, especially in the early period of Aztec expansion, depended on military performance. Warfare, therefore, offered the powerful incentive of upward social mobility. Moreover, defeated peoples had to pay tribute in foodstuffs to support rulers, nobles, warriors, and the imperial bureaucracy. The vanquished supplied laborers for agriculture, the economic basis of Mexica society. Likewise, conquered peoples had to produce workers for the construction and maintenance of the entire Aztec infrastructure—roads, dike systems, aqueducts, causeways, and the royal palaces. Finally, merchants also benefited, for war opened new markets for traders' goods in subject territories.

When the Spaniards under Hernando Cortés (1485–1547) arrived in central Mexico in 1519, the sacred cult of Huitzilopochtli had created a combination of interrelated problems for the emperor Montezuma II. The thirty-eight provinces of the empire, never really assimilated into the Mexica state and usually governed by members of the defeated dynasty, seethed with rebellion. Population increases at the capital Tenochtitlán had forced the emperor to lay increasingly heavier tribute on conquered provinces, which in turn, murdered the tribute collectors. Invasion and reconquest followed. "The provinces were being crushed beneath a cycle of imperial oppression: increases in tribute, revolt, reconquest, retribution, higher tribute, resentment, and repeated revolt."[12] By causing the death in battle and by sacrifice of thousands of food producers, Mexica religion destroyed the very economic basis of the empire.

Faced with grave crisis, Montezuma attempted to solve the problem by freezing social positions. He purged the court of many officials, drastically modified the dress and behavior of the merchant class, and severely limited the honors given to low-born warriors and all but the highest nobility. These reforms provoked great resentment, reduced incentive, and virtually ended social mobility. Scholars have traditionally portrayed Montezuma as weak-willed and indecisive when faced by the Spaniards. But recent research has shown that he was a very determined, even autocratic ruler. Terrible domestic problems whose roots lay in a religious cult requiring appalling human slaughter offer the fundamental explanation for the Mexica collapse.[13]

The Life of the People

A wealth of information has survived about fifteenth- and sixteenth-century Mexico. The Aztecs were deeply interested in their own past, and in their pictographic script they wrote many books recounting their history, geography, and religious practices. They loved making speeches, and every public or social occasion gave rise to lengthy orations, which scribes copied down. The Aztecs also preserved records of their legal disputes, which alone amounted to vast files. The Spanish conquerors subsequently destroyed much of this material. But enough documents remain to construct a picture of the Mexica people at the time of the Spanish intrusion.

No sharp social distinctions existed among the Aztecs during their early migrations. All were equally poor. The head of a family was both provider and warrior, and a sort of tribal democracy prevailed in which all adult males participated in important decision making. By the early sixteenth century, however, Aztec society had changed. A stratified social structure had come into being, and the warrior aristocracy exercised great authority.

Scholars do not yet understand precisely how this change evolved. According to Aztec legend, the Mexicans admired the Toltecs and chose their first king, Acamapichti, from among them. The many children he fathered with Mexica women formed the nucleus of the noble class. At the time of the Spanish intrusion into Mexico, men who had distinguished themselves in war occupied the highest military and social positions in the state. Generals, judges, and governors of provinces were appointed by the emperor from among his servants who had earned reputations as war heroes. These great lords, or *tecuhtli,* dressed luxuriously and lived in palaces. Like feudal lords, the provincial governors exercised full political, judicial, and military authority on the emperor's behalf. In their territories they maintained order, settled disputes, and judged legal cases; oversaw the cultivation of land; and made sure that tribute—in food or gold—was paid. The governors also led troops in wartime. These functions resembled those of feudal lords in western Europe during the Middle

Ages (see pages 413–414). Just as only nobles of France and England could wear fur and carry a sword, just as gold jewelry and elaborate hairstyles for women distinguished royal and noble classes in African kingdoms, so in Mexica societies only the tecuhtli could wear jewelry and embroidered cloaks.

Beneath the great nobility of soldiers and imperial officials was the class of warriors. Theoretically every freeman could be a warrior, and parents dedicated their male children to war, burying a male child's umbilical cord with some arrows and a shield on the day of his birth. In actuality the sons of nobles enjoyed advantages deriving from their fathers' position and influence in the state. At the age of six, boys entered a school that trained them for war. Future warriors were taught to fight with a *macana,* a paddle-shaped wooden club edged with bits of obsidian (a volcanic rock similar to granite but as sharp as glass). This weapon could be brutally effective: during the Spanish invasion, Aztec warriors armed with macanas slashed off horses' heads with one blow. Youths were also trained in the use of spears, bows and arrows, and lances fitted with obsidian points. They learned to live on little food and sleep and to accept pain without complaint. At about age eighteen a warrior fought his first campaign. If he captured a prisoner for ritual sacrifice, he acquired the title *iyac,* or warrior. If in later campaigns he succeeded in killing or capturing four of the enemy, he became a *tequiua*—one who shared in the booty and thus was a member of the nobility. Warriors enjoyed a privileged position in Mexica society because they provided the state with the victims necessary for its survival. If a young man failed in several campaigns to capture the required four prisoners, he joined the *maceualtin,* the plebeian or working class.

The maceualtin were the ordinary citizens—the backbone of Aztec society and the vast majority of the population. The word *maceualti* means "worker" and implied boorish speech and vulgar behavior. Members of this class performed all sorts of agricultural, military, and domestic services and carried heavy public burdens not required of noble warriors. Government officials assigned the maceualtin work on the temples, roads, and bridges. Army officers called them up for military duty, but Mexicans considered this an honor and a religious rite, not a burden. Unlike nobles, priests, orphans, and slaves, maceualtin paid taxes. Maceualtin in the capital, however, possessed certain rights: they

❈ **Coronation Stone of Montezuma**   Originally located within the ritual center at Tenochtitlán, this quadrangular stone, carved with hieroglyphics in the Nahual language of the Aztecs, commemorates the start of Montezuma's reign, July 15, 1503, the date of his coronation. The sculpture associates his rule with the cycle of birth, death, and renewal. (*Source: Art Institute of Chicago, Major Acquisitions Centennial Endowment*)

held their plots of land for life, and they received a small share of the tribute paid by the provinces to the emperor.

Beneath the maceualtin were the *thalmaitl,* the landless workers or serfs. Some social historians speculate that this class originated during the "Time of Troubles," a period of migrations and upheavals in which weak and defenseless people placed themselves under the protection of strong warriors. The thalmaitl provided agricultural labor at times of planting and harvesting, paid rents in kind, and were bound to the soil—they could not move off the land. The thalmaitl resembled in many ways the serfs of western Europe, but unlike serfs they performed military service when called on to do so. They enjoyed some rights as citizens and generally were accorded more respect than slaves.

Slaves were the lowest social class. Like Asian, European, and African slaves, most were prisoners captured in war or kidnapped from enemy tribes.

But Aztecs who stole from a temple or private house or plotted against the emperor could also be enslaved, and people in serious debt sometimes voluntarily sold themselves into slavery. Female slaves often became their masters' concubines. Mexican slaves, however, differed fundamentally from European ones: "Tlatlocotin slaves could possess goods, save money, buy land and houses and even slaves for their own service."[14] Slaves could purchase their freedom. If a male slave married a free woman, their offspring were free, and a slave who escaped and managed to enter the emperor's palace was automatically free. Most slaves eventually gained their freedom. Mexican slavery, therefore, had humane qualities, in marked contrast with the slavery that the Spanish later introduced into South America and that the English imposed in North America.

Women of all social classes played important roles in Mexica society, but those roles were restricted entirely to the domestic sphere. As the little hands of the new-born male child were closed around a tiny bow and arrow indicating his warrior destiny, so the infant female's hands were wrapped around miniature weaving instruments and a small broom: weaving was a sacred and exclusively female art; the broom signalled a female's responsibility for the household shrines and for keeping the household swept and free of contamination. Almost all of the Mexica people married, a man at about twenty when he had secured one or two captives, a woman a couple years earlier. As in premodern Asian and European societies, parents selected their children's spouse, using neighborhood women as go-betweens. Save for the few women vowed to the service of the temple, marriage and the household was woman's fate; marriage represented social maturity for both sexes. Pregnancy became the occasion for family and neighborhood feasts, and a successful birth launched celebrations lasting from ten to twenty days. The rich foods available, such as frogs stewed with green chilis or gophers with sauce, as well as the many varieites of tamales, suggest that women had a sophisticated knowledge of food preparation. Women also had the care of small children.

Women took no part in public affairs—with a few notable exceptions. As the bearing of children was both a social duty and a sacred act, midwives enjoyed great respect. The number of midwives at a confinement indicated rank: a noblewoman often had two or three midwives. As in the medieval European West, in a very difficult birth midwives sacrificed the life of the child for that of the mother. Mexica society also awarded high status and authority to female physicians and herbalists. They treated men as well as women, setting broken bones and prescribing herbal remedies for a variety of ailments. The sources, though limited, imply that a few women skilled at market trading achieved economic independence. The woman weaver capable of executing complicated designs also had the community's esteem. Prostitutes in the state brothels, not local Mexica but tribute girls from the provinces given to successful warriors as part of their rewards, probably did not enjoy esteem.[15]

Alongside the secular social classes stood the temple priests. Huitzilopochtli and each of the numerous lesser gods had many priests to oversee the upkeep of the temple, assist at religious ceremonies, and perform ritual sacrifices. The priests also did a brisk business in foretelling the future from signs and omens. Aztecs consulted priests on the selection of wives and husbands, on the future careers of newborn babies, and before leaving on journeys or for war. Temples possessed enormous wealth in gold and silver ceremonial vessels, statues, buildings, and land. Fifteen provincial villages had to provide food for the temple at Texcoco and wood for its eternal fires. The priests who had custody of all this property did not marry and were expected to live moral and upright lives. From the temple revenues and resources, the priests supported schools, aided the poor, and maintained hospitals. The chief priests had the ear of the emperor and often exercised great power and influence.

At the peak of the social pyramid stood the emperor. The various Aztec historians contradict one another about the origin of the imperial dynasty, but modern scholars tend to accept the verdict of one sixteenth-century authority that the "custom has always been preserved among the Mexicans (that) the sons of kings have not ruled by right of inheritance, but by election."[16] A small oligarchy of the chief priests, warriors, and state officials made the selection. If none of the sons proved satisfactory, a brother or nephew of the emperor was chosen, but election was always restricted to the royal family.

The Aztec emperor was expected to be a great warrior. He led Mexican and allied armies into battle. All his other duties pertained to the welfare of his people. It was up to the emperor to see that justice was done—he was the final court of appeal. He also held ultimate responsibility for ensuring an adequate food supply. The emperor Montezuma I (r. 1440–1467) distributed twenty thousand loads of stockpiled grain when a flood hit Tenochtitlán. The records show that the Aztec emperors took their public duties seriously.

The Cities of the Aztecs

When the Spanish entered Tenochtitlán (which they called "Mexico City") in November 1519, they could not believe their eyes. According to Bernal Díaz, one of Cortés's companions,

when we saw all those cities and villages built in the water, and other great towns on dry land, and that straight and level causeway leading to Mexico, we were astounded. These great towns and cues (temples)

and buildings rising from the water, all made of stone, seemed like an enchanted vision. . . . Indeed, some of our soldiers asked whether it was not all a dream.[17]

Tenochtitlán had about 60,000 households. The upper class practiced polygamy and had many children, and many households included servants and slaves. The total population probably numbered around 250,000. At the time, no European city and few Asian ones could boast a population even half that size. The total Aztec Empire has been estimated at around 5 million inhabitants.

Originally built on salt marshes, Tenochtitlán was approached by four great highways that connected it with the mainland. Wide straight streets and canals crisscrossed the city. Boats and canoes plied the canals. Lining the roads and canals stood thousands of rectangular one-story houses of mortar faced with stucco. Although space was limited, many small gardens and parks were alive with the

Tenochtitlán The great Mexican archaeologist Ignacio Marquina reconstructed the central plaza of the Aztec capital as it looked in 1519. The huge temple of the god of war dominates the area; royal palaces are on each side. On the right stands the rack with tens of thousands of human skulls; in the center is the platform where captives met sacrificial death. *(Source: Library of Congress)*

colors and scents of flowers. The Mexicans loved flowers and used them in ritual ceremonies.

A large aqueduct whose sophisticated engineering astounded Cortés carried pure water from distant springs and supplied fountains in the parks. Streets and canals opened onto public squares and marketplaces. Tradespeople offered every kind of merchandise. Butchers hawked turkeys, ducks, chickens, rabbits, and deer; grocers sold kidney beans, squash, avocados, corn, and all kinds of peppers. Artisans sold intricately designed gold, silver, and feathered jewelry. Seamstresses offered sandals, loincloths and cloaks for men, and blouses and long skirts for women—the clothing customarily worn by ordinary people—and embroidered robes and cloaks for the rich. Slaves for domestic

service, wood for building, herbs for seasoning and medicine, honey and sweets, knives, jars, smoking tobacco, even human excrement used to cure animal skins—all these wares made a dazzling spectacle.

At one side of the central square of Tenochtitlán stood the great temple of Huitzilopochtli. Built as a pyramid and approached by three flights of 120 steps each, the temple was about 100 feet high and dominated the city's skyline. According to Cortés it was

so large that within the precincts, which are surrounded by a very high wall, a town of some five hundred inhabitants could easily be built. All round inside this wall there are very elegant quarters with very large rooms and corridors where their priests live.[18]

Describing the Aztec way of life for the emperor Charles V, Cortés concluded: "considering that they are barbarous and so far from the knowledge of God and cut off from all civilized nations, it is truly remarkable to see what they have achieved in all things."[19] Certainly Cortés's views reflect his own culture and outlook, but it is undeniable that Mexica culture was remarkable.

THE INCAS OF PERU

In the late 1980s archaeologists working in the river valleys on the west coast of present-day Peru uncovered stunning evidence of complex societies that flourished between 5,000 and 3,000 years ago—roughly the same period as the great pyramids of Egypt. In spite of the altitude and dryness of the semidesert region, scores of settlements existed (Map 14.3). Perhaps the most spectacular was the one at Pampa de las Llamas-Moxeke in the Casma Valley. Stepped pyramids and U-shaped buildings, some more than ten stories high, dominated these settlements. Were these structures warehouses for storing food or cultic temples? Were these settlements connected in some sort of political association? Was there sufficient commercial activity to justify calling them cities? Why did these peoples, who lived on a diet of fish, sweet potatoes, beans, and peanuts, suddenly abandon their settlements and move into the Andean highlands? Scholars have only begun to process these

MAP 14.3 The Inca Empire, 1463–1532
South America, which extends 4,750 miles in length and 3,300 miles from east to west at its widest point, contains every climatic zone and probably the richest variety of vegetation on earth. Roads built by the Incas linked most of the Andean region.

vast remains, but radio carbon dating has already demonstrated that the settlements are older than the Maya and Aztec structures.[20]

Another archaeological discovery is providing scholars with rich information about pre-Columbian society. For some time, the villagers of Sipán in northern Peru supplemented their meager incomes by plundering ancient cemeteries and pyramids. One night in 1987 while digging deep in a pyramid, they broke into one of the richest funerary chambers ever located, and they filled their sacks with ceramic, gold, and silver objects. A dispute about the distribution of the loot led one dissatisfied thief to go to the police. When archaeologists from Lima and the United States arrived, they ranked the discoveries at Sipán with those at Tutankhamen's tomb in Egypt and the terra-cotta statues of the Qin Dynasty warriors near Xian, China.

The treasures from the royal tombs at Sipán derive from the Moche civilization, which flourished along a 250-mile stretch of Peru's northern coast between A.D. 100 and 800. Rivers that flowed out of the Andes Mountains into the valleys allowed the Moche people to develop complex irrigation systems for agricultural development. Each Moche valley contained a large ceremonial center with palaces and pyramids surrounded by settlements of up to 10,000 people. The dazzling gold and silver artifacts, elaborate hairdresses, and ceramic vessels display a remarkable skill in metalwork. Much of later Inca technology seems clearly based on the work of the Moche.[21]

The Aztec civilization of Mexico had already passed its peak when the Spanish landed in America. So too had a greater culture to the south, that of the Incas of Peru. Like the Aztecs, the Incas were "a small militaristic group that came to power late, conquered surrounding groups, and established one of the most extraordinary empires in the world."[22] Gradually, Inca culture spread throughout Peru. Modern knowledge of the Incas is concentrated on the last century before Spanish intrusion (1438–1532); today's scholars know far less about earlier developments.

In the center of Peru rise the cold highlands of the Andes Mountains. Six valleys of fertile and wooded land at altitudes ranging from 8,000 to 11,000 feet punctuate highland Peru. The largest of these valleys are Huaylas, Cuzco, and Titicaca. It was there that Inca civilization developed and flourished.

Portrait Vessel of a Ruler   Artisans of the Moche culture on the northern coast of Peru produced objects representing many aspects of their world, including this flat-bottomed stirrup-spout jar with a ruler's face. The commanding expression conveys a strong sense of power, as does the elaborate headdress with the geometric designs of Moche textiles worn only by elite persons. *(Source: Art Institute of Chicago. Kate S. Buckingham Endowment, 1955.2338)*

Archaeologists still do not understand how people of the Andean region acquired a knowledge of agriculture. Around 2500 B.C. they were relying on fish and mussels for food. Early agriculture seems to have involved cultivating cotton for ordinary clothing, ceremonial dress, and fish nets. Beautifully dyed cotton textiles, swatches of which

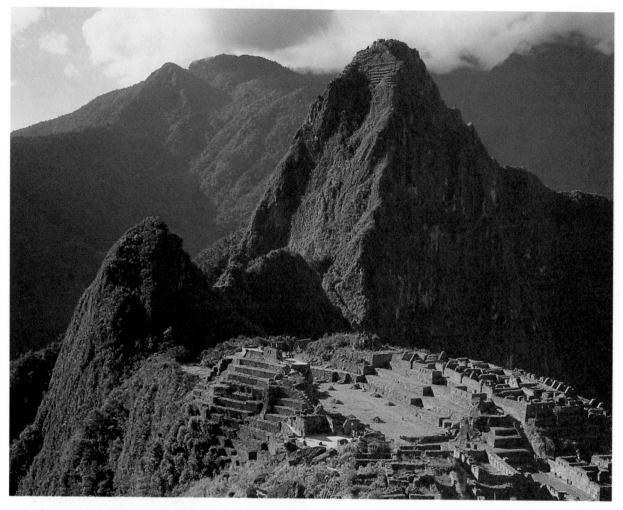

Machu Picchu   The citadel of Machu Picchu, surrounded by mountains in the clouds, clings to a spectacular crag in upland Peru. It was discovered in 1911 by the young American explorer Hiram Bingham. Its origin and the reason for its abandonment remain unknown. *(Source: Photo Researchers)*

have been found in ancient gravesites, may also have served as articles for trade. The central highland region of the Andes is much less well suited to agriculture than is Mesoamerica; in the Andes arable land is scarce. Yet between A.D. 600 and 1000, remarkable agricultural progress was made.

The Incas constructed great terraces along the mountain slopes and shored them up with walls to retain moisture. With only a foot plow, bronze hoe, and *guano* (the dried excrement of sea birds) as fertilizer, the Amerindians of Peru produced bumper crops of white potatoes. Potatoes ordinarily cannot be stored for long periods, but the Inca

of the Andean highlands developed a product called *chuñu,* freeze-dried potatoes made by subjecting potatoes alternately to nightly frosts and daily sun. Chuñu will keep unspoiled for several years. The construction of irrigation channels also facilitated the cultivation of corn. Potatoes and corn required far less labor and time than did the cultivation of wheat in Europe or rice in China.

By the fifteenth century, enough corn, beans, chili peppers, squash, tomatoes, sweet potatoes, peanuts, avocados, and white potatoes were harvested to feed not only the farmers themselves but also massive armies and administrative bureaucracies and thousands of industrial workers. Wild animals had become almost extinct in the region and were the exclusive preserve of the nobility. Common people rarely ate any meat other than guinea pigs, which most families raised. Chicha, a beer fermented from corn, was the staple drink.

Inca Imperialism

Who were the Incas? *Inca* was originally the name of the governing family of an Amerindian group that settled in the basin of Cuzco (see Map 14.3). From that family, the name was gradually extended to all people living in the Andes valleys. The Incas themselves used the word to identify their chief or emperor. Here the term is used for both the ruler and the people.

As with the Aztecs, so with the Incas: religious ideology was the force that transformed the culture. Religious concepts created pressure for imperialist expansion—with fatal consequences.

The Incas believed their ruler descended from the sun-god and that the health and prosperity of the state depended on him. Dead rulers were thought to link the people to the sun-god. When the ruler died, his corpse was preserved as a mummy in elaborate clothing and housed in a sacred and magnificent chamber. The mummy was brought in procession to all important state ceremonies, his advice was sought in time of crisis, and hundreds of human beings were sacrificed to him. In ordinary times, the dead ruler was carried to visit his friends, and his heirs and relatives came to dine with him. Some scholars call this behavior the "cult of the royal mummies" because it was a kind of ancestor worship.

The mummies were not only the holiest objects in the Inca world, but also a powerful dynamic force in Inca society. According to the principle of the "split inheritance," when an Inca ruler died, the imperial office, insignia, and rights and duties of the monarchy passed to the new king. The dead ruler, however, retained full and complete ownership of all his estates and properties. His royal descendants as a group managed his lands and sources of income for him and used the revenues to care for his mummy and to maintain his cult. Thus a new ruler came to the throne land- or property-poor. In order to live in the royal style, strengthen his administration, and reward his supporters, he had to win his own possessions by means of war and imperial expansion.[23]

Around A.D. 1000 the Incas were one of many small groups fighting among themselves for land and water. As they began to conquer their neighbors, a body of religious lore came into being that ascribed divine origin to their earliest king, Manco Capac (ca 1200) and promised warriors the gods' favor and protection. Strong historical evidence, however, dates only from the reign of Pachacuti Inca (1438–1471), who launched the imperialist phase of Inca civilization.

If the cult of ancestor or mummy worship satisfied some Inca social needs, in time it also created serious problems. The desire for conquest provided incentives for courageous (or ambitious) nobles: those who were victorious in battle and gained new territories for the state could expect lands, additional wives, servants, herds of llamas, gold, silver, fine clothes, and other symbols of high status. And even common soldiers who distinguished themselves in battle could be rewarded with booty and raised to noble status. The imperial interests of the emperor paralleled those of other social groups. Thus, under Pachacuti Inca and his successors Topa Inca (1471–1493) and Huayna Capac (1493–1525), Inca domination was gradually extended by warfare to the frontier of present-day Ecuador and Colombia in the north and to the Maule River in present-day Chile in the south (see Map 14.3), an area of about 350,000 square miles. Eighty provinces, scores of ethnic groups, and 16 million people came under Inca control. A remarkable system of roads held the empire together.

Before Inca civilization, each group that entered the Andes valleys had its own distinct language. These languages were not written and have become extinct. Scholars will probably never understand the linguistic condition of Peru before the fifteenth century when Pachacuti made Quechua (pronounced "keshwa") the official language of his people and administration. Conquered peoples were forced to adopt the language, and Quechua spread the Inca way of life throughout the Andes. Though not written until the Spanish in Peru adopted it as a second official language, Quechua had replaced local languages by the seventeenth and eighteenth centuries and is still spoken by most Peruvians today.

Whereas the Aztecs controlled their subject peoples through terror, the Incas governed by means of imperial unification. They imposed not only their language but their entire panoply of gods: the sun-god, divine ancestor of the royal family; his wife the moon-god; and the thunder-god, who brought life-giving rain. Magnificent temples scattered throughout the expanding empire housed idols of these gods and the state-appointed priests who attended them. Priests led prayers and elaborate rituals, and, on such occasions as a terrible natural disaster or a great military victory, they sacrificed human beings to the gods. Subject peoples were required to worship the state gods. Imperial unification was also achieved through the forced participation of local chieftains in the central bureaucracy and through a policy of colonization called *mitima*. To prevent rebellion in newly conquered territories, Pachacuti transferred all their inhabitants to other parts of the empire, replacing them with workers who had lived longer under Inca rule and whose independent spirit had been broken.[24] An excellent system of roads—averaging three feet in width, some paved and others not—facilitated the transportation of armies and the rapid communication of royal orders by runners. The roads followed straight lines wherever possible but also crossed pontoon bridges and tunneled through hills. This great feat of Inca engineering bears striking comparison with ancient Roman roads, which also linked an empire.

Rapid Inca expansion, however, produced stresses. Although the pressure for growth remained unabated, in the reign of Topa Inca open lands began to be scarce. Topa Inca had some success in attacks on the eastern slopes of the Andes, but his attempts to penetrate the tropical Amazon forest east of the Andes led to repeated military disasters. The Incas waged wars with highly trained armies drawn up in massed formation and fought pitched battles on level ground, often engaging in hand-to-hand combat, or they launched formal assaults on fortresses. But in dense jungles, the troops could not maneuver or maintain order against enemies using guerrilla tactics and sniping at them with deadly blowguns. Another source of stress was discontent among subject peoples in conquered territories. Many revolted. It took Huayna Capac several years to put down a revolt in Ecuador. Even the system of roads and trained runners eventually caused administrative problems. The average runner could cover about 50 leagues or 175 miles per day—a remarkable feat of physical endurance, especially at high altitude—but the larger the empire became, the greater the distances to be covered. The round trip from the capital at Cuzco to Quito in Ecuador, for example,

took from 10 to 12 days, so that an emperor might have to base urgent decisions on incomplete or out-of-date information. The empire was overextended. "In short, the cult of the royal mummies helped to drive the Inca expansion, but it also linked economic stress, administrative problems, and political instabilities in a cyclical relationship."[25]

In 1525 the Inca Huayna Capac died of plague while campaigning in Ecuador. Between that date and the arrival of the Spanish conquistador Francisco Pizarro in 1532, the Inca throne was bitterly contested by two of Huayna's sons, the half-brothers Huascar and Atauhualpa. Inca law called for a dying emperor to assign the throne to his most competent son by his principal wife, who had to be the ruler's full sister. Huascar, unlike Atauhualpa, was the result of such an incestuous union and thus had a legitimate claim to the throne. Atauhualpa, who had fought with Huayna Capac in his last campaign, tried to convince Huascar that their father had divided the kingdom and had given him (Atauhualpa) the northern part. Huascar bitterly rejected his half-brother's claim.

When Huascar came to the throne, the problems facing the Inca Empire had become critical: the dead rulers controlled too much of Peru's land and resources. Huascar proposed a radical solution:

annoyed one day with these dead (his ancestors), [he] said that he ought to order them all buried and take from them all that they had, and that there should not be dead men but living ones, because (the dead) had all that was best in the country.[26]

Although Atauhualpa had the grave liability of being born of a nonincestuous union, to the great nobility responsible for the cult of the royal mummies, Huascar's proposal represented a far graver threat to the established order: Huascar intended to insult the mummies who linked the Inca people to the gods, and if his proposals were enacted, the anger of the mummies would ensure a disastrous future. (The nobility did not say the obvious—that if Huascar buried the dead and took their vast properties, the nobles would be deprived of wealth and power.) Not surprisingly, the nobles threw their support behind Atauhualpa.

In the civil war that began in 1532, Atauhualpa's veteran warriors easily defeated Huascar's green recruits. On his way to his coronation at Cuzco,

THE AMERICAS, CA 400–1500

ca 20,000 b.c.	Migration across the Bering Strait to the Americas
ca 1500 b.c.–a.d. 300	Rise of Olmec culture
ca a.d. 400–600	Height of Teotihuacán civilization
ca 600–900	Peak of Maya civilization
ca 800–1000	"Time of Troubles" in Mesoamerica
ca 980–1000	Toltec hegemony
ca 1000	Beginning of Inca expansion
ca 1325	Arrival of the Aztecs in the Valley of Mexico
mid-15th century	Height of Aztec culture
1438–1493	Great Age of Inca imperialism
1519	Arrival of the Spanish
1521	Collapse of the Aztecs
1532	Spanish execution of the Inca king and decline of Inca Empire

Atauhualpa encountered Pizzaro and 168 Spaniards who had recently entered the kingdom. The Spaniards quickly became the real victors in the Inca kingdom (see pages 523–524). The cult of the royal mummies had brought, or at least contributed heavily to, Inca collapse.

Inca Society

The fundamental unit of early Inca society was the *ayllu,* or clan, whose members were all those who claimed a common male ancestor. A village typically consisted of several ayllus. Each had its own farmland and woodland, which all members tended. The chief, or *curacas,* of an ayllu, to whom all members owed allegiance, conducted relations with outsiders.

In the fifteenth century, Pachacuti Inca and Topa Inca superimposed imperial institutions on those of kinship. They ordered allegiance to be paid to the ruler at Cuzco rather than to the curacas. They drafted local men for distant wars and relocated the entire populations of certain regions through the mitima system. Entirely new ayllus were formed, based on residence rather than kinship.

The emperors sometimes gave newly acquired lands to victorious generals, distinguished civil servants, and favorite nobles. These lords subsequently exercised authority previously held by the native curacas. Whether long-time residents or new colonists, common people had the status of peasant farmers, which entailed heavy agricultural or other obligations. Just as in medieval Europe peasants worked several days each week on their lord's lands, so the Inca people had to work on state lands (that is, the emperor's lands) or on lands assigned to the temple. Peasants also labored on roads and bridges; terraced and irrigated new arable land; served on construction crews for royal palaces, temples, and public buildings such as fortresses; acted as runners on the post roads; and excavated in the imperial gold, silver, and copper mines. The imperial government annually determined the number of laborers needed for these various undertakings, and each district had to supply an assigned quota. The government also made an ayllu responsible for the state-owned granaries and for the production of cloth for army uniforms.

The state required everyone to marry and even decided when and sometimes whom a person should marry. Men married around the age of twenty, women a little younger. A young man who wanted a certain girl hung around her father's house and shared in the work. The Incas did not especially prize virginity; premarital sex was common. The marriage ceremony consisted of the joining of hands and the exchange of a pair of sandals. This ritual was followed by a large wedding feast, at which the state presented the bride and groom with two complete sets of clothing, one for everyday wear and one for festive occasions. If a man or woman did not find a satisfactory mate, the provincial governor selected one for him or her. Travel was forbidden, so couples necessarily came from the same region. Like most warring societies with high male death rates, the Incas practiced polygamy, though the cost of supporting many wives restricted it largely to the upper classes.

In many aspects of daily life, the common people were regimented, denied both choice and initiative. The Incas, however, took care of the poor and aged who could not look after themselves, distributed grain in time of shortage and famine, and supplied assistance in natural disasters. Scholars have debated whether Inca society was socialistic, totalitarian, or a forerunner of the welfare state; it may be merely a matter of definition. Although the Inca economy was strictly regulated, there certainly was not an equal distribution of wealth. Everything above and beyond the masses' basic needs went to the emperor and the nobility.

The backbreaking labor of ordinary people in the fields and mines made possible the luxurious lifestyle of the great Inca nobility. The nobles—called *Orejones*, or "Big Ears," by the Spanish because they pierced their ears and distended the lobes with heavy jewelry—were the ruling Inca's kinsmen. Lesser nobles included the curacas, royal household servants, public officials, and entertainers. As the empire expanded in the fifteenth century, there arose a noble class of warriors, governors, and local officials, whose support the ruling Inca secured with gifts of land, precious metals, and llamas and alpacas (llamas were used as beasts of burden; alpacas were raised for their long fine wool). The nobility was exempt from agricultural work and from other kinds of public service.

SUMMARY

Several strong Amerindian civilizations flourished in the Western Hemisphere in the years between 400 and 1500. The Maya are justly renowned for their art and their accomplishments in abstract thought, especially mathematics. The Aztecs built a unified culture based heavily on the Toltec heritage and distinguished by achievements in engineering, sculpture, and architecture. The Incas revealed a genius for organization, and their state was virtually unique in its time for assuming responsibility for all its people. In both the Mexica and the Inca societies religious ideology shaped other facets of the culture. The Mexica cult of war and human sacrifice and the Inca cult of the royal mummies proved fatal weaknesses and contributed to the decline of those societies.

Inca culture did not die with the Spaniard Pizarro's strangulation of Atauhualpa (p. 524). In May 1536 his successor Inca Mancu Yupanki led a massive revolt against the Spanish and then led his people to Machu Picchu deep in the Valcahamba range of the Andes. Inca military resistance to Spanish domination continued throughout the sixteenth to eighteenth centuries. In 1780 Jose Gabriel Kunturkanki, a highly educated businessman and landowner, proclaimed himself Inca Tupac Amaru II and launched a native independence movement that the Spanish put down with the greatest difficulty (p. 919).

NOTES

1. See F. Braudel, *The Structures of Everyday Life: Civilization and Capitalism, 15th–18th Century,* vol. 1, trans. S. Reynolds (New York: Harper & Row, 1981), pp. 160–161.

2. See L. Schele and M. E. Miller, *The Blood of Kings: Dynasty and Ritual in Maya Art* (New York: Braziller, 1986), pp. 14–15, passim.

3. Quoted in I. Bernal, *Mexico Before Cortez: Art, History, and Legend,* rev. ed., trans. Willis Barnstone (New York: Anchor Books, 1975), p. 68.

4. G. W. Conrad and A. A. Demarest, *Religion and Empire: The Dynamics of Aztec and Inca Expansionism* (New York: Cambridge University Press, 1993), p. 71.

5. See I. Clendinnen, *Aztecs: An Interpretation* (New York: Cambridge University Press, 1992), pp. 115–117.

6. J. Soustelle, *Daily Life of the Aztecs on the Eve of the Spanish Conquest,* trans. P. O'Brian (Stan-

ford, Calif.: Stanford University Press, 1970), p. 97.

7. See M. Harris, *Cannibals and Kings* (New York: Random House, 1977), pp. 99–110; the quotation is from p. 106.

8. Ibid., pp. 109–110.

9. See R. Padden, *The Hummingbird and the Hawk* (Columbus: Ohio State University Press, 1967), pp. 76–99.

10. I am relying heavily here on Conrad and Demarest, *Religion and Empire,* pp. 37–44.

11. Ibid., p. 49.

12. Ibid., p. 57.

13. Ibid., pp. 66–70.

14. Soustelle, *Daily Life of the Aztecs,* p. 74.

15. See Clendinnen, pp. 153–173.

16. Quoted in Soustelle, p. 89.

17. B. Díaz, *The Conquest of New Spain,* trans. J. M. Cohen (New York: Penguin Books, 1978), p. 214.

18. Quoted in J. H. Perry, *The Discovery of South America* (New York: Taplinger, 1979), pp. 161–163.

19. Quoted ibid., p. 163.

20. William K. Stevens, "Andean Culture Found to Be as Old as the Great Pyramids," *New York Times,* October 3, 1989, p. C1.

21. John Noble Wilford, "Lost Civilization Yields Its Riches as Thieves Fall Out," *New York Times,* July 29, 1994, pp. C1, C28.

22. J. A. Mason, *The Ancient Civilizations of Peru* (New York: Penguin Books, 1978), p. 108.

23. Conrad and Demarest, *Religion and Empire,* pp. 91–94.

24. Mason, *The Ancient Civilization of Peru,* p. 123.

25. Ibid., p. 132.

26. Ibid., p. 136.

SUGGESTED READING

The titles by Clendinnen, Conrad and Demarest, and Schele and Miller, cited in the Notes, represent some of the most exciting recent research on pre-Columbian Mesoamerican societies. For the Maya, students should also see L. Schele and D. Freidel, *A Forest of Kings: The Untold Story of the Ancient Maya* (1990), a splendidly illustrated work, providing expert treatment of many facets of the Maya world; R. Wright, *Time Among the Maya* (1989), which gives a highly readable account of the important Maya agricultural and religious calendars; M. D. Coe, *The Maya,* 4th ed. (1987), a sound and well-illustrated survey. For the Aztecs, R. F. Townsend, *The Aztecs* (1992), discusses the various classes of Mexica society, as well as expansion, education, and religious ritual in a clearly illustrated study. M. León-Portilla, *The Aztec Image of Self and Society: An Introduction to Nahua Culture* (1992), is perhaps the best appreciation of Aztec religious ritual and symbolism. For warfare, R. Hassig, *Aztec Warfare: Imperial Expansion and Political Control* (1988), is probably the standard work.

Students desiring books exploring the entire hemisphere before the arrival of Columbus might see B. Fagan, *Kingdoms of Gold, Kingdoms of Jade* (1991), a fine work in comparative anthropology, and *America in 1492,* ed. A. M. Josephy (1992), an interesting collection of essays, many written by leading scholars. For the impact of the Spanish on Mesoamerican peoples, see I. Clendinnen, *Ambivalent Conquests: Maya and Spanish in Yucatan, 1517–1570* (1987), a profoundly sensitive, learned, and important study; R. Wright, *Stolen Continents: The Americas through Indian Eyes since 1492* (1992), which emphasizes the persistence and survival of native American cultures and peoples; and *In the Wake of Contact: Biological Responses to Conquest,* ed. C. S. Larsen and G. Milner (1994), a useful collection of articles dealing with many parts of the world.

The following older studies may also prove helpful for particular topics: S. Masuda, I. Shimada, and C. Morris, eds., *Andean Ecology and Civilization* (1985) and E. R. Wolfe, ed., *The Valley of Mexico: Studies in Pre-Hispanic Ecology and Society* (1976), are important for environmental research; L. Baudin, *A Socialist Empire: The Incas of Peru* (1961), which gives a provocative interpretation of the Incas, while V. W. Van Hagen, *Realm of the Incas* (1961), offers a popular account; and F. Katz, *The Ancient American Civilisations* (1972), a standard anthropological work that surveys all the major Mesoamerican cultures, and T. Todorov, *The Conquest of America,* trans. R. Howard (1984), an important, but difficult, study in cross-cultural perceptions.

LISTENING TO THE
PAST

The Installation of the Inca

All societies have special ceremonies in which the head of state, ruler, or king is officially constituted or consecrated. These rites, often involving religious ritual, set the head of state apart from all others.

In 1653 the Spanish Jesuit Bernabe Cobo (1580–1657) completed his Historia del Nuevo Mundi *(History of the New World), a major Spanish source for Inca history and institutions. Cobo's work is not based on firsthand observation. Modern scholars believe it rests on lost sixteenth-century manuscripts, but, taking into account Cobo's period and prejudices, they consider it highly reliable. Here is Cobo's account of an Inca's installation, his majesty and splendor.*

. . . The prince was not crowned until the funeral rites of his father were concluded, and after this, all of the great lords and gentlemen who resided in the court and whoever could comfortably come from all over the kingdom gathered in the plaza of Cuzco for the installation and coronation. . . . The Inca took possession of the kingdom when he put the fringe on his forehead, which was like the royal crown, and after it, he put on the rest of the insignias that the Peruvian kings used; besides the fringe there was the *sunturpaucar*, the *champi*, the rainbow and two serpents, and the other emblems that each one picked out.

The way his vassals installed him and swore allegiance to him is as follows. Once all the lords were together in the plaza and the king was seated in the middle on his *duho*,[1] one by one the lords stood up, first the *orejones*[2] and after them the caciques and lords in charge of the most towns. In their hands they had some little feathers called *tocto* from certain birds . . . . They stood barefooted before the Inca and turned the palms of their hands toward him, showing their reverence. They also swore allegiance by the Sun, raising their faces toward

it, and by the earth, to be loyal to the Inca and serve him in whatever he ordered them to do.

The king was dressed and adorned in the same clothing as the Inca nobles and *orejones*. The king was distinguished only by having larger holes pierced in his ears and larger and more lavish earplugs, by having his hair cut short to the breadth of one or two fingers, and by his *lluato* [headband] which was many-colored. The braided headbands worn by other members of the Inca lineage were of a single color. The Inca wore a cloak and a shirt, with *ojotas* on his feet; in this respect he followed the custom of the common people, but his clothing was . . . made of the finest wool and the best cloth that was woven in his whole kingdom, with more brilliant colors and finer-quality weaving. The *mamaconas*[3] made his clothing for him, and most of it was made from vicuña wool, which is almost as fine as silk. . . .

The fringe (royal insignia that they always wore in place of a crown or diadem) was called *maxcapaycha;* it was made of very fine red wool. They had it sewn to the *llauto* and hanging in the middle of their forehead, and it reached down to their eyebrows. . . . The *sunturpaucar* and the *champi* were two of the king's other insignias, besides the royal standard. The *sunturpaucar* was a staff, a little shorter than a pike, all covered and adorned from top to bottom with short feathers of various colors. . . . The *champi*[4] was a certain kind of weapon with which they fought in wars. In front of the Inca, at the sides of the royal standard, two *champis* on two long staves were held and the Inca himself, instead of a scepter, carried a short *champi*, like a baton with a golden head. The royal banner or standard was a small, square pennant, about ten or twelve palms around the edge, made of cotton or wool cloth; it was fixed on the end of a long pole so as to stand out stiffly and not wave in the wind. Each king had his arms and emblems painted on it. . . .

The Incas made a majestic display both in their personal style of life and adornment and in the pomp and splendor that accompanied them and with which they were served inside and outside of their homes. The multitude of servants that they had in their palace was incredible. Many of these servants were the children of caciques and noblemen. These youngsters were raised in the royal house so that they would learn civil customs. The Incas felt that it was a sign of grandeur to support many servants and have many wives and concubines. They were served all the exquisite, precious, and rare things that the land produced, and they had these things brought for their pleasure from the most distant corners of their empire. . . . Serving women brought him all of his food on gold, silver, and pottery plates and set them before him on some very thin, small green rushes.

Wherever he went, and many times within a town, the Inca was carried on the shoulders of bearers supporting a splendid litter covered on the inside with gold; carrying this litter was a special favor and honor. When the Inca traveled, he had a large following of *orejones*; these were the nobles and military men, who added security as well as authority to the Inca's group.

The riches of these barbarian kings were so immense that it is not easy to describe. They never found that their wealth was insufficient, nor were they ever worried about finding a way to remedy their needs, because they never had any; rather they had peace of mind and abundance of everything, for they were more concerned about how to divest themselves of what was left over from their large income than in seeking new ways to obtain and keep treasures. This was due to the fact that whatever their vassals produced or acquired was at their service and disposal. . . .

The riches that were collected and gathered together just in the city of Cuzco, as the capital and court of the empire, were incredible; in it there were many important houses of the dead kings with all the treasure that each one had accumulated in his life. Since the one who ascended to the throne did not touch his predecessor's property and riches, which were given over to the *guaca* and service of the deceased, the new king had his own house built and acquired silver and gold and all the rest; thus the treasure in the city was immense. . . .

So Cuzco was the richest city that has been found in this New World, and the reason why

Painting of Inca chief (Pretender) Lloque Yupanqui, ca. 1615. *(Source: Collection Musée de l'Homme, Paris)*

it had such a great amount of wealth in silver and gold and precious stones was because the caciques and governors made presents of all of these things to the Inca when they visited him in his court and when he passed through their lands as he was visiting his kingdom. . . .

Questions for Analysis

1. What symbols were used in the installation of the Inca, and what do they represent?

2. Why did the Inca travel by litter? What does this method of conveyance tell us about Inca society and technology?

3. Compare the lifestyle of the Inca and the Chinese emperor K'ang-hsi or the French king Louis XIV. What do they all have in common? How does religious ideology support the rule of each?

4. Why does Cobo dwell on the wealth and riches of the Inca?

Source: *History of the Inca Empire by Father Bernabe Cobo,* trans. and ed. R. Hamilton (Austin: University of Texas Press, 1979), pp. 244–49.

Notes: 1. A low stool or bench, the symbol of the Inca's high office. 2. Nobles distinguished by their big ears, from which heavy jewelry extended. 3. Cloistered women who were dedicated to the service of the Inca gods and who also trained all royal household servants. 4. Similar to a mace and carried by the Inca, in war; like the scepter carried by European monarchs, the *champi* was an emblem of authority and of the Inca's duty to defend his people and extend his empire.

15

European Society in the Age of the Renaissance and Reformation

Michelangelo painted the entire Sistine Chapel ceiling by himself, 1508–1512. *(Source: Nippon Television Network Corporation, Tokyo, 1994)*

While the Four Horsemen of the Apocalypse were carrying war, plague, famine, and death across the continent of Europe, a new culture was emerging in southern Europe. The fourteenth century witnessed the beginnings of remarkable changes in many aspects of Italian society. In the fifteenth century, these phenomena spread beyond Italy and gradually influenced society in northern Europe. These cultural changes have collectively been labeled the Renaissance.

The idea of reform is as old as Christianity itself: the need for reform of the individual Christian and of the institutional church is central to the Christian faith. The Christian humanists of the late fifteenth and early sixteenth centuries called for reform of the church on the pattern of the early church, primarily through educational and social change. These cries for reformation were not new. Men and women of every period believed the early Christian church represented a golden age. What was new were the criticisms of educated lay people whose religious needs were not being met. In the sixteenth century, demands for religious reform became so strong that they became enmeshed with social, political, and economic factors.

- What does the term *Renaissance* mean?
- How did the Renaissance manifest itself in politics, government, art, and social organization?
- Why did the theological ideas of Martin Luther trigger political, social, and economic reactions?
- What response did the Catholic church make to the movements for reform?

This chapter explores these questions.

❀ ECONOMIC AND POLITICAL ORIGINS OF THE ITALIAN RENAISSANCE

The period extending roughly from 1050 to 1300 witnessed phenomenal commercial and financial development, the growing political power of self-governing cities in northern Italy, and great population expansion. The period from the late thirteenth to the late sixteenth century was characterized by an amazing flowering of artistic energies.[1] Scholars commonly use the term *Renaissance* to describe the cultural achievements of the fourteenth through sixteenth centuries. Those achievements rest on the economic and political developments of earlier centuries.

In the great commercial revival of the eleventh century, northern Italian cities led the way. By the middle of the twelfth century, Venice, supported by a huge merchant marine, had grown enormously rich from overseas trade. It profited tremendously from the diversion of the Fourth Crusade to Constantinople (see page 371). Genoa and Milan enjoyed the benefits of a large volume of trade with the Middle East and northern Europe. These cities fully exploited their geographical positions as natural crossroads for mercantile exchange between the East and West.

Florence too possessed enormous wealth despite geographical constraints. It was an inland city without easy access to water transportation. But toward the end of the thirteenth century, Florentine merchants and bankers acquired control of papal banking. From their position as tax collectors for the papacy, Florentine mercantile families began to dominate European banking on both sides of the Alps. The profits from loans, investments, and money exchanges that poured back to Florence were pumped into urban industries, such as the Florentine wool industry, which was the major factor in the city's financial expansion and population increase. Florence purchased the best-quality wool from England and Spain, developed remarkable techniques for its manufacture into cloth, and employed thousands of workers in the manufacturing process. Florentine woolen cloth brought the highest prices in the fairs, markets, and bazaars of Europe, Asia, and Africa. Scholars tend to agree that the first artistic and literary manifestations of the Italian Renaissance appeared in Florence.

In the course of the twelfth century, Milan, Florence, Genoa, Siena, and Pisa fought for and won political and economic independence from surrounding feudal nobles. The nobles, attracted by the opportunities of long-distance and maritime trade, the rising value of urban real estate, the new public offices available in the expanding cities, and the chances for advantageous marriages into rich commercial families, frequently settled within the cities. Marriage vows often sealed business contracts between the rural nobility and the mercantile aristocracy. This merger of the northern Italian feudal nobility and the commercial aristocracy brought into being a new social class—an urban nobility.

467

This new class made citizenship and political participation in the city-states dependent on a property qualification, years of residence within the city, and social connections. Only a tiny percentage of the male population possessed these qualifications. A new group, called the *pòpolo*, disenfranchised and heavily taxed, bitterly resented its exclusion from power. Throughout most of the thirteenth century, in city after city, the pòpolo used armed force and violence to take over the city governments. Members of the pòpolo could not establish civil order within their cities, however. Consequently, these movements for republican government—government in which political power theoretically resides in the people and is exercised by their chosen representatives—failed. By the year 1300 *signori* (despots, or one-man rulers) or *oligarchies* (the rule of merchant aristocracies) had triumphed everywhere.[2]

For the next two centuries, the Italian city-states were ruled by signori or by constitutional oligarchies. In the signories, despots pretended to observe the law while actually manipulating it to conceal their basic illegality. Oligarchic regimes possessed constitutions, but through a variety of schemes a small, restricted class of wealthy merchants exercised the judicial, executive, and legislative functions of government. Thus in 1422 Venice had a population of 84,000, but 200 men held all power; and Florence had about 40,000 people, but 600 men ruled. Oligarchic regimes maintained only a façade of republican government. Nostalgia for the Roman form of government, combined with calculating shrewdness, prompted the leaders of Venice, Milan, and Florence to use the old forms.

In the fifteenth century, political power and elite culture centered at the princely courts of despots and oligarchs. "A court was the space and personnel around a prince as he made laws, received ambassadors, made appointments, took his meals, and proceeded through the streets."[3] The princely court afforded the despot or oligarchs the opportunity to display and assert their wealth and power. They flaunted their patronage of learning and the arts by munificent gifts to writers, philosophers, and artists, and they promoted occasions for magnificent pageantry and elaborate ritual—all designed to assert their wealth and power. The rulers of the city-states governed as monarchs. They crushed urban revolts, levied taxes, and killed their enemies. And they used massive building programs to employ, and the arts to overawe, the masses.

Renaissance Italians had a passionate attachment to their individual city-states. This intensity of local feeling perpetuated the dozens of small states and hindered the development of a unified Italian state.

In the fifteenth century, five powers dominated the Italian peninsula: Venice, Milan, Florence, the Papal States, and the kingdom of Naples. Venice had a sophisticated constitution and was a republic in name, but an oligarchy of merchant-aristocrats actually ran the city. Milan was also called a republic, but despots of the Sforza family ruled harshly and dominated the smaller cities of the north. Likewise in Florence the form of government was republican, but between 1434 and 1494 power in Florence was held by the great Medici banking family. Though not public officers, Cosimo de' Medici (1434–1464) and Lorenzo de' Medici (1469–1492) ruled from behind the scenes. Central Italy consisted mainly of the Papal States, which during the Babylonian Captivity (see page 427) had come under the sway of important Roman families. Pope Alexander VI (r. 1492–1503), aided militarily and politically by his son Cesare Borgia, reasserted papal authority in the papal lands. Cesare Borgia, the inspiration of Machiavelli's *The Prince* (see page 478), began the work of uniting the peninsula by ruthlessly conquering and exacting total obedience from the principalities making up the Papal States. South of the Papal States, the kingdom of Naples had long been disputed by the Aragonese and by the French. In 1435 it passed to Aragon.

The five major Italian city-states competed furiously among themselves for territory. They used diplomacy, spies, paid informers, and any other means to advance their ambitions. While the states of northern Europe were moving toward centralization and consolidation, the world of Italian politics resembled a jungle where the powerful dominated the weak.

In one significant respect, however, the Italian city-states anticipated future relations among competing European states after 1500. Whenever one Italian state appeared to gain a dominant position on the peninsula, the other states joined forces to establish a *balance of power* against the major threat. In forming these shifting alliances, Renaissance Italians invented the machinery of modern diplomacy: permanent embassies with resident ambassadors in capitals where political relations and commercial ties needed continual monitoring. The

✳ **A Bank Scene, Florence**   Originally a "bank" was just a counter; if covered with a carpet like this Ottoman geometric rug with a kufic border, it became a bank of distinction. Moneychangers who sat behind the counter became "bankers," exchanging different currencies and holding deposits for merchants and business people. *(Source: Prato, San Francesco/Scala/Art Resource, NY)*

resident ambassador is one of the great achievements of the Italian Renaissance.

At the end of the fifteenth century, Venice, Florence, Milan, and the Papal States possessed great wealth and represented high cultural achievement. However, their imperialistic ambitions at one another's expense, and their resulting inability to form a common alliance against potential foreign enemies, made Italy an inviting target for invasion. When Florence and Naples entered into an agreement to acquire Milanese territories, Milan called on France for support.

In Florence a Dominican friar, Girolamo Savonarola (1452–1498), had been predicting an invasion by France. In a number of fiery sermons between 1491 and 1494, Savonarola attacked what he considered the paganism and moral vice of the city, the undemocratic government of Lorenzo de' Medici, and the corruption of Pope Alexander VI. For a time he enjoyed wide support among the ordinary people; he became the religious leader of Florence and as such contributed to the fall of the Medicis. Savonarola stands as proof that the common people did not share the worldly outlook of the commercial and intellectual elite. Eventually, however, people wearied of his moral denunciations, and he was excommunicated by the pope and executed.

The invasion of Italy in 1494 by the French king Charles VIII (r. 1483–1498) inaugurated a new period in Italian and European power politics. Italy became the focus of international ambitions and the battleground of foreign armies. Charles swept the peninsula with little opposition. Florence, Rome, and Naples soon bowed before him. When Piero de' Medici, Lorenzo's son, went to the French camp seeking peace, the Florentines exiled the Medicis and restored republican government.

In the sixteenth century, the political and social life of Italy was upset by the relentless competition for dominance between France and the Holy Roman Empire. In 1519 Charles V succeeded his grandfather Maximilian as Holy Roman emperor. When the French returned to Italy in 1521, there began a series of conflicts called the Habsburg-Valois Wars (named for the German and French dynasties), whose battlefield was often Italy. The Italian cities suffered severely from the continual warfare, especially in the frightful sack of Rome in 1527 by imperial forces under Charles V. Thus the failure of the Italian city-states to form a common alliance against foreign enemies led to the continuation of the centuries-old subjection of the Italian peninsula by outside invaders.

INTELLECTUAL HALLMARKS OF THE RENAISSANCE

Some Italians in the fourteenth and fifteenth centuries believed that they were living in a new era. The realization that something new and unique was happening first came to men of letters in the fourteenth century, especially to poet and humanist Francesco Petrarch (1304–1374). Petrarch thought that the Germanic invasions had caused a sharp cultural break with the glories of Rome and had ushered in what he called the "Dark Ages." Medieval people had recognized no cultural division between the world of the Roman emperors and their own times, but in the opinion of Petrarch and many of his contemporaries, the thousand-year period between the fourth and the fourteenth centuries constituted a barbarian, or Gothic, or "middle" age (hence historians' use of the expression "Middle Ages"). The sculptors, painters, and writers of the Renaissance spoke contemptuously of their medieval predecessors and identified themselves with the thinkers and artists of Greco-Roman civilization. Petrarch believed he was witnessing a new golden age of intellectual achievement—a rebirth or, to use the French word that came into English, a *renaissance.*

The division of historical time into periods is often arbitrary and done by historians for their own convenience. In terms of the way most people lived and thought, no sharp division existed between the Middle Ages and the Renaissance. The guild and the parish, for example, continued to provide strong support for the individual and to exercise great social influence. Renaissance intellectuals, however, developed a new sense of historical distance and some important poets, writers, and artists believed they were living in a new age.

The Renaissance also manifested itself in new attitudes towards individuals, learning, and the world at large. There was a renewal of belief in the importance of the individual, a rebirth of interest in the Latin classics and in antique lifestyles, and a restoration of interest in the material world.

Individualism

Though the Middle Ages had seen the appearance of remarkable individuals, recognition of such persons was limited. Saint Augustine in the fifth century and Peter Abélard and Guibert of Nogent in the twelfth—men who perceived themselves as unique and produced autobiographical statements—stand out, for Christian humility discouraged self-absorption. In the fourteenth and fifteenth centuries, however, a large literature presenting a distinctly Renaissance individualism emerged.

Many distinctive individuals gloried in their uniqueness. Italians of unusual abilities were self-consciously aware of their singularity and unafraid to be different from their neighbors; they had enormous confidence in their ability to achieve great things. Leon Battista Alberti (1404–1474), a writer, architect, and mathematician, remarked, "Men can do all things if they will."[4] The Florentine goldsmith and sculptor Benvenuto Cellini (1500–1574) prefaced his *Autobiography* with a sonnet that declares:

My cruel fate hath warr'd with me in vain:
Life, glory, worth, and all unmeasur'd skill,
Beauty and grace, themselves in me fulfill
That many I surpass, and to the best attain.[5]

Certain of his genius, Cellini wrote so that the whole world might appreciate it.

Individualism stressed personality, genius, uniqueness, and the fullest development of capabilities and talents. Artist, athlete, painter, scholar, sculptor, whatever—a person's abilities should be stretched until fully realized. Thirst for fame, a driving ambition, a burning desire for success drove such people to achieve their potential. The quest for glory was a central component of Renaissance individualism.

Humanism

In the cities of Italy, especially Rome, civic leaders and the wealthy populace showed great archaeological zeal for the recovery of manuscripts, statues, and monuments. The Vatican Library, planned in the fifteenth century to house the nine thousand manuscripts collected by Pope Nicholas V (r. 1447–1455), remains one of the richest repositories of ancient and medieval documents. Patrician Italians consciously copied the lifestyle of the ancients and tried to trace their genealogies back to ancient Rome.

The revival of interest in antiquity was also apparent in the serious study of the Latin classics. This feature of the Renaissance became known as the "new learning," or simply "humanism," the term used by the Florentine rhetorician and historian Leonardo Bruni (1370–1444). The words *humanism* and *humanist* derived from the Latin *humanitas,* which Cicero used to refer to the literary culture needed by anyone who wanted to be considered educated and civilized. Humanism focused on human beings—their achievements, interests, and capabilities. Although churchmen supported the new learning, by the later fifteenth century Italian humanism was increasingly a lay phenomenon.

Appreciation of the literary culture of the Romans had never died in the West. Bede and John of Salisbury (see page 368), for example, had studied and imitated the writings of the ancients. But medieval writers had accepted pagan and classical authors uncritically. Renaissance humanists, in contrast, were skeptical of their authority, conscious of the historical distance separating themselves from the ancients, and fully aware that classical writers often disagreed among themselves. Medieval writers looked to the classics to reveal God. Renaissance humanists studied the classics to understand human nature, though from a strongly Christian perspective. For example, in a remarkable essay, *On the Dignity of Man,* the Florentine writer Pico della Mirandola (1463–1494) stressed that man possesses great dignity because he was made as Adam in the image of God before the Fall and as Christ after the Resurrection. According to Pico, man's place in the universe is somewhere between the beasts and the angels, but, because of the divine image planted in him, there are no limits to what man can accomplish. Humanists rejected classical ideas that were opposed to Christianity. Or they sought through reinterpretation an underlying harmony between the pagan and secular and the Christian faith. The fundamental difference between medieval humanists and Renaissance ones is that the latter were more self-conscious about what

they were doing and stressed the realization of human potential.[6]

The leading humanists of the early Renaissance were rhetoricians, seeking effective and eloquent communication, both oral and written. They loved the language of the classics and scorned the corrupt, "barbaric" Latin of the medieval schoolmen. Literary humanists of the fourteenth century wrote each other highly stylized letters imitating ancient authors, and they held witty philosophical dialogues in conscious imitation of Plato's Academy of the fourth century B.C. Renaissance writers were very excited by the purity of ancient Latin. Eventually, however, they became concerned more about form than about content, more about the way an idea was expressed than about the significance and validity of the idea.

Secular Spirit

Secularism is a basic concern with the material world instead of with eternal and spiritual matters. A secular way of thinking tends to find the ultimate explanation of everything and the final end of human beings within the limits of what the senses can discover. Medieval business people ruthlessly pursued profits while medieval monks fought fiercely over property. But medieval society was religious, not secular: the dominant ideals focused on the otherworldly, on life after death. Renaissance people often held strong and deep spiritual beliefs. But Renaissance society was secular: attention is concentrated on the here and now, often on the acquisition of material things. The fourteenth and fifteenth centuries witnessed the slow but steady growth of secularism in Italy.

The economic changes and rising prosperity of the Italian cities in the thirteenth century worked a fundamental change in social and intellectual attitudes and values. Worries about shifting rates of interest, shipping routes, personnel costs, and employee relations did not leave much time for thoughts about penance and purgatory. Wealth made possible greater material pleasures, a more comfortable life, the leisure time to appreciate and patronize the arts. Money could buy many sensual gratifications, and the rich, social-climbing bankers and merchants of the Italian cities came to see life more as an opportunity to be enjoyed than as a painful pilgrimage to the City of God.

In *On Pleasure,* the humanist Lorenzo Valla (1406–1457) defended the pleasures of the senses as the highest good. Scholars praise Valla as a father of modern historical criticism. His study *On the False Donation of Constantine* (1444) demonstrated by careful textual examination that an anonymous eighth-century document supposedly giving the papacy jurisdiction over vast territories in western Europe was a forgery. Medieval people had accepted the Donation of Constantine as valid, and the proof that it was a forgery weakened the foundations of papal claims to temporal authority. Lorenzo Valla's work exemplifies the application of critical scholarship to old and almost-sacred writings, as well as the new secular spirit of the Renaissance.

The tales in *The Decameron* (1353), by the Florentine Giovanni Boccaccio (1313–1375), describe ambitious merchants, lecherous friars, and cuckolded husbands and portray a frankly acquisitive, sensual, and worldly society. Historians, however, must be cautious in basing conclusions solely on literature. Boccaccio's figures were stock literary characters not unknown in the Middle Ages, and writers draw on their imagination as well as on social experience. Nevertheless, *The Decameron* contains none of the "contempt of the world" theme so pervasive in medieval literature.

Renaissance writers justified the accumulation and enjoyment of wealth with references to ancient authors, and church leaders did little to combat the new secular spirit. In the fifteenth and early sixteenth centuries, the papal court and the households of the cardinals were just as worldly as those of great urban patricians. Renaissance popes beautified the city of Rome, patronized artists and men of letters, and expended enormous enthusiasm and huge sums of money. A new papal chancellery, begun in 1483 and finished in 1511, stands as one of the architectural masterpieces of the High Renaissance. Pope Julius II (r. 1503–1513) tore down the old Saint Peter's Basilica and began work on the present structure in 1506. Michelangelo's dome for Saint Peter's is still considered his greatest work.

Although papal interests fostered the new worldly attitude, the broad mass of the people and the intellectuals and leaders of society remained faithful to the Christian church. Few questioned the basic tenets of the Christian religion. The thousands of pious paintings, sculptures, processions, and pilgrimages of the Renaissance period prove that strong religious feeling persisted.

Art and the Artist

No feature of the Renaissance evokes greater admiration than its artistic masterpieces. The 1400s (called *quattrocento* in Italian) and 1500s (*cinquecento*) bore witness to a dazzling creativity in painting, architecture, and sculpture. In all the arts, the city of Florence first led the way. In the period art historians describe as the High Renaissance (1500–1527) Rome took the lead. The main characteristics of High Renaissance art—classical balance, harmony, and restraint—are revealed in the masterpieces of Leonardo da Vinci (1452–1519), Raphael (1483–1520), and Michelangelo (1475–1564), all of whom worked in Rome.

In early Renaissance Italy, art manifested corporate power. Powerful urban groups such as guilds and religious confraternities commissioned works of art. The Florentine cloth merchants, for example, delegated Filippo Brunelleschi (1377–1446) to build the magnificent dome on the cathedral of Florence and selected Lorenzo Ghiberti (1378–1455) to design the bronze doors of the baptistry. These works were signs of the merchants' dominant influence in the community. Corporate patronage is also reflected in the Florentine government's decision to hire Michelangelo to create a sculpture of David, the great Hebrew hero and king. The subject matter of art through the early fifteenth century, as in the Middle Ages, remained overwhelmingly religious.

Increasingly in the later quattrocento, individuals and oligarchs, rather than corporate groups, sponsored works of art. Merchants, bankers, popes, and princes supported the arts as a means of glorifying themselves, their families, and their power. Vast sums were spent on family chapels, frescoes, religious panels, and tombs. Writing about 1470, the Florentine oligarch Lorenzo de' Medici declared that over the past thirty-five years his family had spent the astronomical sum of 663,755 gold florins for artistic and architectural commissions. And, he said, "I think it casts a brilliant light on our estate [public reputation] and it seems to me that the monies were well spent and I am very pleased with this."[7]

As the fifteenth century advanced, the subject matter of art became steadily more secular. Religious topics, such as the Annunciation of the Virgin, remained popular among both patrons and artists, but classical themes and motifs, such as the lives and loves of pagan gods and goddesses, figured increasingly in painting and sculpture. The individual portrait emerged as a distinct artistic genre. People were conscious of their physical uniqueness and wanted their individuality immortalized. In the fifteenth century, members of the newly rich middle class often had themselves painted in a scene of romantic chivalry or in courtly society. Rather than reflecting a spiritual ideal, as medieval painting and sculpture tended to do, Renaissance portraits mirrored reality.

The Florentine painter Giotto (1276–1337) led the way in the use of realism; his treatment of the human body and face replaced the formal stiffness and artificiality that had for so long characterized the representation of the human body. The sculptor Donatello (1386–1466) probably exerted the greatest influence of any Florentine artist before Michelangelo. His many statues express an appreciation of the incredible variety of human nature. Medieval artists had depicted the nude body only in a spiritualized and moralizing context. Donatello revived the classical figure with its balance and self-awareness. The short-lived Florentine Masaccio (1401–1428), sometimes called the father of modern painting, inspired a new style characterized by great realism, narrative power, and effective use of light and dark.

Narrative artists depicted the body in a more scientific and natural manner. The female figure is voluptuous and sensual. The male body, as in Michelangelo's *David* (1501–1504) and *The Last Judgment* (1534–1541), is strong and heroic. This glorification of the human body is a sign of the secular spirit of the age. Brunelleschi and Piero della Francesca (1420–1492) seem to have pioneered *perspective* in painting—the linear representation of distance and space on a flat surface. *The Last Supper* (ca 1495–1498) of Leonardo da Vinci, with its stress on the tension between Christ and the disciples, is a subtle psychological interpretation.

As important as realism was the new "international style," so called because of the wandering careers of influential artists, the close communications and rivalry of princely courts, and the increased trade in works of art. Rich color, decorative detail, curvilinear rhythms, and swaying forms characterized the international style. As the term *international* implies, this style was European, not merely Italian.

The growing secular influences on art are reflected in the improved social status of the artist in the Renaissance. The lower-middle-class medieval master mason had been viewed in the same light as a mechanic. The artist in the Renaissance was considered a free intellectual worker. Artists did not produce unsolicited pictures or statues for the general public; that could mean loss of status. They usually worked on commission from a powerful prince. The artist's reputation depended on the support of powerful patrons, and through them some artists and architects achieved not only economic security but great wealth. All aspiring artists received a practical (not theoretical) education in a recognized master's workshop. For example, Michelangelo was apprenticed at age thirteen to the artist Ghirlandaio (1449–1494), although he later denied that fact to make it appear he never had any formal training. The more famous an artist was, the more he attracted assistants or apprentices.

Renaissance society respected and rewarded the distinguished artist. At a time when a person could live in a princely fashion on 300 ducats a year, Leonardo da Vinci was making 2,000 ducats annually. Michelangelo was paid 3,000 ducats for painting the ceiling of the Sistine Chapel. When he agreed to work on Saint Peter's Basilica, he refused a salary; he was already a wealthy man.[8] In 1537 the prolific letter writer, humanist, and satirizer of princes Pietro Aretino (1492–1556) wrote to Michelangelo while he was painting the Sistine Chapel:

To the Divine Michelangelo:
Sir, just as it is disgraceful and sinful to be unmindful of God so it is reprehensible and dishonourable for any man of discerning judgement not to honour you as a brilliant and venerable artist whom the very stars use as a target at which to shoot the rival arrows of their favour. You are so accomplished, therefore, that hidden in your hands lives the idea of a new king of creation. . . . And it is surely my duty to honour you with this salutation, since the world has many kings but only one Michelangelo.[9]

The Renaissance witnessed the birth of the concept of the artist as genius. In the Middle Ages, people believed that only God created, albeit through individuals; the medieval conception recognized no particular value in artistic originality. Boastful Renaissance artists and humanists came to think that a work of art was the deliberate creation of a unique personality, of an individual who transcended traditions, rules, and theories. A genius had a peculiar gift, which ordinary laws should not inhibit. Cosimo de' Medici described a painter, because of his genius, as "divine," implying that the artist shared in the powers of God. Aretino and others applied the word *divine* to Michelangelo.

But the student must remember that Italian Renaissance culture was that of a small mercantile elite, a business patriciate with aristocratic pretensions. Renaissance culture did not directly affect the broad middle classes, let alone the vast urban proletariat. Renaissance humanists were a smaller and narrower group than the medieval clergy had ever been. In the Middle Ages, high churchmen had commissioned the construction of the Gothic cathedrals, but, once finished, the buildings were for all to enjoy. Nothing comparable was built in the Renaissance. A small, highly educated group of literary humanists and artists created the culture of and for an exclusive elite. They cared little for ordinary people.[10]

The Renaissance in the North

In the last quarter of the fifteenth century, Italian Renaissance thought and ideals penetrated north-

Benozzo Gozzoli: Journey of the Magi Few Renaissance paintings better illustrate art in the service of the princely court, in this case the Medici. Commissioned by Piero de' Medici to adorn his palace chapel, everything in this fresco—the large crowd, the feathers and diamonds adorning many of the personages, the black servant in front—serve to flaunt the power and wealth of the House of Medici. There is nothing especially religious about it; the painting could more appropriately be called "Journey of the Medici." *(Source: Scala/Art Resource, NY)*

ern Europe. Students from the Low Countries, France, Germany, and England flocked to Italy, imbibed the "new learning," and carried it back to their countries. However, cultural traditions of northern Europe tended to remain more distinctly Christian, or at least pietistic, than those of Italy. Italian humanists certainly were strongly Christian, as the example of Pico della Mirandola shows. But in Italy secular and pagan themes and Greco-Roman motifs received more humanistic attention than they received north of the Alps. The Renaissance in northern Europe had a distinctly religious character, and what fundamentally distinguished Italian humanists from northern ones is that the latter had a program for broad social reform based on Christian ideals.

Christian humanists in northern Europe were interested in the development of an ethical way of life. To achieve it, they believed, the best elements of classical and Christian cultures should be combined. For example, the classical ideals of calmness, stoical patience, and broad-mindedness should be joined in human conduct with the Christian virtues of love, faith, and hope. Northern humanists also stressed the use of reason, rather than acceptance of dogma, as the foundation for an ethical way of life. Like the Italians, they were impatient with Scholastic philosophy. Christian humanists had a profound faith in the power of human intellect to bring about moral and institutional reform. They believed that human nature had been corrupted by sin but nevertheless was fundamentally good and capable of improvement through education, which would lead to piety and an ethical way of life.

The Englishman Thomas More (1478–1535) towers above other figures in sixteenth-century English social and intellectual history. More's political stance and his resulting fate later, at the time of the Reformation (see page 501), have tended to obscure his contribution to Christian humanism. More, who practiced law, was deeply interested in the classics; his household served as a model of warm Christian family life and as a mecca for foreign and English humanists. He entered government service during the reign of Henry VIII and was sent as ambassador to Flanders. There More found the time to write *Utopia* (1516), which presented a revolutionary view of society.

Utopia, which literally means "nowhere," describes an ideal socialistic community on an island somewhere off the mainland of the New World. All its children receive a good education, and since the goal of all education is to develop rational faculties, adults divide their days equally between manual labor or business pursuits and various intellectual activities. The profits from business and property are held strictly in common, so there is absolute social equality. The Utopians use gold and silver both to make chamber pots and to prevent wars by buying off their enemies. By this casual use of precious metals, More meant to suggest that the basic problems in society were caused by greed. Utopian law exalts mercy above justice. Citizens of Utopia lead a nearly perfect existence because they live by reason. More punned on the word *Utopia,* which he termed "a good place. A good place which is no place."

More's ideas were profoundly original in the sixteenth century. The long-prevailing view was that vice and violence exist because women and men are basically corrupt. But More maintained that acquisitiveness and private property promote all sorts of vices and civil disorders and that because society protects private property, *society's* flawed institutions are responsible for corruption and war. Today people take this view so much for granted that it is difficult to appreciate how radical it was in the sixteenth century. According to More, the key to improvement and reform of the individual was reform of the social institutions that mold the individual.

Better known by contemporaries than Thomas More was the Dutch humanist Desiderius Erasmus of Rotterdam (1466?–1536), whose life work became the application of the best humanistic learning to the study and explanation of the Bible. As a mature scholar with an international reputation stretching from Cracow to London, a fame that rested largely on his exceptional knowledge of Greek, Erasmus could boast with truth, "I brought it about that humanism, which among the Italians . . . savored of nothing but pure paganism, began nobly to celebrate Christ."[11]

Erasmus's long list of publications includes *The Adages* (1500), a list of Greek and Latin precepts on ethical behavior; *The Education of a Christian Prince* (1504), which combines idealistic and practical suggestions for the formation of a ruler's character; *The Praise of Folly* (1509), a satire of worldly wisdom and a plea for the simple and spontaneous Christian faith of children; and, most important of all, a critical edition of the Greek New Testament (1516). In the preface to the New

Testament, Erasmus explained the purpose of his great work:

Only bring a pious and open heart, imbued above all things with a pure and simple faith. . . . For I utterly dissent from those who are unwilling that the sacred Scriptures should be read by the unlearned translated into their vulgar tongue, as though Christ had taught such subtleties that they can scarcely be understood even by a few theologians. . . . Christ wished his mysteries to be published as openly as possible. I wish that even the weakest woman should read the Gospel—should read the epistles of Paul. And I wish these were translated into all languages, so that they might be read and understood, not only by Scots and Irishmen, but also by Turks and Saracens. . . . Why do we prefer to study the wisdom of Christ in men's writings rather than in the writing of Christ himself?[12]

Two fundamental themes run through all of Erasmus's scholarly work. First, education—study of the Bible and the classics—is the means to reform, the key to moral and intellectual improvement. Second, the essence of Erasmus's thought is, in his own phrase, "the philosophy of Christ." By this Erasmus meant that Christianity is an inner attitude of the heart or spirit. Christianity is not formalism, special ceremonies, or law; Christianity is Christ—his life and what he said and did, not what theologians have written about him.

Whereas the writings of Erasmus and More have strong Christian themes and have drawn the attention primarily of scholars, the stories of the French humanist François Rabelais (1490?–1553) possess a distinctly secular flavor and have attracted broad readership. The most roguishly entertaining Renaissance writer, Rabelais was convinced that "laughter is the essence of manhood." Rabelais's *Gargantua* and *Pantagruel* (serialized between 1532 and 1552) belong among the great comic masterpieces of world literature. These stories' gross and robust humor introduced the adjective *Rabelaisian* into the language.

In *Gargantua* and *Pantagruel* the reader enters a world of Renaissance vitality, ribald joviality, and intellectual curiosity. On his travels Gargantua meets various absurd characters, and within their hilarious exchanges there occur serious discussions on religion, politics, philosophy, and education. Rabelais had received an excellent humanistic education in a monastery, and Gargantua discusses the disorders of contemporary religious and secular life. Like Erasmus, Rabelais satirized hypocritical monks, pedantic academics, and pompous lawyers. But unlike Erasmus, Rabelais applied wild and gross humor. Like Thomas More, Rabelais believed that institutions molded individuals and that education was the key to a moral and healthy life. The aristocratic residents of Rabelais's Thélèma, the abbey that Gargantua establishes, live for the full gratification of their physical instincts and rational curiosity. Thélèma, whose motto is "Do as Thou Wilt," admits women *and* men; allows all to eat, drink, sleep, and work when they choose; provides excellent facilities for swimming, tennis, and football; and encourages sexual experimentation and marriage. Rabelais believed profoundly in the basic goodness of human beings and the rightness of instinct.

The distinctly religious orientation of the literary works of the Renaissance in the north also characterized northern art and architecture. Some Flemish painters, notably Rogier van der Weyden (1399/1400–1464) and Jan van Eyck (1366–1441), were considered the artistic equals of Italian painters, were much admired in Italy, and worked a generation before Leonardo and Michelangelo. One of the earliest artists successfully to use oil-based paints, van Eyck, in paintings such as *Ghent Altarpiece* and the portrait *Giovanni Arnolfini and His Bride,* shows the Flemish love for detail; the effect is great realism and remarkable attention to human personality.

Another Flemish painter, Hieronymous Bosch (ca 1450–1516), frequently used religious themes, but in combination with grotesque fantasies, colorful imagery, and peasant folk legends. Many of Bosch's paintings reflect the confusion and anguish often associated with the end of the Middle Ages. In *Death and the Miser,* Bosch's dramatic treatment of the Dance of Death theme, the miser's gold, increased by usury, is ultimately controlled by diabolical rats and toads, and his guardian angel urges him to choose the crucifix.

A quasi-spiritual aura likewise infuses architectural monuments in the north. The city halls of wealthy Flemish towns such as Bruges, Brussels, Louvain, and Ghent strike the viewer more as shrines to house the bones of saints than as settings for the mundane decisions of politicians and business people. Northern architecture was little influenced by the classical revival so obvious in Renaissance Rome and Florence.

❋ SOCIAL CHANGE DURING THE RENAISSANCE

The Renaissance changed many aspects of Italian and, subsequently, European society. The new developments brought about real breaks with the medieval past in education and political thought, through new printing technology, and in the experience of women and blacks.

Education and Political Thought

Education and moral behavior were central preoccupations of the humanists. Humanists poured out treatises, often in the form of letters, on the structure and goals of education and the training of rulers. In one of the earliest systematic programs for the young, Peter Paul Vergerio (1370–1444) wrote Ubertinus, the ruler of Carrara:

For the education of children is a matter of more than private interest; it concerns the State, which indeed regards the right training of the young as, in certain aspects, within its proper sphere. . . . Above all, respect for Divine ordinances is of the deepest importance; it should be inculcated from the earliest years.

Reverence towards elders and parents is an obligation closely akin.

We call those studies liberal which are worthy of a free man; those studies by which we attain and practice virtue and wisdom; that education which calls forth, trains and develops those highest gifts of body and of mind which ennoble men, and which are rightly judged to rank next in dignity to virtue only.[13]

Part of Vergerio's treatise specifies subjects for the instruction of young men in public life: history teaches virtue by examples from the past; ethics focuses on virtue itself; and rhetoric, or public speaking, trains for eloquence.

No book on education had broader influence than Baldassare Castiglione's *The Courtier* (1528). This treatise sought to train, discipline, and fashion the young man into the courtly ideal, the gentleman. According to Castiglione (1478–1529), the educated man of the upper class should have a broad background in many academic subjects, and his spiritual and physical, as well as intellectual, capabilities should be trained. The courtier should have easy familiarity with dance, music, and the arts. Castiglione envisioned a man who could compose a sonnet, wrestle, sing a song and accompany himself on an instrument, ride expertly, solve difficult mathematical problems, and above all speak and write eloquently (see Listening to the Past). In the sixteenth and seventeenth centuries, the courtier envisioned by Castiglione became the model of the European gentleman.

No Renaissance book on any topic has been more widely read and studied in all the centuries since its publication in 1513 than the short political treatise *The Prince,* by Niccolò Machiavelli (1469–1527). Some political scientists maintain that Machiavelli was describing the actual competitive framework of the Italian states with which he was familiar. Other thinkers praise *The Prince* because it revolutionized political theory and destroyed medieval views of the nature of the state. Still other scholars consider this work a classic because it deals with eternal problems of government and society.

Born to a modestly wealthy Tuscan family, Machiavelli received a good education in the Latin classics. He entered the civil service of the Florentine government and served on thirty diplomatic missions. When the exiled Medicis returned to power in Florence in 1512, they expelled Machiavelli from his position as an officer of the city government. In exile he wrote *The Prince.*

The subject of *The Prince* is political power: how the ruler should gain, maintain, and increase it. A good humanist, Machiavelli explores the problems of human nature and concludes that human beings are selfish and out to advance their own interests. This pessimistic view of humanity leads him to maintain that the prince may have to manipulate the people in any way he finds necessary:

For a man who, in all respects, will carry out only his professions of good, will be apt to be ruined amongst so many who are evil. A prince therefore who desires to maintain himself must learn to be not always good, but to be so or not as necessity may require.[14]

The prince should combine the cunning of a fox with the ferocity of a lion to achieve his goals. Pondering the question of whether it is better for a ruler to be loved or feared, Machiavelli wrote:

It will naturally be answered that it would be desirable to be both the one and the other; but as it is difficult to be both at the same time, it is much more safe to be feared than to be loved, when you have to choose between the two. For it may be said of men in

general that they are ungrateful and fickle, dissemblers, avoiders of danger, and greedy of gain. So long as you shower benefits upon them, they are all yours.[15]

Medieval political theorists and theologians had stressed the way government *ought* to be. They had set high moral and Christian standards for the ruler's conduct. In their opinion, the test of good government was whether it provided justice, law, and order. Machiavelli maintained that the ruler should be concerned not with the way things ought to be but with the way things actually are. The sole test of whether a government was "good" was whether it was effective, whether the ruler increased his power. Machiavelli believed that political action cannot be restricted by moral considerations, but he did not advocate amoral behavior. In the *Discourses of the Ten Books of Titus Livy,* he even showed his strong commitment to republican government. Nevertheless, on the basis of a simplistic interpretation of *The Prince,* the adjective *Machiavellian* entered the language as a synonym for devious, corrupt, and crafty politics in which the end justifies the means. Machiavelli's ultimate significance rests on two ideas: that one permanent social order reflecting God's will cannot be established and that politics has its own laws and ought to be considered a science.[16]

Movable Type and the Spread of Literacy

Sometime in the thirteenth century, paper money and playing cards from China reached the West. They were *block-printed*—that is, each word, phrase, or picture was carved on a separate wooden block to be inked and used for printing. This method of reproduction was extraordinarily expensive and slow. By the middle of the fifteenth century, Europeans had mastered paper manufacture, which also originated in China and was introduced by the Arabs to the West in the twelfth century. Then around 1455, probably through the combined efforts of three men—Johann Gutenberg, Johann Fust, and Peter Schöffer, all experimenting at Mainz—movable type came into being in the West. The mirror image of each letter (rather than entire words or phrases) was carved in relief on a small block. Individual letters, easily movable, were put together to form words in lines of type that made up a page. An infinite variety of texts could be printed by reusing and rearranging pieces of type.

The effects of the invention of movable-type printing were not obvious overnight. But within a half-century of the publication of Gutenberg's Bible of 1456, printing from movable type brought about radical changes. It transformed both the private and the public lives of Europeans. Governments that "had employed the cumbersome methods of manuscripts to communicate with their subjects switched quickly to print to announce declarations of war, publish battle accounts, promulgate treaties or argue disputed points in pamphlet form. Theirs was an effort 'to win the psychological war.'" Printing made propaganda possible, emphasizing differences between opposing groups such as Crown and nobility, church and state. These differences laid the basis for the formation of distinct political parties.

Printing also stimulated the literacy of lay people and eventually came to have a deep effect on their private lives. Although most of the earliest books and pamphlets dealt with religious subjects, students, housewives, businessmen, and upper- and middle-class people sought books on all subjects. Printers responded with moralizing, medical, practical, and travel manuals. Pornography as well as piety assumed new forms. For example, the satirist Pietro Aretino used the shock of sex in pornography as a vehicle to criticize: his *Sonnetti lussuriosi* (1527) and *Ragionamenti* (1534–1536), sonnets accompanying sixteen engravings of as many sexual positions, attacked princely court life, humanist education, and false clerical piety.[17] Broadsides and flysheets allowed great public festivals, religious ceremonies, and political events to be experienced vicariously by the stay-at-home. Since books and other printed materials were read aloud to illiterate listeners, print bridged the gap between written and oral cultures.[18]

Women in Renaissance Society

How did women experience the Renaissance? Did they participate in the intellectual and artistic changes of the period? How did the status of women in the fourteenth to sixteenth centuries compare with that of women in the eleventh to thirteenth centuries?

During the Renaissance the status of upper-class women declined. If women in the High Middle Ages are compared with those of fifteenth- and sixteenth-century Italy with respect to the kind of work they performed, their access to property and

political power, and their role in shaping the outlook of their society, it is clear that ladies in the Renaissance ruling classes generally had less power than comparable ladies in the feudal age.

In the cities of Renaissance Italy, well-to-do girls received an education similar to boys'. Young ladies learned their letters and studied the classics. Many read Greek as well as Latin, knew the poetry of Ovid and Virgil, and could speak one or two "modern" languages, such as French or Spanish. In this respect, Renaissance humanism represented a real educational advance for women. Some women, though a small minority among humanists, acquired great learning and fame. Some Italian women published books, and Sofonisba Anguissola (1530–1625) achieved international renown for her paintings.

Laura Cereta (1469–1499) illustrates the successes and failures of educated Renaissance women. Educated by her father, who was a member of the governing elite of Brescia in Lombardy, she learned languages, philosophy, theology, and mathematics. She also gained self-confidence and a healthy respect for her own potential. By the age of fifteen, when she married, her literary career was already launched, as her letters to several cardinals attest. For Laura Cereta, however, as for all educated women of the period, the question of marriage forced the issue: she could choose a husband, family, and full participation in social life or else study and withdrawal from the world. Cereta chose marriage but was widowed at eighteen and was able to spend the remaining twelve years of her life in study. Responding to the envy of other women and the hostility of men who felt threatened, Laura Cereta criticized "empty women, who strive for no good but exist to adorn themselves . . . these women of majestic pride, fantastic coiffures, outlandish ornament, and necks bound with gold or pearls [which] bear the glittering symbols of their captivity to men." She believed that women's inferior status derived not from the divine order of things but from the choices women were making: "For knowledge is not given as a gift, but through study. . . . The free mind, not afraid of labor, presses on to attain the good."[19] Despite Laura Cereta's faith in women's potential, most men believed that a woman who became learned violated nature and thus ceased to be a woman. Brilliant women such as Laura Cereta were severely attacked by men who feared threats to male dominance in the intellectual realm.

Sofonisba Anguissola: The Artist's Sister Minerva A nobleman's daughter and one of the first Italian women to become a recognized artist, Sofonisba did portraits of her five sisters and of prominent people. The coiffure, elegant gown, necklaces, and rings depict aristocratic dress in the mid-sixteenth century. *(Source: Milwaukee Art Museum)*

Laura Cereta was a prodigy. Ordinary girls of the urban upper middle class received some training in painting, music, and dance, in addition to a classical education. What were they to do with this training? They were to be gracious, affable, charming—in short, decorative. Renaissance women were better educated than their medieval counterparts. But whereas education trained a young man to participate in the public affairs of the city, it prepared a woman for the social functions of the home. An educated lady was supposed to know how to attract artists and literati to her husband's court and how to grace her husband's household. An educated man was supposed to know how to rule and participate in public affairs.

With respect to love and sex, the Renaissance witnessed a downward shift in women's status. In the medieval literature of courtly love—the etiquette books and romances—manners shaped the man to please the woman. According to *The Courtier,* Castiglione's manual on courtesy and good behavior, the woman was to make herself pleasing to the man. In contrast to the medieval tradition of relative sexual equality, Renaissance humanists laid the foundations for the bourgeois double standard. Men, and men alone, operated in the public sphere; women belonged in the home. Castiglione, the foremost spokesman of Renaissance love and manners, completely separated love from sexuality. For women, sex was restricted entirely to marriage. Ladies were bound to chastity, to the roles of wife and mother in a politically arranged marriage. Men, however, could pursue sensual indulgence outside marriage.[20]

Did the Renaissance have an impact on the lives of ordinary women? Women, of course, continued to perform economic functions in the expanding industries. Rural women assisted husbands and fathers in agricultural tasks. Urban women helped in the shops and were heavily involved in the Florentine textile industry, weaving cloth and reeling and winding silk. In the Venetian Arsenal, the state-controlled dock and ship construction area—the largest single industrial plant in Europe—women made sails. Widows frequently ran their husbands' businesses, and in Italy and France some became full members of guilds.

Educational opportunities being severely limited, few girls received an education. Women may have taken civic pride in the new monuments and art works in their localities, as far as they could understand them. But apart from that, the literary and art works of the Renaissance had no effect on ordinary women—or men. Many scholars believe the period of the Renaissance witnessed the emergence of the irreversible divide between an educated elite that participates in a "high culture" of art, music, literature, and learning, and the broad mass whose "popular culture" involves tools, houses, and the man-made environment.[21]

Official attitudes toward rape provide another index of the status of women in the Renaissance. A careful study of the legal evidence from Venice from 1338 to 1358 shows that rape was not considered a particularly serious crime against either the victim or society. The rape of a young girl of marriageable age or a child under twelve was considered a graver crime than the rape of a married woman. Still, the punishment for rape of a noble, marriageable girl was only a fine or about six months' imprisonment. In an age when theft and robbery were punished by mutilation, and forgery and sodomy by burning, this penalty was very mild indeed. In the eleventh century, William the Conqueror had decreed that rapists be castrated, implicitly according women protection and a modicum of respect. But in the early Renaissance, Venetian laws and their enforcement show that the governing oligarchy believed that rape damaged, but only slightly, men's property—women.[22]

Evidence from Florence in the fifteenth century also sheds light on infanticide, which historians are only now beginning to study in the Middle Ages and Renaissance. Early medieval penitentials and church councils legislated against abortion and infanticide. Nevertheless, Pope Innocent III (r. 1198–1216) was moved to establish an orphanage "because so many women were throwing their children into the Tiber."[23] In the fourteenth and early fifteenth centuries, a considerable number of children died in Florence under suspicious circumstances such as exposure or suffocation. These deaths occurred too frequently to have all been accidental, and far more girls than boys died, thus reflecting societal discrimination against girl children as inferior and less useful than boys. Dire poverty led some parents to do away with unwanted children.

The gravity of the problem of infanticide, which violated both the canon law of the church and the civil law of the state, forced the Florentine government to build the Foundling Hospital. Supporters of the institution maintained that, without public responsibility, "many children would soon be found dead in the rivers, sewers, and ditches, unbaptized."[24] The large size of the hospital suggests that great numbers of children were abandoned.

Blacks in Renaissance Society

Ever since the time of the Roman republic, a few black people had lived in western Europe. They had come, along with white slaves, as the spoils of war. Even after the collapse of the Roman Empire, Muslim and Christian merchants continued to import them. The evidence of medieval art attests to the presence of Africans in the West and Europeans' awareness of them. In the twelfth and thirteenth centuries, a large cult surrounded Saint Maurice, who was portrayed as a black knight martyred in the fourth century for refusing to renounce his Christian faith. Saint Maurice received the special veneration of the nobility.

Until the fifteenth century, the number of blacks living in western Europe was small. Then, in the fifteenth century, sizable numbers of black slaves began to enter Europe. Portuguese explorers imported perhaps a thousand a year and sold them at the markets of Seville, Barcelona, Marseilles, and Genoa. By the mid-sixteenth century, blacks, slave and free, constituted about 10 percent of the populations of the Portuguese cities of Lisbon and Évora; other cities had smaller percentages. In all, blacks made up roughly 3 percent of the Portuguese population. The Venetians specialized in the import of white slaves, but blacks were so greatly in demand at the Renaissance courts of northern Italy that the Venetians defied papal threats of excommunication to secure them.

What roles did blacks play in Renaissance society? What image did Europeans have of Africans? The medieval interest in curiosities, the exotic, and the marvelous continued into the Renaissance. Because of their rarity, black servants were highly prized and a symbol of wealth. In the late fifteenth century, Isabella, the wife of Gian Galazzo Sforza, took pride in the fact that she had ten black servants. In 1491 Isabella of Este, duchess of Mantua, instructed her agent to secure a black girl between four and eight years old, "shapely and as black as possible." The duchess saw the child as a source of entertainment: "we shall make her very happy and shall have great fun with her." She hoped that the little girl would become "the best buffoon in the world."[25] The cruel ancient tradition of retaining a professional "fool" for the amusement of a noble family persisted through the Renaissance—and even down to the twentieth century.

Adult black slaves filled a variety of positions. Many served as maids, valets, and domestic servants. The Venetians employed blacks—slave and free—as gondoliers and stevedores on the docks. In Portugal, they supplemented the labor force in virtually all occupations.[26] In Renaissance Spain and Italy, blacks performed as dancers, as actors and actresses in courtly dramas, and as musicians, sometimes making up full orchestras.[27] Slavery during the Renaissance foreshadowed the American, especially the later Brazilian, pattern.

Before the sixteenth-century "discoveries" of the non-European world, Europeans had little concrete knowledge of Africans and their cultures. Europeans knew little about them beyond biblical accounts and their attitude toward Africans was ambivalent.[28] On the one hand, Europeans perceived Africa as a remote place, the home of strange people isolated by heresy and Islam from supposedly superior European civilization. They believed that contact with Christian Europeans could only "improve" black Africans, even slaves. Theologians taught that God was light, and blackness, the opposite of light, was believed to represent the hostile forces of evil, sin, and the devil. Thus in medieval and early Renaissance art the devil was commonly represented as a black man. On the other hand, blackness was also associated with certain positive qualities. It symbolized the emptiness of worldly goods and the humility of the monastic way of life. Black vestments and funeral trappings indicated grief, and Christ had said that those who mourn are blessed. Thus in Renaissance society blacks—like women—were signs of wealth; both were used for display.

❀ POLITICS AND THE STATE IN THE RENAISSANCE (CA 1450–1521)

The High Middle Ages witnessed the beginnings of many of the basic institutions of the modern state. Sheriffs, inquests, juries, circuit judges, professional bureaucracies, and representative assemblies all trace their origins to the twelfth and thirteenth centuries (see pages 375, 377). The linchpin for the development of states, however, was strong monarchy, and during the period of the Hundred Years' War, no ruler in western Europe was able to provide effective leadership. The resurgent power of feudal nobilities weakened the centralizing work begun earlier.

Beginning in the fifteenth century, rulers utilized the aggressive methods implied by Renaissance political ideas to rebuild their governments. First in Italy (see pages 468–469), then in France, England, and Spain, rulers began the work of reducing violence, curbing unruly nobles and troublesome elements, and establishing domestic order. The Holy Roman Empire of Germany, however, remained divided into scores of independent principalities.

The despots and oligarchs of the Italian city-states, together with Louis XI of France, Henry VII of England, and Ferdinand of Aragon, were tough, cynical, calculating rulers. In their ruthless push for power and strong governments, they sub-

ordinated morality to hard results. They preferred to be secure and feared rather than loved. They could not have read Machiavelli's *The Prince,* but their actions were in harmony with its ideas.

Some historians have called Louis XI (r. 1461–1483), Henry VII (r. 1485–1509), and Ferdinand and Isabella in Spain (r. 1474–1516) "new monarchs" because they invested kingship with a strong sense of royal authority and national purpose. They stressed that the monarchy was the one institution that linked all classes and peoples within definite territorial boundaries. They insisted on the respect and loyalty of all subjects and ruthlessly suppressed opposition and rebellion, especially from the nobility. And they loved the business of kingship and worked hard at it.

In other respects, however, the methods of these rulers, which varied from country to country, were not so new. They reasserted long-standing ideas and practices of strong monarchs in the Middle Ages. To advance their authority, they seized on the maxim of the Justinian *Code*: "What pleases the prince has the force of law." Like medieval rulers, Renaissance rulers tended to rely on middle-class civil servants. Using tax revenues, medieval rulers had built armies to crush feudal anarchy. Renaissance townspeople with commercial and business interests wanted a reduction of violence and usually they were willing to pay taxes in order to achieve it.

France

The Hundred Years' War left France badly divided, drastically depopulated, commercially ruined, and agriculturally weak. Nonetheless, the ruler whom Joan of Arc had seen crowned at Reims, Charles VII (r. 1422–1461), revived the monarchy and France. He seemed an unlikely person to do so. Frail, indecisive, and burdened with questions about his paternity (his father was deranged, his mother notoriously promiscuous), Charles VII nevertheless began France's long recovery.

Charles reorganized the royal council, giving increased influence to the middle-class men, and strengthened royal finances through such taxes as the *gabelle* (on salt) and the *taille* (on land). By establishing regular companies of cavalry and archers—recruited, paid, and inspected by the state—Charles created the first permanent royal army. In 1438 he published the Pragmatic Sanction of Bourges, giving the French crown major control over the appointment of bishops, and depriving the pope of French ecclesiastical revenues. The Pragmatic Sanction established the Gallican (or French) liberties because it affirmed the special rights of the French crown over the French church. Greater control over the church and the army helped to consolidate the authority of the French crown.

Charles's son Louis XI (r. 1461–1483), called the "Spider King" by his subjects because of his treacherous and cruel character, was very much a Renaissance prince. Facing the perpetual French problems of unification of the realm and reduction of feudal disorder, he saw money as the answer. Louis promoted new industries, such as silk weaving at Lyons and Tours, and entered into commercial treaties with other countries. The revenues raised through these economic activities and severe taxation were used to improve the army. With the army Louis stopped aristocratic brigandage and slowly cut into urban independence. He was also able to gain territory that furthered his goal of expanding royal authority and unifying the kingdom. Some scholars have credited Louis XI with laying the foundations for later French royal absolutism. Indeed, he worked tirelessly to remodel the government after the disorders of the fourteenth and early fifteenth centuries. In his reliance on finances supplied by the middle classes to fight the feudal nobility, Louis was thought to be typical of the new monarchs.

England

English society suffered severely from the disorders of the fifteenth century. The aristocracy dominated the government and indulged in mischievous violence at the local level. Population, decimated by the Black Death, continued to decline. Then between 1455 and 1471, supporters of the ducal houses of York and Lancaster waged civil war, commonly called the Wars of the Roses because the symbol of the Yorkists was a white rose and that of the Lancastrians a red one. The chronic disorder hurt trade, agriculture, and domestic industry, and the authority of the monarchy sank lower than it had been in centuries.

The Yorkist Edward IV (r. 1461–1483) began re-establishing domestic tranquillity. He defeated the Lancastrian forces and after 1471 began to reconstruct the monarchy and consolidate royal power. Henry VII (r. 1485–1509) of the Welsh house of Tudor advanced the work of restoring royal prestige by crushing the power of the nobility and establishing order and law at the local level.

The Hundred Years' War had cost the nation dearly, and the money to finance it had been raised by Parliament, the arena where the nobility exerted its power. As long as the monarchy was dependent on the Lords and the Commons for revenue, the king had to call Parliament. Thus Edward IV, and subsequently the Tudors except for Henry VIII, conducted foreign policy by means of diplomacy and avoided expensive wars. Unlike the continental countries of Spain and France, England had no standing army or professional civil service bureacracy. The Tudors relied on the support of unpaid local justices of the peace—influential landowners in the shires—to handle the work of local government. From the royal point of view, they were an inexpensive method of government. Thus for a time the English monarchy did not depend on Parliament for money, and the Crown undercut that source of aristocratic influence.

Henry VII did summon several meetings of Parliament in the early years of his reign, primarily to confirm laws, but the center of royal authority while he was king was the royal council, which governed at the national level. The royal council handled any business the king put before it—executive, legislative, judicial. It also dealt with real or potential aristocratic threats through a judicial offshoot, the Court of Star Chamber, so called because of the stars painted on the ceiling of the room in which it met. The court applied principles of Roman law, a system that exalted the power of the Crown as the embodiment of the state. The court's methods were sometimes terrifying: evidence and proceedings were secret, torture could be applied, and juries were not called. These procedures ran directly counter to English common-law precedents, but they effectively reduced aristocratic troublemaking.

The Tudors won the support of the influential upper middle class because the Crown linked government policy with the interests of that class. A commercial or agricultural upper class fears and dislikes few things more than disorder and violence. Grave, secretive, cautious, and always thrify, Henry VII promoted peace and social order, and the gentry did not object to arbitrary methods, like those used by the Court of Star Chamber, because the government had ended the long period of anarchy. At the same time both English exports of wool and the royal export tax on that wool steadily increased. When Henry VII died in 1509, he left a country at peace both domestically and internationally, a substantially augmented treasury, and the dignity and role of the royal majesty much enhanced.

Spain

Political development in Spain followed a pattern different from that of France and England. The central theme in the history of medieval Spain's separate kingdoms was disunity and plurality. Different languages, laws, and religious communities made for a rich cultural diversity shaped by Hispanic, Roman, Visigothic, Muslim, and Jewish traditions.

By the middle of the fifteenth century, the centuries-long *reconquista*—the attempts of the northern Christian kingdoms to control the entire peninsula—was nearing completion. The kingdoms of Castile and Aragon dominated weaker kingdoms, and with the exception of Granada, the Iberian Peninsula had been won for Christianity. The wedding in 1469 of the dynamic and aggressive Isabella, heiress of Castile, and the crafty and persistent Ferdinand, heir of Aragon, was the final major step in the unification and Christianization of Spain.

Ferdinand and Isabella pursued a common foreign policy. Under their rule Spain remained a loose confederation of separate states, but they determined to strengthen royal authority. To curb rebellious and warring aristocrats, they revived an old medieval institution. In the towns, popular groups called *hermandades,* or brotherhoods, were given the authority to act both as local police forces and as judicial tribunals. The hermandades repressed violence with such savage punishments that by 1498 they could be disbanded. The decisive step that Ferdinand and Isabella took to curb aristocratic power was the restructuring of the royal council. The king and queen appointed to the council only people of middle-class background; they rigorously excluded aristocrats and great territorial magnates. The council and various government boards recruited men trained in Roman law.

In the extension of royal authority and the consolidation of the territories of Spain, the church was the linchpin. Through a diplomatic alliance with the Spanish pope Alexander VI, the Spanish

monarchs secured the right to appoint bishops in Spain and in the Hispanic territories in America. This power enabled the "Most Catholic Kings of Spain," a title that the pope granted to Ferdinand and Isabella, to establish, in effect, a national church.[29] Revenues from ecclesiastical estates provided the means to raise an army to continue the reconquista. The victorious entry of Ferdinand and Isabella into Granada on January 6, 1492, signaled the conclusion of eight centuries of Spanish struggle against the Arabs in southern Spain. In 1512 Ferdinand conquered Navarre in the north.

Although the Muslims had been defeated, there still remained a sizable and, in the view of the Catholic sovereigns, potentially dangerous minority, the Jews. Since ancient times, Christian governments had usually suppressed religious faiths that differed from the official state religion, considering them politically dangerous. France and England had expelled their Jewish populations in the Middle Ages, but in Spain Jews had been tolerated and had played a decisive role in the economic and intellectual life of the several Spanish kingdoms. Then, in the late fourteenth century, anti-Semitic riots and pogroms led many Spanish Jews to convert to Christianity; such people were called *conversos.*

By the middle of the fifteenth century, many conversos held high positions in Spanish society as financiers, physicians, merchants, tax collectors, and even officials of the church hierarchy. Numbering perhaps 200,000 in a total population of about 7.5 million, Jews exercised an influence quite disproportionate to their numbers. Aristocratic grandees who borrowed heavily from Jews resented their financial dependence, and churchmen questioned the sincerity of Jewish conversions. At first, Isabella and Ferdinand continued the policy of royal toleration—Ferdinand himself had inherited Jewish blood from his mother. But many conversos apparently reverted to the faith of their ancestors, prompting Ferdinand and Isabella in 1478 to secure Rome's permission to revive the Inquisition, a medieval judicial procedure for the punishment of heretics.

Although the Inquisition was a religious institution established to safeguard the Catholic faith, in Spain it was controlled by the Crown and served primarily as a political unifying force. Because the Spanish Inquisition commonly applied torture to extract confessions, first from lapsed conversos, then from Muslims, and later from Protestants, it

✳ **van Schwanenburgh: The Spinners**   In the late sixteenth century, the prosperity of Leyden in Holland rested on the textile industry, which in turn depended on the import of merino wool from Spain. In this lush scene three large spinning wheels are operated simultaneously. Women composed 30 percent of the work force but earned much less than men. *(Source: Stedelijk Museum, "De Lakenhal," Leiden, Holland)*

gained a notorious reputation. Thus the word *inquisition,* meaning "any judicial inquiry conducted with ruthless severity," came into the English language.

In 1492, Isabella and Ferdinand took a further dire and drastic step against backsliding conversos. They issued an edict expelling all practicing Jews from Spain. Of the community of perhaps 200,000 Jews, 150,000 fled. (Efforts were made, through last-minute conversions, to retain good Jewish physicians.) Absolute religious orthodoxy and purity of blood (untainted by Jews or Muslims) became the theoretical foundation of the Spanish national state.

The diplomacy of the Catholic rulers of Spain achieved a success they never anticipated. Partly out of hatred for the French and partly to gain international recognition for their new dynasty, Ferdinand and Isabella in 1496 married their second daughter, Joanna, heiress to Castile, to the archduke Philip, heir through his mother to the Burgundian Netherlands and through his father to the Holy Roman Empire.

Germany and the Habsburg Dynasty

The marriage in 1477 of Maximilian I of the house of Habsburg and Mary of Burgundy was a decisive event in early modern European history. Burgundy consisted of two parts: the French duchy with its capital at Dijon, and the Burgundian Netherlands with its capital at Brussels. Through this union with the rich and powerful duchy of Burgundy, the Austrian House of Habsburg, the strongest ruling family in the empire, started to become an international power.

In the fifteenth and sixteenth centuries, as in the Middle Ages, relations among states continued to be greatly affected by the connections of royal families. Marriage often determined the diplomatic status of states. The Habsburg-Burgundian marriage angered the French, who considered Burgundy part of French territory. Within the empire, German principalities that resented Austria's preeminence began to see that they shared interests with France. The marriage of Maximilian and Mary inaugurated centuries of conflict between the Austrian House of Habsburg and the kings of France. Germany was to be the chief arena of the struggle.

"Other nations wage war; you, Austria, marry." Historians dispute the origins of the adage, but no one questions its accuracy. The heir of Mary and Maximilian, Philip of Burgundy, married Joanna of Castile, daughter of Ferdinand and Isabella of Spain. Philip and Joanna's son Charles V (1500–1558) fell heir to a vast conglomeration of territories. Through a series of accidents and unexpected deaths, Charles inherited Spain from his mother, together with her possessions in the Americas and the Spanish dominions in Italy, Sicily, Sardinia, and Naples. From his father he inherited the Habsburg lands in Austria, southern Germany, the Low Countries, and Franche-Comté in east-central France.

Charles's inheritance was an incredibly diverse collection of states and peoples, each governed in a different manner and held together only by the person of the emperor (Map 15.1). Charles's Italian adviser, the grand chancellor Gattinara, told the young ruler: "God has set you on the path toward world monarchy." Charles not only believed this; he was convinced that it was his duty to maintain the political and religious unity of Western Christendom. In this respect Charles V was the last medieval emperor.

Charles needed and in 1519 secured the imperial title from the electors. Forward-thinking Germans proposed government reforms. They urged placing the administration in the hands of an imperial council whose president, the emperor's appointee, would have ultimate executive power. They also recommended reforms of the imperial finances, the army, and the judiciary. Such ideas did

not interest the young emperor at all. When he finally arrived in Germany from Spain and opened his first Diet (assembly of the estates of the empire) at Worms in January 1521, he naively announced that "the empire from of old has had not many masters, but one, and it is our intention to be that one." Charles went on to say that he was to be treated as of greater account than his predecessors because he was more powerful than they had been. In view of the long history of aristocratic power in the Holy Roman Empire, Charles's notions were pure fantasy.

Charles continued the Burgundian policy of his grandfather Maximilian. German revenues and German troops were subordinated to the needs of other parts of the empire, first Burgundy and then Spain. Habsburg international interests came before the need for reform in Germany.

Two years before the electors chose as emperor the nineteen-year-old Charles, Martin Luther had launched a movement to reform the church.

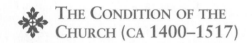

THE CONDITION OF THE CHURCH (CA 1400–1517)

The papal conflict with the German emperor Frederick II in the thirteenth century, followed by the Babylonian Captivity and then the Great Schism (see pages 427–428), badly damaged the prestige of church leaders. In the fourteenth and fifteenth centuries, leaders of the conciliar movement reflected educated public opinion when they called for the reform of the church "in head and members" (see page 428). The humanists of Italy and the Christian humanists of northern Europe denounced corruption in the church. As Machiavelli put it, "We Italians are irreligious and corrupt above others, because the Church and her representatives set us the worst example."[30] In *The Praise of Folly,* Erasmus condemned the absurd superstitions of the parish clergy and the excessive rituals of the monks. The records of episcopal visitations of parishes, civil court records, and even such literary masterpieces as Chaucer's *Canterbury Tales* and Boccaccio's *The Decameron* tend to confirm the perceptions of corruption.

Signs of Disorder

In the early sixteenth century, critics of the church concentrated their attacks on three disorders: cleri-

MAP 15.1 The European Empire of Charles V   Charles V exercised theoretical jurisdiction over more territory than anyone since Charlemagne. This map does not show his Latin American and Asian possessions.

cal immorality, clerical ignorance, and clerical pluralism. There was little pressure for doctrinal change; the emphasis was on moral and administrative reform.

Since the fourth century, church law had required candidates for the priesthood to accept absolute celibacy. The requirement had always been difficult to enforce. Many priests, especially those ministering to country people, had concubines, and reports of neglect of the rule of celibacy were common. Immorality, of course, included more than sexual transgressions. Clerical drunkenness, gambling, and indulgence in fancy dress were frequent charges. There is no way of knowing how many priests were guilty of such behavior. But because such conduct was so much at odds with the church's rules and moral standards, it scandalized the educated faithful.

The bishops enforced regulations regarding the education of priests casually. As a result, standards for ordination were shockingly low. The evidence points consistently to the low quality of the Italian clergy. In northern Europe—in England, for ex-

ample—recent research shows an improvement in clerical educational standards in the early sixteenth century. Nevertheless, parish priests throughout Europe were not as educated as the educated laity. Predictably, Christian humanists, with their concern for learning, condemned the ignorance or low educational level of the clergy. Many priests could barely read and write, and critics laughed at the illiterate priest mumbling Latin words to the Mass that he could not understand.

Pluralism and absenteeism constituted the third major abuse. Many clerics, especially higher ecclesiastics, held several *benefices,* or offices, simultaneously but seldom visited them, let alone performed the spiritual responsibilities those offices entailed.

The Folly of Indulgences This woodcut viciously satirizes the church's sale of indulgences. With one foot in the holy water symbolizing the rite of purification (Psalm 50) and the other foot resting on the coins paid for indulgences, the church, portrayed as a rapacious eagle with its right hand stretched out for offerings, writes out an indulgence with excrement—which represents its worth. Fools with a false sense of security sit in the animal's gaping mouth, representing hell, to which a devil delivers the pope wearing a three-tiered crown and holding the keys to heaven originally given to Saint Peter. *(Source: Kunstsammlungen der Veste Coburg)*

THE CONDITION OF THE CHURCH (CA 1400–1517) **489**

Instead, they collected revenues from each benefice and paid a poor priest a fraction of the income to fulfill the spiritual duties of a particular local church. The French king Louis XII's diplomat Antoine du Prat is perhaps the most notorious example of absenteeism. He was archbishop of Sens, but the first time he entered his cathedral was in his own funeral procession.

Critics condemned pluralism, absenteeism, and the way money seemed to change hands when a bishop entered into his office. Although royal governments strengthened their positions and consolidated their territories in the fifteenth and sixteenth centuries, rulers lacked sufficient revenues to pay and reward able civil servants. The Christian church, with its dioceses and abbeys, possessed a large proportion of the wealth of the countries of Europe. What better way for a ruler to reward government officials, who were usually clerics, than with bishoprics and other high church offices? The practice was sanctioned by centuries of tradition. Thus churchmen who served as royal councilors, diplomats, treasury officials, chancellors, viceroys, and judges were paid by the church for their services to the state. It is astonishing that so many conscientiously tried to carry out their religious duties on top of their public burdens.

In most countries except England, members of the nobility occupied the highest church positions. The spectacle of proud, aristocratic prelates living in magnificent splendor contrasted very unfavorably with the simple fishermen who were Christ's disciples. Nor did the popes of the period 1450 to 1550 set much of an example. They lived like secular Renaissance princes, supporting artists and undertaking building projects, often making the papal court a model of luxury and scandal. Some popes used papal power and wealth to advance the material interests of their own families.

The court of the Spanish pope Rodrigo Borgia, Alexander VI (r. 1492–1503), who publicly acknowledged his mistress and children, reached new heights of impropriety. Because of the prevalence of intrigue, sexual promiscuity, and supposed poisonings, the name Borgia became a synonym for moral corruption. Pope Julius II (r. 1503–1513) donned military armor and personally led papal troops against the French invaders of Italy in 1506. After him, Giovanni de' Medici, the son of Lorenzo de' Medici, carried on as Pope Leo X (r. 1513–1521) the Medicean tradition of being a great patron of the arts.

Signs of Vitality

Calls for reform testify to the spiritual vitality of the church as well as to its problems. In the late fifteenth and early sixteenth centuries, both individuals and groups within the church were working actively for reform. In Spain, for example, Cardinal Francisco Jiménez (1436–1517) visited religious houses, encouraged the monks and friars to obey their rules and constitutions, and set high standards for the training of the diocesan clergy.

In Holland, beginning in the late fourteenth century, a group of pious lay people called Brethren of the Common Life sought to make religion a personal, inner experience. They lived in stark simplicity while daily carrying out the Gospel teaching of feeding the hungry, clothing the naked, and visiting the sick. The Brethren also taught in local schools to prepare devout candidates for the priesthood and the monastic life. The spirituality of the Brethren of the Common Life found its finest expression in the classic *The Imitation of Christ* by Thomas à Kempis, which urges Christians to take Christ as their model and seek perfection in a simple way of life. As Protestants would do later, the Brethren stressed the centrality of Scripture in the spiritual life.[31] In the mid-fifteenth century, the movement had houses in the Netherlands, in central Germany, and in the Rhineland; it was a true religious revival.

If external religious observances are a measure of depth of heartfelt conviction, Europeans in the early sixteenth century remained deeply pious and loyal to the Roman Catholic church. Villagers participated in processions honoring the local saints. Middle-class people made pilgrimages to the great shrines such as Saint Peter's in Rome. The upper classes continued to remember the church in their wills.

The papacy also expressed concern for reform. Pope Julius II summoned an ecumenical, or universal, council, which met in the church of Saint John Lateran in Rome from 1512 to 1517. Most of the bishops were Italian and did not represent a broad cross section of international opinion, so the designation *ecumenical* was not really appropriate. Nevertheless, the bishops and theologians who attended the Lateran Council strove earnestly to reform the church. The council recommended higher standards for education of the clergy and instruction of the common people. The bishops placed the responsibility for eliminating

Lucas Cranach the Younger: Luther and the Wittenberg Reformers The massive figure of John Frederick, elector of Saxony, who protected and supported Luther, dominates this group portrait. Luther is on the far left, his associate Philip Melancthon far right in the front. Luther's face shows a quiet determination. *(Source: The Toledo Museum of Art, Toledo, Ohio; Gift of Edward Drummond Libbey)*

bureaucratic corruption squarely on the papacy and suggested significant doctrinal reforms. But many obstacles stood in the way of ecclesiastical change. Nor did the actions of an obscure German friar immediately force the issue.

MARTIN LUTHER AND THE BIRTH OF PROTESTANTISM

As a result of a personal religious struggle, a German Augustinian friar, Martin Luther (1483–1546) launched the Protestant Reformation of the

sixteenth century. Luther articulated the widespread desire for reform of the Christian church and the deep yearning for salvation that were typical of his time.

Martin Luther was born at Eisleben in Saxony, the second son of a copper miner who later became a mine owner. At considerable sacrifice, his father sent him to school and then to the University of Erfurt. Hans Luther intended his son to study law and have a legal career, which for centuries had been the steppingstone to public office and material success. Badly frightened during a thunderstorm, however, young Luther vowed to become a friar. Without consulting his father, he entered a monastery at Erfurt in 1505. Luther was ordained a priest in 1507 and after additional study earned the doctorate of theology. From 1512 until his death, he served as professor of Scripture at the new University of Wittenberg.

Martin Luther was exceedingly scrupulous in his monastic observances and was devoted to prayer, penances, and fasting; but the doubts and conflicts that trouble any sensitive young person who has just taken a grave step were especially intense in young Luther. He had terrible anxieties about sin, and he worried continually about his salvation. Luther intensified his monastic observances but still found no peace of mind.

Luther's wise and kindly confessor, Staupitz, directed him to the study of Saint Paul's letters. Gradually, Luther arrived at a new understanding of the Pauline letters and of all Christian doctrine. He came to believe that salvation comes not through external observances and penances but through a simple faith in Christ. Faith is the means by which God sends humanity his grace, and faith is a free gift that cannot be earned.

The Ninety-five Theses

An incident illustrative of the condition of the church in the early sixteenth century propelled Martin Luther onto the stage of history and brought about the Reformation in Germany. The University of Wittenberg lay within the archdiocese of Magdeburg. The archbishop of Magdeburg, Albert, held two other high ecclesiastical offices. To hold all three offices simultaneously—blatant pluralism—required papal dispensation. Archbishop Albert borrowed money from the Fuggers, a wealthy banking family of Augsburg, to pay Pope Leo X for the dispensation (the pope wanted the money to complete work on Saint Peter's Basilica). Leo X then authorized Archbishop Albert to sell indulgences in Germany to repay the Fuggers.

Wittenberg was in the political jurisdiction of the elector Frederick of Saxony. When Frederick forbade the sale of indulgences within his duchy, people of Wittenberg, including some of Professor Luther's students, streamed across the border from Saxony into Jütenborg in Thuringia to buy them.

What exactly was an *indulgence*? According to Catholic theology, individuals who sin alienate themselves from God and his love. In order to be reconciled to God, the sinner must confess his or her sins to a priest and do the penance that the priest assigns. The doctrine of indulgence rested on three principles. First, God is merciful, but he is also just. Second, Christ and the saints, through their infinite virtue, established a "treasury of merits" on which the church, because of its special relationship with Christ and the saints, can draw. Third, the church has the authority to grant sinners the spiritual benefits of those merits. Originally an indulgence was a remission of the temporal (priest-imposed) penalties for sin. Beginning in the twelfth century, the papacy and bishops had given Crusaders such indulgences. By the later Middle Ages people widely believed that an indulgence secured total remission of penalties for sin—on earth or in purgatory—and ensured swift entry into heaven.

Archbishop Albert hired the Dominican friar John Tetzel to sell the indulgences. Tetzel mounted an advertising blitz. One of his slogans—"As soon as coin in coffer rings, the soul from purgatory springs"—brought phenomenal success. Men and women bought indulgences not only for themselves but for deceased parents, relatives, or friends.

Luther was severely troubled that ignorant people believed they had no further need for repentance once they had purchased an indulgence. Thus, according to historical tradition, in the academic fashion of the times, on the eve of All Saints' Day (October 31), 1517, he attached to the door of the church at Wittenberg Castle a list of ninety-five theses (or propositions) on indulgences. By this act Luther intended only to start a theological discussion of the subject and to defend the theses publicly.

Luther's theses were soon translated from Latin into German, printed, and read throughout the empire. Immediately, broad theological issues were raised. When questioned, Luther rested his fundamental argument on the principle that there was no biblical basis for indulgences. But, replied Luther's opponents, to deny the legality of indulgences was to deny the authority of the pope who had authorized them. The issue was drawn: where did authority lie in the Christian church?

The papacy responded with a letter condemning some of Luther's propositions, ordering that his books be burned, and giving him two months to recant or be excommunicated. Luther retaliated by publicly burning the letter. By January 3, 1521, when the excommunication was supposed to become final, the controversy involved more than theological issues. The papal legate wrote, "All Germany is in revolution. Nine-tenths shout 'Luther' as their warcry; and the other tenth cares nothing about Luther, and cries 'Death to the court of Rome.'"[32]

In this highly charged atmosphere the twenty-one-year-old emperor Charles V held his first Diet at Worms and summoned Luther to appear before it. When ordered to recant, Luther replied in language that rang all over Europe:

Unless I am convinced by the evidence of Scripture or by plain reason—for I do not accept the authority of the Pope or the councils alone, since it is established that they have often erred and contradicted themselves—I am bound by the Scriptures I have cited and my conscience is captive to the Word of God. I cannot and will not recant anything, for it is neither safe nor right to go against conscience. God help me. Amen.[33]

The emperor declared Luther an outlaw of the empire and denied him legal protection. Duke Frederick of Saxony, however, protected him.

Protestant Thought

Between 1520 and 1530, Luther worked out the basic theological tenets that became the articles of faith for his new church and subsequently for all Protestant groups. At first the word *Protestant* meant "Lutheran," but with the appearance of many protesting sects it became a general term applied to all non-Catholic Christians. Ernst Troeltsch, a German student of the sociology of religion, has defined *Protestantism* as a "modification of Catholicism, in which the Catholic formulation of questions was retained, while a different answer was given to them." Luther provided new answers to four old, basic theological issues.[34]

First, how is a person to be saved? Traditional Catholic teaching held that salvation was achieved by both faith *and* good works. Luther held that salvation comes by faith alone. Women and men are saved, said Luther, by the arbitrary decision of God, irrespective of good works or the sacraments. God, not people, initiates salvation.

Second, where does religious authority reside? Christian doctrine had long maintained that authority rests both in the Bible and in the traditional teaching of the church. Luther maintained that authority rests in the Word of God as revealed in the Bible alone and as interpreted by an individual's conscience. He urged that each person read and reflect on the Scriptures.

Third, what is the church? Medieval churchmen had tended to identify the church with the clergy. Luther re-emphasized the Catholic teaching that the church consists of the entire community of Christian believers.

Finally, what is the highest form of Christian life? The medieval church had stressed the superiority of the monastic and religious life over the secular. Luther argued that all vocations, whether ecclesiastical or secular, have equal merit and that every person should serve God according to his or her individual calling. Protestantism, in sum, represented a reformulation of the Christian heritage.

The Social Impact of Luther's Beliefs

As early as 1521, Luther had a vast following. By the time of his death in 1546, people of all social classes had become Lutheran. What was the immense appeal of Luther's religious ideas?

Historical research on the German towns has shown that two significant late medieval developments prepared the way for Luther's ideas. First, since the fifteenth century, city governments had expressed resentment at clerical privileges and immunities. Religious orders frequently held large amounts of urban property, but priests, monks, and nuns paid no taxes and were exempt from civic responsibilities such as defending the city. City governments were determined to integrate the clergy into civic life by reducing their privileges and giving them public responsibilities.

Second, critics of the late medieval church, especially informed and intelligent townspeople, had condemned the irregularity and poor quality of sermons. As a result, prosperous burghers in many towns had established preacherships. Preachers were men of superior education who were required to deliver about a hundred sermons a year, each lasting about forty-five minutes. Luther's ideas attracted many preachers, and in Stuttgart, Reutlingen, and other towns, preachers became Protestant

❖ **Hans Holbein the Younger: Christ as the Man of Sorrows**   The scriptural basis of this concept is Isaiah 53:3–5: "He was pierced for our offenses, crushed by our sins. Upon him was the chastisement that makes us whole; by his stripes we were healed." Using a theme characteristic of early-sixteenth-century German piety, and placing the subject within a Renaissance architectural structure, Holbein produced this devotional painting in 1520 for the private use of the donor. *(Source: Öffentliche Kunstsammlung Basel)*

leaders. Preacherships also encouraged the Protestant form of worship, in which the sermon, not the Eucharist, was the central part of the service.[35]

In the countryside the attraction of the German peasants to Lutheran beliefs was almost predictable. Luther himself came from a peasant background and admired the peasants' ceaseless toil. Peasants respected Luther's defiance of church authority. Moreover, they thrilled to the words Luther used in his treatise *On Christian Liberty* (1520): "A Christian man is the most free lord of all and subject to none." Taken out of context, these words easily stirred social unrest.

Fifteenth-century Germany had witnessed several peasant revolts. In the early sixteenth century, the economic condition of the peasantry varied from place to place but was generally worse than it had been in the fifteenth century and was deteriorating. Crop failures in 1523 and 1524 aggravated an explosive situation. In 1525 representatives of the Swabian peasants met at the city of Memmingen and drew up twelve articles that expressed their grievances. The peasants complained that nobles had seized village common lands, which traditionally had been used by all; that nobles had imposed new rents and services on the peasants working properties; and that nobles had forced poor peasants to pay unjust death duties in the form of their best horses or cows. Wealthy, socially mobile peasants especially resented these burdens, which, they maintained, were new.[36] The peasants believed their demands conformed to Scripture and cited Luther as a theologian who could prove that they did.

Luther wanted to prevent rebellion. At first he sided with the peasants and in his tract *An Admonition to Peace* blasted the nobles:

We have no one on earth to thank for this mischievous rebellion, except you lords and princes, especially you blind bishops and mad priests and monks. . . . In your government you do nothing but flay and rob your subjects in order that you may lead a life of splendor and pride, until the poor common folk can bear it no longer.[37]

But nothing justified the use of armed force, he warned: "The fact that rulers are unjust and wicked does not excuse tumult and rebellion; to punish wickedness does not belong to everybody, but to the worldly rulers who bear the sword."[38] As for biblical support for the peasants' demands,

he maintained that Scripture had nothing to do with earthly justice or material gain.

Massive revolts first broke out near the Swiss frontier and then swept through Swabia, Thuringia, the Rhineland, and Saxony. The crowds' slogans came directly from Luther's writings. "God's righteousness" and the "Word of God" were invoked in the effort to secure social and economic justice. The peasants who expected Luther's support were soon disillusioned. He had written of the "freedom" of the Christian, but he had meant the freedom to obey the Word of God, for in sin men and women lose their freedom and break their relationship with God. To Luther, freedom meant independence from the authority of the Roman church; it did *not* mean opposition to legally established secular powers. Firmly convinced that rebellion hastened the end of civilized society, he wrote a tract *Against the Murderous, Thieving Hordes of the Peasants:* "Let everyone who can smite, slay, and stab [the peasants], secretly and openly, remembering that nothing can be more poisonous, hurtful or devilish than a rebel."[39] The nobility ferociously crushed the revolt. Historians estimate that over seventy-five thousand peasants were killed in 1525.

Luther took literally these words in Saint Paul's Letter to the Romans: "Let every soul be subject to the higher powers. For there is no power but of God: the powers that be are established by God. Whosoever resists the power, resists the ordinance of God: and they that resist shall receive to themselves damnation."[40] As it developed, Lutheran theology exalted the state, subordinated the church to the state, and everywhere championed "the powers that be." The revolt of 1525 strengthened the authority of lay rulers. Peasant economic conditions, however, moderately improved. For example, in many parts of Germany, enclosed fields, meadows, and forests were returned to common use.

Like the peasants, educated people and humanists were much attracted by Luther's words. He advocated a simpler, personal religion based on faith and the Scriptures, a return to the spirit of the early church, the abolition of elaborate ceremonial—precisely the reforms the northern humanists had been calling for. Ulrich Zwingli (1484–1531), for example, a humanist of Zurich, was strongly influenced by Luther's bold stand. It stimulated Zwingli's reforms in the Swiss city of Zurich and later in Bern.

Luther's linguistic skill, together with his translation of the New Testament in 1523, led to the acceptance of his dialect of German as the standard version of German. His insistence that everyone should read and reflect on the Scriptures attracted the literate and thoughtful middle classes partly because he appealed to their intelligence. Moreover, the business classes, preoccupied with making money, envied the church's wealth, disapproved of the luxurious lifestyle of some churchmen, and resented tithes and ecclesiastical taxation. Luther's doctrines of salvation by faith and the priesthood of all believers not only raised the religious status of the commercial classes but protected their pocketbooks as well.

Hymns, psalms, and Luther's two catechisms (1529)—compendiums of basic religious knowledge—also show the power of language in spreading the ideals of the Reformation. The reformers knew "that rhyme, meter, and melodies could forcefully impress minds and affect sensibilities." Lutheran hymns such as "A Mighty Fortress Is Our God" expressed deep feelings, were easily remembered, and imprinted on the mind central points of doctrine. Luther's *Larger Catechism* contained brief sermons on the main articles of faith; his *Shorter Catechism* gave concise explanations of doctrine in question-and-answer form. Both catechisms stressed the importance of the Ten Commandments, the Lord's Prayer, the Apostle's Creed, and the sacraments for the believing Christian. Though originally intended for the instruction of pastors, these catechisms became powerful tools for the indoctrination of men and women of all ages, especially the young.[41]

What appeal did Luther's message have for women? Luther's argument that all vocations have equal merit in the sight of God gave dignity to those who performed ordinary, routine, domestic tasks. The abolition of monasticism in Protestant territories led to the exaltation of the home, which Luther and other reformers stressed as the special domain of the wife. The Christian home, in contrast to the place of business, became the place for the exercise of the gentler virtues—love, tenderness, reconciliation, the carrying of one another's burdens. The Protestant abolition of private confession to a priest freed women from embarrassing explorations of their sexual lives. Protestants established schools where girls, as well as boys, became literate in the catechism and the Bible. The reformers stressed marriage as the cure for clerical concupiscence. Protestantism thus proved attractive to the many women who had been priests' concubines and mistresses: they became legal and honorable wives.[42]

For his time, Luther held enlightened views on matters of sexuality and marriage. He wrote to a young man, "Dear lad, be not ashamed that you desire a girl, nor you my maid, the boy. Just let it lead you into matrimony and not into promiscuity, and it is no more cause for shame than eating and drinking."[43] Luther was confident that God took delight in the sexual act and denied that original sin affected the goodness of creation. He believed, however, that marriage was a woman's career. A student recorded Luther as saying, early in his public ministry, "Let them bear children until they are dead of it; that is what they are for." A happy marriage to the former nun Katharine von Bora mellowed him, and another student later quoted him as saying, "Next to God's Word there is no more precious treasure than holy matrimony. God's highest gift on earth is a pious, cheerful, God-fearing, home-keeping wife, with whom you may live peacefully, to whom you may entrust your goods, and body and life."[44] Though Luther deeply loved his "dear Katie," he believed that women's principal concerns were children, the kitchen, and the church.

❈ GERMANY AND THE PROTESTANT REFORMATION

The history of the Holy Roman Empire in the later Middle Ages is a story of dissension, disintegration, and debility. Unlike Spain, France, and England, the empire lacked a strong central power. In 1356 the Golden Bull legalized what had long existed—government by an aristocratic federation. Each of seven electors gained virtual sovereignty in his own territory. The agreement ended disputed elections in the empire; it also reduced the central authority of the Holy Roman emperor. The empire was characterized by weak borders, localism, and chronic disorder. The nobility strengthened their territories, while imperial power declined.

The Political Impact of Luther's Beliefs

In the sixteenth century, the practice of religion remained a public matter. Everyone participated in the religious life of the community, just as almost everyone shared in the local agricultural work.

Peasants Sack the Abbey of Weissenau   Convinced that the monks lived idle, luxurious lives on money squeezed from the poor, peasants sacked the abbeys during the great revolt of 1525. (*Source: Château de Waldburg, Archives/Schneiders/Artephot*)

Whatever spiritual convictions individuals held in the privacy of their consciences, the emperor, king, prince, magistrate, or other civil authority determined the official form of religious practice within his jurisdiction. Almost everyone believed that the presence of a faith different from that of the majority represented a political threat to the security of the state. Only a tiny minority, and certainly none of the princes, believed in religious liberty.

Against this background, the religious storm launched by Martin Luther swept across Germany. Several elements in his religious reformation stirred patriotic feelings. Anti-Roman sentiment ran high. Humanists lent eloquent intellectual support. And Luther's translation of the New Testament into German evoked national pride.

For decades devout lay people and churchmen had called on the German princes to reform the church. In 1520 Luther took up the cry in his *Appeal to the Christian Nobility of the German Nation.* Unless the princes destroyed papal power in Germany, Luther argued, reform was impossible. He urged the princes to confiscate ecclesiastical wealth and to abolish indulgences, dispensations, pardons, and clerical celibacy. He told them that it was their public duty to bring about the moral reform of the church. Luther based his argument in part on the papacy's financial exploitation of Germany:

How comes it that we Germans must put up with such robbery and such extortion of our property at the hands of the pope? Why do we Germans let them make such fools and apes of us? It would all be more bearable if in this way they only stole our property; but they lay waste the churches and rob Christ's sheep of their pious shepherds, and destroy the worship and the Word of God.[45]

These words fell on welcome ears and itchy fingers. Luther's appeal to German patriotism gained him strong support, and national feeling influenced many princes otherwise confused by or indifferent to the complexities of the religious issues.

The church in Germany possessed great wealth. And, unlike other countries, Germany had no strong central government to check the flow of gold to Rome. Rejection of Roman Catholicism and adoption of Protestantism would mean the legal confiscation of lush farmlands, rich monasteries, and wealthy shrines. Some German princes were sincerely attracted to Lutheranism, but many civil authorities realized that they had a great deal to gain by embracing the new faith. A steady stream of duchies, margraviates, free cities, and bishoprics did so and secularized church property. The decision reached at Worms in 1521 to condemn Luther and his teaching was not enforced because the German princes did not want to enforce it.

Many princes used the religious issue to extend their financial and political independence. The results were unfortunate for the improvement of German government. The Protestant movement ultimately proved a political disaster for Germany.

Charles V must share blame with the German princes for the disintegration of imperial authority in the empire. He neither understood nor took an interest in the constitutional problems of Germany, and he lacked the material resources to oppose Protestantism effectively there. Throughout his reign he was preoccupied with his Flemish, Spanish, Italian, and American territories. Moreover, the Turkish threat prevented him from acting effectively against the Protestants; Charles's brother Ferdinand needed Protestant support against the Turks who besieged Vienna in 1529.

Five times between 1521 and 1555, Charles V went to war with the Valois kings of France. The issue each time was the Habsburg lands acquired by the marriage of Maximilian and Mary of Burgundy. Much of the fighting occurred in Germany. The cornerstone of French foreign policy in the sixteenth and seventeenth centuries was the desire to keep the German states divided. Thus Europe witnessed the paradox of the Catholic king of France supporting the Lutheran princes in their challenge to his fellow Catholic, Charles V. Habsburg-Valois Wars advanced the cause of Protestantism and promoted the political fragmentation of the German empire.

Finally, in 1555, Charles agreed to the Peace of Augsburg, which, in accepting the status quo, officially recognized Lutheranism. Each prince was permitted to determine the religion of his territory. Most of northern and central Germany became Lutheran; the south remained Roman Catholic. There was no freedom of religion, however.

Princes or town councils established state churches to which all subjects of the area had to belong. Dissidents, whether Lutheran or Catholic, had to convert or leave. The political difficulties Germany inherited from the Middle Ages had been compounded by the religious crisis of the sixteenth century.

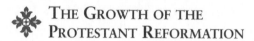

THE GROWTH OF THE PROTESTANT REFORMATION

By 1555 much of northern Europe had broken with the Roman Catholic church. All of Scandinavia, England (except during the reign of Mary Tudor), Scotland, and large parts of Switzerland, Germany, and France had rejected the religious authority of Rome and adopted new faiths. Because a common religious faith had been the one element uniting all of Europe for almost a thousand years, the fragmentation of belief led to profound changes in European life and society. The most significant new form of Protestantism was Calvinism, of which the Peace of Augsburg had made no mention at all.

Calvinism

In 1509, while Luther was studying for the doctorate at Wittenberg, John Calvin (1509–1564) was born in Noyon in northwestern France. Luther inadvertently launched the Protestant Reformation. Calvin, however, had the greater impact on future generations. In 1533 he experienced a religious crisis, as a result of which he converted to Protestantism. His theological writings profoundly influenced the social thought and attitudes of Europeans and English-speaking peoples all over the world, especially in Canada and the United States.

Convinced that God selects certain people to do his work, Calvin believed that God had specifically called him to reform the church. Accordingly, he accepted an invitation to assist in the reformation of the city of Geneva. There, beginning in 1541, Calvin worked assiduously to establish a Christian society ruled by God through civil magistrates and reformed ministers. Geneva, "a city that was a Church," became the model of a Christian community for sixteenth-century Protestant reformers.

To understand Calvin's Geneva, it is necessary to understand Calvin's ideas. These he embodied in *The Institutes of the Christian Religion,* first published in 1536 and definitively issued in 1559. The cornerstone of Calvin's theology was his belief in the absolute sovereignty and omnipotence of God and the total weakness of humanity. Before the infinite power of God, he asserted, men and women are as insignificant as grains of sand.

Calvin did not ascribe free will to human beings, because that would detract from the sovereignty of God. Men and women cannot actively work to achieve salvation; rather, God in his infinite wisdom decided at the beginning of time who would be saved and who damned. This viewpoint constitutes the theological principle called *predestination:*

Predestination we call the eternal decree of God, by which he has determined in himself, what he would have become of every individual of mankind. . . . God has once for all determined, both whom he would admit to salvation, and whom he would condemn to destruction. We affirm that this counsel, as far as concerns the elect, is founded on his gratuitous mercy, totally irrespective of human merit; but that to those whom he devotes to condemnation, the gate of life is closed by a just and irreprehensible, but incomprehensible, judgment. How exceedingly presumptuous it is only to inquire into the causes of the Divine will; which is in fact, and is justly entitled to be, the cause of everything that exists. . . . For the will of God is the highest justice; so that what he wills must be considered just, for this very reason, because he wills it.[46]

Many people have found the doctrine of predestination, which dates back to Saint Augustine and Saint Paul, a pessimistic view of the nature of God, who, they feel, revealed himself in the Old and New Testaments as merciful as well as just. But "this terrible decree," as even Calvin called it, did not lead to pessimism or fatalism. Rather, the Calvinist believed in the redemptive work of Christ and was confident that God had elected (saved) him or her. Predestination served as an energizing dynamic, forcing a person to undergo hardships in the constant struggle against evil.

Calvin aroused Genevans to a high standard of morality. Using his sermons and a program of religious education, God's laws and man's were enforced in Geneva. Using his *Genevan Catechism,* published in 1541, children and adults memorized set questions and answers and acquired a summary of their faith and a guide for daily living. Calvin's sermons and his *Catechism* gave a whole generation of Genevans thorough instruction in the reformed religion.[47]

In the reformation of the city, the Genevan Consistory also exercised a powerful role. This body consisted of twelve laymen, plus the Company of Pastors, of which Calvin was the permanent moderator (presider). The duties of the Consistory were "to keep watch over every man's life [and] to admonish amiably those whom they see leading a disorderly life." Calvin emphasized that the Consistory's activities should be thorough and "its eyes may be everywhere," but corrections were only "medicine to turn sinners to the Lord."[48]

Although all municipal governments in early modern Europe regulated citizens' conduct, none did so with the severity of Geneva's Consistory under Calvin's leadership. Nor did it make any distinction between what we would consider crimes against society and simple unchristian conduct. The Consistory investigated and punished absence from sermons, criticism of ministers, dancing, playing cards, family quarrels, and heavy drinking. The civil authorities handled serious crimes and heresy and, with the Consistory's approval, sometimes used torture to extract confessions. Between 1542 and 1546 alone seventy-six persons were banished from Geneva and fifty-eight executed for heresy, adultery, blasphemy, and witchcraft.

Calvin reserved his harshest condemnation for religious dissenters, declaring them "dogs and swine":

God makes plain that the false prophet is to be stoned without mercy. We are to crush beneath our heel all affections of nature when His honor is concerned. The father should not spare his child, nor brother his brother, nor husband his own wife or the friend who is dearer to him than life. No human relationship is more than animal unless it be grounded in God.[49]

Calvin translated his words into action. He made an example of the Spanish humanist Michael Servetus, who, persecuted by the Spanish Inquisition, escaped to Geneva. In addition to denying the Trinity—which identifies God as three divine persons, Father, Son, and Holy Spirit—Servetus insisted that a person under twenty cannot commit a mortal sin. The city fathers considered this idea dangerous to public morality, "especially in these days when the young are so corrupted." Servetus was burned at the stake.

To many sixteenth-century Europeans, Calvin's Geneva seemed "the most perfect school of Christ since the days of the Apostles." Religious refugees from France, England, Spain, Scotland, and Italy

THE LATER MIDDLE AGES, RENAISSANCE, AND PROTESTANT AND CATHOLIC REFORMATIONS, 1300–1600

1309–1376	Babylonian Captivity of the papacy
1310–1320	Dante, *The Divine Comedy*
1337–1453	Hundred Years' War
1347–1351	The Black Death (returned intermittently until ca 1700)
1356	Golden Bull transforms the Holy Roman Empire into an aristocratic confederation
ca 1376	John Wyclif attacks the church's temporal power and asserts the supremacy of the Scriptures
1378–1417	The Great Schism
1381	Peasants' revolt in England
1387–1400	Chaucer, *Canterbury Tales*
1404	Christine de Pisan, *The City of Ladies*
1414–1418	Council of Constance ends the schism, postpones reform, executes John Hus
1453	Capture of Constantinople by the Ottoman Turks, ending the Byzantine Empire
1455–1471	Wars of the Roses in England
1456	Gutenberg Bible
1492	Unification of Spain under Ferdinand and Isabela; expulsion of Jews and Muslims from Spain Columbus reaches the Americas
1494	France invades Italy, inaugurating sixty years of war on Italian soil
1513	Machiavelli, *The Prince*
1517	Martin Luther publishes the Ninety-five Theses
1523	Luther's translation of the New Testament into German
1525	Peasants' revolt in Germany
1533	Act in Restraint of Appeals inaugurates the English Reformation
1536	Calvin, *The Institutes of the Christian Religion*
1540	Loyola founds the Society of Jesus (Jesuits)
1541	Calvin establishes a theocracy in Geneva
1543	Copernicus, *On the Revolutions of the Heavenly Spheres*
1545–1563	Council of Trent
1555	Peace of Augsburg officially recognized
1588	Spanish Armada
1603	Shakespeare, *Hamlet*
1611	Authorized or King James Version of the Bible

Calvinist Worship   A converted house in Lyons, France, serves as a church for the simple Calvinist service. Although Calvin's followers believed in equality and elected officials administered the church, here men and women are segregated, and some people sit on hard benches while others sit in upholstered pews. Beside the pulpit an hourglass hangs to time the preacher's sermon. (Could the dog sit still for that long?) (*Source: Bibliothèque publique et universitaire, Geneva*)

visited the city. Subsequently, the Reformed church of Calvin served as the model for the Presbyterian church in Scotland, the Huguenot church in France, and the Puritan churches in England and New England. The Calvinist provision for congregational participation and vernacular liturgy helped to satisfy women's desire to belong to and participate in a meaningful church organization. The Calvinist ethic of the "calling" dignified all work with a religious aspect: hard work, well done, was said to be pleasing to God. This doctrine encouraged an aggressive, vigorous activism. In the *Institutes* Calvin provided a systematic theology for Protestantism. The Reformed church of Calvin had a strong and well-organized machinery of government. These factors, together with the social

and economic applications of Calvin's theology, made Calvinism the most dynamic force in sixteenth- and seventeenth-century Protestantism.

The Anabaptists

The name *Anabaptist* derives from a Greek word meaning "to baptize again." The Anabaptists, sometimes described as the left wing of the Reformation, believed that only adults could make a free choice about religious faith, baptism, and entry into the Christian community. Thus they considered the practice of baptizing infants and children preposterous and wanted to rebaptize believers who had been baptized as children. Anabaptists took the Gospel and, at first, Luther's teachings absolutely literally and favored a return to the kind of church that had existed among the earliest Christians—a voluntary association of believers who had experienced an inner light.

Anabaptists maintained that only a few people would receive the inner light. This position meant that the Christian community and the Christian state were not identical. In other words, Anabaptists believed in the separation of church and state and in religious tolerance. They almost never tried to force their values on others. In an age that believed in the necessity of state-established churches, Anabaptist views on religious liberty were thought to undermine that concept.

Each Anabaptist community or church was entirely independent; it selected its own ministers and ran its own affairs. In 1534 the community at Münster in Germany, for example, established a legal code that decreed the death penalty for insubordinate wives. Moreover, the Münster community also practiced polygamy and forced all women under a certain age to marry or face expulsion or execution.

Anabaptists admitted women to the ministry. They shared goods as the early Christians had done, refused all public offices, and would not serve in the armed forces. In fact, they laid great stress on pacifism. A favorite Anabaptist scriptural quotation was "By their fruits you shall know them," suggesting that if Christianity was a religion of peace, the Christian should not fight. With such beliefs Anabaptists were inevitably a minority. Anabaptism later attracted the poor, the unemployed, the uneducated. Geographically, Anabaptists drew their members from depressed urban areas.

Ideas such as absolute pacifism and the distinction between the Christian community and the state brought down on these unfortunate people fanatical hatred and bitter persecution. Zwingli, Luther, Calvin, and Catholics all saw—quite correctly—the separation of church and state as leading ultimately to the complete secularization of society. The powerful rulers of Swiss and German society immediately feared that the combination of religious differences and economic grievances would lead to civil disturbances. In Saxony, in Strasbourg, and in the Swiss cities, Anabaptists were either banished or executed by burning, beating, or drowning. Their community spirit and the edifying example of their lives, however, contributed to the survival of Anabaptist ideas.

The Quakers with their gentle pacifism, the Baptists with their emphasis on an inner spiritual light, the Congregationalists with their democratic church organization, and, in 1787, the authors of the U.S. Constitution with their concern for the separation of church and state—all trace their origins in part to the Anabaptists of the sixteenth century.

The English Reformation

As on the continent of Europe, the Reformation in England had social and economic causes as well as religious ones. As elsewhere, too, Christian humanists had for decades been calling for the purification of the church. When the personal matter of the divorce of King Henry VIII (r. 1509–1547) became enmeshed with political issues, a complete break with Rome resulted.

Demands for ecclesiastical reform dated back at least to the fourteenth century. The Lollards (see page 428) had been driven underground in the fifteenth century but survived in parts of southern England and the Midlands. Working-class people, especially cloth workers, were attracted to their ideas. The Lollards stressed the individual's reading and interpretation of the Bible, which they considered the only standard of Christian faith and holiness. They put no stock in the value of the sacraments and were vigorously anticlerical. Lollards opposed ecclesiastical wealth, the veneration of the saints, prayers for the dead, and all war. Although they had no notion of justification by faith, like Luther they insisted on the individual soul's direct responsibility to God.

Still, traditional Catholicism exerted an enormously strong, diverse, and vigorous hold over the imagination and loyalty of the people. The teachings of Christianity were graphically represented in the liturgy, constantly reiterated in sermons, enacted in plays, and carved and printed on walls, screens, and the windows of parish churches. A zealous clergy, increasingly better educated, engaged in a "massive catechetical enterprise." No substantial gulf existed between the religion of the clergy and educated elite and the broad mass of the English people.[50] The Reformation in England was an act of state, initiated by the king's emotional life.

In 1527, having fallen in love with Anne Boleyn, Henry wanted his marriage to Catherine of Aragon annulled. Catherine had failed to bear a boy child, and Henry claimed that only a male heir to the throne could prevent a disputed succession. He thus petitioned Pope Clement VII (r. 1523–1534) for an annulment. When Henry had married Catherine, he had secured a dispensation from Pope Julius II eliminating all legal technicalities about Catherine's previous union with Henry's late brother, Arthur. Henry now argued that Pope Julius's dispensation had contradicted the law of God—that a man may not marry his brother's widow. The English king's request reached Rome at the very time that Luther was widely publishing tracts condemning the papacy. If Clement had granted Henry's annulment and thereby admitted that Julius II had erred, Clement would have given support to the Lutheran assertion that popes substitute their own evil judgments for the law of God. This Clement could not do, so he delayed acting on Henry's request.[51] The capture and sack of Rome in 1527 by mercenaries working for the emperor Charles V, Queen Catherine's nephew, thoroughly tied the pope's hands.

Since Rome appeared to be thwarting Henry's matrimonial plans, he decided to remove the English church from papal jurisdiction. Henry used Parliament to legalize the Reformation in England. The Act in Restraint of Appeals (1533) declared the king to be the supreme sovereign in England and forbade judicial appeals to the papacy, thus establishing the Crown as the highest legal authority in the land. The Act for the Submission of the Clergy (1534) required churchmen to submit to the king and forbade the publication of ecclesiastical laws without royal permission. The Supremacy Act of 1534 declared the king the supreme head of the Church of England.

An authority on the Reformation Parliament has written that probably only a small number of those who voted for the Restraint of Appeals actually knew they were voting for a permanent break with Rome.[52] Some opposed the king. John Fisher, the bishop of Rochester, a distinguished scholar and humanist, lashed the clergy with scorn for their cowardice. Thomas More, who had written *Utopia* nearly two years before (see page 475), resigned the chancellorship rather than acknowledge the rejection of papal authority. Fisher, More, and other dissenters were beheaded for treason in 1535.

When Anne Boleyn failed twice to produce a male child, Henry VIII charged her with adulterous incest and in 1536 had her beheaded. His third wife, Jane Seymour, gave Henry the desired son, Edward, but died in childbirth. Henry went on to three more wives before he passed to his reward in 1547.

Between 1535 and 1539, under the influence of his chief minister, Thomas Cromwell, Henry decided to dissolve the English monasteries because he wanted their wealth. The king ended nine hundred years of English monastic life, dispersed the monks and nuns, and confiscated their lands. Hundreds of properties were sold to the middle and upper classes and the proceeds spent on war. The closing of the monasteries did not achieve a more equitable distribution of land and wealth. Rather, the "bare ruined choirs where late the sweet birds sang"—as Shakespeare's Sonnet 73 describes the desolate religious houses—testified to the loss of a valuable cultural force in English life. The redistribution of land, however, strengthened the upper classes and tied them to the Tudor Dynasty.

Henry retained such traditional Catholic practices and doctrines as auricular confession, clerical celibacy, and *transubstantiation* (the doctrine that the bread and wine of the Eucharist are transformed into the body and blood of Christ although their appearance does not change). But Protestant literature circulated, and Henry approved the selection of men of Protestant sympathies as tutors for his son.

Did the religious changes have broad popular support? Recent scholarship has emphasized that the English Reformation came from above. The surviving evidence does not allow us to gauge the degree of opposition to (or support for) Henry's break with Rome. Certainly, many lay people wrote to the king, begging him to spare the monasteries. "Most laypeople acquiesced in the Reformation because they hardly knew what was going on, were understandably reluctant to jeopardise life or limb, a career or the family's good name."[53] But not all quietly acquiesced. In 1536 popular opposition in the north to the religious changes led to the Pilgrimage of Grace, a massive multiclass rebellion that proved the largest in English history. In 1546 serious rebellions in East Anglia and in the west, despite possessing economic and Protestant components, reflected considerable public opposition to the state-ordered religious changes.[54]

After Henry's death, the English church shifted left and right. In the short reign of Henry's sickly son Edward VI (r. 1547–1553), strongly Protestant ideas exerted a significant influence on the

Lutheran
Calvinist (Reformed)
Church of England
Roman Catholic
▲ Huguenot centers
→ Spread of Calvinism

0   150   300 Km.
0   150   300 Mi.

ATLANTIC
OCEAN

IRELAND
•Dublin

SCOTLAND
1560
•Edinburgh
John Knox,
1505–1572

ENGLAND
1536
Oxford•   •London
John Wyclif,
1320–1384
•Plymouth

Penetration of Calvinism
to England after 1558

North
Sea

NORWAY
1536/1607
•Bergen

S W E D E N
•Stockholm

Baltic
Sea

•Riga

•Helsinki

LITHUANIA

PRUSSIA

•Warsaw

POLAND

TRANSYLVANIA

DENMARK
Copenhagen•

•Hamburg BRANDENBURG
SAXONY
Amsterdam• •Münster Wittenberg
Birthplace of
Antwerp•   Martin Luther,
NETHERLANDS •Brussels   1483–1546
•Marburg •Leipzig
Birthplace of   Worms Erfurt•
John Calvin,   1521   Eisleben•
•Noyon 1509–1564 •Speyer •Nuremburg
•Paris Edict of Worms Stuttgart• •Augsburg •Munich
Strasbourg•   Basel• Zürich•
Ulrich Zwingli,
1484–1531

HOLY ROMAN
EMPIRE

Prague•   BOHEMIA
John Hus,
1369–1415

MORAVIA
AUSTRIA •Vienna
•Buda •Pest
HUNGARY

Council of Trent,
1545–1563
Geneva• •Trent •Venice
John Calvin,
•Milan
•Pavia
•Genoa   •Florence
Genoa •Pisa

Corsica

Sardinia

ITALY
•Rome
Roman Inquisition
established, 1542

Adriatic
Sea

•Bari

•Naples

Sicily

Mediterranean
Sea

Black
Sea

•Lepanto

OTTOMAN EMPIRE

FRANCE
•Rennes   •Orléans
•Nantes
Edict of Nantes,
1598
•La Rochelle
•Bordeaux

•Avignon
•Marseilles
•Toulouse

•Barcelona

Balearic Is.

•Valencia

•Loyola
Birthplace of
Ignatius Loyola,
1491

SPAIN
•Madrid
•Toledo
•Seville   •Granada

MUSLIM STATES

PORTUGAL

Lisbon•

religious life of the country. Archbishop Thomas Cranmer simplified the liturgy, invited Protestant theologians to England, and prepared the first *Book of Common Prayer* (1549). In stately and dignified English, the *Book of Common Prayer* included, together with the Psalter, the order for all services of the Church of England.

The equally brief reign of Mary Tudor (r. 1553–1558) witnessed a sharp move back to Catholicism. The devoutly Catholic daughter of Catherine of Aragon and Henry, Mary rescinded the Reformation legislation of her father's reign and fully restored Roman Catholicism. Mary's marriage to her cousin Philip of Spain, son of the emperor Charles V, proved highly unpopular in England, and her persecution and execution of several hundred Protestants further alienated her subjects. Mary's death raised to the throne her sister Elizabeth (r. 1558–1603) and inaugurated the beginnings of religious stability.

Elizabeth had been raised a Protestant, but at the start of her reign sharp differences existed in England. Catholics wanted a Roman Catholic ruler, but a vocal number of returning exiles wanted all Catholic elements in the Church of England eliminated. Members of the latter group were called Puritans because they wanted to "purify" the church. Probably one of the shrewdest politicians in English history, Elizabeth chose a middle course between Catholic and Puritan extremes. She insisted on dignity in church services and political order in the land. She did not care what people believed as long as they kept quiet about it. Avoiding precise doctrinal definitions, Elizabeth had herself styled "Supreme Governor of the Church of England, Etc.," and left it to her subjects to decide what the "Etc." meant.

The parliamentary legislation of the early years of Elizabeth's reign—laws sometimes labeled the "Elizabethan Settlement"—required outward conformity to the Church of England and uniformity in all ceremonies. Everyone had to attend Church of England services; those who refused were fined. During Elizabeth's reign, the Anglican church (from the Latin *Ecclesia Anglicana*), as the Church of England was called, moved in a moderately Protestant direction. Services were conducted in English, monasteries were not re-established, and the clergy were allowed to marry. But the bishops remained as church officials, and apart from language, the services were quite traditional.

 THE CATHOLIC AND THE COUNTER-REFORMATIONS

Between 1517 and 1547, the reformed versions of Christianity known as Protestantism made remarkable advances. All of England, Scandinavia, much of Scotland and Germany, and sizable parts of France and Switzerland adopted the creeds of Luther, Calvin, and other reformers. Still, the Roman Catholic church made a significant comeback. After about 1540, no new large areas of Europe, except for the Netherlands, accepted Protestant beliefs (Map 15.2).

Historians distinguish between two types of reform within the Catholic church in the sixteenth and seventeenth centuries. The Catholic Reformation began before 1517 and sought renewal basically through the stimulation of a new spiritual fervor. The Counter-Reformation started in the 1540s as a reaction to the rise and spread of Protestantism. The Counter-Reformation was a Catholic effort to convince or coerce dissidents or heretics to return to the church.

The Renaissance princes who sat on the throne of Saint Peter were not blind to the evils that existed. Modest reform efforts had begun with the Lateran Council that Pope Julius II called in 1512. The Dutch pope Adrian VI (r. 1522–1523) instructed his legate in Germany "to say that we frankly confess that God permits this [Lutheran] persecution of his church on account of the sins of men, especially those of the priests and prelates."[55]

Overall, why did the popes, spiritual leaders of the Western church, move so slowly? The answers lie in the personalities of the popes themselves, in their preoccupation with political affairs in Italy, and in the awesome difficulty of reforming so complicated a bureaucracy as the Roman curia. Clement VII, a true Medici, was far more interested in elegant tapestries and Michelangelo's painting of the Last Judgment than in theological disputes in barbaric Germany or far-off England.

MAP 15.2 The Protestant and the Catholic Reformations The reformations shattered the religious unity of Western Christendom. What common cultural traits predominated in regions where a particular branch of the Christian faith was maintained or took root?

In the Habsburg-Valois conflicts in Italy Clement first backed the emperor Charles. He then switched to the French ruler. Shortly afterward, the emperor's Spanish and German mercenaries sacked and looted Rome and took him captive.

The idea of reform was closely linked to the idea of a general council representing the entire church. Popes such as Clement VII, remembering fifteenth-century conciliar attempts to limit papal authority, resisted calls for a council, fearing loss of power, revenue, and prestige.

The Council of Trent

In the papal conclave that followed the death of Clement VII, Cardinal Alexander Farnese promised two German cardinals that if he were elected pope he would summon a council. He won the election and ruled as Pope Paul III (r. 1534–1549). This Roman aristocrat, humanist, and astrologer, who immediately made his teenage grandsons cardinals, seemed an unlikely person to undertake serious reform. Yet Paul III appointed as cardinals several learned and reform-minded men; established the Inquisition in the Papal States; and called a council, which finally met at Trent, an imperial city close to Italy (see Map 15.2).

The Council of Trent met intermittently from 1545 to 1563. It was called not only to reform the church but to secure reconciliation with the Protestants. Lutherans and Calvinists were invited to participate, but their insistence that the Scriptures be the sole basis for discussion made reconciliation impossible. International politics repeatedly cast a shadow over the theological debates. Charles V opposed discussions on any matter that might further alienate his Lutheran subjects. The French kings worked against any reconciliation of Roman Catholicism and Lutheranism, wanting the German states to remain divided. Portugal, Poland, Hungary, and Ireland sent representatives, but very few German bishops attended.

Another problem was the persistence of the conciliar theory of church government. Some bishops wanted a concrete statement asserting the supremacy of a church council over the papacy. The adoption of the conciliar principle could have led to a divided church. The bishops had a provincial and national outlook; only the papacy possessed an international religious perspective. The centralizing tenet was established that all acts of the council required papal approval.

In spite of the obstacles, the achievements of the Council of Trent are impressive. It dealt with both doctrinal and disciplinary matters. The council gave equal validity to the Scriptures and to tradition as sources of religious truth and authority. It reaffirmed the seven sacraments and the traditional Catholic teaching on transubstantiation, rejecting Lutheran and Calvinist positions.

The council tackled the problems arising from ancient abuses by strengthening ecclesiastical discipline. Tridentine (from *Tridentum,* the Latin word for "Trent") decrees required bishops to reside in their own dioceses, suppressed pluralism and simony, and forbade the sale of indulgences. Clerics who kept concubines were to give them up. In a highly original canon, the council required every diocese to establish a seminary for the education and training of the clergy and insisted that preference for admission be given to sons of the poor. Seminary professors were to determine whether candidates for ordination had *vocations*—genuine callings as evidenced by purity of life, detachment from the broader secular culture, and a steady inclination toward the priesthood. This was a novel idea, since from the time of the early church, parents had determined their sons' (and daughters') religious careers. Also, great emphasis was laid on preaching and instructing the laity, especially the uneducated.

One decision had especially important social consequences for lay people. Since the time of the Roman Empire, many couples had treated marriage as a completely personal matter, exchanged vows privately without witnesses, and thus formed clandestine (secret) unions. This widespread practice frequently led later to denials by one party that a marriage had taken place, to conflicts over property, and to disputes in the ecclesiastical courts that had jurisdiction over marriage. The Tridentine decree *Tametsi* (1563) stipulated that for a marriage to be valid, consent (the essence of marriage) as expressed in the vows had to be given publicly before witnesses, one of whom had to be the parish priest. Trent thereby ended secret marriages in Catholic countries.

The Council of Trent did not bring about reform immediately. But the Tridentine decrees laid a solid basis for the spiritual renewal of the church and for the enforcement of correction. For four centuries, the doctrinal and disciplinary legislation of Trent served as the basis for Roman Catholic faith, organization, and practice.

New Religious Orders and the Inquisition

The establishment of new religious orders within the church reveals a central feature of the Catholic Reformation. These new orders developed in response to the need to raise the moral and intellectual level of the clergy and people. Education was a major goal of them all.

The Ursuline order of nuns, founded by Angela Merici (1474–1540), attained enormous prestige for the education of women. The daughter of a country gentleman, Angela Merici worked for many years among the poor, sick, and uneducated around her native Brescia in northern Italy. In 1535 she established the Ursuline order to combat heresy through Christian education of young girls. The Ursulines sought to re-Christianize society by training future wives and mothers. Approved as a religious community by Paul III in 1544, the Ursulines rapidly grew and spread to France and the New World. Their schools in North America, stretching from Quebec to New Orleans, provided superior education for young women and inculcated the spiritual ideals of the Catholic Reformation.

The Society of Jesus, founded by Ignatius Loyola (1491–1556), a former Spanish soldier, played a powerful international role in resisting the spread of Protestantism, converting Asians and Latin American Indians to Catholicism, and spreading Christian education all over Europe. While recuperating from a severe battle wound to his legs, Loyola studied a life of Christ and other religious books and decided to give up his military career and become a soldier of Christ. His great classic, *Spiritual Exercises,* directed the individual imagination and will to the reform of life and a new spiritual piety.

Loyola was apparently a man of considerable personal magnetism. After study at the universities

Juan de Valdes Leal: Pope Paul III Approves the Jesuit Constitutions Although Paul III devoted considerable energy to advancing the interests of his (Farnese) family, he also tried to meet the challenge of Protestantism—by means of the Council of Trent and new religious orders. When the Jesuit constitutions were read to him, Paul III supposedly murmured, "There is the finger of God." The portrait of Ignatius Loyola (holding the paper) is a reasonable likeness; that of the pope is an idealization: in 1540 he was a very old man. *(Source: MAS, Barcelona)*

in Salamanca and Paris, he gathered a group of six companions and in 1540 secured papal approval of the new Society of Jesus, whose members were called Jesuits. The first Jesuits were recruited primarily from the wealthy merchant and professional classes. They saw the Reformation as a pastoral problem, its causes and cures related not to doctrinal issues but to people's spiritual condition. Reform of the church as Luther and Calvin understood the word *reform* played no role in the future the Jesuits planned for themselves. Their goal was "to help souls." Loyola also possessed a gift for leadership that consisted in spotting talent and "in the ability to see how at a given juncture change is more consistent with one's scope than staying the course."[56]

The Society of Jesus developed into a highly centralized, tightly knit organization. Candidates underwent a two-year novitiate, in contrast to the usual one-year probation required by older religious orders. In addition to the traditional vows of poverty, chastity, and obedience, professed members vowed "special obedience to the sovereign pontiff regarding missions."[57] Thus, as stability—the promise to live one's life in the monastery—was what made a monk, so mobility—the commitment to go anywhere for the help of souls—was the defining characteristic of a Jesuit. Flexibility and the willingness to respond to the needs of time and circumstance formed the Jesuit tradition. In this respect they were very modern, and they attracted many recruits.

The Society of Jesus achieved phenomenal success for the papacy and the reformed Catholic church. Jesuit schools adopted the modern humanist curricula and methods. They first concentrated on the children of the poor but soon were educating the sons of the nobility. As confessors and spiritual directors to kings, Jesuits exerted great political influence. Operating on the principle that the end sometimes justifies the means, they were not above spying. Indifferent to physical comfort and personal safety, they carried Christianity to India and Japan before 1550 and to Brazil, North America, and the Congo in the seventeenth century. Within Europe, the Jesuits brought southern Germany and much of eastern Europe back to Catholicism.

In 1542 Pope Paul III established the Sacred Congregation of the Holy Office with jurisdiction over the Roman Inquisition, a powerful instrument of the Counter-Reformation. A committee of six cardinals, the Roman Inquisition had judicial authority over all Catholics and the power to arrest, imprison, and execute. Under the fanatical Cardinal Caraffa, it vigorously attacked heresy. The Roman Inquisition operated under the principles of Roman law. It accepted hearsay evidence, was not obliged to inform the accused of charges against them, and sometimes used torture. Echoing one of Calvin's remarks about heresy, Cardinal Caraffa wrote, "No man is to lower himself by showing toleration towards any sort of heretic, least of all a Calvinist."[58] The Holy Office published the *Index of Prohibited Books,* a catalogue of forbidden reading.

Within the Papal States, the Roman Inquisition effectively destroyed heresy (and some heretics). Outside the papal territories, its influence was slight. Governments had their own judicial systems for the suppression of treasonable activities, as religious heresy was then considered.[59]

SUMMARY

From about 1050 to 1300, a new economy emerged in Italy, based on Venetian and Genoese shipping and long-distance trade and on Florentine banking and cloth manufacture. The combination of these commercial activities and the struggle of urban communities for political independence from surrounding feudal lords led to the appearance of a new wealthy aristocratic class. With this foundation, Italy was the scene of a remarkable intellectual and artistic flowering. Based on renewed interest in the Greco-Roman world, the Renaissance had a classicizing influence on many facets of culture. Despots or oligarchs ruled the city-states of fifteenth- and sixteenth-century Italy and manipulated Renaissance culture to enhance their personal power. Moving beyond Italy, the individualism, humanism, and secular spirit characteristic of the Italian Renaissance affected the culture of all Europe.

In northern Europe, city merchants and rural gentry allied with rising monarchies. Using taxes provided by business people, kings provided a greater degree of domestic peace and order, conditions essential for trade. In Spain, France, and England, rulers also emphasized royal dignity and authority. Except in the Holy Roman Empire, feudal monarchies gradually evolved in the direction of nation-states.

In the sixteenth century and through most of the seventeenth, religion and religious issues continued to play a major role in the lives of individuals and in the policies and actions of governments. The age of the Reformation presents very real paradoxes. The break with Rome and the rise of Lutheran, Anglican, Calvinist, and other faiths destroyed the unity of Europe as an organic Christian society. The strength of religious convictions caused political fragmentation, and religion, whether Protestant or Catholic, decisively influenced the growth of national states. Although most reformers rejected religious toleration, they helped pave the way for it.

Scholars have maintained that the sixteenth century witnessed the beginnings of the modern world. They are both right and wrong. The sixteenth-century revolt from the church laid the groundwork for the eighteenth-century revolt from the Christian God, one of the strongest supports of life in Western culture. In this respect, the Reformation marks the beginning of the modern world, with its secularism and rootlessness. At the same time, it can be argued that the sixteenth century represents the culmination of the Middle Ages. Martin Luther's anxieties about salvation show him to be very much a medieval man. His concerns had deeply troubled serious individuals since the time of Saint Augustine. Modern people tend to be less troubled by them.

NOTES

1. See L. Martines, *Power and Imagination: City-States in Renaissance Italy* (New York: Vintage Books, 1980), esp. pp. 332–333.
2. Ibid., pp. 22–61.
3. Ibid., pp. 221–237, esp. p. 221.
4. Quoted in J. Burckhardt, *The Civilization of the Renaissance in Italy* (London: Phaidon Books, 1951), p. 89.
5. *Memoirs of Benvenuto Cellini; A Florentine Artist; Written by Himself* (London: J. M. Dent & Sons, 1927), p. 2.
6. See C. Trinkaus, *In Our Image and Likeness: Humanity and Divinity in Italian Humanist Thought,* vol. 2 (London: Constable, 1970), pp. 505–529.
7. See Martines, *Power and Imagination,* Ch. 13, esp. pp. 241, 243.
8. See A. Hauser, *The Social History of Art,* vol. 2 (New York: Vintage Books, 1959), Ch. 3, esp. pp. 60, 68.
9. G. Bull, trans., *Aretino: Selected Letters* (Baltimore: Penguin Books, 1976), p. 109.
10. Hauser, *The Social History of Art,* pp. 48–49.
11. Quoted in E. H. Harbison, *The Christian Scholar and His Calling in the Age of the Reformation* (New York: Charles Scribner's Sons, 1956), p. 109.
12. Quoted in F. Seebohm, *The Oxford Reformers* (London: J. M. Dent & Sons, 1867), p. 256.
13. Quoted in W. H. Woodward, *Vittorino da Feltre and Other Humanist Educators* (Cambridge: Cambridge University Press, 1897), pp. 96–97.
14. C. E. Detmold, trans., *The Historical, Political and Diplomatic Writings of Niccolò Machiavelli* (Boston: J. R. Osgood, 1882), pp. 51–52.
15. Ibid., pp. 54–55.
16. See F. Gilbert, *Machiavelli and Guicciardini: Politics and History in Sixteenth Century Florence* (New York: Norton, 1984), pp. 197–200.
17. See L. Hunt, *The Invention of Pornography: Obscenity and the Origins of Modernity, 1500–1800* (New York: Zone Books, 1993), pp. 10, 93–95.
18. Quoted in E. L. Eisenstein, *The Printing Press as an Agent of Change: Communications and Cultural Transformations in Early Modern Europe,* vol. 1 (New York: Cambridge University Press, 1979), p. 135; for an overall discussion, see pp. 126–159.
19. M. L. King, "Book-lined Cells: Women and Humanism in the Early Italian Renaissance," in *Beyond Their Sex: Learned Women of the European Past,* ed. P. H. Labalme (New York: New York University Press, 1980), pp. 66–81, esp. p. 73.
20. This account rests on J. Kelly-Gadol, "Did Women Have a Renaissance?" in *Becoming Visible: Women in European History,* ed. R. Bridenthal and C. Koontz (Boston: Houghton Mifflin, 1977), pp. 137–161, esp. p. 161.
21. See Peter Burke, "What Is the History of Popular Culture," in *What Is History Today?* ed. J. Gardiner (Atlantic Highlands, N.J.: Humanities Press, 1989), pp. 121–123.
22. G. Ruggerio, "Sexual Criminality in Early Renaissance Venice, 1338–1358," *Journal of Social History* 8 (Spring 1975): 18–31.
23. Quoted in R. C. Trexler, "Infanticide in Florence: New Sources and First Results," *History of Childhood Quarterly* 1 (Summer 1973): 99.
24. Ibid., p. 100.
25. J. Devisse and M. Mollat, *The Image of the Black in Western Art,* trans. W. G. Ryan, vol. 2 (New York: Morrow, 1979), pt. 2, pp. 187–188.
26. See C. M. Saunders, *A Social History of Black Slaves and Freedmen in Portugal, 1441–1555* (New York: Cambridge University Press, 1982), pp. 59, 62–88, 176–179.

27. Ibid., pp. 190–194.

28. Ibid., pp. 255–258.

29. See J. H. Elliott, *Imperial Spain, 1469–1716* (New York: Mentor Books, 1963), esp. pp. 75, 97–108.

30. Quoted in Burckhardt, *The Civilization of the Renaissance in Italy,* p. 262.

31. See R. R. Post, *The Modern Devotion: Confrontation with Reformation and Humanism* (Leiden: E. J. Brill, 1968), esp. pp. 237–238, 255, 323–348.

32. Quoted in O. Chadwick, *The Reformation* (Baltimore: Penguin Books, 1976), p. 55.

33. Quoted in E. H. Harbison, *The Age of Reformation* (Ithaca, N.Y.: Cornell University Press, 1963), p. 52.

34. This discussion is based heavily on Harbison, *The Age of Reformation,* pp. 52–55.

35. See S. E. Ozment, *The Reformation in the Cities: The Appeal of Protestantism to Sixteenth-Century Germany and Switzerland* (New Haven, Conn.: Yale University Press, 1975), pp. 32–45.

36. See S. E. Ozment, *The Age of Reform, 1250–1550: An Intellectual and Religious History of Late Medieval and Reformation Europe* (New Haven, Conn.: Yale University Press, 1980), pp. 273–279.

37. Quoted ibid., p. 280.

38. Quoted ibid., p. 281.

39. Quoted ibid., p. 284.

40. Romans 13:1–2.

41. G. Strauss, *Luther's House of Learning: Indoctrination of the Young in the German Reformation* (Baltimore: Johns Hopkins University Press, 1978), esp. pp. 159–162, 231–233.

42. See R. H. Bainton, *Women of the Reformation in Germany and Italy* (Minneapolis: Augsburg, 1971), pp. 9–10; and Ozment, *The Reformation in the Cities,* pp. 53–54, 171–172.

43. Quoted in H. G. Haile, *Luther: An Experiment in Biography* (Garden City, N.Y.: Doubleday, 1980), p. 272.

44. Quoted in J. Atkinson, *Martin Luther and the Birth of Protestantism* (Baltimore: Penguin Books, 1968), pp. 247–248.

45. *Martin Luther: Three Treatises* (Philadelphia: Muhlenberg Press, 1947), pp. 28–31.

46. J. Allen, trans., *John Calvin: The Institutes of the Christian Religion* (Philadelphia: Westminster Press, 1930), bk. 3, chap. 21, paras. 5, 7.

47. E. W. Monter, *Calvin's Geneva* (New York: Wiley, 1967), pp. 98–108.

48. Ibid., p. 137.

49. Quoted in Bainton, *Women of the Reformation in Germany and Italy,* pp. 69–70.

50. E. Duffy, *The Stripping of the Altars: Traditional Religion in England, 1400–1580* (New Haven, Conn.: Yale University Press, 1992), pp. 2–6, and passim.

51. See R. Marius, *Thomas More: A Biography* (New York: Knopf, 1984), pp. 215–216.

52. See S. E. Lehmberg, *The Reformation Parliament 1529–1536* (Cambridge: Cambridge University Press, 1970), pp. 174–176, 204–205.

53. J. J. Scarisbrick, *The Reformation and the English People* (Oxford: Basil Blackwell, 1984), pp. 81–84, esp. p. 81.

54. Ibid.

55. Quoted in P. Smith, *The Age of the Reformation,* rev. ed. (New York: Henry Holt, 1951), p. 346.

56. See J. W. O'Malley, *The First Jesuits* (Cambridge, Mass.: Harvard University Press, 1993), p. 376.

57. Ibid., p. 298.

58. Quoted in Chadwick, *The Reformation,* p. 270.

59. See P. Grendler, *The Roman Inquisition and the Venetian Press, 1540–1605* (Princeton, N.J.: Princeton University Press, 1977).

SUGGESTED READING

Scores of exciting studies are available on virtually all aspects of the Renaissance. In addition to the titles given in the Notes, the curious student should see P. Burke, *The Italian Renaissance: Culture and Society in Italy* (1986), an important sociological interpretation relating culture and society, and J. H. Plumb, *The Italian Renaissance* (1965), a superbly written book. P. Burke, *The Historical Anthropology of Early Modern Italy* (1987), contains many useful essays on Italian cultural history in a comparative European framework. J. R. Hale, *Renaissance Europe: The Individual and Society, 1480–1520* (1978), is an excellent treatment of individualism by a distinguished authority. Hale's magisterial achievement, *The Civilization of Europe in the Renaissance* (1994) reveals how the very idea of "Europe" crystallized. For Renaissance humanism and education, see P. F. Grendler, *Schooling in Renaissance Italy: Literacy and Learning, 1300–1600* (1989); J. H. Moran, *The Growth of English Schooling, 1340–1548: Learning, Literacy, and Laicization in Pre-Reformation York Diocese* (1985); and J. F. D'Amico, *Renaissance Humanism in Papal Rome: Humanists and Churchmen on the Eve of the Reformation* (1983), which are all highly readable works of outstanding scholarship. For the city where much of it originated, G. A. Brucker, *Renaissance Florence* (1969), gives a good description of Florentine economic, political, social, and cultural history. Learned, provocative, and beautifully written, and a work on which this chapter leans heavily, L. Martines, *Power and Imagination: City-States in Renaissance Italy* (1980), is probably the best broad appreciation of the period produced in several decades. For the Renaissance court, see the splendid achievement of G. Lubkin, *A Renaissance Court: Milan Under Galeazzo Maria Sforza* (1994).

J. R. Hale, *Machiavelli and Renaissance Italy* (1966), is a sound short biography, but advanced students may want to consult the sophisticated intellectual biography of S. de Grazia, *Machiavelli in Hell* (1989). F. Gilbert, *Machiavelli and Guicciardini,* mentioned in the Notes, places the two thinkers in their intellectual and social context.

The best introduction to the Renaissance in northern Europe and a book that has greatly influenced twentieth-century scholarship is J. Huizinga, *The Waning of the Middle Ages: A Study of the Forms of Life, Thought, and Art in France and the Netherlands in the Dawn of the Renaissance* (1954). This book challenges the whole idea of a Renaissance. R. J. Knecht, *Renaissance Warrior and Patron: The Reign of Francis I* (1994), is the standard study of that important French ruler. W. Blockman and W. Prevenier, *The Burgundian Netherlands* (1986) is essential for the culture of the Burgundy. The leading northern humanist is sensitively treated in M. M. Phillips, *Erasmus and the Northern Renaissance* (1956), and J. Huizinga, *Erasmus of Rotterdam* (1952). R. Marius, *Thomas More: A Biography* (1984), is an original study of the great English humanist and statesman. J. Leclercq, trans., *The Complete Works of Rabelais* (1963), is easily available.

The following titles should prove useful for various aspects of Renaissance social history: G. Ruggerio, *Violence in Early Renaissance Venice* (1980), a pioneering study of crime and punishment in a stable society; J. C. Brown, *Immodest Acts: The Life of a Lesbian Nun in Renaissance Italy* (1985), which is helpful for an understanding of the role and status of women; and I. Maclean, *The Renaissance Notion of Women* (1980). The student who wishes to study blacks in medieval and early modern European society should see the rich and original achievement of J. Devisse and M. Mollat, *The Image of the Black in Western Art,* cited in the Notes.

Renaissance art has inspired vast research. M. Baxandall, *Painting and Experience in Fifteenth Century Italy* (1988), is essential, and A. Martindale, *The Rise of the Artist in the Middle Ages and Early Renaissance* (1972), is a splendidly illustrated introduction. One of the finest appreciations of Renaissance art, written by one of the greatest art historians of this century, is E. Panofsky, *Meaning in the Visual Arts* (1955). Both Italian and northern painting are treated in the brilliant study of M. Meiss, *The Painter's Choice: Problems in the Interpretation of Renaissance Art* (1976), a collection of essays dealing with Renaissance style, form, and meaning. L. Steinberg, *The Sexuality of Christ in Renaissance Art and in Modern Oblivion*

(1983), is a brilliant work that relates Christ's sexuality to incarnational theology. J. M. Saslow, *Ganymede in the Renaissance* (1986), which uses images of Ganymede as a metaphor for emotional and sexual relations between men and youths, provides information on social attitudes toward homosexuality. R. Jones and N. Penny, *Raphael* (1983), celebrates the achievements of that great master.

Students interested in the city of Rome might consult P. Partner, *Renaissance Rome, 1500–1559: A Portrait of a Society* (1979), and the elegantly illustrated study of C. Hibbert, *Rome: The Biography of a City* (1985). Da Vinci's scientific and naturalist ideas and drawings are available in I. A. Richter, ed., *The Notebooks of Leonardo da Vinci* (1985). The magisterial achievement of J. Pope-Hennessy, *Cellini* (1985), is a superb evocation of that artist's life and work.

The following works not only are useful for the political and economic history of the Renaissance but also contain valuable bibliographical information: A. J. Slavin, ed., *The "New Monarchies" and Representative Assemblies* (1965), a collection of interpretations, and R. Lockyer, *Henry VII* (1972), a biography with documents illustrative of the king's reign. For Spain, see P. Liss, *Isabel the Queen: Life and Times* (1992); N. Rubin, *Isabella of Castile: The First Renaissance Queen* (1991); J. S. Gerber, *The Jews of Spain: A History of the Sephardic Experience* (1992); H. Kamen, *Inquisition and Society in Spain in the Sixteenth and Seventeenth Centuries* (1985); B. Bennasar, *The Spanish Character: Attitudes and Mentalities from the Sixteenth to the Nineteenth Century,* trans. B. Keen (1979). For the Florentine business classes, see I. Origo, *The Merchant of Prato* (1957); G. Brucker, *Two Memoirs of Renaissance Florence: The Diaries of Buonaccorso Pitti and Gregorio Dati,* trans. J. Martines (1967); and Paul Grendler, ed., *An Italian Renaissance Reader* (1987).

There are many easily accessible and lucidly written general studies of the religious reformations of the sixteenth century. P. Chaunu, ed., *The Reformation* (1989), is a lavishly illustrated anthology of articles by an international team of scholars, a fine appreciation of both theological and historical developments with an up-to-date bibliography. E. Cameron, *The European Reformation* (1991), provides a comprehensive survey based on recent research. A. Pettegree, ed., *The Early Reformation in Europe* (1992), explores the Reformation as an international movement and compares developments in different parts of Europe. L. W. Spitz, *The Protestant Reformation, 1517–1559* (1985), provides a comprehensive survey. For the recent trend in scholarship, interpreting the Reformation against the background of fifteenth-century reforming developments, see the excellent study of J. F. D'Amico, cited above, and J. H. Overfield, *Humanism and Scholasticism in Late Medieval Germany* (1984), which portrays the intellectual life of the

A Universal Man

Some people of the Renaissance believed in the ideal of universality, the achievement of distinction in many different skills and branches of knowledge. As one humanist put it, "A man is able to learn many things and make himself universal in many excellent arts." (Not everyone thought this: while Michelangelo was painting the Sistine Chapel, he complained to his father that "painting is not my profession.") Leon Battista Alberti (1404–1474), the illegitimate son of a family exiled from Florence, strongly believed he could be a universal man. A scholar-humanist, mathematician, and musician, he wrote treatises on domestic morality, the physical remains of antiquity, painting, and architecture. Here is a section of Alberti's autobiography.

And finally he embraced with zeal and forethought everything which pertained to fame. To omit the rest, he strove so hard to attain a name in modeling and painting that he wished to neglect nothing by which he might gain the approbation of good men. His genius was so versatile that you might almost judge all the fine arts to be his. . . .

He played ball, hurled the javelin, ran, leaped, wrestled, and above all delighted in the steep ascent of mountains; he applied himself to all these things for the sake of health rather than sport or pleasure. As a youth he excelled in warlike games. With his feet together, he could leap over the shoulders of men standing by; he had almost no equal among those hurling the lance. An arrow shot by his hand from his chest could pierce the strongest iron breastplate. . . . On horseback, holding in his hand one end of a long wand, while the other was firmly fixed to his foot, he could ride his horse violently in all directions for hours at a time as he wished, and the wand would remain completely immobile. Strange and marvelous! that the most spirited horses and those most impatient of riders would, when he first mounted them, tremble vio-

lently and shudder as if in great fear. He learned music without teachers, and his compositions were approved by learned musicians. He sang throughout his whole life, but in private, or alone. . . . He delighted in the organ and was considered an expert among the leading musicians.

When he had begun to mature in years, neglecting everything else, he devoted himself entirely to the study of letters, and spent some years of labour on canon and civil law. Finally after so many nightly vigils and such great constancy, he fell gravely ill from the exertion of his studies. Since his relatives were neither kind nor humane to him in his illness, by way of consoling himself between his convalescence and cure he wrote the play *Philodoxeos*, putting aside his legal studies—this when he was only twenty years old. And as soon as his health permitted, he resumed his studies, intending to complete the law, but again he was seized by a grave illness. . . .

At length, on the orders of his doctors, he desisted from those studies which were most fatiguing to the memory, just when they were about to flourish. But in truth, because he could not live without letters, at the age of twenty-four he turned to physics and the mathematical arts. . . .

Although he was affable, gentle, and harmful to no one, nevertheless he felt the animosity of many evil men, and hidden enmities, both annoying and very burdensome; in particular the harsh injuries and intolerable insults from his own relatives. He lived among the envious and malevolent with such modesty and equanimity that none of his detractors or rivals, although very hostile towards him, dared to utter a word about him in the presence of good and worthy men unless it was full of praise and admiration. . . .

When he heard that a learned man of any kind had arrived, he would at once work his way into a position of familiarity with him and thus from any source whatsoever he began to learn what he was ignorant of. From craftsmen, architects, shipbuilders, and even from cobblers he sought information to see if by chance they preserved anything rare or unusual or special in their arts; and he would then communicate such things to those citizens who wished to know them. He pretended to be ignorant in many things so that he might observe the talents and habits and skill of others. And so he was a zealous observer of whatsoever pertained to inborn talent of the arts.

He wholly despised the pursuit of material gain. He gave his money and goods to his friends to take care of and to enjoy. Among those by whom he believed himself loved, he was not only outgoing about his affairs and his habits but even about his secrets. He never betrayed the secrets of another but remained silent forever. . . .

He was by nature prone to wrath and bitter in spirit, but he could repress his rising indignation immediately by taking thought. Sometimes he deliberately fled from the verbose and the headstrong because with them he could not subdue his wrath. At other times he voluntarily submitted to the bold, in order to grow in patience. . . .

He wrote some books entitled *On Painting*, and in this very art of painting he created works unheard of and unbelievable to those who saw them. . . .

He had within himself a ray by which he could sense the good or evil intentions of men towards himself. Simply by looking at them, he could discover most of the defects of anyone in his presence. He used all kinds of reasoning and great effort, but in vain, to make more gentle towards himself those whom he had learned at one glance would be inimical. . . .

He could endure pain and cold and heat. When, not yet fifteen, he received a serious wound in the foot, and the physician, according to his custom and skill, drew together the broken parts of the foot and sewed them through the skin with a needle, he scarcely uttered a sound of pain. With his own hands, though in such great pain, he even aided the ministering doctor and treated his own wound though he was burning with fever. . . . By some defect in his nature he loathed garlic and also honey, and the mere sight of them, if by chance they were offered to him, brought on vomiting. But he conquered himself by

Bronze medallion of Leon Battista Alberti, by Matteo di Andrea de' Pasti. *(Source: Alinari/Art Resource, NY)*

force of looking at and handling the disagreeable objects, so that they came to offend him less, thus showing by example that men can do anything with themselves if they will.

He took extraordinary and peculiar pleasure in looking at things in which there was any mark of beauty or adornment. He never ceased to wonder at old men who were endowed with dignity of countenance, and unimpaired and vigorous, and he proclaimed that he honoured them as "delights of nature." He declared that quadrupeds, birds, and other living things of outstanding beauty were worthy of benevolence because by the very distinction of their nature they deserved favour. When his favorite dog died he wrote a funeral oration for him.

Questions for Analysis

1. What distinctively Renaissance traits did Alberti show?

2. According to his own assessment, what personal or human qualities did Alberti possess?

3. Did Alberti appear to have any psychological complexes or difficulties? How would you explain them?

Source: "Self-Portrait of a Universal Man" by Leon Battista Alberti from *The Portable Renaissance Reader*, edited by J. B. Ross and M. M. McLaughlin. Copyright 1968 by Penguin USA.

German universities, the milieu from which the Protestant Reformation emerged. For the condition of the church in the late fifteenth and early sixteenth centuries, see D. Hay, *The Church in Italy in the Fifteenth Century* (1977), and P. Heath, *The English Parish Clergy on the Eve of the Reformation* (1969).

For the central figure of the early Reformation, Martin Luther, students should see the works by Atkinson and Haile mentioned in the Notes, as well as E. Erikson, *Young Man Luther: A Study in Psychoanalysis and History* (1962); G. Brendler, *Martin Luther: Theology and Revolution* (1991), a response to the Marxist interpretation of Luther as the tool of the aristocracy who sold out the peasantry; and H. Boehmer, *Martin Luther: Road to Reformation* (1960), a well-balanced work treating Luther's formative years.

The best study of John Calvin is W. J. Bouwsma, *John Calvin: A Sixteenth-Century Portrait* (1988), an authoritative study that places Calvin within Renaissance culture. R. T. Kendall, *Calvinism and English Calvinism to 1649* (1981), presents English conditions. R. M. Mitchell, *Calvin and the Puritan's View of the Protestant Ethic* (1979), interprets the socioeconomic implications of Calvin's thought. Students interested in the left wing of the Reformation should see the profound though difficult work of G. H. Williams, *The Radical Reformers* (1962). For reform in other parts of Switzerland, see T. Brady, *Turning Swiss* (1990), and L. P. Wendel, *Always Among Us: Images of the Poor in Zwingli's Zurich* (1990).

For various aspects of the social history of the period, see in addition to the titles by Bainton and Ozment cited in the Notes, S. E. Ozment, *Magdalena and Balthasar* (1987), which reveals many features of social life through the letters of a Nuremburg couple; and K. von Greyerz, ed., *Religion and Society in Early Modern Europe, 1500–1800* (1984), both of which contain interesting essays on religion, society, and popular culture. For women, see M. E. Wiesner, *Women and Gender in Early Modern Europe* (1993); L. Roper, *The Holy Household: Women and Morals in Reformation Augsburg* (1991), an important study in local religious history as well as the history of gender; M. Wiesner, *Women in the Sixteenth Century: A Bibliography* (1983), a useful reference tool; and S. M. Wyntjes, "Women in the Reformation Era," in *Becoming Visible: Women in European History,* ed. R. Bridenthal and C. Koonz (1977), an interesting general survey. The best recent treatment of marriage and the family is S. E. Ozment, *When Fathers Ruled: Family Life in Reformation Europe* (1983). Ozment's

edition of *Reformation Europe: A Guide to Research* (1982) contains not only helpful references but valuable articles on such topics as "The German Peasants," "The Anabaptists," and "The Confessional Age: The Late Reformation in Germany." For Servetus, see R. H. Bainton, *Hunted Heretic: The Life and Death of Michael Servetus* (1953), which remains valuable.

For England, in addition to the fundamental work by Duffy cited in the Notes, see A. G. Dickens, *The English Reformation* (1964). K. Thomas, *Religion and the Decline of Magic* (1971), provides a useful treatment of pre-Reformation popular religion. S. J. Gunn and P. G. Lindley, eds., *Cardinal Wolsey: Church, State and Art* (1991), is a useful study of that important prelate. The marital trials of Henry VIII are treated in both the sympathetic study of G. Mattingly, *Catherine of Aragon* (1949), and A. Fraser, *The Wives of Henry VIII* (1992). The legal implications of Henry VIII's divorces have been thoroughly analyzed in J. J. Scarisbrick, *Henry VIII* (1968), an almost definitive biography. On the dissolution of the English monasteries, see D. Knowles, *The Religious Orders in England,* vol. 3 (1959), one of the finest examples of historical prose in English written in the twentieth century. Knowles's *Bare Ruined Choirs* (1976) is an attractively illustrated abridgment of *The Religious Orders in England.* G. R. Elton, *The Tudor Revolution in Government* (1959), discusses the modernization of English government under Thomas Cromwell; the same author's *Reform and Reformation: England, 1509–1558* (1977) combines political and social history in a broad study. Many aspects of English social history are discussed in J. Youings, *Sixteenth Century England* (1984), a beautifully written work that is highly recommended.

P. Janelle, *The Catholic Reformation* (1951), is a comprehensive treatment of the Catholic Reformation from a Catholic point of view, and A. G. Dickens, *The Counter Reformation* (1969), gives the Protestant standpoint in a beautifully illustrated book. The definitive study of the Council of Trent was written by H. Jedin, *A History of the Council of Trent,* 3 vols. (1957–1961). For the Jesuits, see W. W. Meissner, *Ignatius of Loyola: The Psychology of a Saint* (1993), and J. W. O'Malley, *The First Jesuits* (1993); these books are basic not only for the beginnings of the Society of Jesus but for the refutation of many myths about the Jesuits. Perhaps the best recent work on the Spanish Inquisition is W. Monter, Frontiers of Heresy: *The Spanish Inquisition from the Basque Lands to Sicily* (1990).

16 The Age of European Expansion and Religious Wars

A detail from an early 17th-century Flemish painting depiction maps, illustrated travel books, a globe, a compass, and an astrolabe. *(Source: Reproduced by courtesy of the Trustees, The National Gallery, London)*

Between 1450 and 1650 two developments dramatically altered the world: Europeans' overseas expansion and the reformations of the Christian church. Europeans carried their cultures to other parts of the globe. Overseas expansion brought them into confrontation with ancient civilizations in Africa, Asia, and the Americas. These confrontations led first to conquest, then to exploitation, and finally to profound social changes in both Europe and the conquered territories. Likewise, the Renaissance and the religious reformations drastically changed intellectual, political, religious, and social life in Europe. War and religious issues dominated the politics of European states. Although religion was commonly used to rationalize international conflict, wars were fought for power and territory.

- Why, in the sixteenth and seventeenth centuries, did a relatively small number of people living on the edge of the Eurasian landmass gain control of the major sea lanes of the world and establish political and economic hegemony on distant continents?

- How were a few Spaniards, fighting far from home, able to overcome the powerful Aztec and Inca Empires in America?

- What effect did overseas expansion have on Europe and on conquered societies?

- What were the causes and consequences of the religious wars in France, the Netherlands, and Germany?

- How did the religious crises of this period affect the status of women?

- How and why did African slave labor become the dominant form of labor organization in the New World?

- What religious and intellectual developments led to the growth of skepticism?

- What literary masterpieces of the English-speaking world did this period produce?

This chapter addresses these questions.

❄ DISCOVERY, RECONNAISSANCE, AND EXPANSION

Historians of Europe have called the period from 1450 to 1650 the "Age of Discovery," "Age of Reconnaissance," and "Age of Expansion." All three labels are appropriate. "Age of Discovery" refers to the era's phenomenal advances in geographical knowledge and technology, often achieved through trial and error. In 1350 it took as long to sail from the eastern end of the Mediterranean to the western end as it had taken a thousand years earlier. Even in the fifteenth century, Europeans knew little more about the earth's surface than the Romans had known. By 1650, however, Europeans had made an extensive reconnaissance—or preliminary exploration—and had sketched fairly accurately the physical outline of the whole earth. Much of the geographical information they had gathered was tentative and not fully understood—hence the appropriateness of "Age of Reconnaissance."

The designation "Age of Expansion" refers to the migration of Europeans to other parts of the world. This colonization resulted in political control of much of South and North America; coastal regions of Africa, India, China, and Japan; and many Pacific islands. Political hegemony was accompanied by economic exploitation, religious domination, and the introduction of European patterns of social and intellectual life. The sixteenth-century expansion of European society launched a new age in world history. None of the three "Age" labels reflects the experiences of non-European peoples. Africans, Asians, and native Americans had known the geographies of their regions for centuries. They made no "discoveries" and undertook no reconnaissance, and they experienced "expansion" only as forced slave laborers.

Overseas Exploration and Conquest

The outward expansion of Europe began with the Viking voyages across the Atlantic in the ninth and tenth centuries. Under Eric the Red and Leif Ericson, the Vikings discovered Greenland and the eastern coast of North America. They made permanent settlements in, and a legal imprint on, Iceland, Ireland, England, Normandy, and Sicily. The Crusades of the eleventh through thirteenth centuries were another phase in Europe's attempt to explore and exploit peoples on the periphery of the continent. But the lack of a strong territorial base, superior Muslim military strength, and sheer misrule combined to make the Crusader kingdoms short-lived. In the mid-fifteenth century, Europe seemed ill prepared for further international

ARCTIC OCEAN

PACIFIC OCEAN

PACIFIC OCEAN

GREENLAND

NORTH AMERICA

NEW SPAIN

Quebec 1608
Newfoundland 1497
St. Augustine 1565
Cuba · San Salvador 1492
Guanajuato · Puerto Rico 1492
Mexico City · Hispaniola 1492
1519
Zacatecas · Jamaica 1492
Vera Cruz · HONDURAS
1519
Cartagena · Trinidad 1498
Panama · SPANISH MAIN

SOUTH AMERICA

Quito 1534
Lima 1535
PERU
Potosí
BRAZIL
Santiago
Buenos Aires 1535
Rio de Janeiro 1516
Cape Horn
Strait of Magellan

ATLANTIC OCEAN

Azores
Canary Is.
Cape Verde Is. 1456

1493
1492
1497
1519
1520
1522

EUROPE
Amsterdam
Antwerp
Lisbon
Seville
Ceuta 1415
Constantinople

AFRICA
SAHARA
Timbuktu
Niani
GUINEA
CAPE VERDE
GOLD COAST
ETHIOPIA
Mombasa 1498
Mozambique
MADAGASCAR 1500
Cape of Good Hope
1497
1522

ASIA
PERSIA
Ormuz 1507
ARABIA
Muscat
Aden 1513
INDIA
Goa 1510
Calicut 1498
Ceylon 1505
CHINA
Canton 1513
Macao 1517
JAPAN 1542
Kyushu
PHILIPPINES
Malacca 1509
Borneo
Sumatra
Java
MOLUCCAS 1511
New Guinea
AUSTRALIA

INDIAN OCEAN

1498

1521
1522

Magellan and crew
Columbus
Da Gama
Other

Spanish holdings
Portuguese holdings

0   1500   3000 Mi.
0   1500   3000 Km.

ventures. By 1450 a grave new threat had appeared in the East: the Ottoman Turks.

Combining excellent military strategy with efficient administration of their conquered territories, the Turks had subdued most of Asia Minor and begun to settle on the western side of the Bosporus. The Muslim Ottoman Turks under Sultan Mohammed II (r. 1451–1481) captured Constantinople in 1453, pressed northwest into the Balkans, and by the early sixteenth century controlled the eastern Mediterranean. The Turkish menace badly frightened Europeans. In France in the fifteenth and sixteenth centuries, twice as many books were printed about the Turkish threat as about the American discoveries. Yet the fifteenth and sixteenth centuries witnessed a fantastic continuation, on a global scale, of European expansion.

Political centralization in Spain, France, and England helps to explain those countries' outward push. In the fifteenth century, Isabella and Ferdinand had consolidated their several kingdoms to achieve a more united Spain. The Catholic rulers revamped the Spanish bureaucracy and humbled dissident elements, notably the Muslims and the Jews. The Spanish monarchy was stronger than ever before and in a position to support foreign ventures; it could bear the costs and dangers of exploration. But Portugal, situated on the extreme southwestern edge of the European continent, got the start on the rest of Europe. Still insignificant as a European land power despite its recently secured frontiers, Portugal sought greatness in the unknown world overseas.

Portugal's taking of Ceuta, an Arab city in northern Morocco, in 1415 marked the beginning of European exploration and control of overseas territory (Map 16.1). The objectives of Portuguese policy included the historic Iberian crusade to Christianize Muslims and the search for gold, for an overseas route to the spice markets of India, and for the mythical Christian ruler of Ethiopia, Prester John.

In the early phases of Portuguese exploration, Prince Henry (1394–1460), called "the Naviga-

MAP 16.1 Overseas Exploration and Conquest in the Fifteenth and Sixteenth Centuries The voyages of discovery marked another phase in the centuries-old migrations of European peoples. Consider the major contemporary significance of each of the three voyages depicted on this map.

tor" because of the annual expeditions he sent down the western coast of Africa, played the leading role. In the fifteenth century, most of the gold that reached Europe came from the Sudan in West Africa and from the Akan peoples living near the area of present-day Ghana. Muslim caravans brought the gold from the African cities of Niani and Timbuktu and carried it north across the Sahara to Mediterranean ports. Then the Portuguese muscled in on this commerce in gold. Prince Henry's carefully planned expeditions succeeded in reaching Guinea, and under King John II (r. 1481–1495) the Portuguese established trading posts and forts on the Guinea coast and penetrated into the continent all the way to Timbuktu (see Map 16.1). Portuguese ships transported gold to Lisbon, and by 1500 Portugal controlled the flow of gold to Europe. The golden century of Portuguese prosperity had begun.

The spices Europeans wanted, however, came from South Asia and the Moluccan islands, not from African kingdoms. Thus the Portuguese pushed farther south down the west coast of Africa. In 1487 Bartholomew Diaz rounded the Cape of Good Hope at the southern tip, but storms and a threatened mutiny forced him to turn back. On a second expedition (1497–1499), the Portuguese mariner Vasco da Gama reached India and returned to Lisbon loaded with samples of Indian wares. King Manuel (r. 1495–1521) promptly dispatched thirteen ships under the command of Pedro Alvares Cabral, assisted by Diaz, to set up trading posts in India. On April 22, 1500, the coast of Brazil in South America was sighted and claimed for the crown of Portugal. Cabral then proceeded south and east around the Cape of Good Hope and reached India. Half of the fleet was lost on the return voyage, but the six spice-laden vessels that dropped anchor in Lisbon harbor in July 1501 more than paid for the entire expedition. Thereafter, convoys were sent out every March. Lisbon became the entrance port for Asian goods into Europe—but not without a fight.

For centuries the Muslims had controlled the rich spice trade of the Indian Ocean, and they did not surrender it willingly. Portuguese commercial activities were accompanied by the destruction or seizure of strategic Muslim coastal forts, which later served Portugal as both trading posts and military bases. Alfonso de Albuquerque, whom the Portuguese crown appointed as governor of India

The Cantino Map This map (1502) is named for the agent secretly commissioned to design it in Lisbon for the duke of Ferrara, an avid Italian map collector. It reveals such good knowledge of the African continent, of the islands of the West Indies, and of the shoreline of present-day Venezuela, Guiana, and Brazil in South America that modern scholars suspect there may have been clandestine voyages to the Americas shortly after Columbus's. *(Source: Biblioteca Estense Universitaria, Modena)*

(1509–1515), decided that these bases and not inland territories should control the Indian Ocean. Accordingly, his cannon blasted open the ports of Calicut, Ormuz, Goa, and Malacca, the vital centers of Arab domination of south Asian spice trade (see Map 16.1). This bombardment laid the foundation for Portuguese imperialism in the sixteenth and seventeenth centuries—a strange way to bring Christianity to "those who were in darkness." As one scholar wrote about the opening of China to the West, "while Buddha came to China on white elephants, Christ was borne on cannon balls."[1]

In March 1493, between the voyages of Diaz and da Gama, Spanish ships entered Lisbon harbor bearing a triumphant Italian explorer in the service of the Spanish monarchy. Christopher Columbus (1451–1506), a Genoese mariner, had secured Spanish support for an expedition to the East (see Listening to the Past). He sailed from Palos, Spain, to the Canary Islands and crossed the Atlantic to the Bahamas, landing in October 1492 on an island that he named San Salvador and believed to be the coast of India.

Technological Stimuli to Exploration

Technological developments were the key to Europe's remarkable outreach. By 1350 cannon made of iron or bronze and able to fire iron or stone balls had been fully developed in western Europe. This artillery emitted frightening noises and great flashes of fire and could batter down fortresses and even city walls. Sultan Mohammed II's siege of Constantinople in 1453 provides a classic illustration of the effectiveness of cannon fire.

Constantinople had very strong walled fortifications. The sultan secured the services of a Western technician, who built fifty-six small cannon and a gigantic gun that could hurl stone balls weighing about eight hundred pounds. The gun had to be moved by several hundred oxen and could be loaded and fired only by about a hundred men working together. Reloading took two hours. This awkward but powerful weapon breached the walls of Constantinople before it cracked on the second day of the bombardment. Lesser cannon finished the job.

Although early cannon posed serious technical difficulties for land warfare, they could be used at sea. The mounting of cannon on ships and improved techniques of shipbuilding gave impetus to European expansion. Since ancient times, most seagoing vessels had been narrow, open boats called *galleys,* propelled largely by oarsmen: slaves or convicts who had been sentenced to the galleys manned the oars of the cargo and war ships that sailed the Mediterranean (both types of ship carried soldiers for defense). Well suited to the calm and thoroughly explored waters of the Mediterranean, galleys could not withstand the rough winds and uncharted shoals of the Atlantic. The need for sturdier craft, as well as population losses caused by the Black Death, forced the development of a new style of ship that did not require soldiers for defense or a large crew of oarsmen.

In the course of the fifteenth century, the Portuguese developed the *caravel,* a small, light, three-masted sailing ship. Though somewhat slower than the galley, the caravel held more cargo and was highly maneuverable. When fitted with cannon, it could dominate larger vessels, such as the round ships commonly used in commerce. The substitution of windpower for manpower, and artillery fire for soldiers, signaled a great technological advance and gave Europeans navigational and fighting ascendancy over the rest of the world.[2]

Other fifteenth-century developments in navigation helped make possible the conquest of the Atlantic. The magnetic compass enabled sailors to determine their direction and position at sea. The astrolabe, an instrument developed by Muslim navigators in the twelfth century and used to determine the altitude of the sun and other celestial bodies, permitted mariners to plot their latitude, or position north or south of the equator. Steadily improved maps and sea charts provided information about distances, sea depths, and geography.

The Explorers' Motives

The expansion of Europe was not motivated by demographic pressures. The Black Death had caused serious population losses from which Europe had not recovered in 1500. Few Europeans emigrated to North or South America in the sixteenth century. Half of those who did sail to begin a new life in America died en route; half of those who reached what they regarded as the New World eventually returned to their homeland. Why, then,

did explorers brave the Atlantic and Pacific Oceans, risking their lives to discover new continents and spread European culture?

The reasons are varied and complex. People of the sixteenth century were still basically medieval: their attitudes and values were shaped by religion and expressed in religious terms. In the late fifteenth century, crusading fervor remained a basic part of the Portuguese and Spanish national ideal. The desire to Christianize Muslims and pagan peoples played a central role in European expansion. Queen Isabella of Spain, for example, showed a fanatical zeal for converting the Muslims to Christianity and concentrated her efforts on the Muslims in Granada. But after the abortive crusading attempts of the thirteenth century, Isabella and other rulers realized full well that they lacked the material resources to mount the full-scale assault on Islam necessary for victory. Crusading impulses thus shifted from the Muslims to the pagan peoples of Africa and the Americas.

Moreover, after the *reconquista*—the Christian reconquest of Muslim areas—enterprising young men of the Spanish upper classes found economic and political opportunities severely limited. As a study of the Castilian city Ciudad Real shows, the traditional aristocracy controlled the best agricultural land and monopolized urban administrative posts. Great merchants and a few nobles (surprisingly, since Spanish law forbade noble participation in commercial ventures) dominated the textile and leather-glove manufacturing industries. Thus many ambitious men emigrated to the Americas to seek their fortunes.[3]

Government sponsorship and encouragement of exploration also help to account for the results of the various voyages. Individual mariners and explorers could not afford the massive sums needed to explore mysterious oceans and to control remote continents. The strong financial support of Prince Henry the Navigator led to Portugal's phenomenal success in the spice trade. Even the grudging and modest assistance of Isabella and Ferdinand eventually brought untold riches—and complicated problems—to Spain. The Dutch in the seventeenth century, through such government-sponsored trading companies as the Dutch East India Company, reaped enormous wealth, and although the Netherlands was a small country in size, it dominated the European economy in 1650.

Scholars have frequently described the European discoveries as a manifestation of Renaissance curiosity about the physical universe—the desire to know more about the geography and peoples of the world. There is truth to this explanation. Cosmography, natural history, and geography aroused enormous interest among educated people in the fifteenth and sixteenth centuries. Just as science fiction and speculation about life on other planets excite readers today, quasi-scientific literature about Africa, Asia, and the Americas captured the imaginations of Europeans. Oviedo's *General History of the Indies* (1547), a detailed eyewitness account of plants, animals, and peoples, was widely read.

Spices were another important incentive to voyages of discovery. Introduced into western Europe by the Crusaders in the twelfth century, nutmeg, mace, ginger, cinnamon, and pepper added flavor and variety to the monotonous diet of Europeans. Spices were also used in the preparation of medicinal drugs and incense for religious ceremonies. In the late thirteenth century, the Venetian Marco Polo (1254?–1324?), the greatest of medieval travelers, had visited the court of the Chinese emperor. The widely publicized account of his travels in the *Book of Various Experiences* stimulated the trade in spices between Asia and Italy. The Venetians came to hold a monopoly of trade in western Europe.

Spices were grown in India and China, shipped across the Indian Ocean to ports on the Persian Gulf, and then transported by Arabs across the Arabian Desert to Mediterranean ports. But the rise of the Ming Dynasty in China in the late fourteenth century resulted in the expulsion of foreigners. And the steady penetration of the Ottoman Turks into the eastern Mediterranean and of Muslims across North Africa forced Europeans to seek a new route to the Asian spice markets.

The basic reason for European exploration and expansion, however, was the quest for material profit. Mariners and explorers frankly admitted this. As Bartholomew Diaz put it, his motives were "to serve God and His Majesty, to give light to those who were in darkness and to grow rich as all men desire to do." When Vasco da Gama reached the port of Calicut, India, in 1498, a native asked what the Portuguese wanted. Da Gama replied, "Christians and spices."[4] The bluntest of the Spanish conquistadors, Hernando Cortés, announced as he prepared to conquer Mexico, "I have come to win gold, not to plow the fields like a peasant."[5]

A sixteenth-century diplomat, Ogier Gheselin de Busbecq, summed up explorers' paradoxical attitude: in expeditions to the Indies and the Antipodes, he said, "religion supplies the pretext and gold the motive."[6]

The Problem of Christopher Columbus

The year 1992, which marked the quincentenary of Columbus's first voyages to the Americas, spawned an enormous amount of discussion about the significance of his voyages. Journalists, scholars, amateurs, and polemicists debated Columbus's accomplishments and failures. Until the 1980s most writers generally would have agreed with the Harvard historian Samuel Eliot Morison in his 1942 biography of Columbus:

The whole history of the Americas stems from the Four Voyages of Columbus; and as the Greek city-states looked back to the deathless gods as their founders, so today a score of independent nations and dominions unite in homage to Columbus, the stouthearted son of Genoa, who carried Christian civilization across the Ocean Sea.[7]

In 1942, we must remember, the Western Powers believed they were engaged in a life-and-death struggle to defend "Christian civilization" against the evil forces of fascism. As the five hundredth anniversary of his famous voyage approached, however, Columbus underwent severe criticism.

Critics charged that he enslaved and sometimes killed the Indians and was a cruel and ineffective governor of Spain's Caribbean colony. Moreover, they said, he did not discover a previously unknown continent: Africans and other Europeans had been to the Western Hemisphere before him. And not only did he not discover a "new" continent, he not not realize what he had found. In short, according to his harshest critics, he was a fool who didn't know what was going on around him. Some claim that he was the originator of European exploitation of the non-European world and destroyed the paradise that had been the New World.[8]

Because those judgments rest on social and ethical standards that did not exist in Columbus's world, responsible scholars consider them ahistorical. Instead, using the evidence of his journal (sea log) and letters, let us ask three basic questions: (1) What kind of man was Columbus, and what forces or influences shaped him? (2) In sailing westward from Europe, what were his goals? (3) Did he achieve his goals, and what did he make of his discoveries?

Pepper Harvest   To break the monotony of their bland diet, Europeans had a passion for pepper, which—along with cinnamon, cloves, nutmeg, and ginger—was the main object of the Asian trade. Since one kilo of pepper cost 2 grams of silver at the place of production in the East Indies and from 10 to 14 grams of silver in Alexandria, 14 to 18 grams in Venice, and 20 to 30 grams at the markets of northern Europe, we can appreciate the fifteenth-century expression "As dear as pepper." Here natives fill vats, and the dealer tastes a peppercorn for pungency. *(Source: Bibliothèque Nationale, Paris)*

The central feature in the character of Christopher Columbus is that he was a deeply religious man. He began the *Journal* of his voyage to the Americas, written as a letter to Ferdinand and Isabella of Spain, with this recollection:

On 2 January in the year 1492, when your Highnesses had concluded their war with the Moors who reigned in Europe, I saw your Highnesses' banners victoriously raised on the towers of the Alhambra, the citadel of the city, and the Moorish king come out of the city gates and kiss the hands of your Highnesses and the prince, My Lord. And later in that same month, on the grounds of information I had given your Highnesses concerning the lands of India . . . your Highnesses decided to send me, Christopher Columbus, to see these parts of India and the princes and peoples of those lands and consider the best means for their conversion.[9]

He had witnessed the Spanish reconquest of Granada and shared fully in the religious and nationalistic fervor surrounding that event. Just seven months separated Isabella and Ferdinand's entry into Granada on January 6 and Columbus's departure westward on August 3, 1492. In his mind, the two events were clearly linked. Long after Europeans knew something of Columbus's discoveries in the Caribbean, they considered the restoration of Muslim Granada to Christian hands as Ferdinand and Isabella's greatest achievements; for the conquest, in 1494 the Spanish pope Alexander VI (r. 1492–1503) rewarded them with the title of "Most Catholic Kings." Like the Spanish rulers and most Europeans of his age, Columbus understood Christianity as a missionary religion that should be carried to places and peoples where it did not exist. Although Columbus's character certainly included material and secular qualities, first and foremost, as he wrote in 1498, he believed he was a divine agent:

God made me the messenger of the new heaven and the new earth of which he spoke in the Apocalypse of St. John after having spoken of it through the mouth of the prophet Isaiah; and he showed me the post where to find it.[10]

A second and fundamental facet of Columbus the man is that he was very knowledgeable about the sea. He was familiar with fifteenth-century Portuguese navigational aids such as portolans—written descriptions of routes showing bays, coves, capes, ports, and the distances between these places—and the magnetic compass. He had spent years consulting geographers, mapmakers, and navigators. And, as he implies in his *Journal,* he had acquired not only theoretical but practical experience:

I have spent twenty-three years at sea and have not left it for any length of time worth mentioning, and I have seen everything from east to west [meaning he had been to England] and I have been to Guinea" [North and West Africa].[11]

Some of Columbus's calculations, such as his measurement of the distance from Portugal to Japan as 2,760 miles (it is actually 12,000), proved inaccurate. But his successful thirty-three-day voyage to the Caribbean owed a great deal to his seamanship and his knowledge and skillful use of instruments.

What was the object of his first voyage? What did Columbus set out to do? He gives the answer in the very title of the expedition, "The Enterprise of the Indies." He wanted to find a direct ocean route to Asia, which would provide the opportunity for a greatly expanded trade, a trade in which the European economy, and especially Spain, would participate. Two scholars have recently written, "If Columbus had not sailed westward in search of Asia, someone else would have done so. The time was right for such a bold undertaking."[12] Someone else might have done so, but the fact remains that Columbus, displaying a characteristic Renaissance curiosity and restless drive, actually accepted the challenge.

How did Columbus interpret what he had found, and did he think he had achieved what he set out to do? His mind had been formed by the Bible and the geographical writings of classical authors, as were the minds of most educated people of his time. Thus, as people in every age have often done, Columbus ignored the evidence of his eyes; he described what he saw in the Caribbean as an idyllic paradise, a peaceful garden of Eden. When accounts of his travels were published, Europeans' immediate fascination with this image of the New World meant that Columbus's propaganda created an instant myth. But when he sensed that he had not found the spice markets and bazaars of Asia, his goal changed from establishing trade with the (East) Indians and Chinese to establishing the kind of trade the Portuguese were then conducting with Africa and with Cape Verde and other islands in the Atlantic (see Map 16.1). That meant setting up some form of government in the Caribbean islands, even though Columbus had little interest in, or capacity for, governing. In 1496, he forcibly subjugated the island of Hispaniola, enslaved the Indians, and laid the basis for a system of land grants tied to the Indians' labor service. Borrowing practices and institutions from reconquest Spain and the Canary Islands, Columbus laid the foundation for Spanish imperial administration. In all of this, Columbus was very much a man of his times. He never understood, however, that the scale of his discoveries created problems of trade, settlers, relations with the Indians, and, above all, government bureaucracy.[13]

The Conquest of Aztec Mexico and Inca Peru

Technological development also helps to explain the Spanish conquest of Aztec Mexico and Inca Peru.

The strange end of the Aztec nation remains one of the most fascinating events in the annals of human societies. The Spanish adventurer Hernando Cortés (1485–1547) landed at Vera Cruz in February 1519. In November he entered Tenochtitlán (Mexico City) and soon had the emperor Montezuma II (r. 1502–1520) in custody. In less than two years Cortés destroyed the monarchy, gained complete control of the Mexican capital, and extended his jurisdiction over much of the Aztec Empire. Why did a strong people defending its own territory succumb so quickly to a handful of Spaniards fighting in dangerous and completely unfamiliar circumstances? How indeed, since Montezuma's scouts sent him detailed reports of the Spaniards' movements? The answers to these questions lie in the fact that at the time of the Spanish arrival the Aztec and Inca Empires faced grave internal difficulties brought on by their religious ideologies; by the Spaniards' boldness, timing, and technology; and by Aztec and Incan psychology and attitudes toward war.

The Spaniards arrived in late summer, when the Aztecs were preoccupied with harvesting their crops and not thinking of war. From the Spaniards' perspective, their timing was ideal. A series of nat-

DISCOVERY, RECONNAISSANCE, AND EXPANSION **523**

ural phenomena, signs, and portents seemed to augur disaster for the Aztecs. A comet was seen in daytime, a column of fire had appeared every midnight for a year, and two temples were suddenly destroyed, one by lightning unaccompanied by thunder. These and other apparently inexplicable events seemed to presage the return of the Aztec god Quetzalcoatl and had an unnerving effect on the Aztecs. They looked on the Europeans riding "wild beasts" as extraterrestrial forces coming to establish a new social order. Defeatism swept the nation and paralyzed its will.

The Aztec state religion, the sacred cult of Huitzilopochtli, necessitated constant warfare against neighboring peoples to secure captives for religious sacrifice and laborers for agricultural and infrastructural work. Lacking an effective method of governing subject peoples, the Aztecs controlled thirty-eight provinces in central Mexico through terror. When Cortés landed, the provinces were being crushed under a cycle of imperial oppression: increases in tribute provoked revolt, which led to reconquest, retribution, and demands for higher tribute, which in turn sparked greater resentment and fresh revolt. When the Spaniards appeared, the Totonacs greeted them as liberators, and other subject peoples joined them against the Aztecs. Even before the coming of the Spaniards, Montezuma's attempts to resolve the problem of constant warfare by freezing social positions—thereby ending the social mobility that war provided—aroused the resentment of his elite, mercantile, and lowborn classes. Montezuma faced terrible external and internal difficulties.[14]

Montezuma refrained from attacking the Spaniards as they advanced toward his capital and welcomed Cortés and his men into Tenochtitlán. Historians have often condemned the Aztec ruler for vacillation and weakness. But he relied on the advice of his state council, itself divided, and on the dubious loyalty of tributary communities. When Cortés—with incredible boldness—took Montezuma hostage, the emperor's influence over his people crumbled.

The major explanation for the collapse of the Aztec Empire to six hundred Spaniards lies in the Aztecs' notion of warfare and their level of technology. Forced to leave Tenochtitlán to settle a conflict elsewhere, Cortés placed his lieutenant, Alvarado, in charge. Alvarado's harsh rule drove the Aztecs to revolt, and they almost succeeded in destroying the Spanish garrison. When Cortés re-turned just in time, the Aztecs allowed his reinforcements to join Alvarado's besieged force. No threatened European or Asian state would have conceived of doing such a thing: dividing an enemy's army and destroying the separate parts was basic to their military tactics. But for the Aztecs warfare was a ceremonial act in which "divide and conquer" had no place.

Having allowed the Spanish forces to reunite, the entire population of Tenochtitlán attacked the invaders. The Aztecs killed many Spaniards. In retaliation, the Spaniards executed Montezuma. The Spaniards escaped from the city and inflicted a crushing defeat on the Aztec army at Otumba near Lake Texcoco on July 7, 1520. The Spaniards won because "the simple Indian methods of mass warfare were of little avail against the manoeuvring of a well-drilled force."[15] Aztec weapons proved no match for the terrifyingly noisy and lethal Spanish cannon, muskets, crossbows, and steel swords. European technology decided the battle. Cortés began the systematic conquest of Mexico.

From 1493 to 1527 the Inca Huayna Capac ruled as a benevolent despot (the word *Inca* refers both to the ruler of the Amerindians who lived in the valleys of the Andes Mountains in present-day Peru and to the people themselves). His power was limited only by custom. His millions of subjects considered him a god, firm but just to his people, merciless to his enemies. Only a few of the Inca's closest relatives dared look at his divine face. Nobles approached him on their knees, and the masses kissed the dirt as he rode by in his litter. The borders of his vast empire were well fortified and threatened by no foreign invaders. Grain was plentiful, and apart from an outbreak of smallpox in a distant province—introduced by the Spaniards—no natural disaster upset the general peace. An army of fifty thousand loyal troops stood at the Inca's disposal. Why did this powerful empire fall so easily to Francisco Pizarro and his band of 175 men armed with one small, ineffective cannon?

The Incas were totally isolated. They had no contact with other Amerindian cultures and knew nothing at all of Aztec civilization or its collapse to the Spaniards in 1521. Since about the year 1500, Inca scouts had reported "floating houses" on the seas, manned by white men with beards. Tradesmen told of strange large animals with feet of silver (as horseshoes appeared in the brilliant sunshine). Having observed a border skirmish between Indians and white men, intelligence sources advised

Huayna Capac that the Europeans' swords were as harmless as women's weaving battens. A coastal chieftain had poured chicha, the native beer, down the barrel of a gun to appease the god of thunder. These incidents suggest that Inca culture provided no basis for understanding the Spaniards and the significance of their arrival. Moreover, even if the strange pale men planned war, there were very few of them, and the Incas believed that they could not be reinforced from the sea.[16]

At first the Incas did not think that the strangers intended trouble. They believed the old Inca legend that the creator-god Virocha—who had brought civilization to them, become displeased, and sailed away promising to return someday—had indeed returned. Belief in a legend prevented the Incas, like the Aztecs, from taking prompt action.

Religious ideology contributed to grave domestic crisis within the empire. When the ruler died, his corpse was preserved as a mummy. The mummy was both a holy object and a dynamic force in Inca society. It was housed in a sacred chamber and dressed in fine clothing. It was carried in procession to state ceremonies and was asked for advice in times of trouble. This cult of the royal mummies left a new Inca (ruler) with the title and insignia of his office but little else. Because each dead Inca retained possession of the estates and properties he had held in life, each new Inca lacked land. Thus, to strengthen his administration, secure the means to live in the royal style, and reward his supporters, a new Inca had to engage in warfare to acquire land.

In 1525, Huascar succeeded his father Huayna Capac as Inca and was crowned at Cuzco, the Incas' capital city, with the fringed headband symbolizing his imperial office. By this time, the dead rulers controlled most of Peru's land and resources. The nobility managed the estates of the dead Inca rulers. Needing land and other possessions, Huascar proposed burying the mummies of all of the dead Incas and using the profits from their estates for the living.

According to Inca law, the successor of a dead Inca had to be a son by the ruler's principal wife, who had to be the ruler's full sister. Huascar was the result of such an incestuous union. His half-brother Atauhualpa was not. Atauhualpa tried to persuade Huascar to split the kingdom with him, claiming that their father's dying wish was for both sons to rule. Huascar rejected this claim. The great nobles responsible for the cult of the royal mum-

mies, however, were alarmed and outraged by Huascar's proposal to bury the mummies. Not only would Huascar be insulting the dead mummies and thus provoke their anger and retaliation, but the nobility would be deprived of the wealth and power they enjoyed as custodians of the cult. Willing to ignore the fact that Atauhualpa had not been born of an incestuous union, the nobles supported Atauhualpa's claim to rule. Civil war ensued, and Atauhualpa emerged victorious.[17] The five-year struggle may have exhausted him and damaged his judgment.

Francisco Pizarro (ca 1475–1541) landed on the northern coast of Peru on May 13, 1532, the very day Atauhualpa won the decisive battle against his brother. The Spaniard soon learned about the war and its outcome. As Pizarro advanced across the steep Andes toward Cuzco, Atauhualpa was proceeding to the capital for his coronation. Atauhualpa stopped at the provincial town of Cajamarca. He, like Montezuma in Mexico, was kept fully informed of the Spaniards' movements. His plan was to lure the Spaniards into a trap, seize their horses and ablest men for his army, and execute the rest. What had the Inca, surrounded by his thousands of troops, to fear? Atauhualpa thus accepted Pizarro's invitation to meet in the central plaza of Cajamarca with his bodyguards "unarmed so as not to give offense." He rode right into the Spaniard's trap. Pizarro knew that if he could capture that Inca, from whom all power devolved, he would have the "Kingdom of Gold" for which he had come to the New World.

The Inca's litter arrived in the ominously quiet town square. One cannon blast terrified the Indians. The Spaniards rushed out of hiding and slaughtered them. Atauhualpa's fringed headband was instantly torn from his head. He offered to purchase his freedom with a roomful of gold. Pizarro agreed to this ransom, and an appropriate document was drawn up and signed. But after the gold had been gathered from all parts of the empire to fill the room—its dimensions were 17 feet by 22 feet by 9 feet—the Spaniards trumped up charges against Atauhualpa and strangled him. The Inca Empire lay at Pizarro's feet.

The South American Holocaust

In the sixteenth century, about 200,000 Spaniards emigrated to the New World. Soldiers demobilized from the Spanish and Italian campaigns, adventurers and drifters unable to find work in Spain, they did not intend to work in the New World. After assisting in the conquest of the Aztecs and the subjugation of the Incas, these drifters wanted to settle down and become a ruling class. In temperate grazing areas they carved out vast estates and imported Spanish sheep, cattle, and horses for the kinds of ranching with which they were familiar. In the coastal tropics, unsuited for grazing, the Spanish erected huge sugar plantations. Columbus had introduced sugar into the West Indies; Cortés had introduced it into Mexico. Sugar was a great luxury in Europe, and demand for it was high. Around 1550 the discovery of silver at Zacatecas and Guanajuato in Mexico and Potosí in present-day Bolivia stimulated silver rushes. How were the cattle ranches, sugar plantations, and silver mines to be worked? Obviously, by the Indians.

The Spanish quickly established the *encomienda* system, whereby the Crown granted the conquerors the right to employ groups of Indians in a town or area as agricultural or mining laborers or as tribute-payers. Theoretically, the Spanish were forbidden to enslave the Indian natives; in actuality, the encomiendas were a legalized form of slavery. The European demand for sugar, tobacco, and silver prompted the colonists to exploit the Indians mercilessly. Unaccustomed to forced labor, especially in the blistering heat of tropical cane fields or the dark, dank, and dangerous mines, Indians died like flies. Recently scholars have tried to reckon the death rate of the Amerindians in the sixteenth century. Some historians maintain that the Indian population of Peru fell from 1.3 million in 1570 to 600,000 in 1620; central Mexico had 25.3 million Indians in 1519 and 1 million in 1605.[18] Some demographers dispute these figures, but all agree that the decline of the native Indian population in all of Spanish-occupied America amounted to a catastrophe greater in scale than any that has occurred even in the twentieth century.

What were the causes of this devastating slump in population? Students of the history of medicine have suggested the best explanation: disease. The

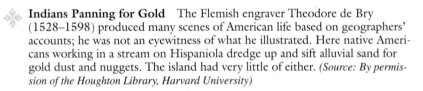

Indians Panning for Gold   The Flemish engraver Theodore de Bry (1528–1598) produced many scenes of American life based on geographers' accounts; he was not an eyewitness of what he illustrated. Here native Americans working in a stream on Hispaniola dredge up and sift alluvial sand for gold dust and nuggets. The island had very little of either. *(Source: By permission of the Houghton Library, Harvard University)*

major cause of widespread epidemics is migration, and those peoples isolated longest from other societies suffer most. Contact with disease builds up bodily resistance. At the beginning of the sixteenth century, Amerindians probably had the unfortunate distinction of longer isolation from the rest of humankind than any other people on earth. Crowded concentrations of laborers in the mining camps bred infection, which the miners carried to their home villages. With little or no resistance to diseases brought from the Old World, the inhabitants of the highlands of Mexico and Peru, especially, fell victim to smallpox. According to one expert, smallpox caused "in all likelihood the most severe single loss of aboriginal population that ever occurred."[19]

Although disease was the prime cause of the Indian holocaust, the Spaniards themselves contributed heavily to the Indians' death rate.[20] According to the Franciscan missionary Bartolomé de Las Casas (1474–1566), the Spanish maliciously murdered thousands:

This infinite multitude of people [the Indians] was . . . without fraud, without subtilty or malice . . . toward the Spaniards whom they serve, patient, meek and peaceful. . . .

To these quiet Lambs . . . came the Spaniards like most c(r)uel Tygres, Wolves and Lions, enrag'd with a sharp and tedious hunger; for these forty years past, minding nothing else but the slaughter of these unfortunate wretches, whom with divers kinds of torments neither seen nor heard of before, they have so cruelly and inhumanely butchered, that of three millions of people which Hispaniola it self did contain, there are left remaining alive scarce three hundred persons.[21]

Las Casas's remarks concentrate on the tropical lowlands, but the death rate in the highlands was also staggering.

The Christian missionaries who accompanied the conquistadors and settlers—Franciscans, Dominicans, and Jesuits—played an important role in converting the Indians to Christianity, teaching them European methods of agriculture, and inculcating loyalty to the Spanish crown. In terms of numbers of people baptized, missionaries enjoyed phenomenal success, though the depth of the Indians' understanding of Christianity remains debatable. Missionaries, especially Las Casas, asserted that the Indians had human rights, and through Las Casas's persistent pressure the emperor Charles

V in 1531 abolished the worst abuses of the encomienda system.

Some scholars offer a psychological explanation for the colossal death rate of the Indians, suggesting that they simply lost the will to survive because their gods appeared to have abandoned them to a world over which they had no control. Hopelessness, combined with abusive treatment and overwork, pushed many men to suicide, many women to abortion or infanticide.

Whatever its precise causes, the astronomically high death rate created a severe labor shortage in Spanish America. As early as 1511, King Ferdinand of Spain observed that the Indians seemed to be "very frail" and that "one black could do the work of four Indians."[22] Thus was born an absurd myth and the massive importation of black slaves from Africa (see pages 665–674).

Colonial Administration

Having seized the great Indian ceremonial centers in Mexico and Peru, the Spanish conquistadors proceeded to subdue the main areas of native American civilization in the New World. Columbus, Cortés, and Pizarro claimed the lands they had "discovered" for the crown of Spain. How were these lands to be governed?

According to the Spanish theory of absolutism, the Crown was entitled to exercise full authority over all imperial lands. In the sixteenth century the Crown divided Spain's New World territories into four *viceroyalties,* or administrative divisions. New Spain, with its capital at Mexico City, consisted of Mexico, Central America, and present-day California, Arizona, New Mexico, and Texas. Peru, with its viceregal seat at Lima, originally consisted of all the lands in continental South America but later was reduced to the territory of modern Peru, Chile, Bolivia, and Ecuador. New Granada, with Bogotá as its administrative center, included present-day Venezuela, Colombia, Panama, and, after 1739, Ecuador. La Plata, with Buenos Aires as its capital, consisted of Argentina, Uruguay, and Paraguay. Within each territory a *viceroy,* or imperial governor, had broad military and civil authority as the Spanish sovereign's direct representative. The viceroy presided over the *audiencia,* twelve to fifteen judges who served as advisory council and as the highest judicial body.

From the early sixteenth century to the beginning of the nineteenth, the Spanish monarchy acted on the mercantilist principle that the colonies existed for the financial benefit of the mother country. The mining of gold and silver was always the most important industry in the colonies. The Crown claimed the *quinto,* one-fifth of all precious metals mined in the Americas. Gold and silver yielded the Spanish monarchy 25 percent of its total income. In return, Spain shipped manufactured goods to the New World and discouraged the development of native industries.

The Portuguese governed their colony of Brazil in a similar manner. After the union of the crowns of Portugal and Spain in 1580, Spanish administrative forms were introduced. Local officials called *corregidores* held judicial and military powers. Mercantilist policies placed severe restrictions on Brazilian industries that might compete with those of Portugal. In the seventeenth century the use of black slave labor made possible the cultivation of coffee, cotton, and sugar. In the eighteenth century Brazil led the world in the production of sugar. The unique feature of colonial Brazil's culture and society was its thoroughgoing mixture of Indians, whites, and blacks.

The Economic Effects of Spain's Discoveries on Europe

The sixteenth century has often been called Spain's golden century. The influence of Spanish armies, Spanish Catholicism, and Spanish wealth was felt all over Europe. This greatness rested largely on the influx of precious metals from the Americas.

The mines at Zacatecas, Guanajuato, and Potosí in Peru poured out huge quantities of precious metals. To protect this treasure from French and English pirates, armed convoys transported it each year to Spain. Between 1503 and 1650, 16 million kilograms of silver and 185,000 kilograms of gold entered Seville's port. Spanish predominance, however, proved temporary.

In the sixteenth century, Spain experienced a steady population increase, creating a sharp rise in the demand for food and goods. Spanish colonies in the Americas also represented a demand for products. Since Spain had expelled some of the best farmers and businessmen—the Muslims and Jews—in the fifteenth century, the Spanish economy was suffering and could not meet the new demands. Prices rose. Because the cost of manufacturing cloth and other goods increased, Spanish products could not compete in the international market with cheaper products made elsewhere. The textile industry was badly hurt. Prices spiraled upward faster than the government could levy taxes to dampen the economy. (Higher taxes would have cut the public's buying power; with fewer goods sold, prices would have come down.)

Did the flood of silver bullion from America cause the inflation? Prices rose most steeply before 1565, but bullion imports reached their peak between 1580 and 1620. Thus there is no direct correlation between silver imports and the inflation rate. Did the substantial population growth accelerate the inflation rate? It may have done so. After 1600, when the population pressure declined, prices gradually stabilized. One fact is certain: the price revolution severely strained government budgets. Several times between 1557 and 1647, Spain's king Philip II and his successors repudiated the state debt, thereby undermining confidence in the government and leading the economy into shambles.

As Philip II paid his armies and foreign debts with silver bullion, Spanish inflation was transmitted to the rest of Europe. Between 1560 and 1600, much of Europe experienced large price increases. Prices doubled and in some cases quadrupled. Spain suffered most severely, but all European countries were affected. People who lived on fixed incomes, such as the continental nobles, were badly hurt because their money bought less. Those who owed fixed sums of money, such as the middle class, prospered: in a time of rising prices, debts had less value each year. Food costs rose most sharply, and the poor fared worst of all.

Seaborne Trading Empires

By 1550, European overseas reconnaissance had led to the first global seaborne trade. For centuries the Muslims had controlled the rich spice trade of the Indian Ocean; Muslim expeditions had been across Asian and African land routes. The Europeans' discovery of the Americas and their exploration of the Pacific for the first time linked the entire world by intercontinental seaborne trade. That trade brought into being three successive commercial empires: the Portuguese, the Spanish, and the Dutch.

In the sixteenth century, naval power and shipborne artillery gave Portugal hegemony over the sea route to India. To Lisbon the Portuguese fleet brought spices, which the Portuguese paid for with

textiles produced at Gujarat and Coromandel in India and with gold and ivory from East Africa (Map 16.2). From their fortified bases at Goa on the Arabian Sea and at Malacca on the Malay Peninsula, ships of Malabar teak carried goods to the Portuguese settlement at Macao in the South China Sea. From Macao, loaded with Chinese silks and porcelains, Portuguese ships sailed to the Japanese port of Nagasaki and to the Philippine port of Manila, where Chinese goods were exchanged for Spanish (that is, Latin American) silver. Throughout Asia, the Portuguese traded in slaves—black Africans, Chinese, and Japanese. The Portuguese imported to India horses from Mesopotamia and copper from Arabia; from India they exported hawks and peacocks for the Chinese and Japanese markets.

Across the Atlantic, Portuguese Brazil provided most of the sugar consumed in Europe in the sixteenth and early seventeenth centuries. African slave labor produced the sugar on the plantations of Brazil, and Portuguese merchants, some of them Jewish, controlled both the slave trade between West Africa and Brazil (see pages 545–546) and the commerce in sugar between Brazil and Portugal. The Portuguese were the first worldwide traders, and Portuguese was the language of the Asian maritime trade.

Spanish possessions in the New World constituted basically a land empire and, as already described, in the sixteenth century the Spaniards devised a method of governing that empire. But across the Pacific the Spaniards also built a seaborne empire, centered at Manila in the Philippines, which had been "discovered" by Ferdinand Magellan in 1521. Between 1564 and 1571, the Spanish navigator Miguel Lopez de Legazpi sailed from Mexico and through a swift and almost bloodless conquest took over the Philippine Islands. Legazpi founded Manila, which served as the trans-Pacific bridge between Spanish America and the extreme Eastern trade.

Chinese silk, sold by the Portuguese in Manila for American silver, was transported to Acapulco in Mexico, from which it was carried overland to Vera Cruz for re-export to Spain. Because hostile Pacific winds prohibited direct passage from the Philippines to Peru, large shipments of silk also went south from Acapulco to Peru (see Map 16.2). Spanish merchants could never satisfy the European demand for silk, so huge amounts of bullion went from Acapulco to Manila. For example, in 1597, 12 million pesos of silver, almost the total value of the transatlantic trade, crossed the Pacific. After about 1640, the Spanish silk trade declined because it could not compete with Dutch imports.

In the latter half of the seventeenth century, the worldwide Dutch seaborne trade predominated. The Dutch Empire was built on spices. In 1599 a Dutch fleet returned to Amsterdam carrying 600,000 pounds of pepper and 250,000 pounds of cloves and nutmeg. Those who had invested in the expedition received a 100 percent profit. The voyage led to the establishment in 1602 of the Dutch East India Company, founded with the stated intention of capturing the spice trade from the Portuguese.

The Dutch fleet, sailing from the Cape of Good Hope and avoiding the Portuguese forts in India, steered directly for the Sunda Strait in Indonesia (see Map 16.2). The Dutch wanted direct access to and control of the Indonesian sources of spices. In return for assisting Indonesian princes in local squabbles and disputes with the Portuguese, the Dutch won broad commercial concessions. Through agreements, seizures, and outright war, they gained control of the western access to the Indonesian archipelago. Gradually, they acquired political domination over the archipelago itself. Exchanging European manufactured goods—armor, firearms, linens, and toys—the Dutch soon had a monopoly on the very lucrative spice trade.[23]

The seaborne empires profited from the geographical reconnaissance and technological developments of the sixteenth century. The empires of Portugal, Spain, and Holland had strong commercial ambitions. They also paved the way for the eighteenth-century mercantilist empires of France and Great Britain.

MAP 16.2 Seaborne Trading Empires in the Sixteenth and Seventeenth Centuries In the sixteenth century, for the first time, the entire globe was linked by seaborne trade. In the seventeenth century American silver paid for Asian silks and spices, and African slaves in Latin America produced sugar for the tables of Europe.

The Chinese and Japanese Discovery of the West

The desire to Christianize pagan peoples was a major motive in Europeans' overseas expansion. The Indians of Central and South America, the

Muslims and polytheistic peoples of the Pacific, and the Confucian, Buddhist, and Shinto peoples of China and Japan became objects of Christianizing efforts. In this missionary activity the new Jesuit Order was dominant and energetic.

In 1582 the Jesuit Matteo Ricci (1552–1610) settled at Macao on the mouth of the Canton River. Like the Christian monks who had converted the Germanic tribes of early medieval Europe, Ricci sought first to convert the emperor and elite groups and then, through gradual assimilation, to win the throngs of Chinese. He tried to present Christianity to the Chinese in Chinese terms. He understood the Chinese respect for learning and worked to win converts among the scholarly class. When Ricci was admitted to the Imperial City at Beijing (Peking), he addressed the emperor Wan-li:

Li Ma-tou [Ricci's name transliterated into Chinese], your Majesty's servant, comes from the Far West, addresses himself to Your Majesty with respect, in order to offer gifts from his country. Despite the distance, fame told me of the remarkable teaching and fine institutions with which the imperial court has endowed all its peoples. I desired to share these advantages and live out my life as one of Your Majesty's subjects, hoping in return to be of some small use.[24]

Ricci presented the emperor with two clocks, one of them decorated with dragons and eagles in the Chinese style. The emperor's growing fascination with clocks gave Ricci the opportunity to display other examples of Western technology. He instructed court scholars about astronomical equipment and the manufacture of cannon and drew for them a map of the world—with China at its center. These inventions greatly impressed the Chinese intelligentsia. Over a century later a Jesuit wrote, "The Imperial Palace is stuffed with clocks, . . . watches, carillons, repeaters, organs, spheres, and astronomical clocks of all kinds—there are more than four thousand pieces from the best masters of Paris and London."[25] The Chinese first learned about Europe from the Jesuits.

But the Christians and the Chinese did not understand one another. Because the Jesuits served the imperial court as mathematicians, astronomers, and cartographers, the Chinese emperors allowed them to remain in Beijing. The Jesuits, however, were primarily interested in converting the Chinese to Christianity. The missionaries thought that

by showing the pre-eminence of Western science, they were demonstrating the superiority of Western religion. This was a relationship that the Chinese did not acknowledge. They could not accept a religion that required total commitment and taught the existence of an absolute. Only a small number of the highly educated, convinced of a link between ancient Chinese tradition and Christianity, became Christians. Most Chinese were hostile to the Western faith. They accused Christians of corrupting Chinese morals because they forbade people to honor their ancestors—and corruption of morals translated into disturbing the public order. They also accused Christians of destroying Chinese sanctuaries, of revering a man (Christ) who had been executed as a public criminal, and of spying on behalf of the Japanese.

The "Rites Controversy," a dispute over ritual between the Jesuits and other Roman Catholic religious orders, sparked a crisis. The Jesuits supported the celebration of the Mass in Chinese and the performance of other ceremonies in terms understandable to the Chinese. The Franciscans and other missionaries felt that the Jesuits had sold out the essentials of the Christian faith in order to win converts.

One burning issue was whether Chinese reverence for ancestors was homage to the good that the dead had done during their lives or an act of worship. The Franciscans secured the support of Roman authorities who considered themselves authorities on Chinese culture and decided against the Jesuits. In 1704 and again in 1742 Rome decreed that Roman ceremonial practice in Latin (not in Chinese) was to be the law for Chinese missions. (This decision continued to govern Roman Catholic missionary activity until the Second Vatican Council in 1962.) Papal letters also forbade Chinese Christians from participating in the rites of ancestor worship. The emperor in turn banned Christianity in China, and the missionaries were forced to flee.

The Christian West and the Chinese world learned a great deal from each other. The Jesuits probably were "responsible for the rebirth of Chinese mathematics in the seventeenth and eighteenth centuries," and Western contributions stimulated the Chinese development of other sciences.[26] From the Chinese, Europeans got the idea of building bridges suspended by chains. The first Western experiments in electrostatics and magnetism in the seventeenth century derived from

Chinese models. Travel accounts about Chinese society and customs had a profound impact on Europeans, making them more sensitive to the beautiful diversity of peoples and manners, as the essays of Montaigne (see pages 546–547) and other Western thinkers reveal.

Initial Japanese contacts with Europeans paralleled those of the Chinese. In 1542, Portuguese merchants arrived in Japan and quickly won large profits carrying goods between China and Japan. Dutch and English ships followed, also enjoying the rewards of the East Asian trade. The Portuguese merchants vigorously supported Christian missionary activity, and in 1547 the Jesuit missionary Saint Francis Xavier landed at Kagoshima, preached widely, and in two years won many converts. From the beginning, however, the Japanese government feared that native converts might have conflicting political loyalties. Divided allegiance could encourage European invasion of the islands—the Japanese authorities had the example of the Philippines, where Spanish conquest followed missionary activity.

Convinced that European merchants and missionaries had contributed to the general civil disorder, which the regime was trying to eradicate, the Japanese government decided to expel the Spanish and Portuguese and to close Japan to all foreign influence. A decree of 1635 was directed at the commissioners of the port of Nagasaki, a center of Japanese Christianity:

If there is any place where the teachings of the padres (Catholic priests) is practiced, the two of you must order a thorough investigation. . . . If there are any Southern Barbarians (Westerners) who propagate the teachings of the padres, or otherwise commit crimes, they may be incarcerated in the prison.[27]

In 1639, an imperial memorandum decreed: "hereafter entry by the Portuguese galeota [galleon or large oceangoing warship] is forbidden. If they insist on coming [to Japan], the ships must be destroyed and anyone aboard those ships must be beheaded.[28]

When tens of thousands of Japanese Christians made a stand on the peninsula of Shimabara, the Dutch lent the Japanese government cannon. The Protestant Dutch hated Catholicism, and as businessmen they hated the Portuguese, their great commercial rivals. Convinced that the Dutch had come only for trade and did not want to prosely-

tize, the imp[...] to remain. F[...] to remove [...] the western [...] Deshima, v[...] The govern[...] year, watch[...] Dutch offic[...] to renew th[...] the Dutch [...] other Euro[...]

Long after Christianity ceased to be a potential threat to the Japanese government, the fear of Christianity sustained a policy of banning Western books on science or religion. Until well into the eighteenth century, Japanese intellectuals were effectively cut off from Western developments. The Japanese opinion of Westerners was not high. What little the Japanese knew derived from the few Dutch businessmen at Deshima. Very few Japanese people ever saw Europeans. If they did, they considered them "a special variety of goblin that bore only a superficial resemblance to a normal human being." The widespread rumor was that when Dutchmen urinated they raised one leg like dogs.[29]

POLITICS, RELIGION, AND WAR

In 1559 France and Spain signed the Treaty of Cateau-Cambrésis, which ended the long conflict known as the Habsburg-Valois Wars. This event marks a watershed in early modern European history. Spain (the Habsburg side) was the victor. France, exhausted by the struggle, had to acknowledge Spanish dominance in Italy, where much of the war had been fought. Spanish governors ruled in Sicily, Naples, and Milan, and Spanish influence was strong in the Papal States and Tuscany. The Treaty of Cateau-Cambrésis ended an era of strictly dynastic wars and initiated a period of conflicts in which politics and religion played the dominant roles.

The wars of the late sixteenth century differed considerably from earlier wars. Sixteenth- and seventeenth-century armies were bigger than medieval ones; some forces numbered as many as fifty thousand men. Because large armies were expensive, governments had to reorganize their administrations to finance them. The use of gunpowder altered both the nature of warfare and popular attitudes toward it. Guns and cannon killed and

wounded from a dis[...]
scorned gunpow[...]
lowed a comm[...]
powder wea[...]
Hundred [...]
was an [...]
lized [...]
a[...]

...ance, indiscriminately. Writers ...er as a coward's weapon that al-...on soldier to kill a gentleman. Gun-...ened the notion, common during the ...Years' War (1337–1453), that warfare ...ennobling experience. Governments uti-...propaganda, pulpits, and the printing press to ...ouse public opinion to support war.[30]

Late sixteenth-century conflicts fundamentally tested the medieval ideal of a unified Christian society governed by one political ruler—the emperor—to whom all rulers were theoretically subordinate, and one church, to which all people belonged. The Protestant Reformation had killed this ideal, but few people recognized it as dead. Catholics continued to believe that Calvinists and Lutherans could be reconverted; Protestants persisted in thinking that the Roman church should be destroyed. Most people believed that a state could survive only if its members shared the same faith. The settlement finally achieved in 1648, known as the Peace of Westphalia, signaled the end of the medieval ideal.

The Origins of Difficulties in France (1515–1559)

In the first half of the sixteenth century, France continued the recovery begun during the reign of Louis XI (r. 1461–1483). The population losses caused by the plague and the disorders accompanying the Hundred Years' War had created such a labor shortage that serfdom virtually disappeared. Cash rents replaced feudal rents and servile obligations. This development clearly benefited the peasantry. Meanwhile, the declining buying power of money hurt the nobility. Domestic and foreign trade picked up; mercantile centers expanded.

The charming and cultivated Francis I (r. 1515–1547) and his athletic, emotional son Henry II (r. 1547–1559) governed through a small, efficient council. In 1539 Francis issued an ordinance that placed the whole of France under the jurisdiction of the royal law courts and made French the language of those courts. This act had a powerful centralizing impact. The *taille*, a tax on land, provided what strength the monarchy had and supported a strong standing army. Unfortunately, the tax base was too narrow to support France's extravagant promotion of the arts and ambitious foreign policy.

Deliberately imitating the Italian Renaissance princes, the Valois monarchs lavished money on a vast building program and on Italian artists. Francis I commissioned the Paris architect Pierre Lescot to rebuild the palace of the Louvre and Michelangelo's star pupil, Il Rosso, to decorate the wing of the Fontainebleau chateau. After acquiring Leonardo da Vinci's painting *Mona Lisa,* Francis brought Leonardo himself to France. Whatever praise Francis I and Henry II deserve for importing Italian Renaissance art and architecture to France, they spent far more than they could afford.

The Habsburg-Valois Wars, which had begun in 1522, also cost more than the government could afford. In addition to the time-honored practices of increasing taxes and heavy borrowing, Francis I tried two new devices to raise revenue: the sale of public offices and a treaty with the papacy. The former proved to be only a temporary source of money. The offices sold tended to become hereditary within a family, and once a man bought an office he and his heirs were tax-exempt. The sale of public offices thus created a tax-exempt class known as the "nobility of the robe."

The treaty with the papacy was the Concordat of Bologna (1516), in which Francis agreed to recognize the supremacy of the papacy over a universal council, thereby accepting a monarchial, rather than a conciliar view of church government. In return, the French crown gained the right to appoint all French bishops and abbots. This understanding gave the monarchy a rich supplement of money and offices and power over ecclesiastical organization that lasted until the Revolution of 1789. The Concordat of Bologna helps to explain why France did not later become Protestant: in effect, it established Catholicism as the state religion. The Concordat, however, perpetuated disorders within the French church. The government used ecclesiastical offices to pay and reward civil servants, who were likely to be worldly priests who possessed few special spiritual qualifications and were not inclined to work to elevate the intellectual and moral standards of the parish clergy. Thus the teachings of Luther and Calvin, spread far and wide because of the invention of printing from movable type some sixty years before, found a receptive audience.

After the publication of Calvin's *Institutes of the Christian Religion* in 1536, sizable numbers of French people were attracted to the "reformed religion," as Calvinism was called. Because Calvin wrote in French rather than Latin, his ideas gained wide circulation. At first, Calvinism drew converts from among reform-minded members of the

Rossi and Primaticcio: The Gallery of Francis I Flat paintings alternating with rich sculpture provide a rhythm that directs the eye down the long gallery at Fontainebleau, constructed between 1530 and 1540. Francis I sought to re-create in France the elegant Renaissance lifestyle found in Italy. *(Source: Art Resource, NY)*

Catholic clergy, the industrious middle classes, and artisan groups. Most Calvinists lived in Paris, Lyons, Meaux, Grenoble, and other major cities.

In spite of condemnation by the universities, government bans, and massive burnings at the stake, the numbers of Protestants in France grew steadily. When Henry II died in 1559, perhaps one-tenth of the population had become Calvinist.

Religious Riots and Civil War in France (1559–1589)

For thirty years, from 1559 to 1589, violence and civil war divided and shattered France. The feebleness of the monarchy was the seed from which the weeds of civil violence germinated. The three weak sons of Henry II could not provide the necessary leadership, and the French nobility took advantage of this monarchial weakness. In the second half of the sixteenth century, between two-fifths and one-half of the nobility at one time or another became Calvinist, frequently adopting the "reformed religion" as a religious cloak for their independence from the monarchy. Armed clashes between Catholic royalist lords and Calvinist antimonarchial lords occurred in many parts of France.

Among the upper classes, the fundamental object of the struggle was power. At lower social levels, however, religious concerns were paramount.

Working-class crowds composed of skilled craftsmen and the poor wreaked terrible violence on people and property. Both Calvinists and Catholics believed that the others' books, services, and ministers polluted the community. Preachers incited violence, and ceremonies like baptisms, marriages, and funerals triggered it. Protestant pastors encouraged their followers to destroy statues and liturgical objects in Catholic churches. Catholic priests urged their flocks to shed the blood of the Calvinist heretics.

In the fourteenth and fifteenth centuries, crowd action—attacks on great nobles and rich prelates—had expressed economic grievances. In contrast, religious rioters of the sixteenth century believed that they could assume the power of public magistrates and rid the community of corruption. Municipal officials criticized the crowds' actions, but the participation of pastors and priests in these riots lent them some legitimacy.[31]

A savage Catholic attack on Calvinists in Paris on August 24, 1572 (Saint Bartholomew's Day), followed the usual pattern. The occasion was a religious ceremony—the marriage of the king's sister Margaret of Valois to the Protestant Henry of Navarre—that was intended to help reconcile Catholics and Huguenots, as French Calvinists were called. The night before the wedding, the leader of the Catholic aristocracy, Henry of Guise, had Gaspard de Coligny, leader of the Huguenot party, attacked. Rioting and slaughter followed. The Huguenot gentry in Paris was massacred, and religious violence spread to the provinces. Between August 25 and October 3, perhaps twelve thousand Huguenots perished at Meaux, Lyons, Orléans, and Paris.

The Saint Bartholomew's Day massacre led to the War of the Three Henrys, a civil conflict among factions led by the Protestant Henry of Navarre, by King Henry III (who succeeded the tubercular Charles IX), and by the Catholic Henry of Guise. The Guises wanted not only to destroy Calvinism but to replace Henry III with a member of the Guise family. France suffered fifteen more years of religious rioting and domestic anarchy. Agriculture in many areas was destroyed; commercial life declined severely; starvation and death haunted the land.

What ultimately saved France was a small group of Catholic moderates called *politiques.* They believed that no religious creed was worth the incessant disorder and destruction and that only the restoration of a strong monarchy could reverse the trend toward collapse. The death of Queen Catherine de' Medici, followed by the assassinations of Henry of Guise and King Henry III, paved the way for the accession of the politique and Protestant Henry of Navarre, who ascended the throne as Henry IV (r. 1589–1610).

This glamorous prince, "who knew how to fight, to make love, and to drink," as a contemporary remarked, knew that the majority of the French were Roman Catholics. Declaring "Paris is worth a Mass," Henry knelt before the archbishop of Bourges and was received into the Roman Catholic church. Henry's willingness to sacrifice religious principles in the interest of a strong monarchy saved France. The Edict of Nantes, which Henry published in 1598, granted to Huguenots liberty of conscience and liberty of public worship in two hundred fortified towns, such as La Rochelle. The reign of Henry IV and the Edict of Nantes prepared the way for French absolutism in the seventeenth century (see page 558) by helping to restore internal peace in France.

The Revolt of the Netherlands and the Spanish Armada

In the last quarter of the sixteenth century, the political stability of England, the international prestige of Spain, and the moral influence of the Roman papacy all became mixed up with a religious crisis in the Low Countries. By this time, the Netherlands was the pivot around which European money, diplomacy, and war revolved. What began as a movement for the reformation of the Catholic church developed into a struggle for Dutch independence from Spanish rule.

The Habsburg emperor Charles V (r. 1519–1556) had inherited the seventeen provinces that compose present-day Belgium and Holland. The French-speaking southern towns produced fine linens and woolens; the wealth of the Dutch-speaking northern cities rested on fishing, shipping, and international banking. In the cities of both regions of the Low Countries, trade and commerce had produced a vibrant cosmopolitan atmosphere.

Each of the seventeen provinces of the Netherlands was self-governing and enjoyed the right to make its own laws and collect its own taxes. Only economic connections and the recognition of a common ruler in the person of the emperor Charles V united the provinces. Delegates from each province met together in the Estates General, but important decisions had to be referred back to each provincial Estate for approval. In the middle of the sixteenth century, the provinces of the Netherlands had a limited sense of federation.

In the Low Countries, as elsewhere, corruption in the Roman church and the critical spirit of the Renaissance provoked pressure for reform. Lutheran tracts and Dutch translations of the Bible flooded the seventeen provinces in the 1520s and 1530s, and Protestant ideas circulated freely in the cosmopolitan atmosphere of the commercial centers. But Charles's Flemish loyalty checked the spread of Lutheranism. Charles had been born in Ghent and raised in the Netherlands; he was Flemish in language and culture. He identified with the Flemish and they with him.

In 1556, however, Charles V abdicated and divided his territories. His younger brother Ferdinand received Austria and the Holy Roman Empire and ruled as Ferdinand I (r. 1558–1564). His son Philip inherited Spain, the Low Countries, Milan and the kingdom of Sicily, and the Spanish possessions in America and ruled as Philip II (r. 1556–1598).

Lutheranism posed no serious threat to Spanish rule in the Low Countries; it was the spread of Calvinism that upset the applecart. By the 1560s,

To Purify the Church The destruction of pictures and statues representing biblical events, Christian doctrine, or sacred figures was a central feature of the Protestant Reformation. Here Dutch Protestant soldiers destroy what they consider idols in the belief that they are purifying the church. *(Source: Fotomas Index)*

there was a strong, militant minority of Calvinists to whom Calvinism appealed because of its intellectual seriousness, moral gravity, and approval of any form of labor well done. Many working-class people converted because Calvinist employers would hire only fellow Calvinists. Well organized and with the backing of rich merchants, Calvinists quickly gained a wide following, and the Calvinist reformed religion tended in the 1570s to encourage opposition to "illegal" civil authorities.

In August of 1566, a year of very high grain prices, fanatical Calvinists, primarily of the poorest classes, embarked on a rampage of frightful destruction. As in France, Calvinist destruction in the Low Countries was incited by popular preaching, and attacks were aimed at religious images as symbols of false doctrines, not at people. The cathedral of Notre Dame at Antwerp was the first target. Begun in 1124 and finished only in 1518, this church stood as a monument to the commercial prosperity of Flanders, the piety of the business classes, and the artistic genius of centuries. On six successive summer evenings, crowds swept through the nave, attacking the greatest concentration of artworks in northern Europe: altars, paintings, books, tombs, ecclesiastical vestments, missals, manuscripts, ornaments, stained-glass windows, and sculptures. Before the havoc was over, thirty more churches had been sacked and irreplaceable libraries burned. From Antwerp the destruction spread to Brussels and Ghent and north to the provinces of Holland and Zeeland.

From Madrid, Philip II sent twenty thousand Spanish troops led by the duke of Alva to pacify the Low Countries. Alva interpreted "pacification" to mean the ruthless extermination of religious and political dissidents. His repressive measures and heavy taxation triggered widespread revolt.

For ten years, between 1568 and 1578, civil war raged in the Netherlands between Catholics and Protestants and between the seventeen provinces and Spain. Spanish generals could not halt the fighting. In 1576 the seventeen provinces united under the leadership of Prince William of Orange, called "the Silent" because of his remarkable discretion. In 1578 Philip II sent his nephew Alexander Farnese, duke of Parma, with an army of German mercenaries to crush the revolt once and for all. Avoiding pitched battles, Farnese fought by patient sieges. One by one the cities of the south fell and finally Antwerp, the financial capital of northern Europe.

Antwerp marked the farthest extent of Spanish jurisdiction and ultimately the religious division of the Netherlands. The ten southern provinces, the Spanish Netherlands (the future Belgium), remained Catholic and under the control of the Spanish Habsburgs. The seven northern provinces were Protestant and, led by Holland, formed the Union of Utrecht and in 1581 declared their independence from Spain. Thus was born the United Provinces of the Netherlands (Map 16.3).

Geography and sociopolitical structure differentiated the two countries. The northern provinces were ribboned with sluices and canals and therefore were highly defensible. Several times the Dutch had broken the dikes and flooded the countryside to halt the advancing Farnese. In the southern provinces the Ardennes Mountains interrupt the otherwise flat terrain. In the north the commercial aristocracy possessed the predominant power; in the south the landed nobility had the greater influence. The north was Protestant; the south remained Catholic.

Philip II and Alexander Farnese did not accept the division of the Low Countries, and the strug-

The Battle of Lepanto   On October 7, 1571, the fleet of the Holy League (Spain, Venice, the papacy), under Don Juan of Austria, met the Ottoman Turkish navy at a bay in the mouth of the Gulf of Patros off Lepanto in western Greece. Since most of the Ottoman sailors had been sent home for the winter, the Turkish fleet was not ready for battle. Superior European numbers and command prevailed, and the Ottomans were routed. The battle broke the spell of complete Turkish supremacy in the Mediterranean, Europe celebrated a great victory, and the Christian galleys gained a huge crop of prisoners to man the oars. But the Turks quickly rebuilt their navy and regained effective control of the Mediterranean. *(Source: National Maritime Museum, London)*

gle continued after 1581. The Protestant United Provinces repeatedly asked the Protestant Queen Elizabeth of England for assistance. But she was reluctant to antagonize Philip II by supporting the Dutch against the Spanish. The Spanish king had the steady flow of silver from the Americas at his disposal, and Elizabeth, lacking such treasure, wanted to avoid war. She realized, however, that if she did not help the Protestant Netherlands and they were crushed by Farnese, the Spanish were likely to invade England.

Three developments forced Elizabeth's hand. First, the wars in the Low Countries—the chief market for English woolens—badly hurt the English economy. When wool was not exported, the Crown lost valuable customs revenues. Second, the murder of William the Silent in July 1584 eliminated not only a great Protestant leader but the chief military check on the Farnese advance. Third, the collapse of Antwerp appeared to signal a Catholic sweep through the Netherlands. The next step, the English feared, would be a Spanish invasion of their island. For these reasons, Elizabeth pumped £250,000 and two thousand troops into the Protestant cause in the Low Countries between 1585 and 1587. Increasingly fearful of plots orchestrated by the Catholic Mary, Queen of Scots, Elizabeth's cousin and probable heir, Elizabeth finally signed her death warrant. Mary was beheaded on February 18, 1587. Sometime between March 24 and 30, the news of Mary's death reached Philip II.

Philip of Spain considered himself the international defender of Catholicism and heir to the medieval imperial power. When Pope Sixtus V (r. 1585–1590) heard of the death of the Queen of Scots, he promised to pay Philip a million gold ducats the moment Spanish troops landed in England. Alexander Farnese had repeatedly warned that, to subdue the Dutch, he would have to conquer England and cut off the source of Dutch support.

In these circumstances Philip prepared a vast fleet to sail from Lisbon to Flanders, fight off Elizabeth's navy *if* it attacked, rendezvous with Farnese, and escort his barges across the English Channel. The expedition's purpose was to transport the Flemish army for a cross-Channel assault. Philip expected to receive the support of English Catholics and anticipated a great victory for Spain.

On May 9, 1588, *la felicissima armada*—"the most fortunate fleet" of 130 vessels as it was called in official documents—sailed from Lisbon harbor.

MAP 16.3 The Netherlands, 1578–1609 Though small in geographical size, the Netherlands held a strategic position in the religious struggles of the sixteenth century.

An English fleet of about 150 ships—smaller, faster, and more maneuverable than the Spanish ships, and many having greater firepower—met the Spanish fleet in the Channel. A combination of storms and squalls, spoiled food and rank water aboard the Spanish ships, inadequate Spanish ammunition, and, to a lesser extent, English fire ships that caused the Spanish to scatter gave England the victory. Many Spanish ships sank on the journey home around Ireland; perhaps 65 managed to reach home ports.

The battle in the Channel had mixed consequences. Spain soon rebuilt its navy, and after 1588 the quality of the Spanish fleet improved. More silver reached Spain from the New World between 1588 and 1603 than in any other fifteen-year period. The war between England and Spain dragged on for years.

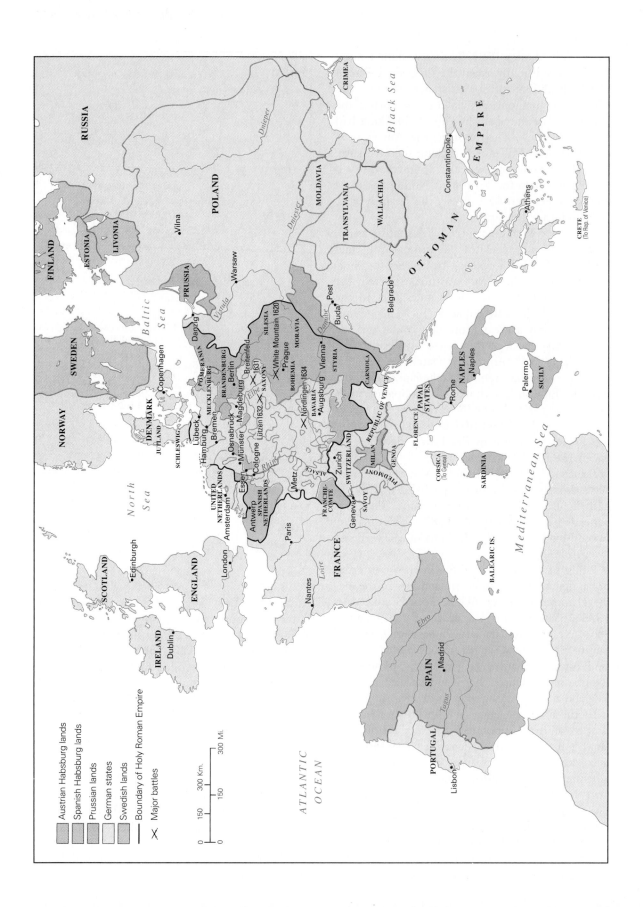

RUSSIA

FINLAND

ESTONIA

LIVONIA

SWEDEN

NORWAY

DENMARK

•Viina

POLAND

•Warsaw

PRUSSIA

Dapzig

Baltic Sea

Dnieper

CRIMEA

Black Sea

MOLDAVIA

TRANSYLVANIA

WALLACHIA

Dniester

OTTOMAN EMPIRE

•Constantinople

•Athens

CRETE
[To Rep. of Venice]

SCOTLAND

•Edinburgh

IRELAND

•Dublin

ENGLAND

•London

North Sea

Copenhagen•

JUTLAND

SCHLESWIG

Lübeck

Hamburg•

Bremen•

POMERANIA

MECKLENBURG

BRANDENBURG

•Berlin

SILESIA

White Mountain 1620

Prague•

BOHEMIA

MORAVIA

Buda•

•Pest

Danube

Belgrade•

Magdeburg

Breitenfeld

1631

SAXONY

Lützen 1632

Elbe

Nördlingen 1634

BAVARIA

Augsburg•

STYRIA

•Vienna

CARNIOLA

Osnabrück•

Münster•

UNITED NETHERLANDS

Amsterdam•

SPANISH NETHERLANDS

Antwerp

Essen•

Cologne•

Rhine

ALSACE

Metz•

SWITZERLAND

Zurich•

Geneva•

SAVOY

FRANCHE-COMTÉ

REPUBLIC OF VENICE

MILAN

PIEDMONT

GENOA

FLORENCE

PAPAL STATES

•Rome

NAPLES

•Naples

•Palermo

SICILY

•Paris

FRANCE

Loire

Nantes•

CORSICA
[To Genoa]

SARDINIA

BALEARIC IS.

Mediterranean Sea

SPAIN

•Madrid

Ebro

Tagus

PORTUGAL

•Lisbon

ATLANTIC OCEAN

Austrian Habsburg lands

Spanish Habsburg lands

Prussian lands

German states

Swedish lands

Boundary of Holy Roman Empire

✕ Major battles

0   150   300 Km.

0   150   300 Mi.

The defeat of the Spanish Armada was decisive, however, in the sense that it prevented Philip II from reimposing unity on western Europe by force. He did not conquer England, and Elizabeth continued her financial and military support of the Dutch. In the Netherlands neither side gained significant territory. The borders of 1581 tended to become permanent. In 1609 Philip III of Spain (r. 1598–1621) agreed to a truce, in effect recognizing the independence of the United Provinces. In seventeenth-century Spain the memory of the defeat of the Armada contributed to a spirit of defeatism. In England the victory gave rise to a David and Goliath legend that enhanced English national sentiment.

The Thirty Years' War (1618–1648)

Meanwhile, the political-religious situation in central Europe deteriorated. An uneasy truce had prevailed in the Holy Roman Empire since the Peace of Augsburg of 1555. The Augsburg settlement, recognizing the independent power of the German princes, had undermined the authority of the central government. According to the Augsburg settlement, the faith of the prince determined the religion of his subjects. There was no freedom of religion. If a prince was Lutheran, his subjects would be Lutheran. If a prince was Catholic, his subjects would be too. Dissidents had to convert or move to an area where their religion was recognized. Later in the century, Catholics grew alarmed because Lutherans, in violation of the Peace of Augsburg, were steadily acquiring German bishoprics. And Protestants were not pleased by militant Jesuits' success in reconverting several Lutheran princes to Catholicism. The spread of Calvinism further confused the issue. Lutherans feared that Catholic and Calvinist gains would totally undermine the Augsburg principles. In an increasingly tense situation, Lutheran princes formed the Protestant Union (1608). Catholics retaliated with the Catholic League (1609). The Holy Roman Empire was divided into two armed camps.

✳ **MAP 16.4 Europe in 1648** Which country emerged from the Thirty Years' War as the strongest European power? What dynastic house was that country's major rival in the early modern period?

Dynastic interests were also at stake. The Spanish Habsburgs strongly supported the goals of the Austrian Habsburgs: the unity of the empire under Habsburg rule and the preservation of Catholicism within the empire.

Violence erupted first in Bohemia (Map 16.4). The Bohemians were Czech and German in nationality, and Lutheran, Calvinist, Catholic, and Hussite in religion; all these faiths enjoyed a fair degree of religious freedom in Bohemia. In 1617 Ferdinand of Styria, the new Catholic king of Bohemia, closed some Protestant churches. In retaliation, on May 23, 1618, Protestants hurled two of Ferdinand's officials from a castle window in Prague. They fell 70 feet but survived: Catholics claimed that angels had caught them; Protestants said the officials fell on a heap of soft horse manure. Called the "defenestration of Prague," this event marked the beginning of the Thirty Years' War (1618–1648).

Historians traditionally divide the war into four phases. The first, or Bohemian, phase (1618–1625) was characterized by civil war in Bohemia, as Bohemians fought for religious liberty and independence from Austrian Habsburg rule. In 1620 Ferdinand, newly elected Holy Roman Emperor Ferdinand II (r. 1619–1637), totally defeated Protestant forces at the Battle of the White Mountain and followed up his victories by wiping out Protestantism in Bohemia.

The second, or Danish, phase of the war (1625–1629)—so called because of the participation of King Christian IV of Denmark (r. 1588–1648), the ineffective leader of the Protestant cause—witnessed additional Catholic victories. The year 1629 marked the peak of Habsburg power. The Jesuits persuaded Ferdinand to issue the Edict of Restitution. It specified that all Catholic properties lost to Protestantism since 1552 were to be restored and only Catholics and Lutherans (*not* Calvinists, Hussites, or other sects) were to be allowed to practice their faiths. Ferdinand appeared to be embarked on a policy to unify the empire. Protestants throughout Europe feared collapse of the balance of power in north-central Europe.

The third, or Swedish, phase of the war (1630–1635) began when Swedish king Gustavus Adolphus (1594–1632) intervened to support the Protestant cause within the empire. In 1631, with French support, Gustavus Adolphus won a brilliant victory at Breitenfeld (see Map 16.4). Again in

1632 he was victorious at Lützen, though he was fatally wounded in the battle. The participation of the Swedes in the Thirty Years' War proved decisive for the future of Protestantism and later German history. The Swedish victories ended the Habsburg ambition of uniting all the German states under imperial authority.

The death of Gustavus Adolphus, followed by the defeat of the Swedes at the Battle of Nördlingen in 1634, prompted the French to enter the war on the side of the Protestants. Thus began the French, or international, phase of the Thirty Years' War (1635–1648). For almost a century, French foreign policy had been based on opposition to the Habsburgs, because a weak Holy Roman Empire enhanced France's international stature. Now, in 1635, France declared war on Spain and again sent financial and military assistance to the Swedes and the German Protestant princes. The war dragged on; neither side had the resources to win a quick, decisive victory. French, Dutch, and Swedes, supported by Scots, Finns, and German mercenaries, burned, looted, and destroyed German agriculture and commerce.

Finally, in October 1648, peace was achieved. The treaties signed at Münster and Osnabrück—the Peace of Westphalia—mark a turning point in European political, religious, and social history. The treaties recognized the sovereign, independent authority of the German princes. Each ruler could govern his particular territory and make war and peace as well. With power in the hands of more than three hundred princes, with no central government, courts, or means of controlling unruly rulers, the Holy Roman Empire as a real state was effectively destroyed.

The independence of the United Provinces of the Netherlands was acknowledged. The political divisions within the empire, and the acquisition of the province of Alsace increased France's size and prestige, and the treaties allowed France to intervene at will in German affairs. Sweden achieved a powerful presence in northeastern Germany (see Map 16.4). The treaties also denied the papacy the right to participate in German religious affairs—a restriction symbolizing the reduced role of the church in European politics.

The Westphalian treaties stipulated that the Augsburg religious agreement of 1555 should stand permanently. The sole modification made Calvinism, along with Catholicism and Lutheranism, a legally permissible creed. In practice, the north German states remained Protestant, the south German states Catholic.

The Thirty Years' War settled little but was a disaster for the German economy and society—probably the most destructive event in German history before the twentieth century. Population losses were frightful. Perhaps one-third of the urban residents and two-fifths of the inhabitants of rural areas died. Entire areas of Germany were depopulated, partly by military actions, partly by disease—typhus, dysentery, bubonic plague, and syphilis (brought to Europe from the Americas) accompanied the movements of armies—and partly by the thousands of refugees who fled to safer areas.

In Germany the European-wide economic crisis caused primarily by the influx of silver from South America was badly aggravated by the war. Scholars still cannot estimate the value of losses in agricultural land and livestock, in trade and commerce. Those losses, compounded by the flood of Spanish silver, brought on severe price increases. Inflation was worse in Germany than anywhere else in Europe.

The population decline caused a rise in the value of labor. Owners of great estates had to pay more for agricultural workers. Farmers who needed only small amounts of capital to restore their lands started over again. Many small farmers, however, lacked the revenue to rework their holdings and became day laborers. Nobles and landlords were able to buy up many small holdings and amass great estates. In some parts of Germany, especially east of the Elbe River in areas like Mecklenburg and Pomerania, peasants' loss of land led to a new serfdom.[32] The Thirty Years' War contributed to the legal and economic decline of the largest segment of German society.

❈ CHANGING ATTITUDES

What were the cultural consequences of the religious wars and of the worldwide discoveries? What impact did the discoveries and wars have on Europeans' attitudes? The clash of traditional religious and geographical beliefs with the new knowledge provided by explorers—combined with decades of devastation and disorder within Europe—bred confusion, uncertainty, and insecurity. Geographical evidence based on verifiable scientific proofs contradicted the evidence of the Scriptures and of the classical authors.

❧ **The Horrors of War**   Following Richelieu's invasion of Lorraine in 1633, the French engraver Jacques Callot (1592/3–1635) produced a series of etchings collectively titled *The Great Miseries of War,* depicting the theft, rape, and brutality for which soldiers of the Thirty Years' War gained an enduring reputation. *(Source: Courtesy of the Trustees of the British Museum)*

The age of religious wars revealed extreme and violent contrasts. It was a deeply religious period in which men fought passionately for their beliefs; 70 percent of the books printed dealt with religious subjects. Yet the times saw the beginnings of religious skepticism. Europeans explored new continents, partly with the missionary aim of Christianizing the peoples they encountered. Yet the Spanish, Portuguese, Dutch, and English proceeded to dominate and enslave the Indians and blacks they encountered. While Europeans indulged in gross sensuality, the social status of women declined. The exploration of new continents reflects deep curiosity and broad intelligence. Yet Europeans believed in witches and burned thousands at the stake. Sexism, racism, and skepticism had all originated in ancient times. But late in the sixteenth century they began to take on their familiar modern forms.

The Status of Women

Did new ideas about women appear in this period? Theological and popular literature on marriage published in Reformation Europe helps to answer this question. Manuals emphasized the qualities expected of each partner. A husband was obliged to provide for the material welfare of his wife and children, to protect his family while remaining steady and self-controlled. He was to rule his household firmly but justly; he was not to behave like a tyrant—a guideline that counselors repeated frequently. A wife was to be mature, a good household manager, and subservient and faithful to her spouse. The husband also owed fidelity. Both Protestant and Catholic moralists rejected the double standard of sexual morality, considering it a threat to family unity. Counselors believed that marriage should be based on mutual respect and trust. Although they discouraged impersonal unions arranged by parents, they did not think romantic attachments—based on physical attraction and love—a sound basis for an enduring relationship.

A woman might assist in her own or her husband's business and do charitable work. But moralists held that involvement in social or public activities was inappropriate because it distracted the wife from her primary responsibility: her household. If a woman suffered under her husband's yoke, writers explained, her submission, like the pain of childbearing, was a punishment inherited from Eve, penance for man's fall. Moreover, they said, a woman's lot was no worse than a man's: he had to earn the family's bread by the sweat of his brow.[33]

Catholics viewed marriage as a sacramental union; validly entered into, it could not be dissolved. Protestants stressed the contractual nature of marriage: each partner promised the other support, companionship, and the sharing of mutual property. Protestants recognized the right of both parties to divorce and remarry for various reasons, including adultery and irreparable breakdown.[34]

Society in the early modern period was patriarchal. Women neither lost their identity nor lacked meaningful work, but the all-pervasive assumption was that men ruled. Leading students of the Lutherans, Catholics, French Calvinists, and English Puritans tend to agree that there was no improvement in women's long-standing subordinate status.

Artists' drawings of plump, voluptuous women and massive, muscular men reveal the contemporary standards of physical beauty. It was a sensual age that gloried in the delights of the flesh. Some people, such as the humanist poet Pietro Aretino (1492–1556), found sexual satisfaction with people of either sex. Reformers and public officials simultaneously condemned and condoned sexual "sins."

Prostitution was common because desperate poverty forced women and young men into it. Since the later Middle Ages, licensed houses of prostitution had been common in urban centers. When in 1566 Pope Pius IV (r. 1559–1565) expelled all the prostitutes from Rome, so many people left and the city suffered such a loss of revenue that in less than a month the pope was forced to rescind the order. Scholars debated Saint Augustine's notion that prostitutes serve a useful social function by preventing worse sins. Civil authorities in both Catholic and Protestant countries licensed houses of public prostitution. These establishments were intended for the convenience of single men, and some Protestant cities, such as Geneva and Zurich, installed officials in the brothels with the express purpose of preventing married men from patronizing them.

Single women of the middle and working classes in the sixteenth and seventeenth centuries worked in many occupations and professions—as butchers, shopkeepers, nurses, goldsmiths, and midwives and in the weaving and printing industries. Most women who were married assisted in their husbands' businesses. What became of the thousands of women who left convents and nunneries during the Reformation? This question pertains primarily to women of the upper classes, who formed the dominant social group in the religious houses of late medieval Europe. Luther and the Protestant reformers believed that celibacy had no scriptural basis and that young girls were forced by their parents into convents and, once there, were bullied by men into staying. Therefore, reformers favored the suppression of women's religious houses and encouraged former nuns to marry. Marriage, the reformers maintained, not only gave women emotional and sexual satisfaction but freed them from clerical domination, cultural deprivation, and sexual repression.[35] It appears that these women passed from clerical domination to subservience to husbands.

Some nuns in the Middle Ages probably did lack a genuine religious vocation, and some religious houses did witness financial mismanagement and moral laxness. Nevertheless, convents had provided women of the upper classes with an outlet for their literary, artistic, medical, or administrative talents if they could not or would not marry. When the convents were closed, marriage became virtually the only occupation available to upper-class Protestant women.

The great European witch scare reveals more about contemporary attitudes toward women.

The Great European Witch-Hunt

The period of the religious wars witnessed a startling increase in the phenomenon of witch-hunting, whose prior history was long but sporadic. "A witch," according to Chief Justice Edward Coke of England (1552–1634), "was a person who hath conference with the Devil to consult with him or to do some act." This definition by the highest legal authority in England demonstrates that educated people, as well as the ignorant, believed in witches. Witches were thought to be individuals who could mysteriously injure other people or animals—by causing a person to become blind or impotent, for instance, or by preventing a cow from giving milk.

Belief in witches dates back to the dawn of time. For centuries, tales had circulated about old women who made nocturnal travels on greased broomsticks to *sabbats,* or assemblies of witches, where they participated in sexual orgies and feasted on the flesh of infants. In the popular imagination witches had definite characteristics. The vast majority were married women or widows between fifty and seventy years old, crippled or bent with age, with pockmarked skin. They often practiced midwifery or folk medicine, and most had sharp tongues and were quick to scold.

Religious reformers' extreme notions of the Devil's powers and the insecurity created by the religious wars contributed to the growth of belief in witches. The idea developed that witches made pacts with the Devil in return for the power to work mischief on their enemies. Since pacts with the Devil meant the renunciation of God, witchcraft was considered heresy, and persecution for it had actually begun in the later fourteenth century when it was so declared. Persecution reached its most virulent stage in the late sixteenth and seventeenth centuries.

Fear of witches took a terrible toll of innocent lives in several parts of Europe. In southwestern Germany, 3,229 witches were executed between 1561 and 1670, most by burning. The communities of the Swiss Confederation in central Europe tried 8,888 persons between 1470 and 1700 and executed 5,417 of them as witches. In all the centuries before 1500, witches in England had been suspected of causing perhaps "three deaths, a broken leg, several destructive storms and some bewitched genitals." Yet between 1559 and 1736, almost 1,000 witches were executed in England.[36]

Historians and anthropologists have offered a variety of explanations for the great European witch-hunt. Some scholars maintain that charges of witchcraft were a means of accounting for inexplicable misfortunes. The English in the fifteenth century had blamed their military failures in France on Joan of Arc's witchcraft. In the seventeenth century the English Royal College of Physicians attributed undiagnosable illnesses to witchcraft. Some scholars think that in small communities, which typically insisted on strict social conformity, charges of witchcraft were a means of attacking and eliminating the nonconformist; witches, in other words, served the collective need for scapegoats. The evidence of witches' trials, some writers suggest, shows that women were not accused because they harmed or threatened their neighbors; rather, people believed such women worshiped the Devil, engaged in wild sexual activities with him, and ate infants. Other scholars argue the exact opposite: that people were tried and executed as witches because their neighbors feared their evil powers. According to still another theory, the unbridled sexuality attributed to witches was a figment of their accusers' imagination—a psychological projection by their accusers resulting from Christianity's repression of sexuality.

Witches Worshiping the Devil In medieval Christian art, a goat symbolizes the damned at the Last Judgment, following Christ's statement that the Son of Man would separate believers from nonbelievers as a shepherd separates the sheep from the goats (Matthew 25:31–32). In this manuscript illustration, a witch arrives at a sabbat and prepares to venerate the Devil in the shape of a goat by kissing its anus. *(Source: The Bodleian Library, Oxford)*

Despite an abundance of hypotheses, scholars cannot fully understand the phenomenon. Specific reasons for the persecution of women as witches probably varied from place to place. Nevertheless, given the broad strand of misogyny (hostility to women) in Western religion, the ancient belief in the susceptibility of women (the so-called weaker vessels) to the Devil's allurements, and the pervasive seventeenth-century belief about women's multiple and demanding orgasms and thus their sexual insatiability, it is not difficult to understand why women were accused of all sorts of mischief and witchcraft. Charges of witchcraft provided a legal basis for the execution of tens of thousands of women. The most important capital crime for women in early modern times, witchcraft has considerable significance for the history and status of women.[37]

NEGROS COMOLOSCRIOLLOS

✳ **African Slave and Indian Woman** A black slave approaches an Indian prostitute. Unable to explain what he wants, he points with his finger; she eagerly grasps for the coin. The Spanish caption above moralizes on the black man using stolen money—yet the Spaniards ruthlessly expropriated all South American mineral wealth. *(Source: New York Public Library)*

European Slavery and the Origins of American Racism

Except for the Aborigines of Australia, almost all peoples in the world have engaged in the enslavement of other human beings at some time in their histories. Since ancient times, victors in battle have enslaved conquered peoples. In the later Middle Ages slavery was deeply entrenched in southern Italy, Sicily, Crete, and Mediterranean Spain. The bubonic plague, famines, and other epidemics created a severe shortage of agricultural and domestic workers throughout Europe, encouraging Italian merchants to buy slaves from the Balkans, Thrace,

southern Russia, and central Anatolia for sale in the West. In 1364 the Florentine government allowed the unlimited importation of slaves as long as they were not Catholics. Between 1414 and 1423, at least ten thousand slaves were sold in Venice alone. The slave trade was a lucrative business enterprise in Italy during the Renaissance. Where profits were high, papal threats of excommunication completely failed to stop it. Genoese slave traders set up colonial stations in the Crimea and along the Black Sea, and according to an international authority on slavery, these outposts were "virtual laboratories" for the development of slave plantation agriculture in the New World.[38] This form of slavery had nothing to do with race; almost all of these slaves were white. How, then, did black African slavery enter the European picture and take root in the New World?

The capture of Constantinople by the Ottoman Turks in 1453 halted the flow of white slaves from the Black Sea region and the Balkans. Mediterranean Europe, cut off from its traditional source of slaves, had no alternative source for slave labor but sub-Saharan Africa. The centuries-old trans-Saharan trade in slaves was greatly stimulated by the existence of a ready market for slaves in the vineyards and sugar plantations of Sicily and Majorca. By the later fifteenth century, before the discovery of America, the Mediterranean had developed an "American" form of slavery.

Meanwhile, the Genoese and other Italians had colonized the Canary Islands in the western Atlantic. And sailors working for Portugal's Prince Henry the Navigator (see page 517) discovered the Madeira Islands and made settlements there. In this stage of European expansion, "the history of slavery became inextricably tied up with the history of sugar."[39] Population increases and monetary expansion in the fifteenth century led to an increasing demand for sugar even though it was an expensive luxury that only the affluent could afford. Between 1490 and 1530, between 300 and 2,000 black slaves arrived annually at the port of Lisbon (Map 16.5). From Lisbon, where African slaves performed most of the manual labor and constituted 10 percent of the city's population, slaves were transported to the sugar plantations of Madeira, the Azores, the Cape Verde Islands, and then Brazil. Sugar and those small Atlantic islands gave slavery in the Americas its distinctive shape. Columbus himself spent a decade in Madeira and took sugar plants on his voyages to "the Indies."

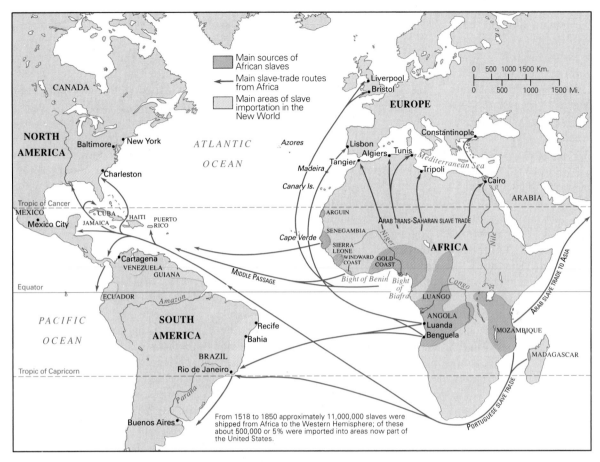

MAP 16.5 The African Slave Trade   Decades before the discovery of America, Greek, Russian, Bulgarian, Armenian, and then black slaves worked the plantation economies of southern Italy, Sicily, Portugal, and Mediterranean Spain—thereby serving as models for the American form of slavery.

As European economic exploitation of the Americas proceeded, the major problem settlers faced was a shortage of labor. As early as 1495, the Spanish solved the problem by enslaving the native Indians. In the next two centuries, the Portuguese, Dutch, and English followed suit.

Unaccustomed to any form of forced labor, certainly not to panning gold for more than twelve hours a day in the broiling sun, the Indians died "like fish in a bucket," as one Spanish settler reported.[40] In 1515 the Spanish missionary Bartolomé de Las Casas (see page 526), who had seen the evils of Indian slavery, urged the future emperor Charles V to end Indian slavery in his American dominions. Las Casas recommended the importation of blacks from Africa, both because church law did not strictly forbid black slavery and

because he thought blacks could better survive under South American conditions. Charles agreed, and in 1518 the African slave trade began. (When the blacks arrived, Las Casas immediately regretted his suggestion.) Columbus's introduction of sugar plants, moreover, stimulated the need for black slaves, and the experience and model of plantation slavery in Portugal and on the Atlantic islands encouraged the establishment of a similar agricultural pattern in the New World.

Several European nations participated in the African slave trade. Portugal brought the first slaves to Brazil; by 1600, 4,000 were being imported annually. After its founding in 1621, the Dutch West India Company, with the full support of the government of the United Provinces, transported thousands of Africans to Brazil and the

Caribbean. Only in the late seventeenth century, with the chartering of the Royal African Company, did the English get involved. Thereafter, large numbers of African blacks poured into the West Indies and North America. In 1790 there were 757,181 blacks in a total U.S. population of 3,929,625. When the first census was taken in Brazil in 1798, blacks numbered about 2 million in a total population of 3.25 million.

European settlers brought to the Americas the racial attitudes they had absorbed in Europe. Their beliefs and attitudes toward blacks derived from two basic sources: Christian theological speculation about the nature of God (light) and the Devil (black), and Muslim ideas. In the sixteenth and seventeenth centuries, the English, for example, were extremely curious about Africans' lives and customs, and slavers' accounts were extraordinarily popular. Travel literature depicted Africans as savages because of their eating habits, morals, clothing, and social customs; as barbarians because of their language and methods of war; and as heathens because they were not Christian. English people saw similarities between apes and Africans; thus the terms *bestial* and *beastly* were frequently applied to Africans. Africans were believed to possess a potent sexuality. One seventeenth-century observer considered Africans "very lustful and impudent, . . . their members' extraordinary greatness is a token of their lust." African women were considered sexually aggressive with a "temper hot and lascivious."[41]

"At the time when Columbus sailed to the New World, Islam was the largest world religion, and the only world religion that showed itself capable of expanding rapidly in areas as far apart and as different from each other as Senegal [in northwest Africa], Bosnia [in the Balkans], Java, and the Philippines."[42] Medieval Arabic literature emphasized blacks' physical repulsiveness, mental inferiority, and primitivism. In contrast to civilized peoples from the Mediterranean to China, some Muslim writers claimed, sub-Saharan blacks were the only peoples who had produced no sciences or stable states. The fourteenth-century Arab historian Ibn Khaldun (1332–1406) wrote that "the only people who accept slavery are the Negroes, owing to their low degree of humanity and their proximity to the animal stage." Though black kings, Khaldun alleged, sold their subjects without even a pretext of crime or war, the victims bore no resentment because they gave no thought to the

future and had "by nature few cares and worries; dancing and rhythm are for them inborn."[43] It is easy to see how such absurd images developed into the classic stereotypes used to justify black slavery in South and North America in the seventeenth, eighteenth, and nineteenth centuries. Medieval Christians and Muslims had similar notions of blacks as inferior and primitive people ideally suited to enslavement. Perhaps centuries of commercial contacts between Muslim and Mediterranean peoples had familiarized the latter with Muslim racial attitudes. The racial beliefs that the Portuguese, Spanish, Dutch, and English brought to the New World, however, derive primarily from Christian theological speculation.

LITERATURE AND ART

The age of religious wars and overseas expansion also witnessed extraordinary intellectual and artistic ferment. This effervescence can be seen in prose, poetry, and drama, in art, and in music. In many ways, the literature, visual arts, music, and drama of the period mirrored the social and cultural conditions that gave rise to them.

The Essay: Michel de Montaigne

Decades of religious fanaticism brought famine, civil anarchy, and death and led both Catholics and Protestants to doubt that any one faith contained absolute truth. The late sixteenth and seventeenth centuries witnessed the beginning of modern *skepticism,* a school of thought founded on doubt that total certainty or definitive knowledge is ever attainable. The skeptic is cautious and critical and suspends judgment. Perhaps the finest representative of early modern skepticism is the Frenchman Michel de Montaigne (1533–1592).

Montaigne came from a bourgeois family that had made a fortune selling salted herring and wine and in 1477 had purchased the title and property of Montaigne in Gascony; his mother descended from a Jewish family that had been forced to flee Spain. Montaigne received a classical education before studying law and securing a judicial appointment in 1554. At the age of thirty-eight, Montaigne resigned his judicial post, retired to his estate, and devoted the rest of his life to study, contemplation, and the effort to understand himself. His wealth provided him the leisure time to do so. Like the Greeks, he believed that the object of life was to "know thyself," for self-knowledge teaches men and women how to live in accordance with nature and God.

Montaigne developed a new literary genre, the essay—from the French word *essayer,* meaning "to test or try"—to express his thoughts and ideas. His *Essays* provide insight into the mind of a remarkably humane, tolerant, and civilized man. Montaigne was a humanist; he loved the Greek and Roman writers and was always eager to learn from them. From the ancient authors, especially the Roman Stoic Seneca, he acquired a sense of calm, inner peace, and patience and broad-mindedness.

Montaigne grew up during the French civil wars—a period when religious ideology had set family against family, even brother against brother. He wrote:

In this controversy . . . France is at present agitated by civil wars. . . . [Even] among the good men . . . we see many whom passion drives outside the bounds of reason, and makes them sometimes adopt unjust, violent, and even reckless courses.[44]

Though he remained a Catholic, Montaigne possessed a detachment and a willingness to look at all sides of a question:

I listen with attention to the judgment of all men; but so far as I can remember, I have followed none but my own. Though I set little value upon my own opinion, I set no more on the opinions of others.

In the book-lined tower where he passed his days, Montaigne became a deeply learned man. Yet he was not ignorant of the world of affairs, and he criticized scholars and bookworms who ignored the life around them. His essay "On Cannibals" reflects the impact of overseas discoveries on Europeans' consciousness. His tolerant mind rejected the notion that one culture is superior to another:

I long had a man in my house that lived ten or twelve years in the New World, discovered in these latter days, and in that part of it where Villegaignon landed [Brazil]. . . .

I find that there is nothing barbarous and savage in [that] nation, by anything that I can gather, excepting, that every one gives the title of barbarism to everything that is not in use in his own country. As, indeed, we have no other level of truth and reason, than the example and idea of the opinions and customs of the place wherein we live.[45]

In his belief in the nobility of human beings in the state of nature, uncorrupted by organized society, and in his cosmopolitan attitude toward different civilizations, Montaigne anticipated many eighteenth-century thinkers.

The thought of Michel de Montaigne marks a sharp break with the past. Faith and religious certainty had characterized the intellectual attitudes of Western society for a millennium. Montaigne's rejection of any kind of dogmatism, his secularism, and his skepticism thus represent a basic change. In his own time and throughout the seventeenth century, few would have agreed with him. Montaigne inaugurated an era of doubt. "Wonder," he said, "is the foundation of all philosophy, research is the means of all learning, and ignorance is the end."[46]

Elizabethan and Jacobean Literature

In addition to the development of the essay as a literary genre, the period fostered remarkable creativity in other branches of literature. England, especially in the latter part of Elizabeth's reign and in the first years of her successor James I (r. 1603–1625), witnessed unparalleled brilliance. The terms *Elizabethan* and *Jacobean* (the latter refers to the reign of James) are used to designate the English music, poetry, prose, and drama of this period. The poetry of Sir Philip Sidney (1554–1586), such as *Astrophel and Stella,* strongly influenced later poetic writing. *The Faerie Queene* of Edmund Spenser (1552–1599) endures as one of the greatest moral epics in any language. Above all, the immortal dramas of Shakespeare and the stately prose of the Authorized or King James Version of the Bible mark the Elizabethan and Jacobean periods as the golden age of English literature.

William Shakespeare (1564–1616), the son of a successful glove manufacturer who rose to the highest municipal office in the Warwickshire town of Stratford-on-Avon, chose a career on the London stage. By 1592 he had gained recognition as an actor and playwright. Between 1599 and 1603, Shakespeare performed in the Lord Chamberlain's Company and became co-owner of the Globe Theatre, which after 1603 presented his plays.

Shakespeare's genius lies in the originality of his characterizations, the diversity of his plots, his understanding of human psychology, and his unexcelled gift for language. Shakespeare was a Renaissance man in his deep appreciation for classical culture, individualism, and humanism. Such plays as *Julius Caesar, Pericles,* and *Antony and Cleopatra* deal with classical subjects and figures. Several of his comedies have Italian Renaissance settings. The nine history plays, including *Richard II, Richard III,* and *Henry IV,* enjoyed the greatest popularity among Shakespeare's contemporaries. Written during the decade after the defeat of the Spanish Armada, the history plays express English national consciousness. Lines such as these from *Richard II* reflect this sense of national greatness with unparalleled eloquence:

This royal Throne of Kings, this sceptre'd Isle,
This earth of Majesty, this seat of Mars,
This other Eden, demi-paradise,
This fortress built by Nature for herself,
Against infection and the hand of war:
This happy breed of men, this little world,
This precious stone, set in the silver sea,
Which serves it in the office of a wall,
Or as a moat defensive to a house,
Against the envy of less happier Lands,
This blessed plot, this earth, this Realm, this
   England.

Shakespeare's later plays, above all the tragedies *Hamlet, Othello,* and *Macbeth,* explore an enormous range of human problems and are open to an almost infinite variety of interpretations. *Othello,* which the nineteenth-century historian Thomas Macaulay called "perhaps the greatest work in the world," portrays an honorable man destroyed by a flaw in his own character and the satanic evil of his supposed friend Iago. The central figure in *Hamlet,* a play suffused with individuality, wrestles with moral problems connected with revenge and with man's relationship to life and death. The soliloquy in which Hamlet debates suicide is perhaps the most widely quoted passage in English literature:

To be, or not to be: that is the question:
Whether 'tis nobler in the mind to suffer
The slings and arrows of outrageous fortune,
Or to take arms against a sea of troubles,
And by opposing end them?

Hamlet's sad cry, "There is nothing either good or bad but thinking makes it so," expresses the anguish and uncertainty of modern man. *Hamlet* has always enjoyed great popularity, because in his many-faceted personality people have seen an aspect of themselves.

In 1929, in lectures at Oxford University, the novelist Virginia Woolf created an imaginary situation. What would have happened, she wondered, if Shakespeare had had a gifted sister who wanted to be an actress and to write poetry or plays? Unlike her brother, she would not have been sent to grammar school. If on her own she learned to read and write and occasionally picked up a book, her parents soon would have interrupted and told her to mend the stockings or mind the stew. Before she was out of her teens, her parents, loving though they were, would have selected a husband for her. If the force of her gift for learning and the stage was strong enough, she would have the choice of obeying her parents or leaving their home. If she succeeded in getting to London, she would discover that the theater did not hire women. Dependent on the kindness of strangers even for food, she probably would have found herself pregnant. And then "who shall measure the heat and violence of the poet's heart when caught and tangled in a woman's body?—she kills herself." Woolf concludes her story:

This may be true or it may be false—who can say?—but what is true in it, so it seemed to me, reviewing the story of Shakespeare's sister as I have made it, is that any woman born with a great gift in the sixteenth century would certainly have gone crazed, shot herself, or ended her days in some lonely cottage outside the village, half witch, half wizard, feared and mocked at.[47]

Unlike her contemporary Montaigne, Shakespeare's sister would not have had "a room of her own"—that is, the financial means to study and to write, even apart from the social and cultural barriers against a woman doing so.

The other great masterpiece of the Jacobean period was the Authorized or King James Version of the Bible (1611). Based on the best scriptural research of the time and divided into chapters and verses, the Authorized Version is actually a revision of earlier versions of the Bible rather than an original work. Yet it provides a superb expression of the mature English vernacular in the early seventeenth century. Thus Psalm 37:

Fret not thy selfe because of evill doers, neither bee
   thou envious against the workers of iniquitie.
For they shall soone be cut downe like the grasse;
   and wither as the greene herbe.

*Trust in the Lord, and do good, so shalt thou dwell in
   the land, and verely thou shalt be fed.*
*Delight thy selfe also in the Lord; and he shall give
   thee the desires of thine heart.*
*Commit thy way unto the Lord: trust also in him, and
   he shall bring it to passe.*
*And he shall bring forth thy righteousness as the
   light, and thy judgement as the noone day.*

The Authorized Version, so called because it was produced under royal sponsorship—it had no official ecclesiastical endorsement—represented the Anglican and Puritan desire to encourage lay people to read the Scriptures. It quickly achieved great popularity and displaced all earlier versions. British settlers carried this Bible to the North American colonies, where it became known as the "King James Bible." For centuries this version of the Bible has had a profound influence on the language and lives of English-speaking peoples.

Baroque Art and Music

Throughout European history, the cultural tastes of one age have often seemed quite unsatisfactory to the next. So it was with the baroque. The term *baroque* may have come from a Portuguese word for an "odd-shaped, imperfect pearl." Late-eighteenth-century art critics used it as an expression of scorn for what they considered an overblown, unbalanced style. The hostility of these critics has long since passed, and modern specialists agree that the triumphs of the baroque mark one of the high points in the history of Western culture.

The early development of the baroque is complex. Most scholars stress the influence of Rome and the revitalized Catholic church of the later sixteenth century. The papacy and the Jesuits encouraged the growth of an intensely emotional, exuberant art. These patrons wanted artists to go beyond the Renaissance focus on pleasing a small, wealthy cultural elite. They wanted artists to appeal to the senses and thereby touch the souls and kindle the faith of ordinary churchgoers while proclaiming the power and confidence of the reformed Catholic church. In addition to this underlying religious emotionalism, the baroque drew its sense of drama, motion, and ceaseless striving from the Catholic Reformation. The interior of the famous Jesuit Church of Jesus in Rome—the Gesù—combined all these characteristics in its lavish, shimmering, wildly active decorations and frescoes.

Taking definite shape in Italy after 1600, the baroque style in the visual arts developed with

Veronese: Feast in the House of Levi Using the story in Mark 2:15, which says that many tax collectors and sinners joined Jesus at dinner, the Venetian painter celebrated patrician wealth and luxury in Venice's golden age. The black servants, dwarfs, and colonnades all contribute to the sumptuous setting. *(Source: Gallerie dell'Accademia/Archivio Cameraphoto Venezia/Art Resource, NY)*

Velázquez: Juan de Pareja This portrait (1650) of the Spanish painter Velázquez's one-time assistant, a black man of obvious intellectual and sensual power and himself a renowned religious painter, suggests the integration of some blacks in seventeenth-century society. The elegant lace collar attests to his middle-class status. *(Source: The Metropolitan Museum of Art)*

exceptional vigor in Catholic countries—in Spain and Latin America, Austria, southern Germany, and Poland. Yet baroque art was more than just "Catholic art" in the seventeenth century and the first half of the eighteenth. True, neither Protestant England nor the Netherlands ever came fully under the spell of the baroque, but neither did Catholic France. And Protestants accounted for some of the finest examples of baroque style, especially in music. The baroque style spread partly because its tension and bombast spoke to an agitated age, which was experiencing great violence and controversy in politics and religion.

In painting, the baroque reached maturity early in the work of Peter Paul Rubens (1577–1640), the most outstanding and representative of baroque painters. Studying in his native Flanders and in Italy, where he was influenced by such masters as Michelangelo, Rubens developed his own rich,

sensuous, colorful style, characterized by animated figures, melodramatic contrasts, and monumental size. Rubens excelled in glorifying monarchs such as Queen Mother Marie de' Medici of France. He was a devout Catholic—nearly half of his pictures treat Christian subjects—yet among his trademarks are the fleshy, sensual nudes who populate his canvases as Roman goddesses, water nymphs, and remarkably voluptuous saints and angels.

In music, the baroque style reached its culmination almost a century later in the dynamic, soaring lines of the endlessly inventive Johann Sebastian Bach (1685–1750), one of the greatest composers of the Western world. Organist and choirmaster of several Lutheran churches across Germany, Bach was equally at home writing secular concertos and sublime religious cantatas. Bach's organ music, the greatest ever written, combines the baroque spirit of invention, tension, and emotion in an unforgettable striving toward the infinite. Unlike Rubens, Bach was not fully appreciated in his lifetime, but since the early nineteenth century his reputation has grown steadily.

SUMMARY

In the sixteenth and seventeenth centuries, Europeans for the first time gained access to large parts of the globe. European peoples had the intellectual curiosity, driving ambition, and scientific technology to attempt feats that were as difficult and expensive then as going to the moon is today. Exploration and exploitation contributed to a more sophisticated standard of living in the form of spices and Asian luxury goods and to a terrible international inflation resulting from the influx of South American silver and gold. Governments, the upper classes, and especially the peasantry were badly hurt by the inflation. Meanwhile, the middle class of bankers, shippers, financiers, and manufacturers prospered for much of the seventeenth century.

Europeans' technological development contributed to their conquest of Aztec Mexico and Inca Peru. Along with technology, Europeans brought disease to the New World and thereby caused a holocaust among the Indians. Overseas reconnaissance led to the first global seaborne commercial empires of the Portuguese, the Spanish, and the Dutch.

European expansion and colonization took place against a background of religious conflict and rising national consciousness. The sixteenth and seventeenth centuries were by no means a secular period. Although the medieval religious framework had broken down, people still thought largely in religious terms. Europeans used religious doctrine to explain what they did politically and economically. Religious ideology served as a justification for a variety of conflicts: the French nobles' opposition to the Crown, the Dutch struggle for political and economic independence from Spain. In Germany, religious pluralism and foreign ambitions added to political difficulties. After 1648 the divisions between Protestants and Catholics tended to become permanent. Sexism, racism, and religious skepticism were harbingers of developments to come.

NOTES

1. Quoted in C. M. Cipolla, *Guns, Sails, and Empires: Technological Innovation and the Early Phases of European Expansion, 1400–1700* (New York: Minerva Press, 1965), pp. 115–116.
2. J. H. Parry, *The Age of Reconnaissance* (New York: Mentor Books, 1963), Chs. 3 and 5.
3. See C. R. Phillips, *Ciudad Real, 1500–1750: Growth, Crisis, and Readjustment in the Spanish Economy* (Cambridge, Mass.: Harvard University Press, 1979), pp. 103–104, 115.
4. Quoted in Cipolla, *Guns, Sails, and Empires,* p. 132.
5. Quoted in F. H. Littell, *The Macmillan Atlas History of Christianity* (New York: Macmillan, 1976), p. 75.
6. Quoted in Cipolla, *Guns, Sails, and Empires,* p. 133.
7. Quoted in S. E. Morison, *Admiral of the Ocean Sea: A Life of Christopher Columbus* (Boston: Little, Brown, 1942), p. 339.
8. T. K. Rabb, "Columbus: Villain or Hero," *Princeton Alumni Weekly,* October 14, 1992, pp. 12–17.
9. J. M. Cohen, ed. and trans., *The Four Voyages of Christopher Columbus* (New York: Penguin Books, 1969), p. 37.
10. Quoted in R. L. Kagan, "The Spain of Ferdinand and Isabella," in *Circa 1492: Art in the Age of Exploration,* ed. J. A. Levenson (Washington, D.C.: National Gallery of Art, 1991), p. 60.
11. Quoted in F. Maddison, "Tradition and Innovation: Columbus' First Voyage and Portuguese Navigation in the Fifteenth Century," ibid., p. 69.
12. W. D. Phillips and C. R. Phillips, *The Worlds of Christopher Columbus* (Cambridge: Cambridge University Press, 1992), p. 273.
13. See ibid.
14. See G. W. Conrad and A. A. Demarest, *Religion and Empire: The Dynamics of Aztec and Inca Expansionism* (New York: Cambridge University Press, 1993), pp. 67–69.
15. G. C. Vaillant, *Aztecs of Mexico* (New York: Penguin Books, 1979), p. 241. Chapter 15, on which this section leans, is fascinating.
16. V. W. Von Hagen, *Realm of the Incas* (New York: New American Library, 1961), pp. 204–207.
17. Conrad and Demarest, *Religion and Empire,* pp. 135–139.
18. N. Sanchez-Albornoz, *The Population of Latin America: A History,* trans. W. A. R. Richardson (Berkeley: University of California Press, 1974), p. 41.
19. Quoted in A. W. Crosby, *The Columbian Exchange: Biological and Cultural Consequences of 1492* (Westport, Conn.: Greenwood, 1972), p. 39.
20. Ibid., pp. 35–59.
21. Quoted in C. Gibson, ed., *The Black Legend: Anti-Spanish Attitudes in the Old World and the New* (New York: Knopf, 1971), pp. 74–75.
22. Quoted in L. B. Rout, Jr., *The African Experience in Spanish America* (Cambridge: Cambridge University Press, 1976), p. 23.
23. See Parry, *The Age of Reconnaissance,* Chs. 12, 14, and 15.
24. Quoted in S. Neill, *A History of Christian Missions* (New York: Penguin Books, 1977), p. 163.
25. Quoted in C. M. Cipolla, *Clocks and Culture: 1300–1700* (New York: Norton, 1978), p. 86.
26. J. Gernet, *A History of Chinese Civilization* (New York: Cambridge University Press, 1982), p. 458.
27. Quoted in A. J. Andrea and J. H. Overfield, *The Human Record,* vol. 1 (Boston: Houghton Mifflin, 1990), pp. 406–407.
28. Ibid., p. 408.
29. See D. Keene, *The Japanese Discovery of Europe,* rev. ed. (Stanford, Calif.: Stanford University Press, 1969), pp. 1–17. The quotation is on page 16.
30. See J. Hale, "War and Public Opinion in the Fifteenth and Sixteenth Centuries," *Past and Present* 22 (July 1962): 29.
31. See N. Z. Davis, "The Rites of Violence: Religious Riot in Sixteenth Century France," *Past and Present* 59 (May 1973): 51–91.
32. H. Kamen, "The Economic and Social Consequences of the Thirty Years' War," *Past and Present* 39 (April 1968): 44–61.
33. This passage is based heavily on S. E. Ozment, *When Fathers Ruled: Family Life in Reformation*

Europe (Cambridge, Mass.: Harvard University Press, 1983), pp. 50–99.

34. Ibid., pp. 85–92.

35. Ibid., pp. 9–14.

36. N. Cohn, *Europe's Inner Demons: An Enquiry Inspired by the Great Witch-Hunt* (New York: Basic Books, 1975), pp. 253–254; K. Thomas, *Religion and the Decline of Magic* (New York: Charles Scribner's Sons, 1971), pp. 450–455.

37. See E. W. Monter, "The Pedestal and the Stake: Courtly Love and Witchcraft," in *Becoming Visible: Women in European History,* ed. R. Bridenthal and C. Koonz (Boston: Houghton Mifflin, 1977), pp. 132–135; and A. Fraser, *The Weaker Vessel* (New York: Random House, 1985), pp. 100–103.

38. C. Verlinden, *The Beginnings of Modern Colonization,* trans. Y. Freccero (Ithaca, N.Y.: Cornell University Press, 1970), pp. 5–6, 80–97.

39. This section leans heavily on D. B. Davis, *Slavery and Human Progress* (New York: Oxford University Press, 1984), pp. 54–62.

40. Quoted in D. P. Mannix with M. Cowley, *Black Cargoes: A History of the Atlantic Slave Trade* (New York: Viking Press, 1968), p. 5.

41. Ibid., p. 19.

42. See P. Brown, "Understanding Islam," *New York Review of Books,* February 22, 1979, pp. 30–33.

43. Davis, *Slavery and Human Progress,* pp. 43–44.

44. D. M. Frame, trans., *The Complete Works of Montaigne* (Stanford, Calif.: Stanford University Press, 1958), pp. 175–176.

45. C. Cotton, trans., *The Essays of Michel de Montaigne* (New York: A. L. Burt, 1893), pp. 207, 210.

46. Ibid., p. 523.

47. V. Woolf, *A Room of One's Own* (New York: Harcourt, Brace & World, 1957), p. 51.

SUGGESTED READING

Perhaps the best starting point for the study of European society in the age of exploration is Parry's *Age of Reconnaissance,* cited in the Notes, which treats the causes and consequences of the voyages of discovery. Parry's splendidly illustrated *The Discovery of South America* (1979) examines Europeans' reactions to the maritime discoveries and treats the entire concept of new discoveries. For the earliest British reaction to the Japanese, see *A World Elsewhere: Europe's Encounter with Japan in the Sixteenth and Seventeenth Centuries* (1990). The urbane studies of C. M. Cipolla present fascinating material on technological

and sociological developments written in a lucid style. In addition to the titles cited in the Notes, see *Cristofano and the Plague: A Study in the History of Public Health in the Age of Galileo* (1973) and *Public Health and the Medical Profession in the Renaissance* (1976). Morison's *Admiral of the Ocean Sea,* also listed in the Notes, is the standard biography of Columbus. The advanced student should consult F. Braudel, *Civilization and Capitalism, 15th–18th Century,* trans. S. Reynolds, vol. 1, *The Structures of Everyday Life* (1981); vol. 2, *The Wheels of Commerce* (1982); and vol. 3, *The Perspective of the World* (1984). These three fat volumes combine vast erudition, a global perspective, and remarkable illustrations. For the political ideas that formed the background of the first Spanish overseas empire, see A. Pagden, *Spanish Imperialism and the Political Imagination* (1990).

For the religious wars, in addition to the references cited in the Notes to this chapter, see J. H. M. Salmon, *Society in Crisis: France in the Sixteenth Century* (1975), which traces the fate of French institutions during the civil wars. A. N. Galpern, *The Religions of the People in Sixteenth-Century Champagne* (1976), is a useful case study in religious anthropology, and W. A. Christian, Jr., *Local Religion in Sixteenth Century Spain* (1981), traces the attitudes and practices of ordinary people.

A cleverly illustrated introduction to the Low Countries is K. H. D. Kaley, *The Dutch in the Seventeenth Century* (1972). The study by J. L. Motley, *The Rise of the Dutch Republic,* vol. 1 (1898), still provides a good comprehensive treatment and is fascinating reading. For Spanish military operations in the Low Countries, see G. Parker, *The Army of Flanders and the Spanish Road, 1567–1659: The Logistics of Spanish Victory and Defeat in the Low Countries' Wars* (1972). The same author's *Spain and the Netherlands, 1559–1659: Ten Studies* (1979), contains useful essays, of which students may especially want to consult "Why Did the Dutch Revolt Last So Long?" For the later phases of the Dutch-Spanish conflict, see J. I. Israel, *The Dutch Republic and the Hispanic World, 1606–1661* (1982), which treats the struggle in global perspective.

Of the many biographies of Elizabeth of England, W. T. MacCaffrey, *Queen Elizabeth and the Making of Policy, 1572–1588* (1981), examines the problems posed by the Reformation and how Elizabeth solved them. J. E. Neale, *Queen Elizabeth I* (1957), remains valuable, and L. B. Smith, *The Elizabethan Epic* (1966), is a splendid evocation of the age of Shakespeare with Elizabeth at the center. The best recent biography is C. Erickson, *The First Elizabeth* (1983), a fine, psychologically resonant portrait.

Nineteenth- and early-twentieth-century historians described the defeat of the Spanish Armada as a great victory for Protestantism, democracy, and capitalism, which those scholars tended to link together. Recent historians have focused on its contemporary significance. For a sympathetic but judicious portrait of the man who launched the Armada, see G. Parker, *Philip II* (1978). The best recent study of the leader of the Armada is P. Pierson, *Commander of the Armada: The Seventh Duke of Medina Sidonia* (1989). D. Howarth, *The Voyage of the Armada* (1982), discusses the expedition largely in terms of the individuals involved, and G. Mattingly, *The Armada* (1959), gives the diplomatic and political background; both Howarth and Mattingly tell very exciting tales. M. Lewis, *The Spanish Armada* (1972), also tells a good story, but strictly from the English perspective. Significant aspects of Portuguese culture are treated in A. Hower and R. Preto-Rodas, eds., *Empire in Transition: The Portuguese World in the Time of Camões* (1985).

C. V. Wedgwood, *The Thirty Years' War* (1961), must be qualified in light of recent research on the social and economic effects of the war, but it is still a good (though detailed) starting point on a difficult period. Various opinions on the causes and results of the war are given in T. K. Rabb's anthology, *The Thirty Years' War* (1981). In addition to the articles by Hale and Kamen cited in the Notes, the following articles, both of which appear in the scholarly journal *Past and Present,* provide some of the latest important findings: J. V. Polisensky, "The Thirty Years' War and the Crises and Revolutions of Sixteenth Century Europe," 39 (1968), and M. Roberts, "Queen Christina and the General Crisis of the Seventeenth Century," 22 (1962).

As background to the intellectual changes instigated by the Reformation, D. C. Wilcox, *In Search of God and Self: Renaissance and Reformation Thought* (1975), contains a perceptive analysis, and T. Ashton, ed., *Crisis in Europe, 1560–1660* (1967), is fundamental. For women, marriage, and the family, see L. Stone, *The Family, Sex, and Marriage in England, 1500–1800* (1977), an important but controversial work; D. Underdown, "The Taming of the Scold," and S. Amussen, "Gender, Family, and the Social Or-

der," in *Order and Disorder in Early Modern England,* ed. A. Fletcher and J. Stevenson (1985); A. Macfarlane, *Marriage and Love in England: Modes of Reproduction, 1300–1848* (1986); C. R. Boxer, *Women in Iberian Expansion Overseas, 1415–1815* (1975), an invaluable study of women's role in overseas immigration; and S. M. Wyntjes, "Women in the Reformation Era," a quick survey of conditions in different countries, in Bridenthal and Koonz's *Becoming Visible.* Ozment's *When Fathers Ruled,* cited in the Notes, is a seminal study concentrating on Germany and Switzerland.

On witches and witchcraft see, in addition to the titles by Cohn and Thomas in the Notes, J. B. Russell, *Witchcraft in the Middle Ages* (1976) and *Lucifer: The Devil in the Middle Ages* (1984); M. Summers, *The History of Witchcraft and Demonology* (1973); and H. R. Trevor-Roper, *The European Witch-Craze of the Sixteenth and Seventeenth Centuries* (1967), an important collection of essays.

As background to slavery and racism in North and South America, students should see J. L. Watson, ed., *Asian and African Systems of Slavery* (1980), a valuable collection of essays. Davis's *Slavery and Human Progress,* cited in the Notes, shows how slavery was viewed as a progressive force in the expansion of the Western world. For North American conditions, interested students should consult W. D. Jordan, *The White Man's Burden: Historical Origins of Racism in the United States* (1974), and the title by Mannix listed in the Notes, a hideously fascinating account. For Caribbean and South American developments, see F. P. Bowser, *The African Slave in Colonial Peru* (1974); J. S. Handler and F. W. Lange, *Plantation Slavery in Barbados: An Archeological and Historical Investigation* (1978); and R. E. Conrad, *Children of God's Fire: A Documentary History of Black Slavery in Brazil* (1983).

The leading authority on Montaigne is D. M. Frame. In addition to his translation of Montaigne's works cited in the Notes, see his *Montaigne's Discovery of Man* (1955).

LISTENING TO THE
PAST

Columbus Describes His First Voyage

On his return voyage to Spain in January 1493, Christopher Columbus composed a letter intended for wide circulation and had copies of it sent ahead to Isabella and Ferdinand and others when the ship docked at Lisbon. Because the letter sums up Columbus's understanding of his achievements, it is considered the most important document of his first voyage. Remember that his knowledge of Asia rested heavily on Marco Polo's Travels, *published around 1298.*

Since I know that you will be pleased at the great success with which the Lord has crowned my voyage, I write to inform you how in thirty-three days I crossed from the Canary Islands to the Indies, with the fleet which our most illustrious sovereigns gave me. I found very many islands with large populations and took possession of them all for their Highnesses; this I did by proclamation and unfurled the royal standard. No opposition was offered.

I named the first island that I found 'San Salvador,' in honour of our Lord and Saviour who has granted me this miracle. . . . When I reached Cuba, I followed its north coast westwards, and found it so extensive that I thought this must be the mainland, the province of Cathay.[1] . . . From there I saw another island eighteen leagues eastwards which I then named 'Hispaniola.'[2] . . .

Hispaniola is a wonder. The mountains and hills, the plains and meadow lands are both fertile and beautiful. They are most suitable for planting crops and for raising cattle of all kinds, and there are good sites for building towns and villages. The harbours are incredibly fine and there are many great rivers with broad channels and the majority contain gold.[3] The trees, fruits and plants are very different from those of Cuba. In Hispaniola there are many spices and large mines of gold and other metals. . . .[4]

The inhabitants of this island, and all the rest that I discovered or heard of, go naked, as their mothers bore them, men and women alike. A few of the women, however, cover a single place with a leaf of a plant or piece of cotton which they weave for the purpose. They have no iron or steel or arms and are not capable of using them, not because they are not strong and well built but because they are amazingly timid. All the weapons they have are canes cut at seeding time, at the end of which they fix a sharpened stick, but they have not the courage to make use of these, for very often when I have sent two or three men to a village to have conversation with them a great number of them have come out. But as soon as they saw my men all fled immediately, a father not even waiting for his son. And this is not because we have harmed any of them; on the contrary, wherever I have gone and been able to have conversation with them, I have given them some of the various things I had, a cloth and other articles, and received nothing in exchange. But they have still remained incurably timid. True, when they have been reassured and lost their fear, they are so ingenuous and so liberal with all their possessions that no one who has not seen them would believe it. If one asks for anything they have they never say no. On the contrary, they offer a share to anyone with demonstrations of heartfelt affection, and they are immediately content with any small thing, valuable or valueless, that is given them. I forbade the men to give them bits of broken crockery, fragments of glass or tags of laces, though if they could get them they fancied them the finest jewels in the world.

I hoped to win them to the love and service of their Highnesses and of the whole Spanish nation and to persuade them to collect and give us of the things which they possessed in abundance and which we needed. They have no religion and are not idolaters; but all believe that power and goodness dwell in the sky and they are firmly convinced that I have come from the sky with these ships and people. In this belief they gave me a good reception everywhere, once they had overcome their fear; and this is not because they are stupid—far from it, they are men of great intelligence, for they navigate all those seas, and give a marvellously good account of everything—but because they have never before seen men clothed or ships like these. . . .

In all these islands the men are seemingly content with one woman, but their chief or king is allowed more than twenty. The women appear to work more than the men and I have not been able to find out if they have private property. As far as I could see whatever a man had was shared among all the rest and this particularly applies to food. . . . In another island, which I am told is larger than Hispaniola, the people have no hair. Here there is a vast quantity of gold, and from here and the other islands I bring Indians as evidence.

In conclusion, to speak only of the results of this very hasty voyage, their Highnesses can see that I will give them as much gold as they require, if they will render me some very slight assistance; also I will give them all the spices and cotton they want . . . I will also bring them as much aloes as they ask and as many slaves, who will be taken from the idolaters. I believe also that I have found rhubarb and cinnamon and there will be countless other things in addition . . .

So all Christendom will be delighted that our Redeemer has given victory to our most illustrious King and Queen and their renowned kingdoms, in this great matter. They should hold great celebrations and render solemn thanks to the Holy Trinity with many solemn prayers, for the great triumph which they will have, by the conversion of so many peoples to our holy faith and for the temporal benefits which will follow, for not only Spain, but all Christendom will receive encouragement and profit.

This is a brief account of the facts.
Written in the caravel off the Canary Islands.[5]

15 February 1493

At your orders
THE ADMIRAL

Questions for Analysis

1. How did Columbus explain the success of his voyage?

❈ German woodcut depicting Columbus's landing at San Salvador. *(Source: John Carter Brown Library)*

2. What was Columbus's view of the native Americans he met?

3. Evaluate Columbus's statements that the Caribbean islands possessed gold, cotton, and spices.

4. Why did Columbus cling to the idea that he had reached Asia?

Source: J. M. Cohen, ed. and trans., *The Four Voyages of Christopher Columbus.* Copyright © 1969 Penguin Books Ltd.

1. Cathay is the old name for China. In the logbook and later in this letter Columbus accepts the native story that Cuba is an island which they can circumnavigate in something more than twenty-one days, yet he insists here and later, during the second voyage, that it is in fact part of the Asiatic mainland. 2. Hispaniola is the second largest island of the West Indies; Haiti occupies the western third of the island, the Dominican Republic the rest. 3. This did not prove to be true. 4. These statements are also inaccurate. 5. Actually Columbus was off Santa Maria in the Azores.

17

Absolutism and Constitutionalism in Europe, ca 1589–1725

The Queen's Staircase is among the grandest of the surviving parts of Louis XIV's palace at Versailles. *(Source: © Photo R.M.N.)*

The seventeenth century in Europe was an age of intense conflict and crisis. The crisis had many causes, but the era's almost continuous savage warfare was probably the most important factor. War drove governments to build enormous armies and levy ever higher taxes on an already hard-pressed, predominately peasant population. Deteriorating economic conditions also played a major role. Europe as a whole experienced an unusually cold and wet climate over many years—a "little ice age" that brought small harvests, periodic food shortages, and even starvation. Not least, the combination of war, increased taxation, and economic suffering triggered social unrest and widespread peasant revolts, which were both a cause and an effect of profound dislocation.

The many-sided crisis of the seventeenth century posed a grave challenge to European governments: how were they to maintain order? The most common response of monarchial governments was to seek more power to deal with the problems and the threats that they perceived. Indeed, European rulers in this period generally sought to attain *absolute*, or complete, power and build absolutist states. Thus monarchs regulated religious sects, and they abolished the liberties long held by certain areas, groups, or provinces. Absolutist rulers also created new state bureaucracies to enhance their power and to direct the economic life of the country in the interest of the monarch. Above all, monarchs fought to free themselves from the restrictions of custom, competing institutions, and powerful social groups. In doing so, they sought freedom from the nobility and from traditional representative bodies—most commonly known as Estates or Parliament—that were usually dominated by the nobility.

The monarchial demand for freedom of action upset the status quo and led to bitter political battles. Nobles and townspeople sought to maintain their traditional rights, claiming that monarchs could not rule at will but rather had to respect representative bodies and follow established constitutional practices. Thus opponents of absolutism argued for *constitutionalism*—the limitation of the state by law. In seventeenth-century Europe, however, advocates of constitutionalism generally lost out and would-be absolutists triumphed in most countries.

There were important national variations in the development of absolutism. The most spectacular example occurred in western Europe, where Louis XIV built on the heritage of a well-developed monarchy and a strong royal bureaucracy. Moreover, when Louis XIV came to the throne, the powers of the nobility were already somewhat limited, the French middle class was relatively strong, and the peasants were generally free from serfdom. In eastern Europe and Russia, absolutism emerged out of a very different social reality: a powerful nobility, a weak middle class, and an oppressed peasantry composed of serfs. Eastern monarchs generally had to compromise with their nobilities as they fashioned absolutist states. Finally, in Holland and England, royal absolutism did not triumph. In England especially, the opponents of unrestrained monarchial authority succeeded in firmly establishing a constitutional state, which guaranteed that henceforth Parliament and the monarch would share power.

Thus in the period between roughly 1589 and 1725, two basic patterns of government emerged in Europe: absolute monarchy and the constitutional state. Almost all subsequent governments in the West have been modeled on one of these patterns, which have also influenced greatly the rest of the world in the last three centuries.

- How and why did Louis XIV of France lead the way in forging the absolute state?

- How did Austrian, Prussian, and Russian rulers in eastern Europe build absolute monarchies—monarchies that proved even more durable than that of Louis XIV?

- How did the absolute monarchs' interaction with artists, architects, and writers contribute to the splendid cultural achievements of both western and eastern Europe in this period?

- How and why did the constitutional state triumph in Holland and England?

This chapter explores these questions.

FRANCE: THE MODEL OF ABSOLUTE MONARCHY

France had a long history of unifying and centralizing monarchy, although the actual power and effectiveness of the French kings had varied enormously over time. Passing through a time of troubles and civil war after the death of Henry II in

1559, both France and the monarchy recovered under Henry IV and Cardinal Richelieu in the early seventeenth century. They laid the foundations for fully developed French absolutism under the "Great Monarch," Louis XIV. Providing inspiration for rulers all across Europe, Louis XIV and the mighty machine he fashioned deserve special attention

The Foundations of French Absolutism

Henry IV, the ingenious Huguenot-turned-Catholic, ended the French religious wars with the Edict of Nantes in 1598 (see page 534). The first of the Bourbon dynasty, Henry IV and his great minister Maximilian de Béthune, duke of Sully (1560–1641), then laid the foundations of later French absolutism.

Henry denied influence on the royal council to the nobility, which had harassed the countryside for half a century. Maintaining that "if we are without compassion for the people, they must succumb and we all perish with them," Henry also lowered taxes paid by the overburdened peasantry. Sully reduced the crushing royal debt accumulated during the era of religious conflict, encouraged French trade, and started a countrywide highway system. Within twelve years, Henry IV and his minister had restored public order in France and laid the foundation for economic prosperity. Unfortunately, the murder of Henry IV in 1610 by a crazed fanatic led to a severe crisis.

After the death of Henry IV, the queen-regent Marie de' Medici led the government for the child-king Louis XIII (r. 1610–1643), but feudal nobles and princes of the blood dominated the political scene. In 1624 Marie de' Medici secured the appointment of Armand Jean du Plessis—Cardinal Richelieu (1585–1642)—to the council of ministers. It was a remarkable appointment. The next year Richelieu became president of the council, and after 1628 he was first minister of the French crown. Richelieu used his strong influence over King Louis XIII to exalt the French monarchy as the embodiment of the French state.

Richelieu's policy was the total subordination of all groups and institutions to the French monarchy. The French nobility, with its selfish and independent interests, had long constituted the foremost threat to the centralizing goals of the Crown and to a strong national state. Now Richelieu crushed aristocratic conspiracies with quick execu-

tions, and he never called a session of the Estates General—the ancient representative body of the medieval orders that was primarily a representative of the nobility.

The genius of Cardinal Richelieu was reflected in the administrative system he established. He extended the use of the royal commissioners called *intendants,* each of whom held authority in one of France's thirty-two *généralités* (districts). The intendants were authorized "to decide, order and execute all that they see good to do." Usually members of the upper middle class or minor nobility, the intendants were appointed directly by the monarch, to whom they were solely responsible. They recruited men for the army, supervised the collection of taxes, presided over the administration of local law, checked up on the local nobility, and regulated economic activities—commerce, trade, the guilds, marketplaces—in their districts. As the intendants' power grew during Richelieu's administration, so did the power of the centralized state.

The cardinal perceived that Protestantism often served as a cloak for the political intrigues of ambitious lords. When the Huguenots revolted in 1625, Richelieu personally supervised the siege of their walled city, La Rochelle, and forced it to surrender. Thereafter, fortified cities were abolished. Huguenots were allowed to practice their faith, but they no longer possessed armed strongholds or the means to be an independent party in the state.

French foreign policy under Richelieu was aimed at the destruction of the fence of Habsburg territories that surrounded France. Consequently, in the Thirty Years' War Richelieu supported the Habsburgs' enemies, like the Lutheran king Gustavus Adolphus (see page 539). French influence became an important factor in the political future of the German Empire.

These new policies, especially war, cost money. Richelieu fully realized the need for greater revenues through increased taxation. But seventeenth-century France remained "a collection of local economies and local societies dominated by local elites." The government's power to tax was limited by the rights of assemblies in some provinces (such as Brittany) to vote their own taxes, the hereditary exemption from taxation of many wealthy members of the nobility and the middle class, and the royal pension system. Therefore, Richelieu—and later Louis XIV—temporarily solved their financial problems by securing the cooperation of local elites. Even in France royal absolutism was restrained by its need to compromise with the financial interests of well-entrenched groups.[1]

In building the French state, Richelieu believed that he had to take drastic measures against persons and groups within France and conduct a tough anti-Habsburg foreign policy. He knew that his actions sometimes seemed to contradict traditional Christian teaching. As a priest and bishop, how did he justify his policies? He developed his own *raison d'état* (reason of state): "What is done for the state is done for God, who is the basis and foundation of it." This being so, Richelieu maintained that, "Where the interests of the state are concerned, God absolves actions which, if privately committed, would be a crime."[2]

Richelieu persuaded Louis XIII to appoint his protégé Jules Mazarin (1602–1661) as his successor. Governing for the child-king Louis XIV, Mazarin became the dominant power in the government. He continued the centralizing policies of Richelieu, but in 1648 his unpopular attempts to increase royal revenues and expand the state bureaucracy resulted in a widespread rebellion known as the Fronde. Bitter civil war ensued between the monarchy and the opposition, led by the nobility and middle class. Riots and turmoil wracked Paris and the nation. Violence continued intermittently for the next twelve years.

Conflicts during the Fronde had a traumatic effect on the young Louis XIV. The king and his mother were frequently threatened and sometimes treated as prisoners by aristocratic factions. This period formed the cornerstone of Louis's political education and of his conviction that the sole alternative to anarchy was to concentrate as much power as possible in his own hands. Yet Louis XIV also realized that he would have to compromise with the bureaucrats and social elites who controlled local institutions and constituted the state bureaucracy. And he did so.

The Monarchy of Louis XIV

In the reign of Louis XIV (r. 1643–1715), the longest in European history, the French monarchy reached the peak of its absolutist development. In the magnificence of his court, in his absolute power, in the brilliance of the culture over which he presided and which permeated all of Europe, and in his remarkably long life, the "Sun King"

Philippe de Champaigne: Cardinal Richelieu
This portrait, with its penetrating eyes, expression of haughty and imperturbable cynicism, and dramatic sweep of red robes, suggests the authority, grandeur, and power that Richelieu wished to convey as first minister of France. (*Source: Reproduced by courtesy of the Trustees, The National Gallery, London*)

dominated his age. It was said that when Louis sneezed, all Europe caught cold.

Born in 1638, king at the age of five, Louis entered into personal, or independent, rule in 1661. Always a devout Catholic, Louis believed that God had established kings as his rulers on earth. The royal coronation consecrated Louis to God's service, and he was certain that although kings were a race apart, they had to obey God's laws and rule for the good of the people.

Louis's education was more practical than formal. He learned statecraft by direct experience.

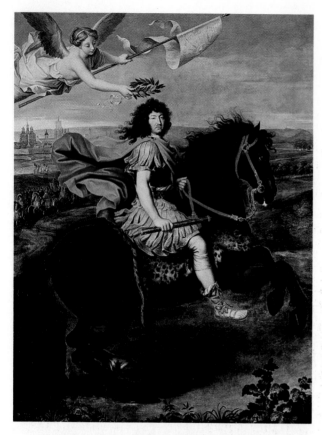

Louis XIV A skilled horseman and an enthusiastic hunter, Louis XIV rode with his armies on their many campaigns. This painting of Louis as a Roman general by Mignard Pierre (1612–1695) captures the king's enormous physical energy and proud self-confidence. *(Source: Galleria Sabauda, Turin/Scala/Art Resource, NY)*

hundreds of candles illuminated the domed ceiling, where allegorical paintings celebrated the king's victories. Louis skillfully used the art and architecture of Versailles to overawe his subjects and visitors and reinforce his power. Many monarchs subsequently imitated Louis XIV's example, and French became the language of diplomatic exchange and of royal courts all across Europe.

Historians have often said that Louis XIV was able to control completely the nobility, which historically had opposed the centralizing goals of the French monarchy. The duke of Saint-Simon, a high-ranking noble and fierce critic of the king, wrote in his memoirs, that Louis XIV

reduced everyone to subjection, and brought to his court those very persons he cared least about. Whoever was old enough to serve did not dare demur. It was still another device to ruin the nobles by accustoming them to equality and forcing them to mingle with everyone indiscriminately. . . .

Upon rising, at bedtime, during meals, in his apartments, in the gardens of Versailles, everywhere the courtiers had a right to follow, he would glance right and left to see who was there; he saw and noted everyone; he missed no one, even those who were hoping they would not be seen. . . .

Louis XIV took great pains to inform himself on what was happening everywhere, in public places, private homes, and even on the international scene. . . . Spies and informers of all kinds were numberless.[3]

As Saint-Simon suggests, the king did use court ceremonial to curb the great nobility. By excluding the highest nobles from his councils, he also weakened their ancient right to advise the king and to participate in government. They became mere instruments of policy, their time and attention occupied with operas, balls, gossip, and trivia.

Recent research, however, has demonstrated that Louis XIV actually secured the active collaboration of the nobility. Thus Louis XIV separated power from status and grandeur at Versailles: he secured the nobles' cooperation, and the nobility enjoyed their status and the grandeur in which they lived. The nobility agreed to participate in projects that both exalted the monarchy and reinforced their own ancient aristocratic prestige. Thus French government in the seventeenth century rested on a social and political structure in which the nobility continued to exercise great influence.[4]

The misery he suffered during the Fronde gave him an eternal distrust of the nobility and a profound sense of his own isolation. Accordingly, silence, caution, and secrecy became political tools for the achievement of his goals. His characteristic answer to requests of all kinds became the enigmatic "Je verrai" ("I shall see").

Louis XIV installed his royal court at Versailles, an old hunting lodge ten miles from Paris. His architects, Le Nôtre and Le Vau, turned what the duke of Saint-Simon called "the most dismal and thankless of sights" into a veritable paradise. Louis XIV required all the great nobility of France—at the peril of social, political, and sometimes economic disaster—to live at Versailles for at least part of the year. Versailles became a model of rational order, the center of France, and the perfect symbol of the king's power. In the gigantic Hall of Mirrors

In day-to-day government Louis utilized several councils of state, which he personally attended, and the intendants, who acted for the councils throughout France. A stream of questions and instructions flowed between local districts and Versailles, and under Louis XIV a uniform and centralized administration was imposed on the country. The councilors of state came from the upper middle class or from the recently ennobled, who were popularly known as "nobility of the robe" (because of the long judicial robes many of them wore). These ambitious professional bureaucrats served the state in the person of the king.

Throughout Louis's long reign and despite increasing financial problems, he never called a meeting of the Estates General. Thus his critics had no means of united action. French government remained highly structured, bureaucratic, centered at Versailles, and responsible to Louis XIV.

Economic Management and Religious Policy

Louis XIV's bureaucracy, court, and army cost a great amount of money, and the French method of collecting taxes consistently failed to produce the necessary revenue. An old agreement between the Crown and the nobility permitted the king to tax the common people if he did not tax the nobles. Because many among the rich and prosperous classes were exempt, the tax burden fell heavily on those least able to pay: the poor peasants.

The king named Jean-Baptiste Colbert (1619–1683), the son of a wealthy merchant-financier, as controller-general of finances. Colbert came to manage the entire royal administration and proved himself a financial genius. His central principle was that the French economy should serve the state, and he rigorously applied to France the system called mercantilism.

Hall of Mirrors, Versailles The grandeur and elegance of the Sun King's reign are reflected in the Hall of Mirrors at the Versailles palace. The king's victories were celebrated in paintings on the domed ceiling. Hundreds of candles lit up the dome. *(Source: Giraudon/Art Resource, NY)*

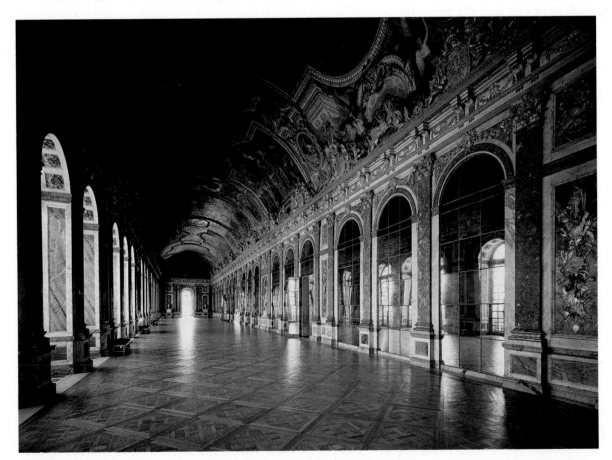

Mercantilism is a collection of government policies for the regulation of economic activities, especially commercial activities, by and for the state. In the seventeenth and eighteenth centuries, a nation's international power was thought to be based on its wealth—specifically on the gold so necessary for fighting wars. To accumulate gold, economic theory suggested, a country should always sell more goods abroad than it bought. Colbert insisted that France should be self-sufficient, able to produce within its borders everything needed by the subjects of the French king. If France were self-sufficient, the outflow of gold would be halted, debtor states would pay in bullion, and, with the wealth of the nation increased, France's power and prestige would be enhanced.

Colbert attempted to accomplish self-sufficiency through state support for both old industries and newly created ones. New factories in Paris manufactured mirrors to replace Venetian imports, for example. To ensure a high-quality finished product, Colbert set up a system of state inspection and regulation. He compelled all craftsmen to organize into guilds, and he encouraged skilled foreign craftsmen and manufacturers to immigrate to France. To improve communications, he built roads and canals. To protect French products, he placed high tariffs on foreign goods. His most important accomplishment was the creation of a powerful merchant marine to transport French goods. Colbert tried to organize and regulate the entire French economy for the glory of the French state as embodied in the king.

Colbert's achievement in the development of manufacturing was prodigious. The commercial classes prospered, and between 1660 and 1700 their position steadily improved. The national economy, however, rested on agriculture. Although French peasants were not serfs, as were the peasants of eastern Europe, they were mercilessly taxed. After 1685 other hardships afflicted them: savage warfare, poor harvests, continuing deflation of the currency, and fluctuation in the price of grain. Many peasants emigrated. A totally inadequate tax base and heavy expenditure for war in the later years of Louis's reign made Colbert's goals unattainable.

Economic policy was complicated in 1685 by Louis XIV's revocation of the Edict of Nantes. The new law ordered the destruction of churches, the closing of schools, the Catholic baptism of Huguenots, and the exile of Huguenot pastors who refused to renounce their faith. Why did Louis, by revoking the edict, persecute some of his most loyal and industrially skilled subjects?

Recent scholarship has convincingly shown that Louis XIV was basically tolerant. He insisted on religious unity not for religious but for political reasons. His goal was "one king, one law, one faith." He hated division within the realm and insisted that religious unity was essential to his royal dignity and to the security of the state. Thus after permitting religious liberty in the early years of his reign, Louis finally decided to crack down on Protestants.

Although France's large Catholic majority applauded Louis XIV, writers in the eighteenth century and later damned him for intolerance and for the adverse impact that revocation had on the economy and foreign affairs. They claimed that tens of thousands of Huguenot craftsmen, soldiers, and business people emigrated, depriving France of their skills and tax revenues and carrying their bitterness to Holland, England, and Prussia. Although the claims of economic damage were exaggerated, the revocation of the Edict of Nantes certainly aggravated Protestant hatred for Louis and for his armies.

French Classicism

Scholars characterize French art and literature during the age of Louis XIV as "French classicism." French artists and writers of the late seventeenth century deliberately imitated the subject matter and style of classical antiquity; their work resembled that of Renaissance Italy. French art possessed the classical qualities of discipline, balance, and restraint. Classicism was the official style of Louis's court.

After Louis's accession to power, the principles of absolutism molded the ideals of French classicism. Individualism was not allowed, and artists glorified the state as personified by the king. Precise rules governed all aspects of culture. Formal and restrained perfection was the goal.

Contemporaries said that Louis XIV never ceased playing the role of grand monarch on the stage of his court, and he used music and theater as a backdrop for court ceremonial. Among composers Louis favored Jean-Baptiste Lully (1632–1687), whose orchestral works and court ballets combine lively animation with the restrained austerity typical of French classicism. His operatic productions were a powerful influence throughout Europe. Louis also supported François Couperin (1668–1733), whose harpsichord and organ works possess the grandeur the king loved, and Marc-Antoine Charpentier (1634–1704), whose solemn religious music entertained him at meals.

Louis XIV loved the stage, and in the plays of Molière and Racine his court witnessed the finest achievements of the French theater. Playwright, stage manager, director, and actor, Molière produced comedies that exposed the hypocrisies and follies of society through brilliant caricature. *Tartuffe* satirized the religious hypocrite; *Les Femmes Savantes (The Learned Women)* mocked the fashionable pseudointellectuals of the day. Molière made the bourgeoisie the butt of his ridicule; he stopped short of criticizing the nobility, thus reflecting the policy of his royal patron.

While Molière dissected social mores, his contemporary Jean Racine (1639–1699) analyzed the power of love. Racine based his tragic dramas on Greek and Roman legends, and his persistent theme is the conflict of good and evil. Several of his plays—*Andromaque, Bérénice, Iphigénie,* and *Phèdre*—bear the names of women and deal with the power of passion in women. For simplicity of language, symmetrical structure, and calm restraint, the plays of Racine represent the finest examples of French classicism.

Jean-Baptiste Poquelin, also known as Molière This is an elegant, sensuous, and romantic portrait of the playwright whose works set the moral tone of Louis's court. Louis basked in Molière's admiration, approved his social criticism, and amply rewarded him. *(Source: Musée de Versailles/Photographie Bulloz)*

The Wars of Louis XIV

Visualizing himself as a great military hero, Louis XIV used almost endless war to exalt himself above the other rulers of Europe. Military glory was his aim. In 1666 Louis appointed François le Tellier (later marquis of Louvois) secretary of war. Louvois created a professional army, which was modern in the sense that the French state, rather than private nobles, employed the soldiers.

A commissariat was established to feed the troops, taking the place of the usual practice of living off the countryside. Uniforms and weapons were standardized. A rational system of recruitment, training, discipline, and promotion was imposed. With this new military machine, one national state, France, was able to dominate the politics of Europe for the first time.

Louis continued on a broader scale the expansionist policy begun by Cardinal Richelieu. In 1667, using a dynastic excuse, he invaded Flanders, part of the Spanish Netherlands, and

Franche-Comté. He thus acquired twelve towns, including the important commercial centers of Lille and Tournai (Map 17.1). Five years later, Louis personally led an army of over a hundred thousand men into Holland. The Dutch ultimately saved themselves only by opening the dikes and flooding the countryside. This war, which lasted six years and eventually involved the Holy Roman Empire and Spain, was concluded by the Treaty of Nijmegen (1678). Louis gained additional Flemish towns and all of Franche-Comté.

Encouraged by his successes, by the weakness of the German Empire, and by divisions among the other European powers, Louis continued his aggression. In 1681 he seized the city of Strasbourg and three years later sent his armies into the province of Lorraine. At that moment the king seemed invincible. In fact, Louis had reached the limit of his expansion at Nijmegen. The wars of the

MAP 17.1 Acquisitions of Louis XIV, 1668–1713   The desire for glory and the weakness of his German neighbors encouraged Louis's expansionist policy. But he paid a high price for his acquisitions.

1680s and 1690s brought him no additional territories. In 1689 the Dutch prince William of Orange, a bitter foe, became king of England. William joined the League of Augsburg—which included the Habsburg emperor, the kings of Spain and Sweden, and the electors of Bavaria, Saxony, and the Palatinate—adding British resources and men to the alliance. Neither the French nor the league won any decisive victories. France lacked the means to win; it was financially exhausted.

At the same time a series of bad harvests between 1688 and 1694 brought catastrophe. Cold, wet summers reduced the harvests by an estimated one-third to two-thirds, and in many provinces the death rate rose to several times the normal figure. Rising grain prices, new taxes, a slump in manufac-

turing, and the constant nuisance of pillaging troops—all these meant great suffering for the French people. France wanted peace at any price. Louis XIV granted a respite for five years while he prepared for the conflict later known as the War of the Spanish Succession.

This struggle (1701–1713) involved the dynastic question of the succession to the Spanish throne. When Charles I (r. 1665–1700) died in 1700, his will left the Spanish crown and the worldwide Spanish Empire to Philip of Anjou, Louis XIV's grandson. By accepting this will, Louis obviously would gain power in Spain; he would also be reneging on an earlier treaty to divide the vast Spanish possessions between himself and the Holy Roman emperor. He accepted the will, thereby provoking a great war.

The Dutch and the English would not accept French acquisition of the Spanish Netherlands and of the rich trade with the Spanish colonies, which would make France too strong in Europe and in North America. Thus in 1701 they joined with the Austrians and Prussians in the Grand Alliance. In the ensuing series of conflicts, Louis suffered major defeats and finally sued for peace.

The war was concluded at Utrecht in 1713, where the principle of partition was applied. Louis's grandson Philip remained the first Bourbon king of Spain on the understanding that the French and Spanish crowns would never be united. France surrendered Newfoundland, Nova Scotia, and the Hudson Bay territory to England, which also acquired Gibraltar, Minorca, and control of the African slave trade from Spain. The Dutch gained little because Austria received the former Spanish Netherlands (Map 17.2).

The Peace of Utrecht represented the balance-of-power principle in operation, setting limits on the extent to which any one power, in this case France, could expand. The treaty completed the decline of Spain as a great power. It vastly expanded the British Empire. The Peace of Utrecht also marked the end of French expansionist policy. In Louis's thirty-five-year quest for military glory, his main territorial acquisition after 1678 was Strasbourg. Even revisionist historians sympathetic to Louis acknowledge "that the widespread misery in France during the period was in part due to royal policies, especially the incessant wars."[5] The news of Louis's death in 1715 brought rejoicing throughout France.

THE DECLINE OF ABSOLUTIST SPAIN IN THE SEVENTEENTH CENTURY

Spanish absolutism and greatness had preceded that of the French. In the sixteenth century, Spain (or, more precisely, the kingdom of Castile) had developed the standard features of absolute monarchy: a permanent professional bureaucracy, a standing army, and national taxes that fell most heavily on the poor. Spain developed its mighty international absolutism on the basis of silver bullion from Peru. But by the 1590s the seeds of disaster were sprouting, and in the seventeenth century Spain experienced a steady decline. The lack of a strong middle class (largely the result of the expul-

sion of the Jews and Moors), agricultural crisis and population decline, failure to invest in productive enterprises, intellectual isolation and psychological malaise—by 1715 all combined to reduce Spain to a second-rate power.

The fabulous flow of silver from Mexico and Peru had led Philip II to assume the role of defender of Roman Catholicism in Europe (see pages 534–539). But when the "Invincible Armada" went down in 1588, a century of Spanish pride and power went with it. After 1590 a spirit of defeatism and disillusionment crippled most reform efforts.

Philip II's Catholic crusade had been financed by the revenues of the Spanish-Atlantic economy. In the early seventeenth century, the Dutch and English began to trade with the Spanish colonies, and Mexico and Peru developed local industries. Between 1610 and 1650, Spanish trade with the colonies fell 60 percent, and the American silver lodes started to run dry. Yet in Madrid royal expenditures remained high. The result was chronic deficits and frequent cancellations of Spain's national debt. These brutal cancellations—a form of bankruptcy—shook public confidence in the state.

Spain, in contrast to the other countries of western Europe, developed only a tiny middle class. Public opinion, taking its cue from the aristocracy, condemned moneymaking as vulgar and undignified. Those with influence or connections sought titles of nobility and social prestige, or they became priests, monks, and nuns. The flood of gold and silver had produced severe inflation, and many businessmen found so many obstacles in the way of profitable enterprise that they simply gave up.

Spanish aristocrats, attempting to maintain an extravagant lifestyle that they could no longer afford, increased the rents on their estates. High rents and heavy taxes in turn drove the peasants from the land. Agricultural production suffered, and the peasants departed for the large cities, where they swelled the ranks of beggars.

Their most Catholic majesties, the kings of Spain, had no solutions to these dire problems. Philip IV (r. 1622–1665) left the management of his several kingdoms to Count Olivares. An able administrator, the count devised new sources of revenue, but he clung to the grandiose belief that the solution to Spain's difficulties rested in a return to the imperial tradition. Unfortunately, the imperial tradition demanded the revival of war with the Dutch in 1622 and a long war with France over Mantua (1628–1659). These conflicts, on top of

RUSSIAN EMPIRE

Moscow

Kiev

Dnieper

Dniester

POLAND

Warsaw

Vistula

LITHUANIA

EAST
PRUSSIA

ESTONIA

LIVONIA

INGRIA

S W E D E N

NORWAY

KINGDOM
OF
DENMARK

DENMARK

Baltic
Sea

North
Sea

WEST
PRUSSIA

BRANDENBURG

Berlin

Oder

SAXONY

SILESIA

HANOVER

Rhine

HOLY ROMAN EMPIRE

PALATINATE

BOHEMIA

BAVARIA

Danube

AUSTRIA

Vienna

Buda

Pest

HUNGARY

MOLDAVIA

WALLACHIA

Danube

OTTOMAN EMPIRE

Constantinople

Black Sea

MOREA
(Rep. of Venice)

CORFU
(Rep. of Venice)

Mediterranean
Sea

SICILY
(Savoy)

KINGDOM
OF
NAPLES

Naples

PAPAL
STATES

Rome

TUSCANY

REPUBLIC OF VENICE

Po

GENOA

MILAN

SAVOY

SWITZERLAND

LORRAINE

Strasbourg

AUSTRIAN
NETHERLANDS

UNITED
NETHERLANDS

Utrecht

Paris

Seine

Loire

FRANCE

Marseilles

Rhône

CORSICA
(Genoa)

SARDINIA
(Austria)

MINORCA
(Gr. Br.)

Balearic Is.

ATLANTIC
OCEAN

GREAT BRITAIN

SCOTLAND

ENGLAND

London

Thames

IRELAND

SPAIN

Madrid

Tagus

PORTUGAL

Lisbon

GIBRALTAR
(Great Britain)

300 Mi.

300 Km.

150

150

0

0

French Bourbon lands
Spanish Bourbon lands
Austrian Habsburg lands
Prussian lands
Great Britain
Boundary of Holy Roman Empire

an empty treasury, brought disaster. The Treaty of the Pyrenees of 1659, which ended the French-Spanish wars, compelled Spain to surrender extensive territories to France. After this treaty, Spain's decline as a great power became irreversible.

Seventeenth-century Spain was the victim of its past. It could not forget the grandeur of the sixteenth century and look to the future. The most cherished Spanish ideals were military glory and strong Roman Catholic faith. In the seventeenth century, Spain lacked the finances and the manpower to fight long, expensive wars. Spain also ignored the new mercantile ideas and scientific methods because they came from heretical nations, Holland and England.

In the brilliant novel *Don Quixote,* the Spanish writer Miguel de Cervantes (1547–1616) produced one of the masterpieces of world literature. *Don Quixote* delineates the whole fabric of sixteenth-century Spanish society. The main character, Don Quixote, lives in a dream world, traveling about the countryside seeking military glory. A leading scholar wrote, "The Spaniard convinced himself that reality was what he felt, believed, imagined. He filled the world with heroic reverberations. Don Quixote was born and grew."[6]

❧ ABSOLUTISM IN EASTERN EUROPE: AUSTRIA, PRUSSIA, AND RUSSIA

The rulers of eastern Europe also labored to build strong absolutist states in the seventeenth century. But they built on social and economic foundations different from those in western Europe. These foundations were laid between 1400 and 1650,

MAP 17.2 Europe in 1715 The Peace of Utrecht ended the War of the Spanish Succession and redrew the map of Europe. A French Bourbon king succeeded to the Spanish throne on the understanding that the French would not attempt to unite the French and Spanish crowns. France surrendered to Austria the Spanish Netherlands (later Belgium), then in French hands; and France recognized the Hohenzollern rulers of Prussia. Spain ceded Gibraltar to Great Britain, for which it has been a strategic naval station ever since. Spain also granted to Britain the *asiento,* the contract for supplying African slaves to America.

when the princes and the landed nobility of eastern Europe rolled back the gains made by the peasantry during the High Middle Ages and reimposed serfdom on the rural masses. The nobility also enhanced its power as the primary social force by reducing the importance of the towns and the middle classes.

Despite the strength of the nobility, strong kings did begin to emerge in many eastern European lands in the course of the seventeenth century. There were endless wars, and in this atmosphere of continuous military emergency monarchs found ways to reduce the political power of the landlord nobility. Cautiously leaving the nobles the unchallenged masters of their peasants, eastern monarchs gradually monopolized political power in three key areas. They imposed and collected permanent taxes without consent. They maintained permanent standing armies, which policed their subjects in addition to fighting abroad. And they conducted relations with other states as they pleased.

There were important variations on the absolutist theme in eastern Europe. The royal absolutism created in Prussia was stronger and more effective than that established in Austria. This advantage gave Prussia a thin edge over Austria in the struggle for power in east-central Europe in the eighteenth century, and it prepared the way for Prussia's unification of the German people in the nineteenth century. As for Russia, it developed its own form of autocratic government at an early date, and its political absolutism was quite different from that of France or even Prussia.

Lords and Peasants

Lords and peasants were the basic social groups in eastern Europe, a vast region including Bohemia, Silesia, Hungary, eastern Germany, Poland, Lithuania, and Russia. Peasants in eastern Europe had done relatively well in the period from roughly 1050 to 1300, a time of gradual economic expansion and population growth. Eager to attract German settlers to their sparsely populated lands, the rulers and nobles of eastern Europe had offered potential newcomers economic and legal incentives. Large numbers of incoming settlers had obtained land on excellent terms and gained much personal freedom. These benefits were gradually extended to the local Slavic populations, even

THE RISE OF WESTERN ABSOLUTISM AND CONSTITUTIONALISM

1581	Formation of the Republic of the United Provinces of the Netherlands
1588	Defeat of the Spanish Armada
1589–1610	Reign of Henry IV of France; economic reforms help to restore public order, lay foundation for absolutist rule
1598	Edict of Nantes: Henry IV ends the French wars of religion
1610–1650	Spanish trade with the New World falls by 60 percent
1618–1648	Thirty Years' War
1624–1642	Richelieu dominates French government
1625	Huguenot revolt in France; siege of La Rochelle
1629–1640	Charles I attempts to rule England without Parliament
1640–1660	Long Parliament in England
1642–1649	English civil war
1643–1715	Reign of Louis XIV
1648–1660	The Fronde: French nobility opposes centralizing efforts of monarchy
1648	Peace of Westphalia confirms Dutch independence from Spain
1649	Execution of Charles I; beginning of the Interregnum in England
1653–1658	Cromwell rules England as military dictator
1659	Treaty of the Pyrenees forces Spain to cede extensive territories to France
1660	Restoration of the English monarchy: Charles II returns from exile
1661	Louis XIV enters into independent rule
ca 1663–1683	Colbert directs Louis XIV's mercantilist economic policy
1667	France invades Holland
1673	Test Act excludes Roman Catholics from public office in England
1685	Louis XIV revokes the Edict of Nantes
1685–1688	James II rules England, attempts to restore Roman Catholicism as state religion
1688	The Glorious Revolution establishes a constitutional monarchy in England under Mary and William III
1689	Enactment of the Bill of Rights in England
1701–1713	War of the Spanish Succession
1713	Peace of Utrecht ends French territorial acquisitions, expands the British Empire, completes decline of Spain as a great power

THE RISE OF ABSOLUTISM IN EASTERN EUROPE

1050–1300	Increasing economic development in eastern Europe encourages decline in serfdom
1054	Death of Prince Iaroslav the Wise, under whom the Kievan state reached its highest development
1054–1237	Kiev is divided into numerous territories ruled by competing princes
1237–1242	Mongol invasion and conquest of Russia
1252	Alexander Nevsky, prince of Moscow, recognizes Mongol overlordship
1327–1328	Suppression of the Tver revolt; Mongol khan recognizes Ivan I as great prince
1400–1650	The nobility reimposes serfdom in eastern Europe
ca 1480	Ivan III rejects Mongol overlordship and begins to use the title of tsar
1533–1584	Rule of Tsar Ivan IV (the Terrible): defeat of the khanates of Kazan and Astrakhan; subjugation of the boyar aristocracy
1598–1613	Time of Troubles in Russia
1613	Election of Michael Romanov as tsar: re-establishment of autocracy
1640–1688	Rule of Frederick William, the Great Elector, in Brandenburg-Prussia
1652	Patriarch Nikon's reforms split the Russian Orthodox church
1670–1671	Cossack revolt of Stenka Razin in Russia
1683	Siege of Vienna by the Ottoman Turks
1682–1725	Rule of Tsar Peter the Great
1683–1699	Habsburg conquest of Hungary and Transylvania
1703	Founding of St. Petersburg
1713–1740	Rule of King Frederick William I in Prussia

those of central Russia. Thus by 1300 serfdom had all but disappeared in eastern Europe. Peasants were able to bargain freely with their landlords and move about as they pleased.

After about 1300, however, as Europe's population and economy declined grievously, mainly because of the Black Death, noble landlords sought to solve their tough economic problems by more heavily exploiting the peasantry. In western Europe this attempt generally failed, but in the vast region east of the Elbe River in Germany the landlords were successful in degrading peasants. By 1500 eastern peasants were on their way to becoming serfs again.

Eastern lords triumphed because they made their kings and princes issue laws that restricted the right of their peasants to move to take advantage of better opportunities elsewhere. In Prussian territories by 1500, the law required that runaway peasants be hunted down and returned to their lords, and a runaway servant was to be nailed to a post by one ear and given a knife to cut himself loose. Moreover, lords steadily took more and more of their peasants' land and arbitrarily imposed heavier and heavier labor obligations. By the early 1500s, lords in many territories could command their peasants to work for them without pay for as many as six days a week.

Punishing Serfs This seventeenth-century illustration from Adam Olearius's *Travels in Moscovy* suggests what eastern serfdom really meant. The scene is eastern Poland. There, according to Olearius, a common command of the lord was, "Beat him till the skin falls from the flesh." Selections from Olearius's book are found in this chapter's Listening to the Past. *(Source: University of Illinois Library, Champaign)*

The gradual erosion of the peasantry's economic position was bound up with manipulation of the legal system. The local lord was also the local prosecutor, judge, and jailer. There were no independent royal officials to provide justice or uphold the common law.

Between 1500 and 1650, the social, legal, and economic conditions of peasants in eastern Europe continued to decline. In Poland, for example, nobles gained complete control over their peasants in 1574. In Russia the right of peasants to move from a given estate was abolished in 1603. In 1649 a new law code completed the legal re-establishment of permanent hereditary serfdom. The common fate of peasants in eastern Europe by the middle of the seventeenth century was serfdom.

The consolidation of serfdom between 1500 and 1650 was accompanied by the growth of estate agriculture, particularly in Poland and eastern Germany. In the sixteenth century, European economic expansion and population growth resumed after the great declines of the late Middle Ages. Eastern lords had powerful economic incentives to increase the production of their estates, and they did so. Generally, the estates were inefficient and technically backward, but they nevertheless succeeded in squeezing sizable surpluses out of the impoverished peasants. These surpluses were sold to foreign merchants, who exported them to the growing cities of wealthier western Europe.

The re-emergence of serfdom in eastern Europe in the early modern period was a momentous human development. Above all, it reflected the fact that eastern lords enjoyed much greater political power than their western counterparts. In the late Middle Ages, when much of eastern Europe was experiencing innumerable wars and general political chaos, the noble landlord class had greatly increased its political power at the expense of the ruling monarchs. Moreover, the western concept and reality of sovereignty, as embodied in a king who protected the interests of all his people, was not well developed in eastern Europe before 1650.

Finally, with the approval of weak kings, the landlords systematically undermined the medieval privileges of the towns and the power of the urban classes. For example, instead of selling their products to local merchants in the towns, as required in the Middle Ages, the landlords often sold directly to foreign capitalists. Eastern towns also lost their medieval right of refuge and were compelled to return runaways to their lords. The population of the towns and the urban middle classes declined greatly. This development both reflected and promoted the supremacy of noble landlords in most of eastern Europe in the sixteenth century.

Austria and the Ottoman Turks

The Habsburgs of Austria emerged from the Thirty Years' War (see pages 539–540) impoverished and exhausted. The effort to root out Protestantism in the German lands had failed utterly, and the authority of the Holy Roman Empire and its Habsburg emperors had declined almost to the vanishing point. Yet defeat in central Europe also opened new vistas. The Habsburg monarchs were forced to turn inward and eastward in an attempt to fuse their diverse holdings into a strong, unified state.

An important step in this direction had actually been taken in Bohemia during the Thirty Years' War. Protestantism had been strong among the Czechs, a Slavic people concentrated in Bohemia. In 1618 the Czech nobles who controlled the Bohemian Estates—the representative body of the different legal orders—had risen up against their Habsburg king. This revolt was crushed, and then the Czech nobility was totally restructured to ensure its loyalty to the monarchy. With the help of this new nobility, the Habsburgs established strong direct rule over reconquered Bohemia. The condition of the enserfed peasantry worsened. Protestantism was also stamped out, and religious unity began to emerge. The reorganization of Bohemia was a giant step toward royal absolutism.

After the Thirty Years' War, Ferdinand III (r. 1637–1657) centralized the government in the hereditary German-speaking provinces, most notably Austria, Styria, and the Tyrol. The king created a permanent standing army ready to put down any internal opposition. The Habsburg monarchy was then ready to turn toward the vast plains of Hungary, in opposition to the Ottoman Turks.

The Ottomans had come out of Anatolia, in present-day Turkey, to create one of history's greatest military empires. Their armies had almost captured Vienna in 1529, and for more than 150 years thereafter the Ottomans ruled all of the Balkan territories, almost all of Hungary, and part of southern Russia. In the late seventeenth century, under vigorous reforming leadership, the Ottoman Empire succeeded in marshaling its forces for one last mighty blow at Christian Europe. A huge Turkish army surrounded Vienna and laid siege to it in 1683. After holding out against great odds for two months, the city was relieved at the last minute, and the Ottomans were forced to retreat. As their Russian and Venetian allies attacked on other fronts, the Habsburgs conquered all of Hungary and Transylvania (part of present-day Romania) by 1699 (Map 17.3).

The Turkish wars and this great expansion strengthened the Habsburg army and promoted some sense of unity in the Habsburg lands. But Habsburg efforts to create a fully developed, highly centralized, absolutist state were only partly successful. The Habsburg state remained a composite of three separate and distinct territories: the old "hereditary provinces" of Austria, the kingdom of Bohemia, and the kingdom of Hungary. Each part had its own laws and political life, for the three noble-dominated Estates continued to exist, though with reduced powers. Above all, the Hungarian nobility effectively thwarted the full development of Habsburg absolutism. Time and again throughout the seventeenth century, Hungarian nobles rose in revolt against the attempts of Vienna to impose absolute rule. They never triumphed decisively, but neither were they ever crushed.

Hungarians resisted because many of them were Protestants, especially in the area long ruled by the more tolerant Turks, and they hated the heavy-handed attempts of the conquering Habsburgs to re-Catholicize everyone. Moreover, the lords of Hungary and even part of the Hungarian peasantry had become attached to a national ideal long before most of the other European peoples. They were determined to maintain as much independence and local control as possible. Thus when the Habsburgs were bogged down in the War of the Spanish Succession (see page 564), the Hungarians rose in one last patriotic rebellion under Prince Francis Rákóczy in 1703. Rákóczy and his forces were eventually defeated, but this time the Habsburgs had to accept many of the traditional privileges of the Hungarian aristocracy in return for Hungarian acceptance of hereditary Habsburg rule. Thus Hungary, unlike Austria or Bohemia,

MAP 17.3 Growth of Austria and Brandenburg-Prussia to 1748   Austria expanded to the southwest into Hungary and Transylvania at the expense of the Ottoman Empire. It was unable to hold the rich German province of Silesia, however, which was conquered by Brandenburg-Prussia.

never came close to being fully integrated into a centralized, absolute Habsburg state.

The Emergence of Prussia

As the status of east German peasants declined steadily after 1400, local princes lost political power, and a revitalized landed nobility became the undisputed ruling class. The Hohenzollern family, which ruled through different branches as the electors of Brandenburg and the dukes of Prussia, were little more than the largest landowners in a landlord society. Nothing suggested that the Hohenzollerns and their territories would ever play an important role in European or even German affairs.

Brandenburg was a helpless spectator in the Thirty Years' War, its territory alternately ravaged by Swedish and Habsburg armies. Yet the country's devastation prepared the way for Hohenzollern absolutism, because foreign armies dramatically weakened the political power of the Estates—the representative assemblies of the realm. The weakening of the Estates helped the very talented young elector Frederick William (r. 1640–1688), later known as the "Great Elector," to ride roughshod over traditional constitutional liberties and to take a giant step toward royal absolutism.

When Frederick William came to power in 1640, the twenty-year-old ruler was determined to unify his three quite separate provinces and to add to them by diplomacy and war. These provinces were Brandenburg itself, the area around Berlin; Prussia, inherited in 1618 when the junior branch of the Hohenzollern family died out; and scattered holdings along the Rhine in western Germany (see Map 17.3). Each province was inhabited by Germans; but each had its own Estates, dominated by the nobility and the landowning classes.

The struggle between the Great Elector and the provincial Estates was long, complicated, and intense. After the Thirty Years' War, the representatives of the nobility zealously reasserted the right of the Estates to vote taxes, a right the Swedish armies of occupation had simply ignored. Yet first in Brandenburg and then in Prussia, the Great Elector eventually had his way. To pay for the permanent standing army that he first established in 1660, Frederick William forced the Estates to accept the introduction of permanent taxation without consent. The soldiers doubled as tax collectors and policemen, becoming the core of the expanding state bureaucracy. The power of the Estates declined rapidly thereafter, and the Great Elector turned the screws of taxation. State revenue tripled and the size of the army leaped about tenfold during his reign.

In accounting for the Great Elector's fateful triumph, two factors appear central. First, as in the formation of every absolutist state, war was a decisive factor. The ongoing struggle between Sweden and Poland for control of the Baltic after 1648 and the wars of Louis XIV in western Europe created an atmosphere of permanent crisis. It was no accident that, except in commercially minded Holland, constitutionalism won out only in England, the only major country to escape devastating foreign invasions in the seventeenth century.

Second, the nobility had long dominated the government through the Estates but only for its own narrow self-interest. When, therefore, the Great Elector reconfirmed the nobility's freedom from taxation and its unlimited control over the peasants in 1653 and after, the nobility accepted a self-serving compromise. While Frederick William reduced the nobility's political power, the bulk of the Great Elector's new taxes fell on towns, and royal authority stopped at the landlords' gates.

By the time of his death in 1688, the Great Elector had created a single state out of scattered principalities. But his new creation was still small and fragile. It was Frederick William I, "the Soldiers' King" (r. 1713–1740), who truly established

A Prussian Giant Grenadier   Frederick William I wanted tall, handsome soldiers. He dressed them in tight, bright uniforms to distinguish them from the peasant population from which most soldiers came. He also ordered several portraits of his favorites from his court painter, J. C. Merk. Grenadiers wore the distinctive mitre cap instead of an ordinary hat so that they could hurl their heavy hand grenades unimpeded by a broad brim. *(Source: Copyright reserved to Her Majesty Queen Elizabeth II)*

Prussian absolutism and gave it its unique character. A dangerous psychoneurotic as well as a talented reformer, Frederick William I created the best army in Europe, for its size, and he infused military values into a whole society.

Frederick William's attachment to the army and military life was intensely emotional. He had, for example, a bizarre, almost pathological love for tall soldiers, whom he credited with superior strength and endurance. Like some fanatical modern-day basketball coach in search of a championship team, he sent his agents throughout both Prussia and all of Europe, tricking, buying, and kidnapping top recruits. Neighboring princes sent him their giants as gifts to win his gratitude. Prussian mothers told their sons: "Stop growing or the recruiting agents will get you."[7] Frederick William's love of the army was also based on a hardheaded conception of the struggle for power and a dog-eat-dog view of international politics. Throughout his long reign he never wavered in his conviction that the welfare of king and state depended above all else on the army.

As in France, the cult of military power provided the rationale for a great expansion of royal absolutism. As the ruthless king himself put it: "I must be served with life and limb, with house and wealth, with honour and conscience, everything must be committed except eternal salvation—that belongs to God, but all else is mine."[8] To make good these extraordinary demands, Frederick William created a strong and exceptionally honest bureaucracy, which administered the country and tried to develop it economically. The last traces of the parliamentary Estates and local self-government vanished.

The king's grab for power brought him into considerable conflict with the noble landowners, the Junkers. In the end the Prussian nobility responded to a combination of threats and opportunities and became the officer caste. By 1739 all but 5 of 245 officers with the rank of major or above were aristocrats. A new compromise had been worked out: the nobility imperiously commanded the peasantry in the army as well as on its estates.

Coarse and crude, penny-pinching and hard working, Frederick William achieved results. Above all, he built a first-rate army out of third-rate resources. Twelfth in Europe in population, Prussia had the fourth largest army by 1740, behind France, Russia, and Austria. Soldier for soldier, the Prussian army became the best in Europe, astonishing foreign observers with its precision,

skill, and discipline. Curiously, the king loved his "blue boys" so much that he hated to "spend" them. This most militaristic of kings was, paradoxically, almost always at peace.

Nevertheless, the Prussian people paid a heavy and lasting price for the obsessions of the royal drillmaster. Civil society became rigid and highly disciplined. Prussia became the "Sparta of the North"; unquestioning obedience was the highest virtue. As a Prussian minister later summed up, "To keep quiet is the first civic duty."[9] Thus the absolutism of Frederick William I combined with harsh peasant bondage and Junker tyranny to lay the foundations for probably the most militaristic country of modern times.

The Rise of Moscow

In the ninth century, the Vikings, those fearless warriors from Scandinavia, appeared in the lands of the eastern Slavs. Called "Varangians" in the old Russian chronicles, the Vikings were interested primarily in international trade. In order to increase and protect their international commerce, they declared themselves the rulers of the eastern Slavs. The Varangian ruler Oleg (r. 878–912) established his residence at Kiev. He and his successors ruled over a loosely united confederation of Slavic territories—the Kievan state—which reached its height under Prince Iaroslav the Wise (r. 1019–1054).

After Iaroslav's death in 1054, Kiev disintegrated into more and more competing units, each ruled by a prince. A given prince owned a certain number of farms or landed estates and had them worked directly by his people, mainly slaves, called *kholops* in Russian. Outside of these estates, the prince exercised limited authority in his principality. Excluding the clergy, two kinds of people lived there: the noble boyars and the commoner peasants.

Like the Germans and the Italians, the eastern Slavs might have emerged from the Middle Ages weak and politically divided had it not been for the Mongol conquest of the Kievan state. Wild nomadic tribes from present-day Mongolia, the Mongols were temporarily unified in the thirteenth century by Jenghiz Khan (1162–1227), one of history's greatest conquerors. In five years his armies subdued all of China. His successors then wheeled westward, smashing everything in their path and reaching the plains of Hungary victorious before they pulled back in 1242. The Mongol army—the

Golden Horde—was savage in the extreme, often slaughtering entire populations of cities before burning them to the ground.

Having devastated and conquered, the Mongols ruled the eastern Slavs for more than two hundred years. They forced all the bickering Slavic princes to submit to their rule and to give them tribute and slaves. If the conquered peoples rebelled, the Mongols were quick to punish with death and destruction. Thus the Mongols unified the eastern Slavs, for the Mongol khan was acknowledged by all as the supreme ruler.

Beginning with Alexander Nevsky in 1252, the previously insignificant princes of Moscow became particularly adept at serving the Mongols. They loyally put down popular uprisings and collected the khan's harsh taxes. By way of reward, the princes of Moscow emerged as hereditary great princes. Eventually the Muscovite princes were able to destroy their princely rivals and even to replace the khan as supreme ruler.

One of the more important Muscovite princes was Ivan I (r. 1328–1341), popularly known as "Ivan the Moneybag." Extremely stingy, Ivan I built up a large personal fortune and increased his influence by loaning money to less frugal princes to pay their Mongol taxes. Ivan's most serious rival was the prince of Tver, who joined his people in 1327 in a revolt against Mongol oppression. Appointed commander of a large Russian-Mongol army, Ivan laid waste to Tver and its lands. For this proof of devotion, the Mongols made Ivan the general tax collector for all the Slavic lands they had subjugated and named him great prince. Ivan also convinced the metropolitan of Kiev, the leading churchman of all eastern Slavs, to settle in Moscow. Ivan I thus gained greater prestige.

In the next hundred-odd years, the great princes of Moscow significantly increased their holdings. Then, in the reign of Ivan III (r. 1462–1505), the process of gathering in the territories around Moscow was largely completed. Of the principalities that Ivan III purchased and conquered, Novgorod with its lands extending almost to the Baltic Sea was most crucial (Map 17.4). Thus the princes of Moscow defeated all rivals to win complete princely authority.

Not only was the prince of Moscow the *unique* ruler, he was the *absolute* ruler, the autocrat, the *tsar*—the Slavic contraction for "caesar," with all its connotations. This imperious conception of absolute power was powerfully reinforced by two de-

velopments. First, about 1480 Ivan III stopped acknowledging the khan as his supreme ruler. There is good evidence to suggest that Ivan and his successors saw themselves as khans. Certainly they assimilated the Mongol concept of kingship as the exercise of unrestrained and unpredictable power.

Second, after the fall of Constantinople to the Turks in 1453, the tsars saw themselves as the heirs of both the caesars and Orthodox Christianity, the one true faith. All the other kings of Europe were heretics: only the tsars were rightful and holy rulers. This idea was promoted by Orthodox churchmen, who spoke of "holy Russia" as the "Third Rome." Ivan's marriage to the daughter of the last Byzantine emperor further enhanced the aura of an imperial inheritance for Moscow. Worthy successor to the mighty khan and the true Christian emperor, the Muscovite tsar was a king claiming unrestricted power as his God-given right. The Mongol inheritance weighed heavily on Russia.

As peasants had begun losing their freedom of movement in the fifteenth century, so had the noble boyars begun losing power and influence. For example, when Ivan III conquered the principality of Novgorod in the 1480s, he confiscated fully 80 percent of the land, executing the previous owners or resettling them nearer Moscow. He then kept more than half of the confiscated land for himself and distributed the remainder to members of a newly emerging service nobility, who held the tsar's land on the explicit condition that they serve in the tsar's army. Moreover, Ivan III began to require boyars outside Novgorod to serve him if they wished to retain their lands.

The rise of the new service nobility accelerated under Ivan IV (r. 1533–1584), the famous "Ivan the Terrible." Having ascended the throne at age three, Ivan suffered insults and neglect at the hands of the haughty boyars after his mother died. But at age sixteen he suddenly pushed aside his hated boyar advisers and crowned himself. Selecting the beautiful and kind Anastasia of the popular Romanov family for his wife and queen, the young tsar soon declared war on the remnants of Mongol power. He defeated the faltering khanates of Kazan and Astrakhan between 1552 and 1556, adding vast new territories to Russia. In the course of these wars, Ivan virtually abolished the old distinction between hereditary boyar private property and land granted temporarily for service. All nobles, old and new, had to serve the tsar in order to hold any land.

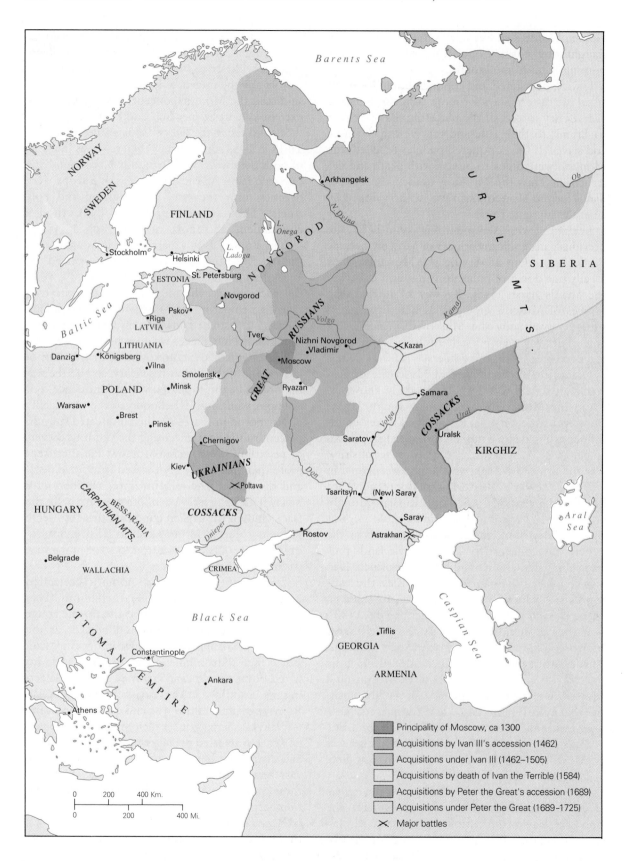

Principality of Moscow, ca 1300

Acquisitions by Ivan III's accession (1462)

Acquisitions under Ivan III (1462–1505)

Acquisitions by death of Ivan the Terrible (1584)

Acquisitions by Peter the Great's accession (1689)

Acquisitions under Peter the Great (1689–1725)

✕ Major battles

0   200   400 Km.

0   200   400 Mi.

Ivan the Terrible   Ivan IV, the first to take the title Tsar of Russia, executed many Muscovite boyars and their peasants and servants. His control of all land, trade, and industry restricted Russian social and economic development. *(Source: National Museum, Copenhagen, Denmark)*

The transformation of the entire nobility into a service nobility was completed in the second part of Ivan the Terrible's reign. In 1557 Ivan turned westward, and for the next twenty-five years Muscovy waged an exhausting, unsuccessful war primarily with the large Polish-Lithuanian state, which controlled not only Poland but much of the Ukraine in the sixteenth century. Quarreling with the boyars over the war and blaming them for the sudden death of his beloved Anastasia in 1560, the increasingly cruel and demented Ivan turned to strike down all who stood in his way.

Above all, he reduced the ancient Muscovite boyar families with a reign of terror. Leading boyars, their relatives, and even their peasants were executed en masse by a special corps of unquestioning servants. Dressed in black and riding black horses, they were forerunners of the modern dictator's secret police. Large estates were confiscated, broken up, and reapportioned to the lower service nobility, which was totally dependent on the autocrat.

Ivan also took giant strides toward making all commoners servants of the tsar. As the service nobles demanded more from their peasants, more and more peasants fled toward the wild, recently conquered territories to the east and south. There they formed free groups and outlaw armies known as Cossacks. The Cossacks maintained a precarious independence beyond the reach of the oppressive landholders and the tsar's hated officials. The solution to this problem was to complete the tying of the peasants to the land, making them serfs perpetually bound to serve the noble landholders, who were bound in turn to serve the tsar.

In the time of Ivan the Terrible, urban traders and artisans were also bound to their towns and

MAP 17.4 Expansion of Russia to 1725   After the disintegration of the Kievan state and the Mongol conquest, the princes of Moscow and their descendants gradually extended their rule over an enormous territory.

jobs so that the tsar could tax them more heavily. The urban classes had no security in their work or property and remained weak and divided. Even the wealthiest merchants were basically dependent agents of the tsar.

As has so often occurred in Russia, the death of an iron-fisted tyrant—in this case, Ivan the Terrible in 1584—ushered in an era of confusion and violent struggles for power. Events were particularly chaotic after Ivan's son Theodore died in 1598 without an heir. The years 1598 to 1613 are aptly called the Time of Troubles.

Close relatives of the deceased tsar intrigued against and murdered each other, alternately fighting and welcoming the invading Swedes and Poles, who even occupied Moscow. Most serious for the cause of autocracy, there was a great social upheaval as Cossacks marched northward, rallying peasants and slaughtering nobles and officials. This social explosion from below, which combined with a belated surge of patriotic opposition to the Polish invaders, brought the nobles to their senses. In 1613 they elected Ivan's sixteen-year-old grand-nephew, Michael Romanov, the new hereditary tsar and rallied around him in the face of common internal and external threats.

Michael's reign saw the gradual re-establishment of tsarist autocracy (see Listening to the Past). The recently rebellious peasants were ground down further, while Ivan's heavy military obligations on the nobility were relaxed considerably, a trend that continued after his death. The result was a second round of mass upheaval and protest.

In the mid-seventeenth century, the unity of the Russian Orthodox church was torn apart by the religious reforms of the patriarch Nikon, a dogmatic purist who wished to bring "corrupted" Russian practices of worship into line with the Greek Orthodox model. The self-serving church hierarchy quickly went along, but the intensely religious common people resisted. Great numbers left the church and formed illegal communities of "Old Believers," who were hunted down and persecuted. After the great split, the Russian masses were alienated from the established church, which became totally dependent on the state for its authority.

Again the Cossacks revolted against the state, which was doggedly trying to catch up with them on the frontiers and reduce them to serfdom. Under the leadership of Stenka Razin they moved up the Volga River in 1670 and 1671, attracting a great undisciplined army of peasants, murdering landlords, and high church officials, and proclaiming freedom from oppression. In response to this rebellion, finally defeated by the government, the thoroughly scared upper classes tightened the screws of serfdom even further.

The Reforms of Peter the Great

It is now possible to understand the reforms of Peter the Great (r. 1682–1725) and his kind of monarchial absolutism. Contrary to some historians' assertions, Peter was interested primarily in military power and not in some grandiose westernization plan. A giant for his time, at six feet seven inches, and possessing enormous energy and determination, Peter was determined to increase Russia's power and to continue the territorial expansion that had gained a large part of the Ukraine in 1667 and had completed the conquest of Siberia in the seventeenth century. Little wonder that the forty-three years of Peter's rule knew only one year of peace.

When Peter took full control in 1689, the heart of his part-time army still consisted of cavalry made up of boyars and service nobility. The Russian army was lagging behind the professional standing armies being formed in Europe in the seventeenth century. The core of such armies was a highly disciplined infantry—an infantry that fired and refired rifles as it fearlessly advanced, before charging with fixed bayonets. Such a large, permanent army was enormously expensive. Given the desire to conquer more territory, Peter's military problem was serious.

Peter's solution was, in essence, to tighten up Muscovy's old service system and really make it work. He put the nobility back in harness with a vengeance. Every nobleman, great or small, was once again required to serve in the army or in the civil administration—for life. Since a more modern army and government required skilled technicians and experts, Peter created schools and even universities. One of his most hated reforms required five years of compulsory education away from home for every young nobleman. Peter established a merit-based military-civilian bureaucracy in which some people of non-noble origin rose to high positions. He also searched out talented foreigners—twice in his reign he went abroad to study and observe—and placed them in his service. These measures combined to make the army and government more powerful and efficient.

Peter also greatly increased the service requirements of the commoners. He established a regular standing army of more than 200,000 soldiers. In addition, special forces of Cossacks and foreigners numbered more than 100,000. The departure of a drafted peasant boy was regarded by his family and village as almost like a funeral, as indeed it was, since the recruit was drafted for life. The peasantry also served with its taxes, which increased threefold during Peter's reign. Serfs were arbitrarily assigned to work in the growing number of factories and mines.

The constant warfare of Peter's reign consumed from 80 to 85 percent of all revenues but brought only modest territorial expansion. Yet after initial losses in the Great Northern War with Sweden, which lasted from 1700 to 1721, Peter's new war machine crushed Sweden's smaller army in the Ukraine at Poltava in 1709, one of the most significant battles in Russian history. Sweden never really regained the offensive. Annexing Estonia and much of present-day Latvia (see Map 17.4), Russia became the dominant power on the Baltic Sea and very much a European Great Power. If victory or defeat is the ultimate historical criterion, Peter's reforms were a success.

There were other important consequences of Peter's reign. Because of his feverish desire to use modern technology to strengthen the army, many Westerners and Western ideas flowed into Russia for the first time. A new class of educated Russians began to emerge. At the same time, vast numbers of Russians, especially among the poor and weak, hated Peter's massive changes. The split between the enserfed peasantry and the educated nobility thus widened, even though all were caught up in the endless demands of the sovereign.

A new idea of state interest, distinct from the tsar's personal interests, began to take hold. Peter claimed to act for the common good, and he attached explanations to his decrees in an attempt to gain the support of the populace. Yet, as before, the tsar alone decided what the common good was.

In sum, Peter built on the service obligations of old Muscovy. His monarchial absolutism was truly the culmination of the long development of a unique Russian civilization. Yet the creation of a more modern army and state introduced much that was new and Western to that civilization. This development paved the way for Russia to move much closer to the European mainstream in its thought and institutions during the Enlightenment under Catherine the Great.

Absolutism and the Baroque

The rise of royal absolutism in eastern Europe had major cultural consequences. Inspired in part by Louis XIV of France, the great and not-so-great rulers called on the artistic talent of the age to glorify their power and magnificence. This exaltation of despotic rule was particularly striking in architecture and city planning.

As soaring Gothic cathedrals expressed the idealized spirit of the High Middle Ages, so dramatic baroque palaces symbolized the age of absolutist power. By 1700 palace building had become an obsession for the rulers of central and eastern Europe. Their baroque palaces were clearly intended to overawe the people with the monarch's strength. One such palace was Schönbrunn, an enormous Viennese Versailles begun in 1695 by Emperor Leopold I to celebrate Austrian military victories and Habsburg might.

Petty princes also contributed mightily to the mania of palace building. The not-very-important elector-archbishop of Mainz, the ruling prince of that city, confessed apologetically that "building is a craze which costs much, but every fool likes his own hat."[10] The archbishop of Mainz's own "hat" was an architectural gem, like that of another churchly ruler, the prince-bishop of Würzburg. In central and eastern Europe, the favorite noble servants of royalty became extremely rich and powerful, and they, too, built grandiose palaces in the capital cities. These palaces were in part an extension of the monarch, for they surpassed the buildings of less favored nobles.

Palaces like Schönbrunn and Würzburg were magnificent examples of the baroque style. They expressed the baroque delight in bold, sweeping statements intended to provide a dramatic emotional experience. To create this experience, baroque masters dissolved the traditional artistic frontiers: the architect permitted the painter and the artisan to cover the undulating surfaces with wildly colorful paintings, graceful sculptures, and fanciful carvings. Space was used in a highly original way, to blend everything together in a total environment.

Not content with fashioning ostentatious palaces, absolute monarchs and baroque architects remodeled existing capital cities or built new ones to

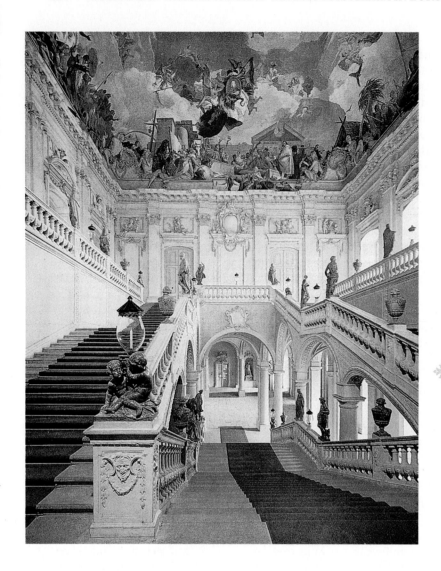

❄ **Würzburg, the Prince-Bishop's Palace** The baroque style brought architects, painters, and sculptors together in harmonious, even playful partnership. This magnificent monumental staircase, designed by Johann Balthasar Neumann in 1735, merges into the vibrant ceiling frescoes by Giovanni Battista Tiepolo. A man is stepping out of the picture, and a painted dog resembles a marble statue. *(Source: Erich Lessing/Art Resource, NY)*

reflect royal magnificence and the centralization of political power. Karlsruhe, founded in 1715 as the capital city of a small German principality, is one extreme example. There, broad, straight avenues radiated out from the palace, so that all roads—like all power—were focused on the ruler. More typically, the monarch's architects added new urban areas alongside the old city, and these areas became the real heart of the expanding capital.

The distinctive features of the new additions were their broad avenues, their imposing government buildings, and their rigorous mathematical layout. Along major thoroughfares the nobles built elaborate townhouses; stables and servants' quarters were built on the alleys behind. Under arcades along the avenues appeared smart and expensive shops, the first department stores, with plate-glass windows and fancy displays. The additions brought reckless speed to the European city. Whereas everyone had walked through the narrow, twisting streets of the medieval town, the high and mighty raced down the broad boulevards in elegant carriages. A social gap opened between the wealthy riders and the gaping, dodging pedestrians.

No city illustrates better than St. Petersburg the close ties among politics, architecture, and urban development in this period. In 1702 Peter the Great's armies seized a desolate Swedish fortress on one of the water-logged islands at the mouth of the Neva River on the Baltic Sea. Within a year the tsar had decided to build a new city there and to make it, rather than ancient Moscow, his capital. The land was swampy and inhospitable. But for Peter it was a future metropolis gloriously bearing his name. After the decisive Russian victory at Poltava in 1709, he moved into high gear. In one imperious decree after another, he ordered his people to build a new city, his "window on Europe."

Peter believed that it would be easier to reform the country militarily and administratively from such a city than from Moscow, and his political goals were reflected in his architectural ideas. First Peter wanted a comfortable, "modern" city. Modernity meant broad, straight, stone-paved avenues, houses built in a uniform line, large parks, canals for drainage, stone bridges, and street lighting. Second, all building had to conform strictly to detailed architectural regulations set down by the government. Finally, each social group—the nobility, the merchants, the artisans, and so on—was to live in a certain section of town. In short, the city

and its population were to conform to a carefully defined urban plan of the baroque type.

Peter used the methods of Russian autocracy to build his modern capital. The creation of St. Petersburg was just one of the heavy obligations he dictatorially imposed on all social groups in Russia. The peasants bore the heaviest burdens. Just as the government drafted peasants for the army, it also drafted from 25,000 to 40,000 men each summer to labor in St. Petersburg for three months, without pay. Peasants hated forced labor in the capital, and each year from one-fourth to one-third of those sent risked brutal punishment and ran away. Many peasant construction workers died each summer from hunger, sickness, and accidents. Beautiful St. Petersburg was built on the shoveling, carting, and paving of a mass of conscripted serfs.

Peter also drafted more privileged groups to his city, but on a permanent basis. Nobles were sum-

St. Petersburg, ca 1760   Rastrelli's remodeled Winter Palace, which housed the royal family until the Russian Revolution of 1917, stands on the left along the Neva River. The Navy Office with its golden spire and other government office buildings are nearby and across the river. Russia became a naval power and St. Petersburg a great port. *(Source: Michael Holford)*

marily ordered to build costly stone houses and palaces in St. Petersburg and to live in them most of the year. Merchants and artisans were also commanded to settle and build in St. Petersburg. These nobles and merchants were then required to pay for the city's avenues, parks, canals, embankments, pilings, and bridges. The building of St. Petersburg was, in truth, an enormous direct tax levied on the wealthy, who in turn forced the peasantry to do most of the work. No wonder so many Russians hated Peter's new city.

Yet the tsar had his way. By the time of his death in 1725, there were at least six thousand houses and numerous impressive government buildings in St. Petersburg. Under the remarkable women who ruled Russia throughout most of the eighteenth century, St. Petersburg blossomed as a majestic and well-organized city, at least in its wealthy showpiece sections. Chief architect Bartolomeo Rastrelli combined Italian and Russian traditions into a unique, wildly colorful St. Petersburg style in many noble palaces and government buildings. All the while St. Petersburg grew rapidly, and its almost 300,000 inhabitants in 1782 made it one of the world's largest cities. A magnificent and harmonious royal city, St. Petersburg proclaimed the power of Russia's rulers and the creative potential of the absolutist state.

❖ ENGLAND: THE TRIUMPH OF CONSTITUTIONAL MONARCHY

In 1588 Queen Elizabeth I of England exercised great personal power, but by 1689 the power of the English monarchy was severely limited. Change in England was anything but orderly. Seventeenth-century England displayed little political stability. It executed one king, experienced a bloody civil war, experimented with military dictatorship, then restored the son of the murdered king, and finally, after a bloodless revolution, established constitutional monarchy. Political stability came only in the 1690s. Yet out of this tumultuous century England built the foundations for a strong and enduring constitutional monarchy.

In the middle years of the seventeenth century, the problem of sovereignty was vigorously debated. In *Leviathan,* the English philosopher and political theorist Thomas Hobbes (1588–1679) maintained that sovereignty is ultimately derived from the people, who transfer it to the monarchy by implicit contract. The power of the ruler is absolute, Hobbes said, but kings do not hold their power by divine right. This abstract theory pleased no one in the seventeenth century, but it did stimulate fruitful thinking about England's great seventeenth-century problem—the problem of order and political power.

The Decline of Absolutism in England (1603–1660)

Elizabeth I's extraordinary success was the result of her political shrewdness and flexibility, her careful management of finances, her wise selection of ministers, her clever manipulation of Parliament, and her sense of royal dignity and devotion to hard work. After her Scottish cousin James Stuart succeeded her as James I (r. 1603–1625), Elizabeth's strengths seemed even greater.

King James was learned and, with thirty-five years' experience as king of Scotland, politically shrewd. But he was not as interested in displaying the majesty and mystique of monarchy as Elizabeth had been, and he lacked the common touch. Moreover, James was a dogmatic proponent of the theory of divine right of kings. "There are no privileges and immunities," said James, "which can stand against a divinely appointed King." This typically absolutist notion implied total royal jurisdiction over the liberties, persons, and properties of English men and women. Such a view ran directly counter to many long-standing English ideas, including the belief that a person's property could not be taken away without due process of law. And in the House of Commons the English had a strong representative body to question these absolutist pretensions.

The House of Commons guarded the state's pocketbook, and James and later Stuart kings badly needed to open that pocketbook. James I looked on all revenues as a windfall to be squandered on a lavish court and favorite courtiers. The extravagance displayed in James's court, as well as the public flaunting of his male lovers, weakened respect for the monarchy. These actions also stimulated the knights and burgesses who sat in the House of Commons at Westminster to press for a thorough discussion of royal expenditures, religious reform, and foreign affairs. In short, the Commons aspired to sovereignty—the ultimate political power in the realm.

During the reigns of James I and his son Charles I (r. 1625–1649) the English House of Commons was very different from the assembly that Henry VIII had manipulated into passing his Reformation legislation. The class that dominated the Commons during the Stuarts' reign wanted political power corresponding to its economic strength. A social revolution had brought about this change. The dissolution of the monasteries and the sale of monastic land had enriched many people. Agricultural techniques like the draining of wasteland had improved the land and increased its yield. In the seventeenth century old manorial common land was enclosed and profitably turned into sheep runs. Many invested in commercial ventures at home, such as the expanding cloth industry, and in foreign trade. Many also made prudent marriages. These developments increased social mobility. The typical pattern was for the commercially successful to set themselves up as country gentry. This elite group possessed a far greater proportion of the land and of the nation's wealth in 1640 than in 1540. Increased wealth resulted in a better-educated and more articulate House of Commons.

In England, unlike France, no social stigma was attached to paying taxes. Members of the House of Commons were willing to tax themselves provided they had some say in state spending and state policies. The Stuart kings, however, considered such ambitions intolerable presumption and a threat to their divine-right prerogative. Consequently, at every Parliament between 1603 and 1640, bitter squabbles erupted between Crown and Commons. Like the Great Elector in Prussia, Charles I tried to govern without Parliament (1629–1640) and to finance his government by arbitrary levies. And as in Prussia these absolutist measures brought intense political conflict.

Religion was another source of conflict. In the early seventeenth century, increasing numbers of English people felt dissatisfied with the Church of England established by Henry VIII and reformed by Elizabeth. Many Puritans (see page 535) remained committed to "purifying" the Anglican church of Roman Catholic elements—elaborate vestments and ceremonies, the position of the altar in the church, even the giving and wearing of wedding rings.

Many Puritans were also attracted by the socioeconomic implications of John Calvin's theology. Calvinism emphasized hard work, sobriety, thrift, competition, and postponement of pleasure, and it tended to link sin and poverty with weakness and moral corruption. These attitudes, which have frequently been called the "Protestant ethic," "middle-class ethic," or "capitalist ethic," fit in precisely with the economic approaches and practices of many (successful) business people and farmers. These "Protestant virtues" represented the prevailing values of members of the House of Commons.

James I and Charles I both gave the impression of being highly sympathetic to Roman Catholicism. Charles supported the policies of Archbishop of Canterbury William Laud (1573–1645), who tried to impose elaborate ritual and rich ceremonial on all churches. People believed that the country was being led back to Roman Catholicism. In 1637 Laud attempted to impose two new elements on the church organization in Scotland: a new prayer book, modeled on the Anglican Book of Common Prayer, and bishoprics, which the Presbyterian Scots firmly rejected. The Scots revolted. To finance an army to put down the Scots, King Charles was compelled to summon Parliament in November 1640. It was a fatal decision.

For eleven years Charles I had ruled without Parliament, financing his government through extraordinary stopgap levies considered illegal by most English people. Most members of Parliament believed that such taxation without consent amounted to absolutist despotism. Thus they were not willing to trust the king with an army. Accordingly, the Parliament summoned in November 1640 (commonly called the Long Parliament because it sat from 1640 to 1660) enacted legislation that limited the power of the monarch and made arbitrary government impossible.

In 1641 the Commons passed the Triennial Act, which compelled the king to summon Parliament every three years. The Commons impeached Archbishop Laud and abolished the House of Lords and the ecclesiastical Court of High Commission. King Charles reluctantly accepted these measures. But understanding and peace were not achieved, and an uprising in Ireland precipitated civil war.

Ever since Henry II had conquered Ireland in 1171, English governors had mercilessly ruled the land, and English landlords had ruthlessly exploited the Irish people. The English Reformation had made a bad situation worse: because the Irish remained Catholic, religious differences united with economic and political oppression. Without an army, Charles I could neither come to terms with the Scots nor put down the Irish rebellion, and the Long Parliament remained unwilling to place an army under a king it did not trust. Charles thus recruited an army drawn from the nobility and the nobility's cavalry staff, the rural gentry, and mercenaries. The parliamentary army that rose in opposition was composed of the militia of the city of London, country squires with business connections, and men with a firm belief that serving was their spiritual duty.

The English civil war (1642–1649) tested whether ultimate political power in England was to reside in the king or in Parliament. The civil war did not resolve that problem, although it ended in 1649 with the execution of King Charles on the charge of high treason and thus dealt a severe blow to the theory of divine-right, absolute monarchy in England. Kingship was abolished in England, and a *commonwealth,* or republican form of government, was proclaimed.

In fact, the army that had defeated the royal forces controlled the government, and Oliver Cromwell controlled the army. Indeed, the period from 1649 to 1660, known as the Interregnum because it separated two monarchial periods, was a transitional time of military dictatorship, and for most of that time Cromwell was head of state.

Oliver Cromwell (1599–1658) came from the country gentry, the class that dominated the House of Commons in the early seventeenth century. He was a member of the Long Parliament. Cromwell rose in the parliamentary army and achieved nationwide fame by infusing the army with his Puritan convictions and molding it into the highly effective military machine, called the New Model Army, that defeated the royalist forces. The army prepared a constitution, the Instrument of Government (1653), that invested executive power in a lord protector (Cromwell) and a council of state. The instrument provided for triennial parliaments and gave Parliament the sole power to raise taxes. But after repeated disputes, Cromwell tore up the document and proclaimed quasi-martial law.

On the issue of religion, Cromwell favored broad toleration, and the Instrument of Government gave all Christians, except Roman Catholics, the right to practice their faith. Cromwell welcomed the immigration of Jews, because of their skills, and they began to return to England after four centuries of absence. As for Irish Catholicism, Cromwell identified it with sedition. In 1649 he crushed rebellion in Ireland with merciless savagery, leaving a legacy of Irish hatred for England. He also rigorously censored the press, forbade sports, and kept the theaters closed in England.

Cromwell pursued mercantilist economic policies similar to those that Colbert established in France. He enforced a navigation act requiring that English goods be transported on English ships. The navigation act was a great boost to the development of an English merchant marine and brought about a short but successful war with the commercially threatened Dutch.

❊ **Periodical Sheet on the English Civil War** Single sheets or broadsides spread the positions of the opposing sides to the nonliterate public. *Mercurius Rusticus,* intended for country people, conveyed the royalist argument. (*Source: The British Library*)

Military government collapsed when Cromwell died in 1658. Fed up with military rule, the English longed for a return to civilian government, restoration of the common law, and social and religious stability. Moreover, the strain of creating a community of puritanical saints proved too psychologically exhausting. Government by military dictatorship was an experiment in absolutism that the English never forgot or repeated. By 1660 they were ready to try a restoration of monarchy.

The Restoration of the English Monarchy

The Restoration of 1660 re-established the monarchy in the person of Charles II (r. 1660–1685), eldest son of Charles I. At the same time both houses of Parliament were also restored, together with the established Anglican church. The Restoration failed to resolve two serious problems. What was to be the attitude of the state toward Puritans, Catholics, and dissenters from the established church? And what was to be the constitutional relationship between the king and Parliament?

Charles II, a relaxed, easygoing, and sensual man, was basically not much interested in religious issues. But the new members of Parliament were, and they proceeded to enact a body of laws that sought to compel religious uniformity. Those who refused to receive the sacrament of the Church of England could not vote, hold public office, preach, teach, attend the universities, or even assemble for meetings, according to the Test Act of 1673.

In politics, Charles II was at first determined to get along with Parliament and share power with it. His method for doing so had profound importance for later constitutional development. The king appointed a council of five men who served both as his major advisers and as members of Parliament, thus acting as liaison agents between the executive and the legislature. It gradually came to be accepted that the council of five was answerable in Parliament for the decisions of the king.

Harmony between the Crown and Parliament rested on the understanding that Charles would summon Parliament frequently and Parliament would vote him sufficient revenues. However, although Parliament believed that Charles should have large powers, it did not grant him an adequate income. Accordingly, in 1670 Charles entered into a secret agreement with Louis XIV. The French king would give Charles £200,000 annually. In return Charles would relax the laws against

Catholics, gradually re-Catholicize England, support French policy against the Dutch, and convert to Catholicism himself.

When the details of this secret treaty leaked out, a wave of anti-Catholic fear swept England. Charles had produced only bastards, and therefore it appeared that his brother and heir, James, duke of York, who had publicly acknowledged his Catholicism, would inaugurate a Catholic dynasty. The combination of hatred for the French absolutism embodied in Louis XIV and hostility to Roman Catholicism led the Commons to pass an exclusion bill denying the succession to a Roman Catholic. But Charles quickly dissolved Parliament, and the bill never became law.

James II (r. 1685–1688) succeeded his brother. Almost at once the worst English anti-Catholic fears, already aroused by Louis XIV's recent revocation of the Edict of Nantes, were realized. In direct violation of the Test Act, James appointed Roman Catholics to positions in the army, the universities, and local government. The king was suspending the law at will and appeared to be reviving the absolutism of his father (Charles I) and grandfather (James I). He went further. Attempting to broaden his base of support with Protestant dissenters and nonconformists, James issued a declaration of indulgence granting religious freedom to all.

Two events gave the signals for revolution. First, seven bishops of the Church of England petitioned the king that they not be forced to read the declaration of indulgence because of their belief that it was an illegal act. They were imprisoned in the Tower of London but subsequently acquitted amid great public enthusiasm. Second, in June 1688 James's second wife produced a male heir. A Catholic dynasty seemed assured. The fear of a Roman Catholic monarchy, supported by France and ruling outside the law, prompted a group of eminent persons to offer the English throne to James's Protestant daughter, Mary, and her Dutch husband, Prince William of Orange. In December 1688 James II, his queen, and their infant son fled to France and became pensioners of Louis XIV. Early in 1689, William and Mary were crowned king and queen of England.

The English call the events of 1688 to 1689 the "Glorious Revolution." The revolution was indeed glorious in the sense that it replaced one king with another with a minimum of bloodshed. It also represented the destruction, once and for all, of the idea of divine-right absolutism in England. William and Mary accepted the English throne from Parliament and in so doing explicitly recognized the supremacy of Parliament.

The men who brought about the revolution quickly framed their intentions in the Bill of Rights, the cornerstone of the modern British constitution. The basic principles of the Bill of Rights were formulated in direct response to Stuart absolutism. Law was to be made in Parliament; once made, it could not be suspended by the Crown. Parliament had to be called at least every three years. Both elections to and debate in Parliament were to be free, in the sense that the Crown was not to interfere in them. Judges would hold their offices "during good behavior," a provision that assured judicial independence.

In striking contrast to the states of continental Europe, there was to be no standing army that could be used against the English population in peacetime. Moreover, the Bill of Rights granted Protestants the right to possess firearms. Additional legislation granted freedom of worship to Protestant dissenters and nonconformists and required that the English monarch always be Protestant.

The Glorious Revolution found its best defense in John Locke's *Second Treatise of Civil Government* (1690). The political philosopher Locke (1632–1704) maintained that people set up civil governments in order to protect life, liberty, and property. A government that oversteps its proper function —protecting the natural rights of life, liberty, and property—becomes a tyranny. (By "natural" rights, Locke meant rights basic to all men because all have the ability to reason.) Under a tyrannical government, the people have the natural right to rebellion. Recognizing the close relationship between economic and political freedom, Locke linked economic liberty and private property with political freedom.

Locke served as the great spokesman for the liberal English revolution of 1688 to 1689 and for representative government. His idea, inherited from ancient Greece and Rome, that there are natural or universal rights equally valid for all peoples and societies, played a powerful role in eighteenth-century Enlightenment thought. His ideas on liberty and tyranny were especially popular in colonial America.

The events of 1688 to 1689 did not constitute a *democratic* revolution. The revolution formalized

Parliament's great power, and Parliament represented the upper classes. The great majority of English people had little say in their government. The English revolution established a constitutional monarchy; it also inaugurated an age of aristocratic government.

In the course of the eighteenth century, the cabinet system of government evolved out of Charles II's old council-of-five system. The term *cabinet* derives from the small private room in which English rulers consulted their chief ministers. In a cabinet system, the leading ministers formulate common policy and conduct the business of the country. During the administration of one royal minister, Sir Robert Walpole, who led the cabinet from 1721 to 1742, the idea developed that the cabinet was responsible to the House of Commons. Walpole enjoyed the favor of the monarchy and of the House of Commons and came to be called the king's first, or "prime," minister. In the English cabinet system, both legislative and executive power are held by the leading ministers, who form the government.

 ## THE DUTCH REPUBLIC IN THE SEVENTEENTH CENTURY

In the late sixteenth century, the seven northern provinces of the Netherlands, of which Holland and Zeeland were the most prosperous, had thrown off Spanish domination (see pages 534–539). The seventeenth century then witnessed an unparalleled flowering of Dutch scientific, artistic, and literary achievement. In this period, often called the golden age of the Netherlands, Dutch ideas and attitudes played a profound role in shaping a new and modern world-view.

The Republic of the United Provinces of the Netherlands represents a variation in the development of the modern constitutional state. Within each province an oligarchy of wealthy merchants called regents handled domestic affairs in the local Estates. The provincial Estates held virtually all the power. A federal assembly, or States General, handled matters of foreign affairs, such as war, but all issues had to be referred back to the local Estates for approval. The regents in each province jealously guarded local independence and resisted efforts at centralization. Nevertheless, Holland, which had the largest navy and the most wealth, dominated the republic and the States General.

The government of the United Provinces conforms to none of the standard categories of seventeenth-century political organization. The Dutch were not monarchial but fiercely republican. The government was controlled by wealthy merchants and financiers. Though rich, their values were not aristocratic but strongly middle class. The political success of the Dutch rested on the phenomenal commercial prosperity of the Netherlands. The moral and ethical bases of that commercial wealth were thrift, hard work, and simplicity in living.

John Calvin had written, "From where do the merchant's profits come except from his own diligence and industry." This attitude undoubtedly encouraged a sturdy people who had waged a centuries-old struggle against the sea. Louis XIV's hatred of the Dutch was proverbial. They represented all that he despised—middle-class values, religious toleration, and independent political institutions.

Alone of all European peoples in the seventeenth century, the Dutch practiced religious toleration. Peoples of all faiths were welcome within their borders. Jews enjoyed a level of acceptance and absorption in Dutch business and general culture unique in early modern Europe. It is a testimony to the urbanity of Dutch society that in a century when patriotism was closely identified with religious uniformity, the Calvinist province of Holland allowed its highest official, Jan van Oldenbarneveldt, to continue to practice his Roman Catholic faith. As long as business people conducted their religion in private, the government did not interfere with them.

Toleration paid off. It attracted a great amount of foreign capital and business expertise. The Bank of Amsterdam became Europe's best source of cheap credit and commercial intelligence and the main clearing-house for bills of exchange. People of all races and creeds traded in Amsterdam, at whose docks on the Amstel River five thousand ships were berthed. Joost van den Vondel, the poet of Dutch imperialism, exulted:

Rembrandt: The Jewish Bride Holland's greatest painter, Rembrandt (1606–1669) combined an expressive mastery of technique, emotional depth, psychological penetration, and enormous range—religious scenes, still lifes, portraits. The so-called Jewish Bride (ca 1665), perhaps a wedding portrait of two wealthy people, reveals the artist's unsurpassed handling of light, so characteristic of his later work. *(Source: Rijksmuseum-Stichting)*

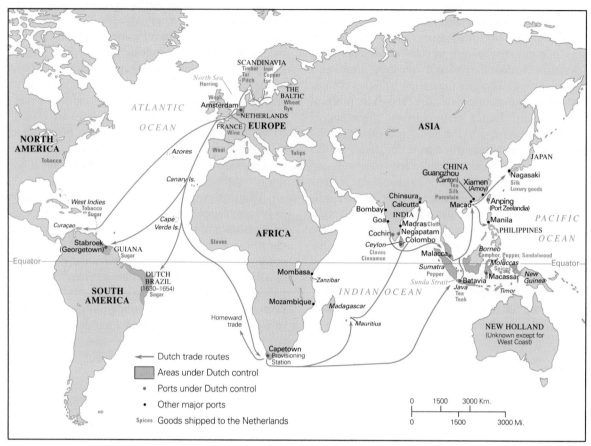

MAP 17.5 Seventeenth-Century Dutch Commerce Dutch wealth rested on commerce, and commerce depended on the huge Dutch merchant marine, manned by perhaps forty-eight thousand sailors. The fleet carried goods from all parts of the globe to the port of Amsterdam.

God, God, the Lord of Amstel cried, hold every
* conscience free;*
And Liberty ride, on Holland's tide, with billowing
* sails to sea,*
And run our Amstel out and in; let freedom gird the
* bold,*
And merchant in his counting house stand elbow deep
* in gold.*[11]

The fishing industry was a cornerstone of the Dutch economy. For half of the year, from June to December, fishing fleets combed the dangerous English coast and the North Sea, raking in tiny herring. Profits from herring stimulated shipbuilding, and even before 1600 the Dutch were offering the lowest shipping rates in Europe. In 1650 the Dutch merchant marine was the largest in Europe,

comprising roughly half of the European total. All the wood for these ships had to be imported: the Dutch bought whole forests from Norway. They controlled the Baltic grain trade, buying entire wheat and rye crops in Poland, east Prussia, and Swedish Pomerania. Foreign merchants coming to Amsterdam could buy anything from precision lenses for the newly invented microscope to muskets for an army of five thousand.

In 1602 a group of the regents of Holland formed the Dutch East India Company, a joint stock company. Each investor received a percentage of the profits proportional to the amount of money he had put in. Within a half-century, the Dutch East India Company had cut heavily into Portuguese trading in East Asia. The Dutch seized the Cape of Good Hope, Ceylon, and Malacca and established trading posts in each place. In the 1630s the Dutch East India Company was paying its investors about a 35 percent annual return on their investments. The Dutch West India Company, founded in 1621, traded extensively with Latin America and Africa (Map 17.5).

Trade and commerce brought the Dutch prodigious wealth. In the seventeenth century, the Dutch enjoyed the highest standard of living in Europe, perhaps in the world. Amsterdam and Rotterdam built massive granaries where the surplus of one year could be stored against possible shortages the next. Thus food prices fluctuated very little, except during the 1650s when several bad harvests reduced supplies. By the standards of Cologne, Paris, or London, salaries were high for all workers, except women. All classes of society, including unskilled laborers, ate well. The low price of bread meant that, compared with other places in Europe, a higher percentage of a worker's income could be spent on fish, cheese, butter, vegetables, even meat. A scholar recently described the Netherlands as "an island of plenty in a sea of want."[12]

Dutch economic leadership was eventually sapped by wars, beginning with those with France and England in the 1670s. The long War of the Spanish Succession, in which the Dutch supported England against France, was a costly drain on Dutch manpower and financial resources. The peace signed in 1713 to end that war marked the beginning of Dutch economic decline.

SUMMARY

War, religious strife, economic depression, and peasant revolts were all aspects of a deep crisis in seventeenth-century Europe. Rulers responded by aggressively seeking to expand their power, which they claimed was essential to meet emergencies and quell disorders. Claiming also that they ruled by divine right, monarchs sought the freedom to wage war, levy taxes, and generally make law as they saw fit. Although they were limited by technology and inadequate financial resources, monarchial governments on the European continent succeeded to a large extent, overpowering organized opposition and curbing the power of the nobility and the traditional representative institutions.

The France of Louis XIV led the way to royal absolutism. France developed a centralized bureaucracy, a professional army, a state-directed economy, all of which Louis personally supervised. The king saw himself as the representative of God on earth and accountable to no one here below. His majestic bearing and sumptuous court dazzled contemporaries. Yet behind the grand façade of unchallenged personal rule and obedient bureaucrats working his will there stood major limitations on Louis XIV's power. Most notable were the financial independence of some provinces and the nobility's traditional freedom from taxation, which Louis himself was compelled to reaffirm.

Within a framework of resurgent serfdom and entrenched nobility, Austrian and Prussian monarchs also fashioned absolutist states in the seventeenth and early eighteenth centuries. These monarchs won absolutist control over standing armies, permanent taxes, and legislative bodies. But they did not question the underlying social and economic relationships. Indeed, they enhanced the privileges of the nobility, which furnished the leading servitors for enlarged armies and growing government bureaucracies.

In Russia, social and economic trends were similar to those in Austria and Prussia. Unlike those two states, however, Russia had a long history of powerful princes. Tsar Peter the Great succeeded in tightening up Russia's traditional absolutism and modernizing it by reforming the army, the bureaucracy, and the defense industry. In Russia and throughout eastern Europe, war and the needs of the state in time of war weighed heavily in the triumph of absolutism.

Triumphant absolutism interacted spectacularly with the arts. It molded the ideals of French classicism, which glorified the state as personified by Louis XIV. Baroque art, which had grown out of the Catholic Reformation's desire to move the faithful and exalt the faith, admirably suited the secular aspirations of eastern European rulers. Thus baroque art attained magnificent heights in eastern Europe, symbolizing the ideal and harmonizing with the reality of imperious royal absolutism.

Holland and England defied the general trend toward absolute monarchy. While Holland prospered under a unique republican confederation that placed most power in the hands of the different provinces, England—fortunately shielded from continental armies and military emergencies by its navy and the English Channel—evolved into the first modern constitutional state. The bitter conflicts between Parliament and the first two Stuart rulers, James I and Charles I, tested where supreme power would rest in the state. The resulting civil war deposed the king, but it did not settle the question. A revival of absolutist tendencies under James II brought on the Glorious Revolution of 1688, and the people who made that revolution settled three basic issues. Power was divided between king and Parliament, with Parliament enjoying the greater share. Government was to be based on the rule of law. And the liberties of English people were to be made explicit in written form, in the Bill of Rights. This constitutional settlement marked an important milestone in world history, although the framers left to later generations the task of making constitutional government work.

NOTES

1. J. B. Collins, *Fiscal Limits of Absolutism: Direct Taxation in Early Seventeenth Century France* (Berkeley: University of California Press, 1988), pp. 1, 3–4, 215–222.
2. Quoted in J. H. Elliot, *Richelieu and Olivares* (Cambridge: Cambridge University Press, 1984), p. 135; and in W. F. Church, *Richelieu and Reason of State* (Princeton, N.J.: Princeton University Press, 1972), p. 507.
3. S. de Gramont, ed., *The Age of Magnificence: Memoirs of the Court of Louis XIV by the Duc de Saint Simon* (New York: Capricorn Books, 1964), pp. 141–145.
4. See W. Beik, *Absolutism and Society in Seventeenth Century France: State Power and Provincial Aristocracy in Languedoc* (Cambridge: Cambridge University Press, 1985), pp. 279–302.
5. W. F. Church, *Louis XIV in Historical Thought: From Voltaire to the Annales School* (New York: Norton, 1976), p. 92.
6. B. Bennassar, *The Spanish Character: Attitudes and Mentalities from the Sixteenth to the Nineteenth Century,* trans. B. Keen (Berkeley: University of California Press, 1979), p. 125.
7. Quoted in R. Ergang, *The Potsdam Fuhrer: Frederick William I, Father of Prussian Militarism* (New York: Octagon Books, 1972), pp. 85, 87.
8. Quoted in R. A. Dorwart, *The Administrative Reforms of Frederick William I of Prussia* (Cambridge, Mass.: Harvard University Press, 1953), p. 226.
9. Quoted in H. Rosenberg, *Bureaucracy, Aristocracy, and Autocracy: The Prussian Experience,* 1660–1815 (Boston: Beacon Press, 1966), p. 38.
10. Quoted in J. Summerson, in *The Eighteenth Century: Europe in the Age of Enlightenment,* ed. A. Cobban (New York: McGraw-Hill, 1969), p. 80.
11. Quoted in D. Maland, *Europe in the Seventeenth Century* (New York: Macmillan, 1967), pp. 198–199.
12. S. Schama, *The Embarrassment of Riches: An Interpretation of Dutch Culture in the Golden Age* (New York: Knopf, 1987), pp. 165–170.

SUGGESTED READING

Students who wish to explore the problems presented in this chapter will find a rich and exciting literature. G. Parker, *Europe in Crisis, 1598–1618* (1980), provides a sound introduction to the social, economic, and religious tensions of the period, as does R. S. Dunn, *The Age of Religious Wars, 1559–1715,* 2d ed. (1979). T. Aston, ed., *Crisis in Europe, 1560–1660* (1967), contains essays by leading historians. P. Anderson, *Lineages of the Absolutist State* (1974), is a stimulating Marxist interpretation of absolutism in western and eastern Europe.

Louis XIV and his age have attracted the attention of many scholars. J. Wolf, *Louis XIV* (1968), remains the best available biography. Two works of W. H. Lewis, *The Splendid Century* (1957) and *The Sunset of the Splendid Century* (1963), make delightful light reading. The advanced student will want to consult the excellent historiographical analysis by W. F. Church mentioned in the Notes, *Louis XIV in Historical Thought.* Perhaps the best works of the Annales school on the period are P. Goubert, *Louis XIV and Twenty Million Frenchmen* (1972), and Goubert's heavily detailed *The Ancien Régime: French Society, 1600–1750,* 2 vols. (1969–1973), which contains invaluable material on the lives and work of ordinary people. R. Bonney, *The King's Debts: Finance and Politics in France, 1589–1661* (1981), and A. Trout, *Jean-Baptiste Colbert* (1978), consider economy and financial conditions. R. Hatton, *Europe in the Age of Louis XIV* (1979), is a splendidly illustrated survey of many aspects of seventeenth-century European culture.

For Spain, M. Defourneaux, *Daily Life in Spain in the Golden Age* (1976), is extremely useful. See also C. R. Phillips, *Ciudad Real, 1500–1750: Growth, Crisis, and Readjustment in the Spanish Economy* (1979), a significant case study. V. L. Tapie, *The Age of Grandeur: Baroque Art and Architecture* (1960), emphasizes the relationship between art and politics with excellent illustrations. Art and architecture are also treated admirably in E. Hempel, *Baroque Art and Architecture in Central Europe* (1965), and G. Hamilton, *The Art and Architecture of Russia* (1954).

The best study on early Prussian history is still F. L. Carsten, *The Origin of Prussia* (1954). Rosenberg, *Bureaucracy, Aristocracy, and Autocracy,* cited in the Notes, is a masterful analysis of the social context of Prussian absolutism. Ergang, *The Potsdam Fuhrer,* also cited in the Notes, is an exciting and critical biography of ramrod Frederick William I. G. Craig, *The Politics of the Prussian Army, 1640–1945* (1964), expertly traces the great influence of the military on the Prussian state over three hundred years. R. J. Evans, *The Making of the Habsburg Empire, 1550–1770* (1979), analyzes the development of absolutism in Austria, as does A. Wandruszka, *The House of Habsburg* (1964). D. McKay and H. Scott, *The Rise of the Great Powers, 1648–1815* (1983), is a good general account. R. Vierhaus, *Germany in the Age of Absolutism* (1988), offers a thorough survey of the different German states.

On eastern European peasants and serfdom, D. Chirot, ed., *The Origins of Backwardness in Eastern Europe: Economics and Politics from the Middle Ages Until the Twentieth Century* (1989), is a wide-ranging introduction. E. Levin, *Sex and Society in the World of the Orthodox Slavs, 900–1700* (1989), carries family history to eastern Europe. J. Blum, *Lord and Peasant in Russia from the Ninth to the Nineteenth Century* (1961), provides a good look at conditions in rural Russia, and P. Avrich, *Russian Rebels, 1600–1800* (1972), treats some of the violent peasant upheavals that those conditions produced. R. Hellie, *Enserfment and Military Change in Muscovy* (1971), is outstanding. In addition to the fine survey by N. V. Riasanovsky, *A History of Russia* (1963), J. Billington, *The Icon and the Axe* (1970), is a stimulating history of early Russian intellectual and cultural developments. B. H. Sumner, *Peter the Great and the Emergence of Russia* (1962), is a good brief introduction, which may be compared with N. V. Riasanovsky, *The Image of Peter the Great in Russian History and Thought* (1985).

English political and social issues of the seventeenth century are considered by M. Ashley, *The House of Stuart: Its Rise and Fall* (1980); C. Hill, *A Century of Revolution* (1961); and K. Wrightson, *English Society, 1580–1680* (1982). Comprehensive treatments of Parliament include C. Russell's *Crisis of Parliaments, 1509–1660* (1971), and *Parliaments and English Politics, 1621–1629* (1979). L. Stone, *The Causes of the English Revolution* (1972), and B. Manning, *The English People and the English Revolution* (1976), are recommended. D. Underdown, *Revel, Riot, and Rebellion* (1985), discusses the extent of popular involvement. For English intellectual currents, see J. O. Appleby, *Economic Thought and Ideology in Seventeenth Century England* (1978). Other recommended works include P. Collinson, *The Religion of Protestants* (1982); R. Thompson, *Women in Stuart England and America* (1974); and A. Fraser, *The Weaker Vessel* (1985). For Cromwell and the Interregnum, A. Fraser, *Cromwell, the Lord Protector* (1973), is valuable. C. Hill, *The World Turned Upside Down* (1972), discusses radical thought during the period. For the Restoration and the Glorious Revolution, see R. Hutton, *Charles II: King of England, Scotland and Ireland* (1989); J. Childs, *The Army, James II, and the Glorious Revolution* (1980); and L. G. Schwoerer, *The Declaration of Rights, 1689* (1981), a fine assessment of that fundamental document. The ideas of John Locke are analyzed by J. P. Kenyon, *Revolution Principles: The Politics of Party, 1689–1720* (1977).

On Holland, K. H. D. Haley, *The Dutch Republic in the Seventeenth Century* (1972), is a splendidly illustrated appreciation of Dutch commercial and artistic achievements, and Schama, *The Embarrassment of Riches,* cited in the Notes, is a lively recent synthesis. R. Boxer, *The Dutch Seaborne Empire* (1980), is useful for Dutch overseas expansion. V. Barbour, *Capitalism in Amsterdam in the Seventeenth Century* (1950), and D. Regin, *Traders, Artists, Burghers: A Cultural History of Amsterdam in the Seventeenth Century* (1977), focus on the leading Dutch city. The leading statesmen of the period may be studied in these biographies: H. H. Rowen, *John de Witt, Grand Pensionary of Holland, 1625–1672* (1978); S. B. Baxter, *William the III and the Defense of European Liberty, 1650–1702* (1966); and J. den Tex, *Oldenbarnevelt,* 2 vols. (1973).

A Foreign Traveler in Russia

Russia in the seventeenth century remained a remote and mysterious land for western and even central Europeans, who had few direct contacts with the tsar's dominion. Knowledge of Russia came mainly from occasional travelers who had visited Muscovy and sometimes wrote accounts of what they had seen.

The most famous of these accounts was by the German Adam Olearius (ca 1599–1671), who was send to Moscow by the duke of Holstein on three diplomatic missions in the 1630s. These missions ultimately proved unsuccessful, but they provided Olearius with a rich store of information for his Travels in Moscovy, *from which the following excerpts are taken. Published in German in 1647 and soon translated into several languages (but not Russian), Olearius's unflattering but well-informed study played a major role in shaping European ideas about Russia.*

The government of the Russians is what political theorists call a "dominating and despotic monarchy," where the sovereign, that is, the tsar or the grand prince who has obtained the crown by right of succession, rules the entire land alone, and all the people are his subjects, and where the nobles and princes no less than the common folk—townspeople and peasants—are his serfs and slaves, whom he rules and treats as a master treats his servants. . . .

If the Russians be considered in respect to their character, customs, and way of life, they are justly to be counted among the barbarians. . . . The vice of drunkenness is so common in this nation, among people of every station, clergy and laity, high and low, men and women, old and young, that when they are seen now and then lying about in the streets, wallowing in the mud, no attention is paid to it, as something habitual. If a cart driver comes upon such a drunken pig whom he happens to know, he shoves him onto his cart and drives him home, where he is paid his fare. No one ever refuses an opportunity to drink and to get drunk, at any time and in any place, and usually it is done with vodka. . . .

The Russians being naturally tough and born, as it were, for slavery, they must be kept under a harsh and strict yoke and must be driven to do their work with clubs and whips, which they suffer without impatience, because such is their station, and they are accustomed to it. Young and half-grown fellows sometimes come together on certain days and train themselves in fisticuffs, to accustom themselves to receiving blows, and, since habit is second nature, this makes blows given as punishment easier to bear. Each and all, they are slaves and serfs. . . .

Because of slavery and their rough and hard life, the Russians accept war readily and are well suited to it. On certain occasions, if need be, they reveal themselves as courageous and daring soldiers. . . .

Although the Russians, especially the common populace, living as slaves under a harsh yoke, can bear and endure a great deal out of love for their masters, yet if the pressure is beyond measure, then it can be said of them: "Patience, often wounded, finally turned into fury." A dangerous indignation results, turned not so much against their sovereign as against the lower authorities, especially if the people have been much oppressed by them and by their supporters and have not been protected by the higher authorities. And once they are aroused and enraged, it is not easy to appease them. Then, disregarding all dangers that may ensue, they resort to every kind of violence and behave like madmen. . . . They own little; most of them have no feather beds; they lie on cushions, straw, mats, or their clothes; they sleep on benches and, in winter, like the non-Germans [i.e., natives] in Livonia, upon the oven, which serves them for cooking and is flat on the top; here husband, wife, children, servants, and maids huddle together. In some houses in the countryside we saw chickens and pigs under the benches and the ovens. . . .

Russians are not used to delicate food and dainties; their daily food consists of porridge, turnips, cabbage, and cucumbers, fresh and pickled, and in Moscow mostly of big salt fish which stink badly, because of the thrifty use of salt, yet are eaten with relish. . . .

The Russians can endure extreme heat. In the bathhouse they stretch out on benches and let themselves be beaten and rubbed with bunches of birch twigs and wisps of bast (which I could not stand); and when they are hot and red all over and so exhausted that they can bear it no longer in the bathhouse, men and women rush outdoors naked and pour cold water over their bodies; in winter they even wallow in the snow and rub their skin with it as if it were soap; then they go back into the hot bathhouse. And since bathhouses are usually near rivers and brooks, they can throw themselves straight from the hot into the cold bath. . . .

Generally noble families, even the small nobility, rear their daughters in secluded chambers, keeping them hidden from outsiders; and a bridegroom is not allowed to have a look at his bride until he receives her in the bridal chamber. Therefore some happen to be deceived, being given a misshapen and sickly one instead of a fair one, and sometimes a kinswoman or even a maidservant instead of a daughter; of which there have been examples even among the highborn. No wonder therefore that often they live together like cats and dogs and that wife-beating is so common among Russians. . . .

In the Kremlin and in the city there are a great many churches, chapels, and monasteries, both within and without the city walls, over two thousand in all. This is so because every nobleman who has some fortune has a chapel built for himself, and most of them are of stone. The stone churches are round and vaulted inside. . . . They allow neither organs nor any other musical instruments in their churches, saying: Instruments that have neither souls nor life cannot praise God. . . .

In their churches there hang many bells, sometimes five or six, the largest not over two hundredweights. They ring these bells to

V. Vasnetsou (1848–1926), Red Square in the late seventeenth century. *(Source: Sovfoto/Eastfoto)*

summon people to church, and also when the priest during mass raises the chalice. In Moscow, because of the multitude of churches and chapels, there are several thousand bells, which during the divine service create such a clang and din that one unaccustomed to it listens in amazement.

Questions for Analysis

1. In what ways were all social groups in Russia similar, according to Olearius?

2. How did Olearius characterize the Russians in general? What supporting evidence did he offer for his judgment?

3. Did Olearius find any positive or admirable traits in the Russian people? What were they?

4. On the basis of these representative passages, why do you think Olearius's book was so popular and influential in central and western Europe?

Source: G. Vernadsky and R. T. Fisher Jr., eds., *A Source Book for Russian History.* Copyright © 1972 by Yale University Press. Reprinted by permission.

18

Toward a New World-View in the West

Painting by Jean-Honoré Fragonard (1732–1806) of Denis Diderot, one of the editors of the *Encyclopedia,* the greatest intellectual achievement of the Enlightenment. *(Source: Louvre © Photo R.M.N.)*

Most people are not philosophers, but they nevertheless have a basic outlook on life, a more or less coherent world-view. At the risk of oversimplification, one may say that the world-view of medieval and early modern Europe was primarily religious and theological. Not only did Christian or Jewish teachings form the core of people's spiritual and philosophical beliefs, but religious teachings also permeated all the rest of human thought and activity. Political theory relied on the divine right of kings, for example, and activities ranging from marriage and divorce to eating habits and hours of business were regulated by churches and religious doctrines.

In the course of the eighteenth century, this religious and theological world-view underwent a fundamental transformation among the European upper and comfortable classes. Economically secure and increasingly well educated, these privileged groups of preindustrial Europe often came to see the world primarily in secular and scientific terms. And while few individuals abandoned religious beliefs altogether, the role of churches and religious thinking in earthly affairs and in the pursuit of knowledge was substantially reduced. Among many in the aristocracy and solid middle classes, a new critical, scientific, and very modern world-view took shape.

- Why did this momentous change occur?
- How did this new world-view affect the way people thought about society and human relations?
- What impact did this new way of thinking have on political developments and monarchial absolutism?

This chapter will focus on these questions.

❖ THE SCIENTIFIC REVOLUTION

The foremost cause of the change in world-view was the scientific revolution. Modern science—precise knowledge of the physical world based on the union of experimental observations with sophisticated mathematics—crystallized in the seventeenth century. Whereas science had been secondary and subordinate in medieval intellectual life, it became independent and even primary for many educated people in the eighteenth century.

The emergence of modern science was a development of tremendous long-term significance. A noted historian has even said that the scientific revolution of the late sixteenth and seventeenth centuries "outshines everything since the rise of Christianity" and was "the real origin both of the modern world and the modern mentality."[1] This statement is an exaggeration, but not much of one. Of all the great civilizations, only that of the West developed modern science. With the scientific revolution Western society began to acquire its most distinctive traits. Let us examine the milestones on the fateful march toward modern science first and then search for the nonscientific influences along the route.

Scientific Thought in 1500

Since developments in astronomy and physics were at the heart of the scientific revolution, one must begin with the traditional European conception of the universe and movement within it. In the early 1500s, traditional European ideas about the universe were still based primarily on the ideas of Aristotle, the great Greek philosopher of the fourth century B.C. These ideas had been recovered gradually during the Middle Ages and then brought into harmony with Christian doctrines by medieval theologians. According to this revised Aristotelian view, a motionless earth was fixed at the center of the universe. Around it moved ten separate transparent crystal spheres. In the first eight spheres were embedded, in turn, the moon, the sun, the five known planets, and the fixed stars. Then followed two spheres that theologians added during the Middle Ages to account for slight changes in the positions of the stars over the centuries. Beyond the tenth sphere was heaven, with the throne of God and the souls of the saved. Angels kept the spheres moving in perfect circles.

Aristotle's views, suitably revised by medieval philosophers, also dominated thinking about physics and motion on earth—the sublunar world. The sublunar world was made up of four imperfect, changeable elements. The "light" elements (air and fire) naturally moved upward; the "heavy" elements (water and earth) naturally moved downward. These natural directions of motion did not always prevail, however, for elements were often mixed together and could be affected by an outside force such as a human being. Aristotle and his

The Copernican Hypothesis

The desire to explain and thereby glorify God's handiwork led to the first great departure from the medieval system. This departure was the work of the Polish clergyman and astronomer Nicolaus Copernicus (1473–1543). As a young man, Copernicus studied church law and astronomy in various European universities. He saw how professional astronomers still depended for their most accurate calculations on the work of Ptolemy, the last great ancient astronomer, who had lived in Alexandria in the second century A.D. Ptolemy's achievement had been to work out complicated rules to help stargazers and astrologers to track the planets with greater precision. Many people then (and now) believed that the changing relationships between planets and stars influenced and even determined the future.

The young Copernicus was uninterested in astrology and felt that Ptolemy's cumbersome and occasionally inaccurate rules detracted from the majesty of a perfect Creator. He preferred an old Greek idea being discussed in Renaissance Italy— the idea that the sun, rather than the earth, was at the center of the universe. Working on his hypothesis from 1506 to 1530, Copernicus indeed theorized that the stars and planets, including the earth, revolve around a fixed sun. Yet Copernicus was a cautious man. Fearing the ridicule of other astronomers, he did not publish his *On the Revolutions of the Heavenly Spheres* until 1543, the year of his death.

Copernicus's theory had enormous scientific and religious implications, many of which the conservative Copernicus did not anticipate. Perhaps most significant from a religious standpoint was that by characterizing the earth as just another planet in an immense universe, Copernicus destroyed the basic idea of Aristotelian physics—the idea that the earthly world was quite different from the heavenly one. Where was the realm of perfection? Where were heaven and the throne of God?

The Copernican theory quickly brought sharp attacks from religious leaders, especially Protestants. Hearing of Copernicus's work even before it was published, Martin Luther spoke of him as the "new astrologer who wants to prove that the earth moves and goes round. . . . The fool wants to turn the whole art of astronomy upside down." Luther noted that "as the Holy Scripture tells us, so did Joshua bid the sun stand still and not the earth."[2]

✳ **Ptolemy's System**   This 1543 drawing shows how the changing configurations of the planets moving around the earth form the twelve different constellations, or "signs," of the zodiac. The learned astronomer on the right is using his knowledge to predict the future for the king on the left. (*Source: Mary Evans Picture Library/Photo Researchers*)

followers also believed that a uniform force moved an object at a constant speed and that the object would stop as soon as that force was removed.

Aristotle's science as interpreted by Christian theologians fit neatly with Christian doctrines. It established a home for God and a place for Christian souls. It put human beings at the center of the universe and made them the critical link in a "great chain of being" that stretched from the throne of God to the most lowly insect on earth. Thus science was primarily a branch of theology, and it reinforced religious thought.

John Calvin also condemned Copernicus. Catholic reaction was milder at first, but in 1616 the church officially declared the Copernican theory false.

Other events were almost as influential in creating doubts about traditional astronomical ideas. In 1572 a new star appeared and shone very brightly for almost two years. The new star, which was actually a distant exploding star, made an enormous impression on people. It seemed to contradict the idea that the heavenly spheres were unchanging and therefore perfect. In 1577 a new comet suddenly moved through the sky, cutting a straight path across the supposedly impenetrable crystal spheres. It was time, as a typical scientific writer put it, for "the radical renovation of astronomy."[3]

From Brahe to Galileo

One astronomer who agreed was Tycho Brahe (1546–1601) of Denmark. He established himself as Europe's leading astronomer with his detailed observations of the new star of 1572. For twenty years thereafter he meticulously observed the stars and planets with the naked eye. An imposing man who had lost a piece of his nose in a duel and replaced it with a special bridge of gold and silver alloy, Brahe was a noble who exploited his peasants arrogantly and approached the heavens humbly. His great contribution was his mass of data. His limited understanding of mathematics, however, prevented him from making much sense out of his data. That was left to his brilliant young assistant, the German Johannes Kepler (1571–1630).

Working and reworking Brahe's mountain of observations in a staggering sustained effort, Kepler formulated three famous laws of planetary motion. First, building on Copernican theory, he demonstrated in 1609 that the orbits of the planets around the sun are elliptical rather than circular. Second, he demonstrated that the planets do not move at a uniform speed in their orbits. Third, in 1619 he showed that the time a planet takes to make its complete orbit is precisely related to its distance from the sun. Kepler's contribution was monumental. Whereas Copernicus had speculated, Kepler proved mathematically the precise relations of a sun-centered (solar) system. His work demolished the old system of Aristotle and Ptolemy, and in his third law he came close to formulating the idea of universal gravitation.

While Kepler was unraveling planetary motion, a young Florentine named Galileo Galilei (1564–1642) was challenging all the old ideas about motion. Like so many early scientists, Galileo was a poor nobleman first marked for a religious career. However, he soon became fascinated by mathematics. A brilliant student, Galileo became a professor of mathematics in 1589 at age twenty-five. He proceeded to examine motion and mechanics in a new way. Indeed, his great achievement was the elaboration and consolidation of the modern experimental method: rather than speculate about what might or should happen, Galileo conducted controlled experiments to find out what actually *did* happen.

In his famous acceleration experiment, by rolling brass balls down an inclined plane, he showed that a uniform force—in this case, gravity—produces a uniform acceleration. With this and other experiments, Galileo went on to formulate the law of inertia: rather than rest being the natural state of objects, an object continues in motion forever unless stopped by some external force. Aristotelian physics was in a shambles.

On hearing details about the invention of the telescope in Holland, Galileo made one for himself and trained it on the heavens. He quickly discovered the first four moons of Jupiter, providing new evidence for the Copernican theory, in which Galileo already believed. Galileo then pointed his telescope at the moon. He wrote in 1610 in *Siderus Nuncius:*

I feel sure that the moon is not perfectly smooth, free from inequalities, and exactly spherical, as a large school of philosophers considers with regard to the moon and the other heavenly bodies. On the contrary, it is full of inequalities, uneven, full of hollows and protuberances, just like the surface of the earth itself, which is varied. . . . The next object which I have observed is the essence or substance of the Milky Way. By the aid of a telescope anyone may behold this in a manner which so distinctly appeals to the senses that all the disputes which have tormented philosophers through so many ages are exploded by the irrefutable evidence of our eyes, and we are freed from wordy disputes upon the subject. For the galaxy is nothing else but a mass of innumerable stars planted together in clusters.[4]

Reading these famous lines, one feels a crucial corner in Western civilization being turned. The traditional religious and theological world-view, which rested on identifying and accepting the proper established authority, was beginning to give way in certain fields to a critical, scientific method. This new method of learning and investigating was the greatest accomplishment of the entire scientific revolution, for it proved capable of great extension. A historian investigating documents of the past, for example, is not so different from a Galileo studying stars and rolling balls.

Galileo's work eventually aroused the ire of some theologians. After the publication in Italian of his widely read *Dialogue on the Two Chief Systems of the World* in 1632, which openly lampooned the traditional views of Aristotle and Ptolemy and defended those of Copernicus, Galileo was tried for heresy by the papal Inquisition. Imprisoned and threatened with torture, the aging Galileo recanted, "renouncing and cursing" his Copernican errors. Of minor importance in the development of science, Galileo's trial later became for some writers the perfect symbol of the inherent conflict between religious belief and scientific knowledge.

Newton's Synthesis

The accomplishments of Kepler, Galileo, and other scientists had taken effect by about 1640. The old astronomy and physics were in ruins, and several fundamental breakthroughs had been made. The fusion of the new findings in a new synthesis, a single explanatory system that would comprehend motion both on earth and in the skies, was the work of Isaac Newton (1642–1727).

Newton was born into lower English gentry and attended Cambridge University. Fascinated by alchemy, he sought the elixir of life and a way to change base metals into gold and silver. Not without reason did the twentieth-century economist John Maynard Keynes call him the "last of the magicians." Newton was also intensely religious. He

 Galileo's Paintings of the Moon When Galileo published the results of his telescopic observations of the moon, he added these paintings to illustrate the marvels he had seen with his telescopes. *(Source: Biblioteca Nazionale Centrale, Florence/Scala/Art Resource, NY)*

had a highly suspicious nature, lacked interest in women and sex, and in 1693 suffered a nervous breakdown from which he later recovered. He was far from being the perfect rationalist so endlessly eulogized by writers in the eighteenth and nineteenth centuries.

Of his intellectual genius and incredible powers of concentration there can be no doubt, however. Arriving at some of his most basic ideas about physics in 1666 at age twenty-four, but unable to prove these theories mathematically, he attained a professorship and studied optics for many years. In 1684 Newton returned to physics for eighteen extraordinarily intensive months. Seldom leaving his room, he neglected even the meals sent up, his mind fastened like a vise on the laws of the universe. He opened the third book of his immortal *Principia,* published in Latin in 1687, with these lines: "In the preceding books I have laid down the principles . . . [that] are the laws of certain motions, and powers or forces. . . . It remains that from the same principles I now demonstrate the frame of the System of the World."

Newton made good his grandiose claim. He integrated the astronomy of Copernicus, as corrected by Kepler's laws, with the physics of Galileo and his predecessors. Newton did this by means of a set of mathematical laws that explain motion and mechanics. These laws of dynamics are complex, and it took scientists and engineers two hundred years to work out all their implications. Nevertheless, the key feature of the Newtonian synthesis was the law of universal gravitation. According to this law, every body in the universe attracts every other body in the universe in a precise mathematical relationship, based on mass and distance. The whole universe—from Kepler's elliptical orbits to Galileo's rolling balls—was unified in one majestic system.

Causes of the Scientific Revolution

With a charming combination of modesty and self-congratulation, Newton once wrote, "If I have seen further [than others], it is by standing on the shoulders of Giants."[5] Surely the path from Copernicus to Newton confirms the "internal" view of the scientific revolution as the product of towering individual genius. Yet there were certainly broader causes as well.

First, the long-term contribution of medieval intellectual life and medieval universities to the scien-

Isaac Newton   This portrait suggests the depth and complexity of the great genius. Is the powerful mind behind those piercing eyes thinking of science or of religion, or perhaps of both? *(Source: Scala/Art Resource, NY)*

tific revolution was much more considerable than historians unsympathetic to the Middle Ages once believed. By the thirteenth century, permanent universities with professors and large student bodies had been established in western Europe to train the lawyers, doctors, and church leaders that society required. By 1300 philosophy had taken its place alongside law, medicine, and theology. Medieval philosophers developed a limited but real independence from theologians and a sense of free inquiry. They nobly pursued a body of knowledge and tried to arrange it meaningfully by means of abstract theories.

Within this framework, science was able to emerge as a minor but distinct branch of philosophy. In the fourteenth and fifteenth centuries, first in Italy and then elsewhere in Europe, leading universities established new professorships of mathematics, astronomy, and physics (natural philosophy) within their faculties of philosophy. Although the prestige of the new fields was low among both professors and students, rational, critical thinking was applied to scientific problems by a permanent community of scholars. And an outlet existed for the talents of a Galileo or a Newton: all the great pathfinders either studied or taught at universities.

Second, the Renaissance also stimulated scientific progress. The recovery of the finest works of Greek mathematics—a byproduct of Renaissance humanism's ceaseless search for the knowledge of antiquity—greatly improved European mathematics well into the early seventeenth century. Finally, in the Renaissance pattern of patronage, especially in Italy, various rulers and wealthy business people supported scientific investigations, as the Medicis of Florence, for instance, did those of Galileo.

The navigational problems of long sea voyages in the age of overseas expansion were a third factor in the scientific revolution. As early as 1484, the king of Portugal appointed a commission of mathematicians to perfect tables to help seamen find their latitude. This resulted in the first European navigation manual.

The problem of fixing longitude was much more difficult. In England the government and the great capitalistic trading companies turned to science and scientific education in an attempt to solve this pressing practical problem. At Gresham College in London, the main center of scientific activity in England in the first half of the seventeenth century, the professor of astronomy was directed to teach courses on the science of navigation. Scientists at Gresham College enjoyed close ties with top officials of the Royal Navy and with leading merchants and shipbuilders. The close tie between practical men and scientists also led to the establishment in 1662 of the Royal Society of London, which published scientific papers and sponsored scientific meetings.

Navigational problems were also critical in the development of many new scientific instruments, such as the telescope, barometer, thermometer, pendulum clock, microscope, and air pump. Better instruments, which permitted more accurate observations, were part of a fourth factor in the scientific revolution, the development of better ways of obtaining knowledge about the world. Two important thinkers, Francis Bacon (1561–1626) and René Descartes (1596–1650), represented key aspects of this improvement in scientific methodology.

The English politician and writer Francis Bacon was the greatest early propagandist for the new experimental method, as Galileo was its greatest early practitioner. Rejecting the Aristotelian and medieval method of using speculative reasoning to build general theories, Bacon argued that new knowledge had to be pursued through empirical, experimental research. A researcher who wants to learn more about leaves or rocks should not speculate about the subject but rather collect a multitude of specimens and then compare and analyze them. Thus freed from sterile medieval speculation, the facts will speak for themselves, and important general principles will then emerge. Knowledge will increase. Bacon's contribution was to formalize the empirical method, which had already been used by Brahe and Galileo, into the general theory of inductive reasoning known as *empiricism.*

Bacon claimed that the empirical method would result not only in more knowledge but also in highly practical, useful knowledge. According to Bacon, scientific discoveries would bring about much greater control over the physical environment and make people rich and nations powerful. Thus Bacon helped provide a radically new and effective justification for private and public support of scientific inquiry.

The French philosopher René Descartes was a true genius who made his first great discovery in mathematics. As a twenty-three-year-old soldier serving in the Thirty Years' War, he experienced on a single night in 1619 a life-changing intellectual vision. Descartes saw that there was a perfect correspondence between geometry and algebra and that geometrical, spatial figures could be expressed as algebraic equations and vice versa. A major step forward in the history of mathematics, Descartes' discovery of analytic geometry provided scientists with an important new tool. But his greatest achievement was to develop his initial vision into a whole philosophy of knowledge and science.

Like Bacon, Descartes scorned traditional science and had great faith in the powers of the human mind. Yet Descartes was much more systematic and mathematical than Bacon. He decided it was necessary to doubt everything that could reasonably be doubted and then, as in geometry, to use deductive reasoning from self-evident principles to ascertain scientific laws. Descartes' reasoning ultimately reduced all substances to "matter" and "mind"—that is, to the physical and the spiri-

Descartes in Sweden   Queen Christina of Sweden (r. 1632–1654) encouraged art and science and invited many foreign artists and scholars to visit her court. She speaks here with French mathematician and philosopher René Descartes in 1649. The strong-minded daughter of Protestant hero Gustavus Adolphus, Christina rejected marriage, abdicated in 1654, converted to Catholicism, and died in Rome. *(Source: Versailles/Photographie Bulloz)*

tual. His view of the world as consisting of two fundamental entities is known as *Cartesian dualism.* Descartes was a profoundly original and extremely influential thinker.

Bacon's inductive experimentalism and Descartes' deductive, mathematical rationalism are combined in the modern scientific method, which began to crystallize in the late seventeenth century. Neither man's extreme approach was sufficient by itself. Thus the modern scientific method has joined precise observations and experimentalism with the search for general laws that may be expressed in rigorously logical, mathematical language.

Finally, there is the question of the role of religion in the development of science. Just as some historians have argued that Protestantism led to the rise of capitalism, others have concluded that Protestantism, by supposedly making scientific inquiry a question of individual conscience and not of religious doctrine, was a fundamental factor in the rise of modern science. However, all religious authorities in the West—Catholic, Protestant, and Jewish—opposed the Copernican system to a greater or lesser extent until about 1630, by which time the scientific revolution was definitely in progress. The Catholic church was initially less hostile than Protestant and Jewish religious leaders. This early Catholic toleration and the scientific interests of Renaissance Italy helped account for the crucial role that Italian scientists played in scientific progress right up to the trial of Galileo in 1633. Thereafter, the Counter-Reformation church became more hostile to science, a change that helped account for the decline of science in Italy (but not in Catholic France) after 1640. At the same time, some Protestant countries became quite proscience, especially if the country lacked a strong religious authority capable of imposing religious orthodoxy on scientific questions, as did Protestant England after 1630. English religious conflicts became so intense that the authorities could not impose religious unity on anything, including science. Neutral and useful, science became an accepted part of life and developed rapidly in England after about 1640.

Some Consequences of the Scientific Revolution

The rise of modern science had many consequences, some of which are still unfolding. First, it went hand in hand with the rise of a new and expanding social group—the international scientific community. Members of this community were linked together by common interests and shared values as well as by journals and the learned scientific societies founded in many countries in the later seventeenth and the eighteenth centuries. Expansion of knowledge was the primary goal of this community, and scientists' material and psychological rewards depended on their success in this endeavor. Thus science became quite competitive, and even more scientific advance was inevitable.

Second, the revolutionary modern scientific method, in addition to being both theoretical and experimental, was highly critical, and it differed profoundly from the old way of getting knowledge about nature. It refused to base its conclusions on tradition and established sources, on ancient authorities and sacred texts.

The scientific revolution had few consequences for economic life and the living standards of the masses until the late eighteenth century at the very earliest. True, improvements in the techniques of navigation facilitated overseas trade and helped enrich leading merchants. But science had relatively few practical economic applications, and the hopes of the early Baconians were frustrated. The close link between theoretical, or pure, science and applied technology, which we take for granted today, simply did not exist before the nineteenth century. Thus the scientific revolution of the seventeenth century was first and foremost an intellectual revolution. For more than a hundred years its greatest impact was on how people thought and believed.

❀ THE ENLIGHTENMENT

The scientific revolution was the single most important factor in the creation of the new world-view of the eighteenth-century Enlightenment. This world-view, which has played a large role in shaping the modern mind, grew out of a rich mix of ideas. These ideas were diverse and often conflicting, for the talented (and not-so-talented) writers who espoused them competed vigorously for the attention of a growing public of well-educated but fickle readers, who remained a small minority of the population. Despite this diversity, three central concepts stand at the core of Enlightenment thinking.

The most important and original idea of the Enlightenment was that the methods of natural science could and should be used to examine and understand all aspects of life. This was what intellectuals meant by *reason,* a favorite word of Enlightenment thinkers. Nothing was to be accepted on faith. Everything was to be submitted to the rational, critical, scientific way of thinking. This approach often brought the Enlightenment into a head-on conflict with established churches, which rested their beliefs on the special authority of the Bible and Christian theology. A second important Enlightenment concept was that the scientific method was capable of discovering the laws of human society as well as those of nature. Thus was social science born. Its birth led to the third key idea, that of progress. Armed with the proper method of discovering the laws of human existence, Enlightenment thinkers believed it was at least possible for human beings to create better societies and better people. Their belief was strengthened by some modest improvements in economic and social life during the eighteenth century.

The Enlightenment was therefore profoundly secular. It revived and expanded the Renaissance concentration on worldly explanations. In the course of the eighteenth century, the Enlightenment had a profound impact on the thought and culture of the urban middle classes and the aristocracy. It did not, however, have much appeal for the urban poor and the peasants, who were preoccupied with the struggle for survival and who often resented the Enlightenment attack on traditional popular beliefs (see Chapter 19).

The Emergence of the Enlightenment

Loosely united by certain key ideas, the European Enlightenment was a broad intellectual and cultural movement that gained strength gradually and did not reach its maturity until about 1750. Yet it was the generation that came of age between the publication of Newton's *Principia* in 1687 and the death of Louis XIV in 1715 that tied the crucial knot between the scientific revolution and a new outlook on life. Talented writers of that generation popularized hard-to-understand scientific achievements for the educated elite.

The most famous and influential popularizer was a versatile French man of letters, Bernard de Fontenelle (1657–1757). He set out to make science witty and entertaining for a broad nonscientific audience—as easy to read as a novel. This was a tall order, but Fontenelle largely succeeded. His most famous work, *Conversations on the Plurality of Worlds* (1686), begins with two elegant figures walking in the gathering shadows of a large park. One is a woman, a sophisticated aristocrat, and the other is her friend, perhaps even her lover. They gaze at the stars, and their talk turns to a passionate discussion of . . . astronomy! He confides that "each star may well be a different world," then gently stresses how error is giving way to truth. At one point he explains:

There came on the scene . . . one Copernicus, who made short work of all those various circles, all those solid skies, which the ancients had pictured to themselves. . . . Fired with the noble zeal of a true astronomer, he took the earth and spun it very far away from the center of the universe, where it had been installed, and in that center he put the sun, which had a far better title to the honor.[6]

Rather than despair at this dismissal of traditional understanding, Fontenelle's lady rejoices in the knowledge that the human mind is capable of making great progress.

Fontenelle and other writers of his generation were instrumental in bringing science into conflict with religion. Many seventeenth-century scientists, both Catholic and Protestant, believed that their work exalted God. They did not draw antireligious implications from their scientific findings. Fontenelle, in contrast, was skeptical about absolute truth and cynical about the claims of organized religion. In *Eulogies of Scientists,* Fontenelle exploited with endless variations the basic theme of rational, progressive scientists versus prejudiced, reactionary priests.

The progressive and antireligious implications that writers such as Fontenelle drew from the scientific revolution reflected a crisis in European thought at the end of the seventeenth century. This crisis had its roots in several intellectual uncertainties and dissatisfactions, of which the demolition of Aristotelian-medieval science was only one.

A second uncertainty involved the whole question of religious truth. The destructive wars of religion had been fought, in part, because religious freedom was an intolerable idea in Europe in the early seventeenth century. Both Catholics and Protestants had believed that religious truth was absolute and therefore worth fighting and dying for. Most Catholics and Protestants also believed that a strong state required unity in religious faith. Yet the disastrous results of the many attempts to impose such religious unity led some people to ask if it was really necessary. Others skeptically asked if religious truth could ever be known with absolute certainty and concluded that it could not.

The most famous of these skeptics was Pierre Bayle (1647–1706), a French Huguenot who despised Louis XIV and found refuge in the Netherlands. Critically examining the religious beliefs and

 Popularizing Science   The frontispiece illustration of Fontenelle's *Conversations on the Plurality of Worlds* invites the reader to share the pleasures of astronomy with an elegant lady and an entertaining teacher. The drawing shows the planets revolving around the sun. *(Source: University of Illinois Library, Champaign)*

persecutions of the past, Bayle demonstrated that human beliefs had been extremely varied and very often mistaken. He concluded that nothing can ever be known beyond all doubt and that in religion, as in philosophy, humanity's best hope was open-minded toleration. Bayle's skeptical views were very influential. Many eighteenth-century writers mined his inexhaustible vein of critical skepticism for ammunition in their attacks on superstition and theology.

The rapidly growing travel literature on non-European lands and cultures was a third cause of uncertainty. In the wake of the great discoveries, Europeans were learning that the peoples of China, India, Africa, and the Americas all had their own very different beliefs and customs. Europeans shaved their faces and let their hair grow. Turks shaved their heads and let their beards grow. In Europe a man bowed before a woman to show respect. In Siam a man turned his back on a woman when he met her because it was disrespectful to look directly at her. Countless similar examples discussed in the travel accounts helped change the perspective of educated Europeans. They began to look at truth and morality in relative, rather than absolute, terms. If anything was possible, who could say what was right or wrong?

A fourth cause and manifestation of European intellectual turmoil was John Locke's epoch-making *Essay Concerning Human Understanding.* Published in 1690—the same year Locke published his *Second Treatise of Civil Government* (see page 586) —Locke's essay brilliantly set forth a new theory about how human beings learn and form their ideas. In doing so, he rejected the prevailing view of Descartes, who had held that all people are born with certain basic ideas and ways of thinking. Locke insisted that all ideas are derived from experience. The human mind at birth is like a blank tablet (*tabula rasa*) on which the environment writes the individual's understanding and beliefs. Human development is therefore determined by education and social institutions, for good or for evil. Locke's *Essay* was, along with Newton's *Principia,* one of the dominant intellectual inspirations of the Enlightenment.

The Philosophes and the Public

By the time Louis XIV died in 1715, many of the ideas that would soon coalesce into the new world-view had been assembled. Yet Christian Europe was still strongly attached to its traditional beliefs, as witnessed by the powerful revival of religious orthodoxy in the first half of the eighteenth century (see Chapter 19). By the outbreak of the American Revolution in 1775, however, a large portion of western Europe's educated elite had embraced many of the new ideas. This acceptance was the work of one of history's most influential groups of intellectuals, the philosophes. It was the philosophes who proudly and effectively proclaimed that they, at long last, were bringing the light of knowledge to their ignorant fellow creatures in a great age of enlightenment.

Philosophe is the French word for "philosopher," and it was in France that the Enlightenment reached its highest development. The French philosophes were indeed philosophers, asking fundamental philosophical questions about the meaning of life, God, human nature, good and evil, and cause and effect. But in the tradition of Bayle and Fontenelle, they were not content with abstract arguments or ivory-tower speculations. They were determined to reach and influence all the economic and social elites, whom they perceived as the educated or enlightened public, or simply the "public."

As a wealth of recent scholarship has shown, this public was quite different from the great majority of the population, which was known as the common people, or simply the "people." French philosophe Jean le Rond d'Alembert (1717–1783) characteristically made a sharp distinction between "the truly enlightened public" and "the blind and noisy multitude."[7] The philosophes believed that the great majority of the common people was doomed to superstition and confusion because it lacked the money and leisure to look beyond its bitter struggle with grinding poverty (see Chapter 19).

The great philosophes and their imitators were not free to write as they wished, for it was illegal in France to criticize openly either church or state. Their most radical works had to circulate in manuscript form. Knowing that direct attacks would probably be banned or burned, the philosophes wrote novels and plays, histories and philosophies, dictionaries and encyclopedias, all filled with satire and double meanings to spread their message to the public.

One of the greatest philosophes, the baron de Montesquieu (1689–1755), brilliantly pioneered this approach in *The Persian Letters,* an extremely influential social satire published in 1721. Montesquieu's work consisted of amusing letters supposedly written by Persian travelers, who see European customs in unique ways and thereby cleverly criticize existing practices and beliefs. Having gained fame by using wit as a weapon against cruelty and superstition, Montesquieu settled down on his family estate to study history and politics. He was also inspired by the example of the physical sciences, and he set out to apply the critical method to the problem of government in *The Spirit of Laws* (1748). The result was a complex comparative study of republics, monarchies, and despotisms.

Dismayed by the triumph of royal absolutism under Louis XIV, Montesquieu focused on the conditions that would promote liberty and prevent tyranny. He argued that despotism could be avoided if political power was divided and shared by a variety of classes and legal orders holding unequal rights and privileges. A strong, independent upper class was especially important, according to Montesquieu, because in order to prevent the abuse of power, "it is necessary that by the arrangement of things, power checks power." Admiring greatly the English balance of power among the king, the houses of Parliament, and the independent courts, Montesquieu believed that in France the thirteen high courts—the *parlements*—were front-line defenders of liberty against royal despotism. Apprehensive about the uneducated poor, Montesquieu was clearly no democrat, but his theory of separation of powers had a great impact on France's wealthy, well-educated elite. The constitutions of the young United States in 1789 and of France in 1791 were based in large part on this theory.

The most famous and in many ways most representative philosophe was François Marie Arouet, who was known by the pen name Voltaire (1694–1778). In his long career, this son of a comfortable middle-class family wrote more than seventy witty volumes, hobnobbed with kings and queens, and died a millionaire because of shrewd business speculations. His early career, however, was turbulent. In 1717 Voltaire was imprisoned for eleven months in the Bastille in Paris for insulting the regent of France. In 1726 a barb from his sharp tongue led a great French nobleman to have him beaten and arrested. This experience made a deep impression on Voltaire. All his life he struggled against legal injustice and unequal treatment be-

Madame du Châtelet Fascinated by the new world system of Isaac Newton, this aristocratic woman helped to spread Newton's ideas in France by translating his *Principia* into French and by influencing Voltaire, her companion for fifteen years until her death. (*Source: Private Collection/Photographie Bulloz*)

fore the law. Released from prison after promising to leave the country, Voltaire lived in England for three years and came to share Montesquieu's enthusiasm for English institutions.

Returning to France and soon threatened again with prison in Paris, Voltaire had the great fortune of meeting Gabrielle-Emilie Le Tonnelier de Breteuil, marquise du Châtelet (1706–1749), an intellectually gifted woman from the high aristocracy with a passion for science. Inviting Voltaire to live in her country house at Cirey in Lorraine and becoming his long-time companion (under the eyes of her tolerant husband), Madame du Châtelet studied physics and mathematics and published scientific articles and translations.

Perhaps the finest representative of a small number of elite French women and their scientific accomplishments during the Enlightenment, Madame du Châtelet suffered nonetheless because of her gender. Excluded on principle from the Royal

Academy of Sciences and from stimulating interchange with other scientists because she was a woman, she depended on private tutors for instruction and became uncertain of her ability to make important scientific discoveries. Madame du Châtelet therefore concentrated on spreading the ideas of others, and her translation with an accompanying commentary of Newton's *Principia* into French for the first (and only) time was her greatest work. But she had no doubt that women's limited scientific contributions in the past were due to limited and unequal education. Imagining a scientific experiment that she would make if she were a ruler, Madame du Châtelet wrote, "I would reform an abuse which cuts off, so to speak, half the human race. I would make women participate in all the rights of humankind, and above all in those of the intellect."[8]

While living at Cirey, Voltaire wrote various works praising England and popularizing English scientific progress. Newton, he wrote, was history's greatest man, for he had used his genius for the benefit of humanity. In the true style of the Enlightenment, Voltaire mixed the glorification of science and reason with an appeal for better individuals and institutions. Yet like almost all of the philosophes, Voltaire was a reformer, not a revolutionary, in social and political matters. He was eventually appointed royal historian in 1743, and his *Age of Louis XIV* portrayed Louis as the dignified leader of his age. Voltaire also began a long correspondence with Frederick the Great and, after the death of his beloved Emilie, accepted Frederick's invitation to come brighten up the Prussian court in Berlin. The two men later quarreled, but Voltaire always admired Frederick as a free thinker and an enlightened monarch.

Unlike Montesquieu, Voltaire pessimistically concluded that the best one could hope for in the way of government was a good monarch since human beings "are very rarely worthy to govern themselves." Nor did he believe in social and economic equality in human affairs. The idea of making servants equal to their masters was "absurd and impossible." The only realizable equality, Voltaire thought, was that "by which the citizen only depends on the laws which protect the freedom of the feeble against the ambitions of the strong."[9]

Voltaire's philosophical and religious positions were much more radical. In the tradition of Bayle, Voltaire's voluminous writings challenged, often indirectly, the Catholic church and Christian the-

ology at almost every point. Though he was considered by many devout Christians to be a shallow blasphemer, Voltaire's religious views were influential and quite typical of the mature Enlightenment. Voltaire clearly believed in a God, but his was a distant, deistic God, a great Clockmaker who built an orderly universe and then stepped aside and let it run. Above all, Voltaire and most of the philosophes hated all forms of religious intolerance, which, they believed, often led to fanaticism and savage, inhuman action. Simple piety and human kindness—as embodied in Christ's great commandments to "love God and your neighbor as yourself"—were religion enough, even Christianity enough, as may be seen in Voltaire's famous essay on religion (see Listening to the Past).

The philosophes' greatest and most representative intellectual achievement was, quite fittingly, a group effort—the seventeen-volume *Encyclopedia: The Rational Dictionary of the Sciences, the Arts, and the Crafts,* edited by Denis Diderot (1713–1784) and Jean le Rond d'Alembert. Diderot and d'Alembert set out to teach people how to think critically and objectively about all matters. As Diderot said, he wanted the *Encyclopedia* to "change the general way of thinking."[10]

The editors of the *Encyclopedia* had to conquer innumerable obstacles. After the appearance in 1751 of the first volume, which dealt with such controversial subjects as atheism, the soul, and blind people, the timid publisher watered down some of the articles in the last ten volumes without the editors' consent. Yet Diderot's unwavering belief in the importance of his mission held the encyclopedists together for fifteen years, and the enormous work was completed in 1765. Hundreds of thousands of articles by leading scientists, famous writers, skilled workers, and progressive priests treated every aspect of life and knowledge.

Not every article was daring or original, but the overall effect was little short of revolutionary. Science and the industrial arts were exalted, religion and immortality questioned. Intolerance, legal injustice, and out-of-date social institutions were openly criticized. The encyclopedists were convinced that greater knowledge would result in greater human happiness, for knowledge was useful and made possible economic, social, and political progress. The *Encyclopedia,* widely read and extremely influential throughout western Europe, summed up the new world-view of the Enlightenment.

figure . 1ʳᵉ

✳ **Canal with Locks**   Articles on science and the industrial arts in the *Encyclopedia*
carried lavish explanatory illustrations. This engraving from the section on water and
its uses shows advances in canal building and reflects the encyclopedists' faith in technical progress. *(Source: University of Illinois Library, Champaign)*

The Later Enlightenment

After about 1770, the harmonious unity of the
philosophes and their thought began to break
down. As the new world-view became increasingly
accepted by the educated public, some thinkers
sought originality by exaggerating certain Enlightenment ideas to the exclusion of others. These
latter-day philosophes often built rigid, dogmatic
systems.

In his *System of Nature* (1770) and other works,
the wealthy German-born but French-educated
Baron Paul d'Holbach (1723–1789) argued that
human beings were machines completely determined by outside forces. Free will, God, and immortality of the soul, he claimed, were foolish
myths. D'Holbach's aggressive atheism and deter-
minism dealt the unity of the Enlightenment
movement a severe blow. Deists such as Voltaire,
who believed in God but not in established

churches, were repelled by the inflexible atheism
they found in the *System of Nature.* They saw in it
the same dogmatic intolerance they had been
fighting all their lives.

Nevertheless, D'Holbach was a generous patron
and witty host of writers and intellectuals. At his
twice-weekly dinner parties, an inner circle of reg-
ulars exchanged ideas with aspiring philosophes
and distinguished visitors. One whose carefully argued skepticism had a powerful long-term influence was the Scottish philosopher David Hume
(1711–1776).

Building on Locke's teachings on learning,
Hume argued that the human mind is really nothing but a bundle of impressions. These impressions
originate only in sense experiences and our habits
of joining these experiences together. Reason,
therefore, cannot tell us anything about questions
that cannot be verified by sense experience (in the
form of controlled experiments or mathematics),

such as the origin of the universe or the existence of God. Paradoxically, Hume's rationalistic inquiry ended up undermining the Enlightenment's faith in the power of reason.

Another French aristocrat, Marie-Jean Caritat, the marquis de Condorcet (1743–1794), transformed the Enlightenment belief in gradual, hard-won progress into fanciful utopianism. In his *Progress of the Human Mind,* written in 1793 during the French Revolution, Condorcet hypothesized and tracked nine stages of human progress that had already occurred, and he predicted that the tenth would bring perfection. Ironically, Condorcet wrote this work while fleeing for his life. Caught and condemned by revolutionary extremists, he preferred death by his own hand to the blade of the guillotine.

Other thinkers and writers after about 1770 began to attack the Enlightenment's faith in reason, progress, and moderation. The most famous of these was the Swiss Jean-Jacques Rousseau (1712–1778), a brilliant and difficult thinker, an appealing but neurotic individual. Born into a poor family of watchmakers in Geneva, Rousseau went to Paris and was greatly influenced by Diderot and Voltaire. Always extraordinarily sensitive and suspicious, Rousseau came to believe that his philosophe friends and the women of the Parisian salons were plotting against him. In the mid-1750s, he broke with them personally and intellectually, living thereafter as a lonely outsider with his uneducated common-law wife and going in his own highly original direction.

Like other Enlightenment thinkers, Rousseau was passionately committed to individual freedom. Unlike them, however, he attacked rationalism and civilization as destroying, rather than liberating, the individual. Warm, spontaneous feeling had to complement and correct cold intellect, he believed. Moreover, the basic goodness of the individual and the unspoiled child had to be protected from the cruel refinements of civilization. These ideas greatly influenced the early romantic movement (see Chapter 25), which rebelled against the culture of the Enlightenment in the late eighteenth century. They also had a powerful impact on the development of child psychology and modern education (see Chapter 19, Listening to the Past).

Rousseau's contribution to political theory in *The Social Contract* (1762) was equally significant. His contribution was based on two fundamental concepts: the general will and popular sovereignty.

According to Rousseau, the general will is sacred and absolute, reflecting the common interests of all the people, who have displaced the monarch as the holder of sovereign power. The general will is not necessarily the will of the majority, however. At times, the general will may be the authentic, long-term needs of the people as correctly interpreted by a farseeing minority. Little noticed before the French Revolution, Rousseau's concept of the general will appealed greatly to democrats and nationalists after 1789. The concept has also been used since 1789 by many dictators claiming that they, rather than some momentary majority of the voters, represent the general will and thus the true interests of democracy and the sovereign masses.

Urban Culture and Public Opinion

The writings and press campaigns of the philosophes were part of a profound cultural transformation. The object of impressive ongoing research and scholarly debate in recent years, this transformation had several interrelated aspects.

Of great importance, the European market for books grew dramatically in the eighteenth century. In Germany the number of new titles appearing annually grew substantially and at an accelerating rate, from roughly six hundred new titles in 1700 to about eleven hundred in 1764 and about twenty-six hundred in 1780. Well-studied France, which was indicative of general European trends, witnessed an explosive growth in book consumption. The solid and upper middle classes, the clergy, and the aristocracy accounted for most of the change. The number of books in the hands of these privileged groups increased eight- to tenfold between the 1690s and the 1780s. Moreover, the number of religious and devotional books published legally in Paris declined precipitously. History and law held constant, while the proportion of legally published books treating the arts and sciences surged.

In addition, France's unpredictable but pervasive censorship caused many books to be printed abroad and then smuggled back into the country for "under-the-cloak" sale. Experts believe that perhaps the majority of French books produced between 1750 and 1789 came from publishing companies located outside France. These publishers also smuggled forbidden books in French and other languages into the absolutist states of central, southern, and eastern Europe. The recently discovered catalogues of some of these foreign publishers reveal a massive presence of the famous French philosophes, reaffirming the philosophes' central role in the spread of critical secular attitudes.

The illegal book trade in France also featured an astonishing growth of scandalmongering denunciations of high political figures and frankly pornographic works. These literary forms frequently came together in scathing pornographic accounts of the moral and sexual depravity of the French court, allegedly mired in luxury, perversion, and adultery. A favorite theme was the way that some beautiful but immoral aristocratic women used their sexual charms to gain power over weak rulers and high officials, thereby corrupting the process of government. Spurred by repeated royal directives, the French police did its best to stamp out this underground literature, but new slanders kept cropping up, like the wild tabloid fantasies at checkout counters in today's supermarkets.

Reading more books on many more subjects, the educated public in France and throughout Europe increasingly approached reading in a new way. The result was what some German scholars have called a "reading revolution." The old style of reading in Europe had been centered on sacred texts read slowly aloud with the audience reverently savoring each word. Now reading involved many texts, which were constantly changing and commanded no special respect. Reading became individual, silent, and rapid. The well-educated classes were reading insatiably, skeptically, and carelessly. Subtle but profound, the reading revolution was closely linked to the rise of a critical world-view.

As the reading public developed, it joined forces with the philosophes to call for the autonomy of the printed word. Outside Prussia, the Netherlands, and Great Britain, however, censorship was the rule. And the philosophes and the public resorted to discussion and social interchange in order to circumvent censorship and create an autonomous cultural sphere. Indeed, sparkling conversation in private homes spread Enlightenment ideas to Europe's upper middle class and aristocracy. Paris set the example, and other French and European cities followed. In Paris a number of talented and often rich women presided over regular social gatherings in their elegant drawing rooms, or *salons*. There they encouraged the exchange of witty, uncensored observations on literature, science, and philosophy.

Elite women also exercised an unprecedented feminine influence on artistic taste. Soft pastels, ornate interiors, sentimental portraits, and starry-eyed lovers protected by hovering Cupids were all hallmarks of the style they favored. This style, known as the rococo, was popular throughout Europe in the eighteenth century. Some philosophes championed greater rights and expanded education for women, claiming that the position and treatment of women were the best indicators of a society's level of civilization and decency.[11] To be sure, to these male philosophes greater rights for women did not mean equal rights, and the philosophes were not particularly disturbed by the fact that elite women remained legally subordinate to men in economic and political affairs. Elite women lacked many rights, but so did most men.

One of the most famous salons was that of Madame Geoffrin, the unofficial godmother of the *Encyclopedia*. Madame Geoffrin was married by arrangement at fifteen to a rich and boring businessman of forty-eight. After dutifully raising her children, and in spite of her husband's loud protests, she developed a twice-weekly salon that counted Fontenelle and Montesquieu among its regular guests. Inheriting a large fortune after her husband's death, Madame Geoffrin gave the encyclopedists generous financial aid and helped save their enterprise from collapse. Corresponding with the king of Sweden and Catherine the Great of Russia, Madame Geoffrin remained her own woman, a practicing Christian who would not tolerate attacks on the church in her house.

The talented Julie de Lespinasse epitomized the skills of the Enlightenment hostess. Her highly informal salon attracted the keenest minds in France and Europe. As one philosophe wrote:

She could unite the different types, even the most antagonistic, sustaining the conversation by a well-aimed phrase, animating and guiding it at will. . . . Politics, religion, philosophy, news: nothing was excluded. Her circle met daily from five to nine. There one found men of all ranks in the State, the Church, and the Court, soldiers and foreigners, and the leading writers of the day.[12]

As that passage suggests, the salons created an independent cultural realm freed from religious dogma and political censorship. There educated members of the intellectual, economic, and social elites could debate issues and form their own ideas.

Enlightenment Culture The culture of the Enlightenment was elegant, intellectual, and international. This painting shows the seven-year-old Austrian child prodigy, Wolfgang Amadeus Mozart (1756–1791), playing his own composition at an "English tea" given by the Princess de Conti near Paris. Mozart's phenomenal creative powers lasted a lifetime, and he produced a vast range of symphonies, operas, and chamber music. (*Source: Versailles/Photographie Bulloz*)

In this gracious atmosphere, the *public* of philosophes, the French nobility, and the prosperous middle classes intermingled and increasingly influenced one another. Critical thinking about almost any question became fashionable and flourished with hopes for human progress through greater knowledge and enlightened public opinion.

THE ENLIGHTENMENT AND ABSOLUTISM

How did the Enlightenment influence political developments? To this important question there is no easy answer. On the one hand, the French philosophes and kindred spirits in most European countries were primarily interested in converting people to critical, scientific thinking and were not particularly concerned with politics. On the other hand, such thinking naturally led to political criticism and interest in political reform as both possible and desirable.

Some Enlightenment thinkers, led by the nobleman Montesquieu, argued for curbs on monarchial power in order to promote liberty. Until the American Revolution, however, most Enlightenment thinkers outside England and the Netherlands believed that political change could best come from above—from the ruler—rather than from below, especially in central and eastern Europe. Royal absolutism was a fact of life, and the kings and queens of Europe's leading states clearly had no intention of giving up their great powers. Therefore, the philosophes and their sympathizers realistically concluded that a benevolent absolutism offered the best opportunities for improving society. Critical thinking was turning the art of good government into an exact science. It was necessary only to educate and "enlighten" the monarch, who could then make good laws and promote human happiness. Enlightenment thinkers also turned toward rulers because rulers seemed to be listening, treating them with respect, and seeking their advice. Finally, the philosophes distrusted "the people," who they believed were deluded by superstitions and driven by violent passions, little children in need of firm parental guidance.

Encouraged and instructed by the philosophes, many absolutist rulers of the later eighteenth century tried to govern in an "enlightened" manner. Yet the actual programs and accomplishments of these rulers varied greatly. Let us therefore examine the evolution of monarchial absolutism at close range before trying to form any overall judgment about the Enlightenment's effect on it.

Absolutism in Central and Eastern Europe

Enlightenment teachings inspired European rulers in small as well as large states in the second half of the eighteenth century. Yet by far the most influential of the new-style monarchs were in Prussia, Russia, and Austria, and they deserve primary attention.

Frederick the Great of Prussia   Frederick II (r. 1740–1786), commonly known as Frederick the Great, built masterfully on the work of his father, Frederick William I (see pages 573–574). This was somewhat surprising, for like many children with tyrannical parents he rebelled against his family's wishes in his early years. Rejecting the crude life of the barracks, Frederick embraced culture and literature, even writing poetry and fine prose in French, a language his father detested. After trying unsuccessfully to run away in 1730 at age eighteen, he was virtually imprisoned and even compelled to watch his companion in flight beheaded at his father's command. Yet like many other rebellious youths, Frederick eventually reached a reconciliation with his father, and by the time he came to the throne ten years later, Frederick was determined to use the splendid army that his father had left him.

Therefore, when the ruler of Austria, Charles VI, also died in 1740 and his young and charismatic daughter, Maria Theresa, inherited the Habsburg dominions, Frederick suddenly and without warning invaded her rich, mainly German province of Silesia. This action defied solemn Prussian promises to respect the Pragmatic Sanction, which guaranteed Maria Theresa's succession. Maria Theresa's ethnically diverse army was no match for Prussian precision. In 1742 as other greedy powers were falling on her lands in the general European War of the Austrian Succession (1740–1748), she was forced to cede almost all of Silesia to Prussia (see Map 17.3). In one stroke Prussia doubled its population to 6 million people. Now Prussia unquestionably towered above all the other German states and stood as a European Great Power.

Though successful in 1742, Frederick had to spend much of his reign fighting against great odds to save Prussia from total destruction. Maria Theresa was determined to regain Silesia, and when the ongoing competition between Britain and France for colonial empire brought renewed conflict in 1756, Austria fashioned an aggressive alliance with France and Russia. During the Seven Years' War (1756–1763), the aim of the alliance was to conquer Prussia and divide up its territory. Frederick led his army brilliantly, striking repeatedly at vastly superior forces invading from all sides. At times he believed all was lost, but he fought on with stoic courage. In the end, he was miraculously saved: Peter III came to the Russian throne in 1762 and called off the attack against Frederick, whom he greatly admired.

In the early years of his reign, Frederick II had kept his enthusiasm for Enlightenment culture strictly separated from a brutal concept of international politics. He wrote:

Of all States, from the smallest to the biggest, one can safely say that the fundamental rule of government is the principle of extending their territories. . . . The passions of rulers have no other curb but the limits of their power. Those are the fixed laws of European politics to which every politician submits.[13]

But the terrible struggle of the Seven Years' War tempered Frederick and brought him to consider how more humane policies for his subjects might also strengthen the state.

Thus Frederick went beyond a superficial commitment to Enlightenment culture for himself and his circle. He tolerantly allowed his subjects to believe as they wished in religious and philosophical matters. He promoted the advancement of knowledge, improving his country's schools and permitting scholars to publish their findings. Moreover, Frederick tried to improve the lives of his subjects more directly. As he wrote his friend Voltaire, "I must enlighten my people, cultivate their manners and morals, and make them as happy as human beings can be, or as happy as the means at my disposal permit." Prussia's laws were simplified, torture of prisoners was abolished, and judges decided cases quickly and impartially. Prussian officials became famous for their hard work and honesty. Frederick himself set a good example. He worked hard and lived modestly, claiming that he was "only the first servant of the state." Thus Frederick justified monarchy in terms of practical results and said nothing of the divine right of kings.

Frederick's dedication to high-minded government went only so far, however. He never tried to

Catherine as Equestrian Catherine took advantage of her intelligence and good looks to overthrow her husband Peter III and become empress of Russia. Strongly influenced by the Enlightenment, she cultivated the French philosophes and instituted moderate reforms only to reverse them in the aftermath of Pugachev's rebellion. Catherine's portrait hangs above her throne. *(Source: Novosti)*

change Prussia's existing social structure. True, he condemned serfdom in the abstract, but he accepted it in practice and did not even free the serfs on his own estates. He accepted and extended the privileges of the nobility, which he saw as his primary ally in the defense and extension of his realm. It became practically impossible for a middle-class person to gain a top position in the government. The Junker nobility remained the backbone of the army and the entire Prussian state.

Catherine the Great of Russia   Catherine the Great of Russia (r. 1762–1796) was one of the most remarkable rulers who ever lived, and the French philosophes adored her. Catherine was a German princess from Anhalt-Zerbst, a totally insignificant principality sandwiched between Prussia and Saxony. Her father commanded a regiment of the Prussian army, but her mother was related to the Romanovs of Russia, and that relationship proved to be Catherine's chance.

Peter the Great had abolished the hereditary succession of tsars so that he could name his successor and thus preserve his policies. This move opened a period of palace intrigue and a rapid turnover of rulers until Peter's youngest daughter, Elizabeth, came to the Russian throne in 1741. A shrewd but crude woman—one of her official lovers was an illiterate shepherd boy—Elizabeth named her nephew Peter heir to the throne and chose Catherine to be his wife in 1744. It was a mismatch from the beginning. The fifteen-year-old Catherine was intelligent and attractive; her husband was stupid and ugly, his face badly scarred by smallpox. Ignored by her childish husband, Catherine carefully studied Russian, endlessly read writers such as Bayle and Voltaire, and made friends at court. Soon she knew what she wanted. "I did not care about Peter," she wrote in her *Memoirs,* "but I did care about the crown."[14]

As the old empress Elizabeth approached death, Catherine plotted against her unpopular husband. She selected as her new lover a tall, dashing young officer named Gregory Orlov, who with his four officer brothers commanded considerable support among the soldiers stationed in St. Petersburg. When Peter came to the throne in 1762, his decision to withdraw Russian troops from the coalition against Prussia alienated the army. Nor did Peter III's attempt to gain support from the Russian nobility by freeing it from compulsory state service succeed. At the end of six months, Catherine and her military conspirators deposed Peter III in a palace revolution. Then the Orlov brothers murdered him. The German princess became empress of Russia.

Catherine had drunk deeply at the Enlightenment well. Never questioning the common assumption that absolute monarchy was the best form of government, she set out to rule in an enlightened manner. She had three main goals. First, she worked hard to bring the sophisticated culture of western Europe to backward Russia. To do so, she imported Western architects, sculptors, musicians, and intellectuals. She bought masterpieces of Western art in wholesale lots and patronized the philosophes. An enthusiastic letter writer, she corresponded extensively with Voltaire and praised him as the "champion of the human race." When the French government banned the *Encyclopedia,* she offered to publish it in St. Petersburg. She sent money to Diderot when he needed it. With these and countless similar actions, Catherine won good press in the West for herself and for her country. Moreover, this intellectual ruler, who wrote plays and loved good talk, set the tone for the entire Russian nobility. Peter the Great westernized Russian armies, but it was Catherine who westernized the thinking of the Russian nobility.

Catherine's second goal was domestic reform, and she began her reign with sincere and ambitious projects. Better laws were a major concern. She appointed a special legislative commission to prepare a new law code. No new unified code was ever produced, but Catherine did restrict the practice of torture and allowed limited religious toleration. She also tried to improve education and strengthen local government. The philosophes applauded these measures and hoped more would follow.

Such was not the case. In 1773 a common Cossack soldier named Emelian Pugachev sparked a gigantic uprising of serfs, very much as Stenka Razin had done a century earlier (see page 578). Proclaiming himself the true tsar, Pugachev issued "decrees" abolishing serfdom, taxes, and army service. Thousands joined his cause, slaughtering landlords and officials over a vast area of southwestern Russia. Pugachev's untrained hordes eventually proved no match for Catherine's noble-led regular army. Betrayed by his own company, Pugachev was captured and savagely executed.

Pugachev's rebellion was a decisive turning point in Catherine's domestic policy. On coming to the throne, she had condemned serfdom in theory, but Pugachev's rebellion put an end to any illusions she might have had about attempting reform. The peasants were clearly dangerous, and her empire rested on the support of the nobility. After 1775 Catherine gave the nobles absolute control of their serfs. She extended serfdom into new areas, such as Ukraine. In 1785 she formalized the nobility's privileged position, freeing nobles forever from taxes and state service. She also confiscated the lands of the Russian Orthodox church and gave them to favorite officials. Under Catherine the Russian nobility attained its most exalted position, and serfdom entered its most oppressive phase.

Catherine's third goal was territorial expansion, and in this she was extremely successful. Her armies subjugated the last descendants of the Mongols, the Crimean Tartars, and began the conquest of the Caucasus. Her greatest coup by far was the partitioning of Poland, whose fate in the late eighteenth century demonstrated the dangers of failing to build a strong absolutist state. All important decisions continued to require the unanimous agreement of all nobles elected to the Polish Diet, which meant that nothing could ever be done to strengthen the state. When Frederick of Prussia proposed that Prussia, Austria, and Russia each take a gigantic slice of Polish territory, Catherine jumped at the chance. The first partition of Poland took place in 1772. Two more partitions, in 1793 and 1795, gave all three powers more Polish territory, and the ancient republic of Poland simply vanished from the map.

Expansion helped Catherine keep the nobility happy, for it provided her with vast new lands to give to her faithful servants and her many lovers. On all the official royal favorites she lavished large estates with many serfs, as if to make sure there were no hard feelings when her interest cooled. Until the end this remarkable woman—who always believed that, in spite of her domestic setbacks, she was slowly civilizing Russia—kept her zest for life. Fascinated by a new twenty-two-year-old flame when she was a roly-poly grandmother in her sixties, she happily reported her good fortune to a favorite former lover: "I have come back to life like a frozen fly; I am gay and well."[15]

The Austrian Habsburgs   In Austria, two talented rulers did manage to introduce major reforms, although traditional power politics was more important than Enlightenment teachings. One was Joseph II (r. 1780–1790), a fascinating individual. For an earlier generation of historians he was the "revolutionary emperor," a tragic hero whose lofty reforms were undone by the landowning nobility he challenged. More recent scholarship has revised this romantic interpretation and stressed how Joseph II continued the state-building work of his mother, the empress Maria Theresa (r. 1740–1780), a remarkable but old-fashioned absolutist.

Emerging from the long War of the Austrian Succession in 1748 with only the serious loss of Silesia, Maria Theresa and her closest ministers were determined to introduce reforms that would make the state stronger and more efficient. Three aspects of these reforms were most important. First, Maria Theresa introduced measures aimed at limiting the papacy's political influence in her realm. Second, a whole series of administrative reforms strengthened the central bureaucracy,

Maria Theresa The empress of Austria and her husband pose with eleven of their sixteen children at Schönbrunn palace in this family portrait by court painter Martin Meytens (1695–1770). Joseph, the heir to the throne, stands at the center of the star pattern. Wealthy women often had very large families, in part because they seldom nursed their babies as poor women usually did. *(Source: Kunsthistorisches Museum, Vienna)*

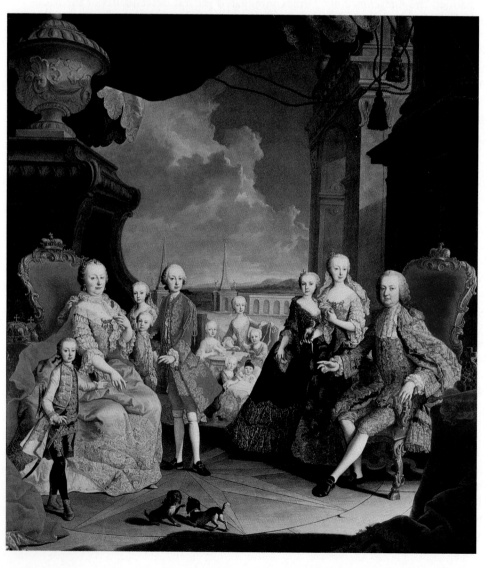

smoothed out some provincial differences, and revamped the tax system, taxing even the lands of nobles without special exemptions. Third, the government sought to improve the lot of the agricultural population, cautiously reducing the power of lords over their hereditary serfs and their partially free peasant tenants.

Coregent with his mother from 1765 onward and a strong supporter of change, Joseph II moved forward rapidly when he came to the throne in 1780. He controlled the established Catholic church even more closely in an attempt to ensure that it produced better citizens. He granted religious toleration and civic rights to Protestants and Jews—a radical innovation that impressed his contemporaries. In even more spectacular peasant reforms, Joseph abolished serfdom in 1781, and in 1789 he decreed that all peasant labor obligations be converted into cash payments. This ill-conceived measure was violently rejected not only by the nobility but also by the peasants it was intended to help, for their primitive barter economy was woefully lacking in money. When a disillusioned Joseph died prematurely at forty-nine, the entire Habsburg Empire was in turmoil. His brother Leopold II (r. 1790–1792) was forced to cancel Joseph's radical edicts in order to re-establish order. Peasants once again were required to do forced labor for their lords.

Absolutism in France

The Enlightenment's influence on political developments in France was complex. The monarchy maintained its absolutist claims, and some philosophes, such as Voltaire, believed that the king was still the best source of needed reform. At the same time, discontented nobles and learned judges drew on thinkers such as Montesquieu for liberal arguments. They sought with some success to limit the king's power, as France diverged from the absolutist states just considered.

When Louis XIV finally died in 1715, to be succeeded by his five-year-old great-grandson, Louis XV (r. 1715–1774), the Sun King's elaborate system of absolutist rule was challenged in a general reaction. Favored by the duke of Orléans (1674–1723), a licentious rake and nephew of Louis XIV who governed as regent until 1723, the nobility made a strong comeback.

Most important, in 1715 the duke restored to the high court of Paris—the Parlement—the an-cient right to evaluate royal decrees publicly before they were given the force of law. The restoration of this right, which had been suspended under Louis XIV, was a fateful step. The judges of the Parlement of Paris had originally come from the middle class, and their high position reflected the way that Louis XIV (and earlier French monarchs) had chosen to use that class to build the royal bureaucracy so necessary for an absolutist state. By the eighteenth century, however, these middle-class judges had risen to become hereditary nobles. Moreover, although Louis XIV had curbed the political power of the nobility, he had never challenged its enormous social prestige. Thus high position in the government continued to bestow the noble status that middle-class officials wanted. The judges of Paris, like many high-ranking officials, actually owned their government jobs and freely passed them on as private property from father to son. By allowing this well-entrenched and increasingly aristocratic group to evaluate the king's decrees, the duke of Orléans sanctioned a counterweight to absolute power.

These implications became clear when the heavy expenses of the War of the Austrian Succession plunged France into financial crisis. In 1748 Louis XV appointed a finance minister who decreed a 5 percent income tax on every individual regardless of social status. Exemption from most taxation had long been a hallowed privilege of the nobility, and other important groups—the clergy, the large towns, and some wealthy bourgeoisie—had also gained special tax advantages over time. The result was a vigorous protest from many sides, led by the Parlement of Paris. The monarchy retreated; the new tax was dropped.

After the disastrously expensive Seven Years' War, the conflict re-emerged. The government tried to maintain emergency taxes after the war ended. The Parlement of Paris protested and even challenged the basis of royal authority, claiming that the king's power had to be limited to protect liberty. Once again the government caved in and withdrew the wartime taxes in 1764. Emboldened by this striking victory, the judicial opposition asserted that the king could not levy taxes without the consent of the Parlement of Paris acting as the representative of the entire nation.

Indolent and sensual by nature, more interested in his many mistresses than in affairs of state, Louis XV finally roused himself for a determined defense of his absolutist inheritance. "The magistrates," he angrily told the Parlement of Paris in a famous face-to-face confrontation, "are my officers. . . . In my person only does the sovereign power rest."[16] In 1768 Louis appointed a tough career official named René de Maupeou as chancellor and ordered him to crush the judicial opposition.

Maupeou abolished the Parlement of Paris and exiled its members to isolated backwaters in the provinces. He created a new and docile Parlement of royal officials, and he began once again to tax the privileged groups. Most philosophes and educated public opinion as a whole sided with the old Parlement, however, and there was widespread criticism of "royal despotism." The illegal stream of scandalmongering, pornographic attacks on the king and his court became a torrent, and some scholars now believe these lurid denunciations ate away at the foundations of royal authority. Yet the monarchy's power was still great enough for Maupeou simply to ride over the opposition, and Louis XV would probably have prevailed—if he had lived to a very ripe old age.

But Louis XV died in 1774. The new king, Louis XVI (r. 1774–1792), was a shy twenty-year-old with good intentions. Taking the throne, he is reported to have said, "What I should like most is to be loved."[17] The eager-to-please monarch decided to yield in the face of such strong criticism from so much of France's educated elite. He dismissed Maupeou and repudiated the strong-willed minister's work. The old Parlement of Paris was reinstated as enlightened public opinion cheered and anticipated moves toward more representative government. But such moves were not forthcoming. Instead, a weakened but unreformed monarchy faced a judicial opposition that claimed to speak for the entire French nation. Increasingly locked in stalemate, the country was drifting toward renewed financial crisis and political upheaval.

The Overall Influence of the Enlightenment

Having examined the evolution of monarchial absolutism in four leading states, we can begin to look for meaningful generalizations and evaluate the overall influence of Enlightenment thought on politics.

France clearly diverged from its eastern neighbors in its political development in the eighteenth century. The capacity of the French monarch to govern in a truly absolutist manner declined substantially. The political resurgence of the French nobility after 1715 and the growth of judicial opposition drew crucial support from educated public opinion, which increasingly made the liberal critique of unregulated royal authority its own.

The situation in eastern and east-central Europe was different. The liberal critique of absolute monarchy remained an intellectual curiosity, and proponents of reform from above held sway. Moreover, despite differences, the leading eastern European monarchs of the later eighteenth century all claimed that they were acting on the principles of the Enlightenment. The philosophes generally agreed with this assessment and cheered them on. Beginning in the mid-nineteenth century, historians developed the idea of a common "enlightened despotism" or "enlightened absolutism," and they canonized Frederick, Catherine, and Joseph as its most outstanding examples. More recent research has raised doubts about this old interpretation and has led to a fundamental reevaluation.

There is general agreement that these absolutists, especially Catherine and Frederick, did encourage and spread the cultural values of the Enlightenment. They were proud of their intellectual accomplishments and good taste, and they supported knowledge, education, and the arts. Historians also agree that the absolutists believed in change from above and tried to enact needed reforms. Yet the results of these efforts brought only very modest improvements, and the life of the peasantry remained very hard in the eighteenth century. Thus some historians have concluded that these monarchs were not really sincere in their reform efforts. Others disagree, arguing that powerful nobilities blocked the absolutists' genuine commitment to reform. (The old interpretation of Joseph II as the tragic revolutionary emperor forms part of this argument.)

The emerging answer to this controversy is that the later eastern absolutists were indeed committed to reform but that humanitarian objectives were of quite secondary importance. Above all, the absolutists wanted reforms that would strengthen the state and allow them to compete militarily with their neighbors. Modern scholarship has therefore stressed how Catherine, Frederick, and Joseph were in many ways simply continuing the state building of their predecessors, reorganizing armies and expanding bureaucracies to raise more taxes and troops. The reason for this continuation was simple. The international political struggle was

THE ENLIGHTENMENT

1686	Fontenelle, *Conversations on the Plurality of Worlds*
1687	Newton, *Principia*
1690	Locke, "Essay Concerning Human Understanding" and "Second Treatise on Civil Government"
1715–1774	Rule of Louis XV in France
1721	Montesquieu, *The Persian Letters*
1740–1748	War of the Austrian Succession
1740–1780	Rule of Maria Theresa in Austria
1740–1786	Rule of Frederick II (the Great) in Prussia
1742	Austria cedes Silesia to Prussia
1743	Voltaire, *Age of Louis XIV*
1748	Montesquieu, *The Spirit of the Laws* Hume, *An Enquiry Concerning Human Understanding*
1751–1765	Publication of the *Encyclopedia,* edited by Diderot and d'Alembert
1756–1763	Seven Years' War
1762	Rousseau, *Social Contract*
1762–1796	Rule of Catherine II (the Great) in Russia
1770	D'Holbach, *The System of Nature*
1771	Maupeou, Louis XV's chancellor, abolishes Parlement of Paris
1772	First partition of Poland among Russia, Prussia, and Austria
1774	Ascension of Louis XVI in France; restoration of Parlement of Paris
1780–1790	Rule of Joseph II in Austria
1781	Abolition of serfdom in Austria
1785	Catherine the Great frees the nobles from taxes and state service
1790–1792	Rule of Leopold II in Austria; serfdom is re-established
1793, 1795	Second and third partitions of Poland, which completes its absorption

brutal, and the stakes were high. First Austria under Maria Theresa and then Prussia under Frederick the Great had to engage in bitter fighting to escape dismemberment. Decentralized Poland was coldly divided and eventually liquidated.

Yet in this drive for more state power, the later absolutists were also innovators, and the idea of an era of enlightened absolutism retains a certain validity. Sharing the Enlightenment faith in critical thinking and believing that knowledge meant power, these absolutists really were more enlightened than their predecessors because they put state-building reforms in a new, broader perspective. Above all, the later absolutists considered how more humane laws and practices could help their populations become more productive and satisfied and thus able to contribute more substantially to the welfare of the state. It was from this perspective that they introduced many of their most progressive reforms, tolerating religious minorities, simplifying legal codes, and promoting practical education. Nevertheless, reforms had to be grafted on to existing political and social structures. Thus each enlightened absolutist sought greater state power, but each believed a different policy would attain it.

The eastern European absolutists of the later eighteenth century combined old-fashioned state building with the culture and critical thinking of the Enlightenment. In doing so, they succeeded in expanding the role of the state in the life of society. Unlike the successors of Louis XIV, they perfected bureaucratic machines that were to prove surprisingly adaptive and capable of enduring into the twentieth century.

Summary

This chapter has focused on the complex development of a new world-view in Western civilization. This new view was essentially critical and secular, drawing its inspiration from the scientific revolution and crystallizing in the Enlightenment.

Decisive breakthroughs in astronomy and physics in the seventeenth century, which demolished the imposing medieval synthesis of Aristotelian philosophy and Christian theology, had only limited practical consequences despite the expectations of scientific enthusiasts. Yet the impact of new scientific knowledge on intellectual life became great. Interpreting scientific findings and Newtonian laws in an antitraditional, antireligious manner, the French philosophes of the Enlightenment extolled the superiority of rational, critical thinking. This new method, they believed, promised not just increased knowledge but even the discovery of the fundamental laws of human society. Although they reached different conclusions when they turned to social and political realities, they did stimulate absolute monarchs to apply reason to statecraft and the search for useful reforms. Above all, the philosophes succeeded in shaping an emerging public opinion and spreading their radically new world-view. These were momentous accomplishments.

Notes

1. H. Butterfield, *The Origins of Modern Science* (New York: Macmillan, 1951), p. viii.
2. Quoted in A. G. R. Smith, *Science and Society in the Sixteenth and Seventeenth Centuries* (New York: Harcourt Brace Jovanovich, 1972), p. 97.
3. Quoted in Butterfield, *The Origins of Modern Science*, p. 47.
4. Quoted in Smith, *Science and Society in the Sixteenth and Seventeenth Centuries*, p. 120.
5. A. R. Hall, *From Galileo to Newton, 1630–1720* (New York: Harper & Row, 1963), p. 290.
6. Quoted in P. Hazard, *The European Mind, 1680–1715* (Cleveland: Meridian Books, 1963), pp. 304–305.
7. Quoted in R. Chartier, *The Cultural Origins of the French Revolution* (Durham, N.C.: Duke University Press, 1991), p. 27.
8. Quoted in L. Schiebinger, *The Mind Has No Sex?: Women in the Origins of Modern Science* (Cambridge, Mass.: Harvard University Press, 1989), p. 64.
9. Quoted in G. L. Mosse et al., eds., *Europe in Review* (Chicago: Rand McNally, 1964), p. 156.
10. Quoted in P. Gay, "The Unity of the Enlightenment," *History* 3 (1960): 25.
11. See E. Fox-Genovese, "Women in the Enlightenment," in *Becoming Visible: Women in European History*, 2d ed., ed. R. Bridenthal, C. Koonz, and S. Stuard (Boston: Houghton Mifflin, 1987), esp. pp. 252–259 and 263–265.
12. Quoted in G. P. Gooch, *Catherine the Great and Other Studies* (Hamden, Conn.: Archon Books, 1966), p. 149.
13. Quoted in L. Krieger, *Kings and Philosophers, 1689–1789* (New York: Norton, 1970), p. 257.
14. Quoted in Gooch, *Catherine the Great and Other Studies*, p. 15.
15. Ibid., p. 53.
16. Quoted in R. R. Palmer, *The Age of Democratic Revolution*, vol. 1 (Princeton, N.J.: Princeton University Press, 1959), pp. 95–96.
17. Quoted in G. Wright, *France in Modern Times*, 4th ed. (New York: Norton, 1987), p. 34.

Suggested Reading

The first three authors cited in the Notes—H. Butterfield, A. G. R. Smith, and A. R. Hall—have written excellent general interpretations of the scientific revolution. These may be compared with an outstanding recent work by M. Jacob, *The Cultural Meaning of the*

Scientific Revolution (1988), which has a useful bibliography. L. Schiebinger, *The Mind Has No Sex?: Women in the Origins of Modern Science* (1989), provides a brilliant analysis of how the new science gradually excluded women interested in science, a question completely neglected in older studies. A. Debus, *Man and Nature in the Renaissance* (1978), is good on the Copernican revolution, whereas M. Boas, *The Scientific Renaissance, 1450–1630* (1966), is especially insightful about the influence of magic on science. S. Drake, *Galileo* (1980), is a good short biography. T. Kuhn, *The Structure of Scientific Revolutions* (1962), is a challenging, much-discussed attempt to understand major breakthroughs in scientific thought over time. E. Andrade, *Sir Isaac Newton* (1958), is a good brief biography, which may be compared with F. Manuel, *The Religion of Isaac Newton* (1974).

The work of P. Hazard listed in the Notes is a classic study of the formative years of Enlightenment thought, and his *European Thought in the Eighteenth Century* (1954) is also recommended. P. Gay has written several major studies on the Enlightenment: *Voltaire's Politics* (1959) and *The Party of Humanity* (1971) are two of the best. J. Sklar, *Montesquieu* (1987), is an engaging biography. I. Wade, *The Structure and Form of the French Enlightenment* (1977), is a major synthesis. F. Baumer, *Religion and the Rise of Skepticism* (1969); H. Payne, *The Philosophes and the People* (1976); and H. Chisick, *The Limits of Reform in the Enlightenment: Attitudes Toward the Education of the Lower Classes in Eighteenth-Century France* (1981), are interesting studies of important aspects of Enlightenment thought. The changing attitudes of the educated public are imaginatively analyzed by R. Chartier in *The Cultural Origins of the French Revolution*, cited in the Notes, and in *French Historical Studies* (Fall 1992). R. Danton, *The Literary Underground of the Old Regime* (1982), provides a fascinating glimpse of low-life publishing. On women, see the stimulating study by E. Fox-Genovese cited in the Notes as well as S. Spencer, ed., *French Women and the Age of Enlightenment* (1984), and K. Rogers, *Feminism in Eighteenth-Century England* (1982). J. Landes, *Women and the Public Sphere in the Age of the French Revolution* (1988), is a fascinating and controversial study of women and politics. Above all, one should read some of the philosophes and let them speak for themselves. Two good anthologies are C. Brinton, ed., *The Portable Age of Reason* (1956), and F. Manuel, ed., *The Enlightenment* (1951). Voltaire's most famous and very amusing novel *Candide* is highly recommended, as is S. Gendzier, ed., *Denis Diderot: The Encyclopedia: Selections* (1967). A. Wilson's biography, *Diderot* (1972), is long but rewarding.

In addition to the works mentioned in the Suggested Reading for Chapter 17, the monarchies of Europe are carefully analyzed in H. Scott, *Enlightened Absolutism* (1990); in C. Tilly, ed., *The Formation of National States in Western Europe* (1975); and in J. Gagliardo, *Enlightened Despotism* (1967), all of which have useful bibliographies. M. Anderson, *Historians and Eighteenth-Century Europe* (1979), is a valuable introduction to modern scholarship, and C. Behrens, *Society, Government, and the Enlightenment: The Experience of Eighteenth-Century France and Prussia* (1985), is a stimulating comparative study. A recommended study on the struggle for power and reform in France is F. Ford, *Robe and Sword* (1953), which discusses the resurgence of the French nobility after the death of Louis XIV. J. Lynch, *Bourbon Spain, 1700–1808* (1989), and R. Herr, *The Eighteenth-Century Revolution in Spain* (1958), skillfully analyze the impact of Enlightenment thought in Spain. Important works on Austria include C. Macartney, *Maria Theresa and the House of Austria* (1970); P. Bernard, *Joseph II* (1968); and T. Blanning, *Joseph II and Enlightened Absolutism* (1970). There are several fine works on Russia. J. Alexander, *Catherine the Great: Life and Legend* (1989), is the best biography of the famous ruler, which may be compared with the empress's own story, *The Memoirs of Catherine the Great*, edited by D. Maroger (1961). I. de Madariaga, *Russia in the Age of Catherine the Great* (1981); and P. Dukes, *The Making of Russian Absolutism, 1613–1801* (1982), are strongly recommended. The ambitious reader should also look at A. N. Radishchev, *A Journey from St. Petersburg to Moscow* (English trans., 1958), a famous 1790 attack on Russian serfdom and an appeal to Catherine the Great to free the serfs, for which Radishchev was exiled to Siberia.

The culture of the time may be approached through A. Cobban, ed., *The Eighteenth Century* (1969), a richly illustrated work with excellent essays, and C. B. Behrens, *The Ancien Régime* (1967). T. Crow, *Painters and Public Life in Eighteenth-Century Paris* (1985), examines artists and cultural politics. C. Rosen, *The Classical Style: Haydn, Mozart, Beethoven* (1972), brilliantly synthesizes music and society, as did Mozart himself in his great opera *The Marriage of Figaro,* where the count is the buffoon and his servant the hero.

Voltaire on Religion

Voltaire was the most renowned and probably the most influential of the French philosophes. His biting, satirical novel Candide *(1759) is still widely assigned in college courses, and his witty yet serious* Philosophical Dictionary *remains a source of pleasure and stimulation. The* Dictionary *consists of a series of essays on topics ranging from Adam to Zoroaster, from certainty to circumcision. The following passage is taken from the essay on religion.*

Voltaire began writing the Philosophical Dictionary *in 1752, at the age of fifty-eight, after arriving at the Prussian court in Berlin. Frederick the Great applauded Voltaire's efforts, but Voltaire put the project aside after leaving Berlin. The first of several revised editions was published anonymously in 1764. It was an immediate, controversial success. Snapped up by an "enlightened" public, it was denounced by religious leaders as a threat to the Christian community and was burned in Geneva and Paris.*

I meditated last night; I was absorbed in the contemplation of nature; I admired the immensity, the course, the harmony of those infinite globes which the vulgar do not know how to admire.

I admired still more the intelligence which directs these vast forces. I said to myself: "One must be blind not to be dazzled by this spectacle; one must be stupid not to recognize its author; one must be mad not to worship the Supreme Being. What tribute of worship should I render Him? Should not this tribute be the same in the whole of space, since it is the same Supreme Power which reigns equally in all space?

Should not a thinking being who dwells on a star in the Milky Way offer Him the same homage as a thinking being on this little globe of ours? Light is the same for the star Sirius as for us; moral philosophy must also be the same. If a feeling, thinking animal on Sirius is born of a tender father and mother who have been occupied with his happiness, he owes them as much love and care as we owe to our parents. If someone in the Milky Way sees a needy cripple, and if he can aid him and does not do so, then he is guilty toward all the globes.

Everywhere the heart has the same duties: on the steps of the throne of God, if He has a throne; and in the depths of the abyss, if there is an abyss."

I was deep in these ideas when one of those genii who fill the spaces between the worlds came down to me. I recognized the same aerial creature who had appeared to me on another occasion to teach me that the judgments of God are different from our own, and how a good action is preferable to a controversy.

The genii transported me into a desert all covered with piles of bones. . . . He began with the first pile. "These," he said, "are the twenty-three thousand Jews who danced before a calf, together with the twenty-four thousand who were killed while fornicating with Midianitish women. The number of those massacred for such errors and offences amounts to nearly three hundred thousand.

"In the other piles are the bones of the Christians slaughtered by each other because of metaphysical disputes. They are divided into several heaps of four centuries each. One heap would have mounted right to the sky; they had to be divided."

"What!" I cried, "brothers have treated their brothers like this, and I have the misfortune to be of this brotherhood!"

"Here," said the spirit, "are the twelve million native Americans killed in their own land because they had not been baptized."

"My God! . . . Why assemble here all these abominable monuments to barbarism and fanaticism?"

"To instruct you. . . . Follow me now." [The genii takes Voltaire to the "heroes of humanity, who tried to banish violence and plunder from the world," and tells Voltaire to question them.]

[At last] I saw a man with a gentle, simple face, who seemed to me to be about thirty-five years old. From afar he looked with compassion upon those piles of whitened bones, through which I had been led to reach the sage's dwelling place. I was astonished to find his feet swollen and bleeding, his hands likewise, his side pierced, and his ribs laid bare by the cut of the lash. "Good God!" I said to him, "is it possible for a just man, a sage, to be in this state? I have just seen one who was treated in a very hateful way, but there is no comparison between his torture and yours. Wicked priests and wicked judges poisoned him; is it by priests and judges that you were so cruelly assassinated?"

With great courtesy he answered, "Yes."

"And who were these monsters?"

"They were hypocrites."

"Ah! that says everything; I understand by that one word that they would have condemned you to the cruelest punishment. Had you then proved to them, as Socrates did, that the Moon was not a goddess, and that Mercury was not a god?"

"No, it was not a question of planets. My countrymen did not even know what a planet was; they were all arrant ignoramuses. Their superstitions were quite different from those of the Greeks."

"Then you wanted to teach them a new religion?"

"Not at all; I told them simply: 'Love God with all your heart and your neighbor as yourself, for that is the whole of mankind's duty.' Judge yourself if this precept is not as old as the universe; judge yourself if I brought them a new religion." . . .

"But did you say nothing, do nothing that could serve them as a pretext?"

"To the wicked everything serves as pretext."

"Did you not say once that you were come not to bring peace, but a sword?"

"It was a scribe's error; I told them that I brought peace and not a sword. I never wrote anything; what I said can have been changed without evil intention."

"You did not then contribute in any way by your teaching, either badly reported or badly

Voltaire dining at Sans Souci palace.
(Source: Bildarchiv Preussischer Kulturbesitz)

interpreted, to those frightful piles of bones which I saw on my way to consult with you?"

"I have only looked with horror upon those who have made themselves guilty of all these murders."

. . . [Finally] I asked him to tell me in what true religion consisted.

"Have I not already told you? Love God and your neighbor as yourself."

"Is it necessary for me to take sides either for the Greek Orthodox Church or the Roman Catholic?"

"When I was in the world I never made any difference between the Jew and the Samaritan."

"Well, if that is so, I take you for my only master." Then he made a sign with his head that filled me with peace. The vision disappeared, and I was left with a clear conscience.

Questions for Analysis

1. Why did Voltaire believe in a Supreme Being? How does this passage reflect the influence of Isaac Newton's scientific system?

2. Was Voltaire trying to entertain or teach or do both? Was he effective? Explain.

3. If Voltaire was trying to convey serious ideas about religion and morality, what were those ideas? What was he attacking?

4. If a person today thought and wrote like Voltaire, would that person be called a defender or a destroyer of Christianity? Why?

Source: F. M. Arouet de Voltaire, *Oeuvres completes* (Paris: Firmin-Didot, 1875), vol. 8, pp. 188–190; translated into English by John McKay.

19

The Changing Life of the People in Europe

The Spanish artist Francisco de Goya y Lucientes painted *The Stilts (Los Zacos)* in 1791–1792. *(Source: Museo del Prado, Madrid)*

The world of European absolutism and aristocracy, a combination of raw power and elegant refinement, was a world apart from that of common people. Weakness and uncertainty, poverty and pain—these enduring realities weighed heavily on the vast majority. Yet the common people in Western societies were by no means helpless victims of fate, ignorance, and inequality. With courage and intelligence, with hard work and family loyalties, ordinary men and women struggled and survived. There is a dignity in these efforts that is deeply moving.

This, then, is the story of those ordinary lives at a time when the idea of far-reaching scientific and material progress was only the sweet dream of a privileged elite in fashionable salons.

- How did the common people of Europe wring a living out of the land, and how was cottage industry growing to complement these efforts?
- What changes occurred in marriage and the family in the course of the eighteenth century?
- What was life like for children, and how did attitudes toward children evolve?
- What did people eat, and how did changes in diet and medical care affect their lives?
- What were the patterns of popular religion and culture? How did these patterns come into contact—and conflict—with the critical world-view of the educated public and thereby widen the cultural divide between rich and poor in the era of the Enlightenment?

Such questions help us better understand how the peasant masses and urban poor really lived in western Europe before the age of revolution opened at the end of the eighteenth century. These questions will be the focus of this chapter.

❖ AGRICULTURE AND POPULATION

At the end of the seventeenth century, at least 80 percent of the people of all western European countries, with the possible exception of Holland, drew their livelihood from agriculture. In eastern Europe the percentage was considerably higher. Men and women lavished their attention on the land, and the land repaid their efforts, yielding the food and most of the raw materials for industry that made life possible. But the land was stingy and capricious. Yields were low even in good years, finding enough to eat was an endless challenge, and disease or starvation was the price of failure. As a result, most peasant communities had learned to keep family size under control. If total population grew even modestly, as it did in the eighteenth century, people had to find new sources of food and income.

Working the Land

The greatest accomplishment of medieval agriculture was the open-field system of village agriculture developed by European peasants. That system divided the land to be cultivated by the peasants into a few large fields that in turn were cut up into long narrow strips. The fields and strips were not enclosed. An individual peasant family—if it was fortunate—held a number of strips scattered throughout the large fields. The land of those who owned but did not till—primarily the nobility, the clergy, and wealthy townsmen—was also in scattered strips. The peasants farmed each large field as a community, plowing, sowing, and harvesting in accordance with tradition and the village leaders.

The ever-present problem was exhaustion of the soil. If a community planted wheat year after year in the same field, the nitrogen in the soil was soon depleted, and crop failure and starvation were certain. Since the supply of manure for fertilizer was limited, the only way for land to recover its life-giving fertility was for a field to lie fallow for a period of time. In the early Middle Ages, a year of fallow was alternated with a year of cropping, so that in any given year half of the land stood idle. Eventually, three-year rotations were introduced. This system permitted a year of wheat or rye followed by a year of oats or beans or peas and then a year of fallow. The results of this change were modest, however. In a rich agricultural region like the Po Valley in northern Italy, every bushel of wheat sown yielded on average only five or six bushels of grain at harvest during the seventeenth century. Such yields were no more than those attained in fertile, well-watered areas in the thirteenth century or in ancient Greece. By modern standards, output in 1700 was distressingly low. (Today an American or French farmer with similar land can expect roughly fifty bushels of wheat for each bushel of wheat sown.) Only awareness of the tragic consequences of continuous cropping forced undernourished populations to let a third of their land lie idle at any given time.

Traditional rights reinforced the traditional pattern of farming. In addition to rotating the field crops in a uniform way, villages held open meadows in common to provide animals with hay and natural pasture. After the harvest, the people of the village also pastured their animals on the wheat or rye stubble. In many places such pasturing followed a brief period, also established by tradition, for the gleaning of grain. Poor women would go through the fields picking up the few single grains that had fallen to the ground in the course of the harvest. This backbreaking labor provided the slender margin of survival for some people in the winter months.

In the age of absolutism and nobility, state and landlord levied heavy taxes and high rents as a matter of course. In so doing, they stripped the peasants of much of their meager earnings. Generally speaking, the peasants of eastern Europe were worst off. As discussed in Chapter 18, they were serfs, bound to their lords in hereditary service. Five or six days of unpaid work per week on the lord's land was not uncommon. Well into the nine-

Millet: The Gleaners   Poor French peasant women search for grains and stalks that the harvesters (in the background) have missed. The open-field system seen here could still be found in parts of Europe in 1857, when this picture was painted. Jean-François Millet is known for his great paintings expressing social themes. *(Source: Louvre © Photo R. M. N.)*

teenth century, individual Russian serfs and serf families were regularly sold with and without land. Serfdom was often very close to slavery.

Social conditions were considerably better in western Europe. Peasants were generally free from serfdom. In France and western Germany, they owned land and could pass it on to their children. Yet life was hard and poverty was the great reality for most people. In the Beauvais region of France at the beginning of the eighteenth century, only a tenth of the peasants could live satisfactorily off the fruits of their landholdings. Owning less than half of the land, the peasants had to pay heavy royal taxes, the church's tithe, and dues to the lord, as well as set aside seed for the next season. Left with only half of their crop for their own use, they had to toil for others and seek work far afield in a constant scramble for a meager living.

Technological progress offered a possible way for European peasants to improve their difficult position by producing more. The uncultivated fields were the heart of the matter. If peasants could replace the fallow with crops, they could increase the land under cultivation by 50 percent. The secret was to eliminate the fallow by alternating grain with certain nitrogen-storing crops, such as turnips and potatoes, clovers and grasses, which rejuvenate the soil while still giving produce.

Technological progress, however, did not come easily. To wait for the entire village to agree to a new crop rotation might mean waiting forever. Thus an innovating agriculturalist sought to enclose and consolidate his scattered holdings into a compact, fenced-in field, and he also sought to enclose his share of the natural pasture—known as the common. But because the common rights, like gleaning, were precious to many rural people, only powerful social and political pressures could overcome the traditionalism of rural communities. The old system of open fields held on tenaciously. Indeed, until the end of the eighteenth century, the promise of the new system was extensively realized only in the Low Countries and in England. Across the rest of Europe, technological progress was limited largely to the introduction of a single new but extremely important crop—the potato (see page 614).

The Balance of Numbers

Until 1700 the total population of Europe grew slowly much of the time and by no means con-

 FIGURE 19.1   The Growth of Population in England, 1000–1800   England is a good example of both the uneven increase of European population before 1700 and the third great surge of growth, which began in the eighteenth century. *(Source: Data from E. A. Wrigley,* Population and History, *McGraw-Hill, New York, 1969)*

stantly (Figure 19.1). In seventeenth-century Europe, births and deaths were in a crude but effective balance. The birthrate—annual births as a proportion of the population—was fairly high but far lower than it would have been if all women had been having as many children as biologically possible. The death rate in normal years was also high, though somewhat lower than the birthrate. As a result, the population grew modestly in normal years at a rate of perhaps 0.5 to 1 percent. Yet even fairly modest population growth of 1 percent per year produces a large increase over a long period— a fourfold increase in 150 years, for example. Such gigantic increases did not occur in agrarian Europe because in certain tragic periods, many more people died than were born; total population fell sharply, even catastrophically.

The grim reapers of demographic crisis were famine, epidemic disease, and war. Famine, the inevitable result of poor farming methods and periodic crop failures, was particularly murderous because it was accompanied by disease. With a brutal one-two punch, famine stunned and weakened a population, and disease finished it off. Disease, including epidemics of bubonic plague, dysentery, and smallpox, could also ravage independently, even in years of adequate harvests.

War was another scourge. The indirect effects were more harmful than the organized killing. War spread disease. Soldiers and camp followers passed venereal disease throughout the countryside to scar and kill. Armies requisitioned scarce food

Albrecht Dürer: The Four Horsemen of the Apocalypse Dürer combines emotional power and unsurpassed technical skill in this famous 1498 woodcut. Dürer's terrifying vision of Death and his henchmen periodically became reality in Europe well into the eighteenth century. *(Source: Courtesy of Museum of Fine Arts, Boston)*

supplies for their own use and disrupted the agricultural cycle. The Thirty Years' War (see pages 539–540) witnessed all possible combinations of distress. In the German states, the number of inhabitants declined by more than *two-thirds* in some large areas and by at least one-third almost everywhere else. The great sixteenth-century artist Albrecht Dürer captured the horror of demographic crisis in his chilling woodcut *The Four Horsemen of the Apocalypse.* Death, accompanied by his trusty companions War, Famine, and Conflict, takes his merciless ride of destruction. The narrow victory of life over death that prevails in normal times is being undone.

In the eighteenth century, the population of Europe began to grow markedly. This increase in numbers occurred in all areas of Europe: western and eastern, northern and southern, dynamic and stagnant. Growth was especially dramatic after about 1750, as Figure 19.2 shows. Why was this so? In some areas some women did have more babies than before because new opportunities for employment in rural industry allowed them to marry at an earlier age, as we shall see (pages 633–634). But the basic cause for Europe as a whole was a decline in mortality—fewer deaths.

The bubonic plague mysteriously disappeared. After the Black Death in the fourteenth century, plagues had remained a part of the European experience, striking again and again with savage force, particularly in towns. As late as 1720 an epidemic swept southern France, killing one-third, one-half, even three-fourths of those in the larger towns. Once again an awful fear swept across Europe. But the epidemic passed, and that was the last time plague fell on western and central Europe. The final disappearance of plague was due in part to stricter measures of quarantine in plague-prone Mediterranean ports and along the Austrian border with Turkey. Chance and plain good luck were more important, however.

After 1600, for reasons unknown, a new rat of Asiatic origin—the brown, or wander, rat—began to drive out and eventually eliminate the black rat whose flea is the principal carrier of the plague bacillus. Although the brown rat also carries the plague bacillus, another kind of flea is its main parasite. That flea carries the plague poorly and, for good measure, has little taste for human blood.

Advances in medical knowledge did not contribute much to reducing the death rate in the eighteenth century (see pages 642–645). However, improvements in the water supply and sewerage promoted somewhat better public health and helped reduce such diseases as typhoid and typhus in some urban areas of western Europe. These improvements and the drainage of many swamps and marshes reduced the large population of flies and mosquitoes that helped spread serious epidemics and common diseases, especially those striking children and young adults.

Human beings also became more successful in their efforts to safeguard the supply of food and protect against famine. The eighteenth century was a time of considerable canal and road building in western Europe. These advances in transportation, which were among the more positive aspects of strong absolutist states, lessened the impact of local crop failure and famine. Emergency supplies could be brought in. The age-old spectacle of localized starvation became less frequent. Wars became more gentlemanly and less destructive than in the seventeenth century and spread fewer epidemics. New foods, particularly the potato from South America, were introduced. In short, population grew in the eighteenth century primarily because years of abnormal death rates were less catastrophic. Famines, epidemics, and wars continued to occur, but their severity moderated.

The growth of population in the eighteenth century cannot be interpreted as a sign of human progress, however. Serious population pressures on resources were in existence by 1600 and continued throughout the seventeenth and eighteenth cen-

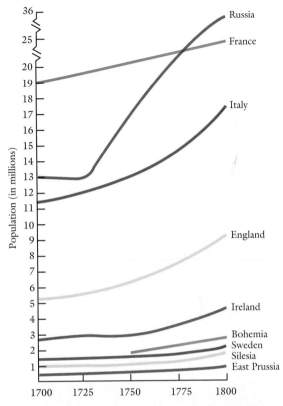

FIGURE 19.2 The Increase of Population in Europe in the Eighteenth Century France's large population continued to support French political and intellectual leadership. Russia emerged as Europe's most populous state because natural increase was complemented by growth from territorial expansion.

turies. Only so much land was available, and tradition slowed the adoption of better farming methods. Thus agriculture could not provide enough work for the rapidly growing labor force, and poor people in the countryside had to look for new ways to make a living.

The Growth of Cottage Industry

The growth of population increased the number of rural workers with little or no land and this in turn contributed to the development of industry in rural areas. To be sure, peasant communities had always made some clothing, processed some food, and constructed some housing for their own use. But in the Middle Ages, peasants did not produce manufactured goods on a large scale for sale in a market. Instead, industry was dominated and organized by urban craft guilds and urban merchants, who jealously regulated handicraft production and sought to maintain it as an urban monopoly. By the eighteenth century, however, the pressures of rural poverty and the need for employment in the countryside had proved too great, and a new system was expanding lustily.

The new system had many names. It has often been called "cottage industry" or "domestic industry," to distinguish it from the factory industry that came later. In recent years, some scholars have preferred to speak of "protoindustrialization," by which they usually mean a stage of rural industrial development with wage workers and hand tools that necessarily preceded the emergence of large-scale factory industry. This focus has sparked renewed interest in Europe's early industrial development and shown again that the mechanized factories grew out of a vibrant industrial tradition. However, the evolving concept of protoindustrialization has different versions; thus the phrase "putting-out system," widely used by contemporaries to describe the key features of eighteenth-century rural industry, still seems an appropriate term for the new form of industrial production.

The two main participants in the *putting-out system* were the merchant-capitalist and the rural worker. The merchant loaned or "put out" raw materials—raw wool, for example—to several cottage workers. Those workers processed the raw material in their own homes, spinning and weaving the wool into cloth in this case, and returned the finished product to the merchant. The merchant

The Weaver's Repose This painting by Decker Cornelis Gerritz (1594–1637) captures the pleasure of release from long hours of toil in cottage industry. The loom realistically dominates the cramped living space and the family's modest possessions. *(Source: Musées Royaux des Beaux-Arts, Brussels. Copyright A.C.I.)*

then paid the workers by the piece and sold the finished products. There were endless variations on this basic relationship. Sometimes rural workers would buy their own materials and work as independent producers before they delivered finished goods to the merchant. Sometimes several workers toiled together in a workshop to perform a complicated process. The relative importance of earnings from the land and from industry varied greatly for handicraft workers. In all cases, however, the putting-out system was a kind of capitalism. Merchants sold finished goods in distant markets, seeking to make profits and increase their capital in their businesses.

The putting-out system grew because it offered competitive advantages. Underemployed rural labor was abundant, and poor peasants and landless laborers would work for low wages. Since production in the countryside did not need to meet rigid guild standards, which maintained quality but discouraged the development of new methods, workers and merchants could change procedures and experiment as they saw fit. Textiles and all manner of everyday articles such as knives, forks, housewares, buttons and gloves, and clocks and musical instruments could be produced quite satisfactorily in the countryside.

Rural manufacturing did not spread across Europe at an even rate. It appeared first in England and developed most successfully there, particularly for the spinning and weaving of woolen cloth. Continental countries developed rural industry more slowly. In France at the time of Louis XIV, Colbert had revived the urban guilds and used them as a means to control the cities and collect taxes (see page 562). But the pressure of rural poverty proved too great. In 1762 the special privileges of urban manufacturing were severely restricted in France, and the already-developing rural industries were given free rein from then on. Thus in France, as in Germany and other areas, the later part of the eighteenth century witnessed a remarkable expansion of rural industry in certain densely populated regions (Map 19.1). The pattern established in England was spreading to the European continent.

Cottage industry, like peasant agriculture from which it evolved, was based on family enterprise. All the members of the family helped in the work, especially in textiles, the most important cottage industry. Children and aged relatives carded and combed the cotton or wool, women and older daughters spun the thread, and the man of the house wove the cloth. The availability of work for everyone, even the youngest, encouraged cottage workers to marry early and have large families. After the dirt was beaten out of the raw material, for example, it had to be thoroughly cleaned with strong soap in a tub, where tiny feet took the place of the agitator in a washing machine. A famous English textile inventor recalled that "soon after I was able to walk I was employed in the cotton manufacture. . . . My mother tucked up my petticoats about my waist, and put me into the tub to tread upon the cotton at the bottom."[1] Each family member had a task, and family life overlapped with the work experience.

 ## MARRIAGE AND THE FAMILY

The family is the basic unit of social organization. It is within the structure of the family that human beings love, mate, and reproduce themselves. It is primarily the family that teaches each child, imparting values and customs that condition an individual's behavior for a lifetime. The family is also an institution woven into the web of history.

Extended and Nuclear Families

In many traditional Asian and African societies, the typical family has often been an extended family. A newly married couple, instead of establishing a home, goes to live with either the bride's or the groom's family. The wife and husband raise their children while living under the same roof with their own brothers and sisters, who may also be married. The extended family is a big, three- or four-generation clan, headed by a patriarch or perhaps a matriarch and encompassing everyone from the youngest infant to the oldest grandparent.

Extended families, it is often said, provide security for adults and children in traditional agrarian peasant economies. Everyone has a place within the extended family, from cradle to grave. Sociologists frequently assume that the extended family gives way to the nuclear family with the advent of industrialization and urbanization. In a society characterized by nuclear families, couples establish their own households when they marry, and they raise their children apart from their parents. A similar process has indeed been occurring in much of

MAP 19.1 Industry and Population in Eighteenth-Century Europe The growth of cottage manufacturing in rural areas helped country people to increase their income and contributed to increases in the population. This putting-out system began in England. Most of the work was in the textile industry. Cottage industry was also strong in the Low Countries—modern-day Belgium and Holland.

Asia and Africa today. And since Europe was once agrarian and preindustrial, it has often been believed that the extended family must also have prevailed in Europe before being destroyed by the Industrial Revolution.

In recent years, innovative historians, analyzing previously neglected parish registers of births, deaths, and marriages, have greatly increased knowledge about the details of family life for the great majority of people before the nineteenth century. It seems clear that the extended, three-generation family was a rarity in western and central Europe by 1700. Indeed, the extended family may

never have been common in Europe, although it is hard to know about the early Middle Ages because relatively few records survive. When young European couples married, they normally established their own households and lived apart from their parents. When a three-generation household came into existence, it usually resulted from a parent moving in with a married child rather than a newly married couple moving in with either set of parents.

Most people did not marry young in the seventeenth and early eighteenth centuries. The average person, who was neither rich nor aristocratic, married surprisingly late, many years after reaching adulthood and many more after beginning to work. In one well-studied, apparently typical English village, both men and women married for the first time at an average age of twenty-seven or older in the seventeenth and eighteenth centuries. A similar pattern existed in early-eighteenth-century France. Moreover, a substantial portion of men and women never married at all.

The custom of late marriage in combination with a nuclear-family household was a distinctive characteristic of European society. It seems likely that the aggressiveness and creativity that have characterized European society have been due in part to a pattern of marriage and family that fosters and requires self-reliance and independence. In preindustrial western Europe in the sixteenth through eighteenth centuries, marriage normally joined a mature man and a mature woman—two adults who had already experienced a great deal of life and could transmit self-reliance and real skills to the next generation.

Why was marriage delayed? The main reason was that couples normally could not marry until they could support themselves economically. The land was still the main source of income. The peasant son often needed to wait until his father's death to inherit the family farm and marry his sweetheart. Similarly, the peasant daughter and her family needed to accumulate a small dowry to help her fiancé buy land or build a house.

There were also laws and community controls to temper impetuous love and physical attraction. In some areas, couples needed the legal permission or tacit approval of the local lord or landowner in order to marry, and poor couples had particular difficulty securing the approval of local officials. These officials believed that freedom to marry for the lower classes would mean more landless paupers, more abandoned children, and more money for welfare. Village elders often agreed. Thus prudence, law, and custom combined to postpone the march to the altar. This pattern helped society maintain some kind of balance between the number of people and the available economic resources.

Work Away from Home

Many young people worked within their families until they could start their own households. Boys plowed and wove; girls spun and tended the cows.

Many others left home temporarily to work elsewhere. In the towns, a lad might be apprenticed to a craftsman for seven or fourteen years to learn a trade. During that time, he would not be permitted to marry. In most trades he earned little and worked hard, but if he was lucky, he might eventually be admitted to a guild and establish his economic independence. More often, a young man would drift from one tough job to another: hired hand for a small farmer, wage laborer on a new road, carrier of water in a nearby town. He was always subject to economic fluctuations, and unemployment was a constant threat.

Girls also temporarily left their families to work, at an early age and in large numbers. The range of opportunities open to them was more limited, however. Service in another family's household was

Chardin: The Kitchen Maid   Lost in thought as she pauses in her work, perhaps this young servant is thinking about her village and loved ones there. Jean-Baptiste Chardin was one of eighteenth-century France's greatest painters. His scenes from everyday life provide valuable evidence for the historian. (*Source: National Gallery of Art, Washington, D.C. Samuel H. Kress Collection*)

by far the most common job, and even middle-class families often sent their daughters into service. Thus a few years away from home as a servant were often a normal part of growing up.

The legions of young servant girls worked hard but had little real independence. Sometimes the employer paid the girl's wages directly to her parents. Constantly under the eye of her mistress, the servant girl found her tasks were many—cleaning, shopping, cooking, caring for the baby. Often the work was endless, for there were no laws to limit exploitation. Rarely were girls so brutalized that they snapped under the strain of such treatment like Varka—the Russian servant girl in Anton Chekhov's chilling story "Sleepy"—who, driven beyond exhaustion, finally quieted her mistress's screaming child by strangling it in its cradle. But court records are full of complaints by servant girls of physical mistreatment by their mistresses. There were many others like the fifteen-year-old English girl in the early eighteenth century who told the judge that her mistress had not only called her "very opprobrious names, as Bitch, Whore and the like," but also "beat her without provocation and beyond measure."[2]

There was also the pressure of seducers and sexual attack. In theory, domestic service offered protection and security within a new family for a young girl leaving home. But in practice, she was often the easy prey of a lecherous master or his sons or his friends. Indeed, "the evidence suggests that in all European countries, from Britain to Russia, the upper classes felt perfectly free to exploit sexually girls who were at their mercy."[3] If the girl became pregnant, she was quickly fired and thrown out in disgrace to make her own way. Prostitution and petty thievery were often the harsh consequences of unwanted pregnancy. "What are we?" exclaimed a bitter Parisian prostitute. "Most of us are unfortunate women, without origins, without education, servants and maids for the most part."[4]

Premarital Sex and Community Controls

Did the plight of some former servant girls mean that late marriage in preindustrial Europe went hand in hand with premarital sex and many illegitimate children? For most of western and central Europe until at least 1750, the answer seems to have been no. English parish registers seldom listed more than one bastard out of every twenty

children baptized. Some French parishes in the seventeenth century had extraordinarily low rates of illegitimacy: less than 1 percent of all babies were born out of wedlock. Illegitimate babies were apparently a rarity, at least as far as the official church records are concerned.

At the same time, premarital sex was clearly commonplace. In one well-studied English village, 33 percent of all first children were conceived before the couple was married, and many were born within three months of the marriage ceremony. In the mid-eighteenth century, 20 percent of the French women in the village of Auffay, in Normandy, were pregnant when they got married, although only 2 percent of all babies in the village were born to unwed mothers.

The combination of very low rates of illegitimate birth and large numbers of pregnant brides reflected the powerful social controls of the traditional village. The prospect of an unwed (and therefore poor) mother with an illegitimate child was inevitably viewed as a grave threat to the economic, social, and moral stability of the closely knit community. Irate parents and anxious village elders, indignant priests and authoritative landlords, all combined to pressure any young people who wavered about marriage in the face of unexpected pregnancy. In the countryside, premarital sex was not entered into lightly, and it was generally limited to those contemplating marriage.

The concerns of the village and the family weighed heavily on most aspects of a couple's life, both before and after marriage. One leading authority describes the traditional French peasant household in these terms:

The individuality of the couple, or rather, its tendency towards individuality, was crushed by the family institutions, and also by the social pressures exercised by the village community as a whole, and by the neighborhood in particular. Anything that might endanger the [couple's] household might also prejudice the village community, and the community reacted, occasionally violently, to punish those who contravened the rules. The intrusion of the community into every aspect of family life was very noticeable.[5]

Thus whereas uninvolved individuals today are inclined to ignore the domestic disputes and marital scandals of others, the people in peasant communities gave such affairs the loudest and most unfavorable publicity, either at the time of the event or during the Carnival season (see page 000). Re-

David Allan: The Penny Wedding (1775) The spirited merry-making of a peasant wedding was a popular theme of European artists. In rural Scotland "penny weddings" were common. Guests paid a fee for the food and fun; the money left over went to the newlyweds to help them get started. The dancing, feasting, and drinking that took place at these community parties led the stern elders of the Presbyterian church to oppose them and hastened their decline. *(Source: National Gallery of Scotland)*

lying on degrading public rituals, the young men of the village would typically gang up on the person they wanted to punish and force him or her to sit astride a donkey facing backward and holding up the donkey's tail. They would parade the overly brutal spouse-beating husband (or wife), or the couple whose adultery had been discovered, all around the village, loudly proclaiming the offender's misdeeds with scorn and ridicule. The donkey ride and similar colorful humiliations ranging from rotten vegetables splattered on the doorstep to obscene and insulting midnight serenades were common punishments throughout much of Europe. They epitomized the community's far-reaching effort to police personal behavior and maintain community standards.

Community controls did not extend to family planning, however. Once a man and woman married they generally had several children. Birth con-

trol within marriage was not unknown in western and central Europe before the nineteenth century, but it was primitive and quite undependable. The most common method was *coitus interruptus*— withdrawal by the male before ejaculation. Mechanical and other means of contraception were also used in the eighteenth century, but mainly by certain sectors of the urban population. The "fast set" of London used the "sheath" regularly, though primarily to protect against venereal disease, not pregnancy. Prostitutes used various contraceptive techniques to prevent pregnancy, and such information was available in large towns if a person really sought it.

New Patterns of Marriage and Illegitimacy

In the second half of the eighteenth century, the pattern of late marriage and few births out of wedlock began to change and break down. The number of illegitimate births soared between about 1750 and 1850 as much of Europe experienced an "illegitimacy explosion." In Frankfurt, Germany, for example, illegitimate births rose steadily from about 2 percent of all births in the early 1700s to a peak of about 25 percent around 1850. In Bordeaux, France, 36 percent of all babies were being born out of wedlock by 1840. Small towns and villages experienced less startling climbs, but increases from a range of 1 to 3 percent initially to 10 to 20 percent between 1750 and 1850 were commonplace. Fewer young women were abstaining from premarital intercourse, and, more important, fewer young men were marrying the women they got pregnant. Thus a profound sexual and cultural transformation took place.

Historians are still debating the meaning of this transformation, but two interrelated ideas dominate most interpretations. First, the growth of cottage industry created new opportunities for earning a living, opportunities not tied to the land. Young people attained greater independence and did not have to wait to inherit a farm in order to get married and have children. A scrap of ground for a garden and a cottage for the loom and spinning wheel could be quite enough for a modest living. These circumstances worked against the businesslike, calculating peasant marriage that was often dictated by the needs of the couple's families. After 1750, courtship became more extensive and freer as cottage industry grew. It was easier to yield to the attraction of the opposite sex and fall in love. Sexual activity might follow, and in most cases marriage for love rather than economic considerations also did, as cottage workers blazed a path that factory workers would follow in the nineteenth century.

Second, the needs of a growing population sent many young villagers to towns and cities in search of temporary or permanent employment. Mobility in turn encouraged new sexual and marital relationships, which were less subject to village tradition and resulted in more illegitimate births. Yet most young women in urban areas found work only as servants or textile workers. Poorly paid, insecure, and with little possibility of living truly independent, "liberated" lives, they looked mainly to marriage and family life as an escape from hard work and as the foundation of a satisfying life.

Promises of marriage from a man of the working

girl's own class led naturally enough to sex, which was widely viewed as part of serious courtship. In one medium-size French city from 1787 to 1788, the great majority of unwed mothers stated that sexual intimacy had followed promises of marriage. Their sisters in rural Normandy reported again and again that they had been "seduced in anticipation of marriage."[6] Many soldiers, day laborers, and male servants were no doubt sincere in their proposals. But their lives were also insecure, and many hesitated to take on the heavy economic burdens of wife and child.

Thus it became increasingly difficult for a woman to convert pregnancy into marriage, and in a growing number of cases the intended marriage did not take place. The romantic yet practical dreams and aspirations of many young working men and women in towns and villages were frustrated by low wages, inequality, and changing economic and social conditions. Old patterns of marriage and family were breaking down among the common people. Only in the late nineteenth century would more stable patterns reappear.

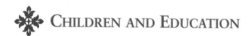 **CHILDREN AND EDUCATION**

In the traditional framework of agrarian Europe, women married late but then began bearing children rapidly. If a woman married before she was thirty, and if both she and her husband lived to forty-five, the chances were roughly one in two that she would give birth to six or more children. The newborn child entered a dangerous world. Infant mortality was high. One in five was sure to die, and one in three was quite likely to die in the poorest areas. Newborn children were very likely to catch mysterious infectious diseases of the chest and stomach, and many babies died of dehydration brought about by a bad bout of ordinary diarrhea. Even in rich families little could be done for an ailing child. Childhood itself was dangerous because of adult indifference, neglect, and even abuse.

Schools and formal education played only a modest role in the lives of ordinary children, and many boys and many more girls never learned to read. Nevertheless, basic literacy was growing among the popular classes, whose reading habits have been intensively studied in recent years. Attempting to peer into the collective attitudes of the common people and compare them with those of the book-hungry cultivated public, historians have produced some fascinating insights.

Child Care and Nursing

Women of the lower classes generally breast-fed their infants and for a much longer period than is customary today. Breast-feeding decreases the likelihood of pregnancy for the average woman by delaying the resumption of ovulation. By nursing their babies, women limited their fertility and spaced their children—from two to three years apart. If a newborn baby died, nursing stopped and a new life could be created. Nursing also saved lives: an infant who was breast-fed and received precious immunity-producing substances with its mother's milk was more likely to survive than an infant who was given any other food. In many areas of Russia, where the common practice was to give a new child a sweetened (and germ-laden) rag to suck on for its subsistence, half of the babies did not survive the first year.

In contrast to the laboring poor, the women of the aristocracy and upper middle class seldom nursed their own children. The upper-class woman felt that breast-feeding was crude, common, and undignified. Instead, she hired a wet nurse to suckle her child. The urban mother of more modest means—the wife of a shopkeeper or an artisan—also commonly used a wet nurse in order to facilitate full-time work in the shop.

Wet-nursing was a very widespread and flourishing business in the eighteenth century, a dismal business within the framework of the putting-out system. The traffic was in babies rather than in wool and cloth, and two or three years often passed before the wet-nurse worker finished her task. In the process the poor wet-nurse worker was often exploited and abused. For example, she had little contact with the family that hired her and could be dismissed on a whim by the mother or the family doctor.

Many observers stressed the flaws of wet nurses. It was a common belief that with her milk a nurse passed her bad traits to a baby. When a child turned out poorly, it was assumed that "the nurse had changed it." Many observers charged that nurses were often negligent and greedy. They claimed that there were large numbers of "killing nurses" with whom no child ever survived. Such a nurse let a child die quickly so that she could take another child and another fee.

Foundlings and Infanticide

In the ancient world it was not uncommon to allow or force newborn babies, particularly girl babies, to die when there were too many mouths to feed. To its great and eternal credit, the early medieval church, strongly influenced by Jewish law, denounced infanticide as a pagan practice and insisted that every human life was sacred. The willful destruction of newborn children became a crime

Abandoned Children At this Italian foundlings' home a frightened mother could discreetly deposit her baby on a revolving table, turn the table to move the baby into the home, and hurry away without being seen. *(Source: The Bettmann Archive)*

punishable by death. And yet, as the previous reference to killing nurses suggests, direct and indirect methods of eliminating unwanted babies did not disappear. There were, for example, many cases of "overlaying"—parents rolling over and suffocating the child placed between them in their bed. Such parents claimed they had been drunk and had acted unintentionally. In Austria in 1784, suspicious authorities made it illegal for parents to take children under five into bed with them. Severe poverty, on the one hand, and increasing illegitimacy, on the other, conspired to force the very poor to thin their own ranks.

The young girl—very likely a servant—who could not provide for her child had few choices. If she would not have an abortion or employ the services of a killing nurse, she could bundle up her baby and leave it on the doorstep of a church. In the late seventeenth century, Saint Vincent de Paul was so distressed by the number of babies brought to the steps of Notre Dame in Paris that he established a home for foundlings. Others followed his example. In England the government acted on a petition calling for a foundling hospital "to prevent the frequent murders of poor, miserable infants at birth" and "to suppress the inhuman custom of exposing newborn children to perish in the streets."

In much of Europe in the eighteenth century, foundling homes emerged as a favorite charity of the rich and powerful. Great sums were spent on them. The foundling home in St. Petersburg, perhaps the most elaborate and lavish of its kind, occupied the former palaces of two members of the high nobility. In the early nineteenth century it had twenty-five thousand children in its care and was receiving five thousand new babies a year. At their best, foundling homes in the eighteenth century were a good example of Christian charity and social concern in an age of great poverty and inequality.

Yet the foundling home was no panacea. By the 1770s one-third of all babies born in Paris were immediately abandoned to the foundling home by their mothers. Fully one-third of all those foundlings were abandoned by married couples, a powerful commentary on the standard of living among the working poor, for whom an additional mouth to feed often meant tragedy.

Furthermore, great numbers of babies entered the foundling homes, but few left. Even in the best of these homes, 50 percent of the babies normally died within a year. In the worst, fully 90 percent did not survive. They succumbed to long journeys over rough roads, the intentional and unintentional neglect of their wet nurses, and the customary childhood illnesses. So great was the carnage that some contemporaries called the foundling hospitals "legalized infanticide."

Attitudes Toward Children

What were the typical circumstances of children's lives? Did the treatment of foundlings reflect the attitudes of typical parents? Although some scholars argue otherwise, it seems that the young child was often of little concern to its parents and to society in the eighteenth century. This indifference toward children was found in all classes; rich children were by no means exempt. The practice of using wet nurses, who were casually selected and often negligent, is one example of how even the rich and the prosperous put the child out of sight and out of mind. One French moralist, writing in 1756 about how to improve humanity, observed that "one blushes to think of loving one's children." It has been said that the English gentleman of the period "had more interest in the diseases of his horses than of his children."[7]

Feelings toward children were greatly influenced by the terrible frequency of death among children of all classes. Doctors and clergymen urged parents not to become too emotionally involved with their children, who were so unlikely to survive. Mothers especially did not always heed such warnings, but the risk of emotional devastation was very real for them. The great eighteenth-century English historian Edward Gibbon (1737–1794) wrote that "the death of a new born child before that of its parents may seem unnatural but it is a strictly probable event, since of any given number the greater part are extinguished before the ninth year, before they possess the faculties of the mind and the body." Gibbon's father named all his boys Edward after himself, hoping that at least one of them would survive to carry his name. His prudence was not misplaced. Edward the future historian and eldest survived. Five brothers and sisters who followed him all died in infancy.

The medical establishment was seldom interested in the care of children. One contemporary observer quoted a famous doctor as saying that "he never wished to be called to a young child because he was really at a loss to know what to offer for it." There were "physicians of note who make no scruple to assert that there is nothing to be done for children when they are ill." The best hope for children was often treatment by women healers and midwives, who helped many women deliver their babies and provided advice on child care. Nevertheless, children were still caught in a vicious circle: they were neglected because they were very likely to die, and they were likely to die because they were neglected.

Emotional detachment from children often shaded off into abuse. When parents and other adults did turn toward children, it was normally to discipline and control them. The novelist Daniel Defoe (1660?–1731), who was always delighted when he saw very young children working hard in cottage industry, coined the axiom "Spare the rod and spoil the child." He meant it. So did Susannah Wesley (1669–1742), mother of John Wesley, the founder of Methodism. According to her, the first task of a parent toward her children was "to conquer the will, and bring them to an obedient temper." She reported that her babies were "taught to fear the rod, and to cry softly."[8]

It was hardly surprising that when English parish officials dumped their paupers into the first factories late in the eighteenth century, the children were beaten and brutalized. That was part of the child-rearing pattern—considerable indifference, on the one hand, and strict physical discipline, on the other—that prevailed throughout most of the eighteenth century.

From the middle of the century, this pattern came under increasing attack and began to change. Critics, led by Jean-Jacques Rousseau in his famous treatise *Emile* (see Listening to the Past), called for greater love, tenderness, and understanding toward children. In addition to supporting foundling homes to discourage infanticide and urging wealthy women to nurse their own babies, these new voices ridiculed the practice of swaddling: wrapping youngsters in tight-fitting clothes and blankets was generally believed to form babies properly by "straightening them out." By the end of the eighteenth century, small children were often being dressed in simpler, more comfortable clothing, allowing much greater freedom of movement. More parents expressed a delight in the love and intimacy of the child and found real pleasure in raising their offspring. These changes were part of the general growth of humanitarianism and cautious optimism about human potential that characterized the eighteenth-century Enlightenment.

Schools and Popular Literature

The role of schools and formal education outside the home was also growing more important. The aristocracy and the rich had led the way in the sixteenth century with special colleges, often run by Jesuits. But schools charged specifically with elementary education of the children of the common people usually did not appear until the seventeenth century. Unlike medieval schools, which mingled all age groups, these elementary schools specialized in boys and girls from seven to twelve, who were instructed in basic literacy and religion. The growth of popular education quickened in the eighteenth century, but there was no revolutionary acceleration, and many common people received no formal education.

Prussia led the way in the development of universal education, inspired by the old Protestant idea that every believer should be able to read and study the Bible in the quest for personal salvation and by the new idea of a population capable of effectively serving the state. As early as 1717, Prussia made attendance at elementary schools compulsory, and more Protestant German states, such as Saxony and Württemberg, followed in the eighteenth century. Religious motives were also extremely important elsewhere. From the middle of the seventeenth century, Presbyterian Scotland was convinced that the path to salvation lay in careful study of the Scriptures, and it established an effective network of parish schools for rich and poor alike. The Church of England and the dissenting congregations established "charity schools" to instruct the children of the poor, and in 1682 France began setting up Christian schools to teach the catechism and prayers as well as reading and writing. In 1774 Habsburg empress Maria Theresa established a general system of elementary education that called for compulsory education and a school in every community. Thus some elementary education was becoming a reality for European peoples, and schools were of growing significance in the life of the child.

The result of these efforts was a remarkable growth in basic literacy between 1600 and 1800, especially after 1700. Whereas in 1600 only one male in six was barely literate in France and Scotland, and one in four in England, by 1800 almost nine out of ten Scottish males, two out of three males in France, and more than half of English males were literate. In all three countries the bulk of the jump occurred in the eighteenth century. Women were also increasingly literate, although they lagged behind men in most countries.

The growth in literacy promoted a growth in reading, and historians have carefully examined what the common people read in an attempt to discern what they were thinking. One thing seems certain: the major philosophical works of the Enlightenment had little impact on peasants and workers, who could neither afford nor understand those favorites of the book-hungry educated public.

Although the Bible remained the overwhelming favorite, especially in Protestant countries, the staple of popular literature was short pamphlets known as chapbooks. Printed on the cheapest paper available, many chapbooks dealt with religious subjects. They featured Bible stories, prayers, devotions, and the lives of saints and other exemplary Christians. Promising happiness after death, devotional literature was also intensely practical. It gave the believer moral teachings and a confidence in God that helped in daily living.

Entertaining, often humorous stories formed a second element of popular literature. Fairy tales, medieval romances, fictionalized history, and fantastic adventures—these were some of the delights that filled the peddler's pack as he approached a village. Both heroes and villains possessed superhuman powers in this make-believe world, a world of

A Peasant Family Reading the Bible Praised by the philosophe Diderot for its moralistic message, this engraving of a painting by Jean-Baptiste Greuze (1725–1805) captures the power of sacred texts and the spoken word. The peasant patriarch reads aloud from the massive family Bible, and the close-knit circle of absorbed listeners concentrates on every word. Only the baby is distracted by the dog. (*Source: Bibliothèque Nationale/Giraudon/Art Resource, NY*)

danger and magic, of fairy godmothers and evil trolls. But the good fairies always triumphed over the evil ones in the story's marvelous resolution. The significance of these entertaining stories for the peasant reader is not clear, however. Many scholars see them reflecting a desire for pure escapism and a temporary flight from harsh everyday reality. Others see these tales reflecting ancient folk wisdom and counseling prudence in a world full of danger and evil, where wolves dress up like grandmothers and eat Little Red Riding Hoods.

Some popular literature was highly practical, dealing with rural crafts, household repairs, useful plants, and similar matters. Much of such lore was stored in almanacs. With calendars listing secular, religious, and astrological events mixed in with agricultural schedules, bizarre bits of information, and jokes, the almanac was universal, noncontroversial, and highly appreciated, even by many in the comfortable classes. "Anyone who could would read an almanac."9

In general, however, the reading of the common people had few similarities with that of educated elites. Popular literature was simple and it was practical, both as devotional self-help and as how-to instruction. It was also highly escapist. Yet the common people were apparently content with works that reinforced traditional values and did not foster social or religious criticism. These results fit well with the modest educational objectives of rulers and educated elites. They believed that carefully limited instruction stressing religion and morals was useful to the masses and that too much study would disorient them and foster discontent.

✤ FOOD AND MEDICAL PRACTICE

The European population increased rapidly in the eighteenth century. Plague and starvation gradually disappeared, and Europeans lived longer lives. What were the characteristics of diets and nutrition in this era of improving health and longevity? Although it played only a small part, what was medical practice like in the eighteenth century? What does a comparison of rich and poor reveal?

Diets and Nutrition

At the beginning of the eighteenth century, ordinary men and women depended on grain as fully as they had in the past. Bread was quite literally the staff of life. Peasants in the Beauvais region of France ate two pounds of bread a day, washing it down with water, green wine, beer, or a little skimmed milk. Their dark bread was made from a mixture of roughly ground wheat and rye—the standard flour of the common people. The poor also ate grains in soup and gruel. In rocky northern Scotland, for example, people depended on oatmeal, which they often ate half-cooked so that it would swell in their stomachs and make them feel full.

Not surprisingly, an adequate supply of grain and an affordable price for bread loomed in the popular imagination. Peasants, landless laborers, and urban workers all believed in the old medieval idea of the "just price"—that is, a price that was "fair" to both consumers and producers. But in the later eighteenth century, this traditional, moral view of prices and the economy clashed repeatedly with the emerging free-market philosophy of unregulated supply and demand, which government officials, large landowners, and early economists increasingly favored. In years of poor harvests and soaring prices, this clash often resulted in food riots and popular disturbances. Peasants and workers would try to stop wagons loaded with grain from leaving their region, or they would seize grain held by speculators and big merchants accused of hoarding and rigging the market. (Usually the tumultuous crowd paid what it considered to be a fair price for what it took.) Governments were keenly aware of the problem of adequate grain supplies, and they would sometimes try to control prices to prevent unrest in crisis years.

Although breadstuffs were all-important for the rural and urban poor, they also ate a fair quantity of vegetables. Indeed, vegetables were considered "poor people's food." Peas and beans were probably the most common and were eaten fresh in late spring and summer. Dried, they became the basic ingredients in the soups and stews of the long winter months. In most regions, other vegetables appeared in season on the tables of the poor—primarily cabbages, carrots, and wild greens. Fruit was uncommon and limited to the summer months.

The common people of Europe loved meat and eggs, but they seldom ate their fill. Indeed, as the population surged in the sixteenth century, meat became more expensive, and the poor ate less meat in 1700 than in 1500. Moreover, in most European countries harsh game laws deprived the poor of the right to hunt and eat edible game such as rabbits, deer, and partridges. Only nobles and large landowners could legally kill game. Few laws were more bitterly resented—or more frequently broken—by ordinary people than those governing hunting.

Milk was rarely drunk. Perhaps because some individuals do suffer seriously from dairy allergies, it was widely believed that milk caused sore eyes, headaches, and a variety of ills, except among the very young and very old. Milk was used primarily to make cheese and butter, which the poor liked but could afford only occasionally. Medical and popular opinion considered whey, the watery liquid left after milk was churned, "an excellent temperate drink."

The diet of the rich—aristocrats, officials, and the comfortable bourgeoisie—was traditionally quite different from that of the poor. The men and women of the upper classes were rapacious carnivores. A truly elegant dinner among the great and powerful consisted of one rich meat after another: a chicken pie, a leg of lamb, a grilled steak, for example, perhaps followed by three fish courses, all complemented with sweets, cheeses, and nuts of all kinds. Fruits and vegetables were not often found on the tables of the rich.

There was also an enormous amount of overdrinking among the rich. The English squire who loved to hunt with his hounds loved to drink with a similar passion. With his dinner he drank red wine from France or white wine from the Rhineland, and with his dessert he took sweet but strong port or Madeira from Portugal. Sometimes he ended the evening under the table in a drunken stupor.

The diet of small traders, master craftsmen, minor bureaucrats—the people of the towns and cities—was generally less monotonous than that of the peasantry. The markets, stocked by market gardens on the outskirts, provided a substantial variety of meats, vegetables, and fruits, although bread and beans still formed the bulk of such families' diet.

There were also regional dietary differences in 1700. Generally speaking, northern, Atlantic Europe ate better than southern, Mediterranean Europe. The poor of England probably ate best of all. The Dutch were also considerably better fed than the average European, in large part because of their advanced agriculture and diversified gardens.

The Impact of Diet on Health

How were the poor and the rich served by their quite different diets? At first glance, the diet of the laboring poor, relying as it did on grains and vegetables, might seem low in protein. However, the whole-grain wheat or rye flour used in eighteenth-century bread retained most of the bran—the ground-up husk—and the all-important wheat germ, which contains higher proportions of some minerals, vitamins, and good-quality proteins than does the rest of the grain. In addition, the field peas and beans eaten by poor people since the early Middle Ages contained protein that complemented the proteins in whole-grain bread. The proteins in whey, cheese, and eggs, which the poor ate at least occasionally, also supplemented the bread and vegetables.

The basic bread-and-vegetables diet of the poor *in normal times* was adequate. But a key dietary problem in some seasons, particularly in the late winter and early spring, was probably getting enough green vegetables (or milk) to ensure adequate supplies of vitamins A and C. A severe deficiency of vitamin C produces scurvy, a disease that leads to rotting gums, swelling of the limbs, and great weakness. Before the season's first vegetables, many people had used up their bodily reserves of vitamin C and were suffering from mild cases of scurvy. (Scurvy was an acute problem for sailors on long voyages and by the end of the sixteenth century was being controlled on ships by a daily ration of lime juice for crew members.)

The practice of gorging on meat, sweets, and spirits caused the rich their own nutritional problems. Because of their great disdain for fresh vegetables, they, too, were very often deficient in vitamins A and C. Gout was a common affliction of the overfed and underexercised rich. No wonder they were often caricatured as dragging their flabby limbs and bulging bellies to the table to stuff their swollen cheeks and poison their livers. People of moderate means, who could afford some meat and dairy products with fair regularity but who had not abandoned the bread and vegetables of the poor, were probably best off from a nutritional standpoint.

Patterns of food consumption changed rather markedly as the century progressed. More varied diets associated with new methods of farming were confined largely to the Low Countries and Eng-

✤ Royal Interest in the Potato   Frederick the Great of Prussia, shown here supervising cultivation of the potato, used his influence and position to promote the new food on his estates and throughout Prussia. Peasants could grow potatoes with the simplest hand tools. But doing so was backbreaking labor, as this painting by R. Warthmüller suggests. *(Source: Private Collection, Hamburg/Archiv für Kunst und Geschichte, Berlin)*

land, but a new food—the potato—came to the aid of the poor everywhere. Introduced into Europe from the Americas—along with corn, squash, tomatoes, and many other useful plants—the humble potato is an excellent food. Containing a good supply of carbohydrates, calories, and vitamins A and C (especially if it is not overcooked and the skin is eaten), the potato offset the lack of vitamins from green vegetables in the poor person's winter and early spring diet, and it provided a much higher caloric yield than grain for a given piece of land.

For some desperately poor peasants who needed to get every possible calorie from a tiny plot of land, the potato replaced grain as the primary food in the eighteenth century. This happened first in Ireland, where English (Protestant) repression and exploitation forced large numbers of poor (and Catholic) peasants to live off tiny scraps of rented ground. Elsewhere in Europe, potatoes took hold

more slowly because many people did not like them. Thus potatoes were first fed to pigs and livestock, and there was even debate about whether they were fit for humans. In Germany the severe famines caused by the Seven Years' War settled the matter: potatoes were edible and not just "famine food." By the end of the century, the potato had become an important dietary supplement in much of Europe.

There was also a general growth of market gardening, and a greater variety of vegetables appeared in towns and cities. In the course of the eighteenth century, the large towns and cities of maritime Europe began to receive semitropical fruits, such as oranges and lemons, from Portugal and the West Indies, although they were not cheap.

Not all changes in the eighteenth century were for the better, however. Bread began to change, most noticeably for the English and for the comfortable groups on the European continent. Rising incomes and new tastes led to a shift from whole-grain black or brown bread to "bread as white as snow" and started a decline in bread's nutritional value. The high-roughage bran and some of the dark but high-vitamin germ were increasingly sifted out by millers. This foretold further "improvements" in the nineteenth century, which would leave bread perfectly white and greatly reduced in nutritional value.

Another sign of nutritional decline was the growing consumption of sugar. Initially a luxury, sugar dropped rapidly in price as slave-based production increased in the Americas, and the sweetener was much more widely used in the eighteenth century. This development probably led to an increase in cavities and to other ailments as well, although the greater or lesser poverty of the laboring poor still protected most of them from the sugar-tooth virus of the rich and well-to-do.

Medical Practitioners

Although sickness, pain, and disease—intractable challenges built into the human condition—permeated the European experience in the eighteenth century, medical science played a very small part in improving the health of most people. Yet the Enlightenment's growing focus on discovering the laws of nature and on human problems did give rise to a great deal of research and experimentation. The century also saw a remarkable rise in the number of medical practitioners, and a high value was placed on their services. Therefore, when the great breakthroughs in knowledge came in the middle and late nineteenth century, they could be rapidly evaluated and diffused.

Care of the sick in the eighteenth century was the domain of several competing groups: faith healers, apothecaries (or pharmacists), surgeons, and physicians. Since the great majority of common ailments have a tendency to cure themselves, each group could point to successes and win adherents. When a doctor's treatment made the patient worse, as it often did, the original medical problem could always be blamed.

Faith healers, who had been among the most important kinds of physicians in medieval Europe, remained active. They and their patients believed that demons and evil spirits caused disease by lodging in people and that the proper treatment was to exorcise, or drive out, the offending devil. This demonic view of disease was strongest in the countryside, where popular belief placed great faith in the healing power of religious relics, prayer, and the laying on of hands. Faith healing was particularly effective in the treatment of mental disorders such as hysteria and depression, where the link between attitude and illness is most direct.

Apothecaries sold a vast number of herbs, drugs, and patent medicines for every conceivable "temperament and distemper." Early pharmacists were seldom regulated, and they frequently diagnosed freely. Their prescriptions were incredibly complex—a hundred or more drugs might be included in a single prescription—and often very expensive. Some of the drugs and herbs undoubtedly worked. For example, strong laxatives were given to the rich for their constipated bowels. Indeed, the medical profession continued to believe that regular "purging" of the bowels was essential for good health and the treatment of illness. Much purging was harmful, however, and only bloodletting for the treatment of disease was more effective in speeding patients to their graves.

Surgeons, in contrast, made considerable medical and social progress. Long considered as ordinary artisans comparable to butchers and barbers, surgeons began studying anatomy seriously and improved their art. With endless opportunities to practice, army surgeons on gory battlefields led the way. They learned that a soldier with an extensive wound, such as a shattered leg or arm, could perhaps be saved if the surgeon could obtain above the wound a flat surface that could be cauterized with fire. Thus if a soldier (or a civilian) had a broken limb and the bone stuck out, the surgeon amputated so that the remaining stump could be cauterized and the likelihood of death reduced.

The eighteenth-century surgeon (and patient) labored in the face of incredible difficulties. Almost all operations were performed without any painkiller, for the anesthesias of the day were hard to control and were believed too dangerous for general use. The terrible screams of people whose limbs were being sawed off echoed across battlefields and through hospitals. Many patients died from the agony and shock of such operations. Surgery was also performed in the midst of filth and dirt, for there simply was no knowledge of bacteriology and the nature of infection. The simplest wound treated by a surgeon could fester and lead to death.

Physicians, the fourth major group, were apprenticed in their teens to a practicing physician for several years of on-the-job training. This training was then rounded out with hospital work or some university courses. Because such prolonged training was expensive, physicians continued to come mainly from prosperous families, and they usually concentrated on urban patients from similar social backgrounds. They had little contact with urban workers and even less with peasants.

To their credit, physicians in the eighteenth century were increasingly willing to experiment with new methods, but time-honored practices lay heavily on them. Physicians, like apothecaries, laid great stress on purging. And bloodletting was still considered a medical cure-all. It was the way "bad blood," the cause of illness, was removed and the balance of humors necessary for good health was restored. According to a physician practicing medicine in Philadelphia in 1799, bleeding was proper at the onset of all inflammatory fevers, in all inflammations, and for "asthma, sciatic pains, coughs, head-aches, rheumatisms, the apoplexy, epilepsy, and bloody fluxes."[10] It was also necessary after all falls, blows, and bruises.

While ordinary physicians were bleeding, apothecaries purging, surgeons sawing, and faith healers praying, the leading medical thinkers were attempting to pull together and assimilate all the information and misinformation they had been accumulating. The attempt was ambitious: to systematize medicine around simple, basic principles, as Newton had done in physics. But the schools of thought resulting from such speculation and theorizing did little to improve medical care.

Hospitals and Medical Experiments

Hospitals were terrible places throughout most of the eighteenth century. There was no isolation of patients. Operations were performed in a patient's bed. Nurses were old, ignorant, greedy, and often drunk women. Fresh air was considered harmful, and infections of every kind were rampant. Diderot's article in the *Encyclopedia* on the Hôtel-Dieu in Paris, the "richest and most terrifying of all French hospitals," vividly describes normal conditions of the 1770s:

Imagine a long series of communicating wards filled with sufferers of every kind of disease who are some-times packed three, four, five or even six into a bed, the living alongside the dead and dying, the air polluted by this mass of unhealthy bodies, passing pestilential germs of their afflictions from one to the other, and the spectacle of suffering and agony on every hand. That is the Hôtel-Dieu.[11]

No wonder the poor of Paris hated hospitals and often saw confinement there as a plot to kill paupers.

In the last years of the century, the humanitarian concern already reflected in Diderot's description of the Hôtel-Dieu led to a movement for hospital reform throughout western Europe. Efforts were made to improve ventilation and eliminate filth in the belief that bad air caused disease. The theory was wrong, but the results were beneficial, for the spread of infection was somewhat reduced.

Mental hospitals, too, were incredibly savage institutions. The customary treatment for mental illness was bleeding and cold water, administered more to maintain discipline than to effect a cure. Violent persons were chained to the wall and forgotten. A breakthrough of sorts occurred in the 1790s when William Tuke founded the first humane sanatorium in England. In Paris an innovative warden, Philippe Pinel, took the chains off the mentally disturbed in 1793 and tried to treat them as patients rather than as prisoners.

In the eighteenth century, all sorts of wildly erroneous ideas about mental illness circulated. One was that moonlight caused madness, a belief reflected in the word *lunatic*—someone harmed by lunar light. Another mid-eighteenth-century theory, which lasted until at least 1914, was that masturbation caused madness, not to mention acne, epilepsy, and premature ejaculation. Thus parents, religious institutions, and schools waged relentless war on masturbation by males, although they were curiously uninterested in female masturbation.

In the second half of the eighteenth century, medicine in general turned in a more practical and experimental direction. Some of the experimentation was creative quackery involving the recently discovered phenomenon of electricity. One magnificent quack in London promoted sleep on a cure-all Celestial Bed, which was lavishly decorated with magnets and electrical devices. A single night on the bed cost a small fortune. The rich could buy expensive treatments, but the prevalence of quacks and the general lack of knowledge meant they often got little for their money. Because so

❄ **Hospital Life**   Patients crowded into hospitals like this one in Hamburg in 1746 had little chance of recovery. A priest by the window administers last rites, while in the center a surgeon coolly saws off the leg of a man who has received no anesthesia. (*Source: Germanisches Nationalmuseum, Nuremberg*)

many treatments were harmful, the common people were probably much less deprived by their reliance on faith healers and folk medicine than one might think.

Experimentation and the intensified search for solutions to human problems led to some real advances in medicine after 1750, however. The eighteenth century's greatest medical triumph was the conquest of smallpox. With the progressive decline of bubonic plague, smallpox became the most terrible of the infectious diseases. In the words of historian Thomas Macaulay, "Smallpox was always present, filling the churchyard with corpses, tormenting with constant fears all whom it had not stricken." It is estimated that 60 million Europeans died of smallpox in the eighteenth century. Fully 80 percent of the population was stricken at some point in life, and 25 percent of the total population was left permanently scarred. If ever a human problem cried out for solution, it was smallpox.

Inoculation against smallpox was already practiced in China and the Muslim lands of western Asia. Something approaching mass inoculation took place in England in the 1760s and the practice spread to the continent of Europe. By the later years of the century, smallpox inoculation was playing some part in the decline of the death rate and the general increase in European population. However, the method of inoculation—using active smallpox to stimulate immunity—could cause a mild, and potentially infectious, case of the disease.

The final breakthrough against smallpox came at the end of the century. Edward Jenner (1749–1823), a talented country doctor, noted that in the English countryside there was a long-standing belief that dairy maids who had contracted cowpox did not get smallpox. Cowpox produces sores on the cow's udder and on the hands of the milker. The sores resemble those of smallpox, but the disease is mild and not contagious. In 1796, using matter taken from a milkmaid with cowpox, Jenner performed his first vaccination on a young boy. In the next two years, he performed twenty-three successful vaccinations and in 1798 published his findings. After Austrian medical authorities replicated Jenner's results, the new method of treatment spread rapidly. Smallpox soon declined to the point of disappearance in Europe and then throughout the world. For his great discovery, Jenner eventually received prizes totaling £30,000 from the British government, a fitting recompense for a man who gave an enormous gift to humanity and helped lay the foundation for the science of immunology in the nineteenth century.

❊ RELIGION AND POPULAR CULTURE

Though the critical spirit of the Enlightenment spread among the educated elite in the eighteenth century, the majority of ordinary men and women remained firmly committed to the Christian religion, especially in rural areas. Religion offered answers to life's mysteries and gave comfort and courage in the face of sorrow and fear. Religion also remained strong because it was usually embedded in local traditions, everyday social experience, and popular culture.

Yet the popular religion of village Europe was everywhere enmeshed in a larger world of church hierarchies and state power. These powerful outside forces sought to regulate religious life at the local level. Their efforts created tensions that helped set the scene for a vigorous religious revival in Germany and England. Similar tensions arose in Catholic countries, where powerful elites criticized and attacked popular religious practices that their increasingly rationalistic minds deemed foolish and superstitious.

The Institutional Church

As in the Middle Ages, the local parish church remained the basic religious unit all across Europe. Still largely coinciding with the agricultural village, the parish fulfilled many needs. Whether Catholic or Protestant, the parish church was the focal point of religious devotion and much more. Villagers came together at services and gossiped and swapped stories afterward, and neighbors joined in church for baptisms, marriages, funerals, and other special events. Thus the parish church was woven into the very fabric of community life.

Moreover, the local church had important administrative tasks. It is because priests and parsons kept such complete parish registers that historians have learned so much about population and family life. Parishes also normally distributed charity to the destitute, looked after orphans, and provided whatever primary education was available for the common people.

The many tasks of the local church were usually the responsibility of a resident priest or pastor, a full-time professional working with assistants and lay volunteers. All clerics—whether Roman Catholic, Protestant, or Orthodox—also shared the fate of middlemen in a complicated institutional system. Charged most often with ministering to poor peasants, the priest or parson was the last link in a powerful church-state hierarchy that was everywhere determined to control religion down to the grassroots. However, the regulatory framework of belief, which went back at least to the fourth century when Christianity became the official religion of the Roman Empire, had undergone important changes since 1500.

The Protestant Reformation had burst forth as a culmination of medieval religiosity and a desire to purify Christian belief. Martin Luther, the greatest of the reformers, preached that all men and women were saved from their sins and God's damnation only by personal faith in Jesus Christ. The individual could reach God directly, without need of priestly intermediaries. This was the revolutionary meaning of Luther's "priesthood of all believers," which broke forever the monopoly of the priestly class over medieval Europe's most priceless treasure—eternal salvation.

As the Reformation gathered force, with peasant upheaval and doctrinal competition, German princes and monarchs in northern Europe put themselves at the head of official churches in their territories. Protestant authorities, with generous assistance from state-certified theologians, then proceeded to regulate their "territorial churches" strictly, selecting personnel and imposing detailed rules. They joined with Catholics to crush the Anabaptists, who, with their belief in freedom of conscience and separation of church and state, had become the real revolutionaries. Thus the Reformation, initially so radical in its rejection of Rome and its stress on individual religious experience, eventually resulted in a bureaucratization of the church and local religious life in Protestant Europe.

The Reformation era also increased the practical power of Catholic rulers over "their" churches, but

A Religious Festival in Urban France This vibrant painting suggests how religious life interacted with powerful institutions in Catholic Europe. Moving past crowds and through the city, this procession is celebrating the Blessed Sacrament on the Feast of Corpus Christi (the Body of Christ). Church dignitaries are grouped in the center; the colorful nobility is on the left; and the middle orders, with their sober black suits, are on the right. Both participation and hierarchical inequality are the rule. *(Source: Bibliothèque des Arts Décoratifs/Jean-Loup Charmet)*

it was only in the eighteenth century that some Catholic monarchs began to impose striking reforms. These reforms, which had their counterparts in Orthodox Russia, had a very "Protestant" aspect. They increased state control over the Catholic church, making it less subject to papal influence. For instance, Spain, a deeply Catholic country with devout rulers, took firm control of ecclesiastical appointments. Papal proclamations could not even be read in Spanish churches without prior approval from the government. Spain also asserted state control over the Spanish Inquisition, which had been ruthlessly pursuing heresy as an independent agency under Rome's direction for two hundred years. In sum, Spain went far toward creating a "national" Catholic church, as France had done earlier.

Some Catholic rulers also turned their reforming efforts on certain religious orders and monasteries and convents. Following the earlier example of

Portugal, the French king ordered the politically influential Jesuits out of France in 1763 and confiscated their property. Believing that the large monastic clergy should make a more practical contribution to social and religious life, Maria Theresa of Austria (see page 000) sharply restricted entry into "unproductive" orders, and her son Joseph II abolished contemplative orders, henceforth permitting only orders that were engaged in teaching, nursing, or other practical work. The state also expropriated the dissolved monasteries and used their great wealth for charitable purposes and higher salaries for ordinary priests.

Protestant Revival

In their attempt to recapture the vital core of the Christian religion, the Protestant reformers had rigorously suppressed all the medieval practices that they considered nonessential or erroneous because they were not founded on Scripture. Relics and crucifixes had been permanently removed from crypt and altar. Stained-glass windows had been smashed, walls and murals covered with whitewash, and processions and pilgrimages eliminated. Such revolutionary changes had often troubled ordinary churchgoers, but by the late seventeenth century the vast reforms of the Reformation had been completed and thoroughly routinized in most Protestant churches.

Indeed, official Protestant churches had generally settled into a smug complacency. In the Reformation heartland, one concerned German minister wrote that the Lutheran church "had become paralyzed in forms of dead doctrinal conformity" and badly needed a return to its original inspiration.[12] This voice was one of many that would prepare and then guide a powerful Protestant revival, which was largely successful because it answered the intense but increasingly unsatisfied needs of common people.

The Protestant revival began in Germany. It was known as Pietism, and three aspects account for its powerful appeal. First, Pietism called for a warm, emotional religion that everyone could experience. Enthusiasm—in prayer, in worship, in preaching, in life itself—was the key concept. "Just as a drunkard becomes full of wine, so must the congregation become filled with spirit," declared one exuberant writer. Another said simply, "The heart must burn."[13]

Second, Pietism reasserted the earlier radical stress on the priesthood of all believers, thereby reducing the wide gulf between the official clergy and the Lutheran laity. Bible reading and study were enthusiastically extended to all classes, and this provided a powerful spur for popular education as well as individual religious development. Third, Pietists believed in the practical power of Christian rebirth in everyday affairs. Reborn Christians were expected to lead good, moral lives and come from all social classes.

Pietism had a major impact on John Wesley (1703–1791), who served as the catalyst for popular religious revival in England. Wesley, who came from a long line of ministers, mapped a fanatically earnest "scheme of religion." As a teaching fellow at Oxford University, he organized a Holy Club for similarly minded students. They were soon known contemptuously as "Methodists" because they were so methodical in their devotion. Yet like the young Luther, Wesley remained intensely troubled about his own salvation, even after his ordination as an Anglican priest in 1728.

Wesley's anxieties related to grave problems of the faith in England. The government shamelessly used the Church of England to provide favorites with high-paying jobs and sinecures. The building of churches practically stopped even though the population was growing and in many parishes there was a grave shortage of pews. Services and sermons had settled into an uninspiring routine, while the skepticism of the Enlightenment was making inroads among the educated classes and deism was becoming popular. Some bishops and church leaders acted as if they believed that doctrines such as the Virgin Birth or the Ascension were little more than elegant superstitions.

Spiritual counseling from a sympathetic Pietist minister from Germany prepared Wesley for a mystical, emotional "conversion" in 1738. He described this critical turning point in his *Journal*:

In the evening I went to a [Christian] society in Aldersgate Street where one was reading Luther's preface to the Epistle to the Romans. About a quarter before nine, while he was describing the change which God works in the heart through faith in Christ, I felt my heart strangely warmed. I felt I did trust in Christ, Christ alone for salvation; and an assurance was given me that he had taken away my sins, even mine, and saved me from the law of sin and death.[14]

Wesley's emotional experience resolved his intellectual doubts. Moreover, he was convinced that any person, no matter how poor or uneducated, might have a similarly heartfelt conversion and gain the same blessed assurance.

Wesley took the good news to the people, traveling some 225,000 miles by horseback and preaching more than forty thousand sermons in fifty years. Since existing churches were often overcrowded and the church-state establishment was hostile, Wesley preached in open fields. People came in large numbers. Of critical importance was Wesley's rejection of Calvinist predestination—the doctrine of salvation granted only to a select few. Expanding on earlier Dutch theologians' views, he preached that *all* men and women who earnestly sought salvation might be saved. It was a message of hope and joy, of free will and universal salvation. Wesley's ministry won converts and eventually resulted in a new denomination.

And as Wesley had been inspired by Pietist revival in Germany, so evangelicals in the Church of

A Midsummer Afternoon with a Methodist Preacher This detail from a painting by Philippe de Loutherbourg portrays in a humorous manner how John Wesley and his followers took their optimistic Christianity to the people of England. Methodist ministers championed open-air preaching and week-long revivals. *(Source: Royal Ontario Museum)*

England and the old dissenting groups followed his example, giving impetus to an even broader awakening among the lower classes. In Protestant countries religion remained a vital force in the lives of the people.

Catholic Piety

Religion also flourished in Catholic Europe around 1700, but there were important differences with Protestant practice. First of all, the visual contrast was striking. Baroque artists had lavished rich and emotionally exhilarating figures and images on Catholic churches; Protestants excluded such works from their places of worship. Catholics in Europe remained intensely religious. More than 95 percent of the Catholic population probably attended church for Easter Communion, the climax of the Catholic church year.

The tremendous popular strength of religion in Catholic countries reflected religion's integral role in community life and popular culture. Thus although Catholics reluctantly confessed their sins to priests, they enthusiastically joined together in religious festivals to celebrate the passage of the liturgical year. In addition to the great processional days—such as Palm Sunday, the joyful re-enactment of Jesus' triumphal entry into Jerusalem, or Rogations, with its chanted supplications and penances three days before the bodily ascent of Jesus into heaven on Ascension Day—each parish had its own saints' days, processions, and pilgrimages. Led by its priest, a congregation might march around the village or across the countryside to a local shrine or chapel, perhaps closing the event with an enormous picnic. Before each procession or feast day, the priest explained its religious significance to kindle group piety. But processions were also part of folklore and tradition, an escape from work, and a form of recreation. A holiday atmosphere sometimes reigned on longer processions. People drank and danced, and couples disappeared into the woods.

Indeed, devout Catholics had many religious beliefs that were marginal to the Christian faith, often of obscure or even pagan origin. On the feast of Saint Anthony, for example, priests were expected to bless salt and bread for farm animals to protect them from disease. One saint's relics could help cure a child of fear, and there were healing springs for many ailments. Ordinary people combined a strong Christian faith with a wealth of time-honored superstitions.

Inspired initially by the fervor of the Catholic Counter-Reformation and then to some extent by the critical rationalism of the Enlightenment, parish priests and Catholic hierarchies sought increasingly to "purify" popular religious practice and to detach that purified religion from everyday life in the eighteenth century. Thus one parish priest in France lashed out at his parishioners, claiming that they were "more superstitious than devout . . . and sometimes appear as baptized idolators."[15] French priests particularly denounced the "various remnants of paganism" found in popular bonfire ceremonies during Lent in which young men, "yelling and screaming like madmen," tried to jump over the bonfires in order to help the crops grow and protect themselves from illness. One priest saw rational Christians regressing into pagan animals—"the triumph of Hell and the shame of Christianity."[16]

In contrast with Protestant reformers, who had already used the power of the territorial state to crush such practices, many Catholic priests and bishops preferred a compromise between theological purity and the people's piety, perhaps realizing that the line between divine truth and mere superstition is not easily drawn. Thus the severity of the formal attack on popular Catholicism varied widely by country and region. Where authorities pursued purification vigorously, as in Austria under Joseph II, pious peasants saw only an incomprehensible attack on the true faith and drew back in anger. Their reaction dramatized the growing tension between the educated elites and the common people.

Leisure and Recreation

The combination of religious celebration and popular recreation seen in festivals and processions was most strikingly displayed at Carnival, a time of reveling and excess in Catholic and Mediterranean Europe. Carnival preceded Lent—the forty days of fasting and penitence before Easter—and for a few days in January or February a wild release of drinking, masquerading, and dancing reigned. A combination of plays, processions, and rowdy spectacles turned the established order upside-down. Peasants became nobles, fools turned into philosophers, and the rich were humbled. These once-a-year rituals gave people a much-appreciated chance to release their pent-up frustrations and aggressions before life returned to the usual pattern of leisure and recreation.

That pattern featured socializing in groups, for despite the spread of literacy the culture of the common people was largely oral rather than written. In the cold dark winter months families gathered around the fireplace to talk, sing, tell stories, do craftwork, and keep warm. In some parts of Europe, women gathered together in groups in someone's cottage to chat, sew, spin, and laugh. Sometimes a few young men would be invited so that the daughters (and mothers) could size up potential suitors in a supervised atmosphere. A favorite recreation of men was drinking and talking with buddies in public places. It was a sorry village that had no tavern. In addition to old favorites such as beer and wine, the common people turned with gusto toward cheap and potent hard liquor, which in the eighteenth century fell in price because of the greatly improved techniques for distilling grain.

Towns and cities offered a wide range of amusements. Participants had to pay for many of these because the eighteenth century saw a sharp increase in the commercialization of leisure-time activities—a trend that continues to this day. Urban fairs featured prepared foods, acrobats, freak shows, open-air performances, optical illusions, and the like. Such entertainments attracted a variety of social classes. So did the growing number of commercial, profit-oriented spectator sports. These ranged from traveling circuses and horse races to boxing matches and bullfights. Sports heroes such as hefty heavyweight champions and haughty matadors made their appearance on the historical scene.

"Blood sports," such as bullbaiting and cockfighting, remained popular with the masses. In bullbaiting, a bull, usually chained to a stake in the courtyard of an inn, was attacked by ferocious dogs for the amusement of the innkeeper's guests. Eventually the maimed and tortured animal was slaughtered by a butcher and sold as meat. In a cockfight, two roosters, carefully trained by their owners and armed with razor-sharp steel spurs, slashed and clawed each other in a small ring until the victor won—and the loser died. An added attraction of cockfighting was that the screaming spectators could bet on the lightning-fast combat and its uncertain outcome.

In trying to place the vibrant popular culture of the common people in broad perspective, historians have stressed the growing criticism levied against it by the educated elites in the second half of the eighteenth century. These elites, which had previously shared the popular enthusiasm for religious festivals, Carnival, drinking in taverns, blood sports, and the like, now tended to see only superstition, sin, disorder, and vulgarity.[17] The resulting attack on popular culture, which had its more distant origins in the Protestant clergy's efforts to eliminate frivolity and superstition, was intensified as educated elites embraced the critical world-view of the Enlightenment. This shift in cultural attitudes was yet another aspect of the widening separation between the common people and the educated public. The mutual hostility that this separation engendered played an important role in the emergence of sharp class conflict in the era of the French and the Industrial Revolutions.

Cockfighting in England This engraving by William Hogarth (1697–1764) satirizes the popular taste for blood sports, which Hogarth despised and lampooned in his famous *Four Stages of Cruelty*. The central figure in the wildly excited gathering is a blind nobleman, who actually existed and seldom missed a fight. Notice the steel spurs on the birds' legs. (*Source: Courtesy of Trustees of the British Museum*)

SUMMARY

In recent years, imaginative research has greatly increased the specialist's understanding of ordinary life and social patterns in the past. The human experience as recounted by historians has become richer and more meaningful, and many mistaken ideas have fallen by the wayside. This has been particularly true of eighteenth-century, predominately agrarian Europe, which combined a fascinating mixture of continuity and change.

The life of the people remained primarily rural and oriented toward the local community. Tradition, routine, and well-established codes of behavior framed much of the everyday experience of the typical villager. Thus just as the three-field agricultural cycle and its pattern of communal rights had determined traditional patterns of grain production, so did community values in the countryside strongly encourage a late age for marriage, a low rate of illegitimate births, and a strict attitude toward children. Patterns of recreation and leisure, from churchgoing and religious festivals to sewing and drinking in groups, also reflected and reinforced community ties and values. Many long-standing ideas and beliefs, ranging from obscure religious customs to support for fair prices, remained strong forces and sustained continuity in popular life.

Yet powerful forces also worked for change. Many of these came from outside and above, from the aggressive capitalists, educated elites, and government officials discussed in the last two chapters. Closely knit villages began to lose control over families and marital practices, as could be seen in the earlier, more romantic marriages of cottage workers and in the beginning of the explosion in illegitimate births. Although the new, less rigorous attitudes toward children that were emerging in elite culture did not reach the common people, the elite belief in the usefulness of some education did result in growing popular literacy. The grain-based diet became more varied with the grudging acceptance of the potato, and the benefits of the spectacular conquest of smallpox began to reach the common people in the late eighteenth century. Finally, the common people found that their beliefs and customs were being increasingly attacked by educated elites, which thought they knew best. The popular reaction to these attacks generally remained muted in the eighteenth century, but the common people and their advocates would offer vigorous responses and counterattacks in the revolutionary era (see Chapter 23).

NOTES

1. Quoted in S. Chapman, *The Lancashire Cotton Industry* (Manchester, Eng.: Manchester University Press, 1903), p. 13.
2. Quoted in J. M. Beattie, "The Criminality of Women in Eighteenth-Century England," *Journal of Social History* 8 (Summer 1975): 86.
3. W. L. Langer, "Infanticide: A Historical Survey," *History of Childhood Quarterly* 1 (Winter 1974): 357.
4. Quoted in R. Cobb, *The Police and the People: French Popular Protest, 1789–1820* (Oxford: Clarendon Press, 1970), p. 238.
5. M. Segalen, *Love and Power in the Peasant Family: Rural France in the Nineteenth Century* (New York: Basil Blackwell, 1983), p. 41. The passage cited here has been edited into the past tense.
6. G. Gullickson, *Spinners and Weavers of Auffay: Rural Industry and the Sexual Division of Labor in a French Village, 1750–1850* (Cambridge: Cambridge University Press, 1986), p. 186. See also L. A. Tilly, J. W. Scott, and M. Cohen, "Women's Work and European Fertility Patterns," *Journal of Interdisciplinary History* 6 (Winter 1976): 447–476.
7. Quoted in B. W. Lorence, "Parents and Children in Eighteenth-Century Europe," *History of Childhood Quarterly* 2 (Summer 1974): 1–2.
8. Quoted ibid., pp. 13, 16.
9. E. Kennedy, *A Cultural History of the French Revolution* (New Haven, Conn.: Yale University Press, 1989), p. 47.
10. Quoted in L. S. King, *The Medical World of the Eighteenth Century* (Chicago: University of Chicago Press, 1958), p. 320.
11. Quoted in R. Sand, *The Advance to Social Medicine* (London: Staples Press, 1952), pp. 86–87.
12. Quoted in K. Pinson, *Pietism as a Factor in the Rise of German Nationalism* (New York: Columbia University Press, 1934), p. 13.
13. Quoted ibid., pp. 43–44.
14. Quoted in S. Andrews, *Methodism and Society* (London: Longmans, Green, 1970), p. 327.
15. Quoted in I. Woloch, *Eighteenth-Century Europe: Tradition and Progress, 1715–1789* (New York: Norton, 1982), p. 292.
16. Quoted in T. Tackett, *Priest and Parish in Eighteenth-Century France* (Princeton, N.J.: Princeton University Press, 1977), p. 214.

17. Woloch, *Eighteenth-Century Europe,* pp. 220–221; see also pp. 214–220.

SUGGESTED READING

Though long ignored in many general histories of the world, social topics of the kind considered in this chapter have come into their own in recent years. The reader is strongly advised to take time to look through recent volumes of journals such as *Journal of Social History, Past and Present, History of Childhood Quarterly,* and *Journal of Interdisciplinary History.* In addition, the number of book-length studies has expanded rapidly and continues to do so.

Two fine books on the growth of population are C. Cipolla's short and lively *The Economic History of World Population* (1962) and T. McKeown's scholarly *The Modern Rise of Population* (1977). W. McNeill, *Plagues and Peoples* (1976), is also noteworthy. B. H. Slicher van Bath, *The Agrarian History of Western Europe, A.D. 500–1850* (1963), is a wide-ranging general introduction to the gradual transformation of European agriculture. J. Blum, *The End of the Old Order in Rural Europe* (1978), is an impressive comparative study. Two recommended and complementary studies on landowning nobilities are R. Forster, *The Nobility of Toulouse in the Eighteenth Century* (1960), and G. E. Mingay, *English Landed Society in the Eighteenth Century* (1963). E. L. R. Ladurie, *The Peasants of Languedoc* (1976), a brilliant and challenging study of rural life in southern France for several centuries, complements J. Goody et al., eds., *Family and Inheritance: Rural Society in Western Europe, 1200–1800* (1976). Life in small-town preindustrial France comes alive in P. Higonnet, *Pont-de-Montvert: Social Structure and Politics in a French Village, 1700–1914* (1971), and O. Hufton deals vividly and sympathetically with rural migration, work, women, and much more in *The Poor in Eighteenth-Century France* (1974). F. Braudel, *Civilization and Capitalism, 15th–18th Century* (1981–1984), is a monumental and highly recommended three-volume synthesis of social and economic development. Another exciting work is J. Nef, *War and Human Progress* (1968), which examines the impact of war on economic and industrial development in European history between about 1500 and 1800 and may be compared with M. Gutmann, *War and Rural Life in the Early Modern Low Countries* (1980).

Among general introductions to the history of the family, women, and children, J. Casey, *The History of the Family* (1989), is recommended. P. Laslett, *The World We Have Lost* (1965), is an exciting, pioneering

investigation of England before the Industrial Revolution, though further research has weakened some of his conclusions. L. Stone, *The Family, Sex and Marriage in England, 1500–1800* (1977), is a provocative general interpretation, and L. Tilly and J. Scott, *Women, Work and Family* (1978), is excellent. Two valuable works on women, both with good bibliographies, are M. Boxer and J. Quataert, eds., *Connecting Spheres: Women in the Western World, 1500 to the Present* (1987), and R. Bridenthal, C. Koonz, and S. Stuard, eds., *Becoming Visible: Women in European History,* 2d ed. (1987). P. Ariès, *Centuries of Childhood: A Social History of Family Life* (1962), is another stimulating study. E. Shorter, *The Making of the Modern Family* (1975), is a lively, controversial interpretation, which should be compared with the excellent study by M. Segalen, *Love and Power in the Peasant Family: Rural France in the Nineteenth Century* (1983). T. Rabb and R. I. Rothberg, eds., *The Family in History* (1973), is a good collection of articles dealing with both Europe and the United States. A. MacFarlane, *The Family Life of Ralph Josselin* (1970), is a brilliant re-creation of the intimate family circle of a seventeenth-century English clergyman who kept a detailed diary; MacFarlane's *Origins of English Individualism: The Family, Property and Social Transition* (1978) is a major work. I. Pinchbeck and M. Hewitt, *Children in English Society* (1973), is a good introduction. B. Lorence-Kot, *Child-Rearing and Reform: A Study of Nobility in Eighteenth-Century Poland* (1985), stresses the harshness of parental discipline.

Various aspects of sexual relationships are treated imaginatively by M. Foucault, *The History of Sexuality* (1981), and R. Wheaton and T. Hareven, eds., *Family and Sexuality in French History* (1980). L. Moch, *Moving Europeans: Migration in Western Europe Since 1650* (1992), offers a rich, human, and highly recommended account of the movements of millions of ordinary people. J. Burnett, *A History of the Cost of Living* (1969), has a great deal of interesting information about what people spent their money on in the past, and complements J. C. Drummond and A. Wilbraham, *The Englishman's Food: A History of Five Centuries of English Diet,* 2d ed. (1958). J. Knyveton, *Diary of a Surgeon in the Year 1751–1752* (1937), gives a contemporary's unforgettable picture of both eighteenth-century medicine and social customs, as do D. Porter and R. Porter, *Patient's Progress: Doctors and Doctoring in Eighteenth-Century England* (1989), and M. Romsey, *Professional and Popular Medicine in France, 1770–1830: The Social World of Medical Practice* (1988). Good introductions to the evolution of medical practices are B. Ingles, *History of Medicine* (1965); O. Bettmann, *A Pictorial History of Medicine* (1956); and L. King, *The Medical World of the Eight-*

eenth Century (1958). W. Boyd, *History of Western Education* (1966), is a standard survey; R. Houston, *Literacy in Early Modern Europe: Culture and Education, 1500–1800* (1988), is brief and engaging.

The study of popular culture is expanding. Among older studies, M. George, *London Life in the Eighteenth Century* (1965), is a delight, and D. Roche, *The People of Paris: An Essay in Popular Culture in the 18th Century* (1987), presents an unforgettable portrait of the Paris poor. I. Woloch, *Eighteenth-Century Europe: Tradition and Progress, 1715–1789* (1982), includes a survey of popular culture and a good bibliography; E. Kennedy, *A Cultural History of the French Revolution* (1989), beautifully captures rural and urban attitudes in France before and during the French Revolution. R. Malcolmson, *Popular Recreation in English Society, 1700–1850* (1973), provides a colorful account of boxers, bettors, bullbaiting, and more. L. Hunt, *The New Cultural History* (1989), provides an engaging discussion of conceptual issues. G. Rude, *The Crowd in History, 1730–1848* (1964), is an influential effort to see politics and popular protest from below. An important series edited by R. Forster and O. Ranuum considers neglected social questions such as diet, abandoned children, and deviants, as does P. Burke's excellent study, *Popular Culture in Early Modern Europe* (1978). J. Gillis, *For Better, for Worse: Marriage in Britain Since 1500* (1985), and R. Philips, *Untying the Knot: A Short History of Divorce* (1991), are good introductions to institutional changes.

Good works on religious life include Tackett, cited in the Notes; J. Delumeau, *Catholicism Between Luther and Voltaire: A New View of the Counter-Reformation* (1977); B. Semmel, *The Methodist Revolution* (1973); and J. Bettey, *Church and Community: The Parish Church in English Life* (1979).

LISTENING TO THE
PAST

A New Way to Educate Children

Emile, by Jean-Jacques Rousseau, is one of history's most original books. Sometimes called a declaration of rights for children, Emile *challenged existing patterns of child rearing and pleaded for humane treatment of children.*

Rousseau's work also had a powerful impact on theories of education. As the following passage suggests, Emile *argued that education must shield the unspoiled child from the corrupting influences of civilization and allow the child to develop naturally and spontaneously. It is eloquent testimony to Rousseau's troubled life that he neglected his own children and placed all five of them in orphanages.*

Rousseau believed that the sexes were by nature intended for different occupations. Thus Emile might eventually tackle difficult academic subjects, but Sophie, his future wife in the book, needed to learn only how to manage the home and be a good mother and an obedient wife. The idea that girls and boys should be educated to operate in "separate spheres" was to gain wide acceptance in the nineteenth century.

A man must know many things which seem useless to a child, but need the child learn, or can he indeed learn, all that the man must know? Try to teach the child what is of use to a child and you will find that it takes all his time. Why urge him to the studies of an age he may never reach, to the neglect of those studies which meet his present needs? "But," you ask, "will it not be too late to learn what he ought to know when the time comes to use it?" I cannot tell; but this I do know, it is impossible to teach it sooner, for our real teachers are experience and emotion, and man will never learn what befits a man except under its own conditions. A child knows he must become a man; all the ideas he may have as to man's place in life are so many opportunities for his instruction, but he should remain in complete ignorance of those ideas which are beyond his grasp. My whole book is one continued argument in support of this fundamental principle of education.

As soon as we have contrived to give our pupil [Emile] an idea of the word "useful," we have got an additional means of controlling him, for this word makes a great impression on him, provided that its meaning for him is a meaning relative to his own age, and provided he clearly sees its relation to his own well-being. . . . "What is the use of that?" In the future this is the sacred formula, the formula by which he and I test every action of our lives. . . .

I do not like verbal explanations. Young people pay little heed to them, nor do they remember them. Things! Things! I cannot repeat it too often. We lay too much stress upon words; we teachers babble, and our students follow our example.

Suppose we are studying the course of the sun and the way to find our bearings, when all at once Emile interrupts me with the question, "What is the use of that?" What a fine lecture I might give [going on and on]! . . . When I have finished I shall have shown myself a regular pedant, I shall have made a great display of learning, and not one single idea has he understood. . . .

But Emile is educated in a simpler fashion. We take so much pains to teach him a difficult idea that he will have heard nothing of all this. At the first word he does not understand, he will run away, he will prance about room, and leave me to speechify by myself. Let us seek a more commonplace explanation; my scientific learning is of no use to him.

We were observing the position of the forest to the north of Montmorency when he interrupted me with the usual question, "What is the use of that?" "You are right," I said. "Let us take time to think it over, and if we find it is no use we will drop it, for we only want useful games." We find something else to do and geography is put aside for the day.

Next morning I suggest a walk; there is nothing he would like better; children are always ready to run about, and he is a good walker. We climb up to the forest, we wander through its clearings and lose ourselves. . . . At last we [are exhausted and] sit down to rest and to consider our position. I assume that Emile has been educated like an ordinary child. He does not think, he begins to cry; he has no idea we are close to Montmorency, which is hidden from our view by a mere thicket. . . .

Jean-Jacques. "My dear Emile, what shall we do to get out?"

Emile. "I am sure I do not know. I am tired, I am hungry, I am thirsty, I cannot go any further."

Jean-Jacques. "Do you suppose I am any better off? I would cry too if I could make my lunch off tears. Crying is no use, we must look about us. What time is it?"

Emile. "It is noon and I am so hungry!"

Jean-Jacques. "I am so hungry too. . . . Unluckily my dinner won't come to find me. It is twelve o'clock. This time yesterday we were observing the position of the forest from Montmorency. If only we could see the position of Montmorency from the forest—"

Emile. "But yesterday we could see the forest, and here we cannot see the town."

Jean-Jacques. "That is just it. If we could only find it without seeing it. . . . Did not we say the forest was—"

Emile. "North of Montmorency."

Jean-Jacques. "Then Montmorency must lie—"

Emile. "South of the forest."

Jean-Jacques. "We know how to find the north at midday."

Emile. "Yes, by the direction of the shadows."

Jean-Jacques. "But the south?"

Emile. "What shall we do?"

Jean-Jacques. "The south is opposite the north."

Emile. "That is true; we need only find the opposite of the shadows. That is the south! That is the south! Montmorency must be over there! Let us look for it there!"

Jean-Jacques. "Perhaps you are right; let us follow this path through the wood."

✳ This illustration depicts children learning about the five senses. (*Source: Caroline Buckler*)

Emile. (Clapping his hands.) "Oh, I can see Montmorency! there it is, quite plain, just in front of us! Come to lunch, come to dinner, make haste! Astronomy is some use after all."

Be sure that he thinks this if he does not say it; no matter which, provided I do not say it myself. He will certainly never forget this day's lesson as long as he lives, while if I had only led him to think of all this at home, my lecture would have been forgotten the next day. Teach by doing whenever you can, and only fall back upon words when doing is out of the question.

Questions for Analysis

1. What criticism did Rousseau direct at the social and educational practices of his time?

2. How did Rousseau propose to educate his pupil?

3. Do you think Rousseau's plan appealed to peasants and urban workers in the eighteenth century? Why or why not?

4. In what ways did Rousseau's plan of education and his assumptions about human nature reflect some major ideas of the Enlightenment?

Source: Slightly adapted from J.-J. Rousseau, *Emile, or Education,* trans. B. Foxley (New York: E. P. Dutton, 1911), pp. 141–144.

20

Africa, 1400–1800

This bronze figure of a hornblower was created by a royal artisan for the court of Benin (A.D. 1500–1700). *(Source: Courtesy of the Trustees of the British Museum)*

frican states and societies of the fifteenth through eighteenth centuries comprised a wide variety of languages, cultures, and kinds of economic and political development. Modern European intrusion into Africa beginning in the fifteenth century led to the transatlantic slave trade, one of the great forced migrations in world history. Africa made a substantial, though involuntary, contribution to the building of the West's industrial civilization. In the seventeenth century, an increasing desire for sugar in Europe resulted in an increasing demand for slave labor in South America and the West Indies. In the eighteenth century, Western technological changes created a demand for cotton and other crops that required extensive human labor. As a result, the West's "need" for slaves from Africa increased dramatically.

Africa's relationship with Asia, the Islamic world, and the West stretches back a very long time, but only recently have anthropologists, economists, and historians begun to ask critical questions about African societies in early modern times.

- What kinds of economic and social structures did African societies have?
- What impact did Islam have on African societies?
- What kinds of literary sources survive?
- What role did slavery play in African societies before European intrusion?
- What were the geographical and societal origins of the slaves involuntarily shipped to America and to Asia?

This chapter explores these questions.

❖ SENEGAMBIA AND BENIN

In Africa in the mid-fifteenth century, there were societies held together by family or kinship ties, and there were kingdoms and states ruled by princes who governed defined areas through bureaucratic hierarchies. Along the 2,000-mile west coast between Senegambia and the northeastern shore of the Gulf of Guinea, a number of kingdoms flourished. Because much of that coastal region is covered by tropical rain forest, in contrast to the western Sudan, it is called the West African Forest Region (Map 20.1). The Senegambian states in the north possessed a homogeneous culture and a common history. For centuries Senegambia—named for the Senegal and Gambia Rivers—had served as an important entrepôt for desert caravan contact with the Islamic civilizations of North Africa and the Middle East. Through the transatlantic slave trade, Senegambia contributed heavily to New World population in the early seventeenth century. That trade brought Senegambia into contact with the Americas and Europe. Thus Senegambia felt the impact of Islamic culture to the north and of European influences from the maritime West.

In the thirteenth century, the kingdoms of Ghana and Mali had incorporated parts of Senegambia. Mali's influence disintegrated after 1450, and successor kingdoms that were independent but connected to one another through family ties emerged. Stronger states rose and temporarily exercised power over weaker ones.

Scholars are still exploring the social and political structures of the various Senegambian states. The peoples of Senegambia spoke Wolof, Serer, and Pulaar, which are all members of the West African language group. Both the Wolof-speakers and the Serer-speakers had clearly defined social classes: royalty, nobility, warriors, peasants, low-caste artisans such as blacksmiths and leatherworkers, and slaves. Slaves were individuals who were pawned for debt, house servants who could not be sold, and people who were acquired through war or purchase. Senegambian slavery varied from society to society but generally was not a benign institution. In some places the treatment of slaves was as harsh as treatment in the Western world later would be. However, many Senegambian slaves were not considered property to be bought and sold, and some served as royal advisers and enjoyed great power and prestige.[1]

The king of the Wolof was elected by the nobility. After his election the king immediately acquired authority and a special religious charisma. He commanded contingents of soldier-slaves and appointed village chiefs. The king gained his revenue from the chiefs, from merchants, and from taxes levied on defeated peoples.[2] The Wolof had a well-defined government hierarchy.

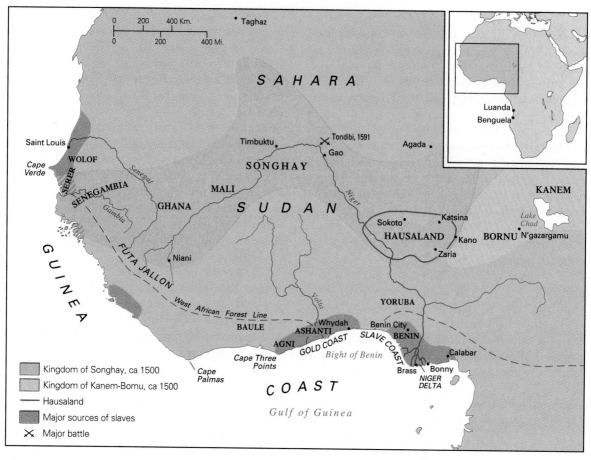

MAP 20.1 West African Kingdoms and the Slave Trade from ca 1500 to 1800
Consider the role that rivers and other geographical factors played in the development of the West African slave trade. Why were Luanda and Benguela the logical Portuguese source for slaves?

Among the stateless societies of Senegambia, where kinship and lineage groups tended to fragment communities, age-grade systems evolved. Age-grades were groups of men and women whom the society initiated into adulthood at the same time. Age-grades cut across family ties, created community-wide loyalties, and provided a means of local law enforcement, because the group was responsible for the behavior of all its members.

The typical Senegambian community was a small self-supporting agricultural village of closely related families. Custom assigned a high value to cultivation of the land—the shared objective of the group. Fields were cut from the surrounding forest, and the average farm of six or eight acres supported a moderate-size family. Often the family worked the land for a common harvest; sometimes individuals had their own private fields. Millet and sorghum were the staple grains in northern Senegambia; farther south, forest dwellers cultivated yams as a staple. Senegambians supplemented their diet with plantains, beans, and bananas, fish, oysters, and small game such as rabbits and monkeys. Along the Guinea coast rice was the basic cereal, and okra, onions, melons, and pepper spiced the regular diet. Frequent fairs in neighboring villages served as markets for the exchange of produce and opportunities for receiving outside news and social diversion. As one scholar has put it, "Life was simple, government largely limited to the settlement

The Oba of Benin   The walls of the Oba's palace were decorated with bronze plaques that may date to the period from the sixteenth to the eighteenth century. This plaque vividly conveys the Oba's power, majesty, and authority. The necklace (or choker) is his symbol of royalty. Attendants hold up his hands, and warriors raise shields over his head as sunshades. *(Source: The Metropolitan Museum of Art, The Michael C. Rockefeller Memorial Collection, Gift of Nelson A. Rockefeller, 1965)*

of disputes by family heads or elders . . . social life centered on the ceremony accompanying birth, death, and family alliance."[3]

The fifteenth and sixteenth centuries saw the emergence of the great forest kingdom of Benin (see Map 20.1) in what is now southern Nigeria. Although scholars still know little about Benin's origins, its history seems to have been characterized by power struggles between the king and the nobility that neither side ever completely won. An elaborate court ceremonial exalted the position of the *oba,* or king, and brought stability to the state. In the later fifteenth century, the oba Ewuare played off his palace chiefs against the village chiefs and thereby maintained a balance of power. A great warrior, Ewuare strengthened his army and pushed Benin's borders as far as the Niger River on the east, westward into Yoruba country, and south to the Gulf of Guinea. During the late sixteenth and seventeenth centuries the office of the oba evolved from a warrior kingship to a position of spiritual leadership.

At its height in the late sixteenth century, Benin controlled a vast territory, and European visitors described a sophisticated society. According to a modern historian, the capital, Benin City, "was a stronghold twenty-five miles in circumference, protected by walls and natural defenses, containing an elaborate royal palace and neatly laid-out houses with verandas and balustrades, and divided by broad avenues and smaller intersecting streets."[4] Visitors also noted that Benin City was kept scrupulously clean and had no beggars and that public security was so effective that theft was unknown. The period also witnessed remarkable artistic creativity in ironwork, in carved ivory, and especially in bronze portrait busts. Over nine hundred brass plaques survive, providing important information about Benin court life, military triumphs, and cosmological ideas.

In 1485 the Portuguese and other Europeans in pursuit of trade began to appear in Benin. A small exchange in pepper and slaves developed but never acquired importance in the Benin economy. Nor did the Portuguese have much success in converting the staunchly animistic people to Christianity. Europe's impact on Benin was minimal. In the early eighteenth century, as tributary states and stronger neighbors nibbled at Benin's frontiers, the kingdom underwent a crisis. Benin, however, survived as an independent entity until the British conquered and burned Benin City in 1898.

✤ THE SUDAN: SONGHAY, KANEM-BORNU, AND HAUSALAND

The kingdom of Songhay, a successor state of Ghana and Mali, dominated the whole Niger region of the western and central Sudan (see Map 20.1). Muhammad Toure (1492–1528) completed the expansionist and administrative consolidation begun by his predecessors. Muhammad Toure's power rested on his successful military expeditions. From his capital at Gao he extended his lordship as far north as the salt-mining center at Taghaz in the mid-Sahara and as far east as Agada and Kano. A convert to Islam, Muhammad made a pilgrimage to Mecca. Impressed by what he saw there, he tried to bring about greater centralization in his own territories. In addition to building a strong army and improving taxation procedures, he re-

placed local Songhay officials with more efficient Arab ones in an effort to substitute royal institutions for ancient kinship ties.

What kind of economy existed in the Songhay Empire? What social structures? What role did women play in Songhay society? What is known of Songhay education and culture? The paucity of written records and of surviving artifacts prevent scholars from satisfactorily exploring these questions. Some information is provided by Leo Africanus (ca. 1465–1550), a Moroccan captured by pirates and given as a slave to Pope Leo X. Leo Africanus became a Christian, taught Arabic in Rome, and in 1526 published an account of his many travels, including a stay in the Songhay kingdom.

As a scholar Leo was naturally impressed by Timbuktu, the second city of the empire, which he visited in 1513. "Here [is] a great store of doctors, judges, priests, and other learned men, that are bountifully maintained at the King's court," Leo reported.[5] Many of these Islamic scholars had studied in Cairo and other centers of Muslim learning. They gave Timbuktu a reputation for intellectual sophistication, religious piety, and moral justice.

Songhay under Muhammad Toure seems to have enjoyed economic prosperity. Leo Africanus noted the abundant food supply, which was produced in the southern savanna and carried to Timbuktu by a large fleet of canoes controlled by the king. The Sudanese had large amounts of money to spend, and expensive North African and European luxuries were much in demand: clothes, copperware, glass and stone beads, perfumes, and horses. The existence of many shops and markets implies the development of an urban culture. At Timbuktu, merchants, scholars and judges, and artisans constituted a distinctive bourgeoisie. The presence of many foreign merchants, including Jews and Italians, gave the city a cosmopolitan atmosphere. Jews largely controlled the working of gold.

Slaves played a very important part in the economy of Songhay. On the royal farms scattered throughout the kingdom, slaves produced rice—the staple crop—for the royal granaries. Although slaves could possess their own slaves, land, and cattle, they could not bequeath any of this property; the king inherited all of it. Muhammad Toure greatly increased the number of royal slaves through raids on the pagans (non-Muslims). He

Queen Mother and Attendants   As in Ottoman, Chinese, and European societies, so the mothers of rulers in Africa sometimes exercised considerable political power because of their influence on their sons. African kings granted the title "Queen Mother" as a badge of honor. The long beaded cap, called "chicken's beak," symbolizes her rank as do her elaborate neck jewelry and attendants. *(Source: Metropolitan Museum of Art. Gift of Mr. and Mrs. Klaus G. Perls, 1991)*

gave slaves to favorite Muslim scholars, who thus gained a steady source of income. Or the slaves were sold at the large market at Gao. Traders from North Africa bought them for sale in Cairo, Constantinople, Lisbon, Naples, Genoa, and Venice.

The kingdom of Songhay had considerable economic and cultural strengths, but it also had serious internal problems. Islamic institutions never took root in the countryside, and Muslim officials alienated the king from his people. Muhammad Toure's reforms were a failure. He governed a diverse group of peoples—Tuareg, Malinke, Fulani, as well as Songhai—who were often hostile to one another, and no cohesive element united them. Finally, the Songhai never developed an effective method of transferring power. Revolts, conspira-

cies, and palace intrigues followed the deaths of every king, and only three of the nine rulers in the dynasty begun by Muhammad Toure died natural deaths. Muhammad himself was murdered by one of his sons. His death began a period of political instability that led to the slow disintegration of the kingdom.[6]

In 1582 the sultanate of Morocco began to press southward in search of a greater share of the trans-Saharan trade. The people of Songhay, lacking effective leadership and believing the desert to be a sure protection against invasion, took no defensive precautions. In 1591 a Moroccan army of three thousand soldiers—many of whom were slaves of European origin equipped with European muskets—crossed the Sahara and inflicted a

"Africa, 1829" For most of the nineteenth century, what Americans learned of African geography derived from "maps" such as this one, a perfect example of abysmal Western ignorance—or carelessness, since even seventeenth–century Portuguese and British traders knew that Luanda and Benguela are in Angola. Because of its errors, this "map" is now a collector's item. By comparing it to Maps 20.1 and 20.2, you should be able to discover at least ten serious mistakes. *(Source: A private collection)*

crushing defeat on the Songhai at Tondibi. This battle spelled the end of the Songhay Empire. Although a moderate-size kingdom lingered on in the south for a century or so and weak political units arose, not until the eighteenth century did kingdoms able to exercise wide authority emerge again.

To the east of Songhay lay the kingdoms of Kanem-Bornu and Hausaland (see Map 20.1). Under the dynamic military leader Idris Alooma (1571–1603), Kanem-Bornu subdued weaker peoples and gained jurisdiction over an extensive area. Well drilled and equipped with firearms, camel-mounted cavalry and a standing army decimated warriors fighting with spears and arrows. Idris Alooma perpetuated the feudal pattern of government in which lands were granted to able fighters in return for loyalty and the promise of future military assistance. Meanwhile, agriculture occupied most people, peasants and slaves alike. Kanem-Bornu shared in the trans-Saharan trade, shipping eunuchs and young girls to North Africa in return for horses and firearms. A devout Muslim, Idris Alooma elicited high praise from Ibn Fartura, who wrote a history of his reign called *The Kanem Wars:*

So he made the pilgrimage and visited Medina with delight. . . . Among the benefits which God . . . conferred upon the Sultan Idris Alooma was the acquisition of Turkish musketeers and numerous household slaves who became skilled in firing muskets. . . .

Among the most surprising of his acts was the stand he took against obscenity and adultery, so that no such thing took place openly in his time. Formerly the people had been indifferent to such offences. . . . In fact he was a power among his people and from him came their strength.

The Sultan was intent on the clear path laid down by the Qur'an . . . in all his affairs and actions.[7]

Idris Alooma built mosques at his capital city of N'gazargamu and substituted Muslim courts and Islamic law for African tribunals and ancient customary law. His eighteenth-century successors lacked his vitality and military skills, however, and the empire declined.

Between Songhay and Kanem-Bornu were the lands of the Hausa. An agricultural people living in small villages, the Hausa grew millet, sorghum, barley, rice, cotton, and citrus fruit and raised livestock. Some Hausa merchants carried on a heavy trade in slaves and kola nuts with North African communities across the Sahara. Obscure trading posts evolved into important Hausa city-states like Kano and Katsina, through which Islamic influences entered the region. Kano and Katsina became Muslim intellectual centers and in the fifteenth century attracted scholars from Timbuktu. The Muslim chronicler of the reign of King Muhammad Rimfa of Kano (r. 1463–1499) records that Muhammad introduced the Muslim practices of *purdah,* or seclusion of women, of the *idal-fitr,* or festival after the fast of Ramadan, and of assigning eunuchs to the high offices of state.[8] As in Songhay and Kanem-Bornu, however, Islam made no strong imprint on the mass of the Hausa people until the nineteenth century.

❧ ETHIOPIA

At the beginning of the sixteenth century, the powerful East African Christian kingdom of Ethiopia extended from Massawa in the north to several tributary states in the south (Map 20.2). The ruling Solomonid Dynasty, however, faced serious troubles. Adal, a Muslim state along the southern base of the Red Sea, began incursions into Ethiopia, and in 1529 the Adal general Ahmad ibn-Ghazi inflicted a disastrous defeat on the Ethiopian emperor Lebna Dengel (r. 1508–1540). Ahmad followed up his victory with systematic devastation of the land, destruction of many Ethiopian artistic and literary works, and the forced conversion of thousands to Islam. Lebna Dengel fled to the mountains and appealed to Portugal for assistance. The Portuguese, eager for a share in the wealth of the East African coast and interested in the conversion of Ethiopia to Roman Catholicism, responded with a force of musketeers. In 1541 they decisively defeated the Muslims near Lake Tana.

No sooner had the Muslim threat ended than Ethiopia encountered three more dangers. The Galla, Cushitic-speaking peoples, moved northward in great numbers, occupying portions of Harar, Shoa, and Amhara. The Ethiopians could not defeat them militarily, and the Galla were not interested in assimilation. For the next two centuries the two peoples lived together in an uneasy truce. Simultaneous with the Galla migrations was the Ottoman Turks' seizure of Massawa and other coastal cities. Then the Jesuits arrived, eager to capitalize on earlier Portuguese support, and attempted to force Roman Catholicism on a proud people whose Coptic form of Christianity long antedated the European version. The overzealous Jesuit missionary Alphonse Mendez tried to revamp the Ethiopian liturgy, rebaptize the people, and replace ancient Ethiopian customs and practices with Roman ones. Since Ethiopian national sentiment was closely tied to Coptic Christianity, violent rebellion and anarchy ensued.

In 1633 the Jesuit missionaries were expelled. For the next two centuries hostility to foreigners, weak political leadership, and regionalism characterized Ethiopia. Civil conflicts between the Galla and the Ethiopians erupted continually. The Coptic church, though lacking strong authority, survived as the cornerstone of Ethiopian national identity.

❧ THE SWAHILI CITY-STATES

The word *Swahili,* meaning "People of the Coast," refers to the people living along the East African coast and on the nearby islands. Their history, unlike that of most African peoples, exists in writing. By the eleventh century, the Swahili had accepted

MAP 20.2 East Africa in the Sixteenth Century In early modern times, the Christian kingdom of Ethiopia, first isolated and then subjected to Muslim and European pressures, played an insignificant role in world affairs. But the East African city-states, which stretched from Sofola in the south to Mogadishu in the north, had powerfully important commercial relations with Mughal India, China, the Ottoman world, and southern Europe.

Islam, and "its acceptance was the factor that marked the acquisition of 'Swahili' identity: Islam gave the society coherent cultural form."[9] The Swahili language is studied today by North Americans who want to identify themselves as having African ancestry, but slaves shipped from East Africa came from inland, not from Swahili-speaking coastal peoples; virtually no Swahili people went to North America. As a people living on the shores of the Indian Ocean, the Swahili felt the influences of Indians, Indonesians, Persians, and especially Arabs.

Swahili civilization was overwhelmingly maritime. A fertile, well-watered, and intensely cultivated stretch of land no more than ten miles wide extends down the coast: it yielded rice, grains, citrus fruit, and cloves. The sea provided fish. But the considerable prosperity of the region rested on trade and commerce. The Swahili acted as middlemen in an Indian Ocean–East African protocapitalism, exchanging ivory, rhinoceros horn, tortoise shells, inlaid ebony chairs, copra (dried coconut meat that yields coconut oil), and inland slaves for Arabian and Persian perfumes and toilet articles, ink and paper, and for Indian textiles, beads, and iron tools. In the fifteenth century, the city-states of Mogadishu, Pate, Lamu, Mombasa, and especially Kilwa enjoyed a worldwide reputation for commercial prosperity.[10] These cities were cosmopolitan, and their standard of living was very high.

The arrival of the Portuguese explorer Vasco da Gama (see Map 16.1, page 517) in 1498 spelled the end of the Swahili cities' independence. Da Gama, lured by the spice trade, wanted to build a Portuguese maritime empire in the Indian Ocean, and between 1502 and 1507 the southern ports of Kilwa, Zanzibar, and Sofala fell before Portuguese guns and became Portuguese tributary states. The better-fortified northern cities, such as Mogadishu, survived as important entrepôts for goods to India.

The Portuguese victory in the south proved hollow, however. Rather than accept Portuguese commercial restrictions, the residents deserted the towns, and the town economies crumbled. Large numbers of Kilwa's people, for example, immigrated to northern cities. The flow of gold from inland mines to Sofala slowed to a trickle. Swahili passive resistance successfully prevented the Portuguese from gaining control of the local coastal trade.

After the intermittent bombardment of several cities, Portugal finally won an administrative

Saint George in Ethiopian Art   This image of a black Saint George slaying a dragon from a seventeenth-century Ethiopian manuscript attests to the powerful and pervasive Christian influence in Ethiopian culture. *(Source: The British Library)*

stronghold near Mombasa in 1589. Called Fort Jesus, it remained a Portuguese base for over a century. In the late seventeenth century, pressures from the northern European maritime powers—the Dutch, French, and English—aided greatly by the Arabs of Oman, combined with local African rebellions to bring about the collapse of Portuguese influence in Africa. A Portuguese presence remained only at Mozambique in the far south.

The Portuguese made no religious or cultural impact on the Swahili cities. Their sole effect was the cities' economic decline.

THE SLAVE TRADE

Slavery had a long history within Africa, and the transatlantic slave trade that began in the late fifteenth century is properly understood against that background. "Slavery was . . . fundamental to the social, political, and economic order of parts of the northern savanna, Ethiopia and the East African coast. . . . Enslavement was an organized activity, sanctioned by law and custom. Slaves were a principal commodity in trade, including the export

Dutch Colony, Cape of Good Hope Founded in 1657, by the mid-eighteenth century the Cape Colony had fifteen thousand inhabitants and may have been the largest European settlement on the African continent. Crews took on fresh provisions there, repaired their ships, and awaited favorable winds for crossing the Indian Ocean. *(Source: William Fehr Collection)*

sector, and slaves were important in the domestic sphere" as concubines, servants, soldiers, and ordinary laborers.[11]

Islam had heavily influenced African slavery. African rulers justified enslavement with the Muslim argument that prisoners of war could be sold; and, since captured peoples were considered chattel, they could be used in the same positions that prevailed in the Muslim world. Between 650 and 1600, black as well as white Muslims transported perhaps as many as 4.82 million black slaves across the trans-Saharan trade route.[12] When the transatlantic slave trade began, it represented little that was new.

The African slave trade, extending from the sixteenth to the nineteenth century and involving the forced migration of millions of human beings, represents one of the most inhumane, unjust, and tragic blots on the histories of human societies. The African diaspora immediately provokes a host of questions. What regions of Africa were the sources of slaves? What goods and business procedures were involved in the exchange of slaves? What were the economic, social, political, and demographic effects of the slave trades on African societies? In a period when the enslavement of peoples was dying out in Asian and European societies, when serfdom was declining in western Europe, why were *African* peoples enslaved, when land was so widely available and much of the African continent had a labor *shortage?*

The answer to the last question seems to lie in a technical problem related to African agriculture. Partly because of the tsetse fly, which causes sleeping sickness and other diseases, partly because of easily leached lateritic soils (containing high concentrations of oxides), farmers had great difficulty using draft animals. Tropical soils responded poorly to plowing, and most work had to be done with the hoe. Productivity, therefore, was low. Economists maintain that in most societies the value of a worker's productivity determines the value of his or her labor. In precolonial Africa, the individual's agricultural productivity was low, so his or her economic value to society was less than the economic value of a European peasant in Europe. *Slaves* in the Americas were more productive than free producers in Africa. And European slave dealers were very willing to pay a price higher than the value of an African's productivity in Africa.

The incidence of disease in the Americas also helps to explain the enslavement of Africans. Smallpox took a terrible toll on native Americans (see page 525), and between 30 percent and 50 percent of Europeans exposed to malaria succumbed to that sickness. Africans had developed some immunity to both diseases, and in the New World they experienced the lowest mortality rate of any people. Europeans wanted workers for mines and sugar cane plantations. A coerced (or slave) labor force proved easier to exploit than a wage labor force.[13] As the demand for sugar increased, as the technology for sugar production improved and shipping rates declined, the pressure for slave labor accelerated.

The search for a sea route to India led the Portuguese in the fifteenth century to explore the West African coast. Having "discovered" Brazil in 1500, the Portuguese founded a sugar colony at Bahia in 1551. Between 1551 and 1575, before the traffic to North America had gotten under way, the Portuguese delivered more African slaves to Brazil than would ever reach British North America (Table 20.1). Portugal essentially monopolized the slave trade until 1600 and continued to play a large role in the seventeenth century, though increasingly threatened by the Dutch, French, and English. From 1690 until the House of Commons abolished the slave trade in 1807, England was the leading carrier of African slaves.

Population density and supply conditions along the West African coast and the sailing time to New World markets determined the sources of slaves. As

TABLE 20.1 ESTIMATED SLAVE IMPORTS BY DESTINATION, 1451–1870

Destination	Estimated Total Slave Imports
British North America	399,000
Spanish America	1,552,100
British Caribbean	1,665,000
French Caribbean	1,600,200
Dutch Caribbean	500,000
Danish Caribbean	28,000
Brazil	3,646,800
Old World	175,000
	9,566,100

Source: P. D. Curtin, The Atlantic Slave Trade: A Census *(Madison, Wis.: University of Wisconsin Press, 1969), p. 268. Used with permission.*

the demand for slaves rose, slavers moved down the West African coast from Senegambia to the more densely populated hinterlands of the Bight of Benin and the Bight of Biafra (see Map 16.5, page 545). In the sixteenth and early seventeenth centuries, the Senegambian coast and the area near the mouth of the Congo River yielded the greatest numbers. By the late seventeenth century the British found the Ivory Coast region the most profitable territory. A century later the Bight of Benin and the Gold Coast had become the largest suppliers. The abundant supply of slaves in Angola, the region south of the Congo River, however, and the quick passage from Angola to Brazil and the Caribbean established that region as the major coast for Portuguese slavers.

Transatlantic wind patterns partly determined the routes of exchange. Shippers naturally preferred the swiftest crossing—that is, from the African port nearest the latitude of the intended

American destination. Thus Portuguese shippers carried their cargoes from Angola to Brazil, and British merchants sailed from the Bight of Benin to the Caribbean. The great majority of slaves were intended for the sugar and coffee plantations extending from the Caribbean islands to Brazil.[14]

Angola produced 26 percent of all African slaves and 70 percent of all Portuguese slaves. Trading networks extending deep into the interior culminated at two major ports on the Angolan coast, Luanda and Benguela (see inset to Map 20.1). Between the 1730s and 1770s Luanda shipped between 8,000 and 10,000 slaves each year; at the end of the eighteenth century Benguela's numbers equaled those of Luanda. In 1820, the peak year, 18,957 blacks left Luanda. The Portuguese acquired a few slaves through warfare but secured the vast majority through trade with African dealers. Whites did not participate in the inland markets.

Almost all Portuguese shipments went to satisfy the virtually insatiable Brazilian demand for slaves.[15] The transatlantic slave trade lasted for almost four centuries and involved the brutalization and exploitation of millions of human beings. Here is an excerpt from the report in 1793 of a Portuguese doctor with experience on the Middle Passage between Angola and Brazil:

When the slaves coming from many different parts of the interior reach the maritime ports of Africa, they are there once more traded for goods and merchandise. . . .

Here takes place the second round of hardships that these unlucky people are forced to suffer. . . . They are terribly handled and most scantily provided for . . . their human nature entirely overlooked. The dwelling place of the slave is simply the dirt floor of the compound, and he remains there exposed to harsh conditions and bad weather, and at night there are only a lean-to and some sheds . . . which they are herded into like cattle.

Their food continues scarce as before . . . limited at times to badly cooked beans, at other times to corn. . . . They also add to the diet a small amount of salted fish. . . .

They suffer in other ways. When they are first traded, they are made to bear the brand mark of the backlander who enslaved them, so that they can be recognized in case they run away. And when they reach a port . . . , they are branded on the right breast

with the coat of arms of the king and nation, of whom they have become vassals. . . . This mark is made with a hot silver instrument in the act of paying the king's duties, and this brand mark is called a carimbo.

They are made to bear one more brand mark. This one is ordered by their private master, under whose name they are transported to Brazil. . . .

In this miserable and deprived condition the terrified slaves remain for weeks and months, and the great number of them who die is unspeakable. With some ten or twelve thousand arriving at Luanda each year, it often happens that only six or seven thousand are finally transported to Brazil. . . .

Shackled in the holds of ships, the black slaves . . . are far more deprived than when on land. First of all, with two or three hundred slaves placed under the deck, there is hardly room enough to draw a breath. . . . The captains, aware of their own (financial) interests, recognize the seriousness of the problem, and they try to remedy it to some extent. . . . Each day they order a certain number of slaves brought on deck in chains to get some fresh air, not allowing more because of their fear of rebellion. . . .

Second, the slaves are afflicted with a very short ration of water, of poor quality and lukewarm because of the climate—hardly enough to water their mouths. The suffering that this causes is extraordinary, and their dryness and thirst cause epidemics which, beginning with one person, soon spread to many others. Thus, after only a few days at sea, they start to throw the slaves into the ocean.

Third, they are kept in a state of constant hunger. Their small ration of food, brought over from Brazil on the outward voyage, is spoiled and damaged. . . . They add to each ration a small portion of noxious fish from the Atlantic Ocean, which decays during the voyage.[16]

Unlike Great Britain, France, and the Netherlands, Portugal did not have a strong mercantile class involved in slaving in the eighteenth century. Instead, the Portuguese colony of Brazil provided the ships, capital, and goods for the slave trade. Credit played a major role in the trade: Brazilian-controlled firms in Luanda extended credit to African operators, who had to make payments in slaves six or eight months later. Portuguese ironware and wine, Brazilian tobacco and brandies, European and Asian textiles, firearms, and beads were the main goods exchanged for slaves. All commodities entered Angola from Brazil. The Luandan (or Benguelan) merchants pegged the value of the goods to the value of prime young slaves but then undervalued the worth of the slaves and overpriced the goods. As a result, the African operators frequently ended up in debt to the merchants.

Although the demand was great, Portuguese merchants in Angola and Brazil sought to maintain only a steady trickle of slaves from the African interior to Luanda and across the ocean to Bahia and Rio de Janeiro: a flood of slaves would have depressed the American market. Rio, the port capital through which most slaves passed, commanded the Brazilian trade. Planters and mine operators from the provinces traveled to Rio to buy slaves. Between 1795 and 1808, approximately 10,000 An-golans per year stood in the Rio slave market. In 1810 the figure rose to 18,000; in 1828 it reached 32,000.[17]

The English ports of London, Bristol, and particularly Liverpool dominated the British slave trade. In the eighteenth century Liverpool was the world's greatest slave-trading port. In all three cities, small and cohesive merchant classes exercised great public influence. The cities also had huge stores of industrial products for export, growing shipping industries, and large amounts of ready cash for investment abroad. Merchants generally formed partnerships to raise capital and to share the risks; each voyage was a separate enterprise or venture.

City of Luanda, Angola   Founded by the Portuguese in 1575, Luanda was a center of the huge slave trade to Brazil. In this eighteenth-century print, offices and warehouses line the streets, and (right foreground) slaves are dragged to the ships for transportation to America. (*Source: New York Public Library, Astor, Lenox, and Tilden Foundations*)

Ashanti Staff Top In the early eighteenth century, the Ashanti of central Ghana expanded northward, subdued various peoples, and established a powerful successor state to the medieval African kingdoms of Ghana and Mali. The gold trade was the linchpin of its economic and political power. A splendid example of the Ashanti's superb skill in goldworking, this staff top reflects the region's proverbial wealth. *(Source: Lee Boltin Picture Library)*

Slaving ships from Bristol searched the Gold Coast, the Bight of Benin, Bonny, and Calabar. The ships of Liverpool drew slaves from Gambia, the Windward Coast, and the Gold Coast. To Africa, British ships carried textiles, gunpowder and flint, beer and spirits, British and Irish linens, and woolen cloth. A collection of goods was grouped together into what was called the "sorting." An English sorting might include bolts of cloth, firearms, alcohol, tobacco, and hardware; this batch of goods would be traded for an individual slave or a quantity of gold, ivory, or dyewood. When Europeans added a markup for profit, Africans followed suit. Currency was not exchanged; it served as a standard of value and a means of keeping accounts.[18]

European traders had two systems for exchange. First, especially on the Gold Coast, they established factory-forts. These fortified trading posts were expensive to maintain but proved useful for fending off rival Europeans. In the second, or shore, method of trading, European ships sent boats ashore or invited African dealers to bring traders and slaves out to the ships. The English captain John Adams, who made ten voyages to Africa between 1786 and 1800, described the shore method of trading at Bonny:

This place is the wholesale market for slaves, as not fewer than 20,000 are annually sold here; 16,000 of whom are natives of one nation called Ibo. . . . Fairs where the slaves of the Ibo nation are obtained are held every five or six weeks at several villages, which are situated on the banks of the rivers and creeks in the interior, and to which the African traders of Bonny resort to purchase them.

. . . The traders augment the quantity of their merchandise, by obtaining from their friends, the captains of the slave ships, a considerable quantity of goods on credit. . . . Evening is the period chosen for the time of departure, when they proceed in a body, accompanied by the noise of drums, horns, and gongs. At the expiration of the sixth day, they generally return bringing with them 1,500 or 2,000 slaves, who are sold to Europeans the evening after their arrival, and taken on board the ships. . . .

It is expected that every vessel, on her arrival at Bonny, will fire a salute the instant the anchor is let go, as a compliment to the black monarch who soon afterwards makes his appearance in a large canoe, at which time, all those natives who happen to be alongside the vessel are compelled to proceed in their canoes to a respectful distance, and make way for his Majesty's barge. After a few compliments to the captain, he usually enquires after brother George, meaning the King of England, George III, and hopes he and his family are well. He is not pleased unless he is re-

*galed with the best the ship affords. . . . His power is
absolute; and the surrounding country, to a considerable distance, is subject to his dominion.*[19]

The shore method of buying slaves allowed the
ship to move easily from market to market. The final prices of the slaves depended on their ethnic
origin, their availability when the shipper arrived,
and their physical health when offered for sale in
the West Indies or the North or South American
colonies.

Meanwhile, according to one scholar, the north-
bound trade in slaves across the Sahara "continued
without serious disruption until the late nineteenth
century, and in a clandestine way and on a much
reduced scale it survived well into the twentieth
century."[20] The present scholarly consensus is that
the trans-Saharan slave trade in the seventeenth
and eighteenth centuries was never as important as
the transatlantic trade.

The Savanna and the Horn regions of East
Africa experienced a great expansion of the slave
trade in the late eighteenth century, and in the first
half of the nineteenth century, slave exports from
these areas and from the eastern coast amounted
to perhaps 30,000 a year. Why this demand? Merchants and planters wanted slaves to work the
sugar plantations on the Mascarene Islands, located east of Madagascar, the clove plantations on
Zanzibar and Pemba, the food plantations along
the Kenya coast. The eastern coast also exported
slaves for the Americas, when Brazilian businessmen significantly increased their purchases. Thus,
in the late eighteenth and early nineteenth centuries, precisely when the slave trade to North
America and the Caribbean declined, the Eastern
and Asian markets expanded. Only with colonial
conquest by Great Britain, Germany, and Italy after 1870 did suppression begin. Slavery, however,
persists. Recent reports (1994) by the United Nations International Labor Organization, the British
Anti-Slavery Society, and the U.S. Department of
State reveal slavery on an extensive scale in Mauritania (northwestern Africa) and in the Sudan (eastern Africa).[21] The past isn't dead; it's not even past.

Supplying slaves for the foreign market was in
the hands of a small wealthy merchant class or was
a state monopoly. Gathering a band of raiders and
the capital for equipment, guides, tolls, and supplies involved considerable expense. By contempo-

rary standards, slave raiding was a costly operation.
Only black entrepreneurs with sizable capital and
labor could afford to finance and direct raiding
drives. They exported slaves because the profits on
exports were greater than the profits to be made
from using labor in the domestic economy:

*The export price of slaves never rose to the point
where it became cheaper for Europeans to turn to alternative sources of supply, and it never fell to the
point where it caused more than a temporary check to
the trade. . . . The remarkable expansion of the slave
trade in the eighteenth century provides a horrific illustration of the rapid response of producers in an un-
derdeveloped economy to price incentives.*[22]

Other factors that might result in slavery were
kidnapping; judicial enslavement by the state for
serious crimes, such as murder or threats to royal
authority; state demand for slaves as tribute from
subject peoples; destitution following a natural disaster, such as famine or plague, which might force
parents to sell "surplus" children; and, as in Russia
or China, severe debt, which might lead a person
to surrender his or her freedom in return for settlement of the debt. Europeans initiated the Atlantic
slave trade, but its continuation was made possible
through an alliance between European shippers
and African suppliers.

African peoples, captured and forcibly brought
to the Americas, played an integral part in the formation of the Atlantic world. They had an enormous impact on the economics of the Portuguese
and Spanish colonies of South America and in the
Dutch, French, and British colonies of the Caribbean and North America. For example, in the
sugar plantations of Mexico and the Caribbean, on
the cotton, rice, and tobacco plantations of North
America, in the silver and gold mines of Peru and
Mexico, slaves of African descent not only worked
in the mines and fields, they filled skilled, supervi-
sory, and administrative positions, as well as per-
forming domestic service. African slaves also transmitted their cultures to the Americas. Through
language, religion, music, and art they contributed
to the cultures of their particular regions and to
the development of an Afro-Atlantic civilization.[23]

What economic impact did European trade have
on African societies? Africans possessed technology well suited to their environment. Over the

centuries they had cultivated a wide variety of plant foods, developed plant and animal husbandry techniques, and mined, smelted, and otherwise worked a great variety of metals. Apart from firearms, American tobacco and rum, and the cheap brandy brought by the Portuguese, European goods presented no novelty to Africans. What made foreign products desirable to Africans was their price. Traders of hand-woven Indian cotton textiles, Venetian imitations of African beads, and iron bars from European smelters could undersell African manufacturers. Africans exchanged slaves, ivory, gold, pepper, and animal skins for those goods. Their earnings usually did not remain in Africa. African states eager to expand or to control commerce bought European firearms, although the difficulty of maintaining guns often gave gun owners only marginal superiority over skilled bowmen.[24] The kingdom of Dahomey, however, built its power on the effective use of firearms.

The African merchants who controlled the production of exports gained from foreign trade. The king of Dahomey, for example, had a gross income in 1750 of £250,000 from the overseas export of slaves. A portion of his profit was spent on goods that improved the living standards of his people.

Three Traders   This sixteenth–century brass plaque shows three traders, probably appointed to deal with Europeans. The one in the center carries his staff of office; the two on the sides hold manillas, an early form of currency. Just as the crocodile holding a fish represents power over the seas, so the traders symbolize royal authority over commerce with outsiders. *(Source: Courtesy of the Trustees of the British Museum)*

Slave-trading entrepôts, which provided opportunities for traders and for farmers who supplied foodstuffs to towns, caravans, and slave ships, prospered. But such economic returns did not spread very far.[25] International trade did not lead to the economic development of Africa. Neither technological growth nor the gradual spread of economic benefits occurred in Africa in early modern times.

The arrival of Europeans did cause basic social changes in some West African societies. In Senegambia, chattel slavery seems to have been unknown before the growth of the transatlantic trade (see page 657). By the late eighteenth century, however, chiefs were using the slave labor of craftsmen, sailors, and farm workers. If the price was right, they were sold off. Those who committed crimes had traditionally paid fines, but because of the urgent demand for slaves, many misdemeanors became punishable by sale to slave dealers. Europeans introduced corn, pineapple, cassava, and sweet potatoes to West Africa, which had important consequences for population growth.

The intermarriage of French traders and Wolof women in Senegambia created a *métis,* or mulatto class. In the emerging urban centers at Saint-Louis, this small class adopted the French language, the Roman Catholic faith, and a French manner of life. The métis exercised considerable political and economic power. When granted French citizenship in the late eighteenth century, its members sent Senegalese grievances to the Estates General of 1789.[26] However, European cultural influences did not penetrate West African society beyond the seacoast.

The political consequences of the slave trade varied from place to place. The trade enhanced the power and wealth of some kings and warlords in the short run but promoted conditions of instability and collapse over the long run. In the kingdom of the Congo the perpetual Portuguese search for slaves undermined the monarchy, destroyed political unity, and led to constant disorder and warfare; power passed to the village chiefs. Likewise in Angola, which became a Portuguese proprietary colony, the slave trade decimated and scattered the population and destroyed the local economy. By contrast, the military kingdom of Dahomey, which entered into the slave trade in the eighteenth century and made it a royal monopoly, prospered enormously from trading in slaves. The economic

TABLE 20.2 THE TRANS-ATLANTIC SLAVE TRADE, 1450–1900

Period	Volume	Percent
1450–1600	367,000	3.1
1601–1700	1,868,000	16.0
1701–1800	6,133,000	52.4
1801–1900	3,330,000	28.5
Total	11,698,000	100.0

Source: P. E. Lovejoy, Transformations in Slavery: A History of Slavery in Africa *(Cambridge: Cambridge University Press, 1983), p. 19. Used with permission.*

strength of the state rested on the slave trade. The royal army raided deep into the interior, and in the late eighteenth century Dahomey became one of the major West African sources of slaves. When slaving expeditions failed to yield sizable catches, and when European demands declined, the resulting depression in the Dahomeyan economy caused serious political unrest. Iboland inland from the Niger Delta, from whose great port cities of Bonny and Brass the British drained tens of thousands of slaves, experienced minimal political effects and suffered no permanent population loss. A high birthrate kept pace with the incursions of the slave trade, and Ibo societies remained demographically and economically strong.

What demographic impact did the slave trade have on Africa? In all, between approximately 1500 and 1900, about 12 million Africans were exported to the Americas, 6 million were exported to Asia, and 8 million were retained within Africa. Tables 20.1 and 20.2 report the somewhat divergent findings of two careful scholars on the number of slaves shipped to the New World. Export figures do not include the approximately 10 to 15 percent who died during procurement or in transit.

Western or American markets wanted young male slaves. The Asian and African markets preferred young females. Women were sought for their reproductive value, as sex objects, and because their economic productivity was not threatened by the possibility of physical rebellion, as might be the case with young men. Consequently, two-thirds of those exported to the Americas were male, one-third female. The population on the western coast of Africa became predominantly female; in the east African Savanna and the Horn regions the population was predominantly male. The slave trade therefore had significant consequences for the institutions of marriage, slavery itself, and the sexual division of labor—topics scholars have yet to explore. Although overall population growth may have shown modest growth from roughly 1650 to 1900, that growth was offset by declines in the Horn and on the eastern and western coasts. While Europe and Asia experienced considerable demographic and economic expansion in the eighteenth century, Africa suffered decline.[27]

Summary

The period between 1400 and 1800 saw the rise of several different African societies. French culture influenced the coastal fringes of Senegambia; the English maintained factories along the Gold Coast; and the Portuguese held Angola as a colony and maintained an insecure grip on Mozambique in East Africa. Yet despite the export of as many as 12 million slaves from Africa to meet the labor needs of South and North America, European influence hardly penetrated the African interior. The overall impact of the slave trade on Africa was devastating for some regions and societies but marginal for others. It appeared around 1810 that Africa's development would be entirely autonomous.

Notes

1. P. D. Curtin, *Economic Change in Precolonial Africa: Senegambia in the Era of the Slave Trade* (Madison: University of Wisconsin Press, 1975), pp. 34–35; and J. A. Rawley, *The Transatlantic Slave Trade: A History* (New York: Norton, 1981), p. 12.

2. R. W. July, *A History of the African People,* 3d ed. (New York: Scribner's, 1980), pp. 128–129.

3. R. W. July, *Precolonial Africa: An Economic and Social History* (New York: Scribner's, 1975), p. 99.

4. July, *A History of the African People,* p. 141.

5. Quoted in R. Hallett, *Africa to 1875* (Ann Arbor: University of Michigan Press, 1970), p. 151.

6. See *The Cambridge History of Africa,* vol. 3, *ca 1050 to 1600,* ed. R. Oliver (Cambridge: Cambridge University Press, 1977), pp. 427–435.

7. A. ibn-Fartura, "The Kanem Wars," in *Nigerian Perspectives,* ed. T. Hodgkin (London: Oxford University Press, 1966), pp. 111–115.

8. "The Kano Chronicle," quoted in Hodgkin, *Nigerian Perspectives,* pp. 89–90.

9. J. Middleton, *The World of Swahili: An African Mercantile Civilization* (New Haven, Conn.: Yale University Press, 1992), p. 27.

10. Ibid., pp. 35–38.

11. P. E. Lovejoy, *Transformations in Slavery: A History of Slavery in Africa* (Cambridge: Cambridge University Press, 1983), p. 19. This section leans heavily on Lovejoy's work.

12. See Table 2.1, "Trans-Saharan Slave Trade, 650–1600," ibid., p. 25.

13. P. Manning, *Slavery and African Life: Occidental, Oriental, and African Slave Trades* (New York: Cambridge University Press, 1990), pp. 31–37.

14. Rawley, *The Transatlantic Slave Trade,* p. 45.

15. Ibid., pp. 41–47.

16. R. E. Conrad, *Children of God's Fire: A Documentary History of Black Slavery in Brazil* (Princeton, N.J.: Princeton University Press, 1983), pp. 20–23.

17. Rawley, *The Transatlantic Slave Trade,* pp. 45–47.

18. July, *A History of the African People,* p. 208.

19. J. Adams, "Remarks on the Country Extending from Cape Palmas to the River Congo," in Hodgkin, *Nigerian Perspectives,* pp. 178–180.

20. A. G. Hopkins, *An Economic History of West Africa* (New York: Columbia University Press, 1973), p. 83.

21. See Lori Grinker, "Disaster in the Sudan," *New York Times,* February 12, 1993, p. A33; Stanley Miller, "U.N. Agency Assails Mauritania on Slavery," *Los Angeles Times,* March 9, 1993, p. 3; Augustine Lado and Betty Hinds, "Where Slavery Isn't History," *Washington Post,* October 17, 1993, section 3, p. 13; and Charles Jacobs and Mohamed Athie, "Bought and Sold," *New York Times,* July 13, 1994, p. A19.

22. Hopkins, *An Economic History of West Africa,* p. 105.
23. J. Thornton, *Africa and Africans in the Making of the Atlantic World* (New York: Cambridge University Press, 1992), pp. 138–142.
24. July, *Precolonial Africa,* pp. 269–270.
25. Hopkins, *An Economic History of West Africa,* p. 119.
26. July, *A History of the African People,* pp. 201–202.
27. Manning, *Slavery and African Life,* pp. 22–23 and Ch. 3, pp. 38–59.

SUGGESTED READING

Students wishing to explore more fully some of the issues raised in this chapter might begin with *African History: Text and Readings:* vol. 1, *Western African History;* vol. 2, *Eastern African History;* and vol. 3, *Central and Southern African History* (1990), all edited by R. O. Collins. This work gives a useful introduction to the geography and history of the continent and brings together a solid collection of primary documents and scholarly commentaries. *African Civilization Revisited,* ed. B. Davidson (1991), also contains interesting source readings on many facets of African history and cultures from antiquity to the present. K. Shillington, *History of Africa* (1989) provides a soundly researched, highly readable, and well-illustrated survey, while R. Oliver, *The African Experience* (1991) traces African history through particular historical problems. Although many of the articles in *The Cambridge History of Africa,* vol. 4, *From 1600–1790,* ed. R. Gray (1975), are now dated, the following articles are still useful: "The Central Sahara and Sudan," "North-West Africa," and "Southern Africa and Madagascar." V. B. Thompson, *Africa and Unity* (1969), offers an African and African-American response to the traditional Eurocentric interpretation of African history and culture.

J. Thornton, *Africa and Africans in the Making of the Atlantic World, 1400–1680* (1992), places African developments in an Atlantic context. Likewise, both *Atlantic American Societies: From Columbus Through Abolition, 1492–1888,* ed. A. L. Karras and J. R. McNeill (1992), and *Slavery and the Rise of the Atlantic System,* ed. B. Solow (1991), contain important and valuable articles on many of the economic and cultural factors that linked Africa and the Western Hemisphere. For Ethiopia, see H. G. Marcus, *A History of Ethiopia* (1994), a concise but highly readable study. The standard study of the Savanna is probably J. Vansina, *Kingdoms of the Savanna* (1966). For East Africa and the Horn region, see J. Middleton, *The World of Swahili: An African Mercantile Civilization* (1992), which provides an expert synthesis of recent scholarly literature by a social anthropologist; the older study of C. S. Nicholls, *The Swahili Coast* (1971), is still useful. J. Knappert, *Four Centuries of Swahili Verse: A Literary History and Anthology* (1979), is a most interesting celebration of literary manifestations of Swahili culture.

The literature of slavery continues to grow. In addition to the titles by P. Manning and J. Middleton cited in the Notes, see P. Manning, *Slavery, Colonialism and Economic Growth in Dahomey, 1640–1960* (1982), an in-depth study of the kingdom of Dahomey, which, after Angola, was the largest exporter of slaves to the Americas. J. F. Searing, *West African Slavery and Atlantic Commerce, 1700–1860* (1993), explores the effects of the Atlantic slave trade on the societies of the Senegal River Valley. The theme of R. L. Stein's *The French Slave Trade in the Eighteenth Century: An Old Regime Business* (1979) is indicated by its title.

Although the emphasis in *Global Dimensions of African Diaspora,* ed. J. E. Harris (1982), is heavily on the U.S. and the Caribbean, with very little on South America, East or South Asia, some of the articles are very important: see, especially, those by J. E. Harris, L. W. Levine, and S. C. Drake.

The Abolition of the Slave Trade

Several Western nations outlawed the slave trade in the early nineteenth century. Great Britain took the lead. Laws, however, cannot be enforced if strong sentiment opposes them. And in the nineteenth century the economies of several African kingdoms rested on the slave trade, which thrived because of demands in the Americas for workers on cotton, coffee, and sugar cane plantations and in East Africa for laborers in the spice fields. Just as today the United States subsidizes the development of agricultural products in Colombia and Turkey in order to encourage farmers to stop growing opium and coca (the sources of heroin and cocaine for American users), so in the nineteenth century the British in Africa promoted farming and the production of nonhuman commodities as alternatives to the slave trade.

In 1839, the British government sent Robert Craigie, a naval officer, to discuss the end of the slave trade with King Pepple of Bonny, an area in the Niger Delta now part of Nigeria. Bonny had continued to export thousands of slaves after Britain abolished the trade in 1807. This document reports the negotiations between King Pepple and Captain Craigie.

King Pepple, of Bonny, accompanied by Anna Pepple,[1] by his Juju man or high priest, and Hee Chee, Anna Pepple's secretary, for the first time went on board a man-of-war, for the purpose of paying a visit to Captain Craigie, where he was received with the usual salutes.

When the King and suite had finished breakfast, Captain Craigie presented to His Majesty a box containing presents from the English Government, which the King desired might be opened. As the bales of scarlet and green broad cloth were being lifted out of the case, the King and Anna Pepple especially were struck with the magnificence of the gifts, and Captain Craigie made a request of His Majesty

to allow Anna Pepple to have one piece of cloth and a shawl, which the King at once complied with.

Captain Craigie then proceeded to read to King Pepple and suite the despatch of Lord Palmerston[2] dated 14th April, 1838, relative to Slave abolition, and strongly impressed upon His Majesty that part which states that treaties had already been made between England and other African Princes for the purpose of putting an end to the Slave Trade, and that in those cases the Articles of Treaty had been faithfully maintained.

Captain Craigie assured the King that England . . . . would send out ships in abundance for their palm-oil and other products; and if the Bonny men directed their attention properly to these, he was certain they could easily get rich without exporting slaves. . . .

The King, Anna Pepple, and the Juju man for some time remained silent; their countenances, however, were indicative of their consternation; the idea of making such a proposal seemed to them to be incomprehensible. At length Anna Pepple said—

"If we cease to sell slaves to foreign ships, our principal source of wealth will be gone; the English were our first customers, and the trade has since been our chief means of support."

Captain Craigie: "How much would you lose if you gave up selling slaves for exportation?"

Anna Pepple: "Too much—very much—we gain more by one slave-ship than by five palm-oil ships."

Hee Chee, Anna Pepple's Secretary: "We depend entirely on selling slaves and palm oil for our subsistence; suppose then the Slave Trade done away with, the consumption of palm-oil in England to stop, the crop to fail, or that the English ships did not come to the Bonny, what are we to do? We must starve, as it is contrary to our religion to cultivate the ground."

Captain Craigie: "There need be no apprehension of the demand for palm-oil in England ceasing, or of English ships not coming out to the Bonny to take from you your products in exchange for British merchandise; but if you can show clearly that your losses will be so great by giving up slave exportation, I think it possible that the Queen of England may in some measure remunerate you for such loss. . . . I only wish to know if you are disposed to treat[4] for the abolition of the Slave Trade."

Juju Man: "Suppose a Spanish ship's coming to Bonny with goods to exchange for slaves; are we to send her away? This morning, if the Spanish ship had things which we stood in need of, it would be equally foolish not to take them."

Captain Craigie: "How would the abolition of the slave exportation so materially affect you?"

King Pepple: "It would affect myself and chiefs thus—

"First, by stopping the revenues arising from slaves being exported.

"Secondly, our own profit on slaves, and that arising from piloting slave-ships up and out of Bonny would be lost."

Captain Craigie: ". . . If your requests are within reasonable limits, to make you an annual 'dash,' or remuneration, for a term of years (perhaps five years), how much would you consider to be sufficient?"

After some consultation among themselves, Hee Chee, Anna Pepple's Secretary, said "The King will take 4,000 dollars yearly."

Captain Craigie: . . . I am certain 4,000 would be considered too much; indeed I would not venture to propose more than 2,000 dollars. If you will say that this sum (for the time above specified) will be sufficient, I shall lay the matter before the English Government."

The King, Anna Pepple, the Juju man, and Hee Chee, had a discussion for some time.

Anti-slavery medallion. *(Source: Josiah Wedgwood and Sons, Limited)*

They for a long while insisted on not naming less than 3,000 dollars, till they at last came down to 2,000. . . .

King Pepple and suite then returned to the shore under the same salute as that with which they were received.

Just as today Colombian and Turkish farmers accept American aid for not producing opium and coca but continue to produce them; so (according to a report to the British Parliament in 1849) did King Pepple accept British aid for not selling slaves but continued to sell them to the Spanish and Portuguese.

Questions for Analysis

1. What arguments does Captain Craigie give for the abolition of the slave trade?

2. What is the reaction of King Pepple to Craigie's remarks?

3. Compare efforts to end slave trade in the nineteenth century with recent government efforts to end the drug trade.

Source: A. J. Andrea and J. H. Overfield, eds., *The Human Record: Sources of Global History*, vol. 2 (Boston: Houghton Mifflin, 1990), pp. 316–318.

Notes: 1. A male relative of the king who held some sort of position in directing the family's slaving operations. 2. Palmerston (1789–1865) was British foreign secretary at the time. 3. Negotiate.

21

The Middle East and India, ca 1450–1800

Wedding Celebrations of Prince Dara Shikoh, 1633, from the Padshah-nama, Mughal, ca. 1645. The marriage of Shah Jahan's favorite son and intended heir. *(Source: The Royal Collection © Her Majesty Queen Elizabeth II)*

Around 1450, the spiritual descendants of the Prophet Muhammad controlled three vast and powerful empires: the Ottoman Empire centered in Anatolia, the Safavid Empire of Persia, and the Mughal Empire of India. From West Africa to central Asia, from the Balkans to Southeast Asia, Muslim armies pursued policies of territorial expansion. Between 1450 and 1800, these powerful Muslim kingdoms reached the zenith of their territorial extension and of their intellectual and artistic vitality. With the conquest of Constantinople in 1453 the Ottoman Turks gained an impregnable capital and the respect of all Islam. The Ottomans soon overran much of Anatolia, North Africa, and the Balkans. Lasting almost five hundred years (1453–1918), the Ottoman Empire was one of the largest and most enduring political entities in world history. In Persia the Safavid Dynasty created a theocracy and presided over a brilliant culture. A theological dispute between the Ottomans and the Safavids brought bitter division in the Islamic world and weakened both powers. Meanwhile, the Mughal leader Babur and his successors conquered the Indian subcontinent, and Mughal rule inaugurated a period of radical administrative reorganization in India and the flowering of intellectual and architectural creativity.

In 1450 all the great highways of international trade were in Muslim hands, and the wealth of the Muslim states derived largely from commerce. By 1750 the Muslims had lost that control, and the Muslim states were declining economically, politically, and culturally.

- Who were the Ottomans and the Safavids?
- What political and religious factors gave rise to the Ottoman and Safavid Empires, and how were the two empires governed?
- What intellectual developments characterized the Ottoman and Safavid cultures?
- What external and domestic difficulties caused the decline of the Ottoman Empire and Safavid Persia?
- How did Muslim government reform and artistic inspiration affect the dominant Hindu population in India?
- What political and social conditions in India enabled the British to expand their empire?

These are the questions explored in this chapter.

THE SPLENDOR OF THE OTTOMAN STATE

The Ottomans took their name from Osman (1299–1326), the ruler of a Turkish-speaking people in western Anatolia who began expansionist moves in the fourteenth century. The Ottomans gradually absorbed other peoples on the Anatolian peninsula, and the Ottoman state emerged as one of many small Turkish states during the breakup of the empire of the Seljuk Turks. The first Ottoman state thus occupied the border between Islam and Byzantine Christendom. The Ottoman ruler called himself "border chief," or leader of the *gazis,* frontier fighters in the *jihad,* or holy war. The earliest Ottoman historical source, a fourteenth-century saga, describes the gazis as the "instrument of God's religion . . . God's scourge who cleanses the earth from the filth of polytheism . . . God's pure sword."[1]

The principle of jihad was the cornerstone of Ottoman political theory and then of the Ottoman state. Europe was the frontier of the Muslim crusading mission. In 1389 in what is today the former Yugoslavia the Ottomans defeated a combined force of Serbs and Bosnians. In 1396, on the Danube River in modern Bulgaria, they crushed King Sigismund of Hungary, who was supported by French, German, and English knights. The reign of Sultan Mehmet II (r. 1451–1481) saw the end of all Turkish dynasties in Anatolia and the Ottoman conquest of Constantinople, capital of the Byzantine Empire, which had lasted a thousand years.

The six-week siege of Constantinople in 1453 remains one of the dramatic events in world history because Constantinople symbolized the continuation of imperial Rome. The Byzantine emperor Constantine IX Palaeologus (r. 1449–1453), with only about 10,000 men, relied on the magnificent system of circular walls and stone fortifications that had protected the city for a thousand years. Mehmet II had over 100,000 men and a large fleet, but iron chains spanning the harbor kept him out of the Golden Horn, the inlet of the Bosporus Strait that connects the Black and Marmona Seas and forms the harbor of Istanbul.

Western technology eventually decided the battle. A Transylvanian cannon founder who deserted the Byzantines for Ottoman service cast huge bronze cannons on the spot (bringing raw materials to the scene of military action was easier than moving guns long distances).[2] When a cannon shot shattered a city gate, the Turks forced an entry. For three days the city suffered looting and rape. The Muslim historian Oruc described the conquest of Constantinople:

Sultan Mehmet, the son of Sultan Murad, inspired by zeal, said "in the cause of God" and commanded plunder. The gazis, entering by force on every side, found a way in through the breaches in the fortress made by the guns and put the infidels in the fortress to the sword. . . . Mounting on the tower they destroyed the infidels who were inside and entered the city. They looted and plundered. They seized their money and possessions and made their sons and daughters slaves. The Muslims took so much booty that the wealth gathered in Istanbul (Constantinople) since it was built 2400 years before became the portion of the gazis. They plundered for three days, and after three days plunder was forbidden.[3]

The conquest of Constantinople inaugurated the imperial phase of the Ottoman military state. The Ottoman emperors considered themselves successors of the Byzantine emperor, as their title *Sultan-i-Rum* ("Sultan of Rome") attests. They renamed the city Istanbul, "city of Islam," though the name was not officially changed until 1930. Mehmet began the transformation of the city into an Ottoman imperial capital. He ordered Constantinople cleaned up and the walls repaired. He appointed Turkish officials to adapt the city administration to Turkish ways, and he nominated a Greek patriarch over the Greek Orthodox church, giving its members virtual freedom of religion as long as they paid the *jitza,* a tax on non-Muslims. Mehmet's installation of the supreme authority over all Orthodox Christians meant that the patriarch acknowledged Turkish rule; Greek resistance to that rule was rendered virtually impossible.

Because the conquest had severely depopulated the city and many survivors had been sold into slavery, inhabitants of territories later conquered by the Ottomans were transplanted to Constantinople. Jews cruelly oppressed in western Europe found Turkey "a paradise." In 1454, one Jewish resident, Isaac Sarfati, sent a circular letter to his coreligionists in the Rhineland, Swabia, Moravia, and Hungary praising the happy conditions of the Jews under the crescent in contrast to the "great torture chamber" under the cross and urging them to come to Turkey.[4] A massive migration to Ottoman lands followed. When Ferdinand and Isabella of Spain expelled the Jews in 1492 (see page 485), many emigrated to Turkey.

The Ottomans also continued to expand. In 1453, they controlled only the northwest quadrant of Anatolia. Mehmet II completed the conquest of Anatolia. From Constantinople, their new capital, the Ottomans pushed down the Aegean and up the Adriatic. They so severely threatened Italy and southeastern Europe that the aged Pope Pius II himself shouldered the cross of the Crusader in 1464. In 1480 an Ottoman fleet took the Italian port of Otranto, and serious plans were laid for the conquest of all Italy. Only a disputed succession following the death of Mehmet II in 1481 caused the postponement of that conquest and, later, the cancellation of those plans. The Ottoman Turks inspired such fear that even in distant Iceland the Lutheran Book of Common Prayer begged God for protection not only from "the cunning of the Pope" but also from "the terror of the Turk."

Selim the Grim (r. 1512–1520) gained the Ottoman throne by forcing his father's abdication and murdering his brother. A bloodthirsty and inflexible despot, Selim was a superb military commander. Under his leadership, the Ottomans added Syria and Palestine (1516) and Egypt (1517) to their empire and extended their rule across North Africa to Cyrenaica, Tripolitania, Tunisia, and Algeria. Selim's reign marks the beginning of four centuries when most Arabs were under Ottoman rule.

Suleiman (r. 1520–1566), who brought to the throne great experience as a provincial administrator and enormous energy as a soldier, extended Ottoman jurisdiction to its widest geographical extent (Map 21.1). With Greece and the Balkans already under Ottoman domination, Suleiman's army crushed the Hungarians at Mohács in 1526, killing the king and thousands of his nobles. Suleiman seems to have taken this victory entirely as his due. Not long after the battle he recorded laconically in his diary, "The emperor, seated on a

MAP 21.1 The Ottoman Empire at Its Height, 1566 The Ottomans, like their great rivals the Habsburgs, rose to rule a vast dynastic empire encompassing many different peoples and ethnic groups. The army and the bureaucracy served to unite the disparate territories into a single state.

golden throne, receives the homage of the viziers and beys: massacre of 2,000 prisoners: the rains fall in torrents." Three years later the Turks besieged the Habsburg capital at Vienna. Only an accident—the army's insistence on returning home before winter—prevented Muslim control of all central Europe.

In virtually every area, the Ottomans' success was due to the weakness and political disunity of

their enemies and to the superiority of Turkish military organization and artillery. Gunpowder, invented by the Chinese and adapted to artillery use by Europeans, played an influential role in the expansion of the Ottoman state.

Though victorious on land, the Ottomans did not enjoy complete dominion on the sea. The middle decades of the sixteenth century witnessed a titanic struggle between the Ottoman and

Habsburg empires for control of the Mediterranean. In September 1538 an Ottoman naval victory at Preveze, the chief Turkish port in Albania, assured Turkish control of the Ionian and Aegean Seas. Meanwhile, attacks from the island of Cyprus by Christian pirates on Ottoman shipping in the eastern Mediterranean provoked the sultan to conquer Cyprus in 1570. He introduced Ottoman administration and settled thousands of Turks from Anatolia there. (Thus began the large Turkish presence on Cyprus that continues to the present day.) In response, Pope Pius V organized the Holy League against the Turks. On October 7, 1571, an armada of over 200 Spanish, Venetian, and papal galleys smashed the Turks at Lepanto at the mouth of the Gulf of Patras in Greece (see Map 21.1). About 15,000 Turks were killed or captured, 10,000 Christian galley slaves were liberated, and the victors lost about 7,000 men. European churches rang with victory celebrations for the first major Ottoman defeat by Christian forces. Lepanto, however, marked no decisive change in Turkish hegemony: the Turks remained supreme on land and quickly rebuilt their entire fleet.

Military organization dominated the Ottoman social and administrative systems, which reached classic form under Suleiman I. The seventeenth-century Ottoman historian Mustafa Naima divided Muslim society into producers of wealth, Muslim and non-Muslim, and the military. In Naima's view there could be no state without the military; wealth was needed to support the military; the state's subjects raised the wealth; subjects could prosper only through justice; and without the state there could be no justice.[5]

The ruling class consisted exclusively of Muslims, theoretically totally loyal to the sultan and fully immersed in the complex Islamic culture. Under Suleiman I, the Ottoman ruling class consisted in part of descendants of Turkish families that had formerly ruled parts of Anatolia. In return for bureaucratic service to the sultan, they held *trimars* (landed estates) on *sipahinek* (property) for the duration of their lifetimes. The ruling class had the usufruct but not the ownership of the land. Since all property belonged to the sultan and reverted to him on the holder's death, Turkish nobles—unlike their European counterparts—could not put down

Procession of Suleiman   In 1533 the Dutch painter and print maker Pieter Coecke van Aelst visited Constantinople, where he sketched the design for this elegant scene. The triumphant procession of the sultan, with his officials and courtiers, through monuments brought from all over the Mediterranean world (notice the column with Egyptian hieroglyphics) captures the power of the Grand Turk. *(Source: The Metropolitan Museum of Art, Harris Brisbane Dick Fund, 1928)*

roots. Because there was no security of landholding and no hereditary nobility, the Ottoman Empire did not develop a feudal structure before 1600.

Slaves who had been purchased from Spain, North Africa, and Venice, captured in battle, and acquired through the system known as *devshirme*—by which the sultan's agents swept the provinces for Christian youths—were recruited for the imperial civil service and the army. Southern Europeans did not shrink from selling people into slavery, and, as the Ottoman jihad advanced in the fifteenth and sixteenth centuries, Albanian, Bosnian, Wallachian, and Hungarian slave boys filled Ottoman imperial needs. Moreover, because devshirme recruitment often meant social advancement, some Christian and Muslim parents bribed government officials to accept their children. All were converted to Islam. (Islamic law forbade the enslavement of Muslims but not of converts.) The brightest 10 percent entered the palace school. There they learned to read and write Arabic, Ottoman Turkish, and Persian, received special religious instruction, and were trained for the civil service. Other boys were sent to Turkish farms, where they acquired physical toughness in preparation for military service. Known as *janissaries* (Turkish for "recruits"), they formed the elite army corps. Thoroughly indoctrinated and absolutely loyal to the sultan, the janissary slave corps eliminated the influence of old Turkish families and played the central role in Ottoman military affairs in the sixteenth century.

All authority theoretically emanated from the sultan and flowed from him to his state servants: police officers, provincial governors, heads of the treasury, generals. The sultan frequently designated these men *pashas,* a title of distinction.

The reign of Suleiman I witnessed an extraordinary artistic flowering and represents the peak of Ottoman influence and culture. In Turkish history Suleiman is known as *Kanuni* ("Lawgiver") because of his profound influence on the civil law. He ordered Lütfi Paşa (d. 1562), a poet of slave origin and juridical scholar, to draw up a new general code of laws. Published in Suleiman's name, this sultanic legal code prescribed penalties for routine criminal acts such as robbery, adultery, and murder. It also sought to reform bureaucratic and financial corruption in areas such as harem interven-

tion in administrative affairs, foreign merchants' payment of bribes to avoid customs duties, imprisonment without trial, and promotion in the provincial administration because of favoritism rather than ability. The legal code also introduced the idea of balanced financial budgets. Suleiman's legal acts influenced many legal codes, including that of the United States. Today, Suleiman's image, along with the images of Solon, Moses, and Thomas Jefferson, and other great lawgivers, appears in the chamber of the U.S. House of Representatives.

Europeans called Suleiman "the Magnificent" because of the grandeur of his court. With annual state revenues of about $80 million (at a time when Elizabeth I of England could expect $150,000 and Francis I of France perhaps $1 million), with thousands of servants to cater to his whims, and with a lifestyle no European monarch could begin to rival, Suleiman was indeed magnificent. He used his fabulous wealth and power to adorn Constantinople with palaces and mosques. Some of his undertakings, such as his reconstruction of the water systems of the great pilgrimage sites at Mecca and Jerusalem, benefited his subjects.

The Ottomans under Suleiman demonstrated splendid creativity in carpet weaving, textiles, ceramics, and, above all, architecture. In the buildings of Pasha Sinan (1491–1588), a Christian slave who rose to become imperial architect, the Ottoman spirit is powerfully expressed. A contemporary of Michelangelo, Sinan designed 312 public buildings—mosques, schools, hospitals, public baths, palaces, and burial chapels. His masterpieces, the Shehzade and Suleimaniye mosques at Constantinople, represented solutions to spatial problems unique to domed buildings and expressed the discipline, power, and devotion to Islam that characterized the Ottoman Empire under Suleiman the Magnificent. With pardonable exaggeration, Suleiman began a letter to the king of France, with whom he was allied against the Habsburgs after 1536, by saying, "I who am the sultan of sultans, the sovereign of sovereigns, the dispenser of crowns to the monarchs on the face of the earth . . . to thee who are Francis, King of the land of France."[6]

The age of Suleiman witnessed a tremendous cultural explosion that may have rivaled the artistic and literary achievements of the European Renaissance. In addition to architecture, Ottoman scholars and artists showed great distinction in poetry, painting, history, mathematics, geographical literature, astronomy, medicine, and the religious sciences.

Poetry, rather than prose, was the main vehicle of Ottoman literary expression. *Diwan* poetry, so called because it consisted of collections of poems, though written by intellectuals in Turkish, followed classical Islamic (Arabic) forms and rules and addressed the ruling class. Şeyhi of Kütahya (d. 1429) compiled a large Diwan collection and in his *Book of the Donkey* used animals to personify and satirize his political enemies. Modern scholars consider Bursah Ahmet Paşa, an imperial judge and confidential adviser to the sultan Mehmet II, to be the greatest Ottoman poet of the fifteenth century. Bursah Ahmet Paşa's beautiful odes and diversified style won him widespread popularity.

Folk literature, produced by traveling troubadours, described the traditions and wisdom of the people in humorous short stories and anecdotes. The folk collection of Dede Korkut, set down in Turkish prose, includes tribal epics describing the conflicts with the Georgians, Circassians, and Byzantines and serves as a major source for the history of the fourteenth century.

Just as Western historical writing in the early modern period often served to justify the rights of ruling dynasties, so Ottoman historical scholarship under Mehmet II and Suleiman promoted the claims of the family of Osman. Perhaps the greatest historian of the early sixteenth century was Ahmet Semseddin Iba-i Kemal, or Kemalpaşazêde (d. 1526), the Muslim judge and administrator whose *History of the House of Osman* gives original source material for the reigns through which he himself lived. Building on the knowledge of earlier Islamic writers and stimulated by Ottoman naval power, the geographer and cartographer Piri Reis produced a map that showed all the known world (1513); another of his maps detailed Columbus's third voyage to the New World. Piri Reis's *Book of the Sea* (1521) contained 129 chapters, each with a map incorporating all Islamic (and Western) knowledge of the seas and navigation and describing harbors, tides, dangerous rocks and shores, and storm areas. Takiyuddin Mehmet (1521–1585), who served as the sultan's chief astronomer, built an observatory at Constantinople. His *Instruments of the Observatory* catalogued astronomical instruments and described an astronomical clock that fixed the location of heavenly bodies with greater precision than ever before.

What medical treatment or health care was available to the sick in the Ottoman world? Muslim medical education was practical, not theoretical: students received their training not in the *madrasas,* or mosque schools, but by apprenticeship to experienced physicians or in the *bimaristans,* the hospitals. Under a senior's supervision, medical students studied the course of various diseases, learned the techniques of surgery, and especially mastered pharmacology—the preparation of drugs from plants. The Muslim knowledge of pharmacology derived from centuries-old traditions, and modern students of the history of medicine believe that pharmacology as an institution is an Islamic invention.

By the fifteenth century, Muslims knew the value of quarantine. Yet when devastating epidemics, such as the bubonic plague, struck the empire during Mehmet II's reign, he and the court fled to the mountains of the Balkans, and the imperial government did little to fight the plague. Under Suleiman, however, the imperial palace itself became a center of medical science, and the large number of hospitals established in Constantinople and throughout the empire testifies to his support for medical research and his concern for the sick. Abi Ahmet Celebi (1436–1523), the chief physician of the empire, produced a study on kidney and bladder stones and supported the research of the Jewish doctor Musa Colinus ul-Israil on the application of drugs. Celebi founded the first Ottoman medical school, which served as a training institution for physicians of the empire.[7] The sultans and the imperial court usually relied on Jewish physicians.

To fight smallpox, the Chinese had successfully practiced inoculation in the sixteenth century, and the procedure spread to Turkey in the seventeenth. Lady Mary Wortley Montague, wife of the British ambassador to Constantinople, had her son inoculated in 1717. Here is her description of the method:

The smallpox, so fatal and so general amongst us (in England), is here entirely harmless by the invention of engrafting. . . . Every autumn . . . people send one another to know if any of their family has a mind to have the smallpox (get inoculated). . . . An old woman comes with a nutshell full of the matter of the best sort of smallpox and asks what veins you please (want) to have opened. She immediately rips open what you offer to her with a large needle (which gives you no more pain than a common scratch) and puts into the vein as much venom as can lie upon the head of the needle, and after binds up the little wound. . . . The children or young patients play together all the rest of the day and are in perfect health till the eighth. Then the fever begins to seize 'em and they keep their beds two days, very seldom three. They have very rarely twenty or thirty (pockmarks) in their faces, which never mark (leave a permanent scar), and in eight days' time they are as well as before their illness. . . . Every year thousands undergo this operation, and the French ambassador says pleasantly that they take the smallpox here by way of diversion as they take the waters in other countries (at spas). . . . There is no example of anyone that has died in it.[8]

This was eighty years before the English physician Edward Jenner (see page 644) tried the procedure using cowpox in England.

Lady Mary Wortley Montague marveled at the splendor of Ottoman culture. Remarkably intelligent and fluent in several languages, a pioneer feminist, Lady Mary also had a mind exceptionally open to different cultures. As an aristocrat, the wife of an official foreign representative, and a woman, she had access to people and places (such as the imperial seraglio or harem) off-limits to ordinary tourists. Her many letters to relatives and friends in England provide a wealth of information about upper-class Ottoman society.

On January 19, 1718, Lady Mary gave birth to a daughter and described the experience in a letter to an English friend:

I was brought to bed of a daughter. . . . I must own that it was not half so mortifying here as in England, there being as much difference as there is between a little cold in the head, which sometimes happens here, and the consumptive coughs so common in London.[9]

The naturalness of childbirth in Turkey, Lady Mary suggests, may have been because Turkish women

 Lady Mary Wortley Montague Famous in her own time for her letters from Constantinople and, after her return to England, for her efforts to educate the English public about inoculation against smallpox, Lady Mary is praised by twentieth-century scholars as a brilliant and urbane woman struggling for emancipation. *(Source: Boston Athenaeum)*

had much more experience of it than English-women:

in this country 'tis more despicable to be married and not fruitful than 'tis with us to be fruitful before marriage. They have a notion that whenever a woman leaves off bearing children, 'tis because she is too old for that business, whatever her face says to the contrary, and this opinion makes the ladies here so ready to make proofs of their youth. . . . Without any exaggeration, all the women of my acquaintance that have been married ten years have twelve or thirteen children, and the old ones boast of having had five and twenty or thirty apiece and are respected according to the number they have produced.[10]

Turkish women's sense of self-worth seems to have been closely tied to their production of children, as was common in many cultures at the time. As for Turkish morality, "'Tis just as 'tis with you; and the Turkish ladies don't commit one sin the less for not being Christians." In other words, Turkish women are neither better nor worse than European ones. Moreover,

'Tis very easy to see that they have more liberty than we have, . . . and their shapes are wholly concealed by a thing they call a ferigee, which no woman of any sort (class) appears without. . . . You may guess how effectively this disguises them, that there is no distinguishing the great lady from her slave, and 'tis impossible for the most jealous husband to know his wife when he meets her, and no man dare either touch or follow a woman in the street.

This perpetual masquerade gives them entire liberty of following their inclinations without danger of discovery. The most usual method of intrigue is to send an appointment to the lover to meet the lady at a Jew's shop, which are as notoriously convenient as our Indian houses. . . .

You may easily imagine the number of faithful wives very small in a country where they have nothing to fear from their lovers' indiscretion. . . . Neither have they much to apprehend from the resentment of their husbands, those ladies that are rich having all their money in their own hands, which they take with 'em upon a divorce with an addition which he is obliged to give 'em. Upon the whole, I look upon the Turkish woman as the only free people in the empire.[11]

In short, in spite of the legal restrictions of the harem, upper-class ladies found ways to go out and even to have affairs.

In the seventeenth and eighteenth centuries, grave political, social, and economic difficulties afflicted the Ottoman Empire. Ottoman government depended heavily on the sultan, and the matter of the dynastic succession posed a major political problem. In earlier centuries heirs to the throne had gained administrative experience as governors of provinces and military experience on the battlefield as part of their education. After Suleiman's reign, however, this tradition was abandoned. To prevent threats of usurpation, heirs were brought up in the harem and were denied a role in government. By the time a prince succeeded his father, years of dissipation were likely to have rendered the prince alcoholic, insane, or exhausted from excessive sexual activity. Selim II (r. 1566–1574), whom the Turks called "Selim the Drunkard," left the conduct of public affairs to his vizier while he pursued the pleasures of the harem. Turkish sources attribute his death to a fall in his bath caused by dizziness when he tried to stop drinking. The Ottomans, moreover, abandoned the system whereby the eldest son inherited and instead gave the throne to the member of the dynasty with the greatest political influence at the time of the sultan's death. As the sultan's brothers and sons formed factions, harem coalitions conspired for the throne.

A series of incompetent rulers enabled the janissaries to destroy the influence of the old Turkish families. Members of the elite army corps secured permanent military and administrative offices for their sons through bribery, making their positions hereditary. The janissaries thus became the powerful feudal class in Ottoman Turkey.

Under the very competent vizier Muhammad Kuprili (ca 1570–1661) Ottoman fortunes revived. Kuprili abolished the corruption pervasive throughout the imperial administration, maintained domestic peace, and pursued a vigorous foreign policy. When Kuprili died, his brother-in-law Kara Mustafa directed the empire's military operations. His objective was an attack on the Habsburg capital, Vienna. When battle came on September 12, 1683, the combination of a strong allied Christian force (see page 571) and Habsburg heavy artillery, which the Turks lacked, gave the Europeans the victory. The Ottomans rallied again, but defeat at Vienna and domestic disorders led to the decline of Ottoman power in the Balkans. In the words of one historian, "The Ottoman state was predicated upon, committed to, and organized for conquest. . . . An end to significant and sustained conquest rocked the entire state structure and sent aftershocks through all its institutions."[12]

The peace treaty signed at Karlowitz (1699) marks a watershed in Ottoman history. By its terms the empire lost (to Austria) the major European provinces of Hungary and Transylvania along with the vast tax revenues they had provided. Karlowitz

Visit to the Lunatic Asylum   Beginning in the ninth century, Islamic hospitals had special wards for the insane. Therapy consisted of baths, massages, bleeding (for the violently agitated), and drugs given as sedatives, stimulants, or antidepressants. Fear that the violent would harm themselves or others led to shackling. In this scene from an album produced for Sultan Ahmed I (r. 1603–1617) three violent patients are chained; the nearly naked appearance of two of them (which would have shocked Muslim sensibilities) is a sure sign of their insanity. The Jewish doctor (right) is threatened with a knife; his assistant is caught in the stocks from which the third lunatic tries to escape. Two visitors observing the mayhem through the window put their forefingers to their mouths, a common gesture in Muslim society indicating astonishment and a defense against evil. *(Source: Topkapi Saray Museum, Istanbul)*

also shattered Ottoman morale. Eighteenth-century wars against European powers—Venice (1714–1718), Austria and Russia (1736–1739), and Russia (1768–1774 and 1787–1792)—proved indecisive but contributed to general Ottoman internal disintegration.

Rising population caused serious social problems. A long period of peace in the later sixteenth century and again in the mid-eighteenth century—while the War of the Austrian Succession (1740–1748) and the Seven Years' War (1756–1763) were preoccupying the European powers (see page 611)—and a decline in the frequency of visits of

the plague led to a doubling of the population. The land could not sustain so many people, nor could the towns provide jobs for the thousands of agricultural workers who fled to them. The return of demobilized soldiers from the West aggravated the situation. Inflation, famine, and widespread revolts resulted.

Inability to respond to European and worldwide economic changes contributed to Ottoman weakness and decline. The empire did not modernize and thus could not compete effectively with European capitalistic powers. European trade with the Americas, Asia, and Africa by means of the Atlantic

Polo Two teams of four on horseback ride back and forth on a grass field 200 by 400 yards trying to hit a 4½-ounce wooden ball with a four-foot mallet through the opponents' goal. Because a typical match involves many high-speed collisions among the horses, each player has to maintain a string of expensive ponies in order to change mounts several times during the game. Students of the history of sports believe the game originated in Persia, as shown in this eighteenth-century miniature, whence it spread to India, China, and Japan. Brought from India to England where it became very popular among the aristocracy in the nineteenth century, polo is a fine example of cross-cultural influences. *(Source: Private Collection)*

Ocean meant that the ancient Middle Eastern trade routes—with their heavy customs duties—were bypassed. The Ottoman state lost vast revenues. Meanwhile, Ottoman guilds set the prices of commodities such as wheat, wool, copper, and precious metals, and European willingness to pay high prices pulled those commodities out of the Ottoman Empire. The result was scarcity, which led to a decline in Turkish industrial production. Likewise in the craft industries, Europeans bought Ottoman raw materials, used them to manufacture textiles and metallurgical goods, and sold them in Turkish lands, thereby destroying Ottoman craft industries in the early nineteenth century. Prices rose; inflation increased; and the government devalued the currency, causing new financial crises.

More than any other single factor, a series of agreements known as capitulations, which the Ottoman government signed with European powers, contributed to the Ottoman decline. A trade compact signed in 1536 and renewed in 1569 virtually exempted French merchants from Ottoman law and allowed them to travel and buy and sell throughout the sultan's dominions and to pay low customs duties on French imports and exports. In 1590, in spite of strong French opposition, a group of English merchants gained the right to trade in Ottoman territory in return for supplying the sultan with iron, steel, brass, and tin for his war with Persia. In 1615, as part of a twenty-year peace treaty, the capitulation rights already given to French and English businessmen were extended to the Habsburgs. These capitulations progressively gave European merchants an economic stranglehold on Ottoman trade and commerce. In the nineteenth century, the Ottoman empire was beset by the loss of territory, the pressures of European capitalistic imperialism, and unresolved internal problems; Tsar Nicholas I of Russia (1825–1855) called it "the sick man of Europe."[13]

THE PERSIAN THEOCRATIC STATE

Describing the Mongol destruction of Persia in the thirteenth century, the Persian historian Juvaini wrote, "With one stroke, a world which billowed with fertility was laid desolate, and the regions thereof became a desert, and the greater part of the living dead, and their skin and bones crumbling dust."[14] Pursuing a scorched-earth policy toward the land and a psychological reign of terror over the people, the Mongols, so modern demographers estimate, reduced the population of Persia, Khurasan, Iraq, and Azerbaijan (Map 21.2) from 2,500,000 to 250,000. Mongol devastation represents the last great sweep of Turkish steppe nomads from central Asia into the European and Islamic heartlands. Turkish tribes in central Asia far outnumbered the ethnic Mongols. The Turks joined Jenghiz Khan partly because he had defeated them, partly because westward expansion with the Mongols offered adventure and rich pasturelands for their herds of sheep and horses.[15]

The rehabilitation of Persia began under Ghazan (r. 1295–1304), the *Ilkhan,* as the Mongol rulers of Persia were called. A descendant of Jenghiz Khan, Ghazan reduced peasants' taxes and thereby encouraged their will to produce. He also worked to improve the fiscal and administrative systems. His declaration of Islam as the state religion had profound political and cultural consequences: native (and Muslim) Persians willingly served the state government; they alone had the literacy needed to run a bureaucracy. Turkish-Mongol soldiers adapted to Persian ways. The court patronized Persian art. Across the central Asian heartlands hundreds of Chinese doctors, engineers, artists, and potterymakers came seeking opportunity in the Persian-Mongol-Turkish capital at Tabriz. Chinese artistic influences left a permanent mark on Persian miniature painting, calligraphy, and pottery design.

But Mongol rule of Persia did not last long. While Mehmet II was extending Ottoman jurisdiction through eastern Anatolia, the Safavid movement advanced in Persia. The Safavid Dynasty, which takes its name from Safi al-Din (1252–1334), a supposed descendant of Ali (the fourth caliph), began as leaders of a contemplative Sufi sect; gradually the dynasty evolved into a militant and heretical Shi'ite regime. The attraction of the masses to Shi'ism perhaps reflects the role of religion as a vehicle for the expression of political feeling—in this case opposition to Mongol domination. In the early sixteenth century, Persia emerged as a powerful Muslim state under the Safavids. (Since 1935 Persia has been known as Iran.)

🌸 **MAP 21.2 The Safavid Empire**   In the late sixteenth century, the power of the Safavid kingdom of Persia rested on its strong military force, its Shi'ite Muslim faith, and its extraordinarily rich trade in rugs and pottery. Many of the cities on the map, such as Tabriz, Qum, and Shiraz, were great rug-weaving centers.

Between 1502 and 1510, Ismail (r. 1502–1524) defeated petty Turkish leaders, united Persia under his sovereignty, and proclaimed himself *shah,* or king.

The strength of the Safavid state rested on three crucial features. First, it had the loyalty and military support of Qizilbash nomadic tribesmen. (*Qizilbash,* a Turkish word meaning "redheads," was applied to these people because of the red hats they wore.) The shah secured the loyalty of the Qizilbash by granting them vast grazing lands, especially on the troublesome Ottoman frontier. In return, the Qizilbash supplied him troops. Second, the Safavid state utilized the skills of urban bureaucrats and made them an essential part of the civil machinery of government.

The third source of Safavid strength was the Shi'ite faith. The Shi'ites claimed descent from Ali, Muhammad's cousin and son-in-law, and believed that leadership among Muslims rightfully belonged to the Prophet's descendants. Ismail claimed descent from a line of twelve infallible *imams* (leaders) beginning with Ali and was officially regarded as their representative on earth. When Ismail conquered Tabriz in 1501, he declared Shi'ism the official and compulsory religion of his new empire under penalty of death. Today, in the late twentieth century, Iran remains the only Muslim state in which Shi'ism is the official religion.

Shi'ism gradually shaped the cultural and political identity of Persia (and later Iran). Recent scholarship asserts that Ismail was not "motivated by cynical notions of political manipulation."[16] Shah Ismail imported Shi'ite *ulema* (scholars outstanding in learning and piety) from other Arab lands to instruct and guide his people. With its puritanical emphasis on the holy law and on self-flagellation in penance for any disloyalty to Ali, the Safavid state represented theocracy triumphant throughout the first half century of its existence.

Safavid power reached its height under Shah Abbas (r. 1587–1629), whose military achievements, support for trade and commerce, and endowment of the arts earned him the epithet "the Great." The Persian army had hitherto consisted of tribal units under tribal leadership. Shah Abbas built a national army on the Ottoman model, composed of Armenian and Georgian recruits paid by and loyal to himself. Shah Abbas campaigned against the Turks and captured Baghdad, Mosul, and Diarbakr in Mesopotamia (see Map 21.2).

Military victories account for only part of Shah Abbas's claim to greatness. Determined to improve his country's export trade, he built the small cottage business of carpet weaving into a national industry. In the capital city of Isfahan alone, factories employed over twenty-five thousand weavers who produced woolen carpets, brocades, and silks of brilliant color, design, and quality. Armenians controlled the carpet industry; the Safavids had brought them to Isfahan to protect them from Turkish persecution. Three hundred Chinese potters were imported to make glazed building tiles, which adorned the great Safavid buildings. They captured much of the European tile market.

The jewel of the empire was Isfahan, whose prosperity and beauty rested on trade and industry. A seventeenth-century English visitor described Isfahan's bazaar as "the surprisingest piece of Greatness in Honour of commerce the world can boast of." Besides splendid rugs, stalls displayed pottery and fine china, metalwork of exceptionally high quality, silks and velvets of stunning weave and design. A city of perhaps 750,000 people, Isfahan contained 162 mosques, 48 schools where future members of the ulema learned the sacred Muslim sciences, 273 public baths, and the vast imperial palace. Private houses had their own garden courts; and public gardens, pools, and parks adorned the wide streets. Tales of the beauty of Isfahan circulated worldwide, attracting thousands of tourists annually in the seventeenth and eighteenth centuries.

Shah Abbas was succeeded by inept rulers whose heavy indulgence in wine and the pleasures of the harem weakened the monarchy and fed the slow disintegration of the state. Internal weakness encouraged increased foreign aggression. In the eighteenth century the Turks, Afghans, and Russians invaded and divided Persia among themselves, and political anarchy and social chaos characterized Persian life.

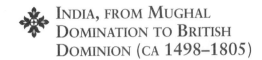

INDIA, FROM MUGHAL DOMINATION TO BRITISH DOMINION (CA 1498–1805)

While powerful Muslim empires developed in Ottoman Turkey and Safavid Persia in the early sixteenth century, the Asian subcontinent of India experienced the intrusion of two vigorous foreign cultures. In 1510 the Portuguese occupied the island of Goa and shortly afterward under Alfonso de Albuquerque (see pages 517–518) extended Portuguese influence on the Indian mainland. The Portuguese soon controlled the trade of the Indian Ocean. On the mainland they used persuasion and force to convert the Indian peoples to Christianity. Fifteen years after the arrival of the Portuguese, an army from Afghanistan and central Asia invaded northern India.

In 1504 Babur (r. 1483–1530), ruler of the small Mughal territory in central Asia, captured Kabul and established a kingdom in Afghanistan. From Kabul he moved southward into India. In 1526 with a force of only twelve thousand men, Babur defeated the decrepit sultan of Delhi at Panipat. Babur's capture of the cities of Agra and Delhi, the key fortresses of the north, paved the way for further conquests in northern India. Thus began Mughal rule, which lasted until the eighteenth century, when domestic disorder and incompetent government opened the door to lengthy European intervention. (*Mughal* refers to the Muslim empire of India. Although the name *Mughal* is a variant of *Mongol,* the founders of the Mughal Empire were mainly Turks and Afghans, not Mongol descendants of Jenghiz Khan.)

The Rule of the Mughals

By the start of the sixteenth century, India had been the object of foreign conquest for almost a millennium. Muslims first invaded India in the seventh century. The Turkish chieftain Mahmud conquered the Punjab in the tenth century, and in the thirteenth century the Turkish Muslim Qutb-ud-din established the sultanate of Delhi, which gained control over most of the subcontinent. In 1398, central Asian armies under Timur the Lame (Tamerlane) swept down through the northwest, looted Delhi, and seized tens of thousands of

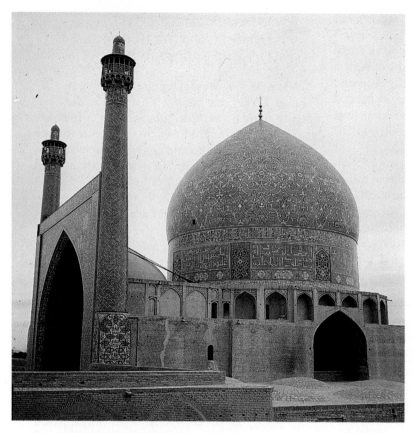

Masji-Shah Mosque   Just as the Gothic cathedrals manifested the civic pride of medieval European towns, so this mosque with its magnificent tile work and delicate stone tracery celebrated the commercial dynamism of Isfahan and the political power of the Safavid Dynasty of Persia. *(Source: Erwin Böhm, Mainz)*

slaves as booty. Timur, Babur's grandfather, left Delhi completely destroyed with "not a bird moving" and all India politically fragmented. Although the vast majority of the people remained Hindu, Islam had a strong impact on the culture of India, especially in art and architecture.

Babur's son Humayun reigned from 1530 to 1540 and from 1555 to 1556. When the Afghans of northern India rebelled, he lost most of the territories that his father had acquired. Humayun went into temporary exile in Persia, where he developed a deep appreciation for Persian art and literature. This interest led to a remarkable flowering of Mughal art under his son Akbar.

The reign of Akbar (r. 1556–1605) may well have been the greatest in the history of India. Under his dynamic leadership the Mughal state took

definite form. A boy of thirteen when he became *badshah,* or imperial ruler, Akbar was ably assisted during his early years by his father's friend Bairam Khan, a superb military leader. In 1555 Bairam Khan had defeated Hindu forces at Panipat and shortly afterward recaptured Delhi and Agra. Before falling from power in 1560, Bairam Khan took the great fortress of Gwalior, annexed the rich city of Janupur, and prepared for war against Malwa. Akbar continued this expansionist policy throughout this time, gradually adding the territories of Malwa, Gondwana, and Gujarat. Because the Afghan tribesmen put up tremendous resistance, it took Akbar several years to acquire Bengal. The Mughal Empire under Akbar eventually included most of the subcontinent north of the Godavari River (see Map 21.3).

To govern this vast region, Akbar developed an efficient bureaucracy staffed by able and well-trained officials, both Muslim and non-Muslim. As in the early modern nations of Europe, solvency in the Mughal state depended on the establishment of a careful system for recording income and expenditures. Under Akbar's finance minister Raja Todar Mal, a Hindu, a *diwan* (bureau of finance) and royal mint came into existence. Raja Todar Mal devised methods for the assessment and collection of taxes, and those methods were applied throughout the empire. To administer the provinces, Akbar appointed about 800 *mansabdars,* imperial officials who performed a wide variety of financial, military, and judicial functions at the local level. The central government, however, rarely interfered in the life of village communities. Akbar's policies laid the basis for all later Mughal administration in India.

A mark of Akbar's cosmopolitanism was his appointment of the Spanish Jesuit Antonio Monserrate (1536–1600) as tutor to his second son, Prince Murad (see Listening to the Past). The cornerstone of Akbar's policies was religious toleration: he sought the peaceful mutual assimilation of Hindus and Muslims, especially in his government. Although this was not a radical innovation—a few Hindus had long been employed in the imperial army and in the administration—very deep prejudices divided the two peoples. When the refusal of many Hindus to serve under a Muslim ruler or to learn Persian (the court language) thwarted Akbar's goal, he took decisive steps to heal the breach, because, according to his principle of *sulahkul* (universal tolerance), the badshah was responsible for all the people, regardless of their religion.

In 1564 the Muslim ruler ended the pilgrim tax and thus won the gratitude of the many Hindus who traveled to various pilgrimage sites. And by abolishing the *jizya,* a tax imposed on non-Muslim adult males, he immediately earned the support of the Hindu warrior class and the goodwill of the general Hindu population. Twice Akbar married Hindu princesses, one of whom became the mother of his heir Jahangir. Hindus eventually accounted for 30 percent of the imperial bureaucracy.

Scholars have heatedly debated Akbar's own religious beliefs. He considered himself an orthodox Muslim and demonstrated great devotion at the shrine of an Islamic mystic at Ajmer. Yet he supported an eclectic assortment of theological ideas, a policy that caused serious domestic difficulties. Orthodox Muslims became alarmed. After 1579 Akbar invited Jains, Zoroastrians, Hindus, and Jesuits to join the Muslim ulema in debate. From these discussions Akbar created the *Din-i-Ilahi* (literally, "divine discipleship"), which some advisers called a syncretic religion (a religion that reconciles different beliefs).

The Din-i-Ilahi borrowed the concept of great respect for animal life from the Jains and reverence for the sun from the Zoroastrians, but it was primarily based on the rationalistic elements in the Islamic tradition and stressed the emperor as a Perfect Man. Some scholars interpret it as a reflection of Akbar's "cult of personality," intended to serve as a common bond for the court nobility. In any case, the Din-i-Ilahi antagonized all sects and provoked serious Muslim rebellions.

Akbar often sought the spiritual advice of the Sufi mystic Shaykh Salim Chishti. The birth of a long-awaited son, Jahangir, which Akbar interpreted as fulfillment of the shaykh's prophecy, inspired Akbar to build a new city, Fatehpur-Sikri, to symbolize the regime's Islamic foundations. He personally supervised the construction of the new city. It combined the Muslim tradition of domes, arches, and spacious courts with the Hindu tradition of flat stone beams, ornate decoration, and solidity. According to Abu-l-Fazl, the historian of Akbar's reign, "His majesty plans splendid edifices, and dresses the work of his mind and heart in the garment of stone and clay."[17] Completed in 1578, the city included an imperial palace, a mosque, lavish gardens, and a hall of worship, as well as thousands of houses for ordinary people. Akbar placed Shaykh Salim Chishti's tomb inside the great mosque in order to draw on its presumed sanctity. Just as medieval European rulers such as Charlemagne and Phillip the Fair sought to strengthen their political power through association with Christian saints, so Akbar tried to identify Mughal authority with a Muslim saint. Along with the ancient cities of Delhi and Agra, Fatehpur-Sikri served as an imperial capital and the center of Akbar's lavish court.

Akbar was gifted with a creative intellect and imagination. He replaced Barlas Turkish with Persian as the offical language of the Mughal Empire; Persian remained the official language until the

British replaced it with English in 1835. He enthusiastically supported artists who produced magnificent paintings and books in the Indo-Persian style. In Mughal India, as throughout the Muslim world, books were regarded as precious objects. Time, talent, and expensive materials went into their production, and they were highly coveted because they reflected wealth, learning, and power.

Akbar reportedly possessed twenty-four thousand books when he died. Abu-l-Fazl, the historian, described the library and Akbar's love of books:

His Majesty's library is divided into several parts. . . . Prose works, poetical works, Hindi, Persian, Greek, Kashmirian, Arabic, are all separately placed. In this order they are also inspected. Experienced people

City of Fatehpur-Sikri In 1569 Akbar founded the city of Fatehpur-Sikri to honor the Muslim holy man Shaikh Salim Chishti, who had foretold the birth of Akbar's son and heir, Jahangir. The red sandstone city, probably the finest example of Mughal architecture still intact, was Akbar's capital for fifteen years. *(Source: Nrupen Madhvani/Dinodia Picture Agency, Bombay)*

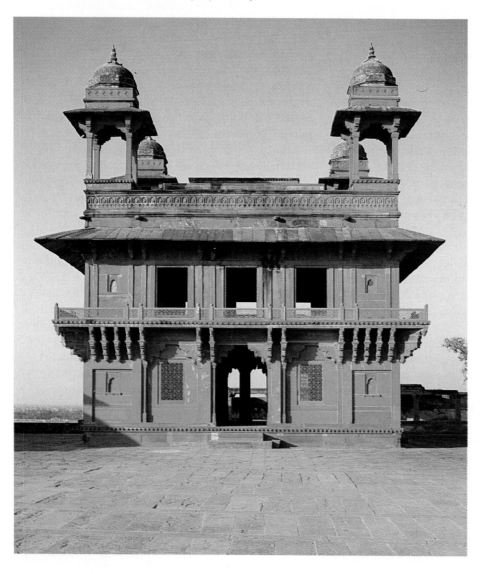

bring them daily and read them before His Majesty, who hears every book from beginning to end . . . and rewards the readers with presents of cash either in gold or silver, according to the number of leaves read out by them. Among books of renown there are few that are not read in His Majesty's assembly hall; and there are no historical facts of past ages, or curiosities of science, or interesting points of philosophy, with which His Majesty, a leader of impartial sages, is unacquainted.[18]

Akbar's son Jahangir (r. 1605–1628) lacked his father's military abilities and administrative genius but did succeed in consolidating Mughal rule in Bengal. His patronage of the arts and lavish court have led scholars to characterize his reign as an "age of splendor."

Jahangir's son Shah Jahan (r. 1628–1658) launched fresh territorial expansion. Faced with dangerous revolts by the Muslims in Ahmadnagar and the resistance of the newly arrived Portuguese in Bengal, Shah Jahan not only crushed them but strengthened his northwestern frontier. He reasserted Mughal authority in the Deccan and Golkunda.

The new capital that Shah Jahan founded at Delhi superseded Agra, Akbar's main capital. Situated on the rich land linking the Indus and Ganges Valleys, Delhi eventually became one of the great cities of the Muslim world. The city boasted one of the finest mosques in Islam, the Juma Masjid, and magnificent boulevards. The Red Fort, named for its red sandstone walls, housed the imperial palace, the headquarters of the imperial administration, the imperial treasury, an arsenal, and a garrison. Subsequent Mughal rulers held their *durbar,* or court, at Delhi.

Shah Jahan ordered the construction of the Peacock Throne. This famous piece, actually a cot resting on golden legs, was encrusted with emeralds, diamonds, pearls, and rubies. It took seven years to fashion and cost the equivalent of $5 million. It served as the imperial throne of India until 1739, when the Persian warrior Nadir Shah seized it as plunder and carried it to Persia.

Shah Jahan's most enduring monument is the Taj Mahal, the supreme example of a garden tomb. The English word *paradise* derives from the old Persian *pairidaeza,* a walled garden. The Mughals sought to bring their vision of paradise alive in the walled garden tombs in which they buried their

Jesuits at the Court of Akbar Akbar considered the creation of a new faith, synthesizing his Muslim beliefs, Hindu, Parsee, and Christian creeds, but the scheme encountered fierce opposition. The Jesuits' black robes fascinated Mughal artists, and the splendor of the imperial court astounded the Jesuits. *(Source: Reproduced by kind permission of the Trustees of the Chester Beatty Library, Dublin)*

dead. Twenty thousand workers toiled eighteen years to build this memorial in Agra to Shah Jahan's favorite wife, Mumtaz Mahal, who died giving birth to their fifteenth child. One of the most beautiful structures in the world, the Taj Mahal is

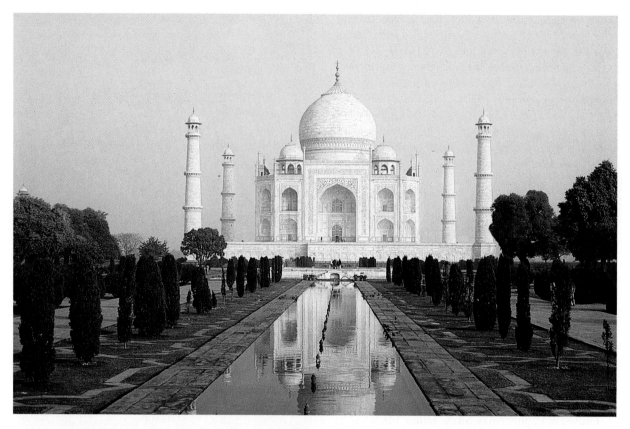

Taj Mahal at Agra   This tomb is the finest example of Muslim architecture in India. Its white marble exterior is inlaid with semiprecious stones in Arabic inscriptions and floral designs. The oblong pool reflects the building, which asserts the power of the Mughal Dynasty. *(Source: Ira Kirschenbaum/Stock, Boston)*

both an expression of love and a superb architectural blending of Islamic and Indian culture. It also asserted the power of the Mughal Dynasty.

The Mughal state never developed a formal procedure for the imperial succession, and a crisis occurred toward the end of Shah Jahan's reign. Competition among his sons ended with the victory of Aurangzeb, who executed his elder brother and locked his father away until death in 1666. A puritanically devout and strictly orthodox Muslim, a skillful general and a clever diplomat, Aurangzeb (r. 1658–1707) ruled more of India than did any previous badshah. His reign witnessed the culmination of Mughal power and the beginning of its decline (Map 21.3).

A combination of religious zeal and financial necessity seems to have prompted Aurangzeb to introduce a number of reforms. He appointed censors of public morals in important cities to enforce Islamic laws against gambling, prostitution, drinking, and the use of narcotics. He forbade *suttee*—the self-immolation of widows on their husbands' funeral pyres—and the castration of boys to be sold as eunuchs. He also abolished all taxes not authorized by Islamic law. This measure led to a serious loss of state revenues. To replace them, Aurangzeb in 1679 reimposed the jizya, the tax on non-Muslims. It fell most on the Hindu majority.

Regulating Indian society according to Islamic law meant modifying the religious toleration and cultural cosmopolitanism instituted by Akbar. Aurangzeb ordered the destruction of some Hindu temples. He required Hindus to pay higher customs duties than Muslims. Out of fidelity to Islamic law, he even criticized his mother's tomb, the Taj Mahal: "The lawfulness of a solid construction

Northern limit of Mughal Empire in 1707
Muslim land in 1765
Muslim land in 1805
Area controlled by Hindus in 1805
Land under British East India Company rule in 1805
✕ Site of important battle

MAP 21.3 India, 1707–1805 In the eighteenth century Mughal power gradually yielded to the Hindu Marathas and to the British East India Company.

over a grave is doubtful, and there can be no doubt about the extravagance involved."[19] Aurangzeb employed more Hindus in the imperial administration than any previous Mughal ruler. But his religious policy proved highly unpopular with the majority of his subjects and created problems that weaker successors could not handle.

Aurangzeb's military ventures also had mixed results. A tireless general, he pushed the conquest of the south and annexed the Golkunda and Bijapur sultanates. The stiffest opposition came from the Marathas, a militant Hindu group centered in the western Deccan. From 1681 until his death in 1707 at the age of ninety, Aurangzeb led repeated sorties through the Deccan. He took many forts and won several battles, but total destruction of the Maratha guerrilla bands eluded him. After his death they played an important role in the collapse of the Mughal Empire.

Aurangzeb's eighteenth-century successors faced formidable problems. Repeated disputes over the succession undermined the stability of the monarchy. Court intrigues replaced the battlefield as the testing ground for the nobility. Mughal provincial governors began to rule independently, giving only minimal allegiance to the badshah at Delhi. The Marathas, who revolted and pressed steadily northward, constituted the gravest threat to Mughal authority. No ruler could defeat them.

In 1739 the Persian adventurer Nadir Shah invaded India, defeated the Mughal army, looted Delhi, and after a savage massacre carried off a huge amount of treasure, including the Peacock Throne. When Nadir Shah withdrew to Afghanistan, he took with him the Mughal government's prestige. Constant skirmishes between the Afghans and the Marathas for control of the Punjab and northern India ended in 1761 at Panipat, where the Marathas were crushingly defeated by the Afghans. At this point, India no longer had any power capable of imposing order on the subcontinent or checking the penetration of the rapacious Europeans.

European Rivalry for the Indian Trade

Shortly before Babur's invasion of India, the Portuguese under the navigator Pedro Alvares Cabral had opened the subcontinent to Portuguese trade. In 1510 they established the port of Goa on the Arabian Sea as their headquarters and through a policy of piracy and terrorism swept the Muslims off the Indian and Arabian Oceans (see Map 21.3). The Portuguese historian Barrões attempted to justify Portugal's seizure of commercial traffic that the Muslims had long dominated:

It is true that there does exist a common right to all to navigate the seas and in Europe we recognize the rights which others hold against us; but the right does not extend beyond Europe and therefore the Portuguese as Lords of the Sea are justified in confiscating the goods of all those who navigate the seas without their permission.[20]

In short, Western principles of international law did not apply in Asia. For almost a century the Portuguese controlled the spice trade over the Indian Ocean.

In 1602 the Dutch formed the Dutch East India Company with the stated goal of wresting the enormously lucrative spice trade from the Portuguese. The scent of fabulous profits also attracted the English. With a charter signed by Queen Elizabeth, eighty London merchants organized the British East India Company. In 1619 Emperor Jahangir granted a British mission important commercial concessions at Surat on the western coast of India. Gifts, medical services, and bribes to Indian rulers enabled the British to set up twenty-seven other coastal forts. Fort St. George on the eastern coast became the modern city of Madras. In 1668 the city of Bombay—given to England when the Portuguese princess Catherine of Braganza married King Charles II—was leased to the company, marking the virtually total British absorption of Portuguese power in India. In 1690 the company founded a fort that became the city of Calcutta. Thus the three places that later became centers of British economic and political imperialism—Madras, Bombay, and Calcutta—existed before 1700. The Dutch concentrated their efforts in Indonesia.

Factory-Fort Societies

The British called their trading post at Surat a "factory," and the word was later used for all European settlements in India. The term did not signify manufacturing; it designated the walled compound containing the residences, gardens, and offices of British East India Company officials and the warehouses where goods were stored before being shipped to Europe. The company president exercised political authority over all residents.

Factory-forts existed to make profits from the Asian-European trade, and they evolved into flourishing centers of economic profit. The British East India Company sold silver, copper, zinc, lead, and fabrics to the Indians and bought cotton goods, silks, pepper and other spices, sugar, and opium from them. By the late seventeenth century the company was earning substantial profits. Profitability increased after 1700 when it began to trade with China. Some Indian merchants in Calcutta and Bombay made gigantic fortunes from trade within Asia.

Because the directors of the British East India Company in London discouraged all unnecessary expenses and financial risks, they opposed any interference in local Indian politics and even missionary activities. Conditions in India, however, brought about a fundamental change in the nature of the company's factories. The violent disorders and political instability that wracked India during Aurangzeb's reign and in the early eighteenth cen-

tury caused the factories to evolve into defensive installations manned by small garrisons of native troops. When warlords appeared or an uprising occurred, people from the surrounding countryside flocked into the fort, and the company factory-forts gradually came to exercise political authority over the territories around them.

Indian and Chinese wares enjoyed great popularity in England and on the European continent in the late seventeenth and early eighteenth centuries. The middle classes wanted Indian textiles,

English Factory at Surat   The factory began as a storage place for goods before they were bought and transported abroad; it gradually expanded to include merchants' residences and some sort of fortification. By 1650, the English had twenty-three factories in India. Surat, in the Gujarat region on the Gulf of Cambay, was the busiest factory and port until it was sacked by the Marathas in 1664. *(Source: The Mansell Collection)*

which were colorful, durable, cheap, and washable. The upper classes desired Chinese wallpaper and porcelains, Indian silks and brocades. In the European economies, however, Asian goods created serious problems. As early as 1695 English manufacturers called for an embargo on Indian cloth, and silk weavers picketed the House of Commons.

Trade with Asia was one-way: Asians had little interest in European manufactured articles. Finding the Siamese completely uninterested in traditional Dutch goods, the Dutch East India Company tried to interest them in collections of pornography. Europeans had to pay for everything they bought from Asia with precious metals. Thus there was insistent pressure in England, France, and the Netherlands against the importation of Asian goods. As one authority explains it: "The root of the argument from which grew a tree of many branches was the old fear of the drain of gold."21

The Rise of the British East India Company

The French were the last to arrive in India. Louis XIV's financial wizard Colbert (see pages 561–562) planned the French East India Company for trade in the Eastern Hemisphere, and in the 1670s the company established factories at Chandernagore in Bengal, Pondicherry, and elsewhere. Joseph Dupleix (1697–1764), who was appointed governor general at Pondicherry in 1742, made allies of Indian princes and built an army of native troops, called *sepoys,* who were trained as infantrymen. The British likewise built an army with Indian surrogates trained in Western military drill and tactics. War broke out at midcentury.

From 1740 to 1763 Britain and France were almost continually engaged in a tremendous global struggle. India, like North America in the Seven Years' War, became a battlefield and a prize. The French won land battles, but English seapower decided the first phase of the war. Then a series of brilliant victories destroyed French power in southern India. By preventing French reinforcements from arriving, British seapower again proved to be the determining factor, and British jurisdiction soon extended over the important northern province of Bengal. The Treaty of Paris of 1763 recognized British control of much of India, and

scholars acknowledge the treaty as the beginning of the British Empire in India.

How was the vast subcontinent to be governed? Parliament believed that the British East India Company had too much power and considered the company responsible for the political disorders in India, which were bad for business. Parliament attempted to solve Indian problems with special legislation. The Regulating Act of 1773 created the office of governor general, with an advisory council, to exercise political authority over the territory controlled by the company. The India Act of 1784 required that the governor general be chosen from outside the company, and it made company directors subject to parliamentary supervision.

Implementation of these reforms fell to Warren Hastings, the governor of Bengal and first governor general (r. 1774–1785) with jurisdiction over Bombay and Madras. Hastings tried to build an effective administrative system and to turn the British East India Company into a government. He laid the foundations for the first Indian civil service, abolished tolls to facilitate internal trade, placed the salt and opium trades under government control, and planned a codification of Muslim and Hindu laws. He sought allies among Indian princes. The biggest problem facing Hastings's administration was a coalition of the rulers of Mysore and the Marathas aimed at the expulsion of the British. Hastings's skillful diplomacy offset this alliance temporarily.

Hastings's successor Lord Charles Cornwallis served as governor general of India from 1786 to 1794. Cornwallis continued the work of building a civil service and the war against Mysore. His introduction of the British style of property relations in effect converted a motley collection of former Mughal officers, tax collectors, and others into English-style landlords. The result was a new system of landholding, in which the rents of tenant farmers supported the landlords.

The third governor general, the marquess Richard Wellesley (r. 1797–1805), defeated Mysore in 1799 and four years later crushed the Marathas at the Battle of Assaye (see Map 21.3). Building on the work of his predecessors, he vastly extended British influence in India. Like most nineteenth-century British governors of India, Wellesley believed that British rule strongly benefited the Indians. With supreme condescension he wrote that

Textile from Kalamkari   Containing a rich variety of Persian, Hindu, Muslim, and Christian motifs, this superb example of seventeenth-century painted cotton suggests the beauty and complexity of Indian textile manufacture as well as the diversity of influences in Indian culture itself. *(Source: The Metropolitan Museum of Art)*

British power should be established over the Indian princes in order

to deprive them of the means of prosecuting any measure or of forming any confederacy hazardous to the security of the British empire, and to enable us to preserve the tranquility of India by exercising a general control over the restless spirit of ambition and violence which is characteristic of every Asiatic government.[22]

By the beginning of the nineteenth century, the authority and power of the British East India Company had yielded to the government in London. Subsequent British rule of India rested on three foundations: the support of puppet Indian princes, who exercised the trappings but not the reality of power; a large army of sepoys of dubious loyalty; and an increasingly effective civil service, staffed largely by Englishmen with Hindus and Muslims in minor positions.

SUMMARY

In the eighteenth century, the Ottoman Turks lived almost entirely within a closed Islamic environment. Very few knew European languages or had firsthand knowledge of Europe. Diplomatic relations with any European power did not exist before 1793. When the Ottomans thought of Europe at all, they believed it inferior to Islamic civilization, despite the plea in 1653 of Katib Chelebi, a renowned Ottoman historian, for greater Muslim knowledge of geography: "Sufficient and compelling proof of the necessity for learning this science is the fact that the unbelievers, by their application to and esteem for those branches of learning, have discovered the New World and have overrun the ports of India and the East Indies."[23] Everyone looked backward to the period of Suleiman the Magnificent, when the empire was at its height. There was little thought of innovation or experimentation. Some scholars believe that Islam's hostility to innovation is traceable to a saying of Muhammad: "The worst things are those that are novelties, every novelty is an innovation, every innovation is an error, and every error leads to Hell-fire." After war with Russia (1736–1739), in which the Turks were largely successful, the Ottomans entered a long period of peace on their western frontier. Not until the reign of Sultan Selim III (r. 1761–1808), during which the imperial administration and the army were restructured, European languages studied, and relations established with European powers, did the Ottoman Empire begin to become a modern state.

In the seventeenth century, the Shi'ite state of Persia enjoyed military success, economic boom, and cultural pre-eminence. The wealth and magnificence of the shah was a legend in sophisticated China and in primitive North America. In the eighteenth century, however, political weakness attracted Russian and Ottoman invasion and led to Persia's dismemberment.

The contemporary Indian writer V. S. Naipaul has called India "a wounded civilization." For centuries the economic prize of European commercial interests, in the 1700s the Indian subcontinent began to experience British political domination. Bitter hostility between Hindus and Muslims persisted as a dominant theme of Indian life.

NOTES

1. Quoted in B. Lewis, *The Muslim Discovery of Europe* (New York: Norton, 1982), p. 29.
2. W. H. McNeill, *The Pursuit of Power: Technology, Armed Force, and Society Since A.D. 1000* (Chicago: University of Chicago Press, 1982), p. 87.
3. Quoted in Lewis, *The Muslim Discovery of Europe*, p. 30.
4. F. Babinger, *Mehmed the Conqueror and His Times*, trans. R. Manheim. (Princeton, N.J.: Princeton University Press, 1978), p. 107.
5. F. Robinson, *Atlas of the Islamic World Since 1500* (New York: Facts on File, 1982), p. 72.
6. Quoted in P. K. Hitti, *The Near East in History* (Princeton, N.J.: Van Nostrand, 1961), p. 336.
7. See S. J. Shaw, *History of the Ottoman Empire and Modern Turkey*, vol. 1, *Empire of the Gazis: The Rise and Decline of the Ottoman Empire, 1208–1808* (Cambridge: Cambridge University Press, 1988), pp. 139–151.
8. *The Selected Letters of Lady Mary Wortley Montagu*, ed. R. Halsband. (London: Longman Group, 1970), pp. 98–99.
9. Ibid., p.106.
10. Ibid., p. 105.
11. Ibid., p. 96–97.
12. N. Itzkowitz, *Ottoman Empire and Islamic Tradition* (Chicago: University of Chicago Press, 1980), p. 95.
13. See Shaw, *Empire of the Gazis*, pp. 171–175, 225, 246–247; V. H. Parry, H. Inalcik, A. N. Kurat, and J. S. Bromley, *A History of the Ottoman Empire to 1715* (New York: Cambridge University Press, 1976), pp. 126, 139–140.
14. Quoted in R. E. Dunn, *The Adventures of Ibn Battuta: A Muslim Traveler of the 14th Century* (Berkeley: University of California Press, 1986), p. 81.
15. Ibid., pp. 83–87.
16. D. Morgan, *Medieval Persia, 1040–1797* (New York: Longman, 1988), pp. 112–113.
17. Quoted in V. A. Smith, *The Oxford History of India* (Oxford: Oxford University Press, 1967), p. 398.
18. Quoted in M. C. Beach, *The Imperial Image: Paintings for the Mughal Court* (Washington, D.C.: Freer Gallery of Art, Smithsonian Institution, 1981), pp. 9–10.
19. Quoted in S. K. Ikram, *Muslim Civilization in India* (New York: Columbia University Press, 1964), p. 202.
20. Quoted in K. M. Panikkar, *Asia and Western*

Domination (London: George Allen & Unwin, 1965), p. 35.
21. Quoted ibid., p. 53.
22. Quoted in W. Bingham, H. Conroy, and F. W. Iklé, *A History of Asia,* vol. 2 (Boston: Allyn and Bacon, 1967), p. 74.
23. Quoted ibid., p. 106.

SUGGESTED READING

The curious student interested in the Ottoman world might begin with A. Wheatcroft, *The Ottomans* (1993), an excitingly written and beautifully illustrated popular account of many facets of Ottoman culture that separates Western myths from Turkish reality; this book also has a helpful bibliography. In addition to the titles by Babinger, Itkowitz, and Shaw cited in the Notes, H. Inalcik, *The Ottoman Empire: the Classical Age, 1300–1600* (1973) and chapters 13, 14, and 15 of A. Hourani, *A History of the Arab Peoples* (1991) should also prove helpful. For Suleiman the Magnificent, E. Atil, *The Age of Sultan Suleyman the Magnificent* (1987) is a splendidly illustrated celebration of the man and his times, while A. Bridge, *Suleiman the Magnificent. Scourge of Heaven* (1972) presents a highly readable, if romantic, view; *Circa 1492. Art in the Age of Exploration,* ed. J. A. Levenson (1991) has several stimulating chapters on the Ottomans and Constantinople. For the later empire, see L. Cassels, *The Struggle for the Ottoman Empire, 1710–1740* (1966) and S. J. Shaw, *Between Old and New: The Ottoman Empire under Sultan Selim III, 1789–1807* (1971).

The literature on women is growing, though still largely restricted to the upper classes. See F. Davis, *The Ottoman Lady: A Social History from 1718 to 1918* (1986); A. L. Croutier, *Harem: The World Behind the Veil* (1989); L. P. Pierce, *The Imperial Harem: Woman and Sovereignty in the Ottoman World* (1993), a fine achievement which treats not only the political roles of Turkish women, but marriage, concubines, and childbirth; and *The Selected Letters of Lady Mary Wortley Montagu,* ed. R. Halsband (1970), which gives the invaluable impressions of a sophisticated Englishwoman.

For slavery in the Ottoman world, see the appropriate pages of B. Lewis, *Race and Slavery in the Middle East* (1990), and E. R. Toledano, *The Ottoman Slave Trade and Its Suppression: 1840–1890* (1982), which although dealing with a period later than this chapter, offers useful references to earlier centuries.

Perhaps the best general introduction to the history and civilization of India is S. Wolpert's elegant appreciation *India* (1990), but see also P. Spears, *A History of India,* vol. II (1986). The titles by V. A. Smith and S. K. Ikram, cited in the Notes, provide broad general treatments, as do P. M. Holt *et al.,* eds., *The Cambridge History of India* 2 vols. (1970), M. Mujeeb, *The Indian Muslims* (1967), and I. Habib, *The Agrarian System of Mughal India, 1556–1707* (1963) whose theme and scope are indicated by the title. Many of the essays in J. F. Richards, *Power, Administration and Finance in Mughal India* (1993) are useful and authoritative. For the decline of imperial authority in eighteenth century India, see the important study of M. Alam, *The Crisis of Empire in Mughal North India: Awadh and the Punjab, 1707–48* (1986). Students wishing to study Indian culture through its architecture, should consult two splendid and recent achievements: C. Tadgell, *The History of Architecture in India: from the Dawn of Civilization to the End of the Raj* (1995) and G. Mitchell, *The Royal Palaces of India* (1995). E. B. Findly, *Nur Jahan. Empress of Mughal India* (1993) provides a vivid picture of one powerful and influential woman. E. Maclagan, *The Jesuits and the Great Mogul* (1932) discusses the Jesuits at the courts of Akbar, Jahangir, and Shah Jahan. B. Gascoigne, *The Great Moghuls* (1971) and G. Hambly, *The Cities of Mughal India: Delhi, Agra, and Fatehpur Sikri* (1968) are well illustrated and highly readable. For the impact of Portuguese, Dutch, and English mercantile activities in India, see M. N. Pearson, *Merchants and Rulers in Gujarat: The Response to the Portuguese in the Sixteenth Century* (1976).

Culture Shock

A keen student of comparative religion, the Mughal emperor Akbar invited Jain teachers, Sikh gurus, and Catholic Jesuits to his court. The Jesuits had recently established a mission and college in Goa. One of the Jesuits, Antonio Monserrate, who eventually served as an adviser to the emperor and accompanied him on several military expeditions, had been ordered by the Superior of the Society of Jesus in India to keep a careful record of his experiences at the Mughal court. Monserrate's Commentary *has proved invaluable to scholars for its picture of Akbar's personality and policies and Westerners' reaction to Indian culture in the late sixteenth century.*

The wives of the Brachmans—a famous class of nobly-born Hindus—are accustomed, in accordance with an ancient tradition of their religion, to burn themselves on the same pyres as their dead husbands. The King ordered the priests to be summoned to see an instance of this. They went in ignorance of what was to take place; but when they found out, they plainly indicated by their saddened faces how cruel and savage they felt that crime to be. Finally Rudolf[1] publicly reprimanded the King for showing openly by his presence there that he approved of such a revolting crime, and for supporting it by his weighty judgment and explicit approbation, (for he was heard to say that such fortitude could only come from God). Such was Zelaldinus'[2] kindness and favour towards the priests that he showed no resentment; and a certain chief, a great favourite of his, a Brachman by birth, who held the office of Superintendent of sacred observances, could no longer persuade him to attend such spectacles. The wretched women are rendered quite insensible by means of certain drugs, in order that they may feel no pain. For this purpose opium is used, or a soporific herb named bang, or—more usually—the herb 'duturo,' which is known to the Indians, although entirely unfamiliar alike to modern Europeans and to the ancients. Sometimes they are half-drugged: and, before they lose their resolution, are hurried to the pyre with warnings, prayers and promises of eternal fame. On arriving there they cast themselves into the flames. If they hesitate, the wretched creatures are driven on to the pyre: and if they try to leap off again, are held down with poles and hooks. The nobles who were present were highly incensed at the Fathers' interference. They did not dare to gainsay the King; but they grumbled loudly amongst themselves, saying, 'Away with you, black-clothed Franks.' The whole city was filled with praise and admiration when news was brought that the Franks had dared to rebuke the King regarding this affair.

On one occasion, the Fathers met a crowd of worthless profligates,[3] some of those who dress and adorn themselves like women. The priests were rightly disgusted at this, and took the first opportunity of privately complaining to the King (since he was so favourable to them) about this disgraceful matter. They declared with the greatest emphasis that they were astonished at his permitting such a class of men to live in his kingdom, let alone in his city, and almost under his eyes. They must be banished, as though they were a deadly plague, to his most distant territories; even better, let them be burnt up by devouring flames. They never would have believed that such men could be found in the court itself and in the royal city, where lived a king of such piety, integrity and prudence. Therefore let him give orders that these libertines should never again be seen in Fattepurum, seeing that his remarkable prophet[4] had guaranteed that good men should never suffer for their good actions. The King laughed at this piece of sarcasm and retired, saying that he would attend to the matter.

Questions for Analysis

1. What does the document reveal about the Jesuits' relations with Akbar?

2. Consider the Jesuits' reactions to the Hindu practice of suttee.[5] Should they have interfered?

3. Contrast the Jesuits' reaction to suttee and to the transvestite prostitutes.

Source: *The Commentary of Father Monserrate, S.J., on His Journey to the Court of Akbar* (London: Oxford University Press, 1922), pp. 61–63.

1. One of the Jesuits.
2. The Jesuits' name for Akbar.
3. Male prostitutes, common in almost all societies.
4. A reference to the Prophet Muhammad. The Jesuits' logic and charity is somewhat faulty here.
5. *Suttee* means "true one" in Sanskrit. The term was used to describe a Hindu widow's self-immolation on the funeral pyre of her dead husband, without whom her life had supposedly lost all meaning. The British abolished suttee in 1829, but even today women whose dowries are not paid are sometimes burned to death.

Antonio at the court of Akbar. *(Source: Reproduced by kind permission of the Trustees of the Chester Beatty Library, Dublin)*

22

China and Japan, ca 1400–1800

Toyotomi Hideyoshi (1530–1598) is represented as a knightly archer in this statue in a niche of the Yomei-mon, a gate leading to the Toshogu Shrine at Nikko. *(Source: Photographer, Martin Hürlimann. Courtesy of Reich Verlag, Switzerland.)*

The period from about 1400 to 1800 witnessed growth and dynamic change in East Asia. In China the native Ming Dynasty (1368–1644) had replaced the Yuan (1271–1368) and in 1644 was replaced by the foreign Manchu Dynasty. The early Ming period was a time of remarkable economic reconstruction and of the establishment of new and original social institutions. Over time, however, the bureaucracy prevented the changes necessary to meet new demands on the empire. The Manchus inaugurated a long period of peace, relative prosperity, and population expansion. In the Manchu period the Chinese Empire reached its greatest territorial extent, and literary and artistic creativity reached their apogee.

In the Japanese islands, united by Nobunaga and later the Tokugawa Shogunate (1600–1867), the feudal military aristocracy continued to evolve. Although Japan developed largely in isolation from outside influences, its sociopolitical system bore striking similarities to medieval European feudalism. The period of the Tokugawa Shogunate, like that of the Ming Dynasty in China, was marked by remarkable agricultural productivity and industrial growth.

- What features characterized the governments of the Ming and Manchu Dynasties in China and the Tokugawa Shogunate in Japan?
- How did agricultural and commercial developments affect Chinese and Japanese societies?
- How did Chinese thinkers interpret and explain the shift from the Ming to the Manchus?

This chapter explores these questions.

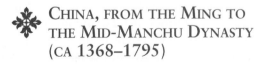

CHINA, FROM THE MING TO THE MID-MANCHU DYNASTY (CA 1368–1795)

Mongol repression under the Yuan Dynasty, rapid inflation of the currency, disputes over succession among the khans, and the growth of peasant secret societies led to the decay of Mongol government in China. By 1368, Hong Wu, the leader of a secret society called the Red Turbans, had pushed the Mongols out of China. Hong Wu (r. 1368–1398), founder of the Ming Dynasty, and Liu Bang (r. 206–195 B.C.), founder of the Han Dynasty, were the only peasants to found major dynasties in China. The Ming Dynasty (1368–1644) was the only dynasty that originated south of the Yangtze River (see Map 22.1).

Under the Ming, China experienced dynamic change. Agricultural development and commercial reconstruction followed a long period of chaos and disorder. Hong Wu introduced far-reaching social and political institutions. By the middle of the fifteenth century, however, his administrative framework had begun to decay. Externally, defeats in Mongolia in the later fifteenth century led to a long period of Chinese withdrawal. Nevertheless, the Ming period stands out because of its social and cultural achievements.

The Ming Agricultural and Commercial Revolutions

Mongol exploitation and the civil disorders that accompanied the breakdown of Yuan rule left China in economic chaos in the mid-fourteenth century. Vast stretches of farmland were laid waste, some entirely abandoned. Damaged dikes and canals proved unusable, causing trade to decline.

Between 1370 and 1398, a profound economic reconstruction occurred. The agricultural revolution that China underwent in the Ming period was part of a gigantic effort at recovery after the disaster of Mongol rule. At the heart of this revolution was radical improvement in methods of rice production.

More than bread in Europe, rice supplied almost the total nourishment of the population in central and south China. (In north China, wheat, made into steamed or baked bread or into noodles, served as the staple of the diet.) Terracing and irrigation of mountain slopes, introduced in the eleventh century, had increased rice harvests. The introduction of drought-resistant Indochinese, or Champa, rice proved an even greater boon. Although Champa rice was of lower nutritional quality than the native rice, it considerably increased the total output of food. Ming farmers experimented with Champa rice that required only sixty days from planting to harvesting instead of the usual hundred days. Peasants soon reaped two harvests a year, an enormous increase in production.

Other innovations also brought good results. Ming-era peasants introduced irrigation pumps worked by pedals. Farmers began to stock the rice paddies with fish, which continuously fertilized the

❀ **Chinese Peasants at Work** The Western artist who sketched this picture in the seventeenth century seems to be telling us that human power in agriculture was as common in China as animal power. Notice that a woman also pulls the plow; she might have been pregnant. Coco palms (left) are not usually found as far north as China. The pigtailed men date the picture from the Manchu period. *(Source: Caroline Buckler)*

rice fields, destroyed malaria-bearing mosquitoes, and enriched the diet. Fish farming in the paddies eventually enabled large, previously uninhabitable parts of southern China to be brought under cultivation. Farmers discovered the possibilities of commercial cropping in cotton, sugar cane, and indigo. And new methods of crop rotation allowed for continuous cultivation and for more than one harvest per year from a single field.

The Ming rulers promoted the repopulation and colonization of devastated regions through massive transfers of people. Immigrants received large plots of land and exemption from taxation for many years. Table 22.1, based on fourteenth-century records of newly reclaimed land, helps tell the story.[1]

Reforestation was a dramatic aspect of the agricultural revolution. In 1391 the Ming government ordered 50 million trees planted in the Nanjing (Nanking) area. Lumber from the trees was intended for the construction of a maritime fleet. In 1392 each family holding colonized land in Anhwei province had to plant 200 each of mulberry, jujube, and persimmon trees. In 1396 peasants in the present-day provinces of Hunan and Hupeh in the east planted 84 million fruit trees. Historians have estimated that 1 billion trees were planted during Hong Wu's reign.[2]

What were the social consequences of agricultural development? Increased food production led to steady population growth. Demographers date the start of the Chinese population boom at about 1550, as a direct result of improved methods of rice production. Increases in total yields differed fundamentally, however, from comparable agricultural growth in Europe: Chinese grain harvests were improved through intensification of peasant labor. This meant lower income per capita.

Population increase seems to have led to the multiplication of towns and small cities. Urbanization in the Ming era (and, later, in the Manchu period) meant the proliferation of market centers and small towns rather than the growth of "large" cities like those in Europe in the High Middle Ages and China in the Song (Sung) period (960–1279). Most people lived in tiny hamlets or villages that had no markets. What distinguished a village from a town was the existence of a market in a town.

Towns held markets twice a week; in southern China, where a week was ten days long, markets were held three times a week. Town markets consisted of little open-air shops that sold essential goods—pins, matches, oil for lamps, candles, paper, incense, tobacco—to country people from surrounding hamlets. The market usually included a tearoom or tavern where tea and rice wine were sold, entertainers performed, and moneylenders and pawnshops sometimes did business.

Tradesmen, who carried their wares on their backs, and craftsmen—carpenters, barbers, joiners, locksmiths—moved constantly from market to market. Itinerant salesmen depended on the city market for their wares. In large towns and cities foodstuffs from the countryside and rare and precious goods from distant places were offered for sale. Cities gradually became islands of sophistication in the highly localized Chinese economy. Nanjing, for example, spread out enormously because the presence of the imperial court and bureaucracy generated a great demand for goods. The concentration of people in turn created demand for goods and services. Industrial development was stimulated. Small businesses manufactured textiles, paper, and luxury goods such as silks and porcelains. Nanjing and Shanghai became centers for the production of cotton and silks; Xiangtan specialized in the grain and salt trade and in silver. Small towns remained embedded in peasant culture, but large towns and cities pursued contacts with the wider world.

The Government of Hong Wu

Hong Wu's government reforms rested on a few strong centralizing principles. Hong Wu established China's capital at Nanjing (literally, "southern capital"), his old base on the Yangtze River. He stripped many nobles of their estates and divided the estates among the peasantry. Although Hong Wu had been a monk, he confiscated many of the temples' tax-exempt lands, thereby increasing the proceeds of the state treasury. In the Song period, commercial taxes had fed the treasury. In the Ming and, later, the Manchu periods, imperial revenues came mainly from agriculture: farmers produced the state's resources.

Hong Wu ordered a general survey of all China's land and several censuses of the population. The data gathered were recorded in official

TABLE 22.1 LAND RECLAMATION IN EARLY MING CHINA

Year	Reclaimed Land (in hectares; 1 hectare = 2.5 acres)
1371	576,000
1373	1,912,000
1374	4,974,000
1379	1,486,000

Source: J. Gernet, A History of Chinese Civilization, trans. J. R. Foster (Cambridge: Cambridge University Press, 1982), p. 391. Used with permission.

registers, which provided valuable information about the taxes that landlords, temples, and peasants owed. According to the registers, the capital was owed 8 million *shih,* or 160,000 tons, of rice per year. Such thorough fiscal information contributed to the efficient operation of the state.

To secure soldiers for the army and personnel for his administration and to generate revenue, Hong Wu adopted the Yuan practice of requiring service to the state. He made all occupations hereditary, classifying the entire Chinese population into three hereditary categories: peasants, artisans, and soldiers. The state ministry that had jurisdiction over a particular category designated an individual's obligations to the state.

The ministry of finance oversaw the peasants, who provided the bulk of the taxes and performed public labor services. The ministry of public works supervised artisans and all people who had special skills and crafts. The ministry of the army controlled the standing army of 2 million men. Each social category prevailed in a particular geographical region. Peasants lived in the countryside. Craftsmen lived mainly in the neighborhoods of the cities for which they produced goods. Army families lived along the coasts and lengthy frontiers that they defended. When a soldier died or proved unable to fight, his family had to provide a replacement.

The Ming emperor wielded absolute and despotic power. Access to his personal favor was the only means of acquiring privilege or some limited derivative power. The complex ceremonial and court ritual surrounding any public appearance by the emperor, the vast imperial palace staffed only by servile women and eunuchs, and the precise procedures of the imperial bureaucracy, which blamed any difficulties on the emperor's advisers—all lent the throne a rarefied aura and exalted the emperor's authority. In addition, Hong Wu demanded that the military nobles (his old rebel comrades-in-arms) live at his court in Nanjing, where he could keep an eye on them. He raised many generals to the nobility, a position that bestowed honor and financial benefits but no political power whatsoever.

Late in his reign Hong Wu executed many nobles and divided China into principalities, putting one of his sons in charge of each. Suspicious even of his sons' loyalty, he carefully limited their power. Positions in the imperial administration were filled in part by means of civil service examinations, which proved to be Hong Wu's most enduring reform. The examination system, which lasted until the twentieth century, later became the exclusive channel for official recruitment. Examinations were given every three years at the district, provincial, and state (imperial) levels; candidates had to pass the lower levels before trying for the imperial level where the success rate in late imperial China was between one and two percent. In the Ming period the examinations required a minute knowledge of the ancient Chinese classics and a formal and precise literary style: they discouraged all originality. In the bureaucrats who passed them, the examinations promoted conservatism and opposition to innovation. To prevent nepotism and corruption, civil service positions were filled according to the "Rule of Avoidance": a candidate could

 An Acrobat Entertains The hard, dull routine of country or town people could be temporarily lightened by a traveling juggler, gymnast, or comedian who performed skits and then passed the hat for payment. Here an acrobat demonstrates his skill with the lance as spectators watch: at the top, a handicapped person, two beggars, and a boy who calls them; at the left, a group of porters with poles for carrying merchandise on their shoulders; on the right, a group of the well-to-do. *(Source: Art Institute of Chicago/Photo: Wan-go Weng)*

not be appointed to a position in his native province, nor could two members of the same family serve in the same province.

After 1426 the eunuch-dominated secret police controlled the palace guards and the imperial workshops, infiltrated the civil service, and headed all foreign missions. Through blackmail, espionage, and corruption, the secret police exercised enormous domestic power. How did eunuchs acquire such power? Without heirs, they had no immediate family concerns. Drawn from the lowest classes of society, viewed with distaste by respectable people, eunuchs had no hope of gaining status except by satisfying every whim of the emperor. They were indifferent to public opinion. Because of their total submission to the emperor, the emperors believed them absolutely trustworthy. Several eunuchs—Wang Chih in the 1470s, Liu Zhi in the 1500s, and Wei Zhong-xian in the 1620s—gained dictatorial power when their emperors lost interest in affairs of state.

Foreign affairs occupied much of Hong Wu's attention. He sought to control all Chinese contacts with the outside world, and he repeatedly invaded Mongolia. But the strengthening and extension of the Great Wall stands as Hong Wu's and his Ming successors' most visible achievement. According to one record, the defense system of the Great Wall throughout the Ming period formed a protective girdle "10,000 *li* (a *li* is about one-third of a mile) in an unbroken chain from the Yalu River in the east to Jiayuguan in the west."[3] The forts, beacon towers, and garrisons that pierced the wall at militarily strategic spots kept in close contact with the central government. Because of the steady pressure of Mongol attacks in the fifteenth century, Hong Wu's successors continued the work of reinforcing the Great Wall.

Hong Wu forbade free commercial contacts along the coasts between Chinese and foreign merchants. He insisted that foreign states eager to trade with China acknowledge his suzerainty by offering tribute. The early Ming emperors displayed greater military and diplomatic efficiency than had Chinese rulers for centuries. By the mid-fifteenth century, however, Mongol raids by land and Japanese piracy at sea, often with the hidden cooperation of the local Chinese, were commonplace. Along the coasts Koreans, Vietnamese, Malays, Sumatrans, and Japanese entered China disguised as merchants. If they were dissatisfied with the official rates of exchange, they robbed and destroyed. Neither fortresses and the transfer of coastal settlements inland nor precautionary attacks on pirate merchant raiders could suppress the problem. The imperial court came to regard foreigners arriving by ship, including Europeans when they arrived in the sixteenth century, as "barbarians."

Maritime Expansion

Another dramatic development of the Ming period was the series of naval expeditions sent out between 1405 and 1433 under Hong Wu's son Yong Lu and Yong Lu's successor. China had a strong maritime history stretching back to the eleventh century, and these early fifteenth-century voyages were a continuation of that tradition. The Ming expeditions established China as the greatest maritime power in the world—considerably ahead of Portugal, whose major seafaring reconnaissances began a half-century later.

In contrast to Hong Wu, Yong Lu broadened diplomatic and commercial contacts within the tribute system. Yong Lu had two basic motives for launching overseas voyages. First, he sent them in search of Jian Wen, a serious contender for the throne whom he had defeated but who, rumor claimed, had escaped to Southeast Asia. Second, he launched the expeditions to explore, to expand trade, and to provide the imperial court with luxury objects. Led by the Muslim eunuch admiral Zheng He and navigating by compass, seven fleets sailed to East and South Asia. The first expedition (which carried 27,800 men) involved 62 major ships, the largest of which was 440 feet in length and 180 feet in the beam and had 9 masts. The expeditions crossed the Indian Ocean to Ceylon, the Persian Gulf, and the east coast of Africa.

These voyages had important consequences. They extended the prestige of the Ming Dynasty throughout Asia. Trade, in the form of tribute from as far as the west coast of southern India, greatly increased. Diplomatic contacts with the distant Middle East led to the arrival in Nanjing of embassies from Egypt. The maritime expeditions also led to the publication of geographical works such as the *Treatise on the Barbarian Kingdoms on the Western Oceans* (1434) and *The Marvels Discovered by the Boat Bound for the Galaxy* (1436). The information acquired from the voyages served as the basis of Chinese knowledge of the maritime world until the nineteenth century. Finally, these expeditions resulted in Chinese emigration to the countries of Southeast Asia and the ports of southern India. The voyages were terminated because Confucian court intellectuals persuaded the emperor that his quest for strange and exotic things signaled the collapse of the dynasty.[4] After 1435, China returned to a policy of isolation.

Decline of the Ming Dynasty

A bitter struggle for the throne ensued when Hong Wu died. The bloody wars that brought his son Yong Lu to the throne devastated the territory between the Yellow and the Yangtze Rivers. Yong Lu (1403–1424) promoted a policy of resettlement there. He continued his father's policies of requiring civil service examinations, controlling the nobility, and trying to restrain pirates. He also transferred the capital back to Beijing (Peking). A former governor *(wang)* of the north, Yong Lu felt he had greater support there than in the south. Beijing was also closer to the northern frontier and thus was a better place for strategic defense against China's ancient enemies, the Mongols. The move pleased the military faction but hurt the new gentry and mercantile groups, whose economic interests centered around Nanjing.

The extravagance of the imperial court caused economic difficulties. Hong Wu had exercised fiscal restraint, but Yong Lu and his successors tried to outdo the splendor and magnificence of the Mongols. The emperor and his court lived in the Forbidden City, a quarter-mile compound filled with palatial buildings, ceremonial halls, marble terraces, and lengthy galleries; their grandeur surpassed that of Louis XIV's Versailles. Surrounding the Forbidden City and occupying some three square smiles was the Imperial City, where, in the words of a modern historian,

there were also supply depots and material-processing plants. Among them was the court of Imperial Entertainments, which had the capacity to serve banquets for up to 15,000 men on short notice. Next to the bakery, distillery, and confectionery were the emperor's stable, armory, printing-office, and book depository.[5]

A century and a half later, in the reign of the emperor Wan-li, everything required for the maintenance of the Imperial City was manufactured or deposited there. Approximately twenty thousand eunuchs worked there, and some three thousand female domestics performed household tasks. The emperor's immediate court—councilors, bodyguards, relatives, official wives, and concubines—numbered several thousand people. Supporting so many people on a lavish scale placed a great burden on the treasury. Financial difficulties thus played a major role in the decline of the Ming.

Yong Lu's successors lacked his drive and ability. The Mongols continued to press on the northern borders, and the Chinese had to yield some territory. In 1450, during an ill-conceived expedition against the Mongols, the inexperienced young emperor Ying-Zoung (r. 1436–1450 and 1457–1464) was captured and remained a prisoner of the Mongols for seven years. In the south, a Chinese army of 200,000 had pressed into northern Vietnam in 1406. This imperialistic move led to temporary Chinese domination of the Red River basin and of much of central Vietnam. A Vietnamese liberation movement retaliated and by 1427 had driven the occupiers out. In the sixteenth century the Japanese accelerated their coastal raids and even sacked the cities of Ningbo (Ningpo) and Yangzhou (Yangchow). Difficulties in collecting taxes hindered the government's ability to strengthen the army. It was commonplace in the eleven hundred counties of Ming China for people to delay or refuse to pay taxes, aware that no magistrate could prosecute thousands of delinquents. Their taxes were eventually written off.

In spite of these pressures, the empire did not fall apart. In fact, southern China enjoyed considerable prosperity in the late sixteenth and early seventeenth centuries. Japanese, Portuguese, and Dutch merchants paid in silver for the Chinese silks and ceramics they bought. However, because of the steady flow of silver into China from the trade with Japan and, later, from the mines of Mexico and Peru by way of Spain, the value of Chinese paper currency, which had been in circulation since the eleventh century, drastically declined. Unable to control either the state economy or local commercial activity, the imperial government had to acquiesce in foreign trade. The emperor also had to recognize the triumph of silver as a medium of exchange.

By the late sixteenth century China was participating in the emerging global economy. Portuguese ships carried Chinese silks and ceramics to Nagasaki and returned with Japanese silver. The huge Ming merchant marine fleet, built from the trees planted by Hong Wu and technically more

Silkworm Culture   Women traditionally handled silkworm culture, though men helped pick the mulberry leaves that fed the worms. At the left, silkworms are cultivated, graded, and harvested. At the right, the cocoons are boiled in a cauldron before the threads can be drawn, and a boy fans the fire under the pot. (*Source: Library of Congress/Laurie Platt Winfrey, Inc.*)

proficient for long sea voyages than were the Spanish and Portuguese fleets, transported textiles, porcelains, silk, and paper to Manila in the Philippines and brought back sweet potatoes, tobacco, firearms, and silver. From Manila the Spanish fleet carried Chinese goods to the markets of Barcelona, Antwerp, and Venice. The Dutch transported tea by the boatload from Fujian (Fukien) and Zhejiang (Chekiang) for the castles and drawing rooms of Europe.[6] Europeans paid for most of their imports with silver. Scholars argue that between one-third and one-half of all the silver mined in the Americas between 1527 and 1821 wound up in China. Spanish galleons carried it from Acapulco to Manila and from there to Chinese ports[7].

In the middle of the sixteenth century, China showed many signs of developing into an urban mercantile society. Merchants and businessmen had large amounts of capital, and they invested it not in land, as in the past, but in commercial and craft industries. Silk making, cotton weaving, porcelain manufacture, printing, and steel production assumed a definite industrial character. So many peasants seeking employment migrated to the towns that agriculture declined. Some businesses employed several hundred workers, many of them women. According to a French scholar, "Peasant women took jobs at Sung-chiang, southwest of Shanghai in the cotton mills. According to contemporary descriptions, in the big workshops the employees were already the anonymous labor force that we regard as characteristic of the industrial age."[8]

Technical treatises reveal considerable progress in manufacturing procedures. Silk looms had three or four shuttle winders. Printers could produce a sheet of paper with three or four different colors, similar to the page of a modern magazine. Chinese ceramics displayed astonishing technology—which helps explain the huge demand for them. Likewise, agricultural treatises described new machines for working the soil, sowing seed, and irrigation. Population, which stood at roughly 70 million at the start of the Ming period, increased to about 130 million by 1600.

With population, technology, and capital, why did China fail to develop something comparable to what Westerners later called an industrial or commercial revolution? The traditional Chinese value system did not esteem commerce, industry, or social change.

China never experienced a scientific revolution or an Enlightenment, as the European West did in the seventeenth and eighteenth centuries (Ch. 18). Lacking a spirit that criticized existing ideas and institutions, China remained culture bound and conservative. The Chinese practice of partible inheritance in which sons divided parents' estates thwarted, or at least slowed, the accumulation of capital. (The English system of primogeniture by which only the eldest son inherited promoted the accumulation of capital.) Likewise, the extensive pursuit of the Confucian civil service examinations as the path to socio-economic advancement diverted capital from industrial, technical, and even agricultural innovation. The fundamental axiom that China, the Central Kingdom of the universe, was superior to other states and contained within its borders all that was needed for a happy existence likewise discouraged change.

Hostility to the artisan and merchant classes had very deep roots in traditional China. The sixth century B.C. scholar Han Fei had listed merchants and craftsmen among "The Five Vermin of the State," writing:

An enlightened ruler will administer his state in such a way as to decrease the number of merchants, artisans and other men who make their living by wandering from place to place, and will see to it that such men are looked down upon. In this way he lessens the number of people who abandon primary pursuits (agriculture) to take up secondary occupations. . . . When wealth and money, no matter how dishonestly gotten, can buy what is in the market, you may be sure that the number of merchants will not remain small. . . . These are the customs of a disordered state.[9]

Revering such classical Confucian texts, officials in the seventeenth and eighteenth centuries looked on merchants with distrust and distaste.

Wealth was based on agriculture, and from agriculture the state derived its taxes and the ruling class its income. Could trade and manufacturing also be taxed? No, they could not. According to Confucian philosophy, any promotion of trade would encourage people to aspire to a different lifestyle and to a higher social status, and such aspirations would bring change and social disorder. Moreover, Chinese thinkers held that merchants produced nothing: they bought something from its grower or maker and sold it at a higher price than they had paid; thus they were parasites living off the labor of others. In addition, the proliferation of luxury goods, which people did not really need, would lead to extravagance and excessive consumption and in turn to moral decay.

Believing that virtue lies in frugality, vice in extravagance, the Ming emperors issued sumptuary laws restricting or prohibiting certain styles of clothing, tableware, means of conveyance, and articles of household decoration. The effect of these laws, however, was *increased* social stratification: the richer became richer, the poor poorer. Nevertheless, the Confucian ideal remained intact: a "successful merchant" was, by definition, one who had stopped trading and had invested his wealth in agriculture.[10] By contrast, in England, and later in western and central Europe, the upper middle classes gained increasing influence in representative assemblies and passed laws that facilitated commerce, business, and industry.

In 1600 the Ming Dynasty faced grave political and economic problems. The Manchus, a Tungusic people from Manchuria, threatened from the north. Wars against the Japanese and Koreans had depleted the imperial treasury. As rich landowners bought up the lands assigned to farm families, the social structures set up by Hong Wu broke down. The military, considered a disreputable profession, attracted the dregs of society, so the government had to hire mercenaries. According to the Italian Jesuit missionary Matteo Ricci (1552–1610), "All those under arms lead a despicable life, for they have not embraced this profession out of love of their country or devotion to their king or love of honour and glory, but as men in the service of a provider of employment."[11] Maintenance of the army placed a heavy burden on the state.

Meanwhile, the imperial court continued to squander vast sums on an ostentatious lifestyle. Under the emperor Wan-li, forty-five princes of the first rank received annual incomes of 10,000 shih (the money equivalent of 10,000 tons of grain), and 21,000 lesser nobles also received large allowances. The emperors increased domestic sales taxes, established customs posts for export-import duties, and laid ever-more-crushing taxes on the peasants. New taxes provoked violent riots in the large commercial centers of Suzhou (Soochow), Hangzhou (Hangchow), and Beijing.

Finally, the emperors became the victims of the bureaucracy and of Confucian ideology. A Ming emperor was taught that his primary duties were to venerate the heavens, the abode of his ancestors who watched over him; and to follow the precedents set by his ancestors. As long as the emperor performed certain time-honored rituals, he retained the Mandate of Heaven, the traditional legitimization of Chinese rulers. Imperial ritual connected the ordinary person to the state by inspiring awe, respect and loyalty. Thus successive emperors spent a large part of each day in the performance of imperial ceremonies which they began to resent.

The dynastic shift from the Ming to the Qing (Ch'ing) Dynasty established by the Manchus seemed to fulfill the Han Confucian doctrine that history operates in a cyclical fashion. The Ming emperor apparently had forfeited the Mandate of Heaven. According to Han Confucian scholars, a wise ruler satisfies Heaven's mandate by observing the proper Confucian rites of social intercourse. If the emperor is respectful to his parents, attentive to his ministers, and concerned for his subjects, then the empire and the civilized world will flourish. The emperor was supposed to be a model. If he was virtuous, his officials were likely to be so too. If he looked to his own self-interest, his civil servants would probably do likewise, to the cost of the general welfare: corruption would spread, taxes would be oppressive, and peasants would revolt.

The reign of Wan-li (r. 1573–1619), who ruled longer than any other member of the Ming Dynasty, illustrates what happened when the emperor was at odds with the system. An intelligent man with some good ideas, Wan-li felt that the bureaucrats opposed everything he wanted to do. When he tried to increase the size of the army and to improve its effectiveness through drills and maneuvers, civil service officials sent him lengthy petitions calling for an end to such exercises. When he wanted to take personal command of the army at a time of foreign invasion, bureaucrats told him that precedent forbade his leaving the Imperial City. Wan-li gradually reached the conclusion that the monarchy had become no more than a set of stylized performances.

Stymied in whatever he wanted to do, he simply refused to make state decisions. He devoted his time to his horses and, though still a young man, to the construction of his tomb. Imperial decisions were postponed. Factional strife among the court eunuchs and bureaucrats increased. The wheels of government ground to a halt.[12] Between 1619 and 1627, greedy court eunuchs helped precipitate a crisis. The eunuch Wei Zhong-xian (1568–1627) exercised a two-year reign of terror and sent hundreds of honest civil servants to their deaths as conspirators. The bureaucracy, which the eunuchs controlled, was so torn by factions that it could not function.

Meanwhile, the Manchus pressed against China's northeastern border. Under their leader Nurhachi (1559–1626), they built a powerful military and administrative organization and gained the allegiance of the Mongols and other tribes. As the Ming government in Beijing floundered, public anger at bureaucratic corruption mounted. The gentry and business classes, centered in the south around Nanjing, had been alienated by the Ming court's fiscal mismanagement and demands for more taxes. Ming troops, their pay in arrears, turned outlaw. Droughts led to crop failures, which in turn caused widespread famines. Starving peasants turned to banditry, and entire provinces revolted. The general decay paved the way for Manchu conquest.

In the popular understanding of the Mandate of Heaven, the natural and political orders were closely linked. Events such as droughts, famines, earthquakes, floods, and volcanic eruptions were considered signs of Heaven's displeasure and signaled that conditions were ripe for the appearance of a new dynasty. Predictably, when it seemed that the Mandate of Heaven had been withdrawn from the Ming emperor and was about to redescend on someone worthy, ambitious generals, bandit warlords, and popular movements appeared. According to a modern historian, "The prospect of a new mandate feverishly excited rebellions, which seemed in turn to prove that the previous dynastic cycle had reached its term."[13] Such events had accompanied the collapse of the Yuan and the rise of the Ming. Similar developments greeted the fall of the Ming and the emergence of the Manchus.

Manchu Rule

Capitalizing on the internal weaknesses of the Ming, in 1644 the Manchus declared a new dynasty, the Qing. They went on to capture Beijing and slowly gained control of all China. Although various Ming princes and local bandit groups had

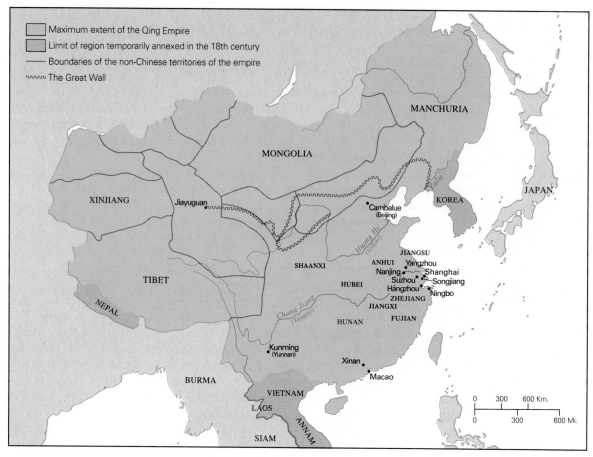

Maximum extent of the Qing Empire
Limit of region temporarily annexed in the 18th century
Boundaries of the non-Chinese territories of the empire
The Great Wall

❋ **MAP 22.1 The Qing Empire, 1759** The sheer size of the Qing Empire in China almost inevitably led to its profound cultural influence on the rest of Asia. What geographical and political factors limited the extent of the empire?

risen against the Manchus, the army lacked good equipment and staying power and gradually collapsed. The entry of the Manchus' imperial armies into Yunnan in 1681 marked their complete military triumph.

By purging the civil service of the old court eunuchs and troublesome factions, and by offering Chinese intellectuals positions in the bureaucracy, the Manchus gained the support of the influential academic and intellectual classes. Chinese scholars flocked to Beijing. The Manchu government, staffed by able and honest Chinese, became much more efficient than the Ming.

The Qing Dynasty—the name adopted by the Manchus means "pure" or "unsullied"—ruled until 1912. In its heyday in the eighteenth century, the Qing Empire covered much of Asia—China proper, Manchuria, Mongolia, Tibet, and Xinjiang

(Sinkiang)—and enjoyed tribute from Burma, Nepal, Laos, Siam, Annam, and Korea (Map 22.1). China had the largest population on earth and achieved an unprecedented degree of prosperity.

How did a million Manchus govern 350 million Chinese? The Qing Dynasty retained the basic structures of Ming and Confucian government. The emperor, possessor of the Mandate of Heaven, governed as a supreme and autocratic ruler. The bureaucracies continued as they had in Ming and earlier times: the imperial household bureaucracy managed the emperor's palaces and households; the central bureaucracy administered his vast empire. Most positions in the empire were assigned on the basis of candidates' performances in the civil service examinations in the Confucian classics. The highest positions in Beijing and in the provinces of China were open to Chinese as well as to Manchus. These measures pacified the Chinese economic and intellectual elites. The Manchus, however, maintained a privileged status in society. They wore distinctive clothes, did not practice footbinding, retained their own language and alphabet, and maintained ethnic separatism by forbidding intermarriage with the Chinese. The Manchus required Chinese males to wear their hair in a pigtail as a sign of subservience.

Along with the agricultural improvements begun in the Ming period, internal peace, relative prosperity, and engineering methods that prevented flooding of the countryside contributed to a population explosion in the eighteenth century, as the statistics in Table 22.2 illustrate. But in the late eighteenth century growth without increased agricultural output led to rebellions and uprisings that eventually weakened the Qing Dynasty.

The reign of the emperor Kang-xi (r. 1662–1722) launched a period of great achievement. A contemporary of the Indian ruler Aurangzeb, the French king Louis XIV, and the Russian tsar Peter the Great, Kang-xi demonstrated exceptional intelligence, energy, and concern for the welfare of his people. He also enjoyed much greater freedom of action than had the Ming emperor Wan-li a century earlier. Whereas Wan-li had been a captive of precedent, incapable of making changes, Kang-xi cut both court expenses and taxes and traveled extensively throughout his domain. On these trips he investigated the conduct of local bureaucrats in an effort to prevent them from oppressing the people. Kang-xi squarely faced and thoroughly crushed a massive rebellion in southern China in 1678. He personally led an army into Mongolia and smashed the forces of the Mongol leader Galdan. This victory permanently eliminated the danger of a reinvigorated Mongolian empire on China's borders.

Kang-xi also cultivated the arts of peace. He invited scholars to his court and subsidized the compilation of a huge encyclopedia and two monumental dictionaries. *The Complete Library of the Four Treasuries,* a collection of all of Chinese literature, required the work of 15,000 calligraphers and 361 editors. It preserved the Chinese literary tradition. Kang-xi's contributions to literature hold a distinguished place in the long history of Chinese culture. Europeans and Americans, however, appreciate this period primarily for its excellent porcelain. An imperial factory at Jiangxi (Kiangsi), directly controlled by Kang-xi's court, produced porcelain masterpieces. Monochrome vases, bowls,

TABLE 22.2 POPULATION OF CHINA, 1578–1989

Year	Government	Population (in millions)	
		Families	Individuals
1578	Ming Dynasty	10.6	60.7
1662	Qing Dynasty	19.2	100.0
1710		23.3	116.0
1729		25.5	127.0
1741			143.4
1754			184.5
1778			243.0
1796			275.7
1814			374.6
1850			414.5
1953	People's Republic		601.9
1974			800.0
1989			1,064.0

and dishes in oxblood, pale green, and dark blue, and polychromes in blue and white, enjoyed great popularity in Paris, London, and New York in the eighteenth century and ever since.

The long reign of the emperor Qian-long (r. 1736–1795) marked the zenith of the Qing Dynasty. The cultivation of new crops from the Americas—white potatoes, corn, peanuts—on marginal lands helped to support the steadily expanding population. Chinese rule was extended into central Asia. The imperial court continued to support arts and letters. In the last two decades of his reign, however, Qian-long showered titles, gifts, and offices on a handsome young Manchu named He-shen. Contemporaries considered He-shen uncultured, greedy, and ambitious. The corruption of the imperial civil service under He-shen, combined with heavy taxation, sparked revolts that continued to the end of the dynasty in 1912.

✺ **The Qianlong Emperor at an Archery Contest**   Executed by the Italian Jesuit Giuseppe Castiglione, whose portraits and panoramas combine Chinese composition with Western perspective and coloration, this painting—with the elegant garden, stately uniforms of the attendants, and dignified image of the emperor—suggests the formal ritual of the imperial court. Castiglione was a special favorite of the Qianlong emperor, who also supported Jesuit architects and designers. *(Source: A private collection/Photo: Wan-go Weng)*

External Pressures

By the middle years of the eighteenth century, Qianlong also faced increasing foreign pressures. In the north and northwest, the region from which invaders had historically entered China, Mongols, Russians, and ethnic minority peoples pressed the borders. Christian missionaries, notably the Jesuits, wanted greater scope for their proselytizing activities. Nearby Asian countries that had many cultural affinities with China—Korea, Burma, Siam, Vietnam—desired greater trade with China. So, too, did European merchants: the European demand for Chinese silk, porcelain, and tea was enormous. The British East India Company, for example, had by 1740 become an international corporation with global activities, backed by eager investors in Great Britain. What was the response of the imperial government to these increasing foreign pressures?

The Qing government had no ministry of foreign affairs. Chinese relations with all foreign countries reflected the Chinese belief that China was the "central kingdom" and that all other countries were "peripheral" and removed from the cultural center of the universe. The Office of Border Affairs conducted relations with peoples in the northwest crescent (Mongols and Russians). It took police action when necessary and used the marriages of imperial daughters as the means of making alliance and maintaining peace in the north. Acting on the theory that religious evangelization by foreigners reflected on the prestige of the emperor, the imperial household itself supervised the activities of Jesuit missionaries. The Ministry of Rituals managed commercial relations with the nations of East Asia. Business delegations from Korea, Burma, Siam were termed "tribute missions." As long as they used a language of subservience to the emperor and his ministers and made the ritual prostrations, they were allowed limited amounts of trade with China in precisely defined times and places—in the port of Canton from October to March.[14] As mentioned above, the Chinese value system did not respect business and commerce and distrusted traders.

Sniffing fat profits to be made from expanded trade, the aggressive merchants of London and Liverpool could not comprehend the Chinese attitude. Accordingly, the British East India Company, with the support of King George III's government, resolved on a personal appeal to Qian-long through a delegation headed by an experienced diplomat, Lord George Macartney. Three ships sailed from Portsmouth in September 1792 carrying rich gifts for the emperor: a huge imperial state coach fashioned after George III's own vehicle; a variety of heavily jeweled pocket, wrist, and neck watches; and a planetarium, a working model of the entire solar system. The dazzling array of gifts was intended to show that England was the most scientifically advanced and economically powerful nation on earth. Delivered in a diamond-encrusted gift box, George III's respectful letter to the emperor stated in part:

His Most Sacred Majesty George III . . . to the Supreme Emperor of China Qianlong, worthy to live tens of thousands and tens of thousands thousand years, sendeth

Greeting . . .

We have been still more anxious to inquire into the arts and manners of countries where civilization has been perfected by the wise ordinances and virtuous examples of their Sovereigns thro a long series of ages; and, above all, Our ardent wish had been to become acquainted with those celebrated institutions of Your Majesty's populous and extensive Empire which have carried its prosperity to such a height as to be the admiration of all surrounding nations. . . .

We have the happiness of being at peace with all the World . . . Many of our subjects have also frequented for a long time past a remote part of your *Majesty's dominions for the purpose of Trade. No doubt the interchange of commodities between Nations distantly situated tends to their mutual convenience, industry, and wealth.*[15]

The letter went on to ask for the establishment of permanent Chinese-British diplomatic relations; broader trade, including the opening of new ports for international commerce; and a fair system of tariffs or customs duties.

The mission that reached Canton in June 1793 (the long journey is an indication of the time involved in eighteenth-century travel) almost floundered over the issue of ritual and procedure. Court officials agreed that Macartney might see the emperor at his summer palace, if the British emissaries acknowledged that they came as a "tributary nation" and performed the *kowtow*—kneeling and striking their heads on the ground nine times in front of the emperor. Macartney protested that he was not required to show such obeisance even to George III. A compromise was finally reached when Macartney agreed to bow on one knee as he would bow to his English sovereign. Qian-long however, was not pleased. The ruler of China considered himself supreme and all other kings his subordinates. Though thoroughly courteous to his guests, he denied all their requests (see Listening to the Past).

The Macartney mission represented the clash of two different cultures. On the one side was China, "an immobile empire," convinced of its superiority, opposed to all innovation, and convinced that the ancient Confucian texts contained the answers to all problems. On the other side was Great Britain, equally convinced of its superiority "because it was modern: founded on science, the free exchange of ideas, and the mastery of commercial exchange."[16] Understanding and communication proved impossible.

The Life of the People

The family is the fundamental unit of every society. In Ming and Qing China, however, the family exercised greater social influence than it did anywhere else—and far more than in Western societies. The family directed the moral education of the child, the economic advancement and marriage of the young, and religious life through ceremonial rites honoring family ancestors. The Chinese family discharged many of the roles that the Christian church performed in Europe in the Middle Ages and that the state carries out today. It assumed total responsibility for the sick, the indigent, and the aged. The family expected and almost invariably received the full devotion and loyalty of its members. A person without a family had no material or psychological support.

Poor families tended to be nuclear: couples established their own households and raised their own children. The educated, the middle class, and the wealthy frequently resided in extended families: several generations of patrilineal relatives and their wives lived together in one large house or compound, individual families occupying different sections. In both kinds of families, the paternal head of the family held autocratic power over all members of the household. Apart from crimes against the emperor and his family, the worst crimes were those committed by children against their parents. Fathers who harmed their sons received lighter punishment than sons who harmed (or even insulted) their fathers. In one instance the Ministry of Punishments reviewed a local governor's sentence that a father be beaten for burying his son alive. The son had used foul language to his father. The ministry concluded that "although the killing (by the father) was done intentionally, it was the killing of a son who had committed a capital crime by reviling his father. The father was acquitted."[17] When a father died, his authority over the household passed to his eldest son.

The father led the family in the ancient Confucian rites honoring the family ancestors. If these ceremonies were not continued by the next generation, the family suffered social disgrace and, it was believed, the dead endured great misery. Thus marriage and childbearing were extremely important.

Almost everyone married. Reverence for one's parents, maintenance of the family, and perpetuation of the line required that sons marry shortly after reaching puberty. The father and family elders discussed the possibilities and employed a local go-between to negotiate with the prospective bride's family. The go-between drew up a marriage contract specifying the property, furniture, clothing, and gifts that the two young people would bring to the union. As elsewhere, parents wanted to make the most economically and socially advantageous union for their children. The couple had no part in these arrangements. Often they had never met each other until the groom lifted the bride's

veil on their wedding day. But they had been brought up to accept this custom.

A Chinese bride became part of her husband's family, subject to him and to her in-laws. Her first duty was to bear sons. If she did not, she might adopt a son. Failure to provide heirs gave her husband grounds for divorce, which brought great disgrace on her family. A woman, however, could not divorce her husband for any reason. Divorce was extremely rare in Chinese society, but a wealthy man with a "nonproductive" wife might bring concubines to live in the house along with his wife.

Men held a much higher position in society than did women. The desperately poor often killed girl babies or sold their daughters as servants or concubines. Young brides came under the direct control of their mothers-in-law, whose severity and cruelty are a common theme in Chinese literature. Once a strong-willed woman had sons, she gained increasing respect as the years went by. The Chinese deeply respected age. Some women of the wealthy classes, with servants to do the household chores, spent their days in semiseclusion nibbling dainties, smoking opium, and gambling. Women who brought large dowries to their marriages could dispose of part of those dowries as they wished. Some invested in profitable business activities. Poor women worked in the fields beside their husbands, in addition to bearing children and managing the household.

The educational system during the Ming and Qing periods had both virtues and weaknesses. Most villages and all towns and cities operated schools that prepared boys for the all-important civil service examinations. Boys learned to write with a brush the approximately three thousand commonly used characters of literary Chinese; and they learned the standard texts of Confucian philosophy, ethics, and history. The curriculum was very limited, and the instructional method stressed memorization and discouraged imagination. The civil service aspirant received no practical training in the work of government. But the system yielded a high percentage of literate men (relative to Europe at the same time) and gave Chinese society cohesion and stability. All educated Chinese shared the same basic ethical and literary culture, much as medieval Europeans were formed by Latin Christian culture.

In China, as in medieval Europe, educational opportunities for girls were severely limited. Rich men occasionally hired tutors for their daughters, and a few women achieved exceptional knowledge. Most women of all classes received training that prepared them for roles as wives and mothers: courteous behavior, submission to their husbands, and the administration of a household.

What of health and medical care in imperial China? Although Egyptian and Babylonian medicine predate Chinese medicine by perhaps a millennium, the Chinese medical tradition is the oldest continuing usage in the world. Chinese medical theory deriving from the Han period (from the third century B.C. to the third century A.D.) attributes all ailments to a lack of harmony in the body; cure, then, rests on restoring harmony. Diagnosis of disease depended on visual observation, studying the case history, auditory symptoms, and taking the pulse. Physicians held that three spots along the wrist gave the pulse readings of different organs, and the experienced physician could diagnose the malfunction of any internal organ by checking the pulse. Two basic forms of therapy (treatment) existed. Medicinal therapy was based on the curative effects of herbs. This treatment entailed taking pills or powders in a boiled broth. The other therapy was acupuncture, the insertion of needles into specific parts of the body.

The theory behind acupuncture was that twelve channels run over the body close to the skin, each channel is related to a specific organ, and the needle stimulates a sluggish or pacifies an overactive organ. The acupuncturist used fine needles and avoided vital organs. Certainly acupuncture was no more dangerous than the widespread European practice of bleeding.

Reliance on acupuncture and the Confucian principle that the body is the sacred gift of parents to child made dissection a terrible violation of filial piety and thus strongly discouraged serious surgery. Another factor militating against surgery was the Chinese culture's disdain for manual work of any kind. A "wise" doctor mastered a body of classical texts, prescribed medicine for treatment, and "did not lower himself to perform manual, surgical operations."[18] Nor should a doctor accept fees for service.

Confucian policy did not allow any experts with specialized knowledge to rise socially as a group: social mobility, it was thought, led to social tensions and demands for restructuring.[19] Thus, while physicians in the Islamic and European worlds enjoyed respect and sometimes modest wealth, the

Ch'en Shu: The White Cockatoo   Like Italy and France in the early modern period, China and Japan can boast of distinguished women artists. This painting in ink and color on a hanging scroll depicts a highly prized species of parrot. The work by Ch'en Shu, a Chinese artist famous in her time, is very much in the Chinese artistic tradition. (*Source: The Metropolitan Museum of Art, 13.220.31*)

position of Chinese doctors was deemed insignificant, and they were considered mere artisans. Rather than consulting medical experts, each person had to acquire sufficient knowledge, including pharmacological knowledge, to help members of his or her family in time of illness.

Several emperors decreed that medical colleges should be established and that annual examinations should test physicians' skills so that the needs of the people, as well as the needs of the imperial court, would be served. But these orders were never implemented. As a result, although the idea of state-supported hospitals was an ancient one in China, the first institutions to provide medical care for the sick of a community were established by

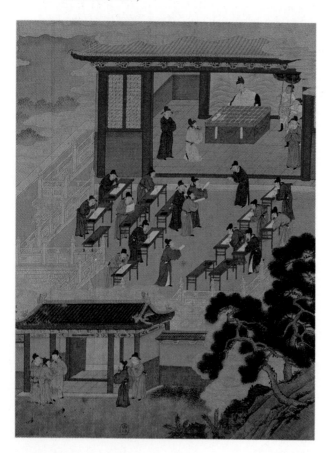

Chinese Scholars The civil service examinations, the chief means of access to government positions and social status, inculcated total submission to the autocratic state. The largest number of candidates took the examinations in general knowledge and literary ability. Here candidates stand at writing desks, composing essays. (*Source: Bibliothèque Nationale, Paris*)

Christian medical missionaries in the nineteenth century.

In sharp contrast to Europe, China had few social barriers. The emperors fought the development of a hereditary aristocracy which could have undermined their absolute monarchy, and they granted very few titles of nobility in perpetuity. Though China had no legally defined aristocracy, she did have an "upper class" based on a *combination* of wealth, education, lineage, and bureaucratic position. Agricultural land remained the most highly prized form of wealth, but silver ingots, jade, libraries of classical works, porcelain, and urban real estate also indicated status. Wealth alone, however, did not bring status. Offices in the state bureaucracy provided opportunities and motivation for upward mobility. Family members encouraged intelligent sons to prepare for the civil service examinations, and the work and sacrifice of parents bore fruit in their sons' success. Positions in the bureaucracy brought salaries and gifts which a family invariably invested in land. The competitive examinations with few exceptions were open to all classes, and that accessibility prevented the formation of a ruling caste. China did not develop a politically articulate bourgeoisie. Because everyone accepted the Confucian principle that the learned and civilized should rule the state, scholars ranked highest in the social order. They, along with Heaven, Earth, the emperor, parents deserved special veneration. With the possible exception of the Jewish people, no people has respected learning as much as the Chinese. Merchants tried to marry into the scholar class in order to rise in the world. At the bottom of society were actors, prostitutes, and beggars.

The Chinese found recreation and relaxation in many ways. All classes gambled at cards and simple numbers games. The teahouse served as the local meeting place for exchanging news and gossip and listening to the tales of professional storytellers, who enjoyed great popularity. The affluent indulged in an alcoholic drink made from fermented and distilled rice, and both men and women liked pipes and tobacco. Everyone who could afford to do so went to the theater. The actors, like their ancient Greek counterparts, wore happy and sad masks, and their gestures were formal and stylized. The plays typically dramatized episodes from Chinese history and literature. The Chinese associated athletics, riding, and horse racing with soldiers, at best a necessary evil, and regarded the active life as

Chinese Cookery Everywhere in the world, until very recently, meat was scarce and thus a luxury. In China, the shortage of meat encouraged great sophistication in the preparation of foods, especially vegetables. Although European travelers interpreted the frequent servings of vegetables and fish as a sign of poverty, the Chinese, if we can trust modern nutritionists, probably had a healthier diet than the Europeans. Notice the variety of dishes. Women obviously ate separately from men. (*Source: Roger-Viollet*)

the direct antithesis of the scholarly contemplation they most valued.

JAPAN (CA 1400–1800)

The Ashikaga Shogunate lasted from the middle of the fourteenth to the late sixteenth century. During this period, Japanese society experienced almost continual violence and civil war. Weak central governments could not maintain order. Throughout the islands, local strongmen took charge. Around 1450, 250 *daimyos,* or lords, held power; by 1600, only 12 survivors could claim descent from daimyo families of the earlier date. Successful military leaders carved out large territories and governed them as independent rulers. Political and social conditions in fifteenth- and sixteenth-century Japan strongly resembled conditions in western Europe in the tenth and eleventh centuries. Political power was in the hands of a small group of military leaders. Historians often use the same term—*feudalism*—to describe the Japanese and the European experience. As in medieval Europe, feudalism paved the way for the rise of a strong centralized state in seventeenth-century Japan.

Feudalism in Japan

Feudalism played a powerful role in Japanese culture until the nineteenth century. The similarities between feudalism in Japan and in medieval Europe have fascinated scholars, as have the very significant differences. In Europe, feudalism emerged out of the fusion of Germanic and Roman social institutions and flowered under the impact of Muslim and Viking invasions. In Japan, feudalism evolved from a combination of the native warrior tradition and Chinese Confucian ethics. Japanese society had adopted the Confucian emphasis on filial respect for the head of the family, for the local civil authorities, and for the supreme authority at the head of the state.

The two constituent elements of Japanese feudalism appeared between the eighth and the twelfth centuries: (1) the *shoen* (private land outside imperial control) with its *shiki* (rights) and (2) the *samurai* (the military warrior clique). Some scholars have equated the shoen with the European manor, but the comparison needs careful qualification. A manor usually corresponded to one composite village; a particular family's shoen was widely scattered. Those who held shoen possessed the shiki there—that is, the right to the income or rice produced by the land. But, just as several persons might hold rights—military, judicial, grazing—on a medieval European manor and all these rights yielded income, so several persons frequently held shiki rights on a Japanese estate.

By the sixteenth century, only a small proportion of samurai had attained the rank of daimyo and possessed a shoen. Most warriors were salaried

Women Husking Rice   Rice was basic to Japanese culture. Farmers paid their taxes to the daimyo's agent in rice, and the daimyo paid the salaries of the samurai in rice. It was the staple of the diet eaten by all classes. Here women husk the rice, separate the grains from the chaff using a primitive machine, and clean and pack the rice in bales made of rice stalks. (*Source: Laurie Platt Winfrey, Inc.*)

fighters with no connection to land. From their daimyos, they received stipends in rice, not in land; and in this respect they resembled European knights, who were supported by cash or money fiefs.

The Japanese samurai warrior resembled the knight of twelfth-century France in other ways as well. Both were armed with expensive weapons, and both fought on horseback. Just as the knight was supposed to live according to the chivalric code, so Japanese samurai were expected to live according to *Bushido,* or "Way of the Warrior," a code that stressed military honor, courage, stoic acceptance of hardship, and, above all, loyalty. Disloyalty brought social disgrace, which the samurai could avoid only through *seppuku,* ritual suicide by slashing his belly. Both samurai and knights were highly conscious of themselves as aristocrats. But knights fought as groups, and samurai fought as individuals.

By the middle of the sixteenth century Japanese feudalism had taken on other distinctive features. As the number of shoen decreased and the powerful daimyos consolidated their territories, the prac-

tice of *primogeniture* became common, keeping an estate intact under the eldest or ablest son. Around 1540 the introduction of the musket from Europe made infantrymen effective against mounted samurai, and the use of Western cannon required more elaborately fortified castles. Thus, in addition to armed cavalrymen, daimyos began to employ large numbers of foot soldiers equipped with spears, and they constructed new castles. These military and social developments occurred during a century of turbulence and chronic disorder, out of which emerged a leader who ended the chaos and began the process of unification, laying the foundation of the modern Japanese national state.

Nobunaga and National Unification

Oda Nobunaga (1534–1582), a samurai of the lesser daimyo class, won control of his native province of Owari in 1559. He began immediately to extend his power, defeating a powerful daimyo in 1560 and eight years later seizing Kyoto, the capital city, where the emperor and his court resided. As a result, Nobunaga became the virtual ruler of central Japan.

Scholars have called the years from 1568 to 1600 the period of "national unification." During this time Japan underwent aggressive and dynamic change. Adopting the motto "Rule the empire by force," Nobunaga set out to subdue all real and potential rivals and to replace them with his vassals. With the support of Toyotomi Hideyoshi (1537–1598), a brilliant general, he subdued first western and then eastern and northern Japan.

The great Buddhist temple-fortresses proved to be Nobunaga's biggest problem. Some of these monasteries possessed vast wealth and armed retainers. During the civil wars the Buddhists had supported various daimyos in their private wars, but Nobunaga would tolerate no such interference. The strategically located monastery on Mount Hiei near Kyoto had long provided sanctuary for political factions. Previous daimyos had refused to attack it because it was sacred. Nobunaga, however, used fire to reduce it, and his men slaughtered thousands of its occupants.

Although Nobunaga won control of most of Japan by the sword, he backed up his conquests with government machinery and a policy of conciliation. He gave lands and subordinate positions in the army to his defeated enemies. Trusted daimyos received complete civil jurisdiction over entire provinces. At strategic points, such as Nijo near Kyoto and Azuchi on the shore of Lake Biwa, Nobunaga built castles to serve as key administrative and defensive centers for the surrounding territories. He opened the little fishing village of Nagasaki to foreign commerce; it soon grew into the nation's largest port. He standardized the currency, eliminated customs barriers, and encouraged the development of trade and industry. In 1582, when Nobunaga was murdered by one of his vassals, his general and staunchest adherent, Hideyoshi, carried on his work.

A peasant's son who had risen to power by his military bootstraps, Hideyoshi advanced the unification and centralization of Japan in two important ways. First, in 1582 he attacked the great fortress at Takamatsu. When direct assault failed, his troops flooded the castle and forced its surrender. When Takamatsu fell, so did the large province of Mori. A successful siege of the town of Kagoshima then brought the southern island of Kyushu under his domination. Hideyoshi soothed the vanquished daimyos as Nobunaga had done—with lands and military positions—but he also required them to swear allegiance and to obey him "down to the smallest particular."[20]

Having reduced his most dangerous adversaries, Hideyoshi ordered a survey of the entire country. The military power of the unified Japanese state depended on a strong agricultural base, and Hideyoshi wanted to exploit the peasantry fully. His agents collected detailed information about the daimyos' lands and about towns, villages, agricultural produce, and industrial output all over Japan. This material enabled Hideyoshi to assess military quotas and taxable property. His surveys tied the peasant population to the land and tightened the collection of the land tax. When Hideyoshi died in 1598, he left a strong centralized state. Brute force had created a unified Japan.

On his deathbed the old soldier had set up a council of regents to govern during the minority of his infant son. The strongest regent was Hideyoshi's long-time supporter Tokugawa Ieyasu (1543–1616), who ruled vast territories around Edo (modern-day Tokyo). Ieyasu quickly eliminated the young ruler and in 1600 at Sekigahara smashed a coalition of daimyo defenders of the heir. This battle was the beginning of the Tokugawa regime.

The Tokugawa Regime

Japanese children are taught that "Ieyasu ate the pie that Nobunaga made and Hideyoshi baked." As the aphorism suggests, Ieyasu took over and completed the work begun by his able predecessors. He took decisive steps to solidify his dynasty and control the feudal nobility and to maintain peace and prosperity in Japan. The Tokugawa regime that Ieyasu fashioned worked remarkably well, lasting until 1867.

Ieyasu obtained from the emperor the title of *shogun,* or general-in-chief. Constitutionally, the emperor exercised sovereign authority. In practice, authority and power—both the legal right and the physical means—were held by the Tokugawa shogun. Ieyasu declared the emperor and his court at Kyoto "very precious and decorative, like gold and silver," and surrounded the imperial court with all the ceremonial trappings but none of the realities of power.

In a scheme resembling the later residency requirements imposed by Louis XIV (see page 560)

✳ **Tokugawa Ieyasu**   A short, stocky man who had spent most of his life on horseback, Ieyasu was sixty-two when he secured appointment as shogun. Having unified Japan and established a peace that lasted 250 years, he ranks with George Washington and Peter the Great of Russia as one of the great nation builders in world history. In this iconic style of Shinto painting, the elderly Ieyasu is depicted as a deity. *(Source: The Tokugawa Foundation)*

and Peter the Great (see page 581), Ieyasu forced the feudal lords to establish "alternate residence" at his capital city of Edo, to spend part of each year there, and to leave their wives and sons there—essentially as hostages. This requirement had obvious

advantages: the shogun could keep close tabs on the daimyos, control them through their children, and weaken them financially with the burden of maintaining two residences. Ieyasu justified this course of action by invoking the *Bushido* code, with its emphasis on loyalty. He forbade members of the nobility to marry without his consent, thus preventing the formation of dangerous alliances.

The early Tokugawa shoguns also restricted the construction of castles—symbols, in Japan as in medieval Europe, of feudal independence. Later, the practice of alternate residence led to considerable castle building, castles that represented demands for goods and services and which turned Edo and other cities into huge commercial centers. Members of the aristocratic class exercised full administrative powers within their domains. In effect, the country was governed by martial law in peacetime. Only warriors could hold official positions in the state bureaucracy. A network of spies kept close watch on those lords whose loyalty the shogun suspected.

As in medieval Europe and early modern China, the agricultural class held a respected position because its members provided Japanese society with sustenance. Even so, farmers had to mind their betters, and they bore a disproportionate share of the tax load. According to the survey made by Hideyoshi, taxes were imposed on villages, not on individuals; the tax varied between 30 and 40 percent of the rice crop. Also as in Europe and China, the commercial classes in Japan occupied the lowest rungs on the social ladder because they profited from the toil of others.

The peace that the Tokugawa Shogunate imposed brought a steady rise in population and prosperity. As demand for goods grew, so did the numbers of merchants. To maintain stability, the early Tokugawa shoguns froze the four ancient social categories: imperial court nobility, samurai, peasants, and merchants. Laws rigidly prescribed what each class could and could not do. Nobles, for example, were "strictly forbidden, whether by day or by night, to go sauntering through the streets or lanes in places where they have no business to be." Daimyos were prohibited from moving troops outside their frontiers, making alliances, and coining money. Designated dress and stiff rules of etiquette distinguished one class from another.[21] As intended, this stratification protected the Tokugawa shoguns from daimyo attack and inaugurated a long era of peace.

MAP 22.2 Tokugawa Japan   Consider the cultural and political significance of the fact that Japan is an island. How did the concentration of shogunate lands affect the shogunate's government of Japan?

In the interests of stability and peace, Ieyasu's descendants also imposed measures called *sakoku*. This "closed country policy" sealed Japan's borders around 1636. Japanese were forbidden to leave the country. Foreigners were excluded.

In 1549 the Jesuit missionary Francis Xavier had landed at Kagoshima. He soon made many converts among the poor and even some among the daimyos. By 1600 there were 300,000 baptized Christians in Japan. Most of them lived on Kyushu, the southernmost island (Map 22.2), where the shogun's power was weakest and the loyalty of the daimyos most doubtful. In 1615 bands of Christian samurai supported Ieyasu's enemies at the fierce Battle of Osaka. In 1637, 30,000 peasants in the heavily Catholic area of northern Kyushu revolted. The shoguns thus came to associate Christianity with domestic disorder and feu-dal rebellion. Accordingly, what had been mild persecution of Christians became ruthless repression after 1639. Foreign priests were expelled or tortured, and thousands of Japanese Christians suffered crucifixion. The "closed country policy" remained in force for almost two centuries. The shogunate kept Japan isolated—but not totally.

Through the Dutch factory on the tiny island of Deshima in Nagasaki harbor (see page 531), a stream of Western ideas and inventions trickled into Japan in the eighteenth century. Western writings, architectural illustrations, calendars, watches, medicine, and paintings deeply impressed the Japanese. Western portraits and other paintings introduced the Japanese to perspective and shading. When the Swedish scientist C. P. Thunberg, physician to the Dutch at Deshima, visited Nagasaki and Edo, the Japanese looked on him as a scientific oracle and plied him with questions. Japanese scholars believed that Western inventions were more efficient than their Japanese equivalents and that these inventions contributed to the prosperity of European nations. Japanese curiosity about things Western gave rise to an intellectual movement known as *rangaku,* foreign studies, which urged that these Western ideas and inventions be adopted by the Japanese.

Japanese understanding of the West was severely limited and often fanciful, as was Western knowledge of Asian civilizations. Like eighteenth-century Europeans who praised Chinese and Persian customs to call attention to shortcomings at home, Japanese scholars idealized Western conditions. Both peoples wanted to create within their countries the desire for reform and progress.[22]

The Life of the People

Two hundred years of peace is no mean achievement in the history of world societies. There is nothing comparable to it in all of medieval and modern times. Moreover, profound social and economic development occurred in spite of Japan's isolation.

The Tokugawa Shogunate subdued the nobility by emasculating it politically. Stripped of power and required to spend part of each year at Edo, the daimyos and samurai passed their lives pursuing pleasure. They spent frantically on fine silks, paintings, concubines, boys, the theater, and the redecoration of their castles. Around 1700 one scholar observed that the entire military class was living "as in an inn, that is, consuming now and pay-

Women Weaving Often working at home, women made an enormous contribution to the Japanese silk industry: their small, delicate hands (in contrast to the larger and possibly callused hands of men) seemed suited to working with fine silk threads. In an age when public-assisted child care was not dreamed of, working mothers relied on the help of female relatives, or, as here, infants were tied to mothers' backs, an added burden for mothers and probably not ideal for the child. Notice the spinning wheel in the corner and various spindles on the floor. *(Source: By kind permission of the East-West Gallery, New Hope, PA)*

A Male Prostitute He writes a poem as a female prostitute massages their patron's back. Notice the elaborate hairstyles, the rich material of the kimonos, and the boxes of writing instruments. *(Source: The Fine Arts Museums of San Francisco. Achenbach Foundation for Graphic Arts purchase, 1969. 32.20)*

ing later."[23] Eighteenth-century Japanese novels, plays, and histories portray the samurai engrossed in tavern brawls and sexual orgies. These frivolities, plus more sophisticated pleasures and the heavy costs of maintaining an alternate residence at Edo, gradually ruined the warrior class.

In traditional Japanese society, women were subordinate to men, and the civil disorders of the sixteenth century strengthened male domination. Parents in the samurai class arranged their daughters' marriages to advance family interests. Once a woman married, her life centered on her children and domestic chores. The management of a large household with several children and many servants imposed heavy responsibilities on women. An upper-class wife rarely left home unchaperoned. "Middle class" women, however, began to emerge from the home. The development of an urban commercial culture in the cities (see page 732) in the Tokugawa period led to the employment of women in silk and textile manufacture, in publishing, in restaurants and various shops, and especially in entertainment.

All major cities contained places of amusement for men—teahouses, theaters, restaurants, houses of prostitution. Desperately poor parents sometimes sold their daughters to entertainment houses, and the most attractive or talented girls, trained in singing, dancing, and conversational arts, became courtesans called *geishas,* or "accomplished persons," in modern times. The Tokugawa period saw the beginnings for men of the separation of family and business life on the one hand, and leisure and amusement on the other. That separation is still evident in Japanese society.[24]

The samurai spent heavily on kabuki theater. An art form created by townspeople, kabuki consisted of crude, bawdy skits dealing with love and romance or aspects of prostitution, an occupation in which many actors and actresses had professional experience. Performances featured elaborate costumes, song, dance, and poetry. Because actresses were thought to be corrupting the public morals, the Tokugawa government banned them from the stage in 1629. From that time on, men played all the parts. Male actors in female dress and makeup performed as seductively as possible to entice the burly samurai who thronged the theaters. Homosexuality, long accepted in Japan, was widely practiced among the samurai, who pursued the actors and spent profligately on them. According to one seventeenth-century writer:

"Youth's kabuki" began with beautiful youths being made to sing and dance, whereupon droll fools . . . had their hearts captivated and their souls stolen. . . . There were many of these men who soon had run through their fortunes.[25]

Some moralists and bureaucrats complained from time to time, but the Tokugawa government decided to accept kabuki and prostitution as necessary evils. The practices provided employment, gratified the tastes of samurai and townspeople, and diverted former warriors from potential criminal and political mischief.[26] The samurai paid for their costly pleasures in the way their European counterparts did—by fleecing the peasants and borrowing from the merchants.

According to Japanese tradition, farmers deserved respect. In practice, peasants were sometimes severely oppressed and led miserable lives. It was government policy to tax them to the level of bare subsistence, and official legislation repeatedly redefined their duties. In 1649 every village in Japan received these regulations:

Peasants are people without sense or forethought. Therefore they must not give rice to their wives and children at harvest time, but must save food for the future. They should eat millet, vegetables, and other coarse food instead of rice. Even the fallen leaves of plants should be saved as food against famine. . . . During the seasons of planting and harvesting, however, when the labor is arduous, the food taken may be a little better. . . .

They must not buy tea or sake [a fermented liquor made from rice] to drink nor must their wives.

The husband must work in the fields, the wife must work at the loom. Both must do night work. However good-looking a wife may be, if she neglects her household duties by drinking tea or sightseeing or rambling on the hillsides, she must be divorced.

Peasants must wear only cotton or hemp—no silk. They may not smoke tobacco. It is harmful to health, it takes up time, and costs money. It also creates a risk of fire.[27]

The conspicuous consumption of the upper classes led them during the seventeenth and eighteenth centuries to increase taxes from 30 or 40 percent of the rice crop to 50 percent. Merchants who bought farm produce fixed the price of rice so low that it seemed to farmers that the more they produced, the less they earned. They found release only by flight or revolt.

After 1704, peasant rebellions were chronic. Oppressive taxation provoked 84,000 farmers in the province of Iwaki to revolt in 1739. After widespread burning and destruction, their demands were met. In other instances the shoguns ordered savage repression.

Natural disasters also added to the peasants' misery. In the 1770s fires, floods, and volcanic eruptions hit all parts of Japan. Drought and torrential rain led to terrible famines between 1783 and 1788 and again between 1832 and 1836. Taxation, disaster, and oppression often combined to make the lot of peasants one of unrelieved wretchedness.

This picture of the Japanese peasantry tells only part of the story, however. Scholarship has demonstrated that in the Tokugawa period peasant society was "a pyramid of wealth and power . . . that rose from the tenant farmer at the bottom through small landholders to wealthy peasants at the top."[28] Agricultural productivity increased substantially, and assessed taxes were fixed, though they remained high. Peasants who improved their lands and increased their yields continued to pay the same assessed tax and could pocket the surplus as profit. Their social situation accordingly improved. By the early nineteenth century there existed a large class of relatively wealthy, educated, and ambitious peasant families who resembled the middle ranks of the warrior class.

Likewise, local economic conditions and family social status shaped the lives of Japanese women. The existence of a rich peasant's wife, daughter, or sister differed considerably from that of poor peasant women. The well-to-do seem to have made few distinctions in the early upbringing of male and female children. Regional prosperity determined the amounts of money spent on the education of both sexes in their early years. In the early nineteenth century the regions around flourishing Edo and Kyoto spent far more than the poor Toh-ku region; and parents in thriving areas devoted considerable sums on their daughters' education. Girls from middle-level peasant families may have had from two to five years of formal schooling. But they were thought incapable of learning the difficult

Kitagawa Utamaro: Ladies at a Tea Shop   Famous for his book of insects reflecting remarkable powers of observation, Utamaro (1753–1806) is best known for his portrayal of women in which he accented their sensuous beauty. First of the great masters of the *ukiyo-e* school, "pictures of the floating world," the dominant movement in Japanese art of the Tokugawa period, Utamaro produced wood-block prints such as this with subjects drawn from everyday life. Notice the dress of the ladies and the various activities of the servants. *(Source: Private Collection)*

Chinese characters, so their education focused on moral instruction intended to instill the virtue of obedience. Daughters of wealthy peasant families learned penmanship, the Chinese classics, poetry, and the proper forms of correspondence, and they rounded off their education with travel.[29]

Scholars of the Japanese family, like students of the late medieval and early modern European family (see pages 632–634), have explored the extent of premarital sex, the age at which people married, the frequency with which they married someone from another village, and the level of divorce. For Tokugawa Japan, considerable regional variations make broad generalizations dangerous; research continues. It is clear, however, that marriage linked families of equal status and class; Japanese marriages, therefore, strengthened economic and social divisions. This practice gave Japanese women an advantage over their Chinese counterparts: the Japanese bride had to learn the special ways of her new household, but she was unlikely to be intimidated by her new family. Chinese women married "up" into families of a higher status and thus tended to be overawed by the wealth and status of their in-laws.

On the Japanese bride fell the responsibility of bringing harmony to the household. Harmony "meant that she had to refrain from quarreling with the members of her new household, do the work expected of her position, and conform to family custom."[30] Both samurai and peasant teaching stressed that "the married couple was the foundation of morality" and that the basis for harmony in the couple rested on good connubial relations. Once the author of *Observations of Agricultural Practices,* a study of rural life, stayed overnight at a farmhouse. Newlyweds in the family went to bed early and, separated from the others by only a screen, began noisy lovemaking. "Outrageous," exclaimed the guest, whereupon the old woman of the family got angry. "Harmony between husband and wife is the basis for prosperity for the descendants. . . . I permit this coupling day and night. People who laugh at their passion are themselves outrageous. Get out!"[31] Domestic harmony and social necessity were closely linked.

A peasant wife shared with her husband responsibility for the family's economic well-being. If of poor or middling status, she worked alongside her husband in the fields, doing the routine work while he did the heavy work. If they were tenant farmers and worked for salaries, the wife invariably earned half or a third less than her husband. Wives of prosperous farmers never worked in the fields, but they spun silk, wove cloth, helped in any family business, and supervised the maids. Whatever their economic status, Japanese women, like women everywhere in the world, tended the children; they were her special responsibility. The production of children, especially sons, strengthened a wife's prestige, but among well-to-do Japanese farm women, the bride's skill in prudent household management was the most desired talent.

How was divorce initiated, and how frequent was it? Customs among the noble class differed considerably from peasant practices. Widows and divorcees of the samurai aristocracy—where female chastity was the core of fidelity—were not expected to remarry. The husband alone could initiate divorce by ordering his wife to leave or by sending her possessions to her natal home. The wife could not prevent divorce or ensure access to her children.

Among the peasant classes, divorce seems to have been fairly common—at least 15 percent in the villages near Osaka in the eighteenth century. Women as well as men could begin the procedure. Wives' reasons were husbands' drunkenness, physical abuse, or failure to support the family. Many women secured divorce from temples whose function was to dissolve marriages: if a married woman entered the temple and performed its rites for three years, her marriage bond was dissolved. Sometimes Buddhist temple priests served as divorce brokers: they went to the village headman and had him force the husband to agree to a divorce. News of the coming of temple officials was usually enough to produce a letter of separation. A poor woman wanting a divorce simply left her husband's home. Opportunities for remarriage were severely limited. Divorce in samurai society carried social stigma; it did not among the peasantry.[32]

The Tokugawa period witnessed a major transformation of agriculture, a great leap in productivity and specialization. The rural population increased, but the agricultural population did not; surplus labor was drawn to other employment and to the cities. In fact, Japan suffered an acute shortage of farm labor from 1720 to 1868. In some villages, industry became almost as important as agriculture. At Hirano near Osaka, for example, 61.7 percent of all arable land was sown in cotton. The peasants had a thriving industry: they ginned the cotton locally before transporting it to wholesalers in Osaka. In many rural places, as many peasants worked in the manufacture of silk, cotton, or veg-

etable oil as in the production of rice.[33] In theory, the urban commercial classes, scorned for benefiting from the misery of the peasants and the appetites of the samurai, occupied the bottom rung of the social ladder. Merchants had no political power, but they accumulated wealth, sometimes great wealth. They also demonstrated the possibility of social mobility and thus the inherent weakness of the regime's system of strict social stratification.

The commercial class grew in response to the phenomenal development of urban life. In the seventeenth century, the surplus rural population, together with underemployed samurai and the ambitious and adventurous, thronged to the cities. All wanted a better way of life than could be found in the dull farming villages. Japan's cities grew tremendously: Kyoto, home to the emperor and his pleasure-loving court; Edo (modern Tokyo), the political capital, with its multitudes of government bureaucrats, daimyos in alternate residence, intellectuals, and police; and Osaka, by this time the greatest commercial city in Japan, with its huge grain exchange and commercial banks. In the eighteenth century, Edo's population of almost a million represented the largest demand for goods and services in the world.

The Tokugawa shoguns turned the samurai into urban consumers by denying them military opportunities. Merchants stood ready to serve them. Towns offered all kinds of luxury goods and catered to every extravagant and exotic taste. By marketing the daimyos' grain, town merchants gave the aristocrats the cash they needed to support their rich establishments. Merchants formed guilds and banks and lent money to the samurai. Those who defaulted on their debts found themselves cut off from further credit.[34]

As the ruling samurai with their fixed stipends became increasingly poorer, the despised merchants grew steadily wealthier. By contemporary standards anywhere in the world, the Japanese "middle" class lived very well. In 1705 the shogunate confiscated the property of a merchant in Osaka "for conduct unbecoming a member of the commercial class." In fact, the confiscation was at the urging of influential daimyos and samurai who owed the merchant gigantic debts. The government seized 50 pairs of gold screens, 360 carpets, several mansions, 48 granaries and warehouses scattered around the country, and hundreds of thousands of gold pieces. This merchant possessed fabulous wealth, but other merchants too enjoyed a rich lifestyle.[35]

SUMMARY

In the eighteenth and early nineteenth centuries China experienced a rapid increase in both prosperity and population. On the basis of highly developed agriculture, the Qing Empire supported a population of 200 million in 1762 and 374 million in 1812, compared with only 193 million in all of Europe in 1800. Qing China was geographically larger than the People's Republic of China today, encompassing some of the present-day Russian federation.

China's political and economic systems began to deteriorate in the late eighteenth and early nineteenth centuries. The country suffered from excessive centralization: all local questions had to be referred to Beijing. The extravagant court was an intolerable drain on the state treasury. Graft and corruption pervaded the imperial bureaucracy, provincial administration, and army. Population explosion led to a severe land shortage, causing tension and revolts in the countryside.

In 1800 Tokugawa Japan was reaping the rewards of two centuries of peace and social order. Steady economic growth and improved agricultural technology had swelled the population. The samurai had been transformed into peaceful city dwellers and civil bureaucrats. The wealth of the business classes grew, and the samurai, dependent on fixed agricultural rents or stipends in rice in a time of rising standards of living, fell into debt. The Tokugawa regime formed submissive citizens whose discipline is apparent even today.

Although the shogunate maintained a policy of national isolation and no foreign power influenced Japan's political or social life, Japan was not really cut off from outside cultural contacts. Through the port of Nagasaki, Western scientific ideas and some Western technology entered Japan in response to the persistent interest of Japanese scholars. The Japanese readily absorbed foreign technological ideas.

NOTES

1. J. Gernet, *A History of Chinese Civilization*, trans. J. R. Foster (New York: Cambridge University Press, 1982), p. 391.
2. Ibid.
3. L. Zewen et al., *The Great Wall* (New York: McGraw-Hill, 1981), p. 140.
4. See E. L. Dreyer, *Early Ming China: A Political History, 1355–1435* (Stanford, Calif.: Stanford University Press, 1982), pp. 194–205.
5. R. Huang, *1587: A Year of No Significance: The Ming Dynasty in Decline* (New Haven, Conn.: Yale University Press, 1981), p. 13.
6. J. E. Wills, Jr., "Maritime China from Wang Chih to Shih Long," in *From Ming to Ch'ing: Conquest, Region, and Continuity in Seventeenth-Century China*, ed. J. D. Spence and J. E. Wills, Jr. (New Haven, Conn.: Yale University Press, 1979), pp. 203–216.
7. F. Braudel, *The Wheels of Commerce: Civilization and Capitalism, 15th–18th Century*, vol. 2, trans. S. Reynolds (New York: Harper & Row, 1982), pp. 198–199.
8. Gernet, *A History of Chinese Civilization*, pp. 425–426.
9. Quoted in C. Clunas, *Superfluous Things: Material Culture and Social Status in Early Modern China* (Urbana: University of Illinois Press, 1991), pp. 141–142.
10. Ibid., pp. 147–165.
11. Quoted in Gernet, *A History of Chinese Civilization*, p. 431.
12. See Huang, *1587*, pp. 120–129.
13. F. Wakeman, Jr., *The Fall of Imperial China* (New York: Free Press, 1975), pp. 58–64.
14. J. D. Spence, *The Search for Modern China* (New York: Norton, 1991), pp. 117–122.
15. Quoted in A. Peyrefitte, *The Immobile Empire*, trans. J. Rothschild (New York: Knopf, 1992), pp. 195–196.
16. Ibid., p. 539.
17. Quoted in Spence, *The Search for Modern China*, p. 125.
18. See R. C. Croizier, *Traditional Medicine in Modern China* (Cambridge, Mass.: Harvard University Press, 1968), pp. 19–27.
19. P. U. Unschuld, *Medicine in China: A History of Pharmaceutics* (Berkeley: University of California Press, 1986), p. 4.
20. See G. B. Sansom, *A History of Japan, 1344–1615*, vol. 2 (Stanford, Calif.: Stanford University Press, 1961), Chs. 20–21.
21. Ibid., Ch. 25.
22. See D. Keene, *The Japanese Discovery of Europe, 1720–1830* (Stanford, Calif.: Stanford University Press, 1969), pp. 24–25, Ch. 4, and passim.
23. Quoted in D. H. Shively, "Bakufu Versus Kabuki," in *Studies in the Institutional History of Early Modern Japan*, ed. J. W. Hall (Princeton, N.J.: Princeton University Press, 1970), p. 236.
24. E. O. Reischauer and A. M. Craig, *Japan: Tradition and Transformation*, rev. ed. (Boston: Houghton Mifflin, 1989), pp. 104–105.
25. Quoted in Shively, "Bakufu Versus Kabuki," pp. 241–242.

LISTENING TO THE
PAST

The Macartney Mission to China

Lord George Macartney's embassy to China (1792–1794) sought to establish permanent diplomatic relations between China and Great Britain and to expand trade between the two countries. The mission failed when the emperor rejected the British proposals for the reasons that he states in the letter that follows. Although Macartney later wrote, "Nothing could be more fallacious than to judge of China by any European standard," the British refused to recognize the right of Chinese civilization to be different. The Macartney mission thus serves as a parading of the cultural clashes between the West and Asia that marked the next two centuries.

You, O King, from afar have yearned after the blessings of our civilization, and in your eagerness to come into touch with our converting influence have sent an Embassy across the sea bearing a memorial.[1] I have already taken note of your respectful spirit of submission, have treated your mission with extreme favor and loaded it with gifts . . . .

Yesterday your Ambassador petitioned my Ministers to memorialize me regarding your trade with China, but his proposal is not consistent with our dynastic usage and cannot be entertained. Hitherto, all European nations, including your own country's barbarian merchants, have carried on their trade with our Celestial Empire at Canton. Such has been the procedure for many years, although our Celestial Empire possesses all things in prolific abundance and lacks no product within its own borders. There was therefore no need to import the manufactures of outside barbarians in exchange for our own produce. But as the tea, silk and porcelain which the Celestial Empire produces, are absolute necessities to European nations and to yourselves, we have permitted, as a signal mark of favor, that foreign *hongs*[2] should be established at Canton, so that your wants might be supplied and your

country thus participate in our beneficence. But your Ambassador has now put forward new requests which completely fail to recognize the Throne's principle to "treat strangers from afar with indulgence," and to exercise a pacifying control over barbarian tribes, the world over. Moreover, our dynasty, swaying the myriad races of the globe, extends the same benevolence towards all. Your England is not the only nation trading at Canton. If other nations, following your bad example, wrongfully importune my ear with further impossible requests, how will it be possible for me to treat them with easy indulgence? Nevertheless, I do not forget the lonely remoteness of your island, cut off from the world by intervening wastes of sea, nor do I overlook your excusable ignorance of the usages of our Celestial Empire. I have consequently commanded my Ministers to enlighten your Ambassador on the subject, and have ordered the departure of the mission. . . .

Your request for a small island near Chusan,[3] where your merchants may reside and goods be warehoused, arises from your desire to develop trade. As there are neither foreign *hongs* nor interpreters in or near Chusan, where none of your ships have ever called, such an island would be utterly useless for your purposes. Every inch of the territory of our Empire is marked on the map and the strictest vigilance is exercised over it all: even tiny islets and far-lying sand-banks are clearly defined as part of the provinces to which they belong. Consider, moreover, that England is not the only barbarian land which wishes to establish . . . trade with our Empire. . . .

The next request, for a small site in the vicinity of Canton city, where your barbarian merchants may lodge or, alternatively, that there be no longer any restrictions over their movements at Aomen,[4] has arisen from the following causes. Hitherto, the barbarian merchants of Europe have had a definite locality assigned to them at Aomen for residence and trade, and have been forbidden to encroach an inch beyond the limits assigned to that locality. . . . If these restrictions were withdrawn, friction would inevitably occur between the Chinese and your barbarian subjects, and the results would militate against the benevolent regard that I feel towards you. From every point of view, therefore, it is best that the regulations now in force should continue unchanged. . . .

Regarding your nation's worship of the Lord of Heaven, it is the same religion as that of other European nations. Ever since the beginning of history, sage Emperors and wise rulers have bestowed on China a moral system and inculcated a code, which from time immemorial has been religiously observed by the myriads of my subjects.[5] There has been no hankering after heterodox doctrines. Even the European (missionary) officials in my capital are forbidden to hold intercourse with Chinese subjects; they are restricted within the limits of their appointed residences, and may not go about propagating their religion. The distinction between Chinese and barbarian is most strict, and your Ambassador's request that barbarians shall be given full liberty to disseminate their religion is utterly unreasonable.

It may be, O King, that the above proposals have been wantonly made by your Ambassador on his own responsibility, or peradventure you yourself are ignorant of our dynastic regulations and had no intention of transgressing them when you expressed these wild ideas and hopes. . . . If, after the receipt of this explicit decree, you lightly give ear to the representations of your subordinates and allow your barbarian merchants to proceed to Chêkiang and Tientsin,[6] with the object of landing and trading there, the ordinances of my Celestial Empire are strict in the extreme, and the local officials, both civil and military, are bound reverently to obey the law of the land. Should your vessels touch the shore, your merchants will assuredly never be permitted to land or to reside there, but will be subject to instant expulsion. In that event your barbarian merchants will have had a long journey for nothing. Do not say that you were not warned in due time! Tremblingly obey and show no negligence! A special mandate!

Lord Macartney tries to impress the emperor Ch'ien-lung with an array of expensive presents. *(Source: National Maritime Museum, London)*

Questions for Analysis

1. Consider the basic premises of eighteenth-century European Enlightenment culture and the premises of Chinese culture.

2. What reasons does the emperor give for denying the British requests? What is the basis for the emperor's position?

3. How does the emperor view China's economic and cultural position in the world?

Source: A. J. Andrea and J. H. Overfield, eds., *The Human Record: Sources of Global History*, vol. 2 (Boston: Houghton Mifflin, 1990), pp. 262–264. Reprinted from E. Backhouse and J. O. P. Brand, *Annals and Memoirs of the Court of Peking* (Boston: Houghton Mifflin, 1914), pp. 325–331.

Notes: **1.** Memorandum. **2.** Groups of merchants. **3.** A group of islands in the East China Sea at the entrance to Hangchow Bay. **4.** A city some 45 miles to the south of Canton, at the lower end of the Pearl (Zhu) River delta. **5.** The reference is to Confucianism. **6.** Two Chinese port cities.

26. Ibid.

27. Quoted in G. B. Sansom, *A History of Japan, 1615–1867,* vol. 3 (Stanford, Calif.: Stanford University Press, 1978), p. 99.

28. T. C. Smith, "The Japanese Village in the Seventeenth Century," in Hall, *Studies in the Institutional History of Early Modern Japan,* p. 280.

29. See A. Walthall, "The Life Cycle of Farm Women in Tokugawa Japan," in *Recreating Japanese Women, 1600–1945,* ed. G. Bernstein (Berkeley: University of California Press, 1991), pp. 42–50.

30. Ibid., p. 55.

31. Ibid., p. 56.

32. Ibid., pp. 60–62.

33. T. C. Smith, *The Agrarian Origins of Modern Japan* (Stanford, Calif.: Stanford University Press, 1959), pp. 78–79.

34. See W. Bingham, H. Conroy, and F. W. Iklé, *A History of Asia,* vol. 2 (Boston: Allyn and Bacon, 1967), pp. 140–142.

35. G. B. Sansom, *Japan: A Short Cultural History,* rev. ed. (New York: Appleton-Century-Crofts, 1962), p. 472.

SUGGESTED READING

Perhaps the best starting point for the weaknesses of Yuan rule and the early development of the Ming is E. L. Dreyer, *Early Ming China, A Political History, 1355–1435* (1982), but see also C. O. Hucker, *The Ming Dynasty: Its Origins and Evolving Institutions* (1978); Hucker's *The Traditional Chinese State in Ming Times, 1368–1644* (1962) is a standard study written in simple, untechnical language. Students interested in Chinese naval explorations should see the rich literature on the Ming voyages of the fifteenth century: J. Needham, *Science and Civilization in China,* IV (1985), a very important study; J. J. L. Duyvendak, *China's Discovering of Africa* (1949); and the recent L. Levathes, *When China Ruled the Seas: The Treasure Fleet of the Dragon Throne, 1405–1433* (1994). For Ming foreign policy, see A. Waldron, *The Great Wall of China: From History to Myth* (1990) and T. Barfield, *The Perilous Frontier: Nomadic Empires and China* (1989), an important revisionist study; and L. Struve, *The Southern Ming, 1644–1662* (1984). For the cultural impact of the sixteenth century economic boom, see E. Rawski, "Economic and Social Foundations of Late Imperial Culture," in D. Johnson, A. Notham, and E. Rawski, eds., *Popular Culture in Late Imperial China* (1985). G. W. Skinner, "Urban Development in Imperial China," in G. W. Skinner, ed., *The City in Late Imperial China* (1977) offers an overview of urban change in the Ming and Qing periods. The literature on other factors of popular culture grows; see, for food, *Food in Chinese Culture. Anthropological and Historical Perspectives,* ed. K. C. Chang (1977); for dress, the comprehensive V. M. Garrett, *Chinese Clothing* (1994); and for shelter, R. G. Knapp, *The Chinese House: Craft, Symbol, and the Folk Tradition* (1991); C. Clunas, *Superfluous Things: Material Culture and Social Status in Early Modern China* (1992) and J. Meskill, *Gentlemanly Interests and Wealth on the Yangtze Delta* (1995). For changing Confucian attitudes, C. F. Yü, *The Renewal of Buddhism in China: Chu-hung and the Late Ming Synthesis* (1991) will prove useful.

The best one-volume survey of Japanese history and culture is E. O. Reischauer, *Japan: The Story of a Nation,* 4th ed. (1990), which combines expert knowledge with superb readability. Sansom's *Japan: A Short Cultural History* (see the Notes) is older but still useful. Craig's *Japan: Tradition and Transformation* (see the Notes), and Sansom's *A History of Japan,* 3 vols. (1958–1978) give detailed treatments of Japanese history, as does C. Totman, *Japan before Perry* (1981), which treats economic and social change over a long time-span. The sophisticated study of H. Ooms, *Tokugawa Ideology: Early Constructs, 1570–1680* (1985) describes how early rulers developed the ideological and military values to create a disciplined and stable society. M. Cooper, ed., *They Came to Japan: An Anthology of European Reports on Japan, 1530–1640* (1981) gives the first European impressions of Japan and the Japanese. G. Elison and B. L. Smith, eds., *Warlords, Artists, and Commoners: Japan in the Sixteenth Century* (1987) is an excellent collection of articles by leading scholars. D. Massarella, *A World Elsewhere: Europe's Encounter with Japan in the Sixteenth and Seventeenth Centuries* (1990) is an almost definitive study of the early English and Dutch in Japan.

The following works are helpful for specific topics: C. Totman, *The Lumber Industry in Early Modern Japan* (1995) for the commercial and environmental history of early modern Japan; H. P. Bix, *Peasant Protest in Japan, 1590–1844* (1986), a Marxist interpretation of peasant uprisings primarily in the eighteenth century; R. P. Dore, *Education in Tokugawa Japan* (1965); A. B. Jannetta, *Epidemics and Mortality in Early Modern Japan* (1986) for disease and health; and M. Colcutt, *Five Mountains: The Zen Monastic Institution in Medieval Japan* (1980); and M. Weidner, ed., *Flowering in the Shadows: Women in the History of Chinese and Japanese Painting* (1990). The standard general studies of the art of the two countries are L. Sickman and A. Soper, *The Art and Architecture of China* (1988) and R. T. Paine and A. Soper, *The Art and Architecture of Japan* (1981).

CHAPTER

23

The Revolution in Western Politics, 1775–1815

The mayor of Rouen protects access to the townhall from the on-slaught of a crowd rioting over the lack of bread, August 29, 1792. *(Source: Musée des Beaux Arts, Rouen/Laurie Platt Winfrey, Inc.)*

The last years of the eighteenth century were a time of great upheaval in the West. A series of revolutions and revolutionary wars challenged the old order of monarchs and aristocrats. The ideas of freedom and equality, ideas that have not stopped shaping the world since that era, flourished and spread. The revolutionary era began in North America in 1775. Then in 1789 France, the most influential country in Europe, became the leading revolutionary nation. It established first a constitutional monarchy, then a radical republic, and finally a new empire under Napoleon. The armies of France also joined forces with patriots and radicals abroad in an effort to establish throughout much of Europe new governments based on new principles. The world of modern domestic and international politics was born.

- What caused this era of revolution?
- What were the ideas and objectives of the men and women who rose up violently to undo the established system?
- What were the gains and losses for privileged groups and for ordinary people in a generation of war and upheaval?

These are the questions underlying this chapter's examination of the revolutionary era.

❈ LIBERTY AND EQUALITY

Two ideas fueled the revolutionary period in both America and Europe: liberty and equality. What did eighteenth-century politicians and other people mean by liberty and equality, and why were those ideas so radical and revolutionary in their day?

The call for liberty was first of all a call for individual human rights. Even the most enlightened monarchs customarily claimed that it was their duty to regulate what people wrote and believed. Liberals of the revolutionary era protested such controls from on high. They demanded freedom to worship according to the dictates of their consciences, an end to censorship, and freedom from arbitrary laws and from judges who simply obeyed orders from the government. The Declaration of the Rights of Man, issued at the beginning of the French Revolution, proclaimed, "Liberty consists in being able to do anything that does not harm another person." In theory, therefore, a citizen's

rights had "no limits except those which assure to the other members of society the enjoyment of these same rights." In the context of the monarchial and absolutist forms of government then dominating Europe, this was a truly radical idea.

The call for liberty was also a call for a new kind of government. Revolutionary liberals believed that the people were sovereign—that is, that the people alone had the authority to make laws limiting an individual's freedom of action. In practice, this system of government meant choosing legislators who represented the people and were accountable to them.

Equality was a more ambiguous idea. Eighteenth-century liberals argued that, in theory, all citizens should have identical rights and civil liberties and that the nobility had no right to special privileges based on the accident of birth. However, liberals accepted some well-established distinctions.

First, most eighteenth-century liberals were *men* of their times, and they generally shared with other men the belief that equality between men and women was neither practical nor desirable. Women played an important political role in the French Revolution at several points, but the men of the French Revolution limited formal political rights—the right to vote, to run for office, to participate in government—to men.

Second, liberals never believed that everyone should be equal economically. Quite the contrary. As Thomas Jefferson wrote in an early draft of the American Declaration of Independence (before he changed "property" to the more noble-sounding "happiness"), everyone was equal in "the pursuit of property." Jefferson and other liberals certainly did not expect equal success in that pursuit. Great differences in wealth and income between rich and poor were perfectly acceptable to liberals. The essential point was that everyone should legally have an equal chance.

In eighteenth-century Europe, however, such equality of opportunity was a truly revolutionary idea. Society was still legally divided into groups with special privileges, such as the nobility and the clergy, and groups with special burdens, such as the peasantry. And in most countries, various middle-class groups—professionals, business people, townspeople, and craftsmen—enjoyed privileges that allowed them to monopolize all sorts of economic activity. Liberals criticized not economic inequality itself but this kind of economic inequality based on artificial legal distinctions.

The ideas of liberty and equality—the central ideas of classical liberalism—had deep roots in Western history. The classical and Judeo-Christian traditions had affirmed for hundreds of years the sanctity and value of the individual human being, as well as personal responsibility on the part of both common folk and exalted rulers. The hounded and persecuted Protestant radicals of the later sixteenth century had died for the revolutionary idea that individuals were entitled to their own religious beliefs.

Although the liberal creed was rooted in the Western tradition, classical liberalism first crystal-lized at the end of the seventeenth century and during the Enlightenment of the eighteenth century. Liberal ideas reflected the Enlightenment's stress on human dignity and human happiness on earth and its faith in science, rationality, and progress. Almost all the writers of the Enlightenment were passionately committed to greater personal liberty and equal treatment before the law.

Certain English and French thinkers were mainly responsible for joining the Enlightenment's concern for personal freedom and legal equality to a theoretical justification of liberal self-government. The two most important were John Locke and the baron de Montesquieu. Locke maintained that England's long political tradition rested on "the rights of Englishmen" and on representative government through Parliament. He admired especially the great Whig nobles who had deposed James II and made the bloodless revolution of 1688–1689, and he argued that if a government oversteps its proper function of protecting the natural rights of life, liberty, and private property, it becomes a tyranny. Montesquieu was also inspired by English constitutional history. He, too, believed that powerful "intermediary groups"—such as the judicial nobility of which he was a proud member—offered the best defense of liberty against despotism.

The belief that representative institutions could defend their liberty and interests appealed powerfully to well-educated, prosperous groups, which historians have traditionally labeled as the bourgeoisie. Yet liberal ideas about individual rights and political freedom also appealed to much of the hereditary nobility, at least in western Europe and as formulated by Montesquieu. Representative government did not mean democracy, which liberal thinkers tended to equate with mob rule. Rather, they envisioned voting for representatives as being restricted to those who owned property—those with "a stake in society." England had shown the way. After 1688 it had combined a parliamentary system and considerable individual liberty with a restricted franchise and unquestionable aristocratic pre-eminence. In the course of the eighteenth century, many leading French nobles, led by a judicial nobility inspired by the doctrines of Montesquieu, were increasingly eager to follow the English example. Thus eighteenth-century liberalism found broad support among the prosperous, well-educated elites in western Europe.

The Marquis de Lafayette   The most famous great noble to embrace the liberal revolution is shown here directing a battle in the American Revolution. He later returned to France to champion liberty and equality there. The elegant black man is Lafayette's servant, a free man in an age of widespread slavery. *(Source: Jean-Loup Charmet)*

What liberalism lacked from the beginning was strong popular support. At least two reasons account for the people's wary attitude. First, for common people, the great questions were not theoretical and political but immediate and economic; getting enough to eat was a crucial challenge. Second, some of the traditional practices and institutions that liberals wanted to abolish were dear to peasants and urban workers. Comfortable elites had already come into conflict with the people in the eighteenth century over the enclosure of common lands and the regulation of food prices. This conflict would sharpen in the revolutionary era as differences in outlook and well-being led to many misunderstandings and disappointments for both groups.

THE AMERICAN REVOLUTION (1775–1789)

The era of liberal political revolution began in the New World. The thirteen mainland colonies of British North America revolted against their home country and then succeeded in establishing a new unified government.

The American revolutionaries believed that they were demanding only the traditional rights of English men and women. But those traditional rights were liberal rights, and in the American context they had very strong democratic and popular overtones that made them quite radical. In founding a government firmly based on liberal principles, the Americans set an example that had a forceful impact on Europe and sped up political development there.

The Origins of the Revolution

The American Revolution had its immediate origins in a squabble over increased taxes. The British government had fought and decisively won the Seven Years' War on the strength of its professional army and navy. The American colonists had furnished little real aid. The high cost of the war to the British, however, had led to a doubling of the British national debt. Anticipating further expense defending its recently conquered western lands from native American uprisings, the British government in London set about reorganizing the empire with a series of bold, largely unprecedented measures. Breaking with tradition, the British decided to maintain a large army in North America after peace was restored in 1763. Moreover, they sought to exercise strict control over their newly conquered western lands and to tax the colonies directly. In 1765 the government pushed through Parliament the Stamp Act, which levied taxes on a long list of commercial and legal documents, diplomas, pamphlets, newspapers, almanacs, dice, and playing cards. A stamp glued to each article indicated the tax had been paid.

This effort to increase taxes as part of a tightening-up of the empire seemed perfectly reasonable to the British. Americans were being asked to pay only a share of their own defense costs. Moreover, Americans had been paying only very low local taxes. The Stamp Act would have doubled taxes to about 2 shillings per person per year. No other people in the European or colonial world (except the Poles) paid so little. In contrast, the British paid the highest taxes in the Western world—26 shillings per person. The colonists protested the Stamp Act vigorously and violently, however, and after rioting and boycotts against British goods, Parliament reluctantly repealed the new tax.

As the fury over the Stamp Act revealed, much more was involved than taxes. The key questions were political. To what extent could the home government reassert its power while limiting the authority of colonial legislatures and their elected representatives? Who had the right to make laws for Americans? While a troubled majority of Americans searched hard for a compromise, some radicals began to proclaim that "taxation without representation is tyranny." The British government replied that Americans were represented in Parliament, albeit indirectly (like most English people themselves), and that the absolute supremacy of Parliament throughout the empire could not be questioned. Many Americans felt otherwise. As John Adams of Massachusetts put it, "A Parliament of Great Britain can have no more rights to tax the colonies than a Parliament of Paris." At risk were Americans' existing liberties and time-honored institutions.

Americans had long exercised a great deal of independence and gone their own way. The colonial assemblies made the important laws, which were seldom overturned by the home government. The right to vote was much more widespread than in England. In many parts of colonial Massachusetts, for example, as many as 95 percent of the adult males could vote. Moreover, greater political

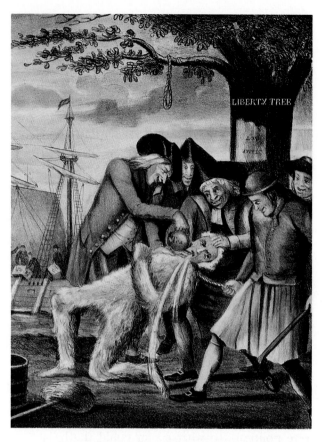

✳ **Toward Revolution in Boston** The Boston Tea Party was one of many angry confrontations between British officials and Boston patriots. On January 27, 1774, a crowd seized and then tarred and feathered a British customs collector. This French engraving from 1784 commemorates the defiant and provocative action. *(Source: The Granger Collection, New York)*

equality was matched by greater social and economic equality. Neither a hereditary nobility nor a hereditary serf population existed, although the slavery of the Americas consigned blacks to a legally oppressed caste. Independent farmers were the largest group in the country and set much of its tone. In short, the colonial experience had slowly formed a people who felt themselves separate and distinct from the home country. The controversies over taxation intensified those feelings of distinctiveness and separation and brought them to the fore.

In 1773 the dispute over taxes and representation flared up again. The British government had permitted the financially hard-pressed East India Company to ship its tea from China directly to its agents in the colonies, rather than through London middlemen who sold to independent colonial merchants. Thus the company secured a monopoly on the tea trade and colonial merchants were suddenly excluded from a highly profitable business. The colonists were quick to protest.

In Boston men disguised as Indians had a rowdy "tea party" and threw the company's tea into the harbor. This action led to extreme measures. Parliament passed the so-called Coercive Acts, which closed the port of Boston, curtailed local elections and town meetings, and greatly expanded the royal governor's power. County conventions in Massachusetts protested vehemently and urged that the acts be "rejected as the attempts of a wicked administration to enslave America." Other colonial assemblies joined in the denunciations. In September 1774, the First Continental Congress met in Philadelphia, where the more radical members argued successfully against concessions to the Crown. Compromise was also rejected by the British Parliament, and in April 1775 fighting began in Massachusetts, at Lexington and Concord.

Independence

The fighting spread, and the colonists moved slowly but inevitably toward open rebellion and a declaration of independence. The uncompromising attitude of the British government and its use of German mercenaries went a long way toward dissolving long-standing loyalties to the home country and rivalries among the separate colonies. *Common Sense* (1775), a brilliant attack by the recently arrived English radical Thomas Paine (1737–1809), also mobilized public opinion in favor of independence. A runaway bestseller, Paine's tract ridiculed the idea of a small island ruling a great continent. In his call for freedom and republican government, Paine expressed Americans' growing sense of separateness and moral superiority.

On July 4, 1776, the Second Continental Congress adopted the Declaration of Independence, which boldly listed the tyrannical acts committed by King George III (r. 1760–1820) and confidently proclaimed the natural rights of mankind and the sovereignty of the American states. Sometimes called the world's greatest political editorial, the Declaration of Independence in effect universalized the traditional rights of English people and made them the rights of all mankind. It stated "that all men are created equal; that they are endowed by their Creator with certain unalienable rights; that among these are life, liberty, and the pursuit of happiness." No other American political document has ever caused such excitement, either at home or abroad.

Many American families remained loyal to Britain; many others divided bitterly. After the Declaration of Independence, the conflict often took the form of a civil war pitting patriots against those who remained loyal to the King. The loyalists tended to be wealthy and politically moderate. Many patriots, too, were wealthy—individuals such as John Hancock and George Washington—but willingly allied themselves with farmers and artisans in a broad coalition. This coalition harassed the loyalists and confiscated their property to help pay for the American war effort. The broad social base of the revolutionaries tended to make the liberal revolution democratic. State governments extended the right to vote to many more men in the course of the war and re-established themselves as republics.

On the international scene, the French sympathized with the rebels from the beginning. They wanted revenge for the humiliating defeats of the Seven Years' War. Officially neutral until 1778, they supplied the great bulk of guns and gunpowder used by the American revolutionaries, very much as foreign great powers have supplied weapons for "wars of national liberation" in our time. By 1777 French volunteers were arriving in Virginia, and a dashing young nobleman, the marquis de Lafayette (1757–1834), quickly became one of Washington's most trusted generals. In 1778 the French government offered a formal alliance to the American ambassador in Paris, Benjamin Franklin, and in 1779 and 1780 the Spanish and Dutch declared war on Britain. Catherine the

The Signing of the Declaration, July 4, 1776 John Trumbull's famous painting shows the dignity and determination of America's revolutionary leaders. An extraordinarily talented group, they succeeded in rallying popular support without losing power to more radical forces in the process. *(Source: Yale University Art Gallery)*

Great of Russia helped organize the League of Armed Neutrality in order to protect neutral shipping rights, which Britain refused to recognize.

Thus by 1780 Great Britain was engaged in an imperial war against most of Europe as well as the thirteen colonies. In these circumstances, and in the face of severe reverses in India, the West Indies, and at Yorktown in Virginia, a new British government decided to cut its losses. American negotiators in Paris were receptive. They feared that France wanted a treaty that would bottle up the new United States east of the Allegheny Mountains and give British holdings west of the Alleghenies to France's ally, Spain. Thus the American negotiators separated themselves from their French allies and accepted the extraordinarily favorable terms Britain offered.

By the Treaty of Paris of 1783, Britain recognized the independence of the thirteen colonies and ceded all its territory between the Allegheny Mountains and the Mississippi River to the Americans. Out of the bitter rivalries of the Old World, the Americans snatched dominion over almost half a continent.

Framing the Constitution

The liberal program of the American Revolution was consolidated by the federal Constitution, the Bill of Rights, and the creation of a national republic. Assembling in Philadelphia in the summer of 1787, the delegates to the Constitutional Convention were determined to end the period of economic depression, social uncertainty, and very weak central government that had followed independence. The delegates decided, therefore, to grant the federal, or central, government important powers: regulation of domestic and foreign trade, the right to levy taxes, and the means to enforce its laws.

Strong rule would be placed squarely in the context of representative self-government. Senators and congressmen would be the lawmaking delegates of the voters, and the president of the republic would be an elected official. The central government would operate in Montesquieu's framework of checks and balances. The executive, legislative, and judicial branches would systematically balance one another. The power of the federal government would in turn be checked by the powers of the individual states.

When the results of the secret deliberations of the Constitutional Convention were presented to the states for ratification, a great public debate began. The opponents of the proposed constitution—the Anti-Federalists—charged that the new document took too much power from the individual states and made the federal government too strong. Moreover, many Anti-Federalists feared for the personal liberties and individual freedoms for which they had just fought. In order to overcome these objections, the Federalists solemnly promised to spell out these basic freedoms as soon as the new constitution was adopted. The result was the first ten amendments to the Constitution, which the first Congress passed shortly after it met in New York in March 1789. These amendments formed an effective bill of rights to safeguard the individual. Most of them—trial by jury, due process of law, right to assemble, freedom from unreasonable search—had their origins in English law and the English Bill of Rights of 1689. Others—the freedoms of speech, the press, and religion—reflected natural-law theory and the American experience.

The American Constitution and the Bill of Rights exemplified the great strengths and the limits of what came to be called classical liberalism. Liberty meant individual freedoms and political safeguards. Liberty also meant representative government but did not necessarily mean democracy, with its principle of one person, one vote. Equality—slaves excepted—meant equality before the law, not equality of political participation or economic well-being. Indeed, economic inequality was resolutely defended by the elite that framed the Constitution. The right to own property was guaranteed by the Fifth Amendment, and if the government took private property, the owner was to receive "just compensation." The radicalism of liberal revolution in America was primarily legal and political, *not* economic or social.

❖ THE FRENCH REVOLUTION (1789–1791)

In Europe, hundreds of books, pamphlets, and articles analyzed and romanticized the American upheaval. Thoughtful Europeans noted, first of all, its enormous long-term implications for international politics. A secret report by the Venetian ambassador to Paris in 1783 stated what many felt: if the new nation survived in unity, it might "become the most formidable power in the world."[1] More generally, American independence fired the imaginations of those aristocrats who were uneasy with their hereditary privileges and those commoners who yearned for equality. Many Europeans believed that the world was advancing and that America was leading the way. As one French writer put it in 1789, "This vast continent which the seas surround will soon change Europe and the universe." The Americans had shown how rational beings could assemble together to exercise sovereignty and write a permanent constitution—a new social contract. All this gave greater reality to the concepts of individual liberty and representative government and reinforced one of the primary ideas of the Enlightenment: that a better world was possible.

No country felt the consequences of the American Revolution more directly than France. Hundreds of French officers served in America and were inspired by the experience. The most famous of these, the young and impressionable marquis de Lafayette, left home as a great aristocrat determined to fight only France's traditional foe, England. He returned with a love of liberty and firm republican convictions. French intellectuals and publicists engaged in passionate analysis of the federal and state constitutions. The American Revolution undeniably hastened upheaval in France.

Yet the French Revolution did not mirror the American example. It was more radical and more complex, more influential and more controversial, more loved and more hated. For Europeans and most of the rest of the world, it was the great revolution of the eighteenth century, *the* revolution that opened the modern era in politics.

The Breakdown of the Old Order

Like the American Revolution, the French Revolution had its immediate origins in the financial difficulties of the government. With both the high court of Paris—the Parlement—and public opinion successfully resisting increased taxes, the government was forced to finance all of its enormous expenditures during the American war with borrowed money. As a result, the national debt and the annual budget deficit soared. By the 1780s, fully 50 percent of France's annual budget went for interest on the ever-increasing debt. Another

25 percent went to maintain the military, while 6 percent was absorbed by the costly and extravagant king and his court at Versailles. Less than 20 percent of the entire national budget was available for the productive functions of the state, such as transportation and general administration. This was an impossible financial situation.

One way out would have been for the government to declare partial bankruptcy, forcing its creditors to accept greatly reduced payments on the debt. Both the Spanish and the French monarchies had done this in earlier times. By the 1780s, however, the French debt was being held by an army of aristocratic and bourgeois creditors, and the French monarchy, though absolute in theory, had become far too weak for such a drastic and unpopular action.

Nor could the king and his ministers, unlike modern governments, print money and create inflation to cover their deficits. Unlike England and Holland, which had far larger national debts relative to their populations, France had no central bank, no paper currency, and no means of creating credit. French money was good gold coin. Therefore, when a depressed economy and a lack of public confidence made it increasingly difficult for the government to obtain new gold loans in 1786, it had no alternative but to try increasing taxes. But since France's tax system was unfair and out-of-date, increased revenues were possible only through fundamental reforms. Such reforms, which would affect all groups in France's complex and fragmented society, opened a Pandora's box of social and political demands.

Legal Orders and Social Realities

As in the Middle Ages, France's 25 million inhabitants were still legally divided into three orders, or *estates*—the Roman Catholic clergy, the nobility, and everyone else. As the nation's first estate, the clergy numbered about 100,000 and had important privileges. It owned about 10 percent of the land and paid only a "voluntary gift," rather than regular taxes, to the government every five years. Moreover, the church levied a tax (the tithe) on landowners, which averaged somewhat less than 10 percent. Much of the church's income was actually drained away from local parishes by political appointees and worldly aristocrats at the top of the church hierarchy—to the intense dissatisfaction of the poor parish priests.

The second legally defined estate consisted of some 400,000 noblemen and noblewomen. The nobles owned outright about 25 percent of the land in France, and they, too, were taxed very lightly. Moreover, nobles continued to enjoy certain manorial rights, or privileges of lordship, that dated back to medieval times and allowed them to tax the peasantry for their own profit. They did this by means of exclusive rights to hunt and fish, village monopolies on baking bread and pressing grapes for wine, fees for justice, and a host of other "useful privileges." In addition, nobles had "honorific privileges," such as the right to precedence on public occasions and the right to wear a sword. These rights conspicuously proclaimed the nobility's legal superiority and exalted social position.

Everyone else was a commoner, legally a member of the third estate. A few commoners—prosperous merchants or lawyers and officials—were well educated and rich, and might even buy up manorial rights as profitable investments. Many more commoners were urban artisans and unskilled day laborers. The vast majority of the third estate consisted of the peasants and agricultural workers in the countryside. Thus the third estate was a conglomeration of vastly different social groups united only by their shared legal status as distinct from the nobility and clergy.

In discussing the long-term origins of the French Revolution, historians have long focused on growing tensions between the nobility and the comfortable members of the third estate, usually known as the *bourgeoisie,* or middle class. A dominant historical interpretation, which has held sway for at least two generations, maintains that the bourgeoisie was basically united by economic position and class interest. Aided by a general economic expansion, the middle class grew rapidly in the eighteenth century, tripling to about 2.3 million persons, or about 8 percent of France's population. Increasing in size, wealth, culture, and self-confidence, this rising bourgeoisie became progressively exasperated by archaic "feudal" laws and customs that restrained the economy and their needs and aspirations. As a result, the French bourgeoisie eventually rose up to lead the entire third estate in a great social revolution, a revolution that destroyed feudal privileges and established a capitalist order based on individualism and a market economy.

In recent years, a flood of new research has challenged these accepted views, and once again the French Revolution is a subject of heated scholarly debate. Above all, revisionist historians have questioned the existence of a growing social conflict between a progressive capitalistic bourgeoisie and a reactionary feudal nobility in eighteenth-century France. Instead, these historians see both bourgeoisie and nobility as highly fragmented, riddled with internal rivalries. Rather than standing as unified blocs against each other, nobility and bourgeoisie formed two parallel social ladders increasingly linked together at the top by wealth, marriage, and Enlightenment culture.

Revisionist historians stress three developments in particular. First, the nobility remained a fluid and relatively open order. Throughout the eighteenth century, substantial numbers of successful commoners continued to seek and obtain noble status through government service and purchase of expensive positions conferring nobility. Thus the nobility continued to attract the wealthiest members of the middle class and to permit social mobility. Second, key sections of the nobility and the prosperous bourgeoisie formed together the core of the book-hungry Enlightenment public. Both groups saw themselves as forming part of the educated elite and standing well above the common people—the peasants and the urban poor. Both groups were also equally liberal until revolution actually began, and they generally supported the judicial opposition to the government. Third, the nobility and the bourgeoisie were not really at odds in the economic sphere. Both looked to investment in land and to government service as their preferred activities, and the goal of the merchant capitalist was to gain enough wealth to live nobly as a large landowner. At the same time, wealthy nobles often acted as aggressive capitalists, investing especially in mining, metallurgy, and foreign trade.

The revisionists have clearly shaken the belief that the bourgeoisie and the nobility were inevitably locked in growing conflict before the French Revolution. But in stressing the similarities between the two groups, especially at the top, revisionists have also reinforced the view, long maintained by historians, that the Old Regime had ceased to correspond with social reality by the 1780s. Legally, society was still based on rigid orders inherited from the Middle Ages. But France had moved far toward being a society based on wealth and education, where an emerging elite that included both aristocratic and bourgeois notables was frustrated by a bureaucratic monarchy that continued to claim the right to absolute power.

The Formation of the National Assembly

The Revolution was under way by 1787, though no one could have realized what was to follow. Spurred by a depressed economy and falling tax receipts, Louis XVI's minister of finance convinced the king to call an assembly of notables to gain support for a general tax on all landed property. The assembled notables, who were mainly important noblemen and high-ranking clergy, ultimately responded that such sweeping tax changes required the approval of the Estates General, the representative body of all three estates, which had not met since 1614.

Facing imminent bankruptcy, the king tried to reassert his authority. He dismissed the notables and established new taxes by decree. In stirring language, the Parlement of Paris promptly declared the royal initiative null and void. When the king tried to exile the judges, a tremendous wave of protest swept the country. Frightened investors also refused to advance more loans to the state. Finally in July 1788, a beaten Louis XVI bowed to public opinion and called for a spring session of the Estates General. Absolute monarchy was collapsing.

What would replace it? Throughout the unprecedented election campaign of 1788 and 1789, that question excited France. All across the country, clergy, nobles, and commoners met together in their respective orders to draft petitions for change and to elect their respective delegates to the Estates General. The local assemblies of the clergy chose two-thirds of the delegates from among the poorer parish priests, who were commoners by birth. Among the nobles, already badly split by wealth and education, a conservative majority was drawn from the poorer and more numerous provincial nobility. But fully one-third of the nobility's representatives were liberals committed to major changes.

As for the third estate, there was great popular participation in the elections. Almost all male commoners twenty-five years or older had the right to vote. Still, most of the representatives finally selected were well-educated, prosperous lawyers and government officials. There were no delegates elected from the great mass of laboring poor, an exclusion that would encourage the peasants and

also the urban artisans to intervene directly and dramatically at numerous points in the Revolution, as we shall see.

The petitions for change coming from the three estates showed a surprising degree of consensus on most issues. There was general agreement that royal absolutism should give way to constitutional monarchy, in which laws and taxes would require the consent of the Estates General meeting regularly. All agreed that in the future individual liberties would have to be guaranteed by law and that the economic position of the parish clergy would have to be improved. It was generally acknowledged that economic development required reforms, such as the abolition of internal trade barriers. The striking similarities in the grievance petitions of the clergy, nobility, and third estate reflected the broad commitment of France's educated elite to liberalism.

Yet an increasingly bitter quarrel undermined this consensus during the intense electoral campaign. *How* would the Estates General vote, and precisely *who* would lead in the political reorganization that was generally desired? The Estates General of 1614 had sat as three separate houses. Any action had required the agreement of at least two branches, a requirement that had virtually guaranteed control by the nobility and the clergy. The aristocratic Parlement of Paris ruled that the Estates General should once again sit separately. Certain middle-class intellectuals and some liberal nobles demanded instead a single assembly dominated by representatives of the third estate. Amid increased political competition and a growing hostility toward aristocratic aspirations, the government agreed that the third estate should have as many delegates as the clergy and the nobility combined. When it then rendered this act meaningless by upholding voting by separate order, middle-class leaders saw fresh evidence of an aristocratic conspiracy.

The Estates General opened in May 1789 at Versailles with twelve hundred delegates. The estates were almost immediately deadlocked. Delegates of the third estate refused to transact any business until the king ordered the clergy and nobility to sit with them in a single body. Finally, after a six-week war of nerves, the third estate on June 17 voted to call itself the National Assembly. On June 20, the delegates of the third estate, excluded from their hall because of "repairs," moved to a large indoor tennis court. There they swore

The Oath of the Tennis Court This painting, based on an unfinished work by Jacques-Louis David (1748–1825), enthusiastically celebrates the revolutionary rupture of June 20, 1789. Locked out of their assembly hall at Versailles and joined by some sympathetic priests, the delegates of the third estate have moved to an indoor tennis court and are swearing never to disband until they have written a new constitution and put France on a firm foundation. *(Source: Musée Carnavalet/Photographie Bulloz)*

the Oath of the Tennis Court, pledging not to disband until they had written a new constitution.

The indecisive king's actions were then somewhat contradictory. On June 23 he made a conciliatory speech urging reforms to a joint session and then ordered the three estates to meet together. Then, apparently following the advice of relatives and court nobles that he dissolve the Estates General by force, the king called an army of eighteen thousand troops toward Versailles. On July 11 he dismissed his finance minister and his other more liberal ministers. Having resigned himself to bankruptcy, Louis XVI belatedly sought to reassert his historic "divine right" to rule. The middle-class delegates and their allies from the liberal nobility had done their best, but they were resigned to being disbanded at bayonet point. One third-estate

delegate reassured a worried colleague, "You won't hang—you'll only have to go back home."[2]

The Revolt of the Poor and the Oppressed

While the educated delegates of the third estate pressed for symbolic equality with the nobility and clergy in a single legislative body at Versailles, economic hardship gripped the common people of France in a tightening vise. Grain was the basis of the diet of ordinary people in the eighteenth century, and in 1788 the harvest had been extremely poor. The price of bread, which had been rising gradually since 1785, began to soar. By July 1789 it had climbed as high as 8 sous per pound in the provinces. In Paris, where bread was regularly subsidized by the government in an attempt to prevent popular unrest, the price rose to 4 sous, a price at which a laborer with a wife and three children had to spend most of his wages to buy the family's bread.

Harvest failure and high bread prices unleashed a classic economic depression of the preindustrial age. With food so expensive and with so much uncertainty, the demand for manufactured goods collapsed, resulting in thousands of artisans and small traders being thrown out of work. By the end of 1789, almost half of the French people were in need of relief. In Paris the situation was so desperate in July 1789 that perhaps 150,000 of the city's 600,000 people were without work.

Against this background of dire poverty and excitement generated by the political crisis, the people of Paris entered decisively onto the revolutionary stage. They believed in a general, though ill-defined, way that the economic distress had human causes. They believed that they should have steady work and enough bread at fair prices to survive. Specifically, they feared that the dismissal of the king's moderate finance minister would put them at the mercy of aristocratic landowners and grain speculators. Stories like that quoting the wealthy financier Joseph François Foulon as saying that the poor "should eat grass, like my horses" and rumors that the king's troops would sack the city began to fill the air. Angry crowds formed, and passionate voices urged action. On July 13 the people began to seize arms for the defense of the city, and on July 14 several hundred of the most determined people marched to the Bastille to search for gunpowder.

Storming the Bastille This representation by an untrained contemporary artist shows civilians and members of the Paris militia—the "conquerors of the Bastille"— on the attack. Their successful action had enormous practical and symbolic significance, and July 14 has long been France's most important national holiday. (*Source: Musée Carnavalet/Photo Hubert Josse*)

The governor of the medieval fortress-prison refused to hand over the powder, panicked, and ordered his men to fire, killing ninety-eight people attempting to enter. Cannons were brought to batter the main gate, and fighting continued until the prison surrendered. The governor of the prison was later hacked to death, and his head was stuck on a pike and paraded through the streets. The next day a committee of citizens appointed the marquis de Lafayette commander of the city's armed forces. Paris was lost to the king, who was forced to recall the finance minister and disperse his troops. The popular uprising had saved the National Assembly.

As the delegates resumed their long-winded and inconclusive debates at Versailles, the people in the countryside sent them a radical and unmistakable message. All across France, peasants began to rise in spontaneous, violent, and effective insurrection against their lords. Neither middle-class landowners nor the larger, more prosperous farmers were spared. In some areas, peasants reinstated traditional village practices, undoing recent enclosures and reoccupying old common lands. Peasants seized forests, and taxes went unpaid. Fear of vagabonds and outlaws—called the Great Fear by contemporaries—seized the countryside and fanned the flames of rebellion.

Faced with chaos yet afraid to call on the king to restore order, some liberal nobles and middle-class delegates at Versailles responded to peasant demands with a surprise maneuver on the night of August 4, 1789. The duke of Aiguillon, one of France's greatest noble landowners, declared that

in several provinces the whole people forms a kind of league for the destruction of the manor houses, the ravaging of the lands, and especially for the seizure of the archives where the title deeds to feudal properties are kept. It seeks to throw off at last a yoke that has for many centuries weighted it down.[3]

He urged equality in taxation and the elimination of feudal dues. In the end, all the old exactions imposed on the peasants—serfdom where it still existed, village monopolies, the right to make peasants work on the roads, and a host of other dues—were abolished. Though a clarifying law passed a week later was less generous, the peasants ignored the "fine print." They never paid feudal dues again. Thus the French peasantry, which already owned about 30 percent of all the land, achieved a great and unprecedented victory in the early days of revolutionary upheaval. Henceforth, the French peasants would seek mainly to protect and consolidate their triumph. As the Great Fear subsided in the countryside, they became a force for order and stability.

A Limited Monarchy

The National Assembly moved forward. On August 27, 1789, it issued the Declaration of the Rights of Man, which stated, "Men are born and remain free and equal in rights." The declaration also maintained that mankind's natural rights are "liberty, property, security, and resistance to oppression" and that "every man is presumed innocent until he is proven guilty." As for law, "it is an expression of the general will; all citizens have the right to concur personally or through their representatives in its formation. . . . Free expression of thoughts and opinions is one of the most precious rights of mankind: every citizen may therefore speak, write, and publish freely." In short, this clarion call of the liberal revolutionary ideal guaranteed equality before the law, representative government for a sovereign people, and individual freedom. This revolutionary credo, only two pages long, was propagandized throughout France and the rest of Europe and around the world.

Moving beyond general principles to draft a constitution proved difficult. The questions of how much power the king should retain led to another deadlock. Once again the decisive answer came from the poor—in this instance, the poor women of Paris.

Women customarily bought the food and managed the poor family's slender resources. In Paris great numbers of women also worked for wages. In the general economic crisis, increasing unemployment and hunger put tremendous pressure on household managers, and the result was another popular explosion.

On October 5 some seven thousand desperate women marched the twelve miles from Paris to Versailles to demand action. This great crowd invaded the National Assembly, "armed with scythes, sticks and pikes." One tough old woman directing a large group of younger women defiantly shouted into the debate, "Who's that talking down there? Make the chatterbox shut up. That's not the point: the point is that we want bread."[4] Hers was the genuine voice of the people, essential to any understanding of the French Revolution.

"To Versailles"   This print is one of many commemorating the women's march on Versailles. Notice on the left that the artist has depicted—and criticized—the fashionable lady from the well-to-do as a most reluctant revolutionary. *(Source: Giraudon/Art Resource, NY)*

The women invaded the royal apartments, slaughtered some of the royal bodyguards, and furiously searched for the queen, Marie Antoinette, who was widely despised for her lavish spending and supposedly immoral behavior. "We are going to cut off her head, tear out her heart, fry her liver, and that won't be the end of it," they shouted, surging through the palace in a frenzy. It seems likely that only the intervention of Lafayette and the National Guard saved the royal family. But the only way to calm the disorder was for the king to go and live in Paris, as the crowd demanded. With this victory, the women clearly emerged as a major and enduring element in the Parisian revolutionary crowd.[5]

The National Assembly followed the king to Paris, and the next two years, until September 1791, saw the consolidation of the liberal Revolution. Under middle-class leadership, the National Assembly abolished the French nobility as a legal order and pushed forward with the creation of a constitutional monarchy, which Louis XVI reluctantly agreed to accept in July 1790. In the final constitution, the king remained the head of state, but all lawmaking power was placed in the hands of the National Assembly, elected by the economic upper half of French males.

New laws broadened women's rights to seek divorce, to inherit property, and to obtain financial support from fathers for illegitimate children. But women were not allowed to vote or hold political office. The great majority of comfortable, well-educated males in the National Assembly believed that women should be limited to child raising and domestic duties and should leave politics and most public activities to men. The delegates to the National Assembly also believed that excluding women from politics would free the political system from the harmful effects of the sexual intrigue common at court; and pure, home-focused wives would raise the high-minded sons needed to govern and defend the nation.

The National Assembly replaced the complicated patchwork of historic provinces with eighty-three departments of approximately equal size. It replaced the jumble of weights and measures that varied from province to province with the simple, rational metric system in 1793. It prohibited monopolies, guilds, and workers' combinations, and it abolished barriers to trade within France in the name of economic liberty. Thus the National Assembly applied the critical spirit of the Enlightenment to reform France's laws and institutions completely.

The National Assembly also nationalized the Catholic church's property and abolished monasteries as useless relics of a distant past. The government sold all former church property in an attempt to put the state's finances on a solid footing. Peasants eventually purchased much of this land when it was subdivided. The purchases strengthened their attachment to the revolutionary state. These actions, however, brought the new government into conflict with the Catholic church and with many sincere Christians, especially in the countryside.

Many delegates to the National Assembly, imbued with the rationalism and skepticism of the eighteenth-century philosophes, harbored a deep distrust of popular piety and "superstitious religion." They were interested in the church only to the extent that they could seize its land and use the church to strengthen the new state. Thus they established a national church, with priests chosen by voters. In the face of widespread resistance, the National Assembly then required the clergy to take a loyalty oath to the new government. The Catholic clergy became just so many more employees of the state. The pope formally condemned this attempt to subjugate the church. Only half of the priests of France took the oath of allegiance, and confusion and hostility among French Catholics were pervasive. The attempt to remake the Catholic church, like the National Assembly's abolition of guilds and workers' combinations, sharpened the division between the educated classes and the common people that had been emerging in the eighteenth century. This policy toward the church was the revolutionary government's first important failure.

WORLD WAR AND REPUBLICAN FRANCE (1791–1799)

When Louis XVI accepted the final version of the completed constitution in September 1791, a young and still obscure provincial lawyer and member of the National Assembly named Maximilien Robespierre (1758–1794) evaluated the work of two years and concluded, "The Revolution is over." Robespierre was both right and wrong. He

was right in the sense that the most constructive and lasting reforms were in place. Nothing substantial in the way of liberty and equality would be gained in the next generation. He was wrong in the sense that a much more radical stage lay ahead. New heroes and new ideologies were to emerge in revolutionary wars and international conflict.

Foreign Reactions and the Beginning of War

The outbreak and progress of revolution in France produced great excitement and a sharp division of opinion in Europe and the United States. Liberals and radicals saw a mighty triumph of liberty over despotism. In Great Britain especially, they hoped that the French example would lead to a fundamental reordering of the political system that had placed Parliament in the hands of the aristocracy and a few wealthy merchants, with the great majority of people having very little say in the government. Conservative leaders such as Edmund Burke (1729–1797) were deeply troubled by the aroused spirit of reform. In 1790 Burke published *Reflections on the Revolution in France,* one of the great intellectual defenses of European conservatism. Defending inherited privileges, he glorified the unrepresentative Parliament and predicted that thoroughgoing reform like that occurring in France would lead only to chaos and tyranny. Burke's work sparked vigorous debate.

One passionate rebuttal came from a young writer in London, Mary Wollstonecraft (1759–1797). Born into the middle class, Wollstonecraft was schooled in adversity by a mean-spirited father who beat his wife and squandered his inherited fortune. Determined to be independent in a society that generally expected women of her class to become homebodies and obedient wives, she struggled for years to earn her living as a governess and teacher—practically the only acceptable careers for single, educated women—before attaining success as a translator and author. Interested in politics and believing that "a desperate disease requires a powerful remedy" in Great Britain as well as France, Wollstonecraft was incensed by Burke's book. She immediately wrote a blistering, widely read attack, *A Vindication of the Rights of Man* (1790).

Then, fired up on controversy and commitment, she made a daring intellectual leap. She developed for the first time the logical implications of natural-law philosophy in her masterpiece, *A Vindication of the Rights of Woman* (1792). To fulfill the still-unrealized potential of the French Revolution and to eliminate the many-sided sexual inequality she had felt so keenly, she demanded that

the Rights of Women be respected . . . [and] JUSTICE for one-half of the human race. . . . It is time to effect a revolution in female manners, time to restore to them their lost dignity, and make them, as part of the human species, labor, by reforming themselves, to reform the world.

Setting high standards for women, Wollstonecraft advocated rigorous coeducation, which would make women better wives and mothers, good citizens, and even economically independent people. Women could manage businesses and enter politics if only men would give them the chance. Men themselves would benefit from women's rights, for Wollstonecraft believed that "the two sexes mutually corrupt and improve each other."[6] Wollstonecraft's analysis testified to the power of the Revolution to excite and inspire outside France. Paralleling ideas put forth independently in France by Olympe de Gouges (1748–1793), a self-taught writer and woman of the people (see Listening to the Past), Wollstonecraft's work marked the birth of the modern women's movement for equal rights, and it was ultimately very influential.

The kings and nobles of continental Europe, who had at first welcomed the revolution in France as weakening a competing power, began to feel no less threatened than Burke and his supporters. At their courts they listened to the diatribes of great court nobles who had fled France and were urging intervention in France's affairs. When Louis XVI and Marie Antoinette were arrested and returned to Paris after trying unsuccessfully to slip out of France in June 1791, the monarchs of Austria and Prussia, in the Declaration of Pillnitz, declared their willingness to intervene in France in certain circumstances.

But the crowned heads of Europe did not deter the revolutionary spirit in France. When the National Assembly disbanded, it sought popular support by decreeing that none of its members would be eligible for election to the new Legislative Assembly. This meant that when the new representative body convened in October 1791, it had a different character. The great majority of the legislators were still prosperous, well-educated, middle-class men, but they were younger and less cautious

Mary Wollstonecraft   Painted by an unknown artist when Mary Wollstonecraft was thirty-two and writing her revolutionary *Vindication of the Rights of Woman,* this portrait highlights the remarkable strength of character that energized Wollstonecraft's brilliant intellect. *(Source: The Board of Trustees of the National Museums and Galleries on Merseyside, Walker Art Gallery)*

than their predecessors. Loosely allied and known as Jacobins, after the name of their political club, the representatives to the Legislative Assembly were passionately committed to liberal revolution.

The Jacobins increasingly lumped "useless aristocrats" and "despotic monarchs" together and easily whipped themselves into a patriotic fury with bombastic oratory. If the courts of Europe were attempting to incite a war of kings against France, then "we will incite a war of people against kings. . . . Ten million Frenchmen, kindled by the fire of liberty, armed with the sword, with reason, with eloquence would be able to change the face of the world and make the tyrants tremble on their thrones."[7] Only Robespierre and a very few others argued that people would not welcome liberation at the point of a gun. Such warnings were brushed aside. France would "rise to the full height of her mission," as one deputy urged. In April 1792 France declared war on Francis II, the Habsburg monarch.

France's crusade against tyranny went poorly at first. Prussia joined Austria in the Austrian Netherlands (present-day Belgium), and French forces broke and fled at their first encounter with armies of this First Coalition. The road to Paris lay open, and it is possible that only conflict between the eastern monarchs over the division of Poland saved France from defeat.

Military reversals and Austro-Prussian threats caused a wave of patriotic fervor to sweep France. In this supercharged wartime atmosphere, rumors of treason by the king and queen spread in Paris. Once again, the common people of Paris acted decisively. On August 10, 1792, a revolutionary crowd captured the royal palace at the Tuileries after heavy fighting. The king and his family fled for their lives to the nearby Legislative Assembly, which suspended the king from all his functions, imprisoned him, and called for a new National Convention to be elected by universal male suffrage. Monarchy in France was on its deathbed, mortally wounded by war and popular upheaval.

The Second Revolution

The fall of the monarchy marked a rapid radicalization of the Revolution, a phase that historians often call the "second revolution." Louis's imprisonment was followed by the September Massacres. Wild stories seized the city that imprisoned counter-revolutionary aristocrats and priests were plotting with the allied invaders. As a result, angry crowds invaded the prisons of Paris and summarily slaughtered half of the men and women they found. In late September 1792, the new, popularly elected National Convention proclaimed France a republic.

The republic sought to create a new popular culture to assure its future and fashioned compelling symbols that broke with the past and glorified the new order. It adopted a brand-new revolutionary calendar, which eliminated saints' days and renamed the days and the months after the seasons of the year. Citizens were expected to address each other with the friendly "thou" of the people rather than with the formal "you" of the rich and powerful. The republic energetically promoted broad, open-air, democratic festivals that sought to redirect the people's traditional enthusiasm for Catholic religious celebrations to secular holidays. Instilling republican virtue and a love of nation, these spectacles were less successful in villages than in cities, where popular interest in politics was greater and Catholicism was weaker.

All of the members of the National Convention were Jacobins and republicans, and the great majority continued to come from the well-educated middle class. But the Convention was increasingly divided into two bitterly competitive groups—the Girondists, named after a department in southwestern France, and the Mountain, led by Robespierre and another young lawyer, Georges Jacques Danton. The Mountain was so called because its members sat on the uppermost left-hand benches of the assembly hall.

This division was clearly apparent after the National Convention overwhelmingly convicted Louis XVI of treason. By a single vote, 361 of the 720 members of the Convention then unconditionally sentenced him to death in January 1793. Louis died with tranquil dignity on the newly invented guillotine. One of his last statements was "I am innocent and shall die without fear. I would that my death might bring happiness to the French, and ward off the dangers which I foresee."[8]

Both the Girondists and the Mountain were determined to continue the "war against tyranny." After stopping the Prussians at the indecisive Battle of Valmy on September 20, 1792, Republican armies successfully invaded Savoy and the German Rhineland. To the north, the revolutionary armies won their first major battle at Jemappes and by November 1792 were occupying the entire Austrian Netherlands. Everywhere they went, French armies of occupation chased the princes, "abolished feudalism," and found support among some peasants and middle-class people.

But the French armies also lived off the land, requisitioning food and supplies and plundering local treasures. The liberators looked increasingly like foreign invaders. International tensions mounted. In February 1793 the National Convention, at war with Austria and Prussia, declared war on Britain, Holland, and Spain as well. Republican France was now at war with almost all of Europe, a great war that would last almost without interruption until 1815.

As the forces of the First Coalition drove the French from the Austrian Netherlands, peasants in western France revolted against being drafted into the army. They were supported and encouraged in their resistance by devout Catholics, royalists, and foreign agents.

In Paris the quarrelsome National Convention found itself locked in a life-and-death political struggle between the Girondists and the Mountain. Both groups hated privilege and wanted to temper economic liberalism with social concern. Yet personal hatreds ran deep. The Girondists feared a bloody dictatorship by the Mountain, and the Mountain was no less convinced that the more moderate Girondists would turn to conservatives and even royalists in order to retain power. With the middle-class delegates so bitterly divided, the laboring poor of Paris emerged as the decisive political factor.

The laboring men and women of Paris always constituted—along with the peasantry in the summer of 1789—the elemental force that drove the Revolution forward. It was they who had stormed the Bastille, marched on Versailles, driven the king from the Tuileries, and carried out the September Massacres. The petty traders and laboring poor were often known as the *sans-culottes,* "without breeches," because the men wore trousers instead of the knee breeches of the aristocracy and the solid middle class. The immediate interests of the sans-culottes were mainly economic, and in the spring of 1793 the economic situation was as bad as the military situation. Rapid inflation, unemployment, and food shortages were again weighing heavily on poor families.

By the spring of 1793, sans-culottes men and women, encouraged by the so-called angry men, were demanding radical political action to guarantee them their daily bread. At first the Mountain joined the Girondists in violently rejecting these demands. But in the face of military defeat, peasant revolt, and hatred of the Girondists, Robespierre's group joined with sans-culottes activists in the city government to engineer a popular uprising, which forced the Convention to arrest thirty-one Girondist deputies for treason on June 2. All power passed to the Mountain.

 The End of Louis XVI   Some cheered and some wept when the executioner showed the crowd the condemned monarch's severed head. The execution of the king was a victory for the radicals in Paris, but it horrified Europe's monarchs and conservatives, and it strengthened their opposition to the French Revolution. *(Source: Musée Carnavalet/Laurie Platt Winfrey, Inc.)*

Robespierre and others from the Mountain joined the recently formed Committee of Public Safety, to which the Convention had given dictatorial power to deal with the national emergency. These developments in Paris triggered revolt in leading provincial cities, such as Lyons and Marseilles, where moderates denounced Paris and demanded a decentralized government. The peasant revolt spread, and the republic's armies were driven back on all fronts. By July 1793 defeat appeared imminent.

Total War and the Terror

A year later, in July 1794, the Austrian Netherlands and the Rhineland were once again in the hands of conquering French armies, and the First Coalition was falling apart. This remarkable change of fortune was due to the revolutionary government's success in harnessing, for perhaps the first time in history, the explosive forces of a planned economy, revolutionary terror, and modern nationalism in a total war effort.

Robespierre and the Committee of Public Safety advanced with implacable resolution on several

fronts in 1793 and 1794. First, in an effort to save revolutionary France, they continued to collaborate with the fiercely patriotic and democratic sans-culottes, who retained the common people's traditional faith in fair prices and a moral economic order and who distrusted most wealthy capitalists and all aristocrats. Thus Robespierre and his co-workers established, as best they could, a planned economy with egalitarian social overtones. Rather than let supply and demand determine prices, the government decreed the maximum allowable prices for a host of key products. Though the state was too weak to enforce all its price regulations, it did fix the price of bread in Paris at levels the poor could afford. Bakers were permitted to make only the "bread of equality"—a brown bread made of a mixture of all available flours. White bread and pastries were outlawed as frivolous luxuries. The poor of Paris may not have eaten well, but at least they ate.

They also worked, mainly to produce arms and munitions for the war effort. Craftsmen and small manufacturers were told what to produce and when to deliver. The government nationalized many small workshops and requisitioned raw

 The Last Roll Call Prisoners sentenced to death by revolutionary courts listen to an official solemnly reading the names of those selected for immediate execution. After being bound, the prisoners will ride standing up in a small cart through the streets of Paris to the nearby guillotine. As this painting highlights, both women and men were executed for political crimes under the Terror. *(Source: Mansell Collection)*

THE FRENCH REVOLUTION

May 5, 1789	Estates General convenes at Versailles
June 17, 1789	Third estate declares itself the National Assembly
June 20, 1789	Oath of the Tennis Court
July 14, 1789	Storming of the Bastille
July–Aug. 1789	The Great Fear in the countryside
August 4, 1789	National Assembly abolishes feudal privileges
August 27, 1789	National Assembly issues Declaration of the Rights of Man
October 5, 1789	Women march on Versailles and force royal family to return to Paris
November 1789	National Assembly confiscates lands held by the Catholic church
July 1790	Civil Constitution of the Clergy establishes a national church Louis XVI reluctantly agrees to accept a constitutional monarchy
June 1791	Arrest of the royal family while attempting to flee France
August 1791	Declaration of Pillnitz by Austria and Prussia
April 1792	France declares war on Austria
August 1792	Parisian mob attacks palace and takes Louis XVI prisoner
September 1792	September Massacres National Convention declares France a republic and abolishes monarchy
January 1793	Execution of Louis XVI
February 1793	France declares war on Britain, Holland, and Spain
March 1793	Bitter struggle in the National Convention between Girondists and the Mountain
April–June 1793	Robespierre and the Mountain organize the Committee of Public Safety Revolts in provincial cities
September 1793	Price controls to aid the sans-culottes and mobilize war effort
1793–1794	Reign of Terror in Paris and the provinces
Spring 1794	French armies victorious on all fronts
July 1794	Execution of Robespierre Thermidorian Reaction begins
1795–1799	The Directory
1795	End of economic controls and suppression of the sans-culottes
1797	Napoleon defeats Austrian armies in Italy and returns triumphant to Paris
1798	Austria, Great Britain, and Russia form the Second Coalition against France
1799	Napoleon overthrows the Directory and seizes power

materials and grain from the peasants. Failures to control and coordinate were failures of means and not of desire: seldom if ever before had a government attempted to manage an economy so thoroughly. The second revolution and the ascendancy of the sans-culottes had produced an embryonic emergency socialism, which thoroughly frightened Europe's properties classes and had great influence on the subsequent development of socialist ideology.

Second, while radical economic measures supplied the poor with bread and the armies with weapons, the Reign of Terror (1793–1794) was solidifying the home front. Special revolutionary courts responsible only to Robespierre's Committee of Public Safety tried rebels and "enemies of the nation" for political crimes. Drawing on popular, sans-culottes support, these local courts ignored normal legal procedures and judged severely. Some 40,000 French men and women were executed or died in prison. Another 300,000 suspects crowded the prisons.

Robespierre's Reign of Terror was one of the most controversial phases of the French Revolution. Most historians now believe that the Reign of Terror was not directed against any single class but was a political weapon directed impartially against all who might oppose the revolutionary government. For many Europeans of the time, however, the Reign of Terror represented a terrifying perversion of the generous ideals that had existed in 1789.

The third and perhaps most decisive element in the French republic's victory over the First Coalition was its ability to continue drawing on the explosive power of patriotic dedication to a national state and a national mission. This is the essence of modern nationalism, and it was something new in history. With a common language and a common tradition newly reinforced by the ideas of popular sovereignty and democracy, the French people were stirred by a common loyalty. The shared danger of foreign foes and internal rebels unified all classes in a heroic defense of the nation. Everyone had to participate in the national effort. According to a famous decree of August 23, 1793:

The young men shall go to battle and the married men shall forge arms. The women shall make tents and clothes, and shall serve in the hospitals; children shall tear rags into lint. The old men will be guided to the public places of the cities to kindle the courage of the young warriors and to preach the unity of the Republic and the hatred of kings.

Like the wars of religion, war in 1793 was a crusade, a life-and-death struggle between good and evil. This war, however, was fought for a secular, rather than a religious, ideology.

Because all unmarried young men were subject to the draft, the French armed forces swelled to a million men in fourteen armies. A force of this size was unprecedented in the history of European warfare. The soldiers were led by young, impetuous generals who had often risen rapidly from the ranks and personified the opportunities the Revolution seemed to offer gifted sons of the people. These generals used mass attacks at bayonet point by their highly motivated forces to overwhelm the enemy. By the spring of 1794, French armies were victorious on all fronts. The republic was saved.

The Thermidorian Reaction and the Directory (1794–1799)

The success of the French armies led Robespierre and the Committee of Public Safety to relax the emergency economic controls, but they extended the political Reign of Terror. Their lofty goal was increasingly an ideal democratic republic where justice would reign and there would be neither rich nor poor. Their lowly means were unrestrained despotism and the guillotine, which struck down any who might seriously question the new order. In March 1794, to the horror of many sans-culottes, Robespierre's Terror wiped out many of the angry men, who had been criticizing Robespierre for being soft on the wealthy. Two weeks later, several of Robespierre's long-standing collaborators, led by the famous orator Danton, marched up the steps to the guillotine. A strange assortment of radicals and moderates in the Convention, knowing that they might be next, organized a conspiracy. They howled down Robespierre when he tried to speak to the National Convention on 9 Thermidor (July 27, 1794). On the following day, it was Robespierre's turn to be shaved by the revolutionary razor.

As Robespierre's closest supporters followed their leader, France unexpectedly experienced a thorough reaction to the despotism of the Reign of Terror. In a general way, this "Thermidorian reaction" recalled the early days of the Revolution.

The respectable middle-class lawyers and professionals who had led the liberal revolution of 1789 reasserted their authority, drawing support from their own class, the provincial cities, and the better-off peasants. The National Convention abolished many economic controls, printed more paper currency, and let prices rise sharply. And all the while, wealthy bankers and newly rich speculators celebrated the sudden end of the Terror with an orgy of self-indulgence and ostentatious luxury, an orgy symbolized by the shockingly low-cut gowns that quickly became the rage among their wives and mistresses.

The collapse of economic controls, coupled with runaway inflation, hit the working poor very hard. The gaudy extravagance of the rich wounded their pride. The sans-culottes accepted private property, but they believed passionately in small business, decent wages, and economic justice. Increasingly disorganized after Robespierre purged radical leaders, the common people of Paris finally revolted against the emerging new order in early 1795. The Convention quickly used the army to suppress these insurrections. For the first time since the fall of the Bastille, bread riots and uprisings by Parisians living on the edge of starvation were effectively put down by a government that made no concessions to the poor. In the face of all these catastrophes, the revolutionary fervor of the laboring poor in Paris finally subsided.

In villages and small towns there arose a great cry for peace and a turning toward religion, especially from women, who had seldom experienced the political radicalization of sans-culottes women in the big cities. Instead, these women had frequently and tenaciously defended their culture and religious beliefs. As the frustrated government began to retreat on the religious question from 1796 to 1801, the women of rural France brought back the Catholic church and the open worship of God. In the words of a leading historian, these women worked constructively and effectively for a return to a normal and structured lifestyle:

Peacefully but purposefully, they sought to re-establish a pattern of life punctuated by a peeling bell and one in which the rites of passage—birth, marriage, and death—were respected and hallowed. The state had intruded too far and women entered the public arena to push it back and won. It was one of the most resounding political statements made by the populace in the entire history of the Revolution.[9]

As for the middle-class members of the National Convention, in 1795 they wrote yet another constitution, which they believed would guarantee their economic position and political supremacy. The mass of the population voted only for electors, who were men of means. Electors then elected the members of a reorganized Legislative Assembly, as well as key officials throughout France. The new assembly also chose a five-man executive—the Directory.

The Directory continued to support French military expansion abroad. War was no longer so much a crusade as a means to meet ever-present, ever-unsolved economic problems. Large, victorious French armies reduced unemployment at home and were able to live off the territories they conquered and plundered.

The unprincipled action of the Directory reinforced widespread disgust with war and starvation, and the national elections of 1797 returned a large number of conservative and even monarchist deputies who favored peace at almost any price. The members of the Directory, fearing for their skins, used the army to nullify the elections and began to govern dictatorially. Two years later, Napoleon Bonaparte ended the Directory in a coup d'état and substituted a strong dictatorship for a weak one. The effort to establish stable representative government had failed.

THE NAPOLEONIC ERA (1799–1815)

For almost fifteen years, from 1799 to 1814, France was in the hands of a keen-minded military dictator of exceptional ability. One of history's most fascinating leaders, Napoleon Bonaparte (1769–1821) realized the need to put an end to civil strife in France in order to create unity and consolidate his rule. And he did. But Napoleon saw himself as a man of destiny, and the glory of war and the dream of universal empire proved irresistible.

Napoleon's Rule of France

In 1799 when he seized power, young General Napoleon Bonaparte was a national hero. Born in Corsica into an impoverished noble family in 1769, Napoleon left home and became a lieutenant in the French artillery in 1785. After a brief and unsuccessful adventure fighting for Corsican independence in 1789, he returned to France as a French patriot and a dedicated revolutionary. Rising rapidly in the new army, Napoleon was placed in command of French forces in Italy and won brilliant victories there in 1796 and 1797. His next campaign, in Egypt, was a failure, but Napoleon made his way back to France before the fiasco was generally known. His reputation remained intact.

Napoleon soon learned that some prominent members of the Legislative Assembly were plotting against the Directory. The dissatisfaction of these plotters stemmed not so much from the fact that the Directory was a dictatorship as from the fact that it was a weak dictatorship. Ten years of upheaval and uncertainty had made firm rule much more appealing than liberty and popular politics to these disillusioned revolutionaries. They wanted a strong military ruler, and the flamboyant thirty-year-old Napoleon was ideal. Thus the conspirators and Napoleon organized a takeover. On November 9, 1799, they ousted the Directors, and the following day soldiers disbanded the Legislative Assembly at bayonet point. Napoleon was named first consul of the republic, and a new constitution consolidating his position was overwhelmingly approved in a plebiscite in December 1799. Republican appearances were maintained, but Napoleon was already the real ruler of France.

The essence of Napoleon's domestic policy was to use his great and highly personal powers to maintain order and put an end to civil strife. He did so by working out unwritten agreements with powerful groups in France. Napoleon's bargain with the solid middle class was codified in the Civil Code of 1804, which reasserted two of the fundamental principles of the liberal and essentially moderate revolution of 1789: equality of all male citizens before the law and absolute security of wealth and private property. Napoleon and the leading bankers of Paris established the privately owned Bank of France, which loyally served the interests of both the state and the financial oligarchy. Napoleon's defense of the new economic order also appealed successfully to the peasants, who had gained both land and status from the revolutionary changes.

At the same time, Napoleon accepted and strengthened the position of the French bureaucracy. Building on the solid foundations that revolutionary governments had inherited from the Old Regime, he perfected a thoroughly centralized state. A network of prefects, subprefects, and centrally appointed mayors depended on Napoleon and served him well. Nor were members of the old nobility slighted. Napoleon granted amnesty to émigrés on the condition that they return to France and take a loyalty oath. Members of this returning elite soon ably occupied many high posts in the expanding centralized state. Napoleon also created a new imperial nobility in order to reward his most talented generals and officials.

Napoleon's great skill in gaining support from important and potentially hostile groups is illustrated by his treatment of the Catholic church in France. Personally uninterested in religion, Napoleon wanted to heal the religious division remaining from the Revolution so that a united Catholic church in France could serve as a bulwark of order and social peace. After long and arduous negotiations, Napoleon and Pope Pius VII (r. 1800–1823) signed the Concordat of 1801. The pope gained for French Catholics the precious right to practice their religion freely, but Napoleon gained political power: his government now nominated bishops, paid the clergy, and exerted great influence over the church in France.

The domestic reforms of Napoleon's early years were his greatest achievement. Much of his legal and administrative reorganization has survived in France to this day. More generally, Napoleon's domestic initiatives gave the great majority of French people a welcome sense of order and stability. And when Napoleon added the glory of military victory, he rekindled a spirit of national unity.

Order and unity had their price: Napoleon's authoritarian rule. Women, who had often participated in revolutionary politics without having legal equality, lost many of the gains they had made in the 1790s under the new Napoleonic Code. Under the law, women were dependents of either their fathers or their husbands, and they could not make contracts or even have bank accounts in their own names. Indeed, Napoleon and his advisers aimed at re-establishing a "family monarch," where the power of the husband and father was as absolute over the wife and the children as that of Napoleon was over his subjects.

Free speech and freedom of the press—fundamental rights of the liberal revolution enshrined in the Declaration of the Rights of Man—were continually violated. Napoleon constantly reduced the number of newspapers in Paris. By 1811 only four were left, and they were little more than organs of government propaganda. The occasional elections were a farce. Later laws prescribed harsh penalties for political offenses.

These changes in the law were part of the creation of a police state in France. Since Napoleon was usually busy making war, this task was largely left to Joseph Fouché, an unscrupulous opportunist who had earned a reputation for brutality during the Reign of Terror. As minister of police, Fouché organized a ruthlessly efficient spy system, which kept thousands of citizens under continual police surveillance. People suspected of subversive activities were arbitrarily detained, placed under house arrest, or even consigned to insane asylums. After 1810 political suspects were held in state prisons, as they had been during the Terror. There were about twenty-five hundred such political prisoners in 1814.

Napoleon's Wars and Foreign Policy

Napoleon was above all a military man, and a great one. After coming to power in 1799, he sent peace feelers to Austria and Great Britain, the two remaining members of the Second Coalition, which had been formed against France in 1798. When these overtures were rejected, French armies led by Napoleon decisively defeated the Austrians. Once more, as in 1797, the British were alone—and war-weary, like the French. Still seeking to consolidate his regime domestically, Napoleon concluded the Treaty of Amiens with Great Britain in 1802. France remained in control of Holland, the Austrian Netherlands, the west bank of the Rhine, and most of the Italian peninsula. The Treaty of Amiens was clearly a diplomatic triumph for Napoleon, and peace with honor and profit increased his popularity at home.

In 1802 Napoleon was secure but unsatisfied. Ever a romantic gambler as well as a brilliant administrator, he could not contain his power drive. Thus he aggressively threatened British interests in the eastern Mediterranean and tried to restrict British trade with all of Europe. Deciding to renew war with Britain in May 1803, Napoleon began making preparations to invade England. But Great Britain remained dominant on the seas. When Napoleon tried to bring his Mediterranean fleet around Gibraltar to northern France, a combined French and Spanish fleet was, after a series of mishaps, virtually annihilated by Lord Nelson at the Battle of Trafalgar on October 21, 1805. A cross-Channel invasion of England was henceforth impossible. Renewed fighting had its advantages, however, for the first consul used the wartime atmosphere to have himself proclaimed emperor in late 1804.

Austria, Russia, and Sweden joined with Britain to form the Third Coalition against France shortly before the Battle of Trafalgar. Actions such as Napoleon's assumption of the Italian crown had convinced both Alexander I of Russia and Francis II of Austria that Napoleon was a threat to their interests and to the European balance of power. Yet the Austrians and the Russians were no match for Napoleon, who scored a brilliant victory over them at the Battle of Austerlitz in December 1805. Alexander I decided to pull back, and Austria accepted large territorial losses in return for peace as the Third Coalition collapsed.

 David: Napoleon Crossing the Alps   Bold and commanding, with flowing cape and surging stallion, the daring young Napoleon Bonaparte leads his army across the Alps from Italy to battle the Austrians in 1797. This painting by the great Jacques-Louis David (1748–1825) is a stirring glorification of Napoleon, a brilliant exercise in mythmaking. *(Source: Louvre © Photo R.M.N.)*

RUSSIAN EMPIRE

Moscow
●Borodino
1812

St. Petersburg●

Smolensk●

●Kiev

Tilsit
Friedland 1807
Königsberg●

Warsaw●

**GRAND DUCHY
OF WARSAW**

**KINGDOM
OF
SWEDEN**

Stockholm●

**KINGDOM OF
NORWAY
AND
DENMARK**

Copenhagen●

Danzig●

PRUSSIA

*Baltic
Sea*

Black Sea

Dnieper

Vistula

Oder

Dniester

Danube

OTTOMAN EMPIRE

Constantinople●

Athens●

Cyprus

Crete

AUSTRIAN EMPIRE

Pest●
Buda●
Pressburg●
Vienna●
Austerlitz
1805
Wagram
1809

ILLYRIAN PROVINCES

**KINGDOM
OF NAPLES**

Rome●

Naples●

**KINGDOM OF
SICILY**

MALTA
(Gr. Br.)

IONIAN IS.
(Gr. Br.)

*Mediterranean
Sea*

Lübeck●
Hamburg●
Bremen●
Berlin●

WESTPHALIA

SAXONY
Leipzig 1813

**CONFEDERATION
OF THE RHINE**

Auerstädt 1806
Jena 1806

WÜRTTEMBERG

BAVARIA

BADEN

Rhine

SWITZERLAND

Zurich●

**KINGDOM
OF
ITALY**

Milan●

Marengo
1800
Genoa●

Elba

Corsica

SARDINIA

HELGOLAND
(Gr. Br.)

Brussels●
Waterloo
1815

Antwerp●

Amiens●

Paris●

Lunéville●

FRANCE

Seine

Loire

Rhône

Marseilles●

SCOTLAND

GREAT BRITAIN

ENGLAND

London●
Thames

IRELAND

*North
Sea*

*ATLANTIC
OCEAN*

SPAIN

Madrid●

Tagus

PORTUGAL

Lisbon●

Trafalgar
1805

GIBRALTAR
(Gr. Br.)

French empire
Dependent states
Allied with Napoleon
At war with Napoleon
✕ Major battles

0   150   300 Mi.
0   150   300 Km.

Victorious at Austerlitz, Napoleon proceeded to reorganize the German states to his liking. He established by decree the German Confederation of the Rhine, a union of fifteen German states minus Austria, Prussia, and Saxony. Naming himself "protector" of the confederation, Napoleon firmly controlled western Germany. His intervention in German affairs alarmed the Prussians, who mobilized their armies after more than a decade of peace with France. Napoleon attacked and won two more brilliant victories in October 1806, at Jena and Auerstädt. The war with Prussia, now joined by Russia, continued into the spring. After Napoleon's larger armies won another victory, Alexander I of Russia wanted peace. In the subsequent treaties of Tilsit, Prussia lost half of its population, while Russia accepted Napoleon's reorganization of western and central Europe. Alexander also promised to enforce Napoleon's recently decreed economic blockade against British goods.

After the victory of Austerlitz and even more after the treaties of Tilsit, Napoleon saw himself as the emperor of Europe and not just of France. The so-called Grand Empire he built had three parts. The core, or first part, was an ever-expanding France, which by 1810 included Belgium, Holland, parts of northern Italy, and much German territory on the east bank of the Rhine. Beyond French borders Napoleon established the second part: a number of dependent satellite kingdoms, on the thrones of which he placed (and replaced) the members of his large family. The third part comprised the independent but allied states of Austria, Prussia, and Russia. Both satellites and allies were expected after 1806 to support Napoleon's continental system and cease trade with Britain.

The impact of the Grand Empire on the peoples of Europe was considerable. In the areas incorporated into France and in the satellites (Map 23.1), Napoleon introduced many French laws, abolishing feudal dues and serfdom where French revolutionary armies had not already done so. Some of the peasants and middle class benefited from these reforms. Yet while he extended progressive measures to his cosmopolitan empire, Napoleon had to

put the prosperity and special interests of France first in order to safeguard his power base. Levying heavy taxes in money and men for his armies, Napoleon came to be regarded more as a conquering tyrant than as an enlightened liberator.

The first great revolt occurred in Spain. In 1808 a coalition of Catholics, monarchists, and patriots rebelled against Napoleon's attempts to make Spain a French satellite with a Bonaparte as its king. French armies occupied Madrid, but the foes of Napoleon fled to the hills and waged uncompromising guerrilla warfare. Spain was a clear warning: resistance to French imperialism was growing. Yet Napoleon pushed on, determined to hold his complex and far-flung empire together.

In 1810 when the Grand Empire was at its height, Britain still remained at war with France, helping the guerrillas in Spain and Portugal. Napoleon's continental system, organized to exclude British goods from the European continent and force that "nation of shopkeepers" to its knees, was a failure. Instead, it was France that suffered from Britain's counter-blockade, which created hard times for French artisans and the middle class. Perhaps looking for a scapegoat, Napoleon turned on Alexander I of Russia, who had been giving only lukewarm support to Napoleon's war of prohibitions against British goods.

Napoleon's invasion of Russia began in June 1812 with a force that eventually numbered 600,000, probably the largest force yet assembled in a single army. Only one-third of this force was French, however; nationals of all the satellites and allies were drafted into the operation. After the great battle of Borodino, a draw from which the Russians retreated in good order, Alexander ordered the evacuation of Moscow, which then burned, and he refused to negotiate. Finally, after five weeks in the burned-out city, Napoleon ordered a retreat. That retreat was one of the great military disasters in history. The Russian army and the Russian winter cut Napoleon's army to pieces. Only 30,000 men returned to their homelands.

Leaving his troops to their fate, Napoleon raced to Paris to raise yet another army. When he refused to accept a France reduced to its historical size— the proposal offered by Austria's foreign minister, Prince Klemens von Metternich—Austria and Prussia deserted Napoleon and joined Russia and Great Britain in the Fourth Coalition. All across Europe patriots called for a "war of liberation"

✳ **Map 23.1 Napoleonic Europe in 1810**   Only Great Britain remained at war with Napoleon at the height of the Grand Empire. Many British goods were smuggled through Helgoland, a tiny but strategic British possession off the German coast.

✳ **Goya: The Third of May, 1808** This famous painting screams in outrage at the horrors of war, which Goya witnessed in Spain. Spanish rebels, focused around the Christ-like figure at the center, are gunned down by anonymous French soldiers, grim forerunners of modern death squads and their atrocities. (*Source: Museo del Prado, Madrid*)

against Napoleon's oppression, and the well-disciplined regular armies of Napoleon's enemies closed in for the kill. Less than a month later, on April 4, 1814, a defeated, abandoned Napoleon abdicated his throne. After this unconditional abdication, the victorious allies granted Napoleon the island of Elba off the coast of Italy as his own tiny state.

The allies also agreed to the restoration of the Bourbon dynasty. The new monarch, Louis XVIII (r. 1814–1824), issued the Constitutional Charter, which accepted many of France's revolutionary changes and guaranteed civil liberties. Indeed, the Charter gave France a constitutional monarchy roughly similar to that established in 1791, al-

though far fewer people had the right to vote for representatives to the resurrected Chamber of Deputies. Moreover, in an attempt to strengthen popular support for Louis XVIII's new government, France was treated leniently by the allies, who agreed to meet in Vienna to work out a general peace settlement (see pages 805–807).

Louis XVIII—old, ugly, and crippled by gout—totally lacked the glory and magic of Napoleon. Hearing of political unrest in France and diplomatic tensions in Vienna, Napoleon staged a daring escape from Elba in February 1815. Landing in France, he issued appeals for support and marched on Paris with a small band of followers. French officers and soldiers who had fought so

THE NAPOLEONIC ERA

November 1799	Napoleon overthrows the Directory
December 1799	French voters overwhelmingly approve Napoleon's new constitution
1800	Napoleon founds the Bank of France
1801	France defeats Austria and acquires Italian and German territories in the Treaty of Lunéville Napoleon signs a concordat with the pope
1802	Treaty of Amiens with Britain
December 1804	Napoleon crowns himself emperor
October 1805	Battle of Trafalgar: Britain defeats the French and Spanish fleets
December 1805	Battle of Austerlitz: Napoleon defeats Austria and Prussia
1807	Treaties of Tilsit: Napoleon redraws the map of Europe
1810	Height of the Grand Empire
June 1812	Napoleon invades Russia with 600,000 men
Winter 1812	Disastrous retreat from Russia
March 1814	Russia, Prussia, Austria, and Britain form the Quadruple Alliance to defeat France
April 1814	Napoleon abdicates and is exiled to Elba
Feb.–June 1815	Napoleon escapes from Elba and rules France until suffering defeat at Battle of Waterloo

long for their emperor responded to the call. Louis XVIII fled, and once more Napoleon took command. But Napoleon's gamble was a desperate long shot, for the allies were united against him. At the end of a frantic period known as the Hundred Days, they crushed his forces at Waterloo on June 18, 1815, and imprisoned him on the rocky island of St. Helena, far off the western coast of Africa. Old Louis XVIII returned again—this time "in the baggage of the allies," as his detractors scornfully put it—and recommenced his reign. The allies now dealt more harshly with the apparently incorrigible French (see page 807). And Napoleon, doomed to suffer crude insults at the hands of sadistic English jailers on distant St. Helena, could take revenge only by writing his memoirs, skillfully nurturing the myth that he had been Europe's revolutionary

liberator, a romantic hero whose lofty work had been undone by oppressive reactionaries. An era had ended.

SUMMARY

The French Revolution left a compelling and many-sided political legacy. This legacy included, most notably, liberalism, assertive nationalism, radical democratic republicanism, embryonic socialism, and self-conscious conservatism. It also left a rich and turbulent history of electoral competition, legislative assemblies, and even mass politics. Thus the French Revolution and conflicting interpretations of its significance presented a whole range of political options and alternative visions of the future. For this reason it was truly *the* revolution in modern European politics.

The revolution that began in America and spread to France was a liberal revolution. Revolutionaries on both sides of the Atlantic wanted to establish civil liberties and equality before the law within the framework of representative government, and they succeeded. In France liberal nobles and an increasingly class-conscious middle class overwhelmed declining monarchial absolutism and feudal privilege, thanks to the intervention of the common people—the sans-culottes and the peasants. France's new political system reflected a social structure based increasingly on wealth and achievement rather than on tradition and legal privileges.

After the establishment of the Republic, the radical phase of the revolution during the Terror, and the fall of Robespierre, the educated elites and the solid middle class reasserted themselves under the Directory. And though Napoleon sharply curtailed representative institutions and individual rights, he effectively promoted the reconciliation of old and new, of centralized bureaucracy and careers open to talent, of noble and bourgeois in a restructured property-owning elite. Louis XVIII had to accept the commanding position of this restructured elite, and in granting representative government and civil liberties to facilitate his restoration to the throne in 1814, he submitted to the rest of the liberal triumph of 1789 to 1791. The liberal core of the French Revolution had successfully survived a generation of war and dictatorship.

The lived experience of the French Revolution and the wars that went with it exercised a pervasive influence on politics and the political imagination in the nineteenth century, not only in France but throughout Europe and even the rest of the world. The radical legacy of the embattled republic of 1793 and 1794, with its sans-culottes democratic republicanism and its egalitarian ideology and embryonic socialism, would inspire republicans, democrats, and early socialists. Indeed, revolutionary upheaval encouraged generations of radicals to believe that political revolution might remake society and even create a new humanity. At the same time, there was a legacy of a powerful and continuing reaction to the French Revolution and to aggressive French nationalism. Monarchists and traditionalists believed that 1789 had been a tragic mistake. They concluded that democratic republicanism and sans-culottes activism led only to war, class conflict, and savage dictatorship. Conservatives and many com-

fortable moderates were profoundly disillusioned by the revolutionary era. They looked with nostalgia toward the supposedly ordered world of benevolent monarchy, firm government, and respectful common people.

NOTES

1. Quoted in R. R. Palmer, *The Age of the Democratic Revolution,* vol. 1 (Princeton, N.J.: Princeton University Press, 1959), p. 239.
2. G. Lefebvre, *The Coming of the French Revolution* (New York: Vintage Books, 1947), p. 81.
3. P. H. Beik, ed., *The French Revolution* (New York: Walker, 1970), p. 89.
4. G. Pernoud and S. Flaisser, eds., *The French Revolution* (Greenwich, Conn.: Fawcett, 1960), p. 61.
5. O. Hufton, *Women and the Limits of Citizenship in the French Revolution* (Toronto: University of Toronto Press, 1992), pp. 3–22.
6. Quotations from Wollstonecraft are drawn from E. W. Sunstein, *A Different Face: The Life of Mary Wollstonecraft* (New York: Harper & Row, 1975), pp. 208, 211; and H. R . James, *Mary Wollstonecraft: A Sketch* (London: Oxford University Press, 1932), pp. 60, 62, 69.
7. L. Gershoy, *The Era of the French Revolution, 1789–1799* (New York: Van Nostrand, 1957), p. 150.
8. Pernoud and Flaisser, *The French Revolution,* pp. 193–194.
9. Hufton, *Women and the Limits of Citizenship in the French Revolution,* p. 130.

SUGGESTED READING

For fascinating eyewitness reports on the French Revolution, see the edited works by Beik and by Pernoud and Flaisser mentioned in the Notes. In addition, A. Young's *Travels in France During the Years 1787, 1788 and 1789* (1969) offers an engrossing contemporary description of France and Paris on the eve of revolution. E. Burke, *Reflections on the Revolution in France,* first published in 1790, is the classic conservative indictment. The intense passions the French Revolution has generated may be seen in nineteenth-century French historians, notably the enthusiastic J. Michelet, *History of the French Revolution;* the hostile H. Taine; and the judicious A. de Tocqueville, whose masterpiece, *The Old Regime and the French Revolution,* was first published in 1856. Important general studies on the entire period include the work of R. R. Palmer, cited in the Notes, which paints a comparative international picture; E. J. Hobsbawm, *The Age of Revolution, 1789–1848* (1962); C. Breunig, *The Age of Revolution and Reaction, 1789–1850* (1970); O. Connelly, *French Revolution—Napoleonic Era* (1979); and L. Dehio, *The Precarious Balance: Four Centuries of the European Power Struggle* (1962).

Recent years have seen a wealth of new scholarship and interpretation. A. Cobban, *The Social Interpretation of the French Revolution* (1964), and F. Furet, *Interpreting the French Revolution* (1981), are major reassessments of long-dominant ideas, which are admirably presented in N. Hampson, *A Social History of the French Revolution* (1963), and in the volume by Lefebvre listed in the Notes. E. Kennedy, *A Cultural History of the French Revolution* (1989), beautifully written and handsomely illustrated, and W. Doyle, *Origins of the French Revolution,* 3d ed. (1988), are excellent on long-term developments. Among recent studies, which generally are often quite critical of revolutionary developments, several are noteworthy: J. Bosher, *The French Revolution* (1988); S. Schama, *Citizens: A Chronicle of the French Revolution* (1989); W. Doyle, *The Oxford History of the French Revolution* (1989); and D. Sutherland, *France, 1789–1815: Revolution and Counterrevolution* (1986).

Two valuable anthologies concisely presenting a range of interpretations are F. Kafker and J. Laux, eds., *The French Revolutions: Conflicting Interpretations,* 4th ed. (1989), and G. Best, ed., *The Permanent Revolution: The French Revolution and Its Legacy, 1789–1989* (1988). G. Rude makes the men and women of the great days of upheaval come alive in his *The Crowd in the French Revolution* (1959), whereas R. R. Palmer studies sympathetically the leaders of the Terror in *Twelve Who Ruled* (1941). Four other particularly interesting, detailed works are D. Jordan, *The Revolutionary Career of Maximilien Robespierre* (1985); J. P. Bertaud, *The Army of the French Revolution: From Citizen-Soldier to Instrument of Power* (1988); C. L. R. James, *The Black Jacobins* (1938, 1980), on black slave revolt in Haiti; and J. C. Herold, *Mistress to an Age* (1955), on the remarkable writer Madame de Staël. Other significant studies on aspects of revolutionary France include P. Jones's pathbreaking *The Peasantry in the French Revolution*

(1979); W. Sewell, Jr.'s imaginative *Work and Revolution in France: The Language of Labor from the Old Regime to 1848* (1980); and L. Hunt's innovative *Politics, Culture, and Class in the French Revolution* (1984).

An ongoing explosion of studies on women in the French Revolution is increasing knowledge and also raising conflicting interpretations. These developments may be seen by comparing two particularly important works: J. Landes, *Women and the Public Sphere in the Age of the French Revolution* (1988), and O. Hufton, listed in the Notes. D. Outram, *The Body and the French Revolution: Sex, Class and Political Culture* (1989), and L. Hunt, *The Family Romance of the French Revolution* (1992), also provide innovative analyses of the gender-related aspects of revolutionary politics and are highly recommended. D. Levy, H. Applewhite, and M. Johnson, eds., *Women in Revolutionary Paris, 1789–1795* (1979), is a valuable collection of contemporary documents with helpful commentaries. Mary Wollstonecraft's dramatic life is the subject of several good biographies, including those by Sunstein and James cited in the Notes.

Two important works placing political developments in a comparative perspective are P. Higonnet, *Sister Republics: The Origins of French and American Republicanism* (1988), and E. Morgan, *Inventing the People: The Rise of Popular Sovereignty in England and America* (1988). B. Bailyn, *The Ideological Origins of the American Revolution* (1967), is also noteworthy.

The best synthesis on Napoleonic France is L. Bergeron, *France Under Napoleon* (1981). P. Geyl, *Napoleon: For and Against* (1949), is a delightful discussion of changing political interpretations of Napoleon, which may be compared with a more recent treatment by R. Jones, *Napoleon: Man and Myth* (1977). Good biographies are J. Thompson, *Napoleon Bonaparte: His Rise and Fall* (1952); F. Markham, *Napoleon* (1964); and V. Cronin, *Napoleon Bonaparte* (1972). Wonderful novels inspired by the period include Raphael Sabatini's *Scaramouche,* a swashbuckler of revolutionary intrigue with accurate historical details; Charles Dickens's fanciful *Tale of Two Cities;* and Leo Tolstoy's monumental saga of Napoleon's invasion of Russia (and much more), *War and Peace.*

Revolution and Women's Rights

The 1789 Declaration of the Rights of Man was a revolutionary call for legal equality, representative government, and individual freedom. But the new rights were strictly limited to men; Napoleon tightened further the subordination of French women.

Among those who saw the contradiction in granting supposedly universal rights to only half of the population was Marie Gouze (1748–1793), known to history as Olympe de Gouges. The daughter of a provincial butcher and peddler, she pursued a literary career in Paris after the death of her husband. Between 1790 and 1793 she wrote more than two dozen political pamphlets under her new name. De Gouges's great work was her "Declaration of the Rights of Women" (1791). Excerpted here, de Gouges's manifesto went beyond the 1789 Rights of Man. It called on males to end their oppression of women and give women equal rights. A radical on women's issues, de Gouges sympathized with the monarchy and criticized Robespierre in print. Convicted of sedition, she was guillotined in November 1793.

. . . Man, are you capable of being just? . . . Tell me, what gives you sovereign empire to oppress my sex? Your strength? Your talents? Observe the Creator in his wisdom . . . and give me, if you dare, an example of this tyrannical empire. Go back to animals, consult the elements, study plants . . . and distinguish, if you can, the sexes in the administration of nature. Everywhere you will find them mingled; everywhere they cooperate in harmonious togetherness in this immortal masterpiece.

Man alone has raised his exceptional circumstances to a principle. . . . He wants to command as a despot a sex which is in full possession of its intellectual faculties; he pretends to enjoy the Revolution and to claim his rights to equality in order to say nothing more about it.

DECLARATION OF THE RIGHTS OF WOMAN AND THE FEMALE CITIZEN

For the National Assembly to decree in its last session, or in those of the next legislature:

PREAMBLE

Mothers, daughters, sisters and representatives of the nation demand to be constituted into a national assembly. Believing that ignorance, omission, or scorn for the rights of woman are the only causes of public misfortunes and of the corruption of governments, [the women] have resolved to set forth in a solemn declaration the natural, inalienable, and sacred rights of woman. . . .

. . . the sex that is as superior in beauty as it is in courage during the sufferings of maternity recognizes and declares in the presence and under the auspices of the Supreme Being, the following Rights of Woman and of Female Citizens:

I. Woman is born free and lives equal to man in her rights. Social distinctions can be based only on the common utility.

II. The purpose of any political association is the conservation of the natural and imprescriptible rights of woman and man; these rights are liberty, property, security, and especially resistance to oppression.

III. The principle of all sovereignty rests essentially with the nation, which is nothing but the union of woman and man. . . .

IV. Liberty and justice consist of restoring all that belongs to others; thus, the only limits on the exercise of the natural rights of woman are perpetual male tyranny; these limits are to be reformed by the laws of nature and reason.

V. Laws of nature and reason proscribe all acts harmful to society. . . .

VI. The law must be the expression of the general will; all female and male citizens must send representatives to its formation; it must be the same for all: male and female citizens, being equal in the eyes of the law, must be equally admitted to all honors, positions, and public employment according to their capacity and without other distinctions besides those of their virtues and talents.

VII. No woman is an exception; she is accused, arrested, and detained in cases determined by law. Women, like men, obey this rigorous law.

VIII. The law must establish only those penalties that are strictly and obviously necessary. . . .

IX. Once any woman is declared guilty, complete rigor is [to be] exercised by the law.

X. No one is to be disquieted for his very basic opinions; woman has the right to mount the scaffold; she must equally have the right to mount the rostrum, provided that her demonstrations do not disturb the legally established public order.

XI. The free communication of thoughts and opinions is one of the most precious rights of woman, since that liberty assures the recognition of children by their fathers. Any female citizen thus may say freely, I am the mother of a child which belongs to you, without being forced by a barbarous prejudice to hide the truth. . . .

XIII. For the support of the public force and the expenses of administration, the contributions of woman and man are equal; she shares all the duties . . . and all the painful tasks; therefore, she must have the same share in the distribution of positions, employment, offices, honors, and jobs. . . .

XIV. Female and male citizens have the right to verify, either by themselves or through their representatives, the necessity of the public contribution. This can only apply to women if they are granted an equal share, not only of wealth, but also of public administration. . . .

XV. The collectivity of women, joined for tax purposes to the aggregate of men, has the right to demand an accounting of his administration from any public agent.

XVI. No society has a constitution without the guarantee of rights and the separation of powers; the constitution is null if the majority of individuals comprising the nation have not cooperated in drafting it.

XVII. Property belongs to both sexes whether united or separate; for each it is an inviolable and sacred right. . . .

❄ Late-eighteenth-century French painting, *La Liberté. (Source: Bibliothèque Nationale/Giraudon/Art Resource, NY)*

POSTSCRIPT

Women, wake up. . . . Discover your rights. . . . Oh women, women! When will you cease to be blind? What advantage have you received from the Revolution? A more pronounced scorn, a more marked disdain. . . . [If men persist in contradicting their revolutionary principles,] courageously oppose the force of reason to the empty pretensions of superiority . . . and you will soon see these haughty men, not groveling at your feet as servile adorers, but proud to share with you the treasure of the Supreme Being. Regardless of what barriers confront you; it is in your power to free yourselves; you have only to want to. . . .

Questions for Analysis

1. On what basis did de Gouges argue for gender equality? Did she believe in natural law?

2. What consequences did "scorn for the rights of women" have for France, according to de Gouges?

3. Did de Gouges stress political rights at the expense of social and economic rights? If so, why?

Source: Olympe de Gouges, "Declaration of the Rights of Woman" in Darline G. Levy, Harriet B. Applewhite, and Mary D. Johnson, eds., *Women in Revolutionary Paris, 1789–1795* (Urbana: University of Illinois Press, 1979), pp. 87–96. Copyright © 1979 by the Board of Trustees, University of Illinois. Used with permission.

❧ TIMELINE

A HISTORY OF WORLD SOCIETIES: A BRIEF OVERVIEW

Period (CA 10,000–CA 400 B.C.)	Africa and the Middle East	The Americas
10,000 B.C.	New Stone Age culture, ca 10,000–3500	Migration into Americas begins, ca 11,000
5000 B.C.	"Agricultural revolution" originates in Tigris-Euphrates and Nile River Valleys, ca 6000 First writing in Sumeria; Sumerian city-states emerge, ca 3500 Egypt unified under Narmer, 3100–2660 Metalworking in Caucasus, 3000	Maize domesticated in Mexico, ca 5000
2500 B.C.	Old Kingdom in Egypt; construction of the pyramids, 2660–2180 Akkadian Empire, 2370–2150 Middle Kingdom in Egypt, 2080–1640 Hyksos "invade" Egypt, 1640–1570 Hammurabi, 1792–1750 Hebrew monotheism, ca 1700	First pottery in Americas, Ecuador, ca 3000 First metalworking in Peru, ca 2000
1500 B.C.	Hittite Empire, ca 1450–1200 Akhenaten institutes worship of Aton, ca 1360 New Kingdom in Egypt; creation of Egyptian Empire, ca 1570–1075 Moses leads Hebrews out of Egypt, ca 1300–1200	Olmec civilization, Mexico, ca 1500 B.C.–A.D. 300
1000 B.C.	Political fragmentation of Egypt; rise of small kingdoms, ca 1100–700 United Hebrew kingdom, 1020–922: Saul, David, Solomon Ironworking spreads throughout Africa, ca 1000 B.C.–A.D. 300 Divided Hebrew kingdom: Israel (922–721), Judah (922–586) Assyrian Empire, 745–612 Zoroaster, ca 600	Olmec center at San Lorenzo destroyed, ca 900; power passes to La Venta in Tabasco Chavin civilization in Andes, ca 1000–200 B.C.
500 B.C.	Babylonian captivity of the Hebrews, 586–539 Cyrus the Great founds Persian Empire, 550 Persians conquer Egypt, 525 Darius and Xerxes complete Persian conquest of Middle East, 521–464	Olmec civilization, ca 1500 B.C.–A.D. 300 Fall of La Venta; Tres Zapotes becomes leading Olmec site
400 B.C.	Spartan Hegemony in Greece 399–371 B.C. Theban Hegemony in Greece 371–362 B.C. Philip of Macedon's Conquest of Greece, 338 B.C.	

East Asia	India and Southeast Asia	Europe
"Agricultural revolution" originates in Yellow River Valley, ca 4000		
Horse domesticated in China, ca 2500	Indus River Valley civilization, ca 2500–1500; capitals at Mohenjo-daro and Harappa	Greek Bronze Age, 2000–1100 Arrival of Greeks in peninsular Greece
Shang Dynasty, first writing in China, ca 1523–ca 1027	Aryans arrive in India; Early Vedic Age, ca 1500–1000 Vedas, oldest Hindu sacred texts	Height of Minoan culture, 1700–1450 Mycenaeans conquer Minoan Crete, ca 1450 Mycenaean Age, 1450–1200
Zhou Dynasty, promulgation of the Mandate of Heaven, ca 1027–221	Later Vedic Age; solidification of caste system, ca 1000–500 Upanishads; foundation of Hinduism, 800–600	Trojan War, ca 1180 Fall of the Mycenaean kingdom, 1100 Greek Dark Age, ca 1100–800 Roman Republic founded, 509 Origin of Greek polis, ca 700 Greek Lyric Age; rise of Sparta and Athens, 800–500
Confucius, 551–479 First written reference to iron, ca 521	Siddhartha Gautama (Buddha), 563–483	Persian Wars, 499–479 Growth of Athenian Empire; flowering of Greek drama, philosophy, and history, 5th century Peloponnesian War, 431–404 Plato, 426–347

Period (CA 300 B.C.–AD 500)	Africa and the Middle East	The Americas
300 B.C.	Alexander the Great extends empire, 334–331 Death of Alexander (323): Ptolemy conquers Egypt, Seleucus rules Asia	
200 B.C.	Scipio Africanus defeats Hannibal at Zama, 202	
100 B.C.	Dead Sea Scrolls Pompey conquers Syria and Palestine, 63	
A.D 100	Jesus Christ, ca 4 B.C.–A.D. 30 Paul, d. ca 65 Bantu migrations begin Jews revolt from Rome, Romans destroy Hebrew temple in Jerusalem: end of the ancient Hebrew state, 70	
A.D 200	Camel first used for trans-Saharan transport, ca 200 Expansion of Bantu peoples, ca 200–900 Axum (Ethiopia) controls Red Sea trade, ca 250	Classic Age of the Maya, ca 300–900 Olmec civilization, ca 1500 B.C.–A.D. 300
A.D 300	Axum accepts Christianity, ca 4th century	Maya civilization in Central America, ca 300–1500 Classic period of Teotihuacán civilization in Mexico, ca 300–900
A.D 500	Political and commercial ascendancy of Axum, ca 6th–7th centuries Muhammad, 570–632; the *hijra*, 622 Extensive slave trade from sub-Saharan Africa to Mediterranean, ca 600–1500 Umayyad Dynasty, 661–750, with capital at Damascus; continued expansion of Islam	Tiahuanaco civilization in South America, ca 600–1000

East Asia	India and Southeast Asia	Europe
Lao-tzu and development of Taoism, 4th century Han Fei-tzu and Li Ssu and development of Legalism, ca 250–208	Alexander invades India, 327–326 Chandragupta founds Mauryan Dynasty, 322–ca 185 Ashoka, 273–232 King Arsaces of Parthia defeats Seleucid monarchy and begins conquest of Persia, ca 250–137	Peloponnesian War, 431–404 Plato, 426–347 Gauls sack Rome, ca 390 Roman expansion, 390–146 Sparton Hegemony in Greece, 399–371 B.C. Theban Hegemony in Greece, 371–362 B.C. Philip of Macedon's Conquest of Greece, 338 B.C. Conquests of Alexander the Great, 334–323 Punic Wars, destruction of Carthage, 264–146
Qin Dynasty and unification of China; construction of the Great Wall, destruction of Confucian literature, 221–210 Han Dynasty, 202 B.C.–A.D. 220	Greeks invade India, ca 183–145 Mithridates creates Parthian Empire, ca 171–131	Late Roman Republic, 133–27
Chinese expansion to South China Sea and Vietnam, ca 111 Silk Road opens to Parthian and Roman Empires; Buddhism enters China, ca 104	First Chinese ambassadors to India and Parthia, ca 140 Bhagavad Gita, ca 100 B.C.–A.D. 100	Formation of First Triumvirate (Caesar, Crassus, Pompey), 60 Julius Caesar killed, 44 Formation of Second Triumvirate, (Octavian, Antony, Lepidus), 43 Octavian seizes power, 31
First written reference (Chinese) to Japan, A.D. 45 Chinese invent paper, 105 Emperor Wu, 140–186	Shakas and Kushans invade eastern Parthia and India, 1st century A.D. Roman attacks on Parthian Empire, 115–211	Octavian rules imperial Rome as Augustus, 27 B.C.–A.D. 14 Roman Empire at greatest extent, 117
Creation of Yamato state in Japan, ca 3d century Buddhism gains popularity in China and Japan, ca 220–590 Fall of Han Dynasty, 220 Three Kingdoms era in China, 221–280	Kushan rule in northwestern India, A.D. 2d–3d centuries Fall of the Parthian Empire, rise of the Sassanids, ca 225	Breakdown of the pax Romana, ca 180–284; civil wars, economic decline, invasions Reforms by Diocletian, 284–305
Barbarian invasions, 4th–5th centuries	Chandragupta I founds Gupta Dynasty in India, ca 320–500 Chandragupta II conquers western India, establishes trade with Middle East and China, ca 400 Huns invade India, ca 450	Reign of Constantine, 306–337; Edict of Milan, 313; founding of Constantinople, 324; Council of Nicaea, 325 Theodosius recognizes Christianity as official state religion, 380 Germanic raids of western Europe, 5th century Clovis unites Franks and rules Gauls, 481–511
Sui Dynasty in China, 580–618; restoration of public order "Constitution" of Shotoku in Japan, 604 Tang Dynasty, 618–907; cultural flowering	Sanskrit drama, ca 600–1000 Muslim invasions of India, ca 636–1206	Saint Benedict publishes his *Rule,* 529 Law Code of Justinian, 529 Synod of Whitby, 664

Period (CA 700–1500)	Africa and the Middle East	The Americas
700	Abbasid Dynasty, 750–1258; Islamic capital moved to Baghdad Decline of Ethiopia, ca 9th century Golden age of Muslim learning, ca 900–1100 Kingdom of Ghana, ca 900–1100 Mahmud of Ghazna, 998–1030	"Time of Troubles" in Mesoamerica, 800–1000
1000	Islam penetrates sub-Saharan Africa, ca 11th century Kingdom of Benin, ca 1100–1897 Kingdom of Mali, middle Niger region, ca 1200–1450 Mongol invasion of Middle East, ca 1220	Inca civilization in South America, ca 1000–1500 Toltec hegemony, ca 1000–1300 Aztecs arrive in Valley of Mexica, ca 1325
1200	Kingdom of Mali, ca 1200–1450 Mongols conquer Baghdad, 1258; fall of Abbasid Dynasty	Maya civilization in Central America, ca 300–1500 Inca civilization in South America, ca 1000–1500 Toltec hegemony, ca 1000–1300
1300	Rise of Yoruba states, West Africa, ca 1300 Height of Swahili (East African) city-states, ca 1300–1500 Mansa Musa rules Mali, 1312–1337	Tenochtitlán (Mexico City) founded by Aztecs, 1325
1400	Zara Yakob rules Ethiopia, 1434–1468 Arrival of Portugese in Benin, ca 1440 Songhay Empire, West Africa, ca 1450–1591 Atlantic slave trade, ca 1450–1850 Ottoman Empire, 1453–1918 Vasco da Gama arrives on East African coast, 1498	Height of Inca Empire, 1438–1493 Reign of Montezuma I, 1440–1468; height of Aztec culture Columbus reaches the Americas, 1492
1500	Portugal dominates East Africa, ca 1500–1650 Safavid Empire in Persia, 1501–1722 Peak of Ottoman power under Suleiman the Magnificent, 1520–1566 Height of Kanem-Bornu under Idris Alooma, 1571–1603 Portuguese found Angola, 1571 Battle of Lepanto, 1571, signals Ottoman naval weakness in the eastern Mediterranean Height of Safavid power under Shah Abbas, 1587–1629	South American holocaust, ca 1500–1600 First African slaves, ca 1510 Cortés arrives in Mexico, 1519; Aztec Empire falls, 1521 Pizarro reaches Peru, 1531; conquers Incas Spanish conquer the Philippines, 1571

East Asia	India and Southeast Asia	Europe
Taika Reform Edict in Japan, 655 Nara era, creation of Japan's first capital, 710–784 Heian era in Japan, 794–1185; literary flowering Era of the Five Dynasties in China, 907–960; warfare, revolt Song Dynasty, 960–1279	Khmer Empire (Kampuchea) founded, 802	Charles Martel defeats Muslims at Tours, 733 Charles the Great (Charlemagne), 768–814 Invasions of Carolingian Empire, 9th–10th centuries Treaty of Verdun divides Carolingian Empire, 843 Cluny monastery founded, 910
Vietnam gains independence from China, ca 1000 China divided between empires of Song (south) and Jin (north), 1127 Kamakura Shogunate, 1185–1333 Mongol conquest of China, 1215–1368	Construction of Angkor Wat, ca 1100–1150 Muslim conquerors end Buddhism in India, 1192 Peak of Khmer Empire in southeast Asia, ca 1200 Turkish sultanate at Delhi, 1206–1526; Indian culture divided into Hindu and Muslim	Yaroslav the Wise, 1019–1054; peak of Kievan Russia Schism between Latin and Greek churches, 1054 Norman Conquest of England, 1066 Investiture struggle, 1073–1122 The Crusades, 1096–1270 Growth of trade and towns, 12th–13th centuries Frederick Barbarossa invades Italy, 1154–1158
Kamakura Shogunate, 1185–1333 Unsuccessful Mongol invasions of Japan, 1274, 1281 Yuan (Mongol) Dynasty, 1279–1368	Peak of Khmer Empire in southeast Asia, ca 1200 Turkish sultanate at Delhi, 1206–1526; Indian culture divided into Hindu and Muslim	Magna Carta, 1215 Thomas Aquinas, *Summa Theologica,* 1253 Prince Alexander Nevsky recognizes Mongol overlordship of Moscow, 1252
Marco Polo arrives at Kublai Khan's court, ca 1275 Ashikaga Shogunate, 1336–1408 Hung Wu drives Mongols from China, 1368; founds Ming Dynasty, 1368–1644	Mongol chieftain Timur the Lame (Tamerlame) conquers the Punjab, 1398	Babylonian Captivity of the papacy, 1309–1376 Tver revolt in Russia, 1327–1328 Hundred Years' War, 1337–1453 Bubonic plague, 1347–1700 Ottoman Turks invade Europe, 1356 Peasants' Revolt in England, 1381
Early Ming policy encourages foreign trade, ca 15th century Ming maritime expeditions to India, Middle East, Africa, 1405–1433	Sultan Mehmed II, 1451–1481 Pasha Sinon, Ottoman architect, 1491–1588 Vasco da Gama reaches India, 1498	Beginnings of representative government, ca 1350–1500 Italian Renaissance, ca 1400–1530 Voyages of discovery, ca 1450–1600 Ottomans capture Constantinople, 1453; end of Byzantine Empire War of the Roses in England, 1455–1485 Unification of Spain completed, 1492
Portuguese trade monopoly in East Asia, ca 16th century Christian missionaries active in China and Japan, ca 1550–1650 Unification of Japan, 1568–1600	Barbur defeats Delhi sultanate, 1526–1527; founds Mughal Empire Akbar expands Mughal Empire, 1556–1605	Martin Luther, Ninety-five Theses, 1517 Charles V elected Holy Roman emperor, 1519 Henry VIII leads English Reformation, 1534 Council of Trent, 1545–1563 Dutch United Provinces declare independence, 1581 Spanish Armada, 1588

Period (CA 1600–1900)	Africa and the Middle East	The Americas
1600	Dutch West India Co. supplants Portuguese in West Africa, ca 1630 Dutch settle Cape Town, 1651 Rise of Ashanti Empire, founded on Gold Coast trade, ca 1700–1750	British settle Jamestown, 1607 Champlain founds Quebec, 1608 Dutch found New Amsterdam, 1624 Black labor allows tenfold increase in production of Carolinian rice and Virginian tobacco, ca 1730–1760 Silver production quadruples in Mexico and Peru, ca 1700–1800
1700	Approximately 11 million slaves shipped from Africa, ca 1450–1850 Dutch found Cape Colony, 1657 Rise of the Ashanti, West Africa, ca 1700 Decline of the Safavid Empire under Nadir Shah, 1737–1747	Spain's defeat in War of the Spanish Succession, 1701–1714, prompts trade reform, leading to colonial dependence on Spanish goods, 18th century
1750	Sultan Selim III introduces administrative and military reforms, 1761–1808 British seize Cape Town, 1795 Napoleon's campaign in Egypt, 1798	"French and Indian Wars," 1756–1763 Quebec Act, 1774 American Revolution, 1775–1783 Comunero revolution, New Granada, 1781
1800	Muhammad Ali founds dynasty in Egypt, 1805–1848 Slavery abolished in British Empire, 1807 Peak year of African transatlantic slave trade, 1820	Latin American wars of independence from Spain, 1806–1825 Brazil wins independence from Portugal, 1822 Monroe Doctrine, 1823 Political instability in most Latin American countries, 1825–1870 Mexican War, 1846–1848
1850	Crimean War, 1853–1856 Suez Canal opens, 1869 Europeans intensify "scramble for Africa," 1880–1900 Battle of Omdurman, 1898 Boer War, 1899–1902	American Civil War, 1861–1865 British North America Act, 1867, for Canada Porfirio Diaz controls Mexico, 1876–1911 United States practices "dollar diplomacy" in Latin America, 1890–1920s Spanish-American War, 1898; United States gains Philippines
1900	Union of South Africa formed, 1910 French annex Morocco, 1912 Ottoman Empire enters World War One on Germany's side Treaty of Sèvres dissolves Ottoman Empire, 1919; Mustafa Kemal mounts nationalist struggle in Turkey	Massive immigration from Europe and Asia to the Americas, 1880–1914 Mexican Revolution, 1910 Panama Canal opens, 1914 United States enters World War One, 1917 Mexico adopts constitution, 1917

East Asia	India and Southeast Asia	Europe
Tokugawa Shogunate, 1600–1867 Japan expels all Europeans, 1637 Manchus establish Qing Dynasty, 1644 Height of Qing Dynasty under K'ang-hsi, 1662–1722 Height of Edo urban culture in Japan, ca 1700	Height of Mughal Empire under Shah Jahan, 1628–1658 British found Calcutta, 1690 Decline of Mughal Empire, ca 1700–1800 Persian invaders sack Delhi, 1739	Romanov Dynasty in Russia, 1613 Thirty Years' War, 1618–1648 Brandenburg-Prussia unified, 1640–1688 English Civil War, 1642–1646 Louis XIV, king of France, 1643–1715 Ottoman Turks besiege Vienna, 1683 Revocation of Edict of Nantes, 1685 The Glorious Revolution in England, 1688 War of Spanish Succession, 1701–1713 Treaty of Utrecht, 1713
Tokugawa regime in Japan, characterized by political stability and economic growth, 1600–1867 Manchus establish Qing Dynasty, 1644–1911 Height of Qing Dynasty under Emperor Ch'ien-lung, 1736–1799	Mughal power contested by Hindus and Muslims, 18th century Persian invaders defeat Mughal army, loot Delhi, 1739 French and British fight for control of India, 1740–1763	Growth of absolutism in central and eastern Europe, ca 1680–1790 The Enlightenment, ca 1680–1800 Development of Cabinet system in England, 1714–1742 Height of land enclosure in England, ca 1760–1810
Maximum extent of Qing Empire, 1759	Battle of Plassey, 1757 Treaty of Paris, 1763; French colonies to Britain Cook in Australia, 1768–1771; first British prisoners to Australia, 1788 East India Act, 1784	Englishman James Watt produces first steam engine, 1769 Louis XVI of France, 1774–1792 Outbreak of French Revolution, 1789 National Convention declares France a republic, 1792
Java War, 1825–1830 Anglo-Chinese Opium War, 1839–1842 Treaty of Nanjing, 1842: Manchus surrender Hong Kong to British	British found Singapore, 1819 British defeat last independent native state in India, 1848	Napoleonic Empire, 1804–1814 Congress of Vienna, 1814–1815 European economic penetration of non-Western countries, ca 1816–1880 Greece wins independence from Ottoman Empire, 1829 Revolutions in France, Prussia, Italy, and Austria, 1848–1849
Taiping Rebellion, 1850–1864 Perry's arrival opens Japan to United States and Europe, 1853 Meiji Restoration in Japan, 1867 Adoption of constitution in Japan, 1890 Sino-Japanese War, 1894–1895 "Hundred Days of Reform" in China, 1898	Great Rebellion in India, 1857–1858 French seize Saigon, 1859 Indian National Congress formed, 1885 French acquire Indochina, 1893	Second Empire and Third Republic in France, 1852–1914 Unification of Italy, 1859–1870 Otto von Bismarck's reign of power in German affairs, 1862–1890 Franco-Prussian War, 1870–1871; foundation of the German Empire Parliamentary Reform Bill, Great Britain, 1867 Second Socialist International, 1889–1914
Boxer Rebellion in China, 1900–1903 Russo-Japanese War, 1904–1905 Chinese Revolution; fall of Qing Dynasty, 1911 Chinese Republic, 1912–1949	Commonwealth of Australia, 1900 Muslim League formed, 1906 Radicals make first calls for Indian independence, 1907 Amritsar massacre in India, 1919 Intensification of Indian nationalism, 1919–1947	Revolution in Russia; Tsar Nicholas II forced to issue October Manifesto, 1905 Triple Entente (Britain, Russia, France), 1914–1918 World War One, 1914–1918 Treaty of Versailles, 1919

Period (CA 1920–1990)	Africa and the Middle East	The Americas
1920	Cultural nationalism in Africa, 1920s Treaty of Lausanne recognizes Turkish Republic, 1923 Reza Shah leads Iran, 1925–1941	U.S. "consumer revolution," 1920s Stock market crash in United States; Great Depression begins, 1929
1930	African farmers organize first "cocoa holdups," 1930–1931 Iraq gains independence, 1932 Syrian-French friendship treaty, 1936	Revolutions in six South American countries, 1930 New Deal begins in United States, 1933
1940	Civil war between Arabs and Jews in Palestine; state of Israel is created, 1948 Apartheid system in South Africa, 1948–1991 Libya gains independence, 1949	Surprise attack by Japan on Pearl Harbor, 1941 United Nations established, 1945 Perón regime in Argentina, 1946–1953
1950	Egypt declared a republic; Nasser named premier, 1954 Morocco, Tunisia, Sudan, and Ghana gain independence, 1956–1957 French-British Suez invasion, 1956	Fidel Castro takes power in Cuba, 1959
1960	Mali, Nigeria, and the Congo gain independence, 1960 Biafra declares independence from Nigeria, 1967 Arab-Israeli Six-Day War, 1967	Cuban missile crisis, 1962 Military dictatorship in Brazil, 1964–1985 United States escalates war in Vietnam, 1964
1970	"Yom Kippur War," 1973 Islamic revolution in Iran, 1979 Camp David Accords, 1979	Military coup in Chile, 1973 U.S. Watergate scandal, 1974 Revolutions in Nicaragua and El Salvador, 1979
1980	Iran-Iraq War, 1980–1988 Reforms in South Africa, 1989 to present	U.S. military buildup, 1980–1988 Argentina restores civilian rule, 1983
1990	Growth of Islamic fundamentalism, 1990 to present Iraq driven from Kuwait by United States and allies, 1991 Israel and Palestinians sign peace agreement, 1993 Nelson Mandela elected president of South Africa, 1994	Canada, Mexico, and United States form free-trade area (NAFTA), 1994 Haiti establishes democratic government, 1994 Permanent extension of Treaty on the Non-Proliferation of Nuclear Weapons, 1995

East Asia	India and Southeast Asia	Europe
Kita Ikki advocates ultranationalism in Japan, 1923 Jiang Jieshi unites China, 1928	Mohandas "Mahatma" Gandhi launches nonviolent resistance campaign, 1920	Mussolini seizes power in Italy, 1922 Stalin takes power in U.S.S.R., 1927 Depths of Great Depression, 1929–1933
Japan invades China, 1931 Mao Zedong's Long March, 1934 Sino-Japanese War, 1937–1945	Mahatma Gandhi's Salt March, 1930 Japanese conquer empire in southeast Asia, 1939–1942	Hitler gains dictatorial power, 1933 Civil War in Spain, 1936–1939 Germany invades Poland, 1939 World War Two, 1939–1945
United States drops atomic bombs on Hiroshima and Nagasaki, 1945 Chinese civil war, 1945–1949; Communists win	Philippines gain independence, 1946 India (Hindu) and Pakistan (Muslim) gain independence, 1947	Yalta Conference, 1945 Marshall Plan, 1947 NATO alliance, 1949 Soviet Union and Red China sign 30-year alliance treaty, 1949
Korean War, 1950–1953 Japan begins long period of rapid economic growth, 1950 Mao Zedong announces Great Leap Forward, 1958	Vietnamese nationalists defeat French; Vietnam divided, 1954 Islamic Republic of Pakistan declared, 1956	Death of Stalin, 1953 Warsaw Pact, 1955 Revolution in Hungary, 1956 Creation of the Common Market, 1957
Sino-Soviet split becomes apparent, 1960 Great Proletarian Cultural Revolution in China, 1965–1969	Indira Gandhi prime minister of India, 1966–1977, 1980–1984	Student revolution in France, 1968 Soviet invasion of Czechoslovakia, 1968
Communist victory in Vietnam War, 1975 China pursues modernization, 1976 to present	India-Pakistan war, 1971 Chinese invade Vietnam, 1979	German Chancellor Willy Brandt's Ostpolitik, 1969–1973 Soviet invasion of Afghanistan, 1979
Japanese foreign investment surge, 1980–1992 China crushes democracy movement, 1989	Sikh nationalism in India, 1984 to present Corazón Aquino takes power in Philippines, 1986	Soviet reform under Mikhail Gorbachev, 1985–1991 Anticommunist revolutions sweep eastern Europe, 1989
Birthrates keep falling Economic growth and political repression in China, 1990 to present Japan and United States reach auto agreement, 1995	Vietnam embraces foreign investment, 1990 to present U.S. military bases closed in Philippines, 1991	Continued high unemployment, 1990 to present Soviet Union ceases to exist, 1991 Civil war in Bosnia, 1991 to present

Index